Budgeting for America

The Politics and Process of Federal Spending

CONGRESSIONAL QUARTERLY INC.
1414 22ND STREET, N.W.
WASHINGTON, D.C. 20037

Congressional Quarterly Inc.

Congressional Quarterly Inc., an editorial research service and publishing company, serves clients in the fields of news, education, business and government. It combines specific coverage of Congress, government and politics by Congressional Quarterly with the more general subject range of an affiliated service, Editorial Research Reports.

Congressional Quarterly was founded in 1945 by Henrietta and Nelson Poynter. Its basic periodical publication was and still is the CQ *Weekly Report*, mailed to clients every Saturday. A cumulative index is published quarterly.

CQ also publishes a variety of books. The CQ *Almanac*, a compendium of legislation for one session of Congress, is published every spring. *Congress and the Nation* is published every four years as a record of government for one presidential term. Other books include paperbacks on public affairs and textbooks for college political science classes.

The public affairs books are designed as timely reports to keep journalists, scholars and the public abreast of developing issues, events and trends.

They include such recent titles as *Environment and Health*, the second edition of *Energy Policy* and the fifth edition of *The Middle East*. College textbooks, prepared by outside scholars and published under the CQ Press imprint, include such recent titles as *Congress and Its Members; Congress Reconsidered, Second Edition;* and *The Politics of Shared Power.*

In addition, CQ publishes *The Congressional Monitor*, a daily report on present and future activities of congressional committees. This service is supplemented by *The Congressional Record Scanner*, an abstract of each day's *Congressional Record*, and *Congress in Print*, a weekly listing of committee publications.

CQ Direct Research is a consulting service that performs contract research and maintains a reference library and query desk for clients.

Editorial Research Reports covers subjects beyond the specialized scope of Congressional Quarterly. It publishes reference material on foreign affairs, business, education, cultural affairs, national security, science and other topics of news interest. Service to clients includes a 6,000-word report four times a month, bound and indexed semi-annually. Editorial Research Reports publishes paperback books in its field of coverage. Founded in 1923, the service merged with Congressional Quarterly in 1956.

Library of Congress Cataloging in Publication Data

Main entry under title:

Budgeting for America.

Bibliography: p.
Includes index.
1. Budget — United States. 2. Taxation — United States. 3. Social Security — United States. 4. United States — Economic policy. 5. Government spending policy — United States. I. Congressional Quarterly, inc.
HJ2051.B775   353.0072'2   81-17376
ISBN 0-87187-214-5   AACR2

Editor: Martha V. Gottron

Associate Editor: Diane C. Hill

Contributing Editors: John L. Moore, Patricia Ann O'Connor

Major Contributors: Thomas J. Arrandale, Christopher R. Conte, Margaret C. Thompson

Contributors: Barbara R. de Boinville, Harrison Donnelly, Ross Evans, Pamela Fessler, Dale Tate

Design: Mary L. McNeil

Cover: Richard A. Pottern, George Rebh

Graphics: Robert O. Redding, Cheryl Rowe

Index: Nancy Nawor Blanpied

Book Department

Congressional Quarterly Inc.

Tables and Charts

Contents

Editor's Note. Ronald Reagan took office in 1981 promising to cut the federal budget and slash income taxes. Within seven months he had succeeded beyond most observers' expectations. But his victories raised important questions not only about the patterns and levels of federal spending but about the governmental process by which spending decisions are made. *Budgeting for America* examines those issues. It looks first at the historical economic context in which Reagan and Congress made their decisions and at the basic constitutional authorities of the executive and legislative branches for shaping the federal budget. The book then traces the use of those authorities, culminating in the contest between President Richard Nixon and Congress for spending control, enactment of the congressional budget control act in 1974 and implementation of that act. Other chapters of the book examine the Social Security system's financial problems, relating them to the present budget crisis, and the effects that Reagan's economic policy is likely to have on the poor and on state and local governments. The book also contains a chronology of budget legislation from 1965 to 1981, a chronology of economic legislation from 1964 to 1981, selected economic speeches of President Reagan, a glossary of budgetary terms, a bibliography and an index. *Budgeting for America* is one of CQ's public affairs books that are designed as timely reports to keep journalists, scholars and the public abreast of issues, events and trends.

Reagan, Congress and the Budget

Republican President Ronald Reagan entered office in Janaury 1981 with one of the clearest electoral mandates in recent decades: to put America's economic house in order. Within seven months, the new president had made impressive strides toward implementing the economic policy he thought would meet that mandate. Congress had enacted the largest spending and tax cuts in its history, slashing fiscal 1982 spending $35 billion below projected levels and reducing personal and corporate income taxes by $37.7 billion.

To secure that victory, Reagan's strategists took advantage of an unusual conjunction of politics and process. What emerged may have altered not only the patterns of federal spending in the immediate future but also the way the federal government decides to spend its resources.

The politics of the situation were relatively simple. Congress as well as the president had received a clear signal from the voters to do something about economic conditions. The stagnant, inflation-ridden economy that had hung on since the mid-1970s did more than just help Reagan evict Jimmy Carter from the White House. It had contributed to a Republican takeover of the Senate and a diminished Democratic majority in the House. Perhaps for the first time since the Depression of the 1930s, Congress was prepared to take extraordinary action to solve the economic woes that, if left unattended, threatened the well-being of the country and the political lives of the president and lawmakers alike.

The process was more complicated. It had its genesis almost a decade earlier when another Republican president, Richard Nixon, angered Congress by his use of executive powers to hold down federal spending and to revise congressionally mandated spending priorities. Acknowledging that it had relinquished much of its authority for making spending decisions to the president, Congress decided to reclaim that power. The Congressional Budget and Impoundment Control Act of 1974 established a new procedure that forced Congress to review the budget as a whole and then to reconcile individual taxing and spending decisions to that overall picture.

Congress began using its new budget procedure in 1975, moving somewhat cautiously as it tentatively explored the power shifts that developed between Congress and the president and between committees and members of Congress. For the most part, Congress over the next five years shied away from making the tough spending decisions that would be required to reverse the upward climb of federal spending. Only once before 1981 did it use the reconciliation process to keep funding for individual federal programs within the overall spending limits Congress had imposed.

In January 1981, then, all this came together: a federal budget that many feared was growing beyond control, a public outcry for a reduction in federal spending, a still untested congressional procedure for shaping the budget and a president who used that procedure in ways Congress had not foreseen. That confluence of events resulted in fulfillment of Reagan's immediate goal — a slowing down of the growth of the federal government. More significantly, it also altered the relationship between the executive and legislative branches, returning to the president the balance of power for directing how federal funds are spent, and raised new questions about the ability of Congress to direct the federal budget.

Power and Responsibility

The Constitution gave Congress the taxing, borrowing and spending powers necessary to conduct the business of government. Initially those purposes were straightforward — raising and maintaining an armed forces, running a postal system, conducting foreign commerce and the like. With the 1930s Depression, however, the federal government assumed a broader responsibility for itself — to ensure the well-being of its citizens during hard times. Income security for the retired, the jobless and the poor were enacted as parts of the same measure in 1935, setting a precedent for future individual aid programs.

Congress added a few new federal aid programs through the 1940s and 1950s, but it was with enactment of President Lyndon B. Johnson's "Great Society" programs that the federal government really expanded its role. In just a few short years Congress put on the lawbooks major new programs providing medical care to the poor and elderly, aid to elementary, secondary and college students, compensation to coal miners afflicted with black lung disease, job training and employment to those unable to get jobs and food for the poor. It expanded existing programs to support farmers when their crops failed or otherwise could not be sold and to encourage small businesses

Reagan's Economic Recovery Plan...

President Reagan's solution to the economic woes of the nation was a largely untested theory called supply-side economics. Simply put, supply siders hold that by returning taxes to businesses and workers and by restricting the growth of government, Americans would have more incentive to work harder and to save more. That would lead to increased investment, higher productivity and a decline in inflation, they said.

To aim the economy in the supply-side direction, Reagan March 10 requested that Congress cut more than $40 billion from fiscal 1982 spending and reduce taxes by $53.9 billion.

Economic Plan

Reagan's ambitious tax cut plan called for a three-year, 30 percent cut in individual income tax rates and faster depreciation write-offs for business investments. According to supply-side theory, such deep cuts would encourage individuals to invest savings and thus set off the spiral that would result in higher productivity and lower inflation. To help control inflation, Reagan proposed significant cuts in scores of federal domestic programs but promised to maintain "social safety net" programs for the truly needy.

Reagan's plan was immediately attacked as unworkable and risky. Many economists warned that the large-scale tax cuts could trigger an increase in spending rather than savings; that would push inflation even higher. Democrats in Congress also claimed that the president's proposals were inequitable. They said the tax cuts would benefit primarily the well-to-do and that, the "safety net" notwithstanding, the spending cuts would hurt the poor.

Reagan had anticipated such criticisms. "Have they an alternative which offers a greater chance of balancing the budget, reducing and eliminating inflation, stimulating the creation of jobs and reducing the tax burden?" he asked at his Feb. 18 address to a joint session of Congress."And if they haven't, are they suggesting we can continue on the present course without coming to a day of reckoning?"

Reagan's challenge haunted his Democratic opponents throughout the debate on both the spending and tax cuts. They were never able to find an answer to their political dilemma: how to assure their constituents — who overwhelmingly supported the president, according to polls — that they were not trying to kill Reagan's economic recovery program and at the same time satisfy their own profound doubts that the Reagan plan would work.

As a result, Congress gave Reagan almost exactly what he wanted in spending reductions — $35.2 billion worth. Slightly less successful with his tax plan, Reagan was forced by the pressures of a tight budget and an unenthusiastic Congress to reduce his tax cut to $37.4 billion and to add some popular "sweeteners," including marriage penalty relief and savings incentives, to win congressional approval.

Little more than a month after he signed the tax and spending cuts, Reagan Sept. 24 returned to Congress asking for a new $2.6 billion round of fiscal 1982 entitlement cuts and for $3 billion in taxes or "revenue enhancers." Another $10.4 billion in savings would come from appropriations cuts; Reagan requested that Congress enact cuts of 12 percent from his March requests in all discretionary spending programs except defense.

This time Congress balked. The new cuts came under fire from Republicans and Democrats alike, who felt they had already cut more than the fat from the budget. Furthermore, they had been confronted with the consequences of making politically unpopular decisions. During consideration of the reconciliation measure Congress voted to eliminate the minimum monthly Social Security benefit. That action met with such public outrage that Congress immediately moved to restore the benefit. Legislators were not anxious to risk a repetition of that episode.

through loan guarantees. And it continued to spend money on defense programs to fight the war in Vietnam and to secure the nation against the threat from the Soviet Union.

At the same time that it was enacting expensive new programs, Congress also was losing more and more control over the federal budget. Spending decisions were made through a piecemeal appropriations process; each year Congress enacted 12 or 13 separate funding bills for the various federal executive agencies. Congress made little effort to relate spending decisions contained in those bills to each other. Nor did it relate the amount of money flowing into the federal government through taxes to the amount of money paid out.

Furthermore, Congress made many of its new social programs entitlements, which meant that anyone who met the eligibility requirements of the program was entitled to its benefits. Congress was required to provide the money to cover those benefits. As the number of people eligible for various entitlements — Social Security, food stamps, college grants and so forth — grew, a greater and greater proportion of the budget was needed to pay the benefits, thus reducing the amount of spending that Congress had any discretion over and further limiting the legislators' ability to direct federal spending policy.

Meanwhile the president had no constitutional authority to set actual spending and revenue figures for the fed-

...From Early Wins to Growing Doubts

Congress also found it painful to contemplate more cuts from domestic programs as its initial cuts were being implemented. No one knew for sure how many people would be adversely affected by those cuts or whether state and local governments would be able to pick up any of the responsibilities dropped by the federal government. Many legislators urged that the deficit be reduced by postponing the August tax cuts instead of making more spending cuts. "How many times can you cut the same piece of the pie?" asked Senate Banking Committee Chairman Jake Garn, R-Utah.

Economic Slump

The political momentum for further spending cuts waned at the same time the economy also sagged. Passage of Reagan's program had not broken the "cycle of negative expectations" about inflation that the president had predicted.

By early November economic indicators were providing clear signals that the economy had entered a recession. The unemployment rate jumped 0.5 percent in October to 8 percent — the highest rate since 1975. The Producer Price Index, which measures increases in wholesale prices, grew a modest 0.6 percent for the month. While economists said that should hold the 1981 rate to the lowest level since 1977, this slackening of inflation was chiefly reflective of a weakening economy. The prime lending rate was dropping — also a reflection of the recession and diminishing demands for credit.

Although it might bring down inflation, a recession was likely to push federal deficits even higher. Tax revenues would fall at the same time the government would be forced to spend more in unemployment benefits and other payments to compensate for lost income.

The president admitted on November 6 that he probably would not be able to balance the budget by 1984 — as he had promised throughout his campaign and often repeated since he took office. "I've never said anything but that it [a balanced budget] was a goal," Reagan told reporters.

Four days later, on Nov. 10, the president retreated from his September call for Congress to trim back the growth in entitlement programs such as Medicare and food stamps and to increase taxes by "enhancing" revenues. Instead he said he would put off decisions on those budget savings until January 1982 and focus on holding fiscal 1982 spending to a minimum through the appropriations process.

At the same time, Reagan's political credibility was damaged by publication of a magazine article in which the president's chief budgetary architect, David A. Stockman, director of the Office of Management and Budget (OMB), expressed his skepticism about the administration's supply-side economics. Stockman was quoted in the December issue of *The Atlantic Monthly* as saying that the main objective of the supply-side theory was to reduce the top income tax bracket from 70 to 50 percent — a goal that clearly favored the rich. Reagan's tax plan, Stockman said, "was always a Trojan Horse to bring down the top rate."

In the commotion that followed disclosure of the article, Stockman offered to resign but Reagan asked him to stay on. "I absolutely believe that that supply-side theory is workable," Stockman later told reporters, adding that he had become "much more realistic about how long it will take."

Given the political and economic situation, Congress appeared willing to put off making any decisions on future spending cuts. Congress seemed prepared to enact a second budget resolution that was a carbon copy of its target resolution adopted in May. It also put off action on individual appropriations bills, enacting instead a stopgap continuing appropriations resolution to provide funding for the federal government while it continued to work on the individual appropriations.

---

eral government; he could only make recommendations to Congress about how money should be raised and spent. But the president did have the apparatus to examine the federal budget as a whole and consequently the ability to shape his budget recommendations to suit his own policy goals. Congress was not required to follow the president's recommendations, but because the president could veto any spending decision Congress made, those decisions more or less reflected presidential policy.

The Budget Process

Because the Constitution was vague on the subject, presidents throughout the nation's history also had assumed the power to refuse to spend funds that Congress had appropriated. It was the extensive use that Nixon made of the impoundment power which so infuriated Congress that it enacted the 1974 budget control law.

The legislation (PL 93-344) was intended to ensure that the president would spend money for the programs that Congress intended and, more importantly, to restore some measure of control over the federal budget to Congress. To that end the law established a congressional apparatus for Congress to relate its individual taxing and spending decisions to overall budget levels it also had set.

Under the provisions of the 1974 act, each spring Congress would review the president's budget proposals for the fiscal year that would begin the following Oct. 1 and then set revenue and spending goals of its own. These target goals would be incorporated in a first budget resolution to be adopted by May 15. Congress then would spend the summer and early fall enacting the regular appropriations bills for the upcoming fiscal year. By Sept. 15 it would adopt a second, binding budget resolution setting final spending and revenue figures.

As part of the budget process, Congress could direct its authorizing and appropriating committees to enact a single omnibus bill making legislative changes in programs already on the books to reconcile their spending and revenue requirements with the levels set out in the budget resolutions. Congress might tighten eligibility for the food stamp program, for example, or boost rent contributions paid by tenants in subsidized housing. The drafters of the 1974 budget act designed the reconciliation procedures in hopes that lawmakers would be more willing to vote for a package of budget savings than for a number of separate spending cut measures.

It was the reconciliation tool that Reagan and Republican strategists in Congress decided to use to achieve Reagan's budget cuts — and to do it quickly before the election zeal had given away to political pressures from individuals and groups who were likely to lose in the budget cutting process.

Using reconciliation to cut billions of dollars from hundreds of federal programs had its advantages. Considering all the programs in one bill short-circuited the lengthy deliberative process of hearings on separate pieces of legislation. It made passage of amendments sought by special interests far more difficult and it strengthened the power of the Budget committees.

It also greatly simplified public perceptions of what was an extraordinarily complex issue, enabling the White House to ask Americans — who then asked their legislators — whether they were "for" or "against" a popular president's budget. In several months of budget work, Congress passed perhaps as many far-reaching changes in basic law as it would in a conventional two-year session.

But by using the budget process to make fundamental changes in federal programs, Congress may have lost sight of the purpose for which its budget process was intended. The framework established for setting overall budget goals and then fitting authorizations and appropriations to those goals was intended to give Congress the time in which to make considered judgments, to determine how each piece of the complicated budget puzzle affected not only that year's budget but also federal spending decisions two and three years in the future.

That deliberation did not occur in 1981 during consideration of the reconciliation measure. The House measure, for example, was passed in such haste that copies of the bill were not available to members before they voted. Rep. Leon E. Panetta, D-Calif., who as chairman of the Budget Committee's reconciliation task force probably knew more than other members about the details and ground rules of reconciliation, told his colleagues: "The fact is, we are rolling the dice with the lives of millions of Americans. Whether they are children, the elderly, the poor, or farmers, whether it is rural areas or urban areas, we do not know what we are doing in terms of impacting on those Americans."

After reconciliation was completed, many predicted it would never again be used in that way. Some also predicted there would be attempts to reform the budget process to cut back the power of both the process and the Budget committees.

Meanwhile, Congress turned its attention to the individual appropriations bills for fiscal 1982 — and found itself in the same old dilemma. Once legislators began to consider spending levels for individual programs, they were again subject to the same constituent and special interest pressures that had caused them to increase spending for those programs in the past. On the other side was President Reagan who had called for a 12 percent decrease from his original budget proposals for all but national security programs.

By mid-November, Congress had cleared only one appropriations bill — funding for the legislative branch itself, a bill that was seldom subject to anyone's budget ax. House and Senate appropriations totals for the remaining 12 regular fiscal 1982 funding bills exceeded President Reagan's requests in almost every instance. In the face of Reagan's threat to "veto any bill that abuses the limited resources of the taxpayers," Congress had slowed action on those appropriations measures.

That meant that virtually every federal program would be funded under a continuing appropriations resolution for at least part of fiscal 1982.

That device had been designed to permit Congress some way of continuing funding for those programs for which new appropriations had not yet been enacted. Spending for each program usually was limited to the lower of the House- or Senate-passed appropriations bill or to the conference agreement amount. If neither chamber had passed an appropriation, the amount usually was limited to the previous year's level or the president's request. No new program could be funded unless Congress specifically permitted it.

Should the resolution apply to most federal spending for an entire fiscal year, Congress in large part would have given up setting priorities for use of federal funds. "Simply put," said Sen. Gary Hart, D-Colo., Nov. 16, "Congress surrendered its budgetary independence from the executive branch."

Whether the balance of power for shaping the budget had tipped permanently toward the president was one of many questions raised by the 1981 debate over federal spending. Others concerned the mechanics of the process itself. Some thought that adjustments — such as converting the system to two-year, rather than one-year, appropriations — might give Congress breathing space to get a new grasp on its constitutional responsibilities.

On a broader scale, it could be asked whether either Congress or the president, even a strong one with popular support, could bring about spending reductions sufficient to slow the growth of government. Spending decisions are made in a political context and decisions to cut spending mean that some groups of people will no longer receive what they once did. David A. Stockman, director of the Office of Management and Budget and Reagan's chief budget architect, made an observation about the federal budget process that few would dispute. The budget, Stockman said in an interview printed in *The Atlantic Monthly*, "isn't something you reconstruct each year. The budget is a sort of rolling history of decisions. All kinds of decisions, made five, ten, fifteen years ago, are coming back to bite us unexpectedly. Therefore, in my judgment, it will take three or four or five years to subdue it. Whether anyone can maintain the political momentum to fight the beast for that long, I don't know."

2

Economic Legacy

The 1980s opened with an upheaval in U.S. economic policy as dramatic as any since the Great Depression of the 1930s. Elected in the first year of this new decade by an impressive majority, President Ronald Reagan mounted the most serious assault on federal spending and tax policies in nearly 50 years.

The post-World-War-II era had seen a steady expansion of the size and role of the federal government. Widespread unemployment during the Depression had shaken the confidence of Americans in their own economy. Out of that experience, and the remarkable economic prosperity that resulted from the government-led war effort of the 1940s, there had emerged a postwar consensus that the government should play a central role in the nation's economic life.

"From our earliest days we had a tradition of substantial government help to our system of private enterprise," said President Franklin D. Roosevelt, who more than any other leader moved the federal government from the sidelines to the center of economic activity. "It is following tradition as well as necessity if government strives to put idle money and idle men to work, to increase our public wealth and to build up the health and strength of the people — and to help our system of private enterprise to function."

It was that philosophy that Reagan directly challenged. The decade of the 1970s, which had brought both severe inflation and uncomfortably high unemployment, had undermined the confidence of the American people in the ability of the government to protect their economic well-being. "The people have not created this disaster in our economy," Reagan said in announcing his candidacy for president in 1979. "The federal government has. It has outspent, overestimated, and overregulated. It has failed to deliver services within the revenues it should be allowed to raise from taxes."

Later, after his election, the new president hit directly at the postwar belief that government intervention could prime the economy to a better performance. The American economic system, he said, "has never failed us." But we have failed it "through a lack of confidence and sometimes through a belief that we could fine-tune the economy and get a tune to our liking."

Reagan promised to cut back the federal government by sharply reducing federal spending, especially for domestic social programs. He also set out to cut taxes substantially, in the process halting the liberal trend toward putting a relatively greater tax burden on the well-to-do. At the same time, the new president embarked on a substantial military buildup.

All of these policies were consistent with the conservative ideology Reagan had been preaching since at least 1964, when he burst onto the national scene with an eloquent speech endorsing the presidential candidacy of Arizona Sen. Barry Goldwater.

But while Goldwater lost by a landslide, Reagan won overwhelmingly. The dramatic turn in conservative fortunes over the 16 years was due at least in part to the public view that traditional economic policies, both liberal and conservative, had failed. Tapping this mood, Reagan sought to engineer his sharp rightward turn in American policy on the basis of a novel theory called "supply-side" economics. Though largely untested, this theory gave conservatism a new appeal in the 1970s because it promised to offer an alternative to the increasingly unattractive implications of conventional economic ideas.

Supply-side theorists challenged the basic assumption of postwar economic policy, which had focused on controlling the demand for goods and services, rather than the supply.

Following the teachings of the British economist John Maynard Keynes, postwar policy was designed largely to eliminate unemployment. Keynes argued that joblessness results from inadequate "demand," which in turn reflects insufficient income in the hands of consumers. The Keynesian remedy for this problem is to increase demand, either by cutting taxes or increasing spending. Once people start spending their additional income, Keynesians said, the demand for goods and services will rise, production will increase and the unemployed will be offered jobs.

The focus of Keynesian theory on unemployment is not surprising; it was born during the 1930s, when joblessness was a chronic problem. Later, when inflation also came to be recognized as an economic worry, Keynes' successors said demand-oriented policies could correct that too.

They argued that, just as unemployment occurs when demand falls short of the economy's productive capacity, inflation results when demand *exceeds* economic capacity. If everybody is producing as much as they can, increasing

5

incomes merely compel consumers to bid up the prices for the limited quantity of goods and services that can be produced, according to this theory. The Keynesian cure for inflation is thus to restrain purchasing power, either by cutting back government spending or raising taxes, until demand again comes into line with supply.

Policy makers found in the 1950s and later that it was not easy to strike a perfect balance between unemployment and inflation. Policies to cure one of those economic ills generally produced at least some of the other. Much of the history of postwar economic policy consisted of a debate over what the balance between the two should be.

Conservatives generally were willing to accept a higher level of unemployment to keep prices stable. That fit with the conservative belief that the economy tends to stabilize itself at a high level of employment anyway. Conservatives argued that there is a "natural" rate of joblessness. Some people simply choose not to work, and efforts to eliminate all unemployment are thus futile, they said.

Liberals, on the other hand, could not accept the notion that some degree of unemployment is voluntary. They argued that the private economy does not automatically perform to its full capacity, and that government policies to assure full employment are much more important than perfect price stability.

While the political winds shifted back and forth during the postwar period, the expansive spirit prevailed much of the time, especially after 1960. Presidents and Congress generally found it easier to pursue policies that were likely to result in inflation than to risk producing the social conflict that comes with high unemployment. That may be because unemployment, though it usually affects fewer people, causes more severe hardship than fairly modest inflation spread out among most people. "Inflation has served as a vent for distributional strife, an escape hatch through which excess demands are automatically channelled," wrote analyst Fred Hirsch.

Successes and Failures

Postwar economic policy succeeded to an impressive degree in tempering recessions and unemployment. Earlier, from 1854 to 1937, business activity expansions lasted an average of 26 months, while the average recession ran 22 months. But from 1945 to 1975 expansions averaged 49 months and recessions only 10 months. The economy spent only 17 percent of the time in recession from 1945 to 1975, compared with 46 percent in the earlier period. It was on the basis of that experience that postwar economists proclaimed that activist government policy had "tamed" the business cycle.

The postwar experience with inflation, however, was a dramatic contrast to that good record. Prices had been remarkably stable prior to World War II. The consumer price level in 1940, for instance, was no higher than the price level in 1778. But the price level in 1980 was more than 400 percent above the 1940 level.

In part, the miserable record of postwar policy on inflation undoubtedly reflects the greater stress the government placed on fighting unemployment during much of the period. In addition, the government sometimes found itself politically unable to use the policies necessary to restrain demand and thus curb inflation.

In most cases, the failure reflected a political reluctance to take purchasing power away from the American public. Other times it resulted from a deadlock between

liberals and conservatives over what to sacrifice in the interest of restraint or over whether to brake the economy by raising taxes or cutting spending. Even when restraint was applied, the public reaction was usually so negative that policy makers were unable to hold the reins long enough to slow inflation.

By the late 1970s, the nation found it increasingly difficult to strike a politically acceptable balance between unemployment and inflation. Rapid inflation had become deeply engrained in the economy, and it resisted conventional methods to defeat it at acceptable political cost. It appeared increasingly that demand restraint would bring inflation down only at the cost of high and sustained joblessness. At the same time, soaring energy prices and a perplexing slowdown in productivity threatened to prevent the rapid economic growth and resulting low unemployment that Keynesian policies were designed to promote.

"The new reality...is the re-emergence during the 1970s of the economics of scarcity — a progressive imbalance between the demands we have been placing on our economy and our capacity to satisfy them," wrote Alfred Kahn, a Cornell University professor who served as President Jimmy Carter's chief inflation adviser.

The inflation of the 1970s had some elements of traditional Keynesian "excess demand" in it. But much of the problem related to the supply side of the economic equation, which demand-oriented policies were ill-equipped to cure. Moreover, most economists of the Keynesian persuasion warned that the solutions to the supply-side problems involved sacrifices that would not pay off for some time.

Keynesians argued, for instance, that the nation had to limit its current level of consumption so that it could afford to invest in new factories and equipment that would permit more efficient production. That meant sacrificing in the short term. "There is no way we can avoid a decline in our standard of living," Kahn said in 1979. "All we can do is adapt to it."

Few politicians enjoy carrying such a message to the public. "To materially reduce standards of living as compelled by low productivity is unthinkable for a Democratic government in peacetime," declared Sen. Jacob K. Javits, R-N.Y. (1957-81), in 1979.

"It is not clear," said economist Robert Solow of the Massachusetts Institute of Technology, "that our political process can deal with solutions whose horizon for success might be 10 years away."

'Supply-Side' Economics

The new supply-side theoreticians claimed they had a way out of the apparent economic impasse. While Keynesian policies cure inflation by reducing demand — a course that sounded to many a lot like accepting a lower standard of living — the supply-siders said they could curb inflation by quickly increasing supply. The key, they said, is to reduce taxes and thus increase the incentives to produce.

The supply-siders disputed the Keynesian notion that once the government maintains an adequate level of demand, supply will be assured. The supply-siders said that people produce not merely in response to demand, but to increase their own income.

The fulcrum of economic activity, according to supply-siders, is the marginal rate of taxation, the rate on the last dollar earned. People continually are deciding between work and leisure, and between saving and consumption. The higher the marginal tax rate, the less incentive a

Key U.S. Economic Statistics, 1929-80

Year	Gross National Product[1]		Percent Change in GNP[2]		GNP Deflator[3] (1972=100)	Unemployment Rate[4] (Percent)	Consumer Price Index (1967=100)
	Current Dollars	1972 Dollars	Current Dollars	1972 Dollars			
1929	103.4	315.7	—	—	32.76	3.2	51.3
1933	55.8	222.1	−4.2	−2.2	25.13	24.9	38.8
1939	90.9	319.8	7.0	7.8	28.43	17.2	41.6
1940	100.0	344.1	10.0	7.6	29.06	14.6	42.0
1945	212.4	560.4	0.9	−1.5	37.91	1.9	53.9
1950	286.5	534.8	10.9	8.7	53.56	5.3	72.1
1955	400.0	657.5	9.0	6.7	60.84	4.4	80.2
1960	506.5	737.2	3.8	2.2	68.70	5.5	88.7
1965	691.1	929.3	8.4	6.0	74.36	4.5	94.5
1970	992.7	1,085.6	5.2	−0.2	91.45	4.9	116.3
1971	1,077.6	1,122.4	8.6	3.4	96.01	5.9	121.3
1972	1,185.9	1,185.9	10.1	5.7	100.00	5.6	125.3
1973	1,326.4	1,255.0	11.8	5.8	105.69	4.9	133.1
1974	1,434.2	1,248.0	8.1	−0.6	114.92	5.6	147.7
1975	1,549.2	1,233.9	8.0	−1.1	125.56	8.5	161.2
1976	1,718.0	1,300.4	10.9	5.4	132.11	7.7	170.5
1977	1,918.0	1,371.7	11.6	5.5	139.83	7.0	181.5
1978	2,156.1	1,436.9	12.4	4.8	150.05	6.0	195.4
1979	2,413.9	1,483.0	12.0	3.2	162.77	5.8	217.4
1980[5]	2,627.4	1,480.7	8.8	−0.2	177.45	7.1	246.8

[1] Billion dollars

[2] Percent change from preceding year

[3] The GNP deflator is the ratio of the GNP in current prices to the GNP in constant dollars.

[4] Percent of civilian labor force

[5] Preliminary figures

Source: Department of Commerce, Bureau of Economic Analysis; Department of Labor, Bureau of Labor Statistics

person has to work rather than be idle, or to save rather than consume, they contended. By reducing marginal tax rates, supply-siders concluded, the government can encourage more work and saving, in the process increasing income and economic well-being.

Reagan economists said the effects of a cut in marginal tax rates would be felt by people at all levels of income. But they also argued that the cut in marginal rates would be effective because the biggest benefits would go to people in the upper income brackets, who can afford to save and invest more.

Tax cuts that redistribute income to poor people are more likely to increase consumption because people in low tax brackets cannot afford to save, they said.

Liberals said that argument merely rationalized a program designed to benefit the well-to-do. But Reagan replied that the nation had grown tired of Democratic programs designed to redistribute income. "The taxing power of government must be used to provide revenues for legitimate government purposes," he said. "It must not be used to regulate the economy or bring about social change."

The 'Laffer Curve'

Modern supply-side thinking emerged basically in the thinking of two economists — Arthur Laffer of the University of Southern California and Robert Mundell of Columbia University. Their ideas captured the attention of Jude Wanniski, then an editorial writer at *The Wall Street Journal*. Wanniski, in turn, found an avid learner in Republican Rep. Jack Kemp of New York, who caught the ear of Reagan early in the 1980 presidential campaign.

Laffer's main contribution was the "Laffer curve." It was based on the proposition that the government would not take in any tax revenues if the tax rate is zero. Similarly, the government would not collect any taxes if the tax rate is 100 percent because people would have no incentive to earn income.

From that Laffer concluded that there must be a point at which tax rates get so high that they discourage work, in turn retarding the growth of supply, reducing income and thus actually reducing the government's revenues. Laffer argued that U.S. taxes had become so high they were starting to have this bad effect.

Components of Gross National Product, 1940-80

In billion dollars

Year	Gross National Product		Personal Consumption Expenditures	Government Purchases of Goods and Services	Gross Private Domestic Investment	Net Exports of Goods and Services
	Current Dollars	1972 Dollars				
1940	$ 100	$ 344	$ 71	$ 14	$ 13	$ 2
1941	125	400	81	25	18	2
1942	159	462	89	60	10	0.2
1943	192	532	99	89	6	−2
1944	211	569	108	97	7	−2
1945	212	560	120	83	11	−0.5
1946	210	478	144	28	31	8
1947	233	470	162	26	34	12
1948	260	490	175	32	46	7
1949	258	492	178	38	35	7
1950	287	535	192	39	54	2
1951	331	579	207	60	59	4
1952	348	601	217	76	52	3
1953	367	624	230	83	53	1
1954	367	616	236	76	53	3
1955	400	658	254	75	68	3
1956	422	672	266	80	71	5
1957	444	684	281	87	69	7
1958	450	681	290	95	62	3
1959	488	722	311	98	78	1
1960	507	737	325	100	76	6
1961	525	757	335	108	75	7
1962	565	800	355	118	85	6
1963	597	833	375	124	91	8
1964	638	876	401	130	97	10
1965	691	929	430	138	114	9
1966	756	985	465	159	126	7
1967	800	1,011	490	180	123	6
1968	873	1,058	537	199	133	4
1969	944	1,088	582	209	149	4
1970	993	1,086	622	220	144	7
1971	1,078	1,122	672	235	166	4
1972	1,186	1,186	737	253	195	1
1973	1,326	1,255	812	270	230	14
1974	1,434	1,248	888	304	229	13
1975	1,549	1,234	976	340	206	27
1976	1,718	1,300	1,084	362	258	14
1977	1,918	1,372	1,206	395	322	−4
1978	2,156	1,437	1,349	433	375	−1
1979	2,414	1,483	1,511	474	416	13
1980	2,627	1,481	1,670	535	395	28

Source: Department of Commerce, Bureau of Economic Analysis

Laffer theorized that the government might never be able to balance the budget by raising taxes, but that a tax cut could spur so much economic growth that revenues would actually rise to balance the budget.

That approach to budget matters had a politically liberating effect on Republicans, who traditionally had placed top priority on balancing the budget. Although Republican Presidents Eisenhower, Nixon and Ford did acquiesce to deficit spending to stimulate the economy during recessions, they sought at other times to achieve surpluses. When inflation appeared to be the biggest threat, their belief in budget surpluses was even stronger.

Kemp argued that Republican devotion to balanced budgets had cost the party repeated electoral defeats. "As Republicans, we must rid ourselves of the perceived political idolatry of balanced budgets," Kemp said. "Republicans must not be bookkeepers for Democratic deficits."

The same idea was also advanced by Irving Kristol, another conservative thinker. "When in office, liberals. . .will always spend generously, regardless of budgetary considerations, until the public permits the conservatives an interregnum in which to clean up the mess — but with liberals retaining their status as the activist party, the party of the 'natural majority,'" Kristol wrote. "The neo-conservatives have decided that two can play at this game — and must, since it is the only game in town. . . .They vigorously advocate [increased defense spending and] tax cuts, with the budget remaining a secondary consideration."

Doubts

Not surprisingly, liberals scoffed at the economic reasoning behind supply-side economics. "Never have so many gambled so much on the basis of so little economic evidence," said Jeremy J. Stone in the liberal *Journal of the Federation of American Scientists*. Economist Lester Thurow warned that Reagan's desire to cut taxes while expanding the nation's military power would "wreck the economy."

Liberals argued that there is little evidence to support the supply-siders' claim that their tax cut would promptly increase economic output without boosting demand. "An across-the-board tax cut is a Keynesian remedy," declared Thurow. "The only thing President Reagan has done is rehabilitate it by calling it 'supply-side.'"

Still torn between fighting inflation and unemployment, liberals were deeply divided over the wisdom of tax cuts in the late 1970s. Those who remained unwilling to fight inflation by increasing unemployment supported instead a tax cut to bolster economic activity, although they doubted such a cut would cure inflation. Others, convinced that inflation had become the nation's biggest problem and that other approaches to curing it had failed, reluctantly resisted cutting taxes.

Criticism of the Reagan approach did not come only from liberals. George Bush, who ran against Reagan and later became his vice president, reflected mainstream Republican thinking during the 1980 campaign, dismissing Reagan's economic proposals as "voodoo economics."

Herbert Stein, who had served as President Nixon's top economic adviser, was more sympathetic, but he still called the Reagan mix of policies "the sharpest change in economic policy since the time of Franklin Roosevelt."

Whether the new conservative doctrine could in fact accomplish its goal remained highly uncertain in late 1981.

But it was clear that supply-side economics had given conservatism more political appeal than it had managed to gain in a generation.

The Role of Monetary Policy

Reagan and the supply-siders adopted one other set of economic ideas that had been outside the mainstream of economic thinking for much of the postwar period — namely, monetarism.

Developed by conservative economist Milton Friedman, monetarism holds that economic stability can be assured simply by holding the rate of growth in the supply of money to the growth rate of the actual economy. That view challenges the assumption of many economists that government can influence income — and thus economic activity — by changing the supply of money, just as it influences income via fiscal policy.

During much of the postwar period, most economists believed that the government could spur economic growth, and thus reduce unemployment, by increasing the money supply. That is because a larger supply of money tends to reduce interest rates, which are basically the cost of money. Lower interest rates encourage investment, which in turn leads to faster economic growth, the theory goes.

Similarly, a decrease in the supply of money is believed to slow the economy by driving interest rates up and discouraging investment. The resulting slowdown in economic activity would then ease inflation.

The Federal Reserve

Monetary policy is set by the Federal Reserve, the nation's central bank. The Fed can influence the money supply through a variety of methods, but its key device is "open market operations," the buying and selling of government securities.

If the Fed wants to increase the money supply, it buys government securities from banks. That puts new cash in the hands of the banks, which they in turn can then lend out. Conversely, if the Fed wants to cut the money supply back, it sells government securities, thus draining cash out of the banking system.

(The Fed can also influence the money supply by directly changing the amount of reserves the banks hold. Increasing the level of mandatory reserves reduces the amount of money in circulation; decreasing the amount of reserves adds to the sums available in the economy.)

It has been widely accepted during the postwar period that monetary policy should be set separately from fiscal policy. Otherwise, the government could simply decide to create more money to pay for its deficits — a practice that obviously would undermine the value of the currency.

"To oversimply only slightly, the question is whether the principal office in charge of paying the government's bills should be entrusted also with the power to create the money to pay them," explained William McChesney Martin Jr., chairman of the Federal Reserve Board in 1964. To be effective, Martin said, monetary management "should be insulated so far as possible from private pressures just as much as political pressures. . ."

The Monetarist View of Inflation

Monetarists concede that fluctuations in the money supply can affect income over the short run, but they contend that income is determined by actual economic output over the long run. When the supply of money rises faster than output, the value of each dollar has to decline because there is more money available to buy relatively fewer goods, they argue. "Inflation," according to Friedman, "is always and everywhere a monetary phenomenon."

Monetarists concede that government surpluses can slow the economy and deficits can accelerate it in the short run. But they say neither surpluses nor deficits have any impact on growth or inflation over time. Instead, they merely influence the mix of public and private spending in the economy.

While generally considered a conservative doctrine, monetarism parts with many postwar theories in rejecting the claim that deficits are inflationary. Deficits cause inflation only if the government increases the supply of money to prevent government borrowing from driving up interest rates, monetarists contend.

"Ongoing inflation is a monetary phenomenon and deficits stimulate inflation only when they are monetized consistently by the Federal Reserve," declared Beryl Sprinkel, Reagan's Treasury under secretary for monetary affairs.

By embracing monetarism, President Reagan put most of the burden for controlling inflation on the Federal Reserve and managed to alleviate some fears within his own party that a large tax cut would be inflationary.

Non-monetarists warned that Reagan's expansive approach to fiscal policy would collide with a monetary policy designed to wring inflation out of the economy. They predicted that the tax cut would require increased federal borrowing to finance the deficit at the same time that a tight money policy by the Fed would diminish the amount of funds available for borrowing. The federal government would thus be a major competitor for a shrinking supply of savings, with the result that interest rates would skyrocket and investment would be retarded, they said.

In 1980 and again in 1981, interest rates did reach the almost unimaginable level of 20 percent. But monetarists said that jump merely reflected fears among investors that the administration would not stick to its anti-inflation monetary policy. Once the public became convinced that the administration would not be swayed, interest rates would fall, they said.

In the meantime, the need to reduce federal competition for limited supplies of credit added to pressures to cut federal spending. Although the Reagan administration was not happy about high interest rates, it did endorse such pressures. The president believed he had a strong mandate to cut social benefit programs, which had accelerated enormously since the mid-1960s.

Kemp and David A. Stockman, Reagan's budget director, complained in 1980 that the federal budget had become "an automatic coast-to-coast soup line that dispenses remedial aid with almost reckless abandon." That sentiment evidently struck a responsive chord with an American public facing the threat of economic stagnation and declining living standards.

"It is unlikely that Congress would have enacted the myriad of transfer payment liberalizations if it had foreseen the apparent resentment of non-beneficiaries," wrote Brookings Institution economist Robert Hartman.

Monetarism had one other important implication for Reagan economic policies. In keeping with the monetarist idea, Reagan argued that the Federal Reserve should pursue a steady monetary policy rather than one designed to counterbalance economic trends. The new administration's recommendation that monetary policy be constant rather than countercyclical mirrored its call for an end to "stop-and-go" fiscal policies.

In embracing monetarism and rejecting the idea that fiscal policy should be countercyclical, Reagan did much to restore the "classical economics" that had prevailed before the 1930s Depression ushered in Keynesian theory.

NEW FEDERAL ROLE: KEYNES TO EISENHOWER

Before Keynes, economists generally viewed the economy as a self-adjusting mechanism that naturally tended to provide full employment. That happy result was produced by the free workings of wages and prices, which were thought to balance supply and demand.

Under this "classical" view, if workers are unemployed (because the supply of workers exceeds the demand for them), wages will fall. Lower wages in turn will make it profitable for business to hire more workers, and unemployment thus will be eliminated. Similarly, prices rise and fall according to demand, so that everything that is produced is consumed.

Interest rates play a key role in classical theory. Analysts believed that they assure a balance between savings and investment, and thus guarantee that whenever people choose to increase the amount of money they set aside there will not be a drop in economic activity.

Under classical theory, an increase in the amount of money people save expands the supply of money available for investment. That in turn reduces the price investors have to pay for money, which is the interest rate. But a drop in interest rates increases investment incentive so that higher investment takes the place of laggard consumer spending in assuring that economic activity continues at a pace guaranteeing full employment.

Classical economics explains recessions as part of the economy's inherent self-adjusting abilities. During boom periods, the classical economists argued, prices or wages sometimes accelerate more quickly than is justified by the underlying relationship of supply and demand. Recessions reduce demand, and thus bring them back into line.

Recessions also were thought to occur when the supply of money gets out of line with the demand for it. If the supply of money falls short of what people want at full employment, it was believed there would be a temporary decline in economic activity, forcing prices to decline. But the drop in prices causes a given amount of money to rise in value, restoring production to its natural state of full employment.

The Depression shattered the confident optimism of classical economics. For the decade of the 1930s, an average of 18 percent of the work force was unemployed. In 1933 the jobless rate totaled 24.9 percent. Seven years after the onset of the Depression, in 1936, 16.9 percent of the labor force — nine million people — were still out of work. Those statistics raised serious doubts about the validity of the view that the free-market behavior of wages and prices can assure economic self-adjustment and full employment.

Keynesian Economics

In 1936 Keynes offered an explanation for why the economy appeared stuck in a condition far short of full employment. The explanation, he said, lies in fluctuations in income, not prices, wages or interest rates.

Keynes noted that people's incomes decline when wages drop because of unemployment. As people lose income, demand falls and production gets cut back. That in turn leads to more layoffs, causing income and then demand to drop further in a frightening downward spiral.

Keynes said the classical economists were wrong to assume that interest rates could come to the rescue in such a situation. He argued that interest rates might never drop low enough to prompt the level of investment needed to start the economy growing again.

Interest rates, he explained, represent the price people receive for exchanging cash for other kinds of assets, such as bonds. Because cash is preferable to other kinds of assets, there is a "floor" for interest rates below which people will be unwilling to exchange their cash for securities, he said.

Keynes concluded that using monetary policy to increase the supply of money and drive interest rates down is like pushing on a string. It won't necessarily bring the economy out of a recession, he argued, because it won't necessarily increase investment.

Moreover, he warned that a drop in incomes could cause savings to dry up so there would be no money available for investment in any case. And he also noted that businesses would be reluctant to invest anyway if consumer income is so diminished that people might be unable to buy whatever is produced.

Keynes' theory suggested that the economy could fall into a recession and stay there. In such circumstances, Keynes said, the only way back to full employment is for the government to bolster consumer purchasing power enough to guarantee sufficient demand. The rub, according to Keynesians, is that the government cannot add to consumer demand if it insists on balancing the budget.

A balanced budget requires that any income pumped into the consumer sector through higher federal spending or lower taxes be offset by the higher taxes or lower spending. Thus, to increase income, government has to incur a deficit.

In Keynes' view, President Hoover made a terrible mistake in 1931 by pushing for a big tax increase to balance the budget despite a painfully high level of unemployment. The tax increase merely reduced already low income further, compounding the economy's weakness, according to Keynes.

Keynes and FDR

During the 1930s, Keynes repeatedly urged President Roosevelt to spend the economy out of the Depression. "The notion that, if the government would retire altogether from the economic field, business, left to itself, would soon work out its own salvation, is, to my mind, foolish," he said in 1934. "I conclude, therefore, that for six months at least, and probably a year, the measure of recovery to be achieved will mainly depend on the degree of the direct stimulus to production deliberately applied by the administration."

President Roosevelt never fully embraced Keynes' ideas, but he did increase government spending to help

U.S. Budget, 1929-82: A Long History of Deficits

Current billion dollars

Fiscal Year	Receipts	Outlays	Surplus or Deficit (−)
1929	3.9	3.1	0.7
1933	2.0	4.6	− 2.6
1939	5.0	8.8	− 3.9
1940	6.4	9.5	− 3.1
1945	45.2	92.7	−47.5
1950	39.5	42.6	− 3.1
1955	65.5	68.5	− 3.0
1960	92.5	92.2	0.3
1965	116.8	118.4	− 1.6
1970	193.7	196.6	− 2.8
1971	188.4	211.4	−23.0
1972	208.6	232.0	−23.4
1973	232.2	247.1	−14.8
1974	265.0	269.6	− 4.7
1975	281.0	326.2	−45.2
1976	300.0	266.4	−66.4
Transition quarter[1]	81.8	94.7	−13.0
1977	357.8	402.7	−44.9
1978	402.0	450.8	−48.8
1979	465.9	493.6	−27.7
1980	520.1	579.6	−59.5
1981	602.6	660.5	−57.9
1982[2]	662.4	704.8	−52.5

[1] *Under the 1974 Congressional Budget Act, the fiscal year for the federal government shifted beginning with fiscal 1977. Through fiscal 1976, the fiscal year was on a July 1-June 30 basis; since Oct. 1976, the fiscal year runs from Oct. 1-Sept. 30. The period from July 1, 1976, through Sept. 30, 1976, is a separate fiscal period.*

[2] *1982 estimates are from President Reagan's* Mid Session Review of the 1982 Budget, *July 1981, Office of Management and Budget.*

Source: Department of the Treasury, Office of Management and Budget, and Council of Economic Advisers

offset the economic hardship caused by the Depression. Federal outlays had edged up to $4.6 billion in 1933 from $3.1 billion in 1929. But due to unemployment relief and a variety of other public works projects, they rose to $6.6 billion in 1934, and to $8.4 billion in 1936.

Still, although the economy did climb out of its Depression lows by the end of the 1930s, it failed to approach anything like full employment. Some believed that was because President Roosevelt was never willing to apply the full dose of deficit spending needed to restore consumer demand. At least through the middle years of the decade, the president remained hopeful that he could balance the federal budget.

More conservative analysts argued that the economy did not recover fully because business investment was stifled by the growth of government during the New Deal. Left to its own devices, these conservatives contended, business investment eventually would have recovered. But, they said, New Deal intrusion of the government into the private sector had the ironic consequence of stifling business and thus preventing the private economy from getting back on its feet.

That was a debate that would recur throughout the postwar period. In any event, in 1939, after more than a decade of depression and stagnation, 9.5 million Americans (more than 17 percent of the labor force) were still unemployed.

Legacy of the War

World War II abruptly pulled the economy out of its Depression doldrums. Federal expenditures skyrocketed, from $8.8 billion in 1939 to $92.7 billion in 1945. Between 1940 and 1944, when government expenditures accounted for one-half of total output, gross national product more than doubled. And by 1944 unemployment had dropped to a mere 670,000, or about 1 percent of the work force.

The sharp contrast between prewar stagnation and wartime prosperity had a profound effect on public perceptions of the role of government in the economy. Full employment —jobs for everyone able and willing to work — became, according to Herbert Stein, the "flag around which everyone could rally." In *The Fiscal Revolution in America*, Stein explained:

> One important lesson of the war was that the benefits of full employment were not confined to those persons who had previously been unemployed. Aside from the direct effects of military service, everyone, or almost everyone, was better off than he had ever been before. Although current consumption had not increased for many and had decreased for some, incomes after tax were very much higher, even after discount for higher prices, and the prospect of incomes at wartime levels without wartime taxes was dizzying. It was not only incomes that full employment provided; it was also opportunity and mobility and freedom of many kinds. Therefore the idea spread that full employment was the important and essential means to deliver what every group wanted for itself and had been seeking by other more limited means. Full employment became the first plank in programs to assist and adjust agriculture. It became the necessary condition, even before tax reform, for reviving business profits and investment opportunities. It became the way to invigorate competition by creating conditions favorable to starting and building new enterprises. It became the surest route to raising incomes of workers, not only by assuring them employment, but also by stimulating their training and upgrading.

The war had more direct economic results as well. The massive conversion of the economy to the war effort created an enormous backlog of demand for business and consumer goods. In addition, extensive federal borrowing to finance the war, combined with the limited supply of consumer goods, left consumers holding large amounts of savings in the form of government securities and bank deposits. That guaranteed consumers would have the means to pay for such goods.

Those forces produced a postwar economic boom. But before the end of the war, that outcome was far from taken for granted. Instead, many analysts feared that demobilization would result in a rise in unemployment and a return to the stagnant conditions of the 1930s.

Policy makers were committed to prevent that economic nightmare from occurring. As early as 1942, the National Resources Planning Board had called "imperative" the development of a "positive program of postwar economic expansion and full employment, boldly conceived and vigorously pursued." In 1944 President Roosevelt endorsed that goal, declaring that every American had "the right to a useful and remunerative job."

The Goal of Full Employment

Congress took up the question of how to assure that right in 1946. The Employment Act of 1946 established the basic framework in which postwar fiscal policy was to be debated.

At the outset, advocates of an aggressive federal program to guarantee full employment proposed that Congress enact a "Full Employment" act committing the federal government to "stimulate and encourage the highest feasible levels" of private investment and spending. To the extent that the private sector failed to provide full employment, they said the government should be required to "provide such volume of federal investment and expenditure as would be needed to assure continuing full employment."

The policy was to be carried out through a "national production and employment budget," which would estimate private investment and propose federal spending to fill any gap between private investment and "full employment."

Conservative critics of the bill complained that "full employment" was impossible to define. And even if it could be defined, they said, it would be impossible to achieve without causing inflation, or at least leading the government to impose wage and price controls. Many of the critics feared that the bill would be used to authorize continual deficit spending. Others complained that it placed too much power in the hands of the president.

After considerable debate, Congress approved a bill that was much less ambitious than its original sponsors had intended.

Gone was the commitment to provide "full employment." The law was renamed simply The Employment Act of 1946. Instead of committing the government to policies to achieve full employment, the law merely gave it the responsibility "to use all practicable means consistent with its needs and obligations and other essential considerations of national policy" to promote "maximum employment, production and purchasing power."

The final version of the act also dropped the notion that the federal budget was to be the prime tool for accomplishing "maximum" employment. Instead, the law simply directed the president to submit an annual economic report — separate from his budget recommendations — on how he intended to achieve the goals of the act. The report was to be prepared by a Council of Economic Advisers, whose three members were to be confirmed by the Senate.

Some conservatives had attempted during the debate on the employment act to include the achievement of "price stability" among the economic responsibilities of the federal government. They were unsuccessful. By inference, the final version of the act assigned greater importance to achieving a low unemployment rate than to maintaining price stability, although it did acknowledge "other essential considerations of national policy."

Truman and Demobilization

When he signed the employment act on Feb. 20, 1946, President Truman described it as "not the end of the road, but rather the beginning." The act, he said, represented a "commitment" by the government "to take any and all of the measures necessary for a healthy economy."

Initially, those measures did not include federal deficit spending to make up for a weak private sector. In a combined State of the Union and budget message on Jan. 21, President Truman already had warned: "Inflation is our greatest immediate domestic problem."

Confounding some pessimistic projections, the economy made a remarkably smooth transition to a peacetime footing. A drastic drop in federal spending (from a peak annual rate of $91 billion in the first quarter of 1945 to $26 billion in the first quarter of 1946) had only a moderately depressing effect on the economy. Rising business and consumer purchases offset about two-thirds of the decrease. Moreover, unemployment did not rise as much as had been anticipated because some 4.3 million workers withdrew from the labor force, leaving room for newly discharged GIs.

President Truman's fears of inflation were based on at least two factors. First, pent-up demand clearly exceeded supply, putting strong upward pressures on prices. That problem was aggravated by shortages of some materials, a rising tide of strikes and some cases of withholding of goods in protest against the continuation of wartime price controls.

In addition, price controls had prevented prices from rising in tandem with the supply of money during the war. As a result, there was a greater supply of money relative to the available goods than there had been before the war. That

U.S. Employment and Unemployment, 1929-80

Civilian labor force

Thousands of persons of working age*

Year	Total Civilian Labor Force	Employment	Unemployment	Unemployment Rate (Percent)
1929	49,180	47,630	1,550	3.2
1933	51,590	38,760	12,830	24.9
1939	55,230	45,750	9,480	17.2
1940	55,640	47,520	8,120	14.6
1945	53,860	52,820	1,040	1.9
1950	62,208	58,918	3,288	5.3
1951	62,017	59,961	2,055	3.3
1952	62,138	60,250	1,883	3.0
1953	63,015	61,179	1,834	2.9
1954	63,643	60,109	3,532	5.5
1955	65,023	62,170	2,852	4.4
1956	66,552	63,799	2,750	4.1
1957	66,929	64,071	2,859	4.3
1958	67,639	63,036	4,602	6.8
1959	68,369	64,630	3,740	5.5
1960	69,628	65,778	3,825	5.5
1961	70,459	65,746	4,714	6.7
1962	70,614	66,702	3,911	5.5
1963	71,133	67,762	4,070	5.7
1964	73,091	69,305	3,786	5.2
1965	74,455	71,088	3,366	4.5
1966	75,770	72,895	2,875	3.8
1967	77,347	74,372	2,975	3.8
1968	78,737	75,920	2,817	3.6
1969	80,734	77,902	2,832	3.5
1970	82,715	78,627	4,088	4.9
1971	84,113	79,120	4,993	5.9
1972	86,542	81,702	4,840	5.6
1973	88,714	84,409	4,304	4.9
1974	91,011	85,935	5,076	5.6
1975	92,613	84,783	7,830	8.5
1976	94,773	87,485	7,288	7.7
1977	97,401	90,546	6,855	7.0
1978	100,420	94,373	6,047	6.0
1979	102,908	96,945	5,963	5.8
1980	104,719	97,270	7,448	7.1

Before 1947, figures include persons 14 years of age and over; after 1947, figures are for 16 years and over.

Source: Department of Labor, Bureau of Labor Statistics

meant that the "real," or inflation-adjusted, value of money had declined. In retrospect, economists believe that once wartime price controls were removed a jump in the price level to correct this imbalance was inevitable.

That is what occurred when all remaining price and wage controls except for ceilings on rents, sugar and rice were eliminated on Nov. 9, 1949.

President Truman tried to fight the upward surge of prices in a variety of ways. He appealed to business and labor groups to exercise price and wage restraint. When that failed to produce demonstrable results, he summoned Congress to enact a special anti-inflation program, little of which was approved.

In fiscal policy, the late 1940s saw a protracted battle between Truman and congressional Republicans over cutting taxes. The Republicans, who by 1946 had been in the minority for 16 years, depicted Democrats as the party of high spending and high taxes. They clamored for a tax cut. Truman, in turn, described the Republicans as the party of inflation. He argued it would be a mistake for the government to cut taxes until wartime spending could be reduced, especially since employment already was full. The president called for a balanced budget, proclaiming the "pay-as-you-go idea" the "soundest principle of financing that I know."

In June and July of 1947, Truman vetoed congressionally approved tax cuts, calling them "the wrong kind of tax reduction at the wrong time." He vetoed a tax cut for the third time in April 1948, but this time Congress overrode him.

That proved to be fortuitous; six months later the economy slipped into its first postwar recession. The 1948-49 recession turned out to be relatively mild. Labeled an "inventory recession," its impact was cushioned both by the tax cut and by the government's willingness to see budget surpluses of fiscal 1947, 1948 and 1949 give way to a deficit in fiscal 1950. As late as January 1949, Truman had sought a tax increase to balance the budget, but he finally dropped the idea in July because of the recession. By 1950 he was able to boast that "we have met and reversed the most significant downturn in economic activity since the war."

Korean War Expansion

Economist Arthur Okun was later to call the Korean War "the best managed military emergency in United States history." When North Korea invaded South Korea on June 24, 1950, the U.S. economy was already in the midst of a healthy recovery. Fearing a return to wartime shortages, consumers rushed to buy all sorts of consumer goods. Upward pressure on prices became severe. Adding a defense boom on top of that — from late 1950 through the second quarter of 1953 government spending on goods and services rose a dramatic 27 percent — threatened to create a classical case of Keynesian "excess demand."

Federal expenditures had risen from $38.8 billion in fiscal 1949 to $42.6 billion in 1950 and $45.5 billion in 1951. Then they shot up to $67.7 billion in 1952 and $76.1 billion in 1953.

Adhering to Keynesian theory, the strong government-led demand reduced unemployment and aggravated inflation. The unemployment rate, which had averaged 5.9 percent of the work force in 1949, dropped to 5.3 percent in 1950, 3.3 percent in 1951, 3 percent in 1952 and 2.9 percent in 1953.

Concern about inflation led to a prompt increase in taxes and imposition of price, wage and credit controls. These actions may have helped produce a pronounced drop in civilian demand. In any event, inflation eased. After rising 5.8 percent in 1950 and 5.9 percent in 1951, the consumer price index increased only 0.9 percent in 1952 and 0.6 percent in 1953.

Freeing Monetary Policy

Perhaps the most important development of the Korean War period involved the freeing of monetary policy to act as a force for economic stabilization. Just as the Employment Act of 1946 established the framework for postwar fiscal policy, the 1951 "accord" between the Treasury and the Federal Reserve established the basis for postwar monetary policy.

At the insistence of the Treasury, the Federal Reserve after World War II had continued a policy of "pegging" interest rates on government bonds. It did that by agreeing to purchase at face value all bonds offered on the open market. The policy served to keep the prevailing interest rate on all Treasury bonds at or below 2.5 percent, which helped minimize the cost of servicing the national debt. But it prevented the Federal Reserve from using monetary policy to offset inflation or recession.

During the period immediately after World War II, when inflation was the nation's main economic problem, the board's stable interest rate policy tended to increase the money supply and aggravate inflation. That was because, as demand mounted, the natural tendency was for interest rates to rise as well. In that climate, investors had little incentive to continue holding the low price government bonds. As a result, they sold their bonds to the Federal Reserve, obtaining cash that they could invest elsewhere.

The perverse effect of that monetary policy worked in the opposite direction during the 1948-49 recession. The economic slowdown led the demand for money to fall and interest rates to decline. When market rates dropped below the "pegged" level on government bonds, investors had an obvious incentive to trade in their cash for the higher-priced bonds. The result was that the supply of money shrank further, exacerbating the effects of the recession.

The Treasury conceded that the policy of pegged interest rates did not make sense during the recession, and it allowed the Fed to move away from its inflexible wartime policy. But when inflation pressures renewed in 1950 and 1951, it resisted allowing the Fed to be as flexible against inflation as it had been in fighting recession.

A lengthy battle between the administration and the Fed followed. In the end, the administration and the Fed announced that they had reached "full accord." It took some time to determine exactly what the agreement was, but it eventually became clear that the Fed had achieved a greater measure of independence. Subsequently, interest rates became more variable, and monetary policy was conducted in ways designed to stabilize the economy.

Eisenhower Economics

When President Eisenhower took office in 1953, the economy had fully recovered from the recession and inflation again appeared to be the nation's biggest economic problem. Accordingly, he sought to reduce federal spending and to defer proposals to cut taxes. The rest of the burden for fighting inflation fell on monetary policy, since wage and price controls had been dropped.

The economy again slipped into recession in 1953, largely as a result of the drop in federal expenditures following the end of the Korean War. Eisenhower said the recession was merely a "minor readjustment," and he opposed congressional proposals to stimulate the economy. "[E]conomic conditions do not call for an emergency program that would justify larger federal deficits and further inflation through large additional tax reductions at this time," he said in 1954. Eisenhower's position was strengthened by the fact that about $6 billion in tax cuts already had taken effect by the end of March with the automatic expiration of the Korean War tax increase and the enactment in 1952 of a cut in excise taxes.

The Eisenhower administration's conservative fiscal policies were attacked by Democrats as a return to Hoover economics. But as even some liberals conceded, that criticism was not fully deserved. In his first economic report to Congress, issued in early 1954, Eisenhower pledged to use the full "arsenal of stabilizing weapons boldly, but not more frequently than is required to help maintain reasonable stability." The new president noted that "minor variations in [economic] activity are bound to occur in a free economy." But he said "flexible policies aiming to minimize economic fluctuations" should not interfere "any more than is necessary" with the goal of "bringing down the scale of federal expenditures, reducing taxes, and arriving at a budgetary balance."

Reviewing the administration's economic policies, liberal economist John Kenneth Galbraith concluded in 1955 that the new president had shown "considerable grace and ease in getting away from the clichés of a balanced budget and the unspeakable evils of deficit spending."

Looking back, economists believe that the willingness of the government to tolerate deficits significantly muted the impact of the 1953-54 recession. When the economy slumped, tax receipts dropped and spending for programs such as unemployment compensation increased. Both had the effect of softening the effect of the economic slowdown. For that reason, economists referred to them as "automatic stabilizers."

"If there was a 'fiscal revolution' in the first postwar decade, it was in the willingness to allow the government budget to move into deficit during recessions, thus allowing the automatic stabilizers to work, in contrast to the destructive tax increases engineered by Herbert Hoover in 1932 under the budget-balancing rulebook of the pre-Keynesian fiscal policy," noted Northwestern University economist Robert Gordon.

Orthodox Conservatism

Eisenhower fought to minimize countercyclical swings in government fiscal policy because he was eager to demonstrate that private business could provide a prosperous economy on its own if government just would not interfere and distort private sector decisions.

In 1955, with the economy growing again, he declared: "Instead of expanding federal enterprises or initiating new spending programs, the basic policy of the government in dealing with the contraction was to take actions that created confidence in the future and stimulated business firms, consumers, and states and localities to increase their expenditures."

U.S. Personal Income, 1929-80

Current billion dollars

Year	Total Personal Income	Less: Personal Tax And Non-tax Payments	Equals: Disposable Personal Income
1929	85.0	2.6	82.4
1933	47.0	1.4	45.6
1939	72.4	2.4	70.0
1940	77.9	2.6	77.9
1942	122.6	5.9	116.6
1945	170.0	20.8	149.1
1950	227.2	20.6	206.6
1955	310.3	35.4	275.0
1960	402.3	50.4	352.0
1965	540.7	64.9	475.8
1970	811.1	115.8	695.3
1971	868.4	116.7	751.8
1972	951.4	141.0	810.3
1973	1,065.2	150.7	914.5
1974	1,168.6	170.2	998.3
1975	1,265.0	168.9	1,096.1
1976	1,391.2	196.8	1,194.4
1977	1,538.0	226.5	1,311.5
1978	1,721.8	258.8	1,462.9
1979*	1,943.8	302.0	1,641.7
1980*	2,160.5	338.7	1,821.7

Preliminary figures

Source: Department of Commerce, Bureau of Economic Analysis

Eisenhower's belief in the private sector also led him to propose, in 1954, business tax cuts to reward investment. Democrats scorned that approach, saying it mainly helped the wealthy, and that the poor would only receive the meager breaks that would "trickle down" to them as a result of greater spending by the wealthy.

In place of the president's plan, the Democrats proposed a tax cut strategy that would concentrate the benefits among low-income people. A stalemate developed and neither approach was adopted.

Second Term Problems

When Eisenhower began his second term, inflation again appeared to be the economy's worst problem. The Consumer Price Index was essentially flat during 1954 and 1955, reflecting the effect of the recession. But, riding a strong business expansion, the CPI rose 2.9 percent in 1956 and 3 percent in 1957. The unemployment rate, in the meantime, fell back to 4.1 percent in 1956 and 4.3 percent in 1957 from 5.5 percent in 1954 and 4.4 percent in 1955.

In 1957 Eisenhower again warned against inflation and urged business and labor to help prevent a wage and price spiral: "Business in its pricing policies should avoid unnecessary price increases especially at a time like the present when demand in so many areas presses hard on short supplies.... Increases in wages and other labor benefits negotiated by labor and management must be reasonably related to improvements in productivity.... Except where necessary to correct obvious injustices, wage increases that outrun productivity... are an inflationary factor."

The attention of the nation shifted back to recession in 1957 and 1958, as the economy again slumped. Again, pressures mounted in Congress for an emergency anti-recession program. And again Eisenhower denounced calls by Democrats and some Republicans for tax cuts or spending increases as "a sudden upsurge in pump-priming schemes."

The 1957-58 recession proved to be sharp though fairly short. The ensuing recovery abruptly halted in 1959. A national steel strike helped cause yet a new recession in which federal fiscal and monetary policy also played a role. The president was determined to balance the budget following the 1957-58 downturn. By cutting back on spending sharply, the government managed to eke out a $269 million surplus in fiscal 1960 following a $12.9 billion deficit the preceding year.

Critics said that the administration had swung budget policy too sharply and that the sudden contraction of the deficit had pulled spending power out of the economy too quickly. Eisenhower replied that ominous underlying economic trends forced his dramatic tightening of fiscal policy. During the 1957-58 recession, he noted, wages and prices had defied traditional patterns and continued to increase despite the downturn. He warned that trend could lead to "real inflationary trouble in a time of prosperity."

One vigorous dissenter from the administration's restrictive fiscal policy was Vice President Richard Nixon, who by that time was running for president himself. Nixon had argued for a more stimulative policy Later he was to say that he lost the 1960 election to John F. Kennedy partly because of Eisenhower's failure to shift to a policy geared at bringing unemployment down.

By the time Eisenhower left office in 1961, he could claim that his policies had achieved some demonstrable success. The Consumer Price Index rose only 12.7 percent from 1953 through 1960, an enviable pace compared with the rates that occurred subsequently. But that success had been achieved at considerable price. At the end of Eisenhower's term, the nation had suffered its longest, most severe bout of unemployment since World War II. The jobless rate had not been below 4 percent in any year since 1953. In 1960 it stood at 5.5 percent, and a year later it averaged 6.7 percent.

'NEW ECONOMICS': KENNEDY-JOHNSON ERA

The debates over economic policy were acrimonious during the Eisenhower era. Senate Majority Leader Lyndon B. Johnson pinned responsibility for economic slack on the "intolerable burden of laggard government" under Eisenhower. Republicans generally countered by posing the issues as a contest of "spenders versus savers." That

strategy struck a responsive chord with the public, and a coalition of Republicans and southern Democrats managed to win most battles during the period.

Although the Democrats believed government should play a bigger role in providing goods and services and in regulating the economy, their main line of attack against Republicans during the 1950s was to recast the debate in the more complex terms of economic theory — much as the "supply-siders" would do in the early 1980s.

In 1960 Democrats recaptured the White House and heralded the beginning of a more activist "new economics."

Democratic Aspirations

The election of President Kennedy marked a victory for those who believed that the private economy was not strong enough by itself to provide full employment and prosperity for all.

At the same time, the election marked the beginning of an era of rising expectations. Democrats took office with a backlog of goals they believed the government could accomplish. These included eliminating poverty, strengthening education, providing increased medical care and rebuilding the nation's cities. In addition, President Kennedy promised to match what was perceived to be the growing Soviet economic and military threat.

The high aspirations of Democrats in the 1960s fundamentally shifted the emphasis of economic policy. Concern for price stability received much less attention than it had in the Eisenhower years. By 1964 James Tobin, a member of Kennedy's Council of Economic Advisers, noted that "in recent years economic growth has come to occupy an exalted position in the hierarchy of goals of economic policy."

In his 1961 State of the Union address Kennedy declared: "The American economy is in trouble. We take office in the wake of seven months of recession, three and one-half years of slack, seven years of diminished economic growth, and nine years of falling farm income."

Claiming than there had never been a "complete recovery" from the 1957-58 recession, Walter Heller, chairman of Kennedy's Council of Economic Advisers, said the administration's goal would be to restore the economy to full employment. The council estimated that in the first quarter of 1961 the economy was actually operating about $50 billion below its potential output.

Despite his expansive promises, Kennedy moved cautiously. The new president wished to avoid political attack as a deficit spender and was reluctant to cut taxes deeply because he had ambitious plans for federal spending.

The thinking of Democrats during the early 1960s was reflected in John Kenneth Galbraith's popular book, *The Affluent Society.* Galbraith argued that the U.S. economy was characterized by an abundance of "private goods" and a scarcity of "public goods."

In 1958 Galbraith argued before a congressional committee that fiscal policy should consist of an increase in spending rather than a cut in taxes. "[W]e now have so many things that need doing...," he said. "Schools and aid to education, research support and facilities, health facilities, urban rental housing, urban redevelopment, resource development, metropolitan communications, are all deficient or lagging. It would surely be a mistake to talk of tax reduction to make jobs when so many of our schools are dirty, rundown, overcrowded, understaffed, on double shifts, or scheduled to become inadequate when the next increase in the school population hits them."

The desire to retain revenues to support such services was so prevalent among Democrats that the 1960 platform of the Democratic Party called for a budget surplus. The job of stimulating the economy to provide full employment should fall to monetary policy, the Democrats said, arguing that a budget surplus would make it possible for the Federal Reserve to maintain low interest rates to stimulate private investment.

To help bolster the private sector, Kennedy did propose a package of tax cuts that resembled the program Eisenhower had urged on a reluctant Democratic Congress, only to be accused of advocating "trickle-down" policies. Among Kennedy's proposals was an 8 percent tax credit on new investment and liberalized depreciation allowances. Congress approved both, but rejected two other tax increases he had requested to offset the lost revenue.

Higher spending and those tax cuts failed to accelerate the pace of economic activity as much as the administration hoped. To the contrary, the economy appeared to be running out of steam in early 1962. Although there was no recession, there was a distinct "pause" in the recovery sufficiently pronounced to renew fears of a recession — a prospect that the Democratic administration found unacceptable.

The 1964 Tax Cut

Seeking an explanation for weakness in business activity, administration economists concluded that the tax system was imposing a serious "fiscal drag" on the economy. As the economy expanded and personal income grew, taxes tended to rise faster, they noted. That was because U.S. income taxes are "progressive," with higher rates being imposed on higher levels of income. With government taxing an increasing share of people's income, it was feared that the economy would come to a halt well before it reached full employment levels.

In June 1962 Kennedy decided to advocate a large cut in individual income tax rates. The decision was a difficult one and it came only after the administration concluded that the private economy would not propel the nation to full employment if left alone.

"The decision taken in June 1962 to cut taxes was not a prompt response to a minor change and uncertain forecasts of further changes in the economy," Herbert Stein wrote later. "It was a delayed response to a chronic condition after hopes of a spontaneous recovery were dimmed."

The tax cuts could not have been approved if there had been no break in the deadlock over tax policy that had occurred during the Eisenhower administration. The Democratic administration, facing a protracted battle with Republicans in Congress over its spending plans, was worried that spending stimulus would be too little too late to strengthen the economy. So it set aside its long-term spending plans in favor of a tax cut that would stimulate the economy.

Republicans, for their part, could not resist the opportunity to vote for a tax cut. However, to protect themselves from sharing any possible political backlash against deficit spending, the Republicans did try, unsuccessfully, to make the tax cuts contingent on reductions in federal spending.

Kennedy, still sensitive to potential criticism, argued that there actually was no conflict between the tax cut and the goal of balancing the budget. Without the cut, he said, the economy could not grow rapidly enough to produce the revenues needed to balance the budget.

"Our present choice is not between a tax cut and a balanced budget," Kennedy said. "The choice, rather, is between chronic deficits arising out of a slow rate of economic growth, and temporary deficits stemming from a tax program designed to promote fuller use of our resources and more rapid economic growth. . . . Unless we release the tax brake which is holding back our economy, it is likely to continue to operate below its potential, federal receipts are likely to remain disappointingly low, and budget deficits are likely to persist."

The supply-siders of the 1970s were later to make the same argument. But Heller denounced their claim to Kennedy's legacy. When Kennedy proposed his tax cut the economy's capacity was severely underutilized and inflation was almost non-existent, Heller said. By the late 1970s, he argued, inflation was a severe problem and tax cuts were no longer so desirable.

Despite the apparent consensus on the tax cut question, lawmakers of different persuasions had varying opinions on what the economic impact of the cuts would be. Liberals believed the cuts would increase personal income, thus boosting demand. But conservatives argued that the main impact would be to increase the incentives of individuals to work, save and invest. By boosting the amount of

U.S. Disposable Personal Income, 1929-80

	Total (Billion dollars)		Per Capita (Dollars)	
	Current Dollars	1972 Dollars	Current Dollars	1972 Dollars
1929	82.4	229.5	676	1,883
1933	45.6	169.6	363	1,349
1939	70.0	229.8	534	1,754
1940	75.3	244.0	570	1,847
1942	116.6	317.5	865	2,354
1945	149.1	338.1	1,066	2,416
1950	206.6	362.9	1,362	2,393
1955	275.0	426.9	1,664	2,583
1960	352.0	489.7	1,947	2,709
1965	475.8	616.3	2,448	3,171
1970	695.3	751.6	3,393	3,668
1971	751.8	779.2	3,630	3,763
1972	810.3	810.3	3,880	3,880
1973	914.5	865.3	4,346	4,112
1974	998.3	858.4	4,710	4,050
1975	1,096.1	875.8	5,132	4,101
1976	1,194.4	907.4	5,550	4,216
1977	1,311.5	939.8	6,046	4,332
1978	1,462.9	981.5	6,688	4,487
1979	1,641.7	1,011.5	7,441	4,584
1980*	1,821.7	1,017.7	8,176	4,567

* Preliminary figures

Source: Department of Commerce, Bureau of Economic Analysis and Bureau of the Census

income a person could keep after taxes, the conservatives argued, the tax cuts would make work and savings more rewarding.

The conservative argument later became the theme of the supply-side economists ushered into government under President Reagan. Kennedy's own view was somewhat ambiguous. In the effort to sell the tax cuts, he made both arguments, emphasizing the incentive aspect before conservative audiences.

A Moment of Triumph

The Kennedy tax cut — enacted in 1964 after the president's death — marked the first time the government had decided to stimulate the economy even though there was no recession. Moreover, it was enacted when the federal budget was in deficit and while federal spending was on the rise.

The amount of stimulus was substantial. When it was fully effective in 1965 the tax cut added more than $11 billion to private purchasing power. Government officials called it the largest stimulative action ever undertaken in peacetime.

The tax cuts initially appeared to be an outstanding success. The unemployment rate, which seemed stuck at 5.7 percent in 1963, dropped to 5.2 percent in 1964 and 4.5 percent in 1965 — close to the 4 percent "interim full employment" goal President Kennedy's advisers had set at the beginning of his term in office. And, at the outset at least, the inflationary costs of the tax cuts seemed acceptable. Consumer prices rose a fairly modest 1.6 percent in 1963, 1.2 percent in 1964 and 1.9 percent in 1965.

Most economists viewed 1965 as a year of triumph. Harvard economist Otto Eckstein, who served on President Johnson's Council of Economic Advisers, was later to look back on the early 1960s as "a golden age for economic policy." Full employment seemed to have been achieved at a fairly modest cost in terms of inflation. Analysts declared that the business cycle had been tamed, and the government had found the way to keep the economy on a long-term growth path.

On the level of theory, economists proclaimed the "neo-Keynesian synthesis," which they said united the Keynesian and classical traditions of economic analysis. Under the synthesis, economists basically accepted the classical theory that prices and wages are determined primarily by the interplay of supply and demand. But they added one Keynesian caveat — that government intervention was needed to assure steady consumer demand.

Unfortunately, the "synthesis" came unraveled almost as soon as it was "achieved." Economic historians attribute its demise to one of the biggest mistakes in postwar economic policy making.

Guns And Butter

While Kennedy had taken a cautious approach to fulfilling the liberal social agenda, Lyndon B. Johnson brought a wave of pent-up liberal aspirations to the White House. ". . . [W]e have the opportunity to move not only toward the rich society and the powerful society, but upward to the Great Society," he said on May 22, 1964.

"In the remainder of this century urban population will double, city land will double, and we will have to build homes, highways and facilities equal to all those built since this country was first settled," Johnson continued. "So in the next 40 years we must rebuild the entire urban United States."

Johnson went on to say that in the Great Society he envisioned "men are more concerned about the quality of

GNP Growth Around the Globe, 1960-80

Country	Annual Average 1960-73	Percent Change from Previous Year						
		1974	1975	1976	1977	1978	1979	1980*
United States	4.2	0.7	−0.5	5.3	3.7	3.9	3.3	1.0
Canada	5.4	3.6	1.2	5.5	2.2	3.4	2.8	−0.5
China	7.1	3.9	6.9	−0.2	8.3	11.5	7.0	5.0
France	5.7	3.2	0.2	5.2	2.8	3.6	3.3	1.8
Italy	5.2	4.1	−3.6	5.9	1.9	2.6	5.0	3.8
Japan	10.5	−0.6	1.5	6.5	5.4	6.0	5.9	5.0
United Kingdom	3.2	−1.2	−0.8	4.2	1.0	3.6	1.5	−2.3
U.S.S.R.	5.0	3.7	1.7	4.7	3.5	3.4	0.6	1.4
West Germany	4.8	0.4	−1.8	5.3	2.6	3.5	4.5	1.8
Oil Exporting Countries	9.0**	8.0	−0.3	12.1	6.2	2.7	2.9	—

Preliminary figures
** *Annual average 1967-72*

Source: Department of Commerce, International Monetary Fund, Organization for Economic Development, and Council of Economic Advisers

their goals than the quantities of their goods." But the proposals he sent Congress clearly demonstrated that the Great Society had plenty of materialistic aspects. The president was committed to a major social program, covering dozens of activities ranging from helping the poor to building new parks.

On top of that, shortly after he was elected president in his own right in 1964, Johnson embarked on an expensive military engagement in Vietnam. The war expenditures put considerable strain on an economy that already was operating near its full capacity as a result of the 1964 tax cuts and a 1965 reduction in excise taxes. Strong government demand quickly bid up prices for goods and services, setting off renewed inflation.

As early as the first months of 1966 many economists, including some of the advocates of the 1964 tax cut, were calling for an increase in taxes or a cut in federal spending to cool the overheating economy.

"I believe that we can continue the Great Society while we fight in Vietnam," President Johnson replied in his 1966 State of the Union message. "But if there are some who do not believe this, then, in the name of justice, let them call for the contribution of those who live in the fullness of our blessing rather than try to strip it from the hands of those that are most in need."

Later, Johnson said that in 1966 he had discussed the possibility of a tax increase with members of Congress and was convinced that it could not be enacted. Finally, on Jan. 10, 1967, he asked for a 6 percent income tax surcharge. On Aug. 3, 1967, with inflation still mounting, he raised the request to 10 percent. But Congress acted slowly on the president's request. The surcharge was not enacted until June 28, 1968, almost 18 months after it had been first requested and almost three years after many economists believed it was needed. By then, the nation was experiencing its worst sustained inflation since World War II.

Policy Failures of the Late 1960s

By some measures, economic policy produced impressive results during the 1960s. The economy posted its longest non-stop expansion in history — 106 consecutive months from February 1961 through February 1969. The gross national product rose from $756.6 billion in early 1961 to just under $1.1 trillion in 1969, after adjustment for inflation. About 11 million jobs were created during the period, permitting the unemployment rate to drop to 3.5 percent by 1969. Disposable personal income per capita — after taxes and adjustment for price increases — increased by 33 percent in the same period. And corporate profits doubled.

But those successes were clouded by steadily worsening inflation. Consumer prices increased 3.4 percent in 1966, 3 percent in 1967, and then jumped 4.7 percent in 1968 and 6.1 percent in 1969.

The price surge of the late 1960s marked the beginning of the spiraling inflation that plagued the 1970s. Price increases achieved a momentum that slowed at times during the middle of the 1970s but never dropped back to the mild pace of the 1950s.

Blessed with hindsight, economists believe the takeoff of inflation during the late 1960s resulted from at least four "mistakes."

For one thing, policy makers failed to respond to the indications that the economy was growing beyond its non-inflationary capacity. Kennedy administration economists

calculated that the GNP had dropped below full employment "potential" after 1955. But by 1965 that gap had been closed. After that, actual growth exceeded potential as unemployment dropped below the 4 percent level.

That was a clear warning that the economy was threatened by inflationary "excess demand," but it was not until 1968 that the fiscal brakes were applied. By then, inflation had accelerated significantly.

The government's failure to restrain the economy in the late 1960s resulted partly from a standoff between Johnson and the Congress over program priorities. Johnson, eager to preserve Great Society programs, initially tried to avoid the unpopular move of seeking a tax increase. When he finally acknowledged the need to cool the economy, he favored raising taxes to cutting spending. Many members of Congress with less attachment to the Great Society, however, preferred to cut spending. While precious time was lost in 1966 and 1967, the two sides were unable to resolve their differences despite the mounting economic problem.

Critics of the post-Depression stabilization policies contend that the Vietnam episode was just an extreme example of the inability of government to take fiscal actions when they are needed. Even analysts sympathetic to the goals of stabilization policy concede these critics have a point. They acknowledge that while the automatic stabilizers in the budget respond instantly to changes in economic currents, discretionary policies do not.

Looking back over the previous four decades, economist Arthur Okun concluded in 1980: "It is fair to conclude that no significant discretionary stimulative fiscal action was adopted while the economy was still in recession. Most of the strongly stimulative fiscal actions were taken in the first year of recovery.

On occasions, these worked effectively to promote the restoration of prosperity; on others, they may have overdone the job — providing a stimulus that was too much too late."

Okun also said that restrictive budget policies were similarly "too much too late." Instead of restraining an economy that was overheating, budget tightening on occasion stifled an economy that already was slowing. At the end of fiscal years 1957 and 1960, for instance, "celebrations on the achievement of federal budgetary surpluses were followed immediately by mourning over the onset of recession," said Okun.

President Kennedy was sensitive to the problem of timing in fiscal policy. In 1962 he asked Congress for standby authority to reduce income tax rates temporarily to head off a recession and to initiate up to $2 billion in public works projects should unemployment rise. Congress was understandably reluctant to cede such power.

Some economists also believe, in retrospect, that economic policy makers of the late 1960s erred in paying too much attention to the federal deficit and too little to the private economy itself. Some of the Kennedy "new economists" assumed that federal budget policy was not overly stimulative because, with the exception of fiscal 1968, deficits during the late 1960s were not large. But some analysts believe that by assuming that the budget would not overheat the economy so long as deficits were manageable, policy makers overlooked the impact of large increases in defense spending.

"[A] sudden and substantial surge in military spending is likely to be inflationary even if taxes do increase in equivalent amount," said Northwestern University economist Robert Eisner in 1979. "For the increased spending represents a demand for real resources which, to be realized in a relatively full-employment economy, entails a bidding up of their prices." Eisner concluded that, contrary to the conventional wisdom of the 1960s, fiscal policy can actually be expansionary even with a balanced budget.

Many economists believe the 1968 income tax surcharge, when it was finally implemented, was a failure. Because the surcharge was explicitly described as "temporary," people realized that the higher tax rates would not continue forever, so they had little incentive to cut their consumption. Instead, they were able to reduce their savings to continue existing levels of consumption, knowing that lower tax rates in the future would enable them to replenish bank accounts.

Recognition of the inadequacies of a temporary tax cut undermined one of the principle tenets of postwar stabilization policy. During the 1960s Milton Friedman, among others, argued that current consumption is determined by many factors other than current income — including savings and ability to borrow. That idea — Friedman called it the "permanent income theory" — implies that transitory increases or decreases in income are unlikely to have much effect on consumption. If that is true, government stabilization policies that alternate between increasing personal income during recessions and decreasing it during periods of inflation are doomed to fail because consumers will realize that neither will have a permanent impact on net income.

THE NIXON YEARS: GROWTH AND INFLATION

President Richard Nixon's five-and-a-half years in office provided dramatic evidence that postwar approaches to fiscal policy were less successful in controlling inflation than in promoting growth.

Having inherited an economy with high inflation and low unemployment, Nixon tried to slow the rate of price increases without substantially increasing joblessness. His initial strategy was to restrain demand gradually by cutting spending and maintaining the revenue base.

That approach proved unable to solve the economic problem in time for the president's re-election campaign, so Nixon abruptly shifted course. He imposed wage and price controls to restrain inflation, while stimulating the economy through fiscal policy.

That proved to be a winning political combination but a very troublesome one economically. By the time his presidency ended as a result of the Watergate scandals, Nixon had scrapped wage and price controls and reverted to his orthodox conservative fiscal policy. Still, inflation showed no sign of relenting.

Shortly after Nixon took office in 1969, Paul McCracken, chairman of the Council of Economic Advisers, said that the administration's fiscal strategy was to "slow down the growth of total demand gradually" to cure inflation without adding to the unemployment rolls. McCracken said that policy should be accompanied by "an appropriate degree of monetary restraint."

The goal was to be achieved with a budget that would produce a $5.8 billion surplus for fiscal 1970. But the surplus never materialized; Congress refused to approve all of the restraints on spending the president recommended and adopted a tax cut that Nixon signed only reluctantly.

Fiscal policy was nevertheless somewhat restrictive for 1969. But monetary policy assumed the main burden of fighting inflation. The Fed held the money supply almost constant through the year, prompting some economists to warn that continuation of that policy might push the economy into a recession. Among the Fed's critics was Milton Friedman. McCracken and George P. Schulz, at the time Nixon's secretary of labor, also joined in criticizing the Fed.

Economists later concluded that a recession began in 1969, but early the next year Nixon again called for a restrictive anti-inflation budget surplus. As the recession deepened, however, the automatic stabilizers in the budget took over. Tax revenues fell $13.7 billion below projections and Nixon was faced with a substantial deficit instead of the surplus he had sought.

In keeping with postwar tradition, Nixon argued that such a deficit was acceptable during a period of economic weakness. "In raising the issue of budget deficits, I am not suggesting that the federal government should necessarily adhere to a strict pattern of a balanced budget every year," he said in July 1970. "At times the economic situation permits — even calls for — a budget deficit. There is one basic guideline for the budget, however, which we should never violate: except in emergency conditions, expenditures must never be allowed to outrun the revenues the tax system would produce at reasonable full employment."

The economic statistics for 1970 proved to be doubly disappointing. Recession drove the unemployment rate up to 4.9 percent. At the same time, consumer price increases slowed only slightly. The rise in the Consumer Price Index for the year was still a hefty 5.5 percent. As the Council of Economic Advisers noted ruefully in February 1971, "Sophisticated econometric analysis of the relationship between the behavior of prices and a large number of variables that might explain it. . . did not generally predict the rate of inflation experienced in 1970, given the actual conditions of 1970."

An 'Incomes Policy'

Even before that report was written, some Nixon administration economists — among them Assistant Treasury Secretary Murray L. Weidenbaum, who in 1981 became chairman of Reagan's Council of Economic Advisers — were warning that the traditional relationship between unemployment and inflation was coming unhinged.

They were joined by Arthur F. Burns, chairman of the Federal Reserve Board. "The excess demand that bedeviled our economy during the past four or five years has been eliminated," Burns said in May 1970. But fiscal and monetary restraint was not succeeding in reducing inflation. The reason, according to Burns, was that inflation no longer resulted from "demand-pull" pressures caused by an overheated economy, but rather from "cost-push" pressures in the form of excessive wage increases that were driving up business costs.

Burns warned that using fiscal restraint to suppress wages would lead to a recession, which in turn would create irresistible pressures for further demand stimulus. As a result, he warned, "our hopes of getting the inflationary problem under control would. . . be shattered."

Weidenbaum and Burns concluded that the administration would have to add some form of "incomes policy" to its economic policy arsenal. That term, which soon came into fashionable use, referred to a broad range of activities designed to influence incomes through wages and prices instead of through fiscal and monetary policy.

During the Kennedy-Johnson years, the government had issued wage and price "guideposts," indicating roughly what wage and price increases it considered economically appropriate. Begun in 1962, the guideposts were intended partly to defray criticism that the expansive fiscal policy Kennedy planned would be inflationary.

The idea of an incomes policy was anathema to the laissez-faire economic philosophy of Republicans. On June 17, 1970, President Nixon repeated a promise that "I will not take this nation down the road of wage and price controls, however politically expedient that may seem." Nixon explained that controls "only postpone a day of reckoning, and in so doing they rob every American of an important part of his freedom."

During this period, Nixon had been fighting a protracted battle with the Democratic-controlled Congress over reducing federal spending. Partly to shift responsibility for inflation back to the president, Congress in August added to a Defense Production Act extension an amendment empowering the president to freeze salaries, rents and prices. The president opposed the amendment and vowed he would never use the authority, but he did sign the bill.

Nixon did change his economic policies somewhat in 1970, though. He moved toward "jawboning" by issuing two "inflation alerts" to publicize excessive wage and price increases. In December he announced measures to offset oil price increases and plans to intervene in wage negotiations in the construction industry if strikes and rising costs were not abated. "Unless the industry wants government to intervene in wage negotiations on federal projects to protect the public interest, the moment is here for labor and management to make their own reforms in that industry," Nixon warned.

Burns noted ominously a few days later that "we are dealing, practically speaking, with a new problem — namely, persistent inflation in the face of substantial unemployment." The Fed chairman cautioned that "classical remedies may not work well enough or fast enough in this case."

Why Don't Wages and Prices Fall?

The failure of economic slowdown to cool inflation significantly during the 1969-70 downturn raised one of the central problems on which postwar economic policy floundered. Even after the excess demand that triggered inflation in the late 1960s was removed, the upward march of prices and wages continued. Inflation, it seemed, had a momentum of its own. The persistence of this phenomenon led to considerable economic research through the 1970s.

The classical economic view, it has been seen, assumed that wages and prices respond primarily to supply and demand. Economists who held this view assumed that fiscal or monetary restraint would slow the rate of price and wage increases by reducing demand for goods and services. Thus, lower demand for goods was thought likely to lead to price cutting, and lower demand for labor to wage reductions.

By the end of the 1970s many economists contended that process had been short-circuited by the success of

Unemployment and the Consumer Price Index

| | | Consumer Price Index Percent Change, Dec. to Dec.[2] | | |
Year	Unemployment Rate[1]	All Items	Food	Energy[3]
1950	5.3	5.8	9.6	—
1951	3.3	5.9	7.4	—
1952	3.0	.9	−1.1	—
1953	2.9	.6	−1.3	—
1954	5.5	− .5	−1.6	—
1955	4.4	.4	− .9	—
1956	4.1	2.9	3.1	—
1957	4.3	3.0	2.8	—
1958	6.8	1.8	2.2	− .7
1959	5.5	1.5	− .8	4.3
1960	5.5	1.5	3.1	1.5
1961	6.7	.7	− .9	−1.1
1962	5.5	1.2	1.5	2.1
1963	5.7	1.6	1.9	− .8
1964	5.2	1.2	1.4	− .2
1965	4.5	1.9	3.4	2.0
1966	3.8	3.4	3.9	1.8
1967	3.8	3.0	1.2	1.4
1968	3.6	4.7	4.3	1.7
1969	3.5	6.1	7.2	3.1
1970	4.9	5.5	2.2	4.5
1971	5.9	3.4	4.3	3.1
1972	5.6	3.4	4.7	2.8
1973	4.9	8.8	20.1	16.8
1974	5.6	12.2	12.2	21.6
1975	8.5	7.0	6.5	11.6
1976	7.7	4.8	.6	6.9
1977	7.0	6.8	8.0	7.2
1978	6.0	9.0	11.8	8.0
1979	5.8	13.3	10.2	37.4
1980	7.1	12.4	10.2	18.1

[1] As a percent of total civilian labor force.
[2] Based on unadjusted indexes.
[3] Fuel oil, coal and bottled gas; gas and electricity; and gasoline, motor oil, coolant, etc.

Source: Department of Labor, Bureau of Labor Statistics

postwar economic policy in averting prolonged recessions. "In the bad old days, any hesitation in economic growth might have been the beginning of a real depression," noted economist Robert Solow in 1980. "Only a brave or overconfident seller of goods or labor would maintain prices and wait for things to improve. In an economy whose recessions are infrequent, mild and short, prices are less likely to plummet when demand weakens. Sellers are more likely to stand pat and cover their costs. If the upturn arrives on schedule, their strategy is vindicated for next time."

As the break between unemployment and inflation became increasingly obvious through the 1970s, economists developed more elaborate theories to explain the independent behavior of wage and price setting. Arthur Okun, for instance, came to explain wage and price behavior as being governed by an "invisible handshake" that prevented either from turning down.

Okun said there is a tacit agreement between business and consumers that prices will be related to costs rather than market forces. The modern marketplace has become so complex that it no longer pays consumers to shop for the best bargains. Thus, for business, it is now more important to build up consumer loyalty than to try to compete by offering the lowest prices. That loyalty has been established by guaranteeing that prices are related to costs.

Okun concluded that businesses have become reluctant to cut prices during periods of economic weakness because they know that such a strategy at best will only win them the temporary loyalty of customers, while price increases following slumps may anger customers. Basing prices on costs prevents sharp price-cutting during recessions, although it may help moderate price increases during periods of economic strength.

Similarly, Okun argued that employers are reluctant to cut wages during a slump because they need to maintain the long-term loyalty of their employees. That is especially true where employers are eager to keep workers who already have the training and experience that makes them highly productive.

Cutting wages at the first sign of a slump would be harmful in the long run because it would undermine the implicit trust between employer and worker, according to Okun. It could lead workers to resign at the first opportunity. Thus, employers tend to maintain wage rates and keep more workers than they need during the early stages of a slump. If the downturn gets worse, they tend to lay off workers according to seniority rather than cut wages generally.

Such behavior makes wages and prices very slow to decline during periods of economic slack, although some economists believe that a long enough period of economic weakness could still slow inflation. But just how long and how severe a recession would have to be is unclear. "The most reasonable reading of the evidence is that it might take a rather long time, maybe more like five years than one or two years," concluded Solow. "During that time, the economy would be depressed, probably severely. A more gradual approach, which would lead to less damage to production and employment, would, naturally, take even longer."

That view is vigorously disputed by a group of conservative economists who in the 1970s developed a theory known as "rational expectations." They argue that wages and prices will adjust rather quickly, with fairly little effect on production and employment, once workers are convinced that the government will not step in to prevent a recession.

Liberals reply that it would be impossible for government to convince the public that it will keep its hands off the economic system. "It is, after all, a political system," noted Brookings Institution economist Barry Bosworth, who served as director of the Council on Wage and Price Stability under President Carter. "People do understand now that the competitive market is not a religious theology.

It's simply a set of rules that we put together to try to govern behavior in as fair a fashion as we can. We've changed the rules repeatedly, and it's bound to happen in the future. You just can't partition the economic arena from the political arena and keep them separate."

The Nixon Controls

In 1971, at least, the government was unwilling to risk a severe recession in order to stabilize wages and prices.

The Republican Party had suffered a net loss in the 1970 congressional and gubernatorial elections. Many politicians interpreted that as a rejection of Nixon's policy of gradualism, which apparently had failed to prevent a recession. By 1971 Nixon also might have been haunted by former President Eisenhower's prediction three years earlier.

"I think Dick's going to be elected president, but I think he's going to be a one-term president," Eisenhower had said. "I think he's really going to fight inflation, and that will kill him politically."

Perhaps with that prediction in mind, Nixon abandoned his orthodox conservative fight on inflation in favor of fiscal stimulus in early 1971. That shift in policy all but assured large federal deficits, but Nixon justified them in much the same terms as John F. Kennedy had nine years earlier. Nixon announced that his new fiscal policy was designed to ensure a "full employment budget," meaning that the deficits he projected for 1971 and 1972 would not have occurred if the economy had been operating at full employment and output. The actual deficits, he said, represented the loss of federal revenues caused by economic performance that was below potential.

To those conservatives who felt betrayed because they saw Nixon backing away from balanced budget principles, Nixon had a ready answer. He told an interviewer in January 1971, "I am now a Keynesian in economics."

Fiscal stimulus may have helped solve the unemployment problem but it only added to concerns about inflation. Unable to solve both problems simultaneously, Nixon, in a dramatic reversal, announced on Aug. 15, 1971, that he would accompany his stimulative policies with a wage and price freeze.

The Nixon controls, which went through four "phases" before Congress allowed them to lapse in 1974, initially were well received by the public. Even Milton Friedman conceded that Nixon, having failed to convince the public there was any other way to end inflation, had acted "the only way a responsible leader in a democracy could."

With controls in place, the economy appeared for a while to have finally accomplished the coveted goal of price stability and full employment. Consumer prices rose only 3.4 percent in both 1971 and 1972, while unemployment averaged 5.9 percent in 1971 and dropped to 5.6 percent in 1972 on its way to a 4.9 percent average in 1973.

Imposition of controls probably helped Nixon win reelection in 1972. Economic policy was not even an issue during the presidential campaign that year. But the controls failed to provide a lasting solution to the nation's economic woes. Instead, Nixon's stimulative fiscal policy the year before the election led to a further buildup of inflationary pressures, which the controls only temporarily capped. That became evident soon after the election.

By 1974 the system of controls was riddled with holes. By preventing prices from mediating between supply and demand, the controls led to serious disruptions in economic activity. As world prices rose above controlled domestic prices, exports surged and domestic shortages appeared for many metals crucial to the nation's defense. Paper products were also in short supply. As paper exports from the United States increased, the U.S. publishing industry found itself short of newsprint.

The Nixon controls provided many examples of the inability of the government, at least without a massive bureaucracy, to manage the economy efficiently. For example, coal production weakened because controls made it unprofitable to produce mine roof bolts. Similarly, meat prices were frozen while feed grain prices were allowed to rise uncontrolled, with the result that production of livestock and poultry became unprofitable. That led farmers to slaughter large numbers of their stock, eventually creating meat shortages that in turn caused sharp price increases in 1978 and 1979.

As pressures and distortions built up, the Nixon administration was forced to grant an increasing number of exemptions from its controls program. By 1974 the list of industries excluded from the controls program included: fertilizer, cement, zinc, aluminum, automobiles, mobile homes, rubber tires and tubes, all retail trade, furniture, paper, coal, shoes and other footwear, canned fruit and vegetables, petrochemicals, prepared feeds and semi-conductors.

Some economists believe that controls did manage to lower the inflation rate in late 1971 and early 1972 by about one percentage point below its previous level. But the rate steadily rose from the second half of 1972 onward, as more and more exemptions were allowed. And when controls were removed entirely, pent-up inflation reasserted itself with a vengeance. Consumer prices rose 8.8 percent in 1973, at that point the most severe for any year since World War II.

The nation's unhappy experience with controls in the early 1970s reaffirmed the free market philosophy of most economists. Later, in 1980, when oppressive inflation again led to pressures for controls, the Democratic administration of President Jimmy Carter led the resistance. Charles L. Schultze, Carter's chief economist, said controls suffered at least two "fatal defects." First, "they cannot be maintained long enough to do the job; and second, they are likely to cause major harm to the economy."

By 1973 and 1974 a penitent Nixon administration had returned to fiscal orthodoxy. The administration proposed a less stimulative fiscal policy in 1973, although Congress resisted most of Nixon's proposed spending reductions. Monetary policy also turned more restrictive. By this time, however, Nixon, faced with the Watergate revelations, was struggling to retain the presidency and economic policy received much less attention.

Supply Shocks of the Early 1970s

The Nixon administration's return to fiscal orthodoxy never had a chance to work. Two unexpected and severe shocks from the outside presented a new set of problems to policy makers. Poor harvests in many countries in 1972, along with a continued rise in international demand, led to a 20 percent jump in U.S. consumer food prices. Worse, energy shortages culminating in the October 1973 Arab oil embargo sent oil prices skyrocketing. The average price of a barrel of oil imported into the United States rose from $3.33 in 1973 to $11.01 in 1974. The total U.S. oil import bill tripled in one year, leaping from $8.4 billion in 1973 to $26.6 billion in 1974.

Traditional economic policies, already unable to deal with the growing rigidity of the U.S. wage and price structure, were also ill-equipped to respond to the problem posed by the supply shocks that occurred in the early 1970s. Strategies designed to deal with demand-induced inflation or unemployment proved unsuited to cure inflation that originated on the supply side of the economic equation — at least at a politically acceptable cost.

Because it is difficult for consumers, at least in the short run, to reduce their demand in response to a rise in prices for necessities such as oil, the dramatic increase in food and energy costs made inevitable a decline in "real" income — the purchasing power of the dollar.

Policy makers thus were confronted with unpleasant choices during this period. If they opted for using conventional demand management strategies to contain the supply-side inflation, they would have been forced to apply restraint to an economy that already was suffering a substantial loss of income. The result could have been a tremendous surge of unemployment.

On the other hand, if they decided to use demand management policies to restore consumer income and prevent a rise in unemployment, they would have increased the amount of income without adding to the supply of oil. There would have been more dollars available to buy the same limited supply of goods. That probably would have contained unemployment, but it inevitably would have produced more inflation as well.

Many economists concluded that the government should bolster income to prevent a drop in economic activity rather than stand by and allow the increase in oil prices to touch off a severe recession. These economists conceded that the result would be more inflation, but they held that would be much better than a rise in unemployment.

Cost to Refiners Of Acquiring Crude Oil

Dollars per barrel

Year	Domestic	Imported	Composite
1974	7.18	12.52	9.07
1975	8.39	13.93	10.38
1976	8.84	13.48	10.89
1977	9.55	14.53	11.96
1978	10.61	14.57	12.46
1979	14.27	21.67	17.72
1980	24.23	33.89	28.07
1981*	36.95	38.35	37.48

* Average through March.

Source: Department of Energy

"There's no sense in shooting ourselves in the foot to show how much we care about inflation," Arthur Okun said in 1979. "Inflation is a terribly serious problem, but it's not going to be cured by deep recession. Or if it is, the cost may not be worth it."

Stalemate Under Ford

Economic policy making during the last half of the 1970s reflected the unhappy choices the nation faced. With economic theory unable to offer a strategy that would achieve price stability and low unemployment simultaneously, politicians fought to a standstill over which of the twin evils should be given top priority.

Nixon, for his part, consistently rejected fighting inflation to the point of producing a sharp rise in joblessness. His last budget proposal, offered in early 1974, proposed "moderate restraint," but he reserved the right "to support the economy if that should be necessary." The president remained prepared "to do whatever is necessary to avoid a recession," explained Frederic V. Malek, assistant director of the Office of Management and Budget. "If it means busting the budget, then he will bust the budget rather than keep people out of jobs."

President Gerald R. Ford sought to adhere to that moderately conservative policy when he took over after Nixon resigned in August 1974. His first economic proposals included a call for conventional economic restraint in the form of a 5 percent tax surcharge and a cut in outlays.

Ford's proposals were quickly overcome by events. Economic statistics later showed that the economy fell into its worst postwar recession in the first half of 1974, as the rapid run-up of oil prices collided with fairly restrictive fiscal and monetary policies. The severity of the collapse was made much worse because of excessive accumulation of inventories resulting from the rapid pace of growth caused by the stimulative policies Nixon had followed during the controls period.

With Ford's support, Congress abruptly shifted to an anti-recession fiscal strategy, rushing through a public service jobs program in its post-election session. The 1974 statistics showed that unemployment was back up to 5.6 percent, while consumer prices rose an uncontrolled 12.2 percent.

For the next two years, Ford and Congress fought to a standstill on economic policy. Democrats in Congress clamored for a more stimulative fiscal policy. Supported by organized labor and many black leaders, liberals pushed for adoption of the Humphrey-Hawkins "full employment" bill, which would commit the government to holding the jobless rate for adult men to 3 percent. Echoing the anti-Eisenhower rhetoric of 20 years earlier, Sen. Hubert H. Humphrey, D-Minn. (1949-64; 1971-78), said in 1976 that adoption of the bill would "reject the discredited economic doctrine of the present administration and replace it with a new economics that puts all of America's resources back to work."

Ford tried to counter the Democrats' attack by calling for even bigger tax cuts. In October 1974 he proposed a $28 billion tax cut — $16 billion more than the Democratic plan. But to prevent that large a reduction from overstimulating the economy and aggravating inflation, Ford said his tax cut would be provided only on the condition that Congress put a lid on federal expenditures.

Ford's demand that tax cuts be matched "dollar for dollar" by spending reductions was attacked by Keynes-ians, who contended that such a policy would provide no net stimulus to the economy. In the end, although Ford did veto one congressionally approved tax cut, he ultimately signed another even though it fell short of his demand for spending restraint.

For the rest of his term in office, Ford continued to struggle with the Democratic Congress over spending policies. The net result was a fairly stimulative policy. The government ran back-to-back deficits of $45.2 billion in fiscal 1975 and $66.4 billion in fiscal 1976. However, even that was not so stimulative as liberals would have liked.

The Federal Reserve, in the meantime, went its own way. Although it had switched to an expansive policy in late 1974, by 1975 it returned to a restrictive stance against inflation. The board did come under congressional pressure to accelerate money supply expansion to accommodate a faster recovery. But the House backed away from proposals by Rep. Henry S. Reuss, D-Wis., for Congress to dictate money supply goals. Nevertheless, Fed Chairman Burns did agree to disclose monetary growth target ranges in periodic House and Senate testimony.

Unemployment continued to rise in 1975, averaging 8.5 percent for the whole year. In 1976 it dropped back to 7.7 percent, not low enough to protect Ford from Democratic complaints that he had not done enough to ease the pain caused by recession. Inflation, in the meantime, slowed to a still-high 7 percent in 1975, and to 4.8 percent in 1976. Worse for Ford, the economic recovery appeared to be sputtering in 1976. After a strong first quarter, the pace of growth slowed later in the year, adding to Democratic calls for more fiscal stimulus.

Democrats emphasized their traditional concerns about unemployment during the 1976 campaign, but candidate Jimmy Carter also exploited the inflation issue. Capitalizing on the Ford administration's inability to find an acceptable combination of unemployment and inflation, Carter spoke of a "misery index" that added the unemployment and inflation rates. Under Ford, Carter said, the "misery index" stood at an all-time high of 12.5 percent. That ploy was to embarrass Carter four years later when candidate Ronald Reagan noted that the "misery index" had climbed above 20 percent during Carter's presidency.

THE CARTER YEARS: INTO THE ERA OF LIMITS

President Ford may have felt vindicated by some of the events of the Carter years. For one thing, his conservative economic policies were partially supported when the Democrats chose, in Carter, the most conservative of their candidates. Despite the longstanding liberal commitment to seeking full employment, for instance, Carter resisted for some time supporting the litmus test of liberalism in the mid-1970s, the Humphrey-Hawkins bill. He finally reluctantly endorsed the bill late in the primary season — perhaps to appease liberals he had offended by speaking favorably about "ethnic purity" in urban neighborhoods. But as president he objected to setting the 3 percent unemployment rate as a goal of government policy. The Humphrey-Hawkins bill that finally passed was toothless.

Ford may also have taken some satisfaction when events forced President Carter, during the early months of his term in office, to perform a Democratic version of the flip-flop Ford did on economic policy. While Ford had recommended an anti-inflation tax increase shortly after he took office only to back off when the economy dipped into recession, Carter began his presidency calling for a one-time $50 tax rebate to stimulate the economy. Within months, Carter was prompted to withdraw the rebate proposal in the face of unexpectedly strong economic growth.

Finally, the strength of the economy in 1977 appeared to vindicate Ford's efforts to resist fiscal stimulus during the final year of his term. And the dramatic slowdown in consumer price inflation made Ford's policies appear successful.

Conservative economists were later to point to the slowdown in inflation in 1976 as evidence that a recession can produce significant price moderation. But many other analysts contended that the easing of inflation, while influenced by the 1974-75 recession, basically reflected two or three other factors: the stabilization of oil prices following

their precipitous rise in 1973 and 1974, a typical surge in productivity during the early phases of economic recovery, and the end of the boom in price increases that followed the lifting of Nixon's controls three years earlier.

Temporary Relief

Economists had not paid a great deal of attention to the productivity problem before Carter's term. That oversight continued immediately after he took office, as the fairly strong productivity performance between 1975 and 1977 obscured what later came to be recognized as one of the economy's most serious problems.

Productivity, defined as output per hour of labor, is the basic source of increases in income in the long run. When productivity improves, wages can increase without cutting into profits or raising prices. But when productivity fails to improve, wage increases either eat away at profits or force businesses to boost prices in order to protect profit margins. A drop in productivity normally leads to higher labor costs. Because most businesses set prices by adding certain markups to cost, higher prices often result.

Productivity in the private sector has declined steadily since 1965. From 1965 through 1973 growth averaged only 2.3 percent, compared with a growth rate of 3 percent between 1947 and 1965. Between 1973 and 1980, productivity rose an average of 0.8 percent a year. This long-term decline in productivity has been one of the most vexing economic mysteries of the postwar period.

Productivity and Private Business, 1948-80

Average annual rate of change

Year	Output[1]	Hours of All Persons[2]	Output per Hour, All Persons	Compensation Per Hour[3]	Unit Labor Cost	Implicit Price Deflator[4]
1948	6.1%	0.7%	5.3%	8.5%	3.0%	7.0%
1950	9.1	1.1	7.9	7.1	−0.8	1.6
1952	3.3	0.1	3.2	6.4	3.0	1.1
1955	7.9	3.8	4.0	2.5	−1.4	1.6
1957	1.0	−1.5	2.5	6.5	3.9	3.5
1960	3.3	0.2	3.1	4.2	1.1	−0.2
1962	5.5	1.6	3.8	4.6	0.7	1.5
1965	6.8	3.2	3.5	3.9	0.3	1.9
1967	2.2	0.0	2.2	5.5	3.2	2.7
1970	−0.8	−1.7	0.9	7.4	6.4	4.5
1971	3.0	−0.5	3.6	6.6	2.9	4.4
1972	6.6	3.0	3.5	6.5	2.9	3.4
1973	6.6	3.9	2.7	8.0	5.2	5.4
1974	−1.9	0.4	−2.3	9.4	11.9	9.4
1975	−1.9	−4.1	2.3	9.6	7.2	9.7
1976	6.3	2.9	3.3	8.6	5.1	4.7
1977	6.3	4.0	2.1	7.7	5.5	5.6
1978	4.7	4.9	−0.2	8.4	8.6	7.4
1979	2.8	3.3	−0.4	9.9	10.4	8.8
1980	−0.8	−0.5	−0.3	10.0	10.3	9.2

[1] *Output refers to gross domestic product in private business sector in 1972 dollars.*

[2] *Hours of all persons engaged in private business, including hours of proprietors and unpaid family workers. Estimates based primarily on establishment data.*

[3] *Wages and salaries of employee plus employers' contributions for social insurance and private benefit plans. Also includes estimates of wages, salaries and supplemental payments for the self-employed.*

[4] *For gross domestic product.*

Source: Department of Labor, Bureau of Labor Statistics

Productivity rose 2.3 percent in 1975, 3.3 percent in 1976 and 2.1 percent in 1977. That growth helped ease inflationary pressures because it temporarily slowed the rise in business costs. Labor costs had climbed 11.9 percent in 1974, but the rate of gain slowed to 7.2 percent in 1975, 5.1 percent in 1976 and 5.5 percent in 1977.

Unfortunately, that was merely a temporary cyclical improvement. Productivity normally rises during the later stage of recessions and the early part of economic recoveries. Typically, businesses are slow to lay off employees at the beginning of recessions because they are reluctant to lose workers and because it takes them some time to be convinced that a downturn is occurring. Thus, in the early phases of recessions, output drops but the level of employment holds fairly steady. As a result, productivity, or output per worker, drops.

As recessions advance, however, employers finally do lay off workers, bringing the level of employment back into line with output. With fewer workers relative to the level of output, productivity improves. Then, just as employers are slow to lay off workers at the beginning of a recession, there is a delay before they hire them back during a recovery. As a result, when the economy first starts to pick up speed, employers try to increase output for a while without adding new jobs. The result is a marked, though temporary, improvement in productivity.

The behavior of productivity assures that inflation will improve late in a recession and early in an economic recovery for reasons that have little to do with the supply of labor itself. President Carter was the beneficiary of that short-term phenomenon during the first part of his term in office — a fact that some economists believe led the new president to be unduly complacent about inflation for a while.

The Productivity Puzzle

By the mid-1970s, economists came to realize that quite apart from such cyclical fluctuations in productivity, the economy was going through a much more worrisome fundamental decline. Between 1947 and 1965, productivity had climbed at an average annual rate of 3 percent. But from 1965 through 1973, the growth averaged only 2.3 percent. And from 1973 through 1980, productivity rose on the average only 0.8 percent a year. Unless a solution to that long-term slowdown could be found, many worried that Americans would have to accept a slower rate of improvement in their standard of living, perpetual inflation or both.

The more fundamental long-term decline in productivity is one of the most vexing mysteries of the postwar period. Economists have offered a variety of explanations for it, although they have found it difficult to quantify the importance of the various factors.

In part, analysts believe the decline reflects population trends in the United States. Some of the big productivity gains between 1948 and 1965 undoubtedly resulted from a shift of large numbers of workers out of agriculture into rapidly expanding manufacturing industries. In the 1970s the fastest economic growth occurred in the service sector, where it is much more difficult to achieve productivity gains because of the labor-intensive nature of services.

Some economists also believe the large influx of the postwar "baby-boom" workers and women into the labor force in the 1960s and 1970s pulled down the productivity rate. Young and inexperienced workers normally are less productive than those who have been working longer. During the 1970s, the overall work force increased 27 percent, to 104.7 million people from 82.7 million. But the number of workers between ages 16 and 24 grew 38 percent, to 24.6 million from 17.8 million. And the number of working women rose 42 percent, to 44.6 million from 31.5 million.

Analysts believe that population surge, which the Carter administration was to call a "demographic tidal wave," contributed significantly to inflation during the late 1960s and the 1970s by helping to slow productivity. During the 1960s productivity had increased at a 3 percent annual rate but increased at only a 1.4 percent pace in the 1970s.

(Economists also claim that the dramatic growth of the labor force probably put continuous pressure on the government to adopt policies designed to reduce unemployment, rather than concentrate on fighting inflation. At least some of the concern during the Kennedy-Johnson era about chronic economic slack may have resulted from the fear that the economy would not grow fast enough to absorb all the new workers.)

Of course, inadequate investment itself had a perverse effect on productivity. By the mid-1970s the rate of investment in the United States was lagging behind that of most Western industrial nations.

Ben Laden, an economist with T. Rowe Price Associates, Inc., estimated in 1981 that new capital investment per worker added to the labor force totaled only $21,600 during the 1970s after adjustment for inflation. That was down from $25,400 in the 1960s.

In part, that phenomenon probably reflected the impact of inflation, which discourages savings and encourages consumption. During periods of inflation, it is preferable to spend money now than to spend it later, when it will be worth less. A decline of savings reduces the amount of money available for investment.

Investment also suffered from the economic instability of the 1970s, which reduced business profits and confidence. And the interaction between inflation and the tax system also tended to retard business investment during the 1970s. Businesses have long been allowed to write off for tax purposes the cost of investment in plant and equipment. During periods of inflation, the size of the write-offs tends to fall short of what is needed for businesses to make new capital investments.

During the 1960s and 1970s business depreciation allowances were based on the historical cost of equipment. Because of inflation, the cost of new equipment usually was higher than the cost of old equipment. So recovery of depreciation costs on the basis of historical costs fell far short of their "replacement" costs.

The sudden rise in energy prices also played a role in the sharp slowdown in productivity after 1973. Analysts believe that the abrupt rise in oil prices made it economically inefficient for industry to use much of the equipment that had been purchased when energy was fairly cheap. To save money, some businesses slowed down the rate at which such equipment was used, hurting productivity.

A simple example illustrates this phenomenon. To help save energy following the 1973 Arab oil embargo, Congress mandated that the speed limit on highways be reduced to 55 miles an hour. If a trucking company were to adhere to that slower speed limit, it would take longer for each truck to cover its route. As a result, it would require more man-hours on the road to transport the same amount of goods the same distance. More man-hours for the same output translates into lower productivity.

Finally, analysts attribute some of the slowdown in productivity during the 1970s to the costs imposed on business by various federal regulations. Businesses were forced to spend more money on environmental quality, occupational safety and health. Such regulation has a dual effect in retarding productivity. First, to the extent that businesses have to adapt existing equipment to new standards, it forces less efficient use of the equipment. With time, as new equipment is designed from the outset to meet the standards, that cost diminishes. Second, while regulations may enhance the quality of life, intangible forms of economic output such as clean air or better health are not measured in calculating productivity. Many regulations thus shifted some portion of the nation's economic output into "goods" that were not counted by traditional measurements of productivity.

Addressing Structural Ills

The loss of income resulting from higher energy prices, the slowdown in productivity and growing concern for the environment all combined to make President Carter's term in office a time of acute awareness of limits. Some popular ideas of the period included the "limits to growth," "small is beautiful" and "zero population growth."

Carter himself proposed a much more limited role for government than his Democratic predecessors had. In sharp contrast to the expansive rhetoric of Great Society days, Carter declared in his inaugural address: "Government cannot solve all our problems, it can't set our goals, it cannot define our vision. Government cannot eliminate poverty, or provide a bountiful economy or reduce inflation or save our cities or cure illiteracy or provide energy, and government cannot mandate goodness."

The president went on to assert that a "only a true partnership between government and the people can ever hope to reach these goals." But the message of diminished expectations was clear.

One indication of the lowered expectations came in Carter's 1979 economic report to Congress. The president told Congress that the decline in productivity meant that estimates of the economy's long-term potential had to be scaled back. It had previously been assumed that between 1968 and 1975 potential economic output had grown about 4 percent annually after inflation and that the potential growth rate had slowed to 3.75 percent per year since then. But Carter said the economy's potential was more like 3.5 percent annually for the future. That implied past policies designed to provide full employment might have been overly stimulative. At the least, it suggested that a less expansive policy was in order for the future.

Carter set out to correct what he considered a major defect in the relationship between the government and the economy. He inherited a budget that had grown from 20.3 percent of GNP in fiscal 1970 to 22.3 percent in fiscal 1976. The fiscal 1976 deficit was a record $66.4 billion. Carter promised to reduce outlays to 21 percent of GNP and eliminate the deficit by fiscal 1981. In part, the growth of the government's share of the economy in the years immediately preceding his presidency reflected the normal rise of the automatic stabilizers during the 1974-75 recession.

Looked at from a broader perspective, some economists argued that federal spending during the 1970s had actually moved in tandem with the economy. Economist Robert Hartman, for instance, estimated in 1981 that during the 1970s federal outlays had climbed about 3 percent a year after inflation, or at about the same rate as the economy itself expanded.

But that general trend masked an important change in the composition of federal spending. Defense outlays declined steeply in real terms during the first part of the decade, according to Hartman, and only started recovering modestly after 1976. But payments to individuals rose at a real 7.1 percent rate during the decade.

Hartman attributed the sharp rise in payments to individuals to four factors: 1) large unemployment compensation benefits during the 1974-75 recession, 2) three large increases in Social Security benefits voted by Congress between 1970 and 1972, 3) increased use of Medicare and Medicaid services, and 4) sharp rises in use of programs such as food stamps and Supplemental Security Income.

During much of his term, Carter tried to blunt the growth of the budget without offending traditional Democratic constituencies. Relations between the president and liberals were strained throughout the four years, but by fiscal 1979 the president appeared to have some success. That year, federal outlays totaled only 20.9 percent of GNP — below his target for fiscal 1981. The federal deficit had dropped to $27.7 billion.

However, the decline in the deficit partially reflected the willingness of government to let inflation increase revenues. Whereas tax cuts between 1970 and 1976 had pretty much offset the inflation-induced growth in the tax bite, federal revenues rose from 18.3 percent of GNP in fiscal 1976 to 19.8 percent in fiscal 1979. At the same time, economic recovery, which had pushed the unemployment rate down to 7 percent in 1977, cut joblessness to 6 percent in 1978 and then to 5.8 percent in 1979.

Moreover, inflation continued to cloud the economic outlook. Following the 1976 respite, consumer prices shot back up 6.8 percent in 1977 and 9 percent in 1978. By 1979 economists again were beginning to warn about the dangers of an overheating economy.

At first reluctant to clamp down hard on the economy, Carter tried to slow the rate of inflation by increasing the government's effort to monitor and publicize price increases. When that proved ineffective, he announced a system of "voluntary" wage and price restraints. These were to be backed up by the government's refusal to allow non-complying firms to bid for government contracts, although that weapon was never actually used.

To make matters worse, the Organization of Petroleum Exporting Countries (OPEC) started pushing oil prices up again. The average price of a barrel of imported oil surged from $13.29 in 1978 to $18.67 in 1979 and to $30.46 in 1980. The total cost of oil imports into the United States jumped from $42.3 billion in 1978 to $60.5 billion in 1979 and to $78.9 billion in 1980.

Consumer prices soared 13.3 percent in 1979. But by that point the Carter administration had concluded that the only long-term solution to the nation's energy problems was to let prices rise and discourage consumption. To prevent the rise in prices from translating into a new general round of inflation, the administration tried to keep wages from rising to offset the higher oil prices. It was at this time that Alfred Kahn warned that a decline in the American standard of living was unavoidable.

Jamming on the Brakes

The worst impact of the 1979 round of OPEC price increases was not felt until the first quarter of 1980. When the higher-priced oil started arriving in the United States, it added to an already high rate of inflation, pushing the Consumer Price Index to annual rates approaching 20 percent. The psychological impact was devastating, forcing Carter to make the second dramatic economic policy reversal of his presidency.

Carter had surprised many analysts in January 1980 by proposing a fairly healthy rise in spending for fiscal 1981. While the president's previous budget proposals had been described as "lean" and "austere," his fiscal 1981 budget appeared to ease up a bit. It called for a decline in the deficit to $15.8 billion, and at the same time included a substantial increase in defense expenditures and a modest rise in non-defense spending as well.

Given the new scare about inflation and the president's failure to deliver on his three-year promise to produce a balanced budget by the end of his first term, financial markets and the public reacted very negatively to the proposal. Carter promptly went back to the drawing board to come up with a much more austere budget.

In addition, Carter and the Federal Reserve agreed that the economy should be tightly restrained. In March the president invoked the Credit Control Act of 1969 to authorize the Fed to place restrictions on consumer credit. At the same time, the administration worked with Congress to adopt a budget that supposedly would be balanced.

The March shift to fiscal and monetary restraint was dramatic. Administration officials quietly conceded that the policy would produce a recession, but said they saw little alternative in light of the sharp acceleration of inflation and the complete failure of other anti-inflation strategies.

Looking back, economists believe the economy already was falling into a recession in January 1980. The credit controls imposed in March struck another blow to an already faltering economy, producing a steep recession. The recession proved to be short-lived, as the Fed abruptly eased up in mid-year and the credit controls were removed by August. The brief recession did little to abate inflation fears, and the Fed again instituted restrictive monetary policies, with the result that the recovery in late 1980 was tepid. By late 1981 the economy had fallen back into recession.

Carter, in the meantime, opposed mounting calls for a tax cut from economists and election-minded politicians eager to check the rise in unemployment. The president said fiscal restraint was required to contain inflation. Carter also argued that a hastily enacted tax cut would merely add to consumer demand and aggravate inflation. What was needed, he argued, was a program carefully designed to increase investment incentives and reduce business costs to ease inflation without unduly stimulating consumer demand.

Even in 1979 that policy struck many liberals as too conservative. In August economist Paul Samuelson complained that political pressures might force Carter to concentrate fiscal policy on reducing inflation by increasing unemployment. "If that occurs, he [President Carter] will eschew the usual election-year pumping-up of the economy," Samuelson said. "Instead he may go out of office in a blaze of glory fighting inflation. That same blaze could scorch a considerable part of the U.S. economy."

Samuelson predicted that if Carter opted for an anti-inflation strategy, the United States might be in for "two or three years of stagnation."

Carter did indeed reject election-year pump-priming. In the absence of a tax cut, inflation drove the federal tax bite to 20.3 percent of GNP by the end of his term in office. In the meantime, the economic slump pushed federal expenditures to 22.6 percent of GNP. The federal deficit in fiscal 1980 totaled $59.6 billion.

Unemployment in 1980 averaged 7.1 percent. Consumer prices rose 12.4 percent. The economy failed to realize any appreciable real growth in 1980 or 1981. Samuelson's prediction was well on the way to being realized. The stage was set for "Reaganomics."

On to 'Reaganomics'

Conservatives were not the only group to offer solutions to the supply-side problems that became apparent during the 1970s. Many liberals also argued that demand management policies could not solve the new set of problems the economy faced.

These liberals proposed a variety of makeshift solutions to the problem of escalating wages and prices. Most were designed to reduce business costs to ease pressure on prices. Some proposed cutting taxes, such as sales and Social Security taxes, that add to prices. Others shared the conservatives' arguments that regulations that add to costs should be reduced. Still others recommended using the tax system to reward wage and price restraint.

Carter himself proposed some of these attacks on inflation, including "real wage insurance," by which the government would award employers and workers who moderated price increases with tax breaks, and proposals to deregulate the airline and trucking industries.

But by this time, the Republicans had captured the image of the party of prosperity and price stability. There were plenty of signs throughout the late 1970s that the Democrats were losing ground to politicians who argued that government was more the cause of problems than the solution. There were, for instance, a variety of popular movements to put a lid on taxes (the Proposition 13 tax ceiling referendum in California, for instance) and to amend the U.S. Constitution to require the government to balance the budget.

President Carter's chief economist, Charles Shultze, acknowledged in 1979 the change in the public mood that would sweep Ronald Reagan into office the next year.

"One of the things that a democratic, civilized government has as its objective is to give its citizens. . . a condition in which they have some sense of control of their own future," Schultze said. "The future is always uncertain, but when the measuring rod by which we do our planning shrinks — not only shrinks, but shrinks in unpredictable amounts — it weakens significantly people's control of their own future.

". . . One of the problems with inflation, quite apart from its economic problem, is the weakening of control of one's future," he continued. "Proposition 13 [and the [proposed] constitutional amendment. . . stem. . . in part from the belief [that] government spending [is] responsible for inflation, but also in part it is just a general sense of loss of control and a blame that 'they' are doing it to me."

—Christopher R. Conte

3

Control of the Purse Strings

The Constitution gave Congress the power to tax and spend. For nearly 200 years, the "power of the purse" has given the legislative branch paramount authority to command national resources and direct them to federal purposes. No other congressional prerogative confers so much control over the goals of government, or so much influence on the nation's well-being.

Since the 1930s Congress had made broad use of its taxing, spending and borrowing powers to vastly enlarge the government and expand its influence over the U.S. economy. Federal spending mounted to $660.5 billion in fiscal 1981, accounting for more than one-fifth of the gross national product. And the way the government spends its money — and raises it through taxes or borrowing — carries enormous consequences for the nation's economic performance and its political and social balance.

Through the years, the House and Senate have jealously guarded most congressional powers to finance the machinery of government. But Congress has had trouble using its tax and spending powers to shape a coherent federal budget policy. The result has been runaway budget deficits, reaching a record $66.4 billion in fiscal 1976, as well as constant battling between Congress and successive presidents for final authority to set federal fiscal policy.

Except for the Vietnam War and the Watergate scandal, no other issue since World War II has so divided Congress and at times paralyzed government decision-making. Directly or indirectly, congressional historian George B. Galloway noted in a 1955 book, "perhaps nine-tenths of the work of Congress is concerned ... with the spending of public money." The preoccupation with budget decisions has been compounded during the following 25 years as federal deficits mounted, inflation ran rampant and Congress and presidents fought for control over total government outlays.

Much as it wanted to control the purse strings, Congress rarely bothered until the mid-1970s to tie its separate legislation to tax and spending totals. Since 1921 it had left to the executive branch the task of drawing up a yearly federal budget proposing fiscal policy and setting forth revenue, outlay and deficit or surplus targets. But in the early 1970s a heavily Democratic Congress fiercely resisted when Republican President Richard Nixon refused to spend billions of dollars already appropriated to federal agencies.

Congress responded in 1974 by limiting the president's power to impound funds and setting up its own elaborate budget-making procedures. But in subsequent years the House and Senate backed away from politically tough decisions to bring the budget closer to balance by cutting spending or raising taxes. It took a determined Republican President Ronald Reagan — and a conservative swing in the 1980 elections that gave Republicans control of the Senate — to ram large cutbacks through Congress using shortcut procedures that bypassed the normal spending process. The precedent dismayed some thoughtful legislators, who feared that through the process Congress would abdicate its constitutional powers.

With more spending battles ahead — and large tax cuts going into effect — Congress and presidents will continue to struggle for control over federal spending. For the budget process is an imprecise instrument, always subject to change by variable economic fortunes and the give-and-take of politics. And in an era of fiscal austerity, partisan infighting is bound to flare up over where federal resources should be directed.

The Constitution, while granting the government impressive financial powers, did not specifically require it to keep an annual budget. Over the last 60 years, presidents have used budget-making powers that Congress conferred to tighten the White House grip on the far-flung departments and agencies of government. The president's annual budget for fiscal 1982, a 1,954-page, four-volume document, lays out in fine print what the government does and where the administration hopes to take the country. More often than not, however, the budget blueprint is changed by events and congressional decisions.

For Congress still holds the power of the purse, and officials cannot spend the government's funds until Congress has approved their use for federal purposes. Through action on the president's annual requests to appropriate funds, the House and Senate determine what federal agencies can spend during the upcoming fiscal year, and often for years thereafter. By commiting the government to meet certain needs of its citizens, moreover, Congress has obligated itself to come up with the money year after year, no matter the state of the Treasury. As a result, more than three-quarters of total federal outlays each year have been spent beyond effective control by Congress or the president.

"We have a hemorrhaging budget," House Budget Committee Chairman Robert N. Giaimo, D-Conn., observed as he retired from Congress in 1980. Even with elaborate new budget-making machinery at work, the House and Senate barely slowed government outlays that were spurting upward by half-a-billion dollars a year as the 1970s ended. The persistent resulting deficits fired inflation and defeated fiscal restraints that presidents tried to build into their budget proposals.

Since 1975 Congress has been trying to re-establish budget control by setting overall revenue and spending targets before considering tax and appropriations legislation. The new procedures compel the House and Senate to make tougher budget choices and go on record with regard to total taxes, spending and deficits. But Congress still left itself a choice between sticking to overall budget targets or bending them to encompass other objectives. As Rep. Richard Bolling, D-Mo., a framer of the 1974 budget law has noted, the congressional budget process "could be viable, if the will is there."

CONGRESS' TRUMP: POWER OF THE PURSE

The congressional power of the purse is firmly rooted in the U.S. Constitution adopted in 1789. That document's first article granted Congress authority to raise revenues through taxes, tariffs and other levies; to direct the spending of the funds raised; and to borrow money on the nation's credit. Galloway, outlining *The Legislative Process in Congress* in 1955, described the spending power as "the constitutional birthright of Congress." That power is spelled out in three clauses:

● **Article I, Section 8, Clause 1** grants power "to lay and collect taxes, duties, imposts and excises, to pay the debts and provide for the common defense and general welfare of the United States...."

● **Article I, Section 8, Clause 2** grants the power "to borrow money on the credit of the United States."

● **Article I, Section 9, Clause 7** declares that "no money shall be drawn from the Treasury, but in consequence of appropriations made by law...."

The taxing power is specific, and it was vastly enlarged in 1913 by the 16th Amendment authorizing a federal tax on incomes. Over the years, Congress has devised a tax system that was expected to raise more than $660 billion in fiscal 1982, mostly from individual income taxes.

The spending power is more vague, but it has been enlarged by expansive interpretation of the other authorities that the Constitution grants to Congress. For fiscal 1982, total federal outlays were expected to swell beyond $700 billion, even after Congress agreed to Reagan's budget-cutting initiatives.

The borrowing power carries no constitutional restrictions at all, allowing Congress to borrow funds in any amounts for any purposes. With the budget in deficit for 43 out of the 50 fiscal years from 1931 through 1981, national debt topped $1 trillion in late 1981.

Those enormous sums may be beyond the comprehension of most Americans, including members of Congress.

But they suggest the power that the congressional tax, spending and borrowing authorities provide — and indicate the economic and social stakes involved in federal budget battles.

The Power to Tax

Without sufficient revenues, no government could function effectively. The Constitution, along with the 16th Amendment, therefore granted Congress the right to enact virtually any taxes, except for duties on exports. In Article I, Section 8, the framers of the Constitution granted authority broad enough to encompass nearly all known forms of taxation, including tariffs on imported goods and excise taxes on the manufacture, sale, use or transfer of property within the United States. And, in general, both Congress and the courts have construed the taxing power liberally to generate additional sources of federal revenue.

The constitutional historian C. H. Pritchett, in his book *The American Constitution,* noted that adequate sources of funds and broad authority to use them were "essential conditions for carrying on an effective government." "Consequently," he observed, "the first rule for judicial review of tax statutes is that a heavy burden of proof lies on anyone who would challenge any congressional exercise of fiscal power. In almost every decision touching the constitutionality of federal taxation, the Supreme Court has stressed the breadth of congressional power and the limits of its own reviewing powers."

The Constitution did set some limits. Article I, Section 9, Clause 5 forbade export duties. Section 9, Clause 4 prohibited direct taxes unless each state paid a share in proportion to its population. And Section 8, Clause 1 directed that "all duties, imposts and excises" be imposed uniformly throughout the nation. Implied limitations, as interpreted by the Supreme Court in *McCulloch v. Maryland* (1819), exempted state and local governments — and income from state and local bonds — from federal taxes.

Early Reliance on Tariffs

The first congressional measure to raise revenue was a tariff act, approved July 4, 1789. Until the Civil War, customs duties produced sufficient revenue to meet most of the government's needs, accounting for more than 90 percent of total federal receipts. Tariffs, in addition to supplying funds for government operations, protected the nation's fledgling industries against competition from foreign imports. Through most of the nation's history, until the early years of the Great Depression in the 1930s, regions and economic interests often fought over tariff policy.

During the first half of the 19th century, the tariff laws offered protection mainly to manufactured goods. Western and Northern farmers supported a protectionist policy for manufacturers on the assumption that industrial development, aided by high tariffs, would create a profitable home market for their products.

The Republican Party, founded in the West in 1854, lined up behind the protectionist principle on the eve of the Civil War, thereby availing itself of a policy that was to ensure it the enduring adherence of Northern and Eastern industrial elements after settlement of the slavery issue. The Democratic Party, on the other hand, generally favored a moderate-or-low tariff policy that helped it to retain the solid support of the agricultural South for years.

After the Civil War, tariff policy was the major issue in many presidential and congressional elections. Before World War I, a change in administrations often led to passage of new tariff laws. Congress devoted an inordinate amount of time to tariff-making, not only because the customs duties were made and remade so frequently but also because tariffs potentially affected the interests of many segments of American commercial life.

Congress finally delegated virtually all of its tariff-making power to the president, beginning with the Reciprocal Trade Agreements Act of 1934. By then, individual and corporate income taxes had begun replacing customs receipts as the main source of government revenue. In 1910 customs duties still brought in more than 49 percent of federal revenues; by the 1970s they contributed less than 1 percent, even though customs receipts had passed the $2 billion level.

Shift to the Income Tax

Since the 16th Amendment was adopted, federal taxes on individual incomes and corporate profits have become the principal revenue sources. That amendment, ratified in 1913, removed an obstacle to income taxes posed by the constitutional prohibition on direct taxes unless apportioned among the states according to population.

Congress in 1862 levied a tax on individual incomes to help finance the Civil War. That tax brought in a total of $376 million, accounting for 25 percent of internal revenue collections in 1866, before expiring by limitation in 1872. The Supreme Court ruled that the income levy was not a direct tax subject to the Constitution's apportionment requirement.

During the 1870s and 1880s, little interest was shown in enactment of a new income tax law. But growth of the country and accumulation of large fortunes began in the 1890s to generate pressure for a return to income taxation. After the depression of 1893 had reduced federal revenues, Congress yielded and in 1894 levied a tax of 2 percent on personal incomes in excess of $3,000. Before the new tax law became operative, it was challenged, and this time the Supreme Court held that an income tax was a direct tax and therefore unconstitutional without apportionment (*Pollock v. Farmers' Loan & Trust Co.*, 1895).

Although the court had blocked the road to this attempted expansion of the tax system, a solution was afforded by the power of Congress and the states to revise the Constitution. A campaign to do so was begun immediately, and on Feb. 23, 1913, the 16th Amendment was officially declared ratified. The one-sentence amendment stated tersely: "The Congress shall have power to lay and collect taxes on incomes from whatever source derived, without apportionment among the several states, and without regard to any census or enumeration."

Thus the problem of apportioning income taxes was swept away and Congress was left free to do what it had tried to do two decades earlier. The new grant of power came at a providential time, for the great expansion of federal revenue soon required by World War I would have been difficult, if not impossible, to achieve by any other means.

Congress imposed a federal income tax the same year the amendment was ratified, applying the tax to wages, salaries, interest, dividends, rents, entrepreneurial income and capital gains. It set the initial rate at 1 percent, plus a surtax of 1 to 6 percent on larger incomes.

The 1913 law exempted income up to $3,000 ($4,000 for a married couple). It allowed deductions for personal interest, tax payments and business expenses. In the ensuing 68 years Congress complicated the federal income tax code with numerous changes that granted tax advantages to encourage specific activities. It also frequently changed rates and the level of exempted income. Maximum marginal rates reached as high as 94 percent during World War II. In 1981 Congress cut the maximum rate on investment income from 70 percent to 50 percent.

Corporate Taxes

Congress did not encounter with a corporate income tax the constitutional difficulty that it had experienced with the tax on individual income. A corporate income tax was levied in 1909 in the guise of "a special excise tax" at a rate of 1 percent of net income in excess of $5,000. That tax, like the 1894 individual income tax, was challenged in the courts, but the Supreme Court let it stand as an excise on the privilege of doing business as a corporation.

Following ratification of the 16th Amendment, an outright corporate income tax at the same rate was made a part of the Revenue Act of 1913 alongside the individual income tax. The two taxes together, broadened and modified through the years as circumstances required, became basic elements of the nation's revenue system.

In most years, corporate taxes have produced less revenue than individual income taxes. But during World War I, World War II and the Korean War, Congress raised additional revenues by imposing an excess profits tax to supplement corporate income taxes. And in 1980 Congress approved President Carter's request to levy a so-called "windfall profits tax" that was expected to raise $20 billion in fiscal 1982 by taxing the rising value of domestically produced crude oil as federal price controls were lifted.

Excise and Other Taxes

Excise taxes have always been a part of the federal tax system; they were mentioned specifically in Article I, Section 8 of the Constitution among the various levies that Congress was authorized to impose. The excises levied upon ratification of the Constitution included taxes on carriages, liquor, snuff, sugar and auction sales. These and similar taxes have been controversial throughout the republic's history, in important part because they were considered unfair and burdensome to the poor. Over the years, excises have been imposed and repealed or lowered; during every major war, the perennial liquor and tobacco taxes were supplemented by taxes on manufactured goods, licenses, financial transactions, services, luxury articles and dozens of other items that lent themselves to this form of taxation.

The power of Congress to tax in other areas has become well established over the years. One of the most important areas has been payroll taxes, which financially underpin the old-age insurance and unemployment compensation systems. Estate taxes date from the Civil War period, and have been a permanent part of the national tax structure since 1916. The gift tax, levied to check avoidance of the estate tax, has been permanent since 1932.

Growth of Federal Revenues

The federal tax system has steadily produced huge increases in government revenues. Even though Congress periodically cut taxes, individual and corporate income tax revenues rose almost without interruption as a growing population and expanding economy enlarged the base on which they were levied.

By fiscal 1981 individual income taxes mounted to an estimated $285.6 billion. Corporate taxes were estimated at $63.3 billion. Together, they accounted for nearly 58 percent of the $602.6 billion in federal revenues for that fiscal year.

For the same year, social insurance payroll taxes and contributions reached about $186.8 billion, nearly 31 percent of revenues. Other estimated federal receipts included $41.7 billion from excise taxes, $6.9 billion from estate and gift taxes, $7.4 billion in customs duties and $13.8 billion in receipts from miscellaneous government activities.

Initial low rates kept revenues from federal income taxes at modest levels until the United States entered World War I. Then Congress sharply increased rates, stepping the revenue yield up from $360 million in fiscal 1917 to $2.3 billion in fiscal 1918. Since then, federal income taxes have produced more annual revenue than all excise and other internal revenue taxes combined — except for nine fiscal years from 1933 through 1941 when the government levied numerous excise taxes to replace revenues as incomes sagged during the Depression.

In World War II high rates and a broadened tax base doubled and redoubled receipts from income and profits taxes. Those revenues fell off after the war and again after the Korean conflict as wartime rates were reduced. During the following three decades, federal income tax revenues climbed year after year even as Congress reduced rates and introduced new tax benefits.

Following the postwar tax reductions, Congress in 1964 approved an $11.6 billion tax cut designed to stimulate a lagging economy. Congress temporarily raised taxes in 1968 by imposing a 10 percent surcharge on personal and corporate income tax liabilities proposed by President Johnson to finance the Vietnam War.

But in 1971, with the economy in recession, Congress agreed to President Nixon's plan for an $8.6-billion-a-year tax cut to renew growth. After the economy went into a deep recession in late 1974, Congress in 1975 approved an emergency $22.8 billion tax cut to bolster consumer and business purchasing power. Those reductions were extended through the end of the decade.

And Congress in 1981 went along with President Reagan's request for massive tax reductions designed to slash individual tax rates 25 percent over 33 months and then, for the first time ever, index the tax system to keep inflation from forcing taxpayers into higher brackets as their incomes kept pace with prices. By fiscal 1986 these reductions were expected to shave federal revenues by $267.6 billion, including $196.1 billion in estimated individual income tax payments.

Before Reagan's tax-cut plan went into effect, the Carter administration had projected that federal revenues would rise to $900 billion in fiscal 1984. That would have tripled the $300 billion the tax system brought in during fiscal 1976, only eight years before.

The 1981 tax reductions trimmed expected fiscal 1984 revenues to about $750 million, but the Reagan administration estimated that receipts still would surpass $900 billion in fiscal 1986, with individual income taxes amounting to $440 billion and corporate income taxes estimated at around $75 billion.

The Power to Spend

In the five decades after the Great Depression began, the growth of federal revenues provided the funds for an even more explosive increase in government spending. Since President Franklin D. Roosevelt launched the New Deal, Congress has made extensive and imaginative use of its constitutional powers to fund an expanding array of federal initiatives that benefit many Americans and touch most parts of the nation's life.

The Constitution gave Congress the basic authority to decide how the government should spend the money it collects. That power is protected by Article I, Section 9, Clause 7, which declares that "No money shall be drawn from the Treasury, but in consequence of appropriations made by law...." As a result, revenue raised through the taxing system is made available for spending by government agencies only after Congress has approved its use for those purposes.

The Constitution set few specific limits on the spending power. Section 9, Clause 7 went on to require that "a regular statement and account of the receipts and expenditures of all public money shall be published from time to time." Elsewhere, Article I, Section 8, Clause 12 prohibited appropriating money "to raise and support armies" for longer than two years.

Mandate for Spending

Besides its explicit powers, the Constitution implies much more authority to spend government funds. It directs the government to perform various functions — establish post offices, roads, armed forces and courts, and take a decennial census — that could be done only by spending money. And by authorizing Congress to collect taxes "to pay the debts and provide for the common defense and general welfare of the United States," the Constitution opened the way for expansive interpretation of the congressional power to make outlays to address a growing nation's changing problems and challenges.

When the Republic was founded, political leaders differed over what spending for the general welfare meant. One strict interpretation, voiced by James Madison in *The Federalist,* insisted that such outlays were limited to the purposes connected with the powers specifically mentioned by the Constitution. A looser construction, advocated by Alexander Hamilton, contended that the general welfare clause conferred upon the government powers separate and different from those specifically enumerated in the Constitution. Under the latter interpretation the federal government was potentially far more powerful than the strict constructionists intended; in fact, it was something more than a government of delegated powers.

Deep disagreement about the extent of congressional spending powers continued well into the 20th century. The broad interpretation came to be the generally accepted view, but it was not until 1936 that the Supreme Court had an opportunity to give its opinion on the meaning of the controversial wording. In a decision that year *(United States v. Butler)* the court invalidated the Agricultural Adjustment Act of 1933, which had provided federal payments to farmers who participated in a program of production control for the purposes of price stabilization. Although this law was held unconstitutional, the court construed the general welfare clause to mean that the congressional power to spend was not limited by the direct grants of legislative power found in the Constitution.

Rather, an expenditure was constitutional "so long as the welfare at which it is aimed can be plausibly represented as national rather than local." The 1933 law was overturned on other grounds but was later re-enacted on a different constitutional basis and was sustained by the court. Decisions in the immediately following years upheld the tax provisions of the Social Security Act, thus confirming the broad scope of the general welfare clause.

Expansion of Federal Outlays

The new national government spent $5 million in fiscal 1792, its fourth year in operation. The United States then had 4 million people, most living on farms or in small towns east of the Mississippi River. The government grew — and its outlays increased — as the country acquired new territories, settlers moved west and the nation fought wars.

"The original role of the federal government was limited both by the precise language of the Constitution and by the prevailing social consensus that powerful central governments should be avoided," Donald G. Ogilvie, associate dean of the Yale University School of Organization and Management, noted in a 1979 American Enterprise Institute symposium. "As a result, federal activities were restricted to those traditional 'public good' functions such as the maintenance of national security forces, management of the monetary system, and the operation of the executive, congressional and judicial branches of the government."

Still, annual federal outlays reached the $1 billion level only in 1865, the last year of the Civil War, then subsided below that mark until the nation entered World War I. The government spent $18.4 billion in fiscal 1919, incurring a $13.4 billion deficit. But as in the decades after the Civil War, outlays again fell off in peacetime, holding steady between $2 billion and $3 billion a year during the 1920s.

But the nation was undergoing rapid change. Its population had soared, and its economy had grown vastly larger and more complex. People crowded into fast-sprawling metropolitan regions and moved more often from one place to another. Life expectancies lengthened, while families grew apart. Those changes "combined to produce new requirements for federal programs," Ogilvie suggested, and "complicated and expanded the role of the public sector in social, economic and political affairs."

The nation's federal system reached a turning point in the 1930s during the Great Depression. President Roosevelt and Congress launched massive federal programs to pull the economy out of the worst downturn in U.S. history. Spending for domestic assistance programs jumped to $7 billion by 1939 as outlays for civil needs surpassed spending on the military, veterans and war-incurred debt.

During World War II federal spending multiplied tenfold, reaching $98.3 billion in fiscal 1945. Postwar spending declined but stayed well above previous peacetime levels. The Korean War buildup doubled outlays from less than $30 billion in fiscal 1948 to $76.1 billion in fiscal 1953. Spending fell below $70 billion for fiscal 1955. The budget has grown steadily since then in every year except fiscal 1965.

In Ogilvie's words: "It took 186 years for the federal budget to exceed $100 billion; it took only nine more years to reach $200 billion; four more to exceed $300 billion; two more to reach $400 billion; and an additional two years to go to $500 billion. Federal spending is increasing at an average rate of almost $500 million a year."

Budget Terminology

The federal budget is the financial plan for the federal government. It accounts for how government funds have been raised and spent, and it proposes financial policies. It covers the **fiscal year**, which begins on Oct. 1 and ends the following Sept. 30.

The budget discusses **revenues**, amounts the government expects to raise in taxes; **budget authority**, amounts agencies are allowed to obligate or lend; and **outlays**, amounts actually paid out by the government in cash or checks during the year. Examples of outlays are funds spent to buy equipment or property, to meet the government's liability under a contract or to pay employees' salaries. Outlays also include net lending — the differences between disbursements and repayments under government lending programs.

The purpose of the budget is to establish priorities and to chart the government's **fiscal policy**, which is the coordinated use of taxes and expenditures to affect the economy.

Congress adopts its own budget in the form of **budget resolutions**. The **first budget resolution**, due May 15, sets overall goals for taxing and spending, broken down among major budget categories, called **functions**. The **second budget resolution**, due Sept. 15, sets binding budget figures.

An **authorization** is an act of Congress that establishes government programs. It defines the scope of programs and sets a ceiling for how much can be spent on them. Authorizations do not actually provide the money. In the case of authority to enter contractual obligations, though, Congress authorizes the administration to make firm commitments for which funds must later be provided. Congress also occasionally includes mandatory spending requirements in an authorization to ensure spending at a certain level. Some authorizations, such as Medicare, are structured so that anyone who meets the eligibility requirements of the program may participate and enough funding must be made available to cover all participants; such authorizations are known as **entitlements**.

An **appropriation** provides money for programs within the limits established in authorizations. An appropriation may be for a single year, a specified period of years (multi-year appropriations), or an indefinite number of years (no-year appropriations). Appropriations generally take the form of budget authority, which often differs from actual outlays. That is because, in practice, funds actually spent or obligated during a year may be drawn partly from the budget authority conferred in the year in question and partly from budget authority conferred in previous years.

The Power to Borrow

As rapidly as federal revenues have grown, they have not kept up with the increasing spending. As a result, the government since the 1930s has broken away from a longstanding practice of keeping the federal budget in balance except in times of war. In the process, Congress has expanded use of its power to borrow money on the nation's credit.

The borrowing power is extensive. In their *Introduction to American Government*, Frederic A. Ogg and P. Orman Ray noted that the "power to borrow not only is expressly conferred in the Constitution, but is one of the very few federal powers entirely unencumbered by restrictions — with the result that Congress may borrow from any lenders, for any purposes, in any amounts, on any terms, and with or without provision for the repayment of loans, with or without interest." Ogg and Ray noted also that the United States has no constitutional debt limit, whereas many state constitutions and state charters for counties and local governments impose debt ceilings. The United States has had a statutory debt ceiling for many decades, but the ceiling can be easily altered by Congress and, in fact, has been raised repeatedly — although seldom without an intense political fight in Congress.

Composition of the Debt

Debt has been incurred by the federal government when it has found it necessary to spend more than it has collected in tax and other forms of revenue. When expenditures outstrip revenues, the deficit must be made up by borrowing. Through much of the nation's history, a surplus resulting from an excess of revenues over expenditures has been used, at least in part, to reduce outstanding debt. Since the long string of federal budget deficits began in fiscal 1931, there have been budget surpluses in only seven years. It was during this period that the bulk of the national debt (estimated to reach $1.0798 trillion by the end of fiscal 1982) was incurred.

The debt consists of various types of obligations. David J. Ott and Attiat F. Ott in *Federal Budget Policy* gave the following definitions:

> The federal debt consists of direct obligations or debts of the U.S. Treasury and obligations of federal government enterprises or agencies. It is broken down into "public debt" — that part issued by the Treasury — and "agency debt" — that part issued by federal agencies. The public debt consists of issues (that is, bonds, notes and bills), which are generally sold to the public (some are held by federal agencies and trust funds), and "special issues," which are held only by government agencies and trust funds. Of the issues sold to the public, some are "marketable," that is, they are traded on securities markets, and some are "non-marketable" and cannot be traded (for example, U.S. savings bonds). The latter may, however, be redeemed in cash or converted into another issue.

Philosophy Prior to 1930s

Throughout most of the nation's history, the principal concern of government in regard to budget policy was to assure that revenues were sufficient to meet expenditure

Public Debt Of U.S. Government

	Gross Debt*		
Fiscal Year	Total (Billion Dollars)	Per capita (Dollars)	Interest Paid (Billion Dollars)
1940	$ 43.0	$ 325	$ 1.1
1941	49.0	367	1.2
1942	72.4	537	1.6
1943	136.7	1,000	2.7
1944	201.0	1,452	3.8
1945	258.7	1,849	5.0
1946	269.4	1,905	5.4
1947	258.3	1,792	5.4
1948	252.3	1,721	5.5
1949	252.8	1,695	5.6
1950	257.4	1,697	5.6
1951	255.2	1,654	5.7
1952	259.1	1,651	6.0
1953	266.1	1,667	6.4
1954	271.3	1,670	6.3
1955	274.4	1,660	6.4
1956	272.8	1,621	6.9
1957	270.5	1,579	7.3
1958	276.3	1,587	7.2
1959	284.7	1,606	8.1
1960	286.3	1,585	9.3
1961	289.0	1,573	8.8
1962	298.2	1,598	9.5
1963	305.9	1,615	10.1
1964	311.7	1,622	10.9
1965	317.3	1,630	11.5
1966	319.9	1,625	12.5
1967	326.2	1,638	13.0
1968	347.6	1,728	15.4
1969	353.7	1,740	17.1
1970	370.9	1,811	20.3
1971	397.3	1,919	21.0
1972	426.4	2,042	21.8
1973	457.3	2,174	24.2
1974	474.2	2,238	29.3
1975	533.2	2,496	32.7
1976	620.4	2,884	37.1
1976[1]	634.7	2,951	8.1
1977	698.8	3,216	41.9
1978	771.5	3,523	48.7
1979	826.5	3,740	59.8
1980	907.7	4,063	74.9

* Public debt is the portion of the federal debt incurred when the Treasury borrows funds from the public — approximately 99 percent of total gross federal debt. The other 1 percent consists of debt incurred by federal agencies that borrow funds directly from the public.

[1] As of Sept. 30.

Source: Department of the Treasury

requirements. This philosophy, which in application meant an approximate balance between receipts and outlays, was generally accepted from the beginning until the early 1930s.

Lewis H. Kimmel wrote in *Federal Budget and Fiscal Policy, 1789-1958:*

> From the beginning of our national history, ideas in public finance have been influenced by the unfolding of events. At the outset acceptance of the balanced budget philosophy was facilitated by the adverse financial experience during the Revolutionary War and under the Articles of Confederation. There was an awareness that the public credit is a valuable resource, especially in an emergency. The experience of the preceding fifteen years suggested to Hamilton and others that the preservation of the public credit depended on the consolidation of existing indebtedness and the provision of adequate revenues for debt service. The thought that the interests of the new nation would be best served if Hamilton's ideas were adopted was soon translated into policy.

Kimmel pointed out that three key ideas were generally accepted by federal officials and economists alike during the period leading up to the Civil War: 1) a low level of public expenditures was desirable; 2) the federal budget should be balanced in time of peace; and 3) the federal debt should be reduced and eventually extinguished. "These ideas," he observed, "were a reflection of views that were deeply rooted in the social fabric."

The Civil War, like major wars of modern times, resulted in a much enlarged national debt. The reported debt in 1866 amounted to almost $2.8 billion in contrast to less than $90.6 million in 1861. The debt was gradually reduced after the war to a low of $961 million in 1893. However, after the Civil War, there was less concern about eliminating the outstanding debt; increasingly, the emphasis was on servicing the debt in an orderly manner. Proposals to liquidate it became fewer and fewer.

From the post-Civil War low point in 1893, the debt increased very slowly for half a dozen years and then hovered between $1.1 billion and $1.2 billion until 1917, when the United States entered World War I. The debt jumped from just under $3 billion in fiscal 1917 to a peak of $25.5 billion at the end of fiscal 1919. In the 1920s the debt receded steadily, year by year, down to $16.2 billion at the end of fiscal 1930.

Rise of the Debt

But during the 1930s Congress approved major federal projects to stimulate economic recovery. In the process, the government began following an economic philosophy, developed by British economist John Maynard Keynes, that justified peacetime deficits when needed to ensure stable economic growth. As a result, the government abandoned the former insistence on balancing revenues and outlays. Kimmel noted of the early years of the Depression:

> A concerted effort was made by the president and the leadership of both parties in Congress to adhere to the balanced-budget philosophy. Yet a balanced federal budget was almost impossible to attain — the annually balanced-budget dogma in effect gave way to necessity. Alternatives were

soon suggested, and within a few years what came to be known as compensatory fiscal theory gained numerous adherents.

The practice of using the federal budget to help solve national economic problems was increasingly accepted. Budget deficits and a rapidly increasing national debt were the result. The debt rose to nearly $50 billion — almost twice the World War I peak — at the end of fiscal 1941. Then came Pearl Harbor. The debt passed the $100 billion mark in fiscal 1943 and exceeded $269 billion in fiscal 1946. No steady reduction followed World War II. The debt total fluctuated for a few years but then began a new rise that took it past the World War II peak in fiscal 1954, past $300 billion in fiscal 1963 and all the way to $475 billion at the end of fiscal 1974.

The debt more than doubled — surpassing the $1 trillion level — as the government ran unprecedented peacetime deficits in fiscal 1975-82.

EXECUTIVE ROLE IN BUDGET MAKING

The enlarging scope of the government after World War I prodded federal officials to develop formal budgeting techniques to manage the nation's finances. Congress from time to time has tinkered with its own procedures for voting funds for federal agencies. But the House and Senate have had trouble disciplining spending decisions, and members usually have left to the executive branch the task of putting a federal budget together.

The government operated 132 years without a formal budget. After the Constitution was ratified, Congress in September 1789 established the Treasury Department and directed the secretary to "prepare and report estimates of the public revenues, and the public expenditures." But efforts by Alexander Hamilton, the first Treasury secretary, to set up an executive budget for the government were frustrated, Kimmel noted, by "congressional jealousy and existing party divisions."

Kimmel contended that "the budget idea ... was clearly in the minds of leading political and financial leaders as early as the Revolutionary and formative periods." But because the government relied on abundant customs receipts for most of its funds throughout the 19th century, officials felt no need to weigh expenditures against revenues. The budget-making efforts deteriorated until after the turn of the century.

Modern Budgeting Procedure

In 1910 President Taft appointed a Commission on Economy and Efficiency to study the need for a federal budget. The commission concluded that the government's haphazard system for determining its financial needs and providing funds for them should be restructured. But Congress at first resisted the commission's proposal; its report was not even considered by the House Appropriations Committee to which it was referred.

But after appropriating $6.5 billion for fiscal 1920, the first year after World War I, Congress decided to reorganize the federal financial machinery both to retrench on spending and to tighten control over the execution of fiscal policy. In the following two years, the House and Senate both gave their respective Appropriations committees exclusive power over federal spending legislation. And, in the Budget and Accounting Act of 1921, Congress gave the executive branch new budget-making structures.

The 1921 law authorized the president to prepare and submit to Congress an annual budget covering actual revenues and expenditures in the most recently completed fiscal year, estimates for the current year and the administration's proposals for the forthcoming year. The law also created a Bureau of the Budget to strenghten presidential control over fiscal management. Operating under the president's direction, the bureau served as a clearinghouse for budget requests by federal agencies. In that way, Congress denied the agencies the right to go directly to Capitol Hill with their requests for whatever amounts their officials wanted.

Budget Circular 49, approved by President Warren G. Harding on Dec. 19, 1921, required that all agency proposals for appropriations be submitted to the president prior to presentation to Congress. Agency proposals were to be studied for their relationship to "the president's financial program" and were to be sent on to Capitol Hill only if approved by the president. The bureau, though placed in the Treasury, was kept under the supervision of the president.

Under Franklin D. Roosevelt and his successors, the bureau became the president's most potent agent in directing the affairs of the executive branch. In 1935 Roosevelt broadened the clearance function to include other legislation as well as the appropriations requests. According to political scientist Richard E. Neustadt, writing in the *American Political Science Review* for September 1954, Roosevelt's new clearance system was not a mere extension of the budget process: "On the contrary ... this was Roosevelt's creation, intended to protect not just his budget, but his prerogatives, his freedom of action, and his choice of policies in an era of fast-growing government and of determined presidential leadership."

Congress in 1939 approved Roosevelt's Reorganization Plan No. 1 creating an executive office of the president. The plan transferred the Budget Bureau from the Treasury to the new White House structure. By presidential directive, Roosevelt also broadened the bureau's clearance function by giving it responsibility for coordinating executive branch views on all legislation, not just appropriations bills, that Congress approved and sent to the president to be signed or vetoed. Roosevelt required that any recommendation to veto legislation be accompanied by a draft veto message or memorandum of disapproval in the case of a pocket veto.

Unified Budget

Before World War II, the president's administrative budget largely accounted for the full extent of federal finances. But in the following decades Congress excluded an increasing proportion of federal outlays by separating them from the president's budget. Congress drew a line between funds that the government owned and those it collected in a fiduciary capacity for the trust funds set up to finance Social Security, civil service retirement, veterans' and other benefits. It also set apart the earnings and expenditures by government-backed enterprises such as

the Post Office Department, Commodity Credit Corporation, Export-Import Bank, Federal National Mortgage Association, Small Business Administration, Tennessee Valley Authority and other ventures established to carry out federal objectives. In addition, the government's role in making direct loans, or guaranteeing or insuring others, was only partially reflected in the budget.

Lyndon B. Johnson in 1968 expanded the president's budget to take account of such activities. For decades, observers had contended that the budget documents were too complex and too easily distorted by the party in power to hide information. Johnson, following recommendations made in 1967 by a study commission he had appointed, adopted what became known as the unified budget incorporating trust fund receipts and outlays in computing the federal deficit.

Roosevelt's successors had strengthened White House budget-making procedures. Then, in 1970, President Nixon tightened presidential control over the budgetary process when he set up the Office of Management and Budget (OMB). Nixon's reorganization plan, accepted by Congress that year, built the new office around the nucleus of Budget Bureau experts. It also gave OMB sweeping authority to coordinate the way federal agencies carried out White House policies.

By creating OMB, Nixon rearranged the president's relationship with Cabinet officers and budget officials for the first time in 30 years. The reorganization plan — suggested by a presidential advisory commission chaired by Litton Industries President Roy L. Ash — transferred to the president himself all statutory authority previously assigned to the Bureau of the Budget. OMB's responsibilities were extended and greater use made of organization and management systems, development of executive talent and a broader career staff, better dissemination of information and appropriate use of modern techniques and equipment. The rationale for these changes was to provide greater executive capability for analyzing, coordinating, evaluating and improving the efficiency of government programs. Major new roles of the office were:

● Assistance in implementing major legislation, under which several agencies shared responsibility for action.

● Coordination of the complex system of federal grants, which often involved not only more than one federal agency in a particular area but also various agencies and government entities at the state and local levels.

● Evaluation of cost effectiveness of particular programs and the relative priority of needs they were designed to meet.

The House Government Operations Committee tried unsuccessfully to block the reorganization plan, protesting that transferring the Budget Bureau authority to the president would give him "almost unlimited power to restructure the administration of those functions ... without any action or review by Congress." Nixon in 1970 appointed George P. Shultz, previously the administration's secretary of labor, as OMB director. Ash took over in 1972 when Shultz was named Treasury secretary. In 1974, after Nixon used OMB to attempt large-scale cutbacks in federal programs, Congress enacted a law making future directors and deputy directors subject to Senate confirmation.

Annual Budget Requests

Usually submitted to Congress in late January, the president's budget proposal serves as a comprehensive

GAO Audits:
The Watchdog's Bite

As it strengthened presidential control over federal budget decisions, Congress in 1921 also tried to improve its own capability to monitor the way federal funds were spent. In the Budget and Accounting Act of 1921, Congress therefore set up the General Accounting Office (GAO) to strengthen oversight of outlays by federal agencies.

The GAO is headed by the comptroller general and assistant comptroller general, appointed for 15 years by the president with the advice and consent of the Senate. They can be removed only by joint resolution of Congress, thus making the agency responsible to Congress rather than the administration. The comptroller general was granted wide powers to investigate all matters relating to the use of public funds and was required to report annually to Congress, including in his report recommendations for greater economy and efficiency.

Many of the auditing powers and duties of the comptroller general had already been established by the Dockery Act of 1894, which assigned them to the new office of the comptroller of the Treasury. But under that act the comptroller and his staff remained executive branch officers, and Congress lacked its own agency for review of executive expenditures.

In their book *Federal Budget Policy,* David J. Ott and Attiat F. Ott describe the three major types of audits made by the GAO.

Recently the *comprehensive audit* has become the most important. This audit concentrates on the accounting and reporting system used by a particular agency and checks transactions selectively. The *general audit* examines the accounts of agency disbursing and certifying officers to determine the legality of each transaction. If illegal or improper handling of receipts or expenditures is discovered, recovery procedures are instituted against the responsible officer. The *commercial audit* is applied to government corporations and enterprises. No recovery is possible in this case, but Congress is informed of questionable or improper practices.

The results of GAO audits are transmitted to Congress by the comptroller general. The results of special investigations of particular agencies and the annual report are referred to the House and Senate Committees on Government Operations.

During the 1970s controversy was generated by congressional proposals to order GAO audits of the semi-autonomous Federal Reserve System. Because the Federal Reserve financed its own operations through assessments on member banks, the GAO had no authority to monitor the bank regulatory agency's operations. But House Banking and Currency Committee Chairman Wright Patman, D-Texas (1929-76), a longtime critic of Federal Reserve monetary policies that he contended drove interest rates too high, for years advocated GAO audits as a way to force congressional review of the sytem's operations.

Federal Reserve Board officials, led by Chairman Arthur F. Burns, objected that GAO investigations might intrude on the board's secretive decisions on sensitive monetary policy. Shortly after Burns resigned from the Fed in 1978, Congress completed action on legislation (HR 2176 — PL 95-320) ordering the audits, limited to the Federal Reserve functions as supervisor of the nation's banking system. The law barred auditors from examining the board's monetary policy decisions and international financial transactions.

statement of the administration's plans for governing the country. Its recommendations, by slashing agency requests or allocating funds for new government initiatives, set out the president's program for defending the nation, conducting foreign affairs and meeting domestic needs. The budget's projected deficit — or, more rarely, its hoped-for surplus — indicates the administration's judgment on the economic state of the country and the need for measures to stimulate growth or retard inflationary pressures.

The complex budget process usually gets under way a year and a half before the fiscal year begins. During the spring before the budget is sent to Congress, the president, OMB and department officials evaluate proposed and ongoing programs and project economic conditions before setting general budget guidelines. The White House then gives policy directions and planning ceilings to federal agencies to govern preparation of their budget requests.

Through fall and early winter, OMB brings together agency estimates of the funds they need to carry out government programs. OMB coordinates those requests with presidential policies and expected revenues. Officials also draw up three-year projections of revenues and outlays to accompany the budget and they prepare a "current services" budget to indicate what the government would spend if ongoing federal programs remained in place and no new initiatives were undertaken.

But, like any other budget, the federal budget is primarily a schedule of estimated receipts and expenditures. It attempts to show, as nearly as can be reliably estimated, what the government will take in and spend during the fiscal year due to commence the following Oct. 1. By the time that fiscal year ends, twenty months after the budget was proposed, actual revenues and outlays may have varied widely from the president's initial projections.

For one thing, the economy's performance can dramatically change budget parameters. If the gross national product rises faster than expected, revenues climb and outlays fall off for countercyclical programs such as unemployment insurance. On the other hand, lagging economic output may undercut revenue estimates while boosting outlays for welfare programs and other government assistance to jobless workers or troubled industries.

For another, Congress holds final authority to alter the president's appropriations requests or to change tax laws to raise or lower revenues. Most often, the administration budget sets the terms for debate and offers starting points for congressional action on agencies' funding requests. Since the early 1970s battles over Nixon's impoundment of appropriated funds, Congress has been more determined than ever to dictate federal spending priorities.

Through the budget procedures it began using in 1975, Congress has set overall spending goals to guide its appropriations deliberations. But on specific agency proposals, Congress never votes on planned expenditures as such. What Congress acts on are requests for new budget authority, the legal permission for agencies to enter into obligations to make immediate or future payments of money from the government's funds. *(Budget terminology, p. 33)*

The House and Senate provide most agency budget authority each year through action on 13 appropriations bills. Most — but not all — of that authority is used by agencies to spend funds during the fiscal year. Some result in outlays only during subsequent years — for example, for construction of aircraft carriers or other projects that require long lead time.

But additional spending during the fiscal year results from unspent budget authority approved by Congress for previous years — or from permanent appropriations or various "backdoor spending" devices that legislators have used to circumvent the annual appropriations process. *(Sources of spending, p. 41)*

CONGRESSIONAL TAX AND SPENDING MEASURES

Since 1975 Congress has set overall revenue and spending goals through its congressional budget process. Those procedures, by requiring the House and Senate to adopt concurrent resolutions setting out budget totals, have forced Congress to weigh spending during the fiscal year against expected government revenues. But Congress still makes acutal decisions on revenues and spending through separate legislation, written by different House and Senate committees. And the budget process still leaves congressional tax, authorizing and appropriations panels considerable power to shape particular programs and make room for them within budget totals.

Because of its committee system, Congress has always had trouble taking an overview of the budget. The House and Senate refer tax and appropriations bills to different panels, while legislative committees draw up authorizing bills creating new spending programs. Both bodies take up and act on committee bills separately, although the level of spending those measures approve must be financed by taxes or deficit borrowing.

Article I, Section 7, Clause 1 of the Constitution requires that the House of Representatives originate tax legislation. By tradition, the House has assumed the privilege of initiating appropriations measures as well, although the Constitution makes no similar provision for spending legislation. Under normal procedures, House panels write tax and spending legislation that the chamber in the past has accepted with few changes on the floor. Senate committees then review House-passed measures, often listening to appeals by agencies whose proposals were changed by House action. The full Senate, with a tradition of unlimited debate, generally has been more likely than the House to revise committee recommendations during floor consideration.

At the end of the 1970s, newly formed House and Senate Budget committees began asserting an indirect role in congressional tax and spending deliberations. Budget panel chairmen more and more took the floor to urge members to keep budget goals in mind while acting on separate legislation. In 1980 and 1981, the Budget committees enforced spending cutbacks by winning House and Senate support to direct othe panels to report budget reconciliation legislation. But the budget panels have no automatic authority to force Congress to adhere to tax and spending limits. "...The president and his budget office are not merely the equals of the agencies they seek to control," Congressional Research Service specialist Allen Schick has noted. "In Congress, the budget committees stand on level ground with the committees subject to budgetary constraint." And those long-established panels, particularly the House and Senate tax and appropriations committees, still wield impressive clout over congressional budget decisions.

Tax Legislation

In both the House and Senate, powerful and prestigious committees control the complicated process of putting tax legislation together. The collection of federal revenues affects virtually all Americans, along with a growing band of labor, industry and public interest organizations. And the Internal Revenue Code over the years has evolved into an elaborate, often-convoluted body of law that even few members of Congress fully understand.

In the past, senators and representatives have been reluctant to go on record by voting on complex and controversial tax-law changes. Most members preferred to let tax-writing committees handle the task of shaping revenue measures. Those committees — Ways and Means in the House and Finance in the Senate — as a result accumulated vast power to shape the federal revenue system and to influence the varied economic interests at stake in tax laws.

In the decades after World War II, the tax committees worked closely with the executive branch in drawing up tax legislation. Before the 1970s, Treasury officials usually packaged tax proposals and Congress acted on their recommendations. Congress itself initiated major tax-revision measures in 1969 and again in 1975. But committee members, congressional staffers and Treasury experts continued to consult throughout the process to reach agreement on tax-code changes.

Tax Procedures

Because revenue measures must originate in the House, the Ways and Means Committee writes the first draft of virtually all tax legislation. The House most often passes Ways and Means measures with few changes, then sends them to the Senate for consideration.

The Finance Committee may rework the House provisions — and often tacks on additional tax revisions. The full Senate customarily approves even more far-reaching changes before passing the measure. As with all legislation, the House and Senate must resolve their differences before sending the bill to the White House for the president's signature.

Both committees are assisted by the Joint Committee on Taxation, which exists largely to provide the staff expertise needed in dealing with complex tax bills.

In both the House and Senate, influential tax committee chairmen have dominated congressional revenue deliberations. Carefully balancing competing interests during committee action, the chairmen usually have held firm backing from panel members to fend off floor amendments that would change the basic legislation. Two former leaders — Ways and Means Chairman Wilbur D. Mills, D-Ark., and Finance Chairman Russell B. Long, D-La. — were especially adept during the 1960s and 1970s at crafting tax measures through committee and floor action and through hard bargaining in House-Senate conferences.

Ways and Means Role

During Mills' tenure as chairman from 1958 through 1974, the Ways and Means Committee held virtually unchallenged control over the crucial legislation in its jurisdiction. The House created Ways and Means in 1802 and gave it authority over spending as well as taxes. In subsequent years, the House gradually reduced the panel's control over spending legislation until it set up a separate Appropriations Committee in 1865.

At present, Ways and Means considers revenue, debt, customs, trade and Social Security legislation. The committee traditionally was composed of senior House members with close ties to party leaders. Between 1911 and 1975, Ways and Means Democrats acted as their party's committee on committees and held political influence within the House by assigning other Democrats to positions on House panels.

Seven chairmen, including five Democrats and two Republicans, have led Ways and Means since 1947. No others matched the extraordinary authority over tax legislation that Mills exercised during 16 years as chairman. Mills' long tenure and command of complex tax laws won wide respect from House members. Mills also kept control over all tax measures by bringing them before the whole committee and refusing to establish permanent subcommittees to consider different issues. Most of all, Mills solidified his power by accurately sensing what House members wanted and drafting legislation to suit them.

Through the years, Ways and Means members took pride in careful, professional work on tax legislation. The committee's conservative leanings and cautious approach to tax-law changes for years reflected majority House sentiment on tax issues. House leaders sent Ways and Means

measures to the floor under closed rules barring amendments, and the full House customarily passed the panel's bills by large margins.

By the mid-1970s, however, the House was changing. Democratic supporters of sweeping tax-law "reforms" grew restless with the power that Mills held over revenue legislation. In 1974 Mills' self-confessed alcoholism and erratic personal behavior forced him to resign as chairman. House Democrats took the opportunity in October and December of that year to make the committee more liberal and break the chairman's grip over tax deliberations.

The changes included:

● Enlarging the committee to 37 from 25 members, bringing 12 middle-level and freshman Democrats onto the panel.

● Requiring the establishment of subcommittees, and giving members of the committee the power to determine the number and jurisdiction of its subcommittees. Subcommittee chairmen and ranking minority members were allowed to hire one staff person to work on their subcommittees.

● Providing that senior members of the committee would be allowed first choice for only one subcommittee slot and could not make a second choice until the junior members had each made one.

● Stripping Ways and Means of its Democratic committee assignment power and transferring it to the Democratic Steering and Policy Committee.

● Transferring revenue sharing from Ways and Means to the Government Operations Committee and export control legislation to the Foreign Affairs Committee.

Rep. Al Ullman, D-Ore., took over from Mills and chaired Ways and Means from 1975 through 1980. But Ullman was considered a weaker leader than Mills, and the expanded committee proved too fragmented and contentious for Ullman to forge the consensus that Mills had constructed behind the panel's legislation. As a result, Ways and Means suffered some embarrassing defeats during floor debate on its measures; and Ullman was unable to match Finance Committee Chairman Long during House-Senate negotiations on tax legislation. When Ullman was defeated in the 1980 congressional elections, House Democrats named Dan Rostenkowski, D-Ill., to chair Ways and Means.

In 1975 Ways and Means set up six subcommittees to handle welfare, trade, Social Security, unemployment compensation and health legislation. But the full committee still considers tax-law proposals, conducting lengthy hearings with testimony from the secretary of the Treasury and other expert witnesses.

After hearings, the committee normally will begin markup sessions to draft the bill. The Treasury Department may have submitted its own bill, but preparation of legal language often is left to congressional and Treasury experts working together after the hearings have delineated the general scope of the proposals to be put into a bill. Until 1973 markups generally were held in executive (closed) session, but following House passage of new rules on committee secrecy in March of that year, most of the markup sessions have been open.

House Floor Action

Changing House procedures have loosened Ways and Means control over the bills it writes and reports to the House floor. Before 1973 the House took up tax measures under special procedures that had become traditional for Ways and Means bills and all but guaranteed acceptance of the committee's work without change. Technically, under House rules, revenue legislation was "privileged" business, which meant that it could be brought up for consideration on the floor ahead of other measures and without a rule. In practice, the committee obtained from the Rules Committee a "closed rule" for floor action. Under this procedure, the bill was not open to amendment in the course of House debate; essentially, the House had to accept or reject the bill as a whole. The minority party had one opportunity, at the end of debate, to try to make changes in the bill, but significant revisions seldom resulted.

There was one exception to the prohibition against floor amendments. Amendments that were approved by the Ways and Means Committee (separately from the bill) could be offered on the floor by a committee member and voted on. This gave the committee an opportunity to backtrack on any provision that appeared to be in danger of drawing unusual House opposition.

Use of a closed rule was justified on the ground that tax, trade and other Ways and Means bills were too complicated to be opened to revision on the floor, particularly because many of the proposed changes probably would be special-interest provisions designed to favor a small number of persons or groups; such floor proposals, it was argued, might upset carefully drafted legislation approved by the committee.

Nonetheless, the closed rule tradition came under attack as members of the House began to criticize the powers of the Ways and Means Committee. Finally, in 1973, Democrats modified the closed rule by adopting a proposal that allowed 50 or more Democrats to bring amendments to Ways and Means bills to the party caucus for debate. If the caucus voted to approve them, the Rules Committee was instructed to write a rule permitting the amendments to be offered on the floor. In 1975 the House went a step further by changing its rules to require that all Ways and Means revenue bills must receive a rule prior to floor action and no longer had "privileged" status.

The impact of these reforms was vividly demonstrated in 1975 during consideration of two tax bills. The House Feb. 27 passed a Ways and Means Committee tax cut bill, but tacked on a provision repealing the oil depletion allowance, despite Chairman Ullman's objections. The issue was forced by the House Democratic Caucus, which voted to allow a floor vote on amendments repealing the depletion allowance offered by dissident Ways and Means members. In a long-sought victory for tax revision advocates, the full House accepted the amendment by a 248-163 vote.

Later that year, to assure committee approval of a tax revision package, Ways and Means Democrats agreed on floor procedures allowing their liberal members to offer floor amendments to tighten some provisions as written by the full panel. The House accepted three proposals, which further tightened the minimum tax provisions, deleted repeal of a withholding tax on foreigners' portfolio investments and removed a controversial provision allowing capital loss carrybacks worth $167 million to wealthy investors.

Senate Finance Committee

The Senate Finance Committee, created in 1816, shares the same jurisdiction as Ways and Means. But its power and influence on revenue matters in the past has

been more limited. Because the House normally drafts basic tax legislation, the Finance panel usually takes on a review or appellate role for interests trying to change House-approved provisions.

Through the years, Finance acquired a reputation as being receptive to special-interest tax schemes. That trait may trace to the Constitution and the second part of Article I, Section 7, which declares that "the Senate may propose . . . amendments . . ." to revenue legislation. At times, the Finance panel has had little to do except tinker with the House-passed bills and add provisions in which individual senators take special interest.

The committee eventually will go into markup session and make changes it deems necessary in the House bill. It may, and sometimes does, write basic changes into the measure sent to it by the House, but its revisions often will be primarily addition of new material. The committee, like Ways and Means, is assisted by congressional and Treasury Department experts. Thus, the bill reported by the Finance Committee can be expected to have the characteristics of a professionally prepared tax measure (even though it may differ in important respects from the House bill).

Senate Floor Debate

Senate floor action on tax legislation often radically departs from the careful consideration that the House and Finance Committee give revenue proposals. The Senate has no procedures or rules to ward off tax-bill amendments on the floor. And at times senators have used their prerogative to offer floor amendments to rewrite House bills or load them with unrelated provisions.

Senate tax-bill debates often have evolved into legislative logrolling and mutual accommodation, particulary late in congressional sessions when members try to push through favorite proposals before adjournment. Senate amendments, called riders because they were germane only because they would amend some Internal Revenue Code provision, have turned many tax measures into "Christmas-tree bills" bestowing benefits on varied economic interests.

The Senate sometimes approves popular amendments in full knowledge that House conferees will insist that they be dropped. Finance Committee leaders sometimes accept amendments out of courtesy to a sponsoring senator. As Finance chairman, Long frequently agreed to take amendments to conference with the House as bargaining chips that could be discarded in trade-offs for other provisions that senators considered essential. Senate floor maneuvering on tax bills often lasts several weeks.

Conference Maneuvers

Like other acts of Congress, most tax legislation is put in final form by a House-Senate conference committee. But tax-bill conferences, because the economic stakes are high, have produced intense and dramatic bargaining. The conference sessions usually have been held in a small room maintained in the Capitol off the House floor by the Ways and Means Committee. The committee is presided over by the Ways and Means chairman. As a rule, there are three members from the majority and two members from the minority of the Ways and Means and the Finance committees. The number may be enlarged for major bills, but a larger number of one side or the other makes no difference because each side votes as a unit with the majority vote controlling each group.

The conference may last from a day or two to several weeks on major or controversial bills. Congressional and Treasury tax experts are present to assist the conferees. Once all differences are resolved, the bill is sent back to each chamber for approval of the conference agreement. The House files a conference report (for both chambers) listing the differences and their resolution. It is a rather technical document and of most use to an expert; simpler explanations of conference decisions are given by senior committee members during floor discussion of the bill in both houses. If the conference agreement is approved by both, the bill is sent to the president to be signed into law.

House action and lengthy Senate debates in some years last most of the congressional session, so conferees have negotiated their differences under tight deadlines as members prepare to leave Washington, D.C., to vacation or campaign for re-election.

Astute conference leaders such as Mills and Long have used the pressures of time to strengthen the case for their positions. The final products, sometimes negotiated in all-night sessions, usually represent careful compromises that take account of House and Senate politics. The legislation that conferees fashion also may determine how much money the government collects for years to come.

During conference negotiations, Treasury officials and Joint Taxation Committee staff aides help members keep track of the revenue impact of their decisions. But in many cases, conferees have given revenue gains or losses only secondary consideration. By the end of the 1970s, however, congressional budget control procedures had started to force House and Senate tax negotiators to trim compromise tax-cut legislation to keep revenue losses within budget resolution targets. *(Budget control chapter, p. 61)*

Appropriations Process

The Constitution gives the House power to originate tax bills, but it contains no specific provision to that effect concerning appropriations (this is true also of tariff policy). However, the House traditionally has assumed the responsibility for initiating all appropriations, as well as tariff, bills and has jealously guarded this self-assumed prerogative whenever the Senate (as it has from time to time) has attempted to encroach upon it. The practical result, as far as appropriations are concerned, is that the House Appropriations Committee is more powerful than its counterpart on the Senate side. The bulk of basic appropriations decisions are made in the House committee. The general shape of any appropriations bill is derived from House consideration of the measure; what the Senate does in effect is to review the House action and hear appeals from agencies seeking changes in the allotments accorded them by the House. The Senate is free to make alterations as it deems necessary, but important changes usually are limited to revisions in the financing for a relatively small number of significant or controversial government programs.

Prior to World War I, neither the expenditures nor the revenues of the federal government exceeded $800 million a year. No comprehensive system of budgeting had been developed, although the methods of handling funds had undergone various shifts within Congress. During the pre-Civil War period, both taxing and spending bills were handled in the House by the Ways and Means Committee. That eventually proved too difficult a task for a single

Sources of Spending

The amount of money the federal government spends in a fiscal year is only partly related to actions that Congress takes in that year. At one time or another, Congress must grant the authority to spend money to the federal agencies that make the actual outlays. Some of that authority comes in the year the outlays are made, but much of it originates in earlier years. The illustration below shows the sources of planned fiscal 1982 outlays.

The illustration shows that the budget authority appropriated by Congress for a fiscal year is more than the obligations or outlays within that year for the following reasons:

● Budget authority for some major procurement and construction covers the estimated full cost at the time programs are started, even though outlays take place over a number of years as the programs move toward completion.

● Budget authority for many loans and guarantee or insurance programs also provides financing for a period of years or represents a contingency backup.

● Budget authority for trust funds represents mainly receipts from special taxes, which are used as needed over a period of years for purposes specified in the law.

As a result, substantial unspent budget authority is always carried over from prior years. Most of it is earmarked for specified purposes and is not available for new programs.

Relation of Budget Authority to Outlays —1982 Budget

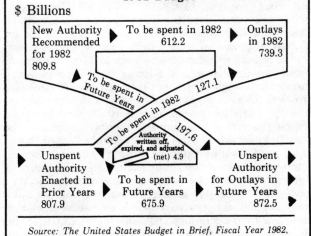

Source: *The United States Budget in Brief, Fiscal Year 1982, Office of Management and Budget*

committee, and in 1865 the House Appropriations Committee was created. A similar situation existed in the Senate, where an Appropriations Committee was created in 1867.

In subsequent years, however, both the House and Senate dispersed appropriations power to other committees as well. Between 1877 and 1885 the House took jurisdiction over eight of 14 annual appropriations bills from the Appropriations Committee and placed those measures with substantive legislative panels. The Senate eventually followed the House lead in reducing the authority of what members considered excessively independent appropriations panels. The division of labor gave committees most familiar with government programs the power over appropriations for them. But that divided responsibility also frustrated any unified control over government financial policy.

After World War I, Congress therefore consolidated appropriations powers while giving the executive branch stronger budgeting capabilities. The House in 1920 restored to the Appropriations Committee exclusive appropriations authority, and the Senate in 1922 similarly concentrated power over spending measures in its Appropriations panel. What evolved from those steps was a two-stage process by which legislative committees draft legislation authorizing federal programs while the Appropriations panels recommend actual funding to carry them out.

Authorization Requirement

By its own rules, Congress cannot consider appropriations for a federal program until the president has signed legislation authorizing its functions during the fiscal year. The House has had a rule since 1837 which provides that "No appropriation shall be reported in any general appropriations bill, or be in order as an amendment thereto, for any expenditure not previously authorized by law. . . ." The Senate had a similar rule but, because appropriations bills originate in the House, the House rule is governing. There are some exceptions, such as a portion of the annual military spending that is authorized by the Constitution, but generally appropriations must await authorizations.

This requirement has led to conflict in Congress on numerous occasions. In the 1950-70 period, Congress required to be authorized annually more and more programs that previously had permanent or multi-year authorization. The trend to annual authorizations represented a victory for the legislative committees — such as the Committee on Education and Labor in the House for matters under its jurisdiction — which felt that they had lost effective control over their programs to the Appropriations committees. The Appropriations committees, particularly in the House, took a dim view of the annual authorizations, in part because they tended in some degree to diminish their power.

In part because Congress must reauthorize programs during each session, the House and Senate seldom have all appropriations in place before the fiscal year begins. With government programs growing in number and becoming more complex, congressional committees needed more time to review their operations and financing needs. Beginning in the late 1950s, Congress rarely finished work on more than one or two appropriations bills before the government's fiscal year began on July 1.

In its 1974 budget law, Congress pushed the fiscal year back three months to start on Oct. 1. The budget measure also set deadlines for legislative committees to report authorization bills by May 15 and for Congress to complete action on final appropriations by mid-September. Even with more time, however, Congress has continued to slip badly behind schedule in considering budget bills.

As a result, the government frequently began the fiscal year without most funding measures in place. Congress has gotten around the problem by adopting continuing resolutions that allow agencies to keep spending money for a specified period, usually at the level that Congress provided for the previous fiscal year. In September 1981, with none of its 13 regular appropriations bills cleared in time for fiscal 1982 to begin Oct. 1, Congress extended funding authority for government agencies for 50 days into the year.

House Appropriations Action

The 1974 budget law gave Congress a process for debating the president's budget as a whole. But the House and Senate still act on budget details in piecemeal fashion, through the 13 regular appropriations bills and often one or two supplemental appropriations measures. And true power to shape actual appropriations remains fragmented among 26 House and Senate subcommittees.

In the House, the Appropriations Committee rivals Ways and Means as a powerful and prestigious panel. Composed largely of senior members elected from safe congressional districts, it has been a conservative body that customarily recommends cuts in the appropriations requests it considers. And its 13 subcommittees traditionally have functioned largely as independent kingdoms.

The subcommittees, organized along functional lines, divide up the president's budget requests soon after Congress receives them. Generally, members of the subcommittees become expert in their assigned areas. The subcommittees, and particularly their chairmen, consequently wield substantial power over spending.

House Appropriations subcommittee hearings were traditionally closed, with testimony almost always restricted to that given by agency officials. A voluminous record of the hearings, along with the parent committee's report, usually was not made public until shortly before House floor action on an appropriation bill. As a result, few if any members not on the subcommittee were prepared to challenge the bill. The Legislative Reorganization Act of 1970 provided that all House committee and subcommittee hearings must be open, but not if a majority determines otherwise. In 1974 the Appropriations Committee opened 90 percent of its hearings, but closed almost half of its markups. Nine of the panel's 13 subcommittees opened all of their markups in 1974, compared with only two in 1973.

The 1970 act provided also that the House Appropriations Committee hold hearings on the president's budget as a whole within 30 days of its receipt; directed the setting up of a standardized data processing system for federal budgetary and fiscal data; and directed the president to send Congress five-year forecasts of the fiscal impact of all federal programs.

At the start of the 94th Congress (1975-77), House Democrats approved steps to weaken the independent power of conservative Appropriations Committee Chairman George Mahon, D-Texas, and other senior Democrats who chaired Appropriations subcommittees. After 1975 the House Democratic Caucus had to approve all subcommittee chairmen. The caucus also voted to limit senior Democrats to serving on only two subcommittees of the same committee. Aimed mainly at the Appropriations Committee, that rule was intended to keep senior members from continuing to dominate key subcommittees that handle defense, agriculture, and health, education and labor funding. Those changes gave committee liberals a stronger voice in subcommittee deliberations.

House procedure on appropriations bills permits amendments from the floor. However, the prestige of the Appropriations Committee is such that few major changes are ever made. By and large, the amounts endorsed by the Appropriations Committee during the post-World-War-II period have been accepted by the House; administration efforts to win "restoration" of cuts in the budget estimates have been concentrated on the Senate.

Senate Appropriations Action

Once an appropriations bill has passed the House, it is sent to the Senate and referred to the Appropriations Committee where a parallel system of subcommittees exists. The Senate subcommittees review the work of the House at hearings that are open to the public. The Senate subcommittees do not attempt to perform the same amount of work on a bill that the House already has gone over thoroughly; the time required (often it is getting late in the year by the time the Senate recieves appropriations bills) and the heavy workload of most senators precludes the same detailed consideration that is given in the House. The Senate subcommittees are viewed more as appellate groups that listen to administration witnesses requesting the restoration of funds cut by the House.

The Senate subcommittees normally will restore some of the House-denied funds, although it may make cuts in other places. The Senate itself may add or restore more when the bill reaches the floor. Most appropriations bills carry larger total amounts when they pass the Senate than when they passed the House. The differences are resolved in conference, generally by splitting the difference between the two chambers.

Federal Debt Limit

Although it holds the power to borrow, Congress generally has sidestepped responsibility for a mounting federal debt. By permanently appropriating funds for interest owed by the government, Congress has spared members the pain of voting each year to set funds aside for that purpose. And only since 1975 have the House and Senate gone on record on the level of deficit for each fiscal year projected by congressional budget resolutions.

The federal government, unlike some states, must obey no constitutional debt limit. Since World War I, Congress from time to time has set statutory limits through legislation. But as the federal debt continued to rise — because Congress continued to provide for more spending than revenue — the House and Senate have had no choice but to raise the ceiling while members lamented deficit spending.

Congress established the first overall debt ceiling in 1917, when the Second Liberty Bond Act fixed a limit at $11.5 billion. By 1945 Congress had amended that act 16 times, lifting the ceiling to $300 billion to accommodate World War II borrowing. In 1946 Congress reduced the limit to a "permanent" $275 billion level. Since then, however, Congress repeatedly has approved a "temporary" debt limit that now has surpassed the $1 trillion mark.

Although Congress actually had little choice but to increase the statutory debt limit, the heated debates — primarily in the House — suggested that the events were milestones in public financial affairs. The controversy over rising debt ceilings flowed essentially from the broader

Debt Limit Depoliticized

To accommodate the government's mushrooming borrowing needs, Congress periodically was forced to raise the federal debt limit. Frequently members in both the Senate and the House played political games by voting against debt limit increases that Congress previously had made necessary by its federal budget decisions. Members also used the presumably "veto-proof" debt ceiling legislation to shield controversial, often non-germane amendments that might have been vetoed if they were enacted separately.

As a result of this politicization of the debt ceiling legislation, the government several times nearly ran out of money as Congress rushed to keep the "temporary" debt ceiling from falling to its permanent $400 billion level. The House finally in 1980 began experimenting with new short-cut procedures to make debt battles unnecessary.

Under that plan, adopted in 1979, the House agreed simply to set the debt limit at whatever level was assumed by the most recently enacted congressional budget resolution. After the House adopted the conference report on a budget resolution, the debt limit would be incorporated into a joint resolution that would be deemed approved by the House and sent on to the Senate without a separate veto.

That strategy presumed that budget resolutions would be enacted on time. In fact, in 1980 action on the first budget resolution fell behind schedule, forcing Congress to consider a stopgap resolution increasing the debt ceiling. Seizing the opportunity, Congress added to that measure a provision overturning President Carter's highly unpopular oil import fee. Carter vetoed the debt limit resolution but Congress promptly overrode the veto.

The House plan also did not apply to the Senate and thus did not prevent that chamber from turning debt limit extensions into political footballs. During consideration of a 1981 measure (H J Res 265 — PL 97-49) to raise the debt ceiling above a trillion dollars for the first time in the nation's history, Democrats offered a series of amendments, several of which involved repealing parts of the recently passed tax cut. The amendments were defeated but the measure faced yet another hurdle — an all-night filibuster. Sen. William D. Proxmore, D-Wis., spoke from early in the evening of Sept. 28 to mid-morning Sept. 29, urging his colleagues to keep the debt limit to $995 million as a means to hold down federal spending.

Proxmire never threatened to hold up passage of the debt limit increase. He did it, he said, because he "wanted some way I could call attention to this very serious economic blunder."

issue of government spending. The proponents of a statutory debt ceiling saw the ceiling as a form of expenditure control. They believed that a firm commitment by Congress not to increase the debt limit would force a halt in spending, especially spending that exceeded the tax revenues.

Officials in the executive branch responsible for paying the government's bills, as well as many members — indeed, a majority — of Congress, were convinced that a debt ceiling could not control expenditures. Throughout the postwar period, secretaries of the Treasury expressed their opposition to use of the debt ceiling for that purpose.

When it came down to actual voting, Congress always has raised the debt limit enough to allow the government to keep borrowing funds to finance daily operations. But congressional conservatives used the debate to throw a spotlight on the public debt and take token stances against rising spending. From time to time, Congress has used debt limit extensions to carry controversial amendments to the president's desk. Presidents have been reluctant to veto debt ceiling measures because the government would be unable to meet its financial obligations and roll over expiring debt if the temporary ceiling expired.

Debt limit extensions were made even more of a charade after Congress began voting on each year's deficit as part of its annual budget resolutions. The House in 1979 finally agreed to a Ways and Means Committee plan to end separate floor votes on debt limit measures. That procedure, first used in 1980, simply assumed that the debt limit would be whatever level was projected by the most recent congressional budget resolution. After the House gave final approval to a budget resolution conference report, it automatically incorporated the debt level into a separate joint resolution that was deemed to have been passed by the chamber and sent to the Senate without a separate vote.

—*Thomas J. Arrandale*

4

Struggle for Spending Control

For nearly two decades, presidents and Congress have struggled to bring the federal budget under control. But even with new congressional budget procedures in place efforts to slow the rate of spending and to bring the federal budget into balance have been singularly unsuccessful.

The government has run chronic deficits since the mid-1960s as Congress expanded financial commitments to defense and domestic programs. Continuous deficits fed inflationary fires and made fiscal policy an ineffective, often counterproductive, tool for managing the U.S. economy. Constant battles to rein in the burgeoning budget corroded relations between Congress and a succession of presidents.

For most of the 1970s, the struggle for spending control dominated congressional deliberations. The Democratic Congress challenged President Nixon's sweeping claims of authority to impound appropriated funds to restrain growth in total outlays. One outcome of that confrontation was realization that Congress was losing control over budget decisions. As a result, the House and Senate devised a new set of budget control procedures in 1974 and put them into use in 1975. But before Republican President Ronald Reagan took office in 1981, Congress still shied away from the politically tough task of cutting back federal spending programs.

By then, the momentum behind budget expansion left it doubtful that Congress could muster the will to make the tough political decisions necessary to bring the budget back into balance. Although Reagan persuaded Congress to cut $36 billion from the fiscal 1982 budget, his call for further cuts had gone unheeded by late 1981. Meanwhile economic conditions and demographic trends pushed spending ever upward, seemingly beyond control by either the legislative or executive branches.

Great national debates over federal taxing and spending occurred throughout the nation's history. But the economic stakes had multiplied after President Franklin D. Roosevelt launched the New Deal to counter a collapsing economy. Since then Congress has used its constitutional powers to enlarge the federal government and assign it ever more complicated roles.

Within a decade, the United States had emerged as a global military power, taking on far-reaching responsibility for the world's and the nation's security. Twice more the country fought wars — in Korea and in Vietnam. And at the same time that it waged an expensive war in Vietnam, the nation launched President Lyndon B. Johnson's "war on poverty" to improve the welfare of its own citizens. Then in the 1970s a stagnant economy marked by high unemployment and even higher inflation pushed federal spending upward at an ever-faster rate.

From the mid-1960s the continuous increase in federal spending intensified traditional partisan divisions over government fiscal policy. A Congress dominated by Democrats continued to expand domestic programs while resisting two Republican presidents' calls for restraint on total spending. Even with Democrat Jimmy Carter occupying the White House the two branches of government were unable to settle on a steady budget policy. In the process the federal budget swelled, reaching beyond $600 billion a year by 1981 and accounting for 23 percent of the nation's economic output.

And even as Congress searched for ways to contain the budget's explosive growth, it forfeited most year-to-year budget control. To ensure that recipients of many of the new domestic programs would be guaranteed the benefits of those programs, Congress removed their funding from the annual appropriations process. Thus by fiscal 1982, with the government spending more than half a trillion dollars a year, Congress effectively had authority to set funding levels for less than one-quarter of the total. David A. Stockman, Reagan's Office of Management and Budget director and a former Republican representative from Michigan, warned that such loss of budget control could reduce Congress to "a green eye-shaded disbursement officer who totes up the bill, writes the check and then trundles off to the chapel to mourn."

Outlays continued to rise almost without restraint as past budget commitments came due. By the late 1970s, outlays were growing by roughly $500 million a year, outpacing monumental revenue increases that the White House and Congress hoped would restore the budget to balance.

Reagan's budget cuts slowed automatic year-to-year growth in spending, at least temporarily. But the simultaneous three-year tax reduction — with its indexing system to limit future inflation-induced tax increases — left the administration and Congress still grappling for ways to keep deficits from widening once more. Fiscal conservatives were exploring new methods of budgetary restraint, including a constitutional cap on government spending or broad presidential powers to withhold funds that Congress appropriated to federal agencies. Meanwhile liberals worried that President Reagan's drive to cut taxes and curb outlays would force Congress to abdicate its constitutional authority to raise revenues and spend public money.

EXPANDING ROLE INCREASES SPENDING

Before the Great Depression of the 1930s, government spending was limited by general concurrence that outlays should not exceed revenues except in times of war. In their study of *Democracy in Deficit*, James M. Buchanan and Richard E. Wagner maintained that the unwritten "fiscal constitution" in the past constrained the government's impulse to launch new spending programs. "Barring extraordinary circumstances," they wrote, "public expenditures were supposed to be financed by taxation, just as private spending was supposed to be financed from income."

When the government began new spending programs to counter the Depression, however, strict adherence to balanced budgets was impossible to follow. During the same period, economists advising the government gave theoretical support to deficit spending during peacetime years to stimulate production. The old link between taxes and spending gradually gave way as Congress approved new programs that spent federal funds for broad and innovative national purposes.

In a 1979 conference sponsored by the American Enterprise Institute for Public Policy Research, a conservative think-tank, Donald G. Ogilvie argued that ending the balanced-budget consensus in the 1930s "stimulated spending by allowing the federal government to avoid the pain of directly imposing the cost of new programs on the people through higher taxes." Ogilvie, associate dean of the Yale University School of Organization and Management, added that in the process "government lost its only yardstick by which to determine how many worthy federal programs the country could afford."

Government's Expanding Role

Roosevelt's New Deal programs marked a fundamental shift away from the limited role that the federal government had previously filled in the nation's economic and social life. During the 1930s, the government first took on responsibility for managing an economy that previous *laissez-faire* policy assumed to be self-regulating. The New Deal also produced a host of programs that redistributed the nation's wealth from one group to another and from some regions to others.

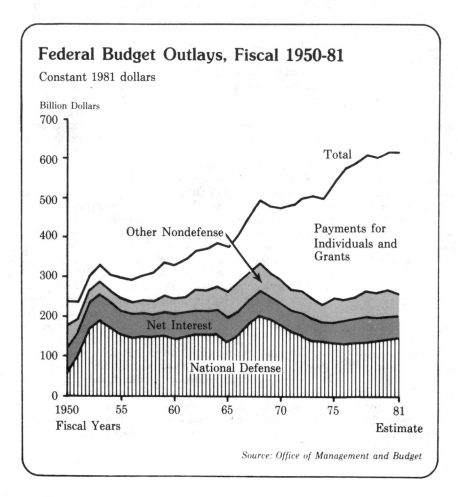

Federal Budget Outlays, Fiscal 1950-81

Constant 1981 dollars

Billion Dollars

Total

Other Nondefense

Payments for Individuals and Grants

Net Interest

National Defense

1950   55   60   65   70   75   81

Fiscal Years   Estimate

Source: Office of Management and Budget

The growth in federal aid to individuals accounts for most of the increase in federal spending since 1965. Defense spending has remained relatively stable but has declined as a percentage of total federal spending.

"Over the next 40 years," Ogilvie noted, "this income redistribution function dramatically changed the structure of the federal budget and increased its share of the national wealth. For the first time, federal officials and elected legislators began to influence the distribution of wealth significantly, initially through the tax system and then increasingly through direct spending programs of the federal government."

Most New Deal initiatives were implemented as countercyclical programs to be phased out as economic conditions improved. Some were terminated within a few years. Others — such as the Social Security system and federal credit assistance for housing, small business and farmers — remain major functions of the government. More significantly, the New Deal set precedents for federal government efforts to provide for the poor and assure economic security for all Americans when times were hard.

After the Depression ended, the federal government continued to expand income transfer programs and take over more and more functions that states, local governments and individuals previously had performed. "In essence, almost without knowing it, we decided to tax ourselves at the federal level and to commission the federal government to provide goods and services that we had historically provided for ourselves," Ogilvie noted.

Those programs, including many providing federal grants to state and local governments to fund specific projects, grew gradually up to the 1960s. Then starting in 1965, with a forceful Lyndon Johnson prodding a heavily Democratic 89th Congress, the government launched a stream of Great Society programs extending its role in providing medical care, education aid, regional development, nutrition, urban renewal, job-training and other services for people and localities. During the 1970s, Congress kept enlarging most of these programs — and adding a few new ones — despite the opposition of Republican presidents.

These new programs translated into increased federal spending. During the 1930s, federal outlays rose from $3.5 billion in fiscal 1931 to $9.5 billion in fiscal 1940. In fiscal 1981 federal outlays reached $660 billion.

A government that spent 3.7 percent of gross national product (GNP) in calendar 1930 was spending 9.1 percent by 1940. The government's contribution to GNP accelerated over the following two decades, reaching 13.9 percent in 1950 and 18.5 percent in 1960. Military buildups for World War II and the Korean War brought sharp temporary spending increases, but the budget resumed steady growth after defense outlays slacked off. The federal share of GNP grew more slowly in the 1960s and 1970s but still climbed past 23 percent. *(Chart, p. 8)*

Changing Budget Priorities

The shifting national priorities resulted not only in increased spending but also in changed spending patterns. Federal outlays grew rapidly for tasks, notably national defense, that the federal government traditionally had performed. But as new social programs came on line they absorbed more and more of the government's resources; the share that the government poured into defense declined as a proportion of the budget.

Annual U.S. military spending peaked at $85 billion during World War II and again at $50 billion during the Korean War. Defense outlays fell off in the mid-1950s but climbed back above $50 million in fiscal 1963. Since then, defense spending has climbed steadily to a Vietnam War peak of $79 billion. After declining slightly, defense outlays accelerated as the country sought to upgrade its military capabilities, reaching an estimated $180 billion for fiscal 1982.

Except for three years during the Vietnam buildup, however, defense purchases of goods and services accounted for a declining share of federal spending as measured by the Commerce Department's national income and product account (NIA). By the early 1980s, defense outlays were expected to average 5.1 percent of gross national product, down from the 9 percent average 20 years before.

At the same time, federal government payments to individuals — the poor, the sick, the elderly, retired government workers — jumped. From $42 billion in the fiscal 1967 budget such payments rose to an estimated $355 billion in President Carter's fiscal 1982 budget proposal, accounting for nearly half of total estimated outlays. And federal grants to state and local governments — for purposes such as highways construction, mass transit, sewage treatment plants, job-training, revenue sharing, community development and welfare services — escalated from $2 billion in 1950 to more than $90 billion 30 years later.

LOSING CONTROL: BACKDOOR SPENDING

Although most of the post-Depression social programs were intended to assist the poor and to improve public services in parts of the nation with hard-pressed regional or local economies, many also benefited middle-income Americans, and even the wealthy. Moreover, state and local governments had grown dependent on federal grants for operating funds. "We have, in effect, created a special interest group that includes a majority of the population," Ogilvie contended.

Congress, a political institution, is obviously attuned to the broad appeal that its benefit programs carried. Beneficiaries of federal programs — such as state and local officials, teachers and students, social workers and welfare recipients, and entrepreneurs who win government contracts — have become adept at lobbying for ever-higher funding. Such lobbying organizations often work with agency officials who run the programs and with congressional committees that authorize them in so-called "iron triangles" to preserve and increase funding.

In political reality, such broad-based and determined support makes any program tough to cut. Congress in some cases has made budget cutting even harder by insulating programs against budget restraint. Through various legislative routes, Congress has exempted more than three-quarters of the money it spends each year from the annual appropriations process.

Congress deliberately authorized some so-called uncontrollable or "backdoor" spending simply because the government must shield certain obligations from political controversy. An example of that kind of spending is the permanent appropriation, passed in 1847, to pay interest as it comes due on the national debt. The government must meet that obligation to retain its borrowing credibility.

For other programs, Congress set up backdoor financing requirements to shield their funding from annual scrutiny from conservative Appropriations committees. Those committees, usually dominated by senior senators and representatives from smaller states and rural districts, often earned reputations as being stingy with taxpayers' money. So other congressional committees, particularly those that authorized social programs providing benefits primarily to urban areas, often bypassed the normal appropriations procedures by writing funding obligations into the original authorizing legislation.

Backdoor spending obligations take several forms. For some programs, Congress authorized agencies to enter contracts, borrow money or guarantee loans that eventually obligate the government to make payments. And Congress excluded some quasi-government agencies — such as the Post Office — from the annual federal budget, effectively exempting them from overall fiscal controls. But by far the largest backdoor outlays resulted from the tremendous growth of federal entitlement programs — so-called because Congress by law entitled their recipients to the benefits the government programs provide.

Backdoor spending devices in effect in 1981 removed more than 75 percent of federal spending from real control by annual appropriations measures. Between 16 percent and 17 percent of the funds that the government spends each fiscal year fulfills contracts and obligations that agencies entered in previous years. And a growing proportion of outlays — 58 percent to 59 percent in the late 1970s and early 1980s — now is set aside to meet open-ended commitments the government has made through fixed provisions that Congress previously wrote into law. *(Chart, p. 49)*

Entitlement Programs

Federal entitlement programs range from massive ones such as Social Security, Medicare and interest on the national debt to ones such as an indemnity program for dairy farmers whose milk is contaminated by chemicals or other toxic substances. Federal programs are entitlements if they provide benefits for which the recipients — individuals or, in some cases, government agencies — have a legally enforceable right.

Each entitlement is a benefit that some past Congress deemed so important that it bound the federal government to pay it, with the threat of judicial action, if necessary, to force Uncle Sam to write the check. Entitlements are not totally uncontrollable; Congress can change the basic laws that set them up. However, such changes generally entail a long and politically difficult process and have been attempted infrequently and seldom successfully.

After several decades of rapid growth — in the number of programs, the number of recipients and costs — entitlements have become the major obligation of federal taxpayers. Most major entitlements were in place by fiscal 1967 as the Great Society programs Congress had approved in 1965 got under way. Entitlements cost $57.1 billion that year, accounting for 36.1 percent of total outlays. Along with 23.4 percent of the budget that went for prior-year contracts and other previous commitments, total uncontrollable spending took up 59.5 percent of the fiscal 1967 budget. By fiscal 1980 entitlement spending alone consumed that much of the budget. In that year 36 major entitlement programs were on the books, committing the government to pay out $342.9 billion.

Federal payments to individuals, the largest category of entitlements, grew from $42 billion in fiscal 1967 to $267.6 billion for fiscal 1980 even though few major new programs were established. Those individual payments — made through Social Security, federal retirement, unemployment compensation, medical care, public assistance, housing, student aid, and food and nutrition programs — expanded from 27 percent of fiscal 1967 outlays to more than 46 percent of what the government spent in fiscal 1980.

Indexing of Benefits

One basic reason that entitlement spending expanded so rapidly was that Congress decided over the years that the federal government should provide more benefits to more people. One way it did that was by expanding government programs into areas, such as health care, that had been beyond the scope of federal efforts. In 1965, the year Medicare was enacted, federal expenses for medical care came to less than $1 billion. By fiscal 1980 the government spent $49 billion on the Medicare-Medicaid system.

An even larger share of the growth in entitlement spending stemmed from Congress' efforts to protect recipients against inflation. Before the 1960s, Congress from time to time raised federal benefit payments to keep pace with rising prices. But by raising benefits on an ad hoc basis, Congress often approved increases that more than compensated for the rate of inflation indicated by the government's Consumer Price Index (CPI). Between 1970 and 1972, for example, Congress increased Social Security benefits by almost 50 percent.

Starting in the early 1960s, Congress began authorizing automatic increases by "indexing" — gearing the benefits paid by many programs to the CPI. In 1962 legislation linked civil service retirement benefits to the CPI. Military retirement pay was indexed in 1963, and federal black lung compensation to disabled coal miners in 1969. Between 1971 and 1975, Congress indexed benefits paid under Social Security, food stamps, railroad retirement, Supplemental Security Income (SSI) and various nutrition programs. Veterans pensions were indexed in 1979, leaving veterans compensation, unemployment benefits and Aid to Families with Dependent Children (AFDC) as the only major cash transfer programs not indexed to inflation. By 1980 benefits that rose automatically with the inflation rate accounted for 30 percent of total federal outlays.

Social Security, Supplemental Security Income and railroad retirement receive annual adjustments equal to the increases in the Consumer Price Index. Until 1981 military and civil service retirement were adjusted twice a year, providing an even greater protection against inflation.

According to a study by the congressional General Accounting Office (GAO), indexing accounted for about half the increase in costs of the Social Security retirement system between 1970 and 1977. However, given the earlier generous record of Congress, indexing actually may have helped to hold down costs by discouraging legislative interference with benefit levels. "On balance, indexation in the Social Security program has probably saved the trust funds money," Office of Management and Budget official W. Bowman Cutter told the House Budget Committee in 1979.

But indexing has compounded the government's difficulty in setting budget and economic policy. Unless Congress undertakes major changes in existing entitlement programs or the economy modifies sharply, inflation will continue to push up the cost of entitlement programs and

Congress' Shrinking Power Over Spending

More than three-fourths of all federal government spending is outside the immediate control of Congress. The chart below shows, in the shaded area, the percent of total federal spending that the government is committed by law to undertake. These outlays can be controlled only if Congress changes the basic law that authorizes the expenditures. The bulk of the uncontrollable expenditures arise from entitlement programs, such as Social Security, Medicare and welfare spending.

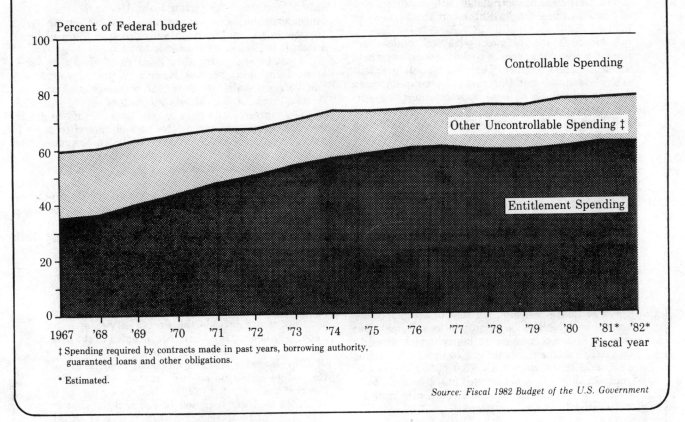

Percent of Federal budget

Controllable Spending

Other Uncontrollable Spending ‡

Entitlement Spending

1967 '68 '69 '70 '71 '72 '73 '74 '75 '76 '77 '78 '79 '80 '81* '82*

Fiscal year

‡ Spending required by contracts made in past years, borrowing authority, guaranteed loans and other obligations.

* Estimated.

Source: Fiscal 1982 Budget of the U.S. Government

Congress will find a larger and larger share of the budget slipping beyond its grasp. With less money under its control, Congress is unlikely to enact new domestic programs, such as national health insurance. And because entitlement programs are so politically difficult to cut, Congress is likely to concentrate cutbacks on programs where spending still is discretionary, including national defense.

Indexing also runs counter to federal efforts to restrain inflationary pressures. Because benefits rise with prices, indexing increases federal spending at precisely the time that traditional fiscal policy calls for budgetary restraint to curtail demand for goods and services. Federal civilian and military retirement programs, by adjusting benefits to inflation twice a year, increase payments more rapidly than if once-a-year adjustments were made. Furthermore, the CPI, the most commonly used index for computing benefit adjustments, overcompensates for inflation by overstating the change in housing costs. The Labor Department's Bureau of Labor Statistics announced in October 1981 that it planned to adjust the CPI beginning in 1983 to correct that overcompensation.

In-Kind Benefits

Other forces drive entitlement spending up, even if benefits are not directly indexed to inflation. Interest on the national debt, for instance, rose from $10 billion in fiscal 1967 to an estimated $67 billion in fiscal 1981 as the government's debt grew and the interest rates it paid mounted steadily.

In addition, the cost to the government for providing direct services has risen in step with costs in the private sector. Medicare and Medicaid are not indexed, but their costs have been pushed up by increases in health care costs.

Such services are known as in-kind benefits. Instead of making cash benefits to recipients, the government provides services through its own employees or by paying bills submitted by private providers, such as doctors, hospitals and pharmacies. In 1960 government in-kind benefits were mostly limited to veterans' medical care and accounted for 1.4 percent of total outlays. Federal in-kind benefits rose to 7 percent of spending in 1970 and to nearly 14 percent by 1980. In-kind programs have been more costly to run than cash benefit programs because of the difficulty of enforcing

Other Forms of Backdoor Spending

Entitlements are not the only form of government spending that is relatively uncontrollable by Congress. While entitlements constitute by far the largest portion of uncontrollable outlays, other forms of "backdoor spending" still take up about one-sixth of the total.

Although the 1974 congressional budget act limited some of the types of backdoor spending, there are still a great number of existing or potential federal obligations that Congress at some point may have to pay off. As a House Appropriations Committee staff report put it, "It is evident that Congress will have to appropriate large sums of liquidating cash in the years ahead to pay off that obligations that will be incurred. . . ."

The main kinds of uncontrollable spending, other than entitlements, are:

Contract Authority

Before passage of the 1974 budget control act, a favorite form of backdoor spending was the use of contract authority, which allows agencies to enter into contracts without immediately providing money to pay the debts thereby incurred. When the bills do come due, the Appropriations committees have no choice but to provide the money.

The budget act required that new contract authority be subject to the appropriations process. But it did not affect existing authority, which agencies can continue to use to enter into contracts. According to a 1976 study, more than $200 billion in existing contract authority could be used in the future. Moreover, the budget act exempted some new contract authorities from appropriations.

Borrowing Authority

A similar type of backdoor spending comes in the form of borrowing authority granted by Congress to federal agencies. Agencies can either borrow from the Treasury or the public; spending is required to pay off the debts incurred.

Like contract authority, new borrowing authority was controlled by the budget act. But there continues to be a large volume of past authorities that can still be used in the future. Federal agencies have about $90 billion in specific unused borrowing authority, which can be used without congressional action. In addition, agencies such as the Farmers Home Administration and Federal Housing Administration can borrow unlimited amounts from the Treasury.

"All told, federal agencies potentially possess several hundred billion dollars of borrowing authority beyond the reach of the budget or the appropriations process," according to a study by Allen Schick of the Congressional Research Service.

Guaranteed Loans

Another type of uncontrollable spending, which has gained in popularity in recent years, is the use of federal guarantees for private loans. Under these arrangements the federal government does not put up any money to begin with, but only promises to repay a loan if the borrower is unable to do so.

Most federal guaranteed loans go to encourage home ownership. Federal Housing Administration and Veterans Administration loan programs account for two-thirds of federal loan guarantees.

Guaranteed loans have appeal because they allow Congress to encourage the flow of capital to a desirable enterprise without any initial cost. Not controlled by the budget act, loan guarantees have become increasingly attractive as a way of getting around spending limits.

However, loan guarantees are particularly uncontrollable, because spending is dependent on the financial health of millions of borrowers, large and small. Each default on a loan creates an unavoidable obligation on the government.

Off-budget Agencies

A different kind of uncontrollable spending involves the off-budget agencies. The budgets for these agencies, which include the Postal Service and the Federal Financing Bank, are not included in the total spending limits established under the budget act.

No clear rule explains why some agencies are on the budget and some are not. In many cases, activities that are carried out off the budget are similar to activiites that are included in the budget. Historically a number of agencies were converted to off-budget status to avoid presidential impoundments.

Although they are not included in the budget and thus are not part of the budget that is uncontrollable, off-budget agency expenditures nevertheless affect the economy. "In terms of their impact on te economy, the financial activities of off-budget agencies have the same effects as those of agencies included in the budget," Schick wrote.

Tax Expenditures

Critics of so-called tax expenditures also claim that they are a form of backdoor spending. Tax expenditures are exemptions or advantages granted through tax law to achieve a specific purpose.

They are not expenditures in the sense of funds actually spent but they do represent revenue deliberately foregone by the government. A popular tax expenditure is the deduction permitted for interest paid on home mortgages enacted to encourage home ownership.

eligibility standards and monitoring service levels. Combined with cash benefits often paid to the same recipients, in-kind services may also overcompensate for inflation.

Population Changes

The changing character of the U.S. population has also contributed to spending growth. Federal outlays, particularly for Social Security, have risen as the nation's workers aged and retired to live on the benefits for which they were eligible.

In the first 20 years after Social Security was set up in 1935, relatively few retirees were covered by the system for all the years they worked. Between 1955 and 1978, however, the number of Social Security recipients more than tripled, from 4.8 percent to 15.8 percent of the U.S. population. And most were eligible for higher benefits because they had been covered for a longer time and earned higher wages than earlier retirees. In addition, by the 1980s most elderly persons lived longer after reaching retirement age. *(Social Security chapter, p. 73)*

Similar demographic trends have driven up costs for military and civil service retirement and disability insurance programs.

State and Local Grants

As it addressed new national problems during the postwar decades, the federal government took on more and more responsibilities previously left to state and local governments. As federal programs proliferated, government grants to state and local governments accelerated in step. From $2 billion in fiscal 1950, federal aid to state and local governments spurted to $91.5 billion in fiscal 1980.

During the 1950s most federal grants were for highway and income security programs administered by states, counties and municipal governments. But during the 1960s Congress established new and expanded grant-in-aid programs that channeled funds through other levels of government. In 1965 alone Congress set up 109 categorical grant programs; the number of such programs doubled from 160 to 379 between 1962 and 1967.

The federal government increasingly used grants-in-aid to encourage state and local action to pursue nationally determined purposes. For most programs, state and local matching fund requirements were reduced from 50 percent to 20 percent or less. Control and direction remained with the federal government through mandates and stipulations that federal assistance carried. Through grants-in-aid, federal officials increasingly shaped state and local policies in education, civil rights, health care, law enforcement and environmental protection.

During the 1970s Congress stepped up fiscal assistance to state and local governments through general revenue sharing and temporary anti-recession (countercyclical) grants to help hard-pressed cities cope with economic downturns that eroded tax bases and pushed spending upward. But grants for human resources programs — education, employment, job-training, social services, health, income security and veterans' assistance — accounted for 63 percent of the increase in federal grants-in-aid between 1972 and 1978.

Federal Credit Programs

Along with the growth in direct outlays, the federal government has vastly increased its role in helping states, localities and private businesses to raise money. Through various forms of credit, the government in 1980 advanced $80.8 billion on U.S. financial markets, 23.2 percent of total funds made available in the nation for borrowing or equity participation.

Federal credit activity rose dramatically in the 1970s, as the volume of direct loans by the government and federal guarantees of private loans increased. During the decade, Congress also authorized use of the government's credit to finance a growing number of projects, such as synthetic fuels, nuclear fuel and Earth-orbiting satellite development and to bail out financially troubled New York City, Lockheed and Chrysler Corp.

The government provides credit in four forms:

● Direct loans of government cash, secured by promises to repay the government.

● Loan guarantees made when a federal agency pledges to use government funds to repay a private lender if a borrower defaults.

● Loan insurance through which a federal agency protects lenders against default by pooling risks and charging premiums.

● Tax-exempt status for interest paid by state and local governments on bonds, often to raise funds for private industrial, housing, hospital and pollution control investments.

Not all federal credit results in government outlays. In some cases, however, borrowers are so likely to default that the granting of credit amounts to direct federal grants. Under many loan programs, the government provides subsidies through below-market interest rates or easy repayment terms that also are the equivalent of outlays. Yet many credit programs are excluded from the annual federal budget, and the impact of others is masked by loan sales and common accounting practices. In 1980 the Carter administration imposed a system of budgetary controls over much of the government's direct loan and loan guarantee programs.

PARTISAN BATTLES ON SPENDING RESTRAINT

Congress created domestic social programs in response to what a majority of senators and representatives saw at the time as a national consensus for federal action. And most of those programs, notably widely disbursed entitlement programs such as Social Security, continue to enjoy broad popular support.

In many cases, however, Congress badly underestimated — or paid no attention to — those programs' future costs. The result, since the mid-1960s, has been a series of sharply partisan battles in Congress over restraining the growth of outlays. Through the mid-1970s battles for budget control were fought largely between Congress and presidents, who tried to rein in outlays by imposing spending ceilings and by impounding appropriated funds.

After 1975 Congress struggled internally for fiscal control as it legislated target and binding spending resolutions required by the 1974 budget control act. None of those approaches accomplished much budget restraint, until

Reagan's aggressive assault on domestic programs in 1981 prodded Congress to begin slowing outlay growth.

Early Budget Experiments

As a deliberative body representing different regions and economic interests, Congress has always been ambivalent about budget control. In the few instances that the House and Senate voted for overall budget restraints, they were unable or unwilling to cut enough from individual programs to meet those goals. Throughout the postwar years, the momentum of those separate spending decisions sooner or later overwhelmed whatever devices Congress has used to try to keep the budget in check.

Immediately after World War II, Congress attempted to use legislative budget procedures to relate appropriations to overall fiscal objectives. In three years of trying, the House and Senate never fully implemented a legislative budget created by the Legislative Reorganization Act of 1946 (PL 79-601). After unsuccessful attempts in 1947, 1948 and 1949, Congress abandoned the experiment as an unqualified failure.

Similar in some respects to the reform procedures later adopted by Congress in 1974, the 1946 act required that Congress approve a concurrent resolution setting a maximum amount to be appropriated for each fiscal year.

That appropriations ceiling was part of a legislative budget based on revenue and spending estimates prepared by a massive Joint Budget Committee composed of all members of the House and Senate Appropriations committees and of the tax-writing House Ways and Means and Senate Finance committees.

In 1947 House-Senate conferees deadlocked over Senate amendments to the budget resolution providing for use of an expected federal surplus for tax reductions and debt retirement. In 1948 Congress appropriated $6 billion more than its own legislative budget ceiling, and in 1949 the legislative budget never was produced as the process broke down completely.

One of the principal reasons the legislative budget failed was the inability of the Joint Budget Committee to make accurate estimates of spending so early in the session and before individual agency requests had been considered in detail. In addition, the committee was said to be inadequately staffed and, with more than 100 members, much too unwieldy for effective operation.

Failure of the legislative budget prompted a serious effort in Congress in 1950 to combine the numerous separate appropriations bills into one omnibus measure. The traditional practice of acting on the separate bills one by one made it difficult to hold total outlays in check.

In 1950 the House Appropriations Committee agreed to give the omnibus-bill plan a trial. The overall bill was passed by Congress about two months earlier than the last of the separate bills had been passed in 1949. The appropriations totaled about $2.3 billion less than the president's budget request. The omnibus approach was praised by many observers and was particularly well received by those seeking reductions in federal spending.

Nevertheless the House Appropriations Committee in January 1951 voted 31-18 to go back to the traditional method of handling appropriations bills separately. Two years later, in 1953, the Senate proposed a return to the omnibus plan, but the House did not respond. The plan was dead. Opponents said the omnibus bill required more time and effort than separate bills. Equally important was

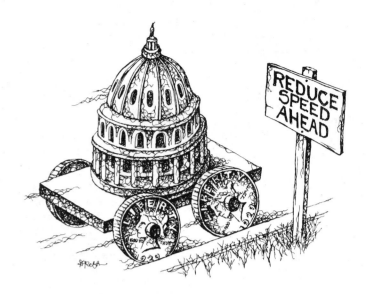

the opposition of the House Appropriations subcommittee chairmen, who feared that their power would be eroded under the omnibus-bill plan.

With the failure of those efforts, Congress' only means of budget restraint was to write into appropriations bills specific restrictions on how funds could be spent. Those provisions provided little overall spending restraint, and during the postwar years Congress discussed but did not try several other plans for restraining outlays. Seven times between 1952 and 1965 the Senate approved creation of a Joint Budget Committee, but the House never acted on the Senate measures. Other spending control measures proposed during that time included a mandatory balanced budget, statutory spending ceilings and a separate congressional budget session to handle only appropriations bills.

Spending Ceilings

In the late 1960s and early 1970s, spending for Great Society programs combined with military outlays in Vietnam to push the budget into deficit. Four times between 1967 and 1970, Congress wrote federal spending limits into law. But those limits proved ineffective.

Distressed by ever-increasing levels of federal spending growth, House Republicans launched an economy drive in 1966. Their first efforts — to cut several annual appropriations bills by 5 percent — were unsuccessful.

Fiscal conservatives were more successful in 1967. In an amendment tacked on to a routine continuing appropriations measure after months of controversy, Congress in December directed federal agencies to cut fiscal 1968 spending on controllable programs by $4 billion. Nonetheless outlays for uncontrollable programs rose about $5 billion, leaving a net spending increase of $1 billion.

A better handle for insisting on spending curbs developed when President Johnson in 1967 proposed a 10 percent tax surcharge. The Ways and Means Committee refused to act on the proposal, however, as Chairman Wilbur D. Mills, D-Ark. (1939-77), held out for expenditure control commitments from the administration before action on raising taxes.

That stalemate finally was broken in June 1968, when the Senate added the surcharge and a $108.1 billion spending ceiling to House-passed excise tax legislation. After lengthy conference deliberations, the House gave in and the measure was enacted into law.

Congress again enacted spending limits in 1969 and 1970, after Republican President Richard Nixon succeeded Johnson. But Congress simply raised both ceilings when they proved too low to accommodate spending required by existing programs.

Congress in 1969 tacked a $191.9 billion fiscal 1970 ceiling on to a supplemental appropriations bill, with provisions adjusting the ceiling to accommodate any congressional action increasing or decreasing spending and allowing the president himself to raise the limit by up to $2 billion to accommodate uncontrollable expenditures.

That cushion proved insufficient, so Congress in 1970 raised the fiscal 1970 ceiling to $197.9 billion, again with allowance for another $2 billion in uncontrollable outlays. In the same bill, Congress set a $200.8 billion fiscal 1971 limit with a cushion for uncontrollables and unlimited additions for spending increases by congressional action.

Nixon Spending Limits

No spending ceiling was enacted for fiscal 1972, but Nixon's request for a $250 billion limit on fiscal 1973 spending provoked a dispute with Congress that was thrashed out amid the 1972 presidential election campaign.

In what Democrats conceded was a masterful political stroke, Nixon in July 1972 asked Congress for authority to trim federal spending as he saw fit to meet a $250 billion ceiling on fiscal 1973 outlays. If such power were denied, Nixon warned, Congress would be responsible for tax increases in 1973.

The House complied by writing the ceiling into a debt limit extension bill. But the Senate balked at giving the president unlimited discretion to cut federal outlays, adding strict guidelines on the size and nature of spending reductions. The ceiling was dropped altogether after the Senate turned down a White House-backed compromise limiting presidential authority to dictate where reductions could be made.

The following year, the House and Senate approved different ceilings on fiscal 1974 outlays as part of bills limiting the president's impoundment authority. Those measures died in conference after Congress decided to include impoundment limitations in budget control legislation. Twice in 1974, the Senate rejected amendments by Sen. William Proxmire, D-Wis., to set a $295 billion ceiling on fiscal 1975 spending. Late in 1974, after Nixon resigned the presidency and was replaced by Gerald R. Ford, the House in an inflation-fighting gesture approved a $300 billion target for fiscal 1975 outlays. But the Senate never acted on the House resolution, which set no binding outlay ceiling.

Ford Proposals

Ford tried to regain the initiative on spending restraint in 1975 by proposing that continuation of tax cuts approved earlier in the year be offset by spending reductions. Offering a $28 billion tax-cut extension, Ford demanded "a clear, affirmative decision" by Congress to hold fiscal 1977 outlays to $395 billion, $28 billion below projections.

But congressional Democrats, just starting to use new House and Senate budget procedures for the first time, balked at binding themselves to steep cutbacks before considering the administration's 1976 budget proposal. At the end of the 1975 session, Congress continued the tax cuts for six months in a compromise measure that included a pledge by Congress to consider offsetting spending reductions if the tax reductions were again extended. But Congress reserved the right to settle on a higher spending total through its budget process.

Nixon, Ford Vetoes

With Congress unwilling to observe spending limitations, both Nixon and Ford resorted to the president's veto power to hold down outlays. Nixon vetoed five bills in 1970, three measures in 1971, 16 in 1972 and five more in 1973 primarily on budgetary grounds. Congress overrode two 1970 vetoes, but the others were sustained. In some cases, threatened vetoes prompted Congress to tailor appropriations measures to fit the president's budget plans.

Ford and Congress fought repeatedly in 1975 and 1976 as the president vetoed measures that the House and Senate approved to step up spending to fight recession. Ford in 1975 vetoed seven measures on budgetary grounds, including four appropriations and three authorization bills Democrats designed to stimulate the economy through increased spending. Congress overrode four of those vetoes. In 1976 Congress overturned Ford's vetoes of legislation authorizing costly public works and countercyclical grants to state and local governments and a separate bill appropriating $4 billion more than the administration requested for the Departments of Labor and Health, Education and Welfare.

Congress in addition steadfastly resisted proposals by both Nixon and Ford to trim government costs by terminating some programs, curtailing others and folding some categorical grants to state and local governments into block grants with fewer administrative requirements. In 1973, after his landslide re-election in 1972, Nixon proposed a fiscal 1974 budget that outlined plans to curtail or eliminate more than 100 federal programs through administrative actions. Concerned by potential erosion of congressional powers and Nixon's sweeping interpretation of presidential authority, House and Senate leaders protested Nixon's claim to a re-election mandate for spending cutbacks. They also pushed ahead with plans to curb the president's power to impound appropriated funds and to set up procedures for Congress to legislate its own budget each year.

IMPOUNDMENTS INTENSIFY CONFLICT

President Nixon's campaign to curb federal spending brought to a head long-simmering differences over whether the government must spend all the money that Congress appropriates.

Enlarging on a practice that most previous presidents had followed, Nixon in the early 1970s impounded billions of dollars Congress had provided for government programs over the administration's objections. By withholding the funds, Nixon set off a legal and political struggle over whether the executive or the legislature held final authority over how the government spent its money.

"... The Nixon administration treated the president's budget as a ceiling on Congress," Louis Fisher, a Congressional Research Service specialist, recalled in a 1979 paper delivered to the American Enterprise Institute conference. "Any funds that Congress added to the president's budget could be set aside and left unobligated." In addition, Nixon administration officials seized on the permissive language that Congress wrote into some authorization and appropriations bills, contending that the provisions gave the president authority to suspend or cancel programs.

House and Senate Democratic leaders contended that Nixon used impoundments to impose his own priorities in defiance of laws passed by Congress. The Nixon impoundments suggested, Fisher went on, that "whatever Congress did during the appropriations phase to fix budget priorities was easily undone by officials during the budget execution phase." The dispute embittered Nixon's relations with Congress and probably contributed to congressional support for 1974 impeachment proceedings that forced the president to resign in the wake of the Watergate scandal.

A 1975 Supreme Court decision subsequently backed the congressional position. Congress in the meantime moved to restrict use of impoundments as part of its landmark 1974 budget law. And in the following years Congress monitored more closely executive branch agencies and policies to make sure that legislative mandates were observed.

Constitutional Ambiguity

The Constitution did not spell out whether the president was required to promptly spend funds appropriated by Congress or whether he could make independent judgments on the timing and even the necessity of putting appropriated funds to use. Despite that constitutional ambiguity, presidents had impounded funds almost from the beginning of the Republic.

Congress even gave some legislative authority for executive impoundments to manage federal finances when it passed the Anti-Deficiency Act of 1950. That measure required the executive branch to subdivide appropriations to ensure that government agencies did not make commitments in excess of amounts appropriated. A 1950 omnibus appropriations act provided additional authority for the executive branch to create reserves for contingencies or to take advantage of savings made possible by developments after appropriations had been voted.

In the post-World-War-II period, presidents more and more began to use impoundment as a fiscal policy tool. Presidents Truman, Eisenhower and Kennedy all got into scrapes with Congress by withholding appropriated funds for defense projects.

In 1966 President Johnson cut back federal spending by $5.3 billion to curb the inflationary impact of the Vietnam War escalation. Major impoundments included $1.1 billion in highway funds, $760 million for housing and urban development, and large amounts for education, agriculture, health and welfare.

Nixon Impoundments

Nixon's extensive use of the power to withhold funds intensified the conflict between a Republican administration pledged to hold domestic spending down and a Democratic Congress determined to preserve the health, welfare, environmental, public works and other programs it had put in place during the preceding decade. Nixon argued that he was withholding funds only as a financial management technique, primarily to slow inflation through temporary reductions in federal spending. Congressional Democrats saw Nixon's impoundments as attempts to emasculate the social programs they wanted to continue.

The conflict took on new urgency when the 93rd Congress convened in 1973. The Senate in October 1972 had killed Nixon's request for a $250 billion fiscal 1973 spending ceiling; but the president set out to meet that goal anyway through liberal use of vetoes and broadly interpreted impoundment authority.

As the controversy gathered, Rep. Joe L. Evins, D-Tenn. (1947-77), chairman of the House Appropriations Subcommittee on Public Works, in mid-January 1973 released estimates that the administration had impounded $12 billion in appropriated funds, including $6 billion of $11 billion in sewage treatment funding that Congress had authorized over Nixon's veto in 1972.

The White House Feb. 5 claimed that the president would impound only $8.7 billion in fiscal 1973, the smallest amount withheld since 1966. A detailed list submitted to Congress excluded the $6 billion in water pollution control funds on the ground that the funds had been authorized but not appropriated.

Congressional Response

Congress responded in 1973 by seeking to limit the president's impoundment authority. In opening Senate hearings on impoundment legislation, Government Operations Committee Chairman Sam J. Ervin Jr., D-N.C. (1954-74), characterized Nixon's use of impoundments as "an item or line veto" — a power the senator said was prohibited by the Constitution — allowing the president to disapprove funding levels for particular programs without vetoing the entire appropriations bill that provided the money. The practice enabled the president to "modify, reshape or nullify completely laws passed by the legislative branch," Ervin contended, "thereby making legislative policy — a power reserved exclusively to the Congress."

Nixon Jan. 31 told a news conference that his constitutional power to impound funds "when the spending of money would mean either increasing prices or increasing taxes ... is absolutely clear." And Deputy Attorney General Joseph T. Sneed told the committee Feb. 6 that the president had "an implied constitutional right" to impound funds.

The bill drafted by the Government Operations Committee and approved by the full Senate would have forced the president to release impounded funds after 60 days unless both the House and Senate approved his action by concurrent resolution. The measure also allowed Congress to force release of funds before the end of 60 days by passing a concurrent resolution disapproving their impoundment.

In the House, the Rules Committee meanwhile drew up separate legislation to empower either the House or the Senate to overrule a presidential impoundment. The bill also set a $267.1 billion fiscal 1974 spending limit.

Before the House passed its measure, Republicans tried without success to make it more difficult for Congress to overturn impoundments. One amendment, requiring both the House and Senate to approve resolutions forcing the release of impounded funds, failed by a single vote.

With Nixon expected to veto impoundment legislation, and the close votes on the Republican amendments underscoring House divisions on the measure, Congress abandoned the legislation. Instead, the House and Senate wrote compromise impoundment procedures into a 1974 congressional budget control law.

New Impoundment Procedures

The 1974 budget law set up two procedures for presidents to follow to delay or cancel the spending of funds. Both were subject to congressional review. The impoundment provisions, a compromise developed from the 1973 House and Senate measures, were tacked on as Title X of the 1974 law creating new congressional procedures for considering the federal budget. *(Details of budget control act, p. 57)*

To simply delay spending temporarily, the president under the law can defer outlays. The deferral stands unless either the House or Senate passes a resolution directing that the money be spent. Congress may act on a deferral at any time.

But if the president believes money should not be spent at all, he must propose that Congress rescind the appropriation making the funds available. In that case, both the House and Senate must approve the rescission within 45 days. If the two houses do not act, the president must release the funds at the end of the 45-day period.

Title X requires the president to keep Congress informed on impoundments by sending deferrals and rescission requests to Capitol Hill. The General Accounting Office may review deferral and rescission messages for accuracy and the comptroller general, who heads that agency, has authority to report to Congress any executive branch action that impounds funds without proper notification of Congress. Such a report from the comptroller general triggers rescission or deferral proceedings as though the president had requested congressional consideration. The comptroller general also may reclassify deferrals as rescissions, or vice versa, and may go to federal court to enforce the law's impoundment requirements.

There is disagreement, even within Congress, about exactly what Title X was intended to accomplish and did accomplish. Congressional and executive branch employees who must deal with Title X generally agree that its language is vague in many respects and is without sufficient legislative history to explain Congress' intent.

Congressional critics find fault with the rescission provision because the president, by asking that appropriations be canceled, can block spending for nearly seven weeks. Even if Congress refuses to approve a rescission measure, the law provides no opportunity for the House and Senate to force the administration to spend the funds before the 45-day period is up.

But the criticisms and the questions go far beyond that. A basic one is whether Title X gives the president new powers to withhold funds and cancel or greatly delay congressionally approved spending. During debate on the provisions, the House asserted that Title X created new authority for fund withholding and allowed the president to propose deferrals for reasons other than administrative housekeeping. Deferring spending for purely managerial reasons was allowed under the old government budgeting procedures that the budget control act replaced.

The Senate argued that Title X did not allow the president to defer spending for policy reasons. After studying this dispute, Comptroller General Elmer B. Staats in late 1974 supported the House view of the matter. The Senate, however, was unconvinced and the issue continued.

Another criticism was that the provisions eroded the president's basic budgetary powers. The argument was that Title X exposed to congressional scrutiny previously hidden budget-juggling maneuvers of the executive branch. This exposure, along with Congress' power to block presidential impoundments, worried some observers — generally officials in the executive branch. They feared that Title X, along with other new congressional budget authority, might tip spending power toward Congress by destroying presidential control over the federal budget. "What we're talking about here is congressional government — and chaos," one executive branch budget official said.

Probably the complaint most often heard in the first years of Title X operation is that the requirements of the law generated a mountain of paperwork by requiring formal action on administrative matters and other minutiae that were never brought through the system in the past. A GAO spokesman estimated that as much as 50 percent of all deferrals fell into this category.

Use of Procedures

Criticisms aside, the congressional authors of the legislation predicted that impoundment proposals for policy reasons would amount to only a few dozen each year. But after the law went into effect, Fisher noted, President Ford requested 330 deferrals and 150 rescissions in less than three years. Fisher classified 120 deferrals and 133 rescissions that Ford sought as policy impoundments rather than routine cost-saving steps. "The large number of policy rescission proposals shows that Ford attempted to continue the presidential custom of reshaping budget priorities enacted by Congress," Fisher contended. ". . . Ford used the rescission-deferral mechanism to frustrate congressional adjustments to his budget."

During Ford's presidency, Congress passed 16 resolutions disapproving deferrals in fiscal 1975, 26 in fiscal 1976 and three in fiscal 1977, Fisher reported. President Jimmy Carter, a Democrat, proposed far fewer policy deferrals, and Congress took exception to fewer impoundment actions. But defense-minded members protested in 1977 when Carter took steps to terminate contracts for the B-1 bomber and Minuteman III missile programs, then requested rescissions two weeks later.

In 1981 President Ronald Reagan used deferrals to hold fiscal 1982 spending to levels he sought while Congress considered his request for 12 percent across-the-board reductions in all spending programs except defense. Reagan made the deferrals effective from Oct. 1 to Nov. 20, the period covered by a continuing resolution providing funds for programs for which Congress had yet to approve fiscal 1982 appropriations when the fiscal year started Oct. 1.

Administrative Oversight

In addition to impoundments, Nixon's other budget-cutting tactics sewed congressional distrust that lingered through the following decade. In response, House and Senate committees and subcommittees began monitoring those executive branch practices that offered opportunities to delay or slow down spending. In particular, members watched carefully how federal agencies reprogrammed funds from one appropriation account to another to take account of changing conditions or new legislation. Members also monitored Office of Management and Budget (OMB) policies imposing personnel ceilings or instructing agencies to absorb pay increases from available funds.

One result has been a tendency by Congress to write administrative restrictions and requirements into law, causing federal officials to object to what they called congressional "meddling" in agency administration. Those initiatives, along with impoundment controls, "all are part of the congressional effort to assure that agencies respect and faithfully carry out legislative priorities," Fisher noted. "Administrators may complain about the intimate involvement of Congress in executive details, but it was administrative behavior in the first place that required Congress to intervene."

REGAINING CONTROL: THE 1974 BUDGET LAW

Frustrated by the impoundment battle and acknowledging that it had forfeited control of the budget through the haphazard way it dealt with presidential spending requests, Congress in 1974 set up a new process, significantly changing the way it handled the federal budget.

Under the Congressional Budget and Impoundment Control Act of 1974, Congress votes each year to set specific spending, tax and deficit limits. Perhaps more importantly for the long-run course of the U.S. economy, Congress also gave itself the machinery necessary to shape the federal budget to the government's fiscal policy objectives.

For the first time since the legislative budget experiments of the postwar years, lawmakers are forced to thoroughly consider the president's fiscal policy goals as they act on separate spending measures. And by requiring Congress to set initial budget targets — and later uphold them or make adjustments — the budget law compels the House and Senate to go on record for each fiscal year on how much the government should spend, how much revenue it should raise and how much money it should borrow to make up for any deficit.

The budget law steered a careful course through the crosscurrents of congressional politics. It left the jurisdictions of previously existing tax and appropriations committees intact and it left legislative committees free to push new and additional spending proposals. The 1974 measure did not require a balanced budget or impose specific spending ceilings but instead superimposed an annual budget review process on top of the yearly congressional procedure for appropriating funds for government agencies.

Genesis of the Process

In revising its budgetary procedures, Congress once again undertook a task that had been tried and abandoned in the legislative budget experiments nearly 25 years earlier. But in the early 1970s, in the midst of angry spending fights with Nixon, congressional leaders finally concluded that the House and Senate had to put their own fiscal procedures in order to hold their own in budget policy struggles.

After a lively political sparring match completed in the month before the 1972 presidential election, Congress denied Nixon's request to set a $250 billion ceiling on fiscal 1973 spending and to give him authority to enforce it. But it did enact a little-noticed provision setting up a joint House-Senate study committee to review the way Congress acted on the budget.

The 32-member panel, composed almost entirely of members from the House and Senate tax-writing and appropriations committees, proposed major changes in congressional procedures in April 1973. Their recommendations included creation of House and Senate budget committees, to be dominated by members from the existing tax and appropriations panels. The panel urged enactment of a concurrent resolution early in each session to set limits on spending and appropriations for the fiscal year, followed by a second resolution later in the session to adjust ceilings and subceilings as necessary to meet unanticipated budget requirements. The joint committee plan called for floor procedures requiring that amendments to budget resolutions raising outlays for one program category be accompanied by equivalent cuts from another category or by tax increases to provide the additional funding. They also proposed that all future backdoor spending programs, including entitlements, be subject to limits set through the annual appropriations process. Other proposals included binding limits on outlays written into appropriations measures and wrap-up appropriations bills to reconcile spending totals at the end of each congressional session.

Congressional Deliberations

What followed during the rest of 1973 and first six months of 1974 turned into a landmark exercise in congressional power brokering. Powerful committee chairmen jockeyed backstage to preserve their panels' existing authority to shape tax and spending decisions. Conservatives sought restrictive budget procedures, while liberals resisted proposals that they felt would squeeze funding for domestic programs. Through the give-and-take of House and Senate deliberations, the process that emerged "was an accommodation to the most salient interests of the affected parties," CRS specialist Allen Schick commented.

In the House serious resistance among liberals both inside and outside Congress forced the Rules Committee to reduce the number of Ways and Means and Appropriations committee members assigned to the new Budget Committee. In general, the liberals suspected that fiscally conservative southern Democrats and Republicans from those panels "would lock the congressional budgetary process into a conservative mold for generations to come," according to a Democratic Study Group report.

In a significant departure from the joint panel proposals, the House bill made the initial budget resolution a flexible guideline that would set targets but not bind subsequent decisions on separate appropriations and spending measures. The Rules Committee report argued that the change would "preserve and enhance the appropriations process which has consistently demonstrated its effectiveness."

The initial Senate version of the budget control legislation was more rigid than the House proposal. But tight budget ceilings, along with provisions making backdoor spending programs subject to the regular appropriations process, aroused concern among the powerful high-ranking members of the existing legislative committees. If committees were subject to a firm initial ceiling that would be difficult to adjust, their power to initiate new programs or step up existing federal efforts would be severely limited. The upshot was a final version with procedures and timetables less stringent than the House bill.

The House passed its version of the bill by a 386-23 vote Dec. 5, 1973. The Senate passed its compromise version without dissent March 22, 1974. Conferees negotiated some further refinements, particularly on impoundment controls, and the conference report won easy approval. The House adopted it by a 401-6 vote on June 18; two Republicans and four Democrats opposed the measure. The Senate gave its approval by a 75-0 roll call on June 21.

President Nixon signed the fnial measure into law (PL 93-344) on July 12, 1974, less than a month before the threat of impeachment forced him to resign the presidency.

Budget-making Procedures

The final budget law set up a permissive, in many ways ambiguous, process for Congress to act on the budget. Following is a description of that process.

To give Congress a more expert perspective on budget totals and on fiscal policy requirements, the budget reform act established House and Senate Budget committees to study and recommend changes in the president's budget.

Assuring that existing House committees concerned with budgetary matters would be represented on the 23-member House Budget Committee, the act assigned five seats to Ways and Means Committee members and five to Appropriations Committee members. The remaining seats are occupied by one member from each of the 11 legislative committees, one member from the majority leadership and one from the minority leadership.

The act rotated House Budget Committee membership by prohibiting any member from serving for more than four years out of a 10-year period. Members on the committee must serve for a full Congress.

The 15-member Senate Budget Committee is picked by normal Senate committee selection procedures. No rotation is required.

The act established an office within Congress to provide the experts and the computers needed to absorb and analyze information that accompanied the president's budget. The act required the Congressional Budget Office to make its staff and resources available to all congressional committees and members, but with priority given to work for the House and Senate Budget committees. The office is run by a director appointed for a four-year term by the Speaker of the House and the president pro tempore of the Senate.

Budget Submission

To give Congress more time to consider the budget during annual sessions starting in January, the law pushed the start of the fiscal year, formerly July 1, back to Oct. 1, effective with fiscal 1977.

To give Congress a quicker start in shaping the budget, the act required the executive branch to submit a "current services" budget by Nov. 10 for the fiscal year that would start the following Oct. 1. Building on the programs and funding levels in effect for the ongoing fiscal year that had started the month before, the November current services budget projects the spending required to maintain those programs at existing commitment levels without policy changes through the following fiscal year. The Joint Economic Committee must review the current services budget outlook and report its evaluation to Congress by Dec. 31.

The president submits his revised federal budget to Congress about Jan. 20. In addition to the customary budget totals and breakdowns, the act requires the budget document to include a list of existing and proposed tax expenditures — revenues lost to the Treasury through preferential tax treatment of certain activities and income.

The measure also requires that the budget include estimates of costs for programs whose funds must be appropriated one full year before they are obligated.

Other provisions direct that the budget figures be presented in terms of national needs, agency missions and basic programs. The budget also must include five-year projections of expected spending under federal programs.

Budget Resolution

After reviewing the president's budget proposals — and considering the advice of the Congressional Budget Office and other committees — the House and Senate Budget committees draw up a concurrent resolution outlining a tentative alternative congressional budget. Under the law's timetable, congressional committees have until March 15 to report their budget recommendations to the budget committees. The budget office report is due on April 1. *(Budget timetable, box, p. 62)*

By April 15 the Budget committees must report concurrent resolutions to the House and Senate floors. By May 15 Congress must clear the initial budget resolution.

The initial resolution, a tentative budget, sets target totals for appropriation, spending, taxes, the budget surplus or deficit and the federal debt. Within those overall targets, the resolution breaks down appropriations and spending among the functional categories — defense, health, income security and so forth — used in the president's budget document. The resolution also includes any recommended changes in tax revenues and in the level of the federal debt ceiling.

Once House and Senate conferees reach agreement on the final version of the first budget resolution, they allocate the targets among those committees in Congress that consider legislation providing the funds to be spent within the total and functional category targets.

The Appropriations committees, which consider the bulk of spending proposals requiring appropriations, further subdivide their allocations among the 13 subcommittees that handle appropriations for different departments and agencies. Each committee also must allocate its share of the spending targets between controllable spending and spending that was beyond immediate congressional control.

Once enacted, the first budget resolution guides but does not bind Congress as it acts on appropriations bills and other measures providing budget authority for spending on federal programs.

No measure appropriating funds, changing taxes or the public debt level or creating a new entitlement program committing the government to pay certain benefits may be considered on the floor before adoption of the first budget resolution. In the Senate, however, that prohibition may be waived by majority vote.

To clear the way for prompt action on appropriations before the fiscal year begins, the law requires that all bills authorizing appropriations be reported by May 15, the deadline for enactment of the budget resolution. That requirement may be waived, however, by majority vote in both the House and the Senate.

There are two exemptions from the May 15 deadline for reporting authorizing legislation: for Social Security legislation dealing with a variety of trust funds and welfare programs, and for entitlement legislation that may not be considered on the floor until the budget resolution is cleared.

Under the terms of the budget control law, the administration must make its request for authorizing legislation a year in advance. Therefore the administration must submit its requests by May 15 for the fiscal year following the fiscal year that begins Oct. 1. That gives congressional committees a full year to study the requests before the following May 15 deadline for reporting authorization bills for the fiscal year in question.

After enactment of the budget resolution, Congress begins processing the 13 regular appropriations bills for the upcoming fiscal year through its customary appropriations process: House Appropriations subcommittee and full committee action, House floor action, Senate Appropriations subcommittee and full committee action, Senate floor action and conference action.

The law directs the House Appropriations Committee to try to complete action on all appropriations measures and submit a report summarizing its decisions before reporting the first bill for floor action.

All appropriations bills have to be cleared by the middle of September — no later than the seventh day after Labor Day. That deadline may be waived, however, for any appropriations bill whose consideration was delayed because Congress had not acted promptly on necessary authorizing legislation.

If Congress so provides in its initial budget resolution, appropriations and entitlement bills may be held up after final action on conference reports. Under that procedure, no appropriations bills would be sent to the president until Congress had completed a September reconciliation of its initial budget targets with its separate spending measures.

Reconciliation

After finishing action on all appropriations and other spending bills in mid-September, Congress takes another overall look at its work on the budget.

By Sept. 15 Congress must adopt a second budget resolution that either affirms or revises the budget targets set by the initial resolution. If separate congressional decisions taken during the appropriations process do not fit the final budget resolution totals, the resolution may dictate changes in appropriations (both for the upcoming fiscal year or carried over from previous fiscal years), entitlements, revenues and the debt limit.

The resolution would direct the committees that had jurisdiction over those matters to report legislation making the required changes.

If all the required changes fall within the jurisdiction of one committee in each house — appropriations changes that the Appropriations committees would consider, for example — those committees then would report a reconciliation bill to the floor.

If the changes involve two committees — appropriations changes by the Appropriations committees and tax changes by the House Ways and Means and Senate Finance committees, for example — those committees would submit recommendations to the Budget committees. The Budget committees then would combine the recommendations without substantial change and report them to the floor as a reconciliation bill.

If Congress withholds all appropriations and entitlement bills from the president, reconciliation may be accomplished by passage of a resolution directing the House clerk and secretary of the Senate to make necessary changes in the bills previously cleared. A reconciliation bill still could be needed, however, to change tax levels or other provisions already enacted into law.

Backdoor Spending

The law attempted to bring most forms of new backdoor spending programs under the appropriations process, but existing backdoor programs remained outside that process. The bill required annual appropriation of funds for new contract authority or borowing authority programs.

The bill also established special procedures for entitlement programs. No entitlements could be enacted until Congress had adopted the first budget resolution, in which it would set guidelines on how much spending would be permissible on new programs.

If an authorizing committee subsequently reported a new entitlement program that exceeded the committee's allocation as established by the first budget resolution, the bill would be referred to the Appropriations Committee. The Appropriations Committee then had 15 days to report an amendment putting a limit on appropriations for the program. If the Appropriations Committee did not act within 15 days, the measure would go on the calendar as reported by the authorization committee.

Exempted from the act's backdoor spending procedures were all Social Security trust funds, all trust funds that received 90 percent or more of their financing from designated taxes rather than from general revenues, general revenue sharing funds, insured and guaranteed loans, federal government and independent corporations, and gifts to the government.

These procedures, if followed, force the full House and Senate to make budget choices for each fiscal year. And, because budget concerns impinge on virtually all other legislation, the law intensified the potential for conflict within Congress as it debates fiscal and budget alternatives.

"All that Congress decided in 1974," Schick said, "was that the disputes are going to be resolved through a process in which the majority rules."

—Thomas J. Arrandale

5

Experiment in Budgeting

The 1974 budget law gave Congress procedural tools for reclaiming control of the federal budget. But through the first six years the process was used, the House and Senate moved uncertainly in legislating budget policy.

Then, with Republican President Ronald Reagan directing from the White House, Congress in 1981 used the budget law to slash $35.2 billion from fiscal 1982 spending, reversing at least momentarily the upward trend of federal outlays. Perhaps more importantly, Congress used its budget procedures, especially reconciliation, to make fundamental policy shifts across a wide range of federal programs.

While some lawmakers hailed the 1981 action as proof that the congressional budget process worked, others warned that Congress once again was relinquishing to the president its responsibiity to shape the budget. By using the 1981 reconciliation measure to make substantive changes in federal law, they contended, Congress went far beyond its original purpose in designing the budget process.

Enacted in 1974 to regain control of the federal budget, the budget law forced Congress to view the federal budget as a whole and to fit individual spending programs into an overall scheme. Each year after the president submitted his budget proposals, Congress was required to devise its own budget targets, projecting revenue, outlay, and surplus or deficit goals. Once those targets were in place Congress would work on its regular authorizations and appropriations bills. Then in mid-September it would establish binding budget totals for the upcoming fiscal year and reconcile individual spending measures to those totals. The 1974 law also cut back the president's authority to refuse to spend already appropriated funds and to otherwise alter the priorities established by the congressional process. (Details, 1974 law, p. 56; budgeting timetable, p. 62)

Ever since the budget process had been approved, Congress had argued over how it should be used. Congressional conservatives, at times allied with Republican presidents, viewed the process as a tool for enforcing wholesale spending cutbacks. Congressional liberals, joined by interest groups lobbying for federal programs, thought the procedures should give Congress greater power to set priorities for the nation by shifting resources from defense to the government's domestic functions.

Within Congress itself, House and Senate committee rivalry fragmented budget debates as authorization panels protected funding for the programs they had helped create. The 1974 act created Budget committees to keep members' attention focused on tax and spending totals. But the law allowed Congress to set maximum spending limits and so left authorizing committees free to press for whatever spending levels could command House and Senate majorities. By devising budget procedures that gave free play to House and Senate conflicts, "Congress institutionalized its own ambivalence over budget policy," Congressional Research Service expert Allen Schick noted.

Through the last half of the 1970s, Congress in its annual budget resolutions generally accommodated political pressures within the House and Senate to leave room for new programs and additional spending. Throughout that period the nation's economy was in slow and halting recovery from a steep 1974-75 recession. Federal fiscal policy, while calling for an eventual balance, gave Congress latitude to add new spending even while budget deficits persisted.

But by the end of the decade the inflation rate soared above 20 percent and federal outlays were growing by roughly $500 million a year, far outpacing revenues. Voters turned out Jimmy Carter in favor of Republican Ronald Reagan, who promised to curb inflation and bring the federal budget into balance through a combination of spending and tax cuts. The 1980 elections also gave Republicans control of the Senate and weakened the Democratic majority in the House.

Reagan's election — and its obvious political message — forced Congress to start disciplining the budget to fiscal scarcity. But faced with the uncomfortable task of drawing the line on federal spending, Congress once again seemingly abdicated to the president. Congress in 1981 cut spending dramatically but those cutbacks generally imposed Reagan's spending priorities and endorsed the president's fiscal policy.

The 1981 reconciliation success gave the process new life, for the time being at least. It strengthened the Budget committees' hand, even in the House, where Republicans and southern Democrats joined to overturn much of the Budget panel's work on the floor. Budget committee leaders were considering changes to further strengthen the process as a way to bind Congress to fiscal limits.

But a backlash also was building among members — particularly from members of still-powerful committees — who felt that reconciliation abused normal congressional procedures. Sen. William Proxmire, D-Wis., warned that "unless we stop short, take stock and revise some of the procedures, the budget reform act itself may die or, worse, may destroy the Senate as a distributive body."

House Rules Committee Chairman Richard Bolling, D-Mo. — in a *Washington Post* article written with John E. Barriere, a Democratic staff assistant who helped write the 1974 law — protested that continued use of reconciliation as it was used in 1981 "will be a gross distortion of the intent of those who wrote the Constitution and the Bill of Rights, as well as the intent of the 1974 Budget Act."

ACCOMMODATION: THE EARLY YEARS

The federal government would not halt in its tracks if Congress simply gave up on legislating budget resolutions. At times, conflicting political pressures threatened congressional faith that the beleaguered system could keep working. Yet, even though the House and Senate often slipped badly behind the timetable that the budget law established, the process functioned more or less intact through its first seven trying sessions.

Between 1975 and 1981, the budget process scored some notable successes and survived some near-disasters. The Senate, with a forceful Budget Committee chairman and tradition of legislating by consensus, used the budget procedures much more smoothly than the deeply divided House. In the House, the rotating membership of the Budget Committee meant that the panel developed less budget expertise. Members' loyalties to the other legislative panels on which they served further limited the Budget Committee's political clout in House maneuvering. House leaders, unable to count on backing from a disgruntled Republican minority, were forced to barter with liberal Democrats and southern fiscal conservatives to gain support.

In its early years, congressional budget making was largely a process of accommodation. House and Senate leaders, anxious to keep the process going, steered away from proposing budget resolutions that would force legislative and appropriations committees to compete openly for budget resources. The House and Senate Budget committees first considered spending needs for each of 19 budget categories before setting an overall total, not the other way around. As Schick pointed out, "At no time during the first five years of budgeting did either committee vote explicitly to take from one function in order to give more to another."

As long as Congress remained in an expansive mood, the House and Senate were able to construct budgets in a piecemeal fashion that satisfied the particular interests of various committees and groups. When Congress tried to shift toward fiscal austerity in mid-1979, it encountered much rougher going.

Revising Ford Budgets

Democrats, eager to rewrite the restrictive budgets that President Ford's Republican administration drew up,

Budget Timetable

Late January: President submits budget (15 days after Congress convenes).

March 15: All legislative committees submit program estimates and reviews to Budget committees.

April 15: Budget committees report first resolution.

May 15: Committees must report authorization bills by this date.

May 15: Congress completes action on first resolution. Before adoption of the first resolution, neither house may consider new budget authority or spending authority bills, revenue changes or debt limit changes.

May 15 through the 7th day after Labor Day: Congress completes action on all budget and spending authority bills.

Sept. 15: Congress completes action on second resolution. Thereafter, neither house may consider any bill, amendment or conference report that results in an increase over outlay or budget authority figures, or a reduction in revenues, beyond the amounts in the second resolution.

Sept. 25: Congress completes action on reconciliation bill or another resolution. Congress may not adjourn until it completes action on the second resolution and reconciliation measure, if any.

Oct. 1: Fiscal year begins.

put the new congressional budget procedures into use in 1975 — a year ahead of schedule.

The budget law mandated that Congress start using the process for fiscal 1977, starting Oct. 1, 1976. The law allowed Congress a year to get the feel of the procedures in 1975, if it chose, by putting the fiscal 1976 budget through a "trial run" process. House and Senate leaders, determined to rework that year's budget to step up stimulative spending to counter a deep 1974-75 recession, agreed to implement key parts of the process during that session.

The 1975 proceedings waived some budget law deadlines and left out potentially controversial budget targets for program categories. But in December legislators cleared a final budget resolution (H Con Res 466) in which Congress for the first time specified the total size of the federal budget. The binding congressional budget figures boosted Ford's initial proposal by $25 billion and projected a $74.1 billion deficit, which would have been the largest in the nation's history. As things turned out, fiscal 1976 outlays fell short of the congressional budget ceiling, but the $66.4 billion deficit still was the largest ever.

The final budget totals dismayed fiscal conservatives and displeased some pro-spending liberals who wanted Congress to take stronger action to reduce unemployment.

In spite of their differences, important conservatives and liberals in both the House and Senate supported the new system at critical points and kept it from collapsing.

Budget Committee leaders were particularly effective in forcing Congress to pay attention to its budget goals. In the Senate, Budget Committee Chairman Edmund S. Muskie, D-Maine (1959-80), gained key support from the committee's top-ranking Republican, Henry Bellmon, Okla. (1969-81), a fiscal conservative. The going was tougher in the House, where Republicans were more resistant to the new process and liberal Democrats challenged the Budget Committee's recommendations as too restrictive.

Brock Adams, D-Wash. (1965-77), had been elected House Budget Committee chairman when Congress convened, as Al Ullman, D-Ore. (1957-81), chose to take over the Ways and Means Committee instead. With strenuous backing from the House Democratic leadership, Adams won narrow House approval of both fiscal 1976 resolutions.

Early in the year, the process was handicapped by lack of a functioning Congressional Budget Office (CBO). House and Senate leaders had been fighting a protracted battle since the budget law was passed over filling the potentially influential post of CBO director. Finally, on Feb. 24, Congress swore in Harvard-trained economist Alice M. Rivlin, a senior fellow at the liberal-leaning Brookings Institution in Washington, D.C., as the first CBO director.

Before the 1975 session ended, Congress stuck by the new process in a dispute with Ford over fiscal 1977 spending. Democrats fended off Ford's demand, backed by House Republicans, that Congress specify a fiscal 1977 spending ceiling without waiting for the budget procedures to operate in 1976.

Ford had proposed a $398 billion spending limit, which would cut estimated fiscal 1977 outlays by about $28 billion, offsetting a $28 billion tax-cut package Ford had also requested. Rejecting the tax package, Congress enacted a six-month extension of 1975 tax cuts and worked that revenue loss into its second fiscal 1976 budget resolution. Because Congress had refused to consider his spending restraints, Ford vetoed the tax-cut extension.

House Republicans, with help from Democratic fiscal conservatives, upheld that veto. But House and Senate leaders, with Muskie and Adams in the forefront, refused to consider a spending limit proposal, contending it would short-circuit the budget process before the president submitted specific reductions in his fiscal 1977 budget.

The issue finally was resolved when Congress won Ford's approval of a six-month tax-cut extension by pledging to consider spending restraints for fiscal 1977. Congressional leaders, who had no intention of accepting all of Ford's spending cut proposals, had protected the freedom of Congress to select a different spending level through its new budget process.

1976 Tax Bill Challenge

The budget law went into full effect in 1976, and Congress met its requirements in approving a $413.1 billion fiscal 1977 budget with a $50.6 billion deficit.

As expected, Congress paid scant attention to Ford's $394.2 billion budget proposal. It nonetheless approved virtually all of the president's $101.1 billion defense spending projection and carved significant amounts from potential and proposed domestic outlays.

Debates on budget resolution figures again produced sharp liberal and fiscal conservative differences with Budget Committee recommendations. But the Senate continued to back up its panel, and the House demonstrated increasing acceptance of the new process by passing its resolutions with more comfortable margins.

And although the outcome was in doubt until the end of the 1976 budget process, Congress fulfilled a self-imposed budget resolution goal by enacting tax revision legislation that raised an additional $1.6 billion despite persistent resistance by powerful Senate Finance Committee Chairman Russell B. Long, D-La.

In May, both the House and Senate gave comfortable approval to an initial resolution setting fiscal 1977 targets. Both the House and Senate versions contemplated extension of the temporary tax cuts through fiscal 1977 and recommended that Congress revise tax laws to pick up $2 billion in additional revenues.

But when Congress tried to follow the first resolution's requirements, it ran into Senate jurisdictional disputes. The Senate Finance Committee set up the most serious showdown in May when it reported a tax revision package that complied with the budget resolution's revenue target only by juggling the expirations dates of specific tax-cut extensions.

Senate Budget Committee Chairman Muskie and ranking minority member Bellmon quickly challenged the cost-trimming device as threatening the fiscal policy assumed in the budget resolution. In a June 16 letter to their colleagues, Muskie and Bellmon argued that revenue losses in subsequent years under the bill's provisions could keep the budget in deficit.

Finance Committee Chairman Long and top-ranking Republican Carl T. Curtis, R-Neb. (1939-54; 1955-79), retorted in their own letter that the bill and accompanying committee amendments provided tax cuts that were consistent with the budget goals. It was the Finance Committee's province, they argued, to decide what specific provisions should be used to meet the budget requirements.

When the Senate took up the Finance Committee bill, Muskie took the dispute to the floor and lost.

But Congress salvaged its fiscal 1977 budget process in September, enacting a second budget resolution calling for $1.6 billion in tax revision revenues and clearing a tax bill conference report which met that requirement.

The budget and tax measures moved simultaneously. As Finance and Ways and Means conferees negotiated a tax revision compromise, the House and Senate Budget committees drew up binding budget resolutions that scaled down the revenue gain anticipated from the tax bill's provisions. Congress completed action on its final fiscal 1977 budget resolution on Sept. 16, the same day it cleared the tax bill.

THE CARTER BUDGETS: UNFULFILLED PROMISES

The 1976 elections turned Ford out of the White House and brought Democrat Jimmy Carter to the presidency in 1977. Carter's election, with continued Democratic majorities in the House and Senate, promised to end nearly a decade of budget battles between Congress and the executive. That never developed. Even though Congress had demonstrated that the budget process could work, Carter and Congress never settled on a tax and spending strategy to fulfill the president's campaign pledge to restore the budget to balance.

The Democrats' opportunity to establish consistent budget policy in the end was wasted. Carter wavered during his four-year term between spending restraints to curb inflation and stimulative measures to fight unemployment. House Democrats remained badly divided over federal budget priorities, while a defense-minded Senate pushed hard to boost military spending to counter a Soviet arms buildup.

The four-year fiscal policy turmoil severely tested the congressional budget process. With Carter in the White House, the House and Senate remained receptive to tax cuts and spending intiatives designed to fine-tune economic growth. But the budget process sputtered — and at times nearly foundered — when changing economic conditions forced Congress to shift toward fiscal restraint through politically difficult spending reductions.

Under Muskie's leadership the Senate committee often forged consensus support for the panel's fiscal policy recommendations. The Senate committee pushed hard for spending cutbacks, although it yielded to senators' demands for stepped-up military spending while the controversial SALT II arms limitation treaty was being debated.

Several times during the four-year period, Muskie took on influential chairmen of other Senate committees, notably Appropriations Committee Chairman Warren G. Magnuson, D-Wash. (1937-44; 1944-81), and Finance Committee Chairman Long, in efforts to force those panels to comply with budget resolution limits. The fight to put teeth into budget goals paid off at the end of 1980, when Congress for the first time put together reconciliation legislation incorporating spending cuts and revenue increases that its first fiscal 1981 budget resolution had ordered congressional committees to prepare. By then, Muskie had resigned from the Senate to serve as Carter's secretary of state.

Continued House Divisions

In the House, however, budget making during Carter's term usually was fractious, even chaotic. Several budget resolutions went down to defeat, opposed by Republicans and liberal Democrats alike. Budget Committee Chairman Robert N. Giaimo, D-Conn. (1959-81), labored to devise budget totals that could satisfy a majority of House Democrats, including conservatives who wanted to spend more on defense and liberals who fiercely resisted cutbacks in the Great Society programs of the 1960s.

Outnumbered House Republicans pushed for spending cutbacks, permanent tax reductions and an end to chronic deficits. On most House votes, Republicans united against budget resolutions, preferring to saddle Democrats with the blame for the deficits they envisioned. That stance probably pushed deficits higher, as House leaders accommodated liberal spending demands to keep the process working.

During the debate on the first budget resolutions in 1975, House Democratic leaders offered floor amendments to make budgets more palatable to liberals. But those tactics put Democrats in the position of openly promoting larger deficits and leaders subsequently focused their efforts on the less-public House Budget Committee mark-up

sessions on budget resolutions. To ease the way in 1977, as the 95th Congress convened, the leadership accordingly changed the Budget panel's membership to give it a more liberal majority. Nonetheless the House committee, in contrast to its Senate counterpart, remained reluctant to challenge other congressional committees by enforcing reconciliation instructions.

By 1980 critics charged that the congressional budget process had turned into a meaningless exercise of adding up separate spending proposals rather than disciplining them to overall budget goals. Congress strengthened that impression during 1980 by approving balanced budget targets in June, then putting off until after the November election the chore of approving final budget limits that showed a growing deficit. In both 1979 and 1980, Congress slipped badly behind the budget law timetable, designed to put final budget limits in place before the fiscal year began Oct. 1. In both years, Congress wound up approving deficits set at unrealistically low levels that had to be revised upwards a few months later.

Congress' budget-making problems were compounded by uncertain, often inaccurate, economic projections. CBO projections frequently were less optimistic than administration economic forecasts, and Congress used CBO assumptions to predict different outlays and revenue figures. Both White House and congressional experts misread economic trends, and Congress in midstream found itself forced to make large changes in budget estimates that dramatically altered the expected deficits. In addition, federal agencies often overestimated outlays, and actual spending fell short of what Congress allowed when it set budget limits.

Expansive Fiscal 1977-78 Budgets

Carter entered office in 1977 with a plan to pump up the sagging economy. Congress responded eagerly, shifting federal fiscal policy toward economic stimulus. In March, the House and Senate adopted an unprecedented third fiscal 1977 budget resolution, adjusting previously approved spending and revenue limits to accommodate the administration's economic proposals. By September, Congress had substantially enlarged the fiscal 1978 budget that Ford submitted three days before his term ended in January.

But in the intervening months sudden Carter policy shifts and deep House divisions nearly threw the budget process into chaos. In May, after Carter abruptly abandoned his proposal for $50 tax rebates, Congress again was forced to change its fiscal 1977 budget assumptions. Along the way, as Congress set targets for fiscal 1978, dissatisfied Democratic liberals and disgruntled Republican conservatives combined in the House to defeat a congressional budget resolution for the first time.

Congress March 3 approved a third fiscal 1977 resolution (S Con Res 10) allowing for outlays of $417.45 billion and a $69.75 billion deficit. S Con Res 10 encompassed Carter's full $13.8 billion tax cut package, even though doubts were growing in Congress about how much stimulus $50 tax rebates would generate. Convinced that direct government spending would create jobs more quickly than the administration's proposal, Congress nearly doubled planned outlay increases for jobs and countercyclical assistance.

Barely a month after Congress put revised fiscal 1977 budget goals in place, Carter abandoned the $50 tax rebates that the administration had proposed for quick stimulative impact. Carter April 14 told reporters that improving economic indicators since the stimulus package was planned in December had made immediate stimulus unnecessary. The administration reversed itself five days before the Senate took up the Finance Committee's tax-cut package in a climate of growing hostility to the $50 rebates from Republicans who favored permanent tax cuts and Democrats who thought spending increases would be more effective in stimulating economic activity.

Carter's surprising withdrawal of the rebate plan — and proposed business tax credits as well — left the third fiscal 1977 budget assumptions far too generous. In writing tentative fiscal 1978 budget targets (S Con Res 19), Congress in May again revised its fiscal 1977 figures, increasing revenue estimates to remove the previously expected cost of the rebate plan. The final revision set the fiscal 1977 deficit estimate at $52.6 billion, just $2 billion more than Congress had approved the previous September.

Revision of the fiscal 1977 budget was not Congress' only problem. Legislators approved fiscal 1978 compromise budget targets only after the House resoundingly rejected initial goals that displeased both liberals and conservatives. House backing for the first budget resolution, usually tenuous at best, unraveled on the floor after adoption of an amendment that restored defense appropriations and outlay figures to Carter's budget proposal. That action undercut the Budget Committee's effort to balance defense and domestic spending and cost moderate and liberal support for the budget resolution.

Budget Committee Chairman Giaimo maintained that those members "felt that the restraint they had showed with respect to spending for urgent domestic needs was not going to produce a similar restraint on the part of the defense establishment." On the other hand, the defense increases failed to win support from Republicans who remained concerned by the high deficit level. The amended resolution satisfied neither side, and it went down to defeat, 84-320, with only five Budget Committee members supporting its approval.

The outcome left in doubt the House commitment to making its budget procedures work. Defense Secretary Harold Brown's lobbying for defense increases angered House leaders, while Carter's abrupt withdrawal of his tax rebate plan stirred discontent about shifting administration policy. OMB re-estimates, which included a projection that fiscal 1977 spending would be $6.1 billion less than previously expected, further confused the budget outlook as the House and Senate committees reworked their target recommendations with the May 15 deadline approaching for approval of the first fiscal 1978 budget resolution. The

administration's policy change, Muskie complained, had "created a crisis of confidence and competence for the budget process."

Congress eventually settled on a revived first budget resolution only after House-Senate conferees spent one full day and half of a second negotiating a compromise defense target that Senate leaders felt was high enough and that House leaders thought was low enough to draw enough liberal votes to pass the measure. The House resolution, adopted 221-177, won support from 29 Republicans; that marked a departure from the minority's nearly unanimous opposition to previous House budget resolutions.

Action on final fiscal 1978 budget totals generated less heated debate over defense spending. But the House and Senate committees, drafting final budget resolutions in August, made important adjustments to accommodate pending energy legislation and higher spending than previously anticipated for farm programs. Both Budget panels were unhappy with congressional decisions that ignored preliminary budget targets in drafting an omnibus farm/food stamp measure. But the Senate committee's attempt to order farm spending restraint was overridden.

Coping With Fiscal Austerity

Congress' expansive mood carried over into the 1978 session, and the House and Senate began writing fiscal 1979 budget resolutions with high unemployment and possible recession in mind. But inflation soared again during the year, and an anti-government spirit took hold in national politics after California voters in June approved a state constitutional amendment slashing property taxes.

By September concern about inflation and high federal spending had eclipsed the early focus on stimulative tax cuts and job-creating measures. As a result, Congress that month approved a $487.5 billion fiscal 1979 budget that sheared Carter's $60.6 billion deficit to less than $39 billion. The binding budget resolution (H Con Res 683) took account of congressional actions reducing tax cuts and federal spending, and reflected smaller-than-previously-expected outlays for defense procurement and for medical and unemployment assistance.

In the process, Congress scaled back its own $50.9 billion deficit target set by a first fiscal 1979 budget resolution (S Con Res 80) in May. And the Senate, demonstrating notable support for its Budget Committee's position, held firm in September against House Democratic leaders' pressure to accept $2 billion in new spending for public works projects. The dispute delayed approval of binding budget totals until Sept. 23, a week after the deadline set by the 1974 budget control law.

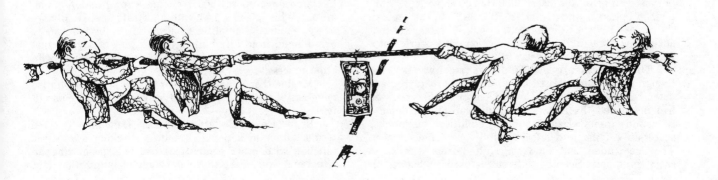

The Senate's stand against increased public works spending again demonstrated its commitment to the budget process. During conference negotiations on the binding fiscal 1979 resolution, Muskie refused to accept House compromise proposals, while House Speaker Thomas P. O'Neill Jr., D-Mass., urged House negotiators to insist on additional public works spending.

With negotiations stalemated, Muskie asked the Senate to back up his stand. By a 63-21 margin, the Senate complied Sept. 14 by instructing its conferees to insist on no new public works spending at all. The impasse blocked a conference agreement for several days, until the conferees accepted a face-saving solution that allowed the House and Senate to interpret the budget limits differently.

As usual, the Senate gave bipartisan support to budget resolutions. But most House Republicans continued to oppose fiscal recommendations by the Democratic majority, and their votes came close to defeating budget proposals. Republicans tried unsuccessfully to amend budget resolutions to make room for deeper tax cuts. They also challenged House Budget Committee procedures that they maintained simply toted up spending requests for different programs without fitting them to previously designed fiscal policy guidelines.

Guns vs. Butter

Congressional budget making faltered badly in 1979 as conflicts between defense and social spending grew. Congress managed to hold its binding fiscal 1980 deficit estimate to less than $30 billion, meeting a goal that President Carter had set the year before. But the fiscal 1980 budget tied Congress in knots, straining longstanding political coalitions and slowing action so that the budget law timetable was seriously breached. Congress finally completed the second budget resolution on Nov. 28, 59 days after fiscal 1980 began and 74 days past the deadline set by the 1974 law.

In the Senate, the Budget Committee continued to make impressive strides in encouraging fiscal discipline. But the House, sharply divided over where spending should be cut, defeated two budget resolutions before settling on a final compromise. As it was, the final budget resolution met Carter's deficit goal only because inflation-generated revenues partly kept pace with rising outlays.

Pressure to balance the budget built up early in the year. Some state legislatures and potential presidential candidates clamored for a constitutional amendment forbidding federal deficits, and conservatives stalled debt limit legislation until congressional leaders assured them a chance to vote for balancing the budget.

Congress responded, after a long and arduous battle, by writing a first budget resolution (H Con Res 107) that promised to bring the fiscal 1980 deficit down to $23 billion, $6 billion less than Carter's proposal. In the process, the Senate Budget Committee laid out a strategy for balancing the fiscal 1981 budget — but only if Congress provided no tax cuts until 1982.

The $23 billion fiscal 1980 deficit target was set even though the Senate insisted on approving most of Carter's defense spending request. House Democratic liberals, who had persuaded the House to include substantial defense reductions in its original budget resolution, mounted a successful campaign to defeat the initial conference report. They demanded that funds be shifted from defense to social programs. Senate conferees refused to budge, al-

though they mollified the House by accepting increased appropriations targets for education, training, employment and social service programs.

In the same resolution, Congress revised the binding fiscal 1979 budget figures it had set the previous September to make room for nearly $7 billion in higher-than-expected outlays and supplemental appropriations for defense and other programs. But because estimated revenues had jumped more than $12 billion, Congress was able to reduce its previous deficit target by $5 billion.

Senate Reconciliation Proposal

The budget process bogged down in the fall as the House and Senate worked on a binding fiscal 1980 budget measure. The House Sept. 19 rejected its Budget Committee's initial binding recommendations, the first time either the House or Senate had turned down a second budget resolution. The House accepted a revised measure eight days later but conferees then haggled a record 23 days before agreeing to increase both defense and social spending.

The final resolution (S Con Res 53), cleared Nov. 28, raised the fiscal 1980 outlay ceiling to $547.6 billion but kept the deficit at $29.8 billion by assuming rising revenues. Work on the budget was finished only after the House rejected the Senate's plan to force Congress for the first time to reconcile separate legislation to the budget resolution limits.

The Senate backed its Budget Committee's plan to invoke the reconciliation process, provided by the 1974 budget law but never before used by Congress, when it approved the binding budget resolution in September. The committee recommended that defense spending should rise dramatically, at least in fiscal 1981 and 1982. But, to keep fiscal policy steady, the panel agreed on budget totals that were lower than the sum of the authorizing and appropriations measures that Congress was likely to approve.

The committee then voted 9-4 to use the reconciliation process to require other congressional committees to report legislation to fit budget limits. The Budget panel proposed instructions to seven Senate committees to reduce fiscal 1980 spending by $4 billion. A likely floor fight on the issue was averted when Muskie negotiated a compromise with other Senate Democratic leaders that settled on $3.6 billion in cuts through reconciliation.

The key to Muskie's success was an agreement he reached with Appropriations Committee Chairman Magnuson. The agreement left the Appropriations panel free to decide later how to achieve the $2.5 billion in spending cuts sought by the Budget Committee. Muskie cemented his agreement with Magnuson by successfully opposing a floor move by Budget Committee Republicans to clamp down more tightly on the Appropriations Committee. While placating Magnuson, Muskie apparently appeased Finance Committee Chairman Long by reducing to $1.4 billion, from $1.7 billion, the amount of savings that panel would be expected to achieve under the reconciliation process.

Muskie then won direct floor battles with disgruntled members of the Agriculture and Veterans' Affairs committees.

In the House, Budget Committee Democrats rejected reconciliation in a Sept. 10 caucus, backing away from tangling with other committees over budget-cutting instructions. But despite their adamant opposition, the

Budget Totals Compared, Fiscal 1977-82

In billion dollars

	Budget Authority	Outlays*	Revenues*	Deficit*
Fiscal Year 1977				
Ford Budget	$433.4	$394.2	$351.3	$−43.0
First Resolution	454.2	413.3	362.5	−50.8
Second Resolution	451.55	413.1	362.5	−50.6
Third Resolution	472.9	417.45	347.7	−69.75
Third Resolution amended	470.2	409.2	356.6	−52.6
Actual	464.4	402.7	357.8	−44.9
Fiscal Year 1978				
Ford Budget	480.4	440.0	393.0	−47.0
Carter Revisions	507.3	459.4	401.6	−57.75
First Resolution	503.45	460.95	396.3	−64.65
Second Resolution	500.1	458.25	397.0	−61.25
Actual	500.4	450.8	402.0	−48.8
Fiscal Year 1979				
Carter Budget	568.2	500.2	439.6	−60.6
First Resolution	568.85	498.8	447.9	−50.9
Second Resolution	555.65	487.5	448.7	−38.8
Revised Second Resolution	559.2	494.45	461.0	−33.45
Actual	556.7	493.6	465.9	−27.7
Fiscal Year 1980				
Carter Budget	615.5	531.6	502.6	−29.0
First Resolution	604.4	532.0	509.0	−23.0
Second Resolution	638.0	547.6	517.8	−29.8
Revised Second Resolution	658.9	572.7	525.7	−47.0
Actual	658.8	579.6	520.1	−59.5
Fiscal Year 1981				
Carter Budget	696.1	615.8	600.0	−15.8
Carter Revisions	691.3	611.5	628.0	+16.5
First Resolution	697.2	613.6	613.8	+ 0.2
Second Resolution	694.6	632.4	605.0	−27.4
Revised Second Resolution	717.5	661.35	603.3	−58.05
Actual	N.A.	660.5	602.6	−57.9
Fiscal Year 1982				
Carter Budget	809.8	739.3	711.8	−27.5
Reagan Revision	772.4	695.3	650.3	−45.0
First Resolution	770.9	695.45	657.8	−37.65

*Actual figures for fiscal 1977-79 are taken from Carter budget for fiscal 1982; fiscal 1980-81 actual figures are from the Reagan administration.

Source: Compiled by Congressional Quarterly from the federal budget and congressional budget resolutions for the appropriate years.

House-Senate conference compromise on the second budget resolution contained reconciliation instructions that directed six authorizing committees to trim $1.8 billion from previously passed legislation, and ordered the House and Senate Appropriations committees to cut fiscal 1980 spending by $2.55 billion.

The Senate approved the conference version. But the House, at the urging of Budget Committee Chairman Giaimo, struck the budget-cutting directions from the resolution in a 205-190 vote. That 15-vote margin was evidence that "I can't take on seven committees in the House" over spending cuts, Giaimo said later. "We've made Congress aware of reconciliation," he added. "But it's just too massive to achieve this year."

The House and Senate subsequently settled on a compromise resolution warning committees that Congress would not bail them out later by covering spending increases through a third fiscal 1980 resolution. But federal spending bumped up against the fiscal 1980 limits by March of 1980. Overlooking that warning, Congress added $19.4 billion to cover the increases by amending the fiscal 1980 resolution.

1980 Reconciliation Success

The budget process all but fell apart in 1980, as Congress dealt with election-year politics rather than with economic reality. Democratic leaders, working with the White House, scrambled in the spring to produce a first fiscal 1981 budget resolution showing a balance between spending and revenues. Congress left to a post-election session the chore of writing a more realistic final budget resolution predicting an inevitable deficit.

But in devising the balanced budget targets, Congress for the first time agreed to make use of the budget law's reconciliation provision. In December, long after springtime zeal for balancing the budget had faded, the House and Senate followed through by passing reconciliation legislation to cut back outlays for federal programs already on the books. And by attaching reconciliation orders to its first budget resolution setting fiscal 1981 budget targets, Congress established a precedent that it was to follow in 1981 to make wholesale budget reductions.

Alarmed by an election-year surge in prices, Congress and Carter worked hard in the spring to produce a fiscal 1981 balance. The president began the year in January by proposing a "prudent and responsible" $15.8 billion deficit. But even as Carter unveiled his budget, the January inflation rate soared to an annual rate of nearly 18.2 percent and U.S. bond markets came close to collapse.

With Republicans blaming a Democratic-controlled government for driving up prices through continued budget deficits, Democratic congressional leaders quickly went to work with Carter officials to chisel the president's budget into balance. Even before the White House revised its requests in mid-March, the House and Senate Budget committees were drafting congressional budget targets to meet Carter's 1976 campaign pledge to balance the budget during his first term in office. Because Democratic lawmakers had taken part in spending cut negotiations, the budget resolutions followed the president's revisions closely on most matters.

Emboldened by budget balancing pressures, the House committee for the first time agreed to try the budget reconciliation process, ordering eight authorizing committees in each chamber to make $9.1 billion in spending cuts to meet budget limits. The reconciliation instructions also directed the House Ways and Means Committee to draw up legislation adding $22.2 billion to fiscal 1981 revenues.

Six liberal Budget Committee Democrats opposed the budget-balancing plan. But the panel's Republicans for the first time backed Giaimo's proposals, assuring approval.

The Senate committee, like its House counterpart, included reconciliation instructions and allowed $10.1 billion for a possible 1981 tax cut. The panel's resolution ordered other committees to save $12.2 billion, including $2.6 billion through curtailed fiscal 1980 appropriations. It warned that the anticipated $10 billion tax cut would be reduced "on a dollar-for-dollar basis" for spending cutbacks that other committees refused to make.

The House and Senate both upheld reconciliation during floor debate. The House adopted its Budget Committee's targets by a 225-193 vote. For the first time since Congress began writing its own budgets in 1975, a majority of House Republicans joined with Democrats to support the resolution.

But final approval of the fiscal 1980 targets was delayed until mid-June after liberal House Democrats defeated a conference agreement that allowed $5.8 billion more for defense spending than the House had approved.

No sooner had the compromise been defeated, however, than the House turned around and instructed its Budget Committee members to insist on retaining the conference report's record-high defense figures. Two weeks later, conferees agreed on a second compromise that increased outlays for transportation and low-income energy assistance by $300 million, cutting the projected budget surplus to $200 million from $500 million. In addition, conferees switched $800 million in budget authority from defense to social programs. The House June 12 accepted those changes, 205-195, and the Senate cleared the resolution by a 61-26 vote the same day.

Within a month, changing economic conditions made it clear that the budget-balancing struggles would prove futile. The administration's July budget re-estimates projected a $29.8 billion deficit as inflation eased and a long-predicted recession took hold. Congress quietly adjusted its binding fiscal 1981 budget resolution accordingly, although it put off action until after the November elections.

The Senate Budget Committee wrote its budget resolution in August, figuring on a $17.9 billion deficit by betting that the downturn would end quickly. House committee Democrats, waiting until Congress convened a November session a week after the election, then put together a revised package that amounted to a political challenge to Reagan to make good on his campaign assaults on federal spending. By a party-line vote, the House approved the Budget Committee resolution built around 2 percent across-the-board cutbacks. The Senate adopted its resolution by an uncharacteristically thin 48-46 margin. House-Senate conferees took only 90 minutes to compromise on a final resolution that predicted a $27.4 billion deficit in fiscal 1981. Both chambers gave perfunctory approval to binding fiscal 1981 totals as Democrats prepared to turn over budget responsibilities to a Republican president and Republican-controlled Senate who were expected to push for quick cutbacks in the budget.

The 96th Congress then wrapped up its budget business by clearing the reconciliation bill that the first fiscal 1981 resolution had ordered.

While falling short of the savings that the first budget resolution had targeted, the reconciliation measure (HR

7765 — PL 96-499) contained $4.6 billion in spending cutbacks and $3.6 billion in revenue increases.

In its final form, the measure cut back spending for federal programs already on the books — for education, transportation, health, federal retirement, unemployment compensation and other services. Its revenue-raising provisions were expected to yield $3.6 billion in added tax receipts through various tax-law changes, duties and excise taxes. HR 7765 combined in one bill provisions that eight House and 10 Senate committees had drafted to meet budget goals. Its approval, despite protests from some powerful congressional committee chairmen, bolstered the House and Senate Budget committees' influence over appropriations and authorization legislation.

THE 1982 BUDGET: REAGAN RECONCILIATION

At the end of 1980, the congressional budget process was being dismissed by some members as irrelevant to fiscal discipline. Democratic leaders' politically motivated delay in considering a final fiscal 1981 resolution gave opponents more fuel for attacking the procedure. They charged that the process had declined into a meaningless exercise producing little change in federal spending. James Hedlund, the House Budget Committee's minority staff director, noted during a conference on the budget that Republicans felt the process "makes very little difference in what Congress would have done anyway."

Still, by putting the reconciliation mechanism to use — at the end of the year in which budget balancing efforts had collapsed — Congress salvaged some hope for the process. By following through on reconciliation, Congress in fact set a precedent for a sweeping 1981 budget-cutting feat that gave the budget process unexpected, some say unintended, power to change the whole course of government.

President Ronald Reagan, after taking office in 1981, asked Congress to cut President Carter's proposed fiscal 1982 budget by $41.4 billion through spending reductions in 83 federal programs. With former Rep. David A. Stockman, R-Mich., Reagan's Office of Management and Budget (OMB) director, masterminding the campaign, Republican leaders who had just taken control of the Senate agreed to consolidate the budget reductions in one reconciliation measure early in the 1981 session. By packaging the budget cuts together, then forcing the House and Senate to vote on a single measure, Republicans hoped to prevent congressional committees and interest groups from chipping away at the president's budget plan.

The strategy worked, far better than many dismayed Democrats could have imagined. By Aug. 13, Reagan signed into law the deepest and farthest-reaching package of budget cuts that Congress had ever approved. The final reconciliation measure, curbing outlays for hundreds of federal programs, was expected to reduce fiscal 1982 spending by nearly $35.2 billion. In all, the package trimmed expected outlays in fiscal years 1981-84 by $130.6 billion.

Sen. Pete V. Domenici, R-N.M., who took over as Budget Committee chairman after Republicans took control of the Senate, proclaimed during final debate that "... the entire reconciliation process has done two crucial things: It has strengthened the legislative process, and it has restored confidence in Congress...."

Reconciliation Struggle

Other members were not convinced that Congress strengthened itself by using swift and severely truncated procedures to reverse federal laws and programs that previous Congresses had constructed over several decades. Reagan's success startled long-time congressional observers who fully expected the House and Senate to pick the administration's budget cuts apart as they moved through committee and floor consideration. The Senate, with its Republican majority, moved smoothly to rubber-stamp the president's requests. The House in contrast went along after momentous floor battles that overturned alternative Democratic budget strategies.

House Democratic leaders, including newly selected Budget Committee Chairman James R. Jones, D-Okla., drew up their own budget plans that scaled down both the spending cuts and Reagan's companion proposal for three-year tax reductions. However, Democratic fiscal conservatives from southern states joined with a united Republican minority to substitute administration-backed measures setting budget targets and implementing the cutbacks that reconciliation had ordered. The outcome shook Democrats' confidence in their own House leaders — and suggested that the drive to cut spending was encouraging fundamental realignments of power in a chamber no longer dominated by liberal, pro-spending sentiments.

The Republican Senate moved out front in making the cuts. The Senate Budget Committee March 23 reported reconciliation instructions (S Con Res 9) requiring 14 Senate committees to cut $36.4 billion in fiscal 1982 and roughly $145 billion for fiscal 1981-84 by altering existing programs. The Senate passed S Con Res 9 on April 2, by an 88-10 vote, ordering $36.9 billion in fiscal 1982 reductions.

The House moved more slowly. Rather than craft separate reconciliation orders, Jones attached them to the first fiscal 1982 budget resolution that the Budget Committee reported April 16 (H Con Res 115). The House committee's plan, following a Democratic prescription, called for $15.8 billion in fiscal 1982 savings and $61.3 billion over fiscal 1982-84. The plan also asked for $23.6 billion in spending cuts through annual appropriations measures.

In a major defeat for Budget panel leaders, the full House overturned the committee's plan May 7, replacing it with a Reagan-backed proposal offered by Delbert L. Latta, R-Ohio, and Phil Gramm, D-Texas, both Budget Committee members. The Gramm-Latta substitute, approved by a 253-176 vote, ordered House authorizing panels to make $36.6 billion worth of cutbacks in fiscal 1982.

The Senate May 12 incorporated its reconciliation instructions in its version of fiscal 1982 budget targets (S Con Res 19). House and Senate conferees May 14 agreed on fiscal 1982 budget goals including $695.45 billion in outlays and a $37.65 billion deficit. The compromise measure (H Con Res 115 — H Rept 97-46), given final approval May 21, included instructions requiring 14 Senate and 15 House committees to make $36 billion in fiscal 1982 cutbacks.

Reconciliation Implemented

In the following month, Congress tackled the revolutionary task of carrying out the reconciliation instructions.

Working separately, House and Senate committees drew up proposals to carve spending by amounts the budget resolution had specified. The House and Senate Budget panels then assembled the separate reductions in reconciliation measures.

The 14 Senate committees reported savings totaling $39.6 billion, $4.5 billion more than the reconciliation instructions required. House panels were more resistant. Some chairmen rebelled at making deep cuts in response to budget directives. House Education and Labor Committee Chairman Carl D. Perkins, D-Ky., who had personally guided many existing social programs through the House, protested that he had "never witnessed an action more ill-advised, more insensitive or more threatening to the rightful operation of the legislative process than these so-called reconciliation instructions."

The House committee proposals, put together by the Budget panel June 17, called for $37.76 billion in fiscal 1982 savings. Republicans and conservative Democrats charged that the authorizing committees had tried to undermine the reconciliation purpose by recommending cutbacks that were "false, counterproductive and unnecessarily severe." Administration allies again took their case to the House floor where 29 hard-core conservative Democrats joined Republicans to engineer a critical procedural victory in late June. By a 217-211 vote, the House adopted a Gramm-Latta reconciliation substitute that cut $37.3 billion from fiscal 1982 outlays according to the administration's blueprint.

It took Congress another month to work out House-Senate differences on reconciliation. More than 250 conferees, meeting in 58 subconferences, shaped a huge conference report on a compromise measure cutting $35.1 billion from the fiscal 1982 budget. Congress cleared the final bill (HR 3982 — H Rept 97-208) on July 31, the House by voice vote and the Senate by an 80-14 margin. It was, Jones noted, "clearly the most monumental and historic turnaround in fiscal policy that has ever occurred."

A BUDGET REVOLUTION OR POLITICAL PHENOMENON

The six-month reconciliation struggle in 1981 left Congress exhausted and unsure of the long-term outlook for its budget-making process. Only time would prove whether the reconciliation battle produced a true budget-making revolution or a transient political phenomenon.

In following months, the House and Senate clearly had little appetite for tackling the second round of budget requests Reagan requested for fiscal 1982. Even the Republican Senate leaders were having difficulty finding politically acceptable ways to reduce spending by the additional $13 billion the president requested in September.

Congressional leaders in the meantime were debating what shifts in power the reconciliation experience brought both inside Congress and in relations with the White House. One consequence already had become clear. As Domenici told reporters Aug. 4: "It [reconciliation] is obviously now a tool — a process for budget restraint, inordinate budget restraint — that you use when you want to do something very different."

"The budget process, as a tool of restraint, absent reconciliation is pretty damn weak," the Senate Budget Committee chairman continued. "With reconciliation, it will have a lot more teeth in it."

Legislative Process

For members deeply involved in the budget process, the swift enactment of massive budget cuts was such a noteworthy accomplishment that they downplayed the significance of the severely truncated legislative process used to consider the bill.

They maintained that the sweep of the legislation included in the measure, involving hundreds of federal programs, did not preclude a well-drafted bill. These members pointed to the marathon meetings of 58 sub-conferences, where more than 250 members worked out final legislative agreements, as proof that the ultimate product was carefully considered.

The bill fell under special rules that apply to budget matters, which made it impossible to filibuster and imposed a 20-hour limit on debate that applied even to the non-budget, substantive and sometimes controversial legislative matters included. Those issues ranged from licensing of radio and television stations to development of product safety standards.

Normally, the public and special interest groups have input in the congressional decision-making process. But because of the scope and constrained time frame, they were for the most part shut out of the reconciliation process.

In the House, Rep. Ted Weiss, D-N.Y., lamented during floor debate July 31, ". . . [W]e are voting today not only on a conference report, but on a process that is out of control."

Congressional Research Service budget expert Schick, in a paper prepared before the 1981 reconciliation action, noted: "Behind the phalanxes of members voting for reconciliation and the budget resolution, there is a deeply rooted feeling that something is awry in the legislative process and resentment that the Budget committees have so much power."

Power in Congress

As a result of reconciliation that power was greatly enhanced. Even in the House, where the Budget Committee had much of its work reversed on the floor, the panel still played a large role in shaping the reconciliation package and shepherding it through Congress.

In the Senate, the power of the Republican-controlled Budget Committee was substantial. Not only did Domenici spearhead the idea of tailoring reconciliation to Reagan's budget-cutting needs, but, with Senate Majority Leader Howard H. Baker Jr., R-Tenn., he saw to it that reconciliation was put on a "fast-track" schedule — ensuring that the GOP could take advantage quickly of the overwhelming popularity of Reagan and public enthusiasm for trimming the federal budget.

With some hefty assistance from Stockman and OMB, the Senate Budget Committee drafted instructions that gave authorizing committees a detailed scenario of what and how they could cut, although the panels were not compelled to adopt their suggestions. In the end, many Senate committees accepted in large measure the suggestions included in the Budget Committee's blueprint.

If the Budget committees gained, other committees had to lose. The Appropriations committees appeared to be the most likely losers in the reconciliation game. Because the package called for reductions below already mandated levels, the Appropriations committees had their actions preordained. The authorizing committees, meanwhile, had much of their work scuttled, though not entirely taken away.

"If the Budget committees wanted and were eager for power, they could take it," concedes House Budget Chairman Jones. "But it would be a short-term power grab that would result in the long-term demise of the budget process."

Reconciliation, Jones added, "ought to allow the authorizing committees to work in a much more orderly fashion in the future." The Appropriations committees, Jones said, have not been singled out. "Reconciliation puts limits on everybody."

In an interview, Schick described reconciliation as just one more step in a continuing change in roles for the Appropriations committees. "When the cuts are being made in advance of the appropriations process," he said, "the Appropriations committees must gravitate to a new role. They must behave more as claimants than guardians and that is particularly true in the House."

Schick pointed out that reconciliation could result in widespread congressional discontent. "While a disadvantaged majority might be subdued for a period of time, it will not endlessly accept its subordinate status. If reconciliation on this year's scale is attempted too often, the process will face strong challenges in the future."

White House Power

Congress set up the budget process in part to defend its tax and spending authority from aggressive presidential claims to broad budget-shaping powers. But after the 1981 reconciliation fight some members feared that the procedure in fact gave the White House an opening to once more usurp control over the drafting of budget legislation. The Reagan reconciliation onslaught brought reminders of the "imperial presidency" and fears that Congress was paving the way for abdicating its power to the executive.

"This is the most excessive use of presidential power and license," House Rules Committee Chairman Bolling declared early in the reconciliation battle. "And reconciliation is the most brutal and blunt instrument used by a president in an attempt to control the congressional process since Nixon used impoundment."

To some observers, Reagan displayed during the 1981 reconciliation and simultaneous tax-cut battles a kind of executive power not seen in Washington since President Lyndon B. Johnson pushed Great Society programs through a compliant Congress. House Ways and Means Committee Chairman Dan Rostenkowski, D-Ill., in a floor speech after Republicans and conservative Democrats had rejected his committee's alternative to Reagan's sweeping tax-cut program, told colleagues: "As one who served in Congress through a succession of administrations, I find it genuinely alarming to see a pattern developing on major pieces of legislation in which the work product of the committee system can be cynically discarded in favor of substitute legislation written in some downtown hideaway."

The result, he maintained, "... leaves the institution [Congress] weaker, for it denies to Republicans and Democrats alike the opportunity to write and take responsibility for our work product."

Schick believed that "reconciliation, as recent experience indicates, improves the president's prospects of getting legislative approval of his budget." More than 75 percent of the reductions approved by the Senate Budget Committee, he said, were initiated by the administration.

Reconciliation, Schick said, "has strengthened the president in that I can't envision him succeeding in making such large budget cuts without it." But the success was in large part a show of the president's "political skill and popularity — that positively made it work," he added.

Budget Process Changes

Budget Committee leaders doubted that Congress would attempt such a massive reconciliation action soon again. Senate Chairman Domenici and House Chairman Jones both were considering possible changes in budget law procedures, including a proposal to make the first budget resolution that Congress adopts in the spring binding on subsequent legislation.

"The budget process is very cumbersome," Domenici said, adding that he does not see why the second budget resolution needs to be "maintained forever." The fact that the first resolution is not binding "makes for frustration," he said.

Jones also doubted the necessity for two budget resolutions. He would like to give consideration to "making the first budget resolution binding and let the second resolution be flexible — used only if economic conditions change or there is some kind of emergency."

When they took over the House and Senate committees at the start of 1981, Jones and Domenici launched studies of other possible budget process changes. Changes under study included:

● Making the aggregate spending figure assigned to each committee binding. Currently, only the overall spending ceiling cannot be breached.

● Reorganizing the budget categories to match Congress' authorizing and appropriating committees. Because the current categories do not match, it is difficult to monitor compliance with budget resolutions.

● Strengthening the "point of order" mechanism that prevents consideration of legislation that breaches the budget.

● Delaying floor action on appropriations bills until reconciliation legislation has been passed.

In the House, many lawmakers contend that the Budget Committee should also be given more prestige by making membership permanent rather than limiting any member to serving four years.

Many Republicans contend that Congress should give the president more discretionary powers over the budget to help control spending levels. They recommended that the president be given power to impound funds in certain situations when he thinks the money should not be spent. House Republicans in 1980 introduced such an impoundment measure as an amendment to the second fiscal 1981 budget resolution, but the proposal failed by a substantial margin, 154-232.

Spending Limitation

An even tougher method of ensuring fiscal responsibility on Capitol Hill would be legislation — or a constitutional amendment — capping federal spending. Jones and Domenici both advocated such a ceiling, and chances for Senate approval of a constitutional amendment improved when Strom Thurmond, R-S.C., took over as Judiciary Committee chairman. Under Democratic leadership in 1980, the panel fell one vote short of reporting a balanced-budget amendment to the full Senate.

Jones hoped to counter any constitutional amendment plan with a legislative ceiling that would limit federal spending to 20 percent of gross national product by 1985. Domenici favored a 1985 cap of 19 percent of GNP.

Whatever changes were made, the congressional budget process was sure to be continually tested in the 1980s as Congress tried to come to grips with competing demands for defense spending, domestic programs, tax cuts and a balanced budget.

—Thomas J. Arrandale

6

Tackling Social Security

The 1980s will be a critical decade for the Social Security system. Faced with both short-term financial problems and a potentially severe crisis in the long run, the system has presented the White House and Congress with one of their biggest challenges.

Few issues are as complex, controversial or politically volatile as Social Security. The debate on the system that took place in 1981 illustrated clearly the difficulties that lie ahead in reaching agreement on the extent of the system's troubles and then forging a consensus on solutions.

The Reagan administration made dire predictions about the Social Security system's future and called for cutbacks in benefits. Democrats on Capitol Hill charged that the administration was overstating the problem and was trying to balance the budget at the expense of America's elderly.

Legislation passed by the Senate in 1981 to provide relief for the system was labeled as "cosmetic" by a key Republican senator, who warned that it was still possible the system would run out of money in 1984. More optimistic Democrats saw the bill as keeping the Social Security system financially sound through the decade.

The Social Security debate was carried on against a highly charged backdrop. The political sensitivity of the issue was brought home to President Reagan when his 1981 cutback proposals triggered a major public outcry and a sharp drop in public confidence in the Social Security system. Democrats, still smarting from Reagan's tax and budget victories and with an eye on the 1982 elections, finally seemed to have an issue on which the Republicans were vulnerable. Talk of cutbacks in programs that directly affect some 35 million beneficiaries does not make for political longevity.

Dimensions of the Program

Social Security is a program of massive dimensions. In 1981 it made up a staggering 25 percent of the federal budget, as compared to 6 percent in its early years in the 1940s.

No federal program directly affects more Americans than Social Security, either through benefits received or payroll taxes deducted from earnings to finance the program. According to the Department of Health and Human Services, in 1981 approximately 114 million workers and their employers were contributing to Social Security through the payroll tax. An anticipated 20.5 million persons aged 65 or over and their dependents — another 3.7 million — would be eligible to receive Social Security benefits in 1982. More than 7 million persons under age 65 would receive benefits as survivors of deceased workers; an additional 5 million would be disabled workers or their dependents. It was estimated that the Social Security system would pay out more than $159 billion in fiscal 1982 to nearly 40 million retired and disabled persons and their dependents.

According to the Carter administration's proposed budget for fiscal 1982, the Old Age, Survivors and Disability Insurance program was one of the costliest and most far-reaching of the "entitlement" programs, accounting for approximately 5 percent of expected gross national product. It has been estimated that Social Security alone may account for somewhere between $4.2 and $5 trillion of the unfunded future public debt.

In January 1981 Social Security monthly payments for retirement, disability and Medicare benefits totaled $10 billion distributed to about 35 million individuals. And that was before the automatic 11.2 percent cost-of-living increase in benefits that took effect in July 1981. That benefit increase cost the already financially beleaguered Social Security system an extra $15.4 billion in 1981 alone, contributing an estimated one-half percentage point to the annual inflation rate. Annual Social Security costs jumped about $1.4 billion every time the CPI increased by 1 percent, according to the Congressional Budget Office.

While benefits had increased 12 times between 1968 and 1981, the payroll tax rate for both employees and employers and the amount of a worker's earnings taxed for the Social Security program had risen 18 times since 1968. In 1981 Social Security taxes were levied on wages up to $29,700, almost four times the taxable wage level in 1968.

Soaring Taxes

Social Security tax rates and the taxable earnings base were scheduled to increase again in January 1982, eating up most of the rebate the average worker received under the first part of President Reagan's three-year across-the-board cut in personal income taxes. The Reagan package was designed to provide tax relief to American workers, but the great majority of workers would actually see their paychecks shrinking because of rising Social Security taxes. In fact, more than half of U.S. workers were paying more each year in Social Security taxes than in federal income taxes.

As provided in the 1977 amendments to the Social Security Act, on Jan. 1, 1982, the maximum tax paid by employees would increase by $195.75, bringing it to a maximum payment of $2,170.80. The average worker — who earned about $14,000 in 1981 and paid about $913 in Social Security taxes — would pay about $1,010 in 1982. Self-employed persons would pay about $267 more in Social Security contributions.

Yet most analysts agreed that those increases and other steeper hikes scheduled for 1985 and 1986 would probably be insufficient and that further action was needed to save the system from bankruptcy. It was this message that President Reagan brought to the American people.

The ensuing debate proved to be a sobering revelation to many Americans that Social Security benefits may be something less than the permanent entitlements they have represented for more than 40 years.

SOCIAL SECURITY: A SOCIAL REVOLUTION

Passage of the Social Security Act of 1935 (PL 74-271) — one of the most comprehensive welfare bills ever cleared by Congress — was a major political event. Enacted at the urgent request of President Franklin D. Roosevelt in the midst of the worst depression in the nation's history, the act changed both the concept of personal economic security in the United States and the nature of federal-state relations in the welfare field.

The heart of the Social Security Act consisted of several "income replacement" programs. They were designed to assure continuation of income to individuals when their normal source of income was cut off by retirement, loss of job, disability or death. The programs were:

● Old Age Insurance, a wholly federal retirement insurance program financed by a federal payroll tax, for persons presumed too old to work;

● Unemployment Insurance, a federal-state system of unemployment compensation programs for persons temporarily unable to find work; and

● Several public assistance programs, basically a system of federal grants to the states to reimburse them for part of the costs of charity aid to the indigent — namely, the aged, the blind and children deprived of the support of a parent — who, for reasons beyond their control, were unable to seek work or support themselves.

Using a variety of approaches, the income replacement programs were to provide individuals with weekly or monthly cash payments from government sources to cover living expenses.

Economic Security

The income replacement programs represented, in many ways, a revolution in American life. Before the 1930s, providing security against old age, unemployment and other economic hardships was considered the function primarily of the individual himself, his family and local private charitable institutions. For isolated groups in the community — federal employees under the civil service system, some state and local government employees, and small numbers of workers covered by private pension plans at their place of employment — relatively dependable retirement pension systems did exist.

But for the bulk of the population there was no systematic program — public or private — to guarantee income after retirement and no organized program at all except charity (where available) to counter economic hazards. The personal economic security afforded the individual by these traditional and uncoordinated sources of aid was often minimal or non-existent. The Depression of the 1930s, which left millions destitute, created both public desire for some sort of economic security program and public willingness to accept action by the federal government.

Other factors leading to passage of the Social Security Act were the personal prestige of President Roosevelt and significant Democratic majorities in both houses of Congress who were ready to follow his lead. The Roosevelt administration's specific proposals for social insurance were viewed by conservatives as relatively moderate compared with other income security schemes that were being considered.

One proposal, named after Dr. Francis Townsend, would have provided a monthly $200 federal pension for everyone aged 60 or older, to be financed by a form of new sales tax. The Townsend plan was a politically potent issue at the time with widespread support among the nation's elderly, but it was considered by many members of Congress to be too costly as well as too extreme a federal role in personal economic security. The Roosevelt proposals, on the other hand, minimized both the breach with tradition and the new tax burden that was to be imposed on business.

By establishing a nationwide program of income security through federal action, the U.S. government for the first time assumed permanent responsibility for functions traditionally reserved for the family and for local governments. The income replacement programs, particularly unemployment insurance, also had the secondary function of stabilizing the national economy by keeping steady the purchasing power of different groups in good and bad economic times. The programs furnishing income to the aged had another function that was important in the context of the Depression: these programs were intended to help clear the labor market of the surplus of older workers competing with younger persons for scarce jobs.

Insurance and Assistance

From the inception of the Social Security system, there was considerable disagreement on how the program would be financed and benefits distributed. A major issue was whether the government should use an assistance approach, an insurance approach, or both, to safeguard the individual against economic misfortunes. In drafting the Social Security legislation in 1935, Congress made a number of key decisions, many of which have indirectly contributed to the system's financial troubles in recent years.

Old Age Insurance

The most important program established by the Social Security Act was Old Age Insurance, a giant national pension system based on social insurance principles. Social Security payments were intended to be the chief method of assuring supplemental income to an individual after retirement. The "replacement rate" — the portion of a worker's final paycheck that Social Security was intended to replace — was originally meant to be about 40 percent for the average worker. Private pensions and savings were expected to make up the remainder of the retiree's income.

The basis of the Old Age Insurance system was a federal payroll tax, imposed on most industrial and white-collar employees and their employers. The tax was to begin at 1 percent each for employers and employees on the first $3,000 annual earnings of the worker, rising to 3 percent each by 1949.

Payroll taxes were first collected in 1937. A special trust fund account was set up in the U.S. Treasury to receive the proceeds of the payroll tax, with funds earmarked for payment of pensions to eligible persons. Assets of the fund were required to be invested in federal securities of various types. An individual became eligible for a monthly cash pension at age 65 if he had worked a specified amount of time in employment subject to the payroll tax and had thus contributed to the costs of his own pension.

Eligibility was a matter of right and did not depend on need. The amount of the monthly pension, subject to upper and lower limits fixed by Congress, was related to the amount of an individual's earnings prior to retirement and was intended to be higher than the subsistence level. Because Old Age Insurance was based on actuarial principles and would require many years before the system built up reserves and large number of workers became eligible, the first monthly benefits were not scheduled to be paid out until 1942. Amendments added in 1939, however, changed the effective date to 1940.

Charity vs. Insurance

In the interim years the main burden of providing income for the aged fell on the traditional charity approach. Congress in the original act created a public assistance program for the aged — Old Age Assistance — which provided matching grants to the states to enable them to give charity aid to the indigent elderly. Need, as determined by the states through a "means test," was the sole criterion of assistance. Payments were meant to be adequate to sustain the indigent person only at or near subsistence levels. Financing came from general revenues at the federal, state and local levels.

President Roosevelt and Congress itself in debate on the Social Security issue made it clear that once the Old Age Insurance system had reached full operation, that program was to be the primary government method of providing supplemental income for the aged. The public assistance program was only a secondary safeguard to protect primarily those ineligible for insurance benefits (or, where the amount of insurance benefits was extremely low, to supplement them). It was expected that eventually, as more individuals built up insured status, the number of elderly requiring public assistance charity would decline proportionately.

These expectations proved correct. In 1940, the first year for monthly retirement insurance benefits, nearly 223,000 workers received benefits, while more than 2 million persons received Old Age Assistance aid. By 1964 the number of beneficiaries under the expanded Old Age, Survivors and Disability Insurance program had swelled to close to 20 million. Of these, about 15 million were age 62 or older; the rest were dependent children, disabled persons and other dependents. Only 2.2 million people were receiving Old Age Assistance benefits in 1964.

Congress relied on the insurance approach to retirement income as the primary method for several reasons. It was generally believed that a self-financing insurance-type mechanism would isolate the Social Security program from the kind of political and economic stresses involved in deciding annual appropriations for government programs. In addition, many experts felt the insurance method would permit benefits at a higher level than the subsistence level, providing better security for the retired individual. By making retirement benefits automatic without consideration of need or the humiliation of a means test, it was hoped that Old Age Insurance would provide surer and truer income security against old age than a charity approach.

Social Security Elsewhere

Although passage of the Social Security Act in 1935 was a revolutionary development in American life, the United States was actually the last major industrial nation to adopt a general social security system covering most of the population. In 1935 some 22 European nations already had such programs. Many dated back to before World War I and were far more comprehensive in scope than the U.S. program — including, for example, sickness, disability, health and maternity benefits. Six non-European nations at that time also had programs covering a sizable portion of their population — Australia, Chile, Japan, New Zealand, South Africa and Uruguay.

Otto Von Bismarck, the "Iron Chancellor" of Germany, is often credited with establishing the world's first old age pension system in 1875. Germany was the first country to adopt a social security program when it set up sickness and maternity insurance in 1883. A contributory old age and disability insurance system was added in 1889 and unemployment insurance in 1927.

With regard to other major industrial nations in Europe, England set up a charity program for the indigent aged in 1908. In 1911 it adopted a contributory social insurance program covering unemployment, disability and health care. A contributory old age insurance system was added in 1925. France established unemployment benefits in 1905, added a contributory old age insurance program in 1910 and sickness and maternity benefits in 1928.

The Growth of Private Pensions

The growth of both government and corporate pension funds since World War II has been explosive. The President's Commission on Pension Policy in February 1981 estimated that current assets and reserves of all funded pension plans totaled $650 billion, almost 17 percent of all financial assets in the country. Most experts agreed that the enormous size of pension plans as a source of capital funding represented a major influence on the U.S. economy.

The years of Social Security expansion were also years of growth for private pensions. In 1940 only 4 million employees were covered by private pensions; estimates of coverage in 1981 ran up to 35 million, or about one-half of the industrial work force. The commission estimated that 56 percent of all workers and 15 percent of the self-employed were covered by some kind of income retirement plan.

Collective bargaining had much to do with this growth. Due to a weak economy during World War II and management's increased resistance to further wage increases, labor unions in the 1940s began pressing for additional benefits in the form of pension funds. The meager benefits that retirees could expect to receive from the still young Social Security system were also an important impetus in the campaign for pension benefits.

Private pension plans officially date from 1875 when the American Express Company established a fund, but the General Motors pension plan set up in 1950 is considered the watershed for private plans. Although many companies had already established retirement plans for their employees, most of them were based on annuities, supported by standard life insurance investments such as government bonds, mortgages and other fixed interest instruments.

In 1950 the Supreme Court ruled that employers had to bargain about pensions with unions. A few months later, General Motors created its innovative fund, intended as an investment trust. GM's fund was widely diversified, with only a small portion of its portfolio in GM stock and most of its money invested in a wide range of U.S. firms. Within a year 8,000 similar funds had been set up by other corporations.

Tax benefits have also encouraged the growth of pension plans. The Revenue Act of 1942 established procedures for the tax deductibility of pension funds. Employers could deduct their contributions to pension funds that met Internal Revenue Service standards. Most wage earners also received a tax advantage; they did not pay taxes on their contributions until they received the benefits in retirement, when they were likely to be in a lower tax bracket. In effect, a large share of these private plans was set up with funds that otherwise would have gone to the federal government as taxes.

Another major tax advantage was granted under the Self-Employed Individuals Retirement Act of 1962 — the Keogh Act. That law permitted the self-employed to place up to 10 percent of their annual income (to a limit of $2,500) in a retirement plan and defer paying taxes on the amount until retirement.

Pension Security

As pension plans grew and became more popular, so did concern for the security of the systems. This concern intensified in 1964 when the Studebaker automobile plant in South Bend, Ind., closed down and terminated its pension plan, jeopardizing the retirement security of more than 10,000 workers. A decade of extensive investigation of private pension plans by several congressional committees and a presidential committee followed. According to Treasury records, in 1972 alone 19,400 workers lost their rights to approximately $49 million in potential pension benefits because plans were terminated without enough funds to meet obligations.

After many efforts to devise legislation to protect worker interests, a compromise was reached in 1974 when Congress approved the Employee Retirement Income Security Act (ERISA). It established standards for the management of private pension funds, guaranteed vesting after a maximum of 10 years of employment and set up a mechanism to assure the financial health of private plans.

ERISA raised the Keogh limits to 15 percent of annual salary to a maximum of $7,500. It also authorized workers not covered by a private pension plan to set up Individual Retirement Accounts (IRAs) with tax-free contributions up to 15 percent of their income, to a limit of $1,500.

1981 Tax Act

The 1981 Economic Recovery Tax Act contained several tax advantages that would encourage more individuals to establish private pension funds. That law extended the right to set up IRAs to all U.S. workers and their spouses, including those protected by other private pension plans. The new law allowed employees who participated in their employer's retirement plan to deduct from their taxes their own voluntary contributions to that plan or contributions to an IRA, subject to the same IRA-type rules and deductions for self-employed IRAs. The amount an individual could deduct for annual contributions was increased to the lesser of $2,000 ($2,250 for a spousal IRA) or 100 percent of income.

The 1981 act also increased from $7,500 to $15,000 the amount the self-employed could deduct for contributions to their Keogh plans.

Financing Concepts

To achieve the long-term financing required for the Social Security Old Age Insurance system, Congress decided to employ a reserve method of financing rather than a strict "pay-as-you-go" method. Under pay-as-you-go financing, revenues would have been provided only in amounts sufficient to meet current obligations, with no allowance for future requirements. Payroll tax rates simply would have been adjusted each year to bring in enough funds to pay for benefits paid out that year. Under the most extreme form of reserve financing, on the other hand, large reserves would have been built up so that the retirement fund at all times would have enough cash available to pay for all current and future benefits earned by individuals on the basis of work already performed.

The Old Age Insurance system as actually set up and amended adopted a less extreme reserve method of financing. Contributions from the payroll tax were to be paid into a fund on a regular basis according to mathematical projections of future need. However, while the system was intended to build up large reserves, there was no real attempt to accumulate reserves great enough to meet all accrued liabilities, only a sizeable portion.

When the system was originally set up, optimistic legislators were convinced that an accumulation of reserve monies would make the Social Security system relatively impregnable to fluctuations in the economy. A reserve system permitted benefit costs to be balanced against income over several decades and payroll taxes to be imposed at a more or less level rate covering the whole period. Moreover, it was believed that annual political fights over the rate of the payroll tax would be eliminated under the reserve method of financing.

Under pay-as-you-go financing, initial benefits costs and tax rates would have been quite low because few persons would be eligible for benefits. But as more people earned eligibility, benefits and also taxes would rise sharply. Thus the reserve approach was believed to afford the individual a surer guarantee that the retirement system's financing was sound and that he would receive benefits as promised.

The theory did not work in practice. In subsequent amendments to the original act, Congress generally raised benefit levels and expanded the program's coverage without providing adequate additional financing. This, along with unforeseen economic strains on the program's trust funds, made Social Security more of a pay-as-you-go financing system, with annual revenues from the payroll tax barely covering current obligations for benefit payments.

The Benefits Explosion

As established, the Old Age Insurance program provided retirement benefits for the insured worker only. Over the years, however, Congress increased benefits and made more people eligible for them. Greater emphasis was placed on assuring an adequate retirement income to an ever-increasing proportion of the population. Even before any benefits had ever been paid out, Congress was already broadening Social Security coverage to include beneficiaries who had never paid into the system.

The first major amendments to the Old Age Insurance program were voted in 1939, when Congress made important structural changes modifying the scope of the original Social Security system. The most significant change authorized monthly benefits to be paid both to the dependents of an insured retiree while he was living and drawing a pension and to his survivors after his death. As a result, the program was renamed Old Age and Survivors Insurance (OASI). The 1939 changes also:

- Set up new eligibility criteria, including the basic requirement of 40 quarter-years in work subject to the payroll tax for insured status for most workers. But the amendments permitted as few as 6 quarters in some cases;
- Moved the first payments of monthly benefits forward from 1942 to 1940; and
- Introduced the concept of basing the amount of a pension on the worker's average monthly wage during covered employment over his or her working lifetime.

Postwar Era

Because of the long-range method of financing and other factors, the Old Age Insurance program was just gearing up when World War II ended. Relatively few people had as yet earned eligibility for benefits, and coverage was still confined largely to urban workers. Only about $274 million was paid out in benefits in fiscal 1945.

As it began to mature the retirement system exerted an ever greater impact on society. By the late 1940s there was a rapid increase in the number of beneficiaries and a corresponding rise in benefits. Whereas in 1940 fewer than a quarter of a million people received Social Security benefits totaling close to $4.1 million each month, by 1950 approximately 3.5 million beneficiaries were receiving monthly payments amounting to $126.9 million.

Despite substantial increases in the cost of living, the OASI system in 1950 still operated under 1939 benefit formulas and coverage rules. As a result, the system was unable to fulfill its anticipated role as the primary mechanism for providing supplemental income after retirement. That led Congress to overhaul and update the entire program in 1950.

The 1950 amendments restored the retirement program to its intended function by:

- Raising the taxable wage base to $3,600 a year and providing a new payroll tax schedule;
- Increasing benefits by an average of 70 percent to compensate for cost-of-living changes;
- Substantially easing eligibility requirements for many currently aged persons; and
- Extending the basic reach of the system beyond urban employees by making the self-employed (except farmers and professionals), many agricultural and domestic service workers, and state and local government workers — about 9.2 million persons — eligible for participation in the social insurance system.

These and later amendments clearly established a benefit bias in favor of persons receiving the lowest retirement benefits. For them, increases in benefits were proportionately higher than for those persons receiving the maximum benefits.

Other changes during the 1950s continued to expand the retirement system by increasing benefits and easing eligibility requirements. In 1952 benefits were raised slightly but amendments were not substantial. In 1954, however, the taxable wage base was increased to $4,200 a year, a new tax schedule was set and benefits were increased somewhat. A potential 7.5 million more persons were brought under Social Security coverage, including self-employed farmers, additional farm and domestic workers, and additional government and non-profit organization employees. After the 1954 amendments, about 80 percent of the paid labor force was covered by the retirement system.

In 1956 there was no increase in general benefits, but Congress did vote small coverage increases and two major changes were made in Social Security law. During postwar debate on Social Security, a continuing controversy had centered on whether the system should assume responsibility for supporting disabled persons below retirement age. A public assistance program, Aid to the Permanently and Totally Disabled, had been set up for the disabled in 1950. Congress linked that program to the retirement insurance system in 1956, establishing a separate Disability Insurance (DI) trust fund to provide benefits to long-term and permanently disabled workers aged 50 to 64. The Social Security program was renamed Old Age, Survivors and Disability Insurance (OASDI).

The 1956 amendments also reduced the minimum benefit age for women from 65 to 62, with actuarially reduced benefits in some cases.

Two years later benefits were again raised slightly, the taxable wage base was increased to $4,800 a year and a new tax schedule, beginning at 2.5 percent, was set. Dependents of workers receiving monthly Disability Insurance payments were also made eligible for monthly dependents benefits.

The 1960s: Medicare Added

During the economic prosperity of the 1950s and 1960s, workers' wages increased at a relatively rapid rate compared to price increases. Between 1950 and 1972, wages increased by an average of 4.7 percent annually, while prices rose only 2.5 percent. As a result, the Social Security trust funds built up a heavy cushion of reserves from the payroll tax levied on the relatively higher earnings and Congress continued to expand Social Security, which was becoming an increasingly popular and politically appealing program for winning votes back home.

In 1960 no general benefit increases were made, but Congress did remove the minimum age of 50 for receipt of Disability Insurance benefits and broadened general eligibility requirements for social insurance. In 1961 eligibility requirements were eased again, a higher tax schedule replaced the one set up in 1958 and benefits increased for some groups of workers. Most importantly, the minimum benefit age for men was dropped to 62, with actuarially reduced benefits if a worker chose to retire at age 62 instead of waiting for "full" retirement at 65.

By the end of 1964, about 90 percent of all employment in the nation was covered by the expanded Old Age, Survivors and Disability Insurance program. Approximately 76 percent of the nation's aged were receiving benefits under the program, with another 8 percent eligible but not drawing benefits because they either had not yet retired or had not applied. The total amount paid out by the Social Security Administration in fiscal 1964 to approximately 20 million people was nearly $16.2 billion, compared with the $274 million paid to beneficiaries in fiscal 1945. The average monthly benefit for a retired worker had climbed from $22.60 when benefits were first distributed in 1940 to $83.92 in 1965.

In short, the Old Age, Survivors and Disability Insurance program had become the nation's single most important welfare program, accounting in fiscal 1964 for 37 percent of all public and private welfare expenditures compared with only 6 percent in fiscal 1950.

The U.S. social insurance system continued to exert an even greater impact on the national economy when Congress in 1965 established a major medical care program for the aged under the Social Security system. The health care issue had come up repeatedly since 1945 when President Harry Truman first proposed adding a health insurance program that would cover a large portion of the entire population. President John F. Kennedy began in 1960 to press for a federally operated health insurance program for the elderly, whose health care bills were high and whose income generally was low.

The 1965 legislation provided a new payroll tax (applied equally to employers, employees and the self-employed) and a taxable earnings base to finance the new Medicare program. General federal tax revenues were to fund the plan for persons not covered by Social Security. The Health Insurance payroll taxes and general revenues earmarked for the plan were placed in a new Health Insurance (HI) trust fund, separate from the system's OASI and DI trust funds. The new law also made other significant changes in Social Security law, including a 7 percent increase in retirement benefits.

There were other important expansions of the original Social Security Act during the Lyndon Johnson administration. Congress raised retirement benefits again in 1967 by 13 percent and continued to ease Social Security eligibility requirements.

Cost-of-Living Increases

Rising inflation in the late 1960s — due in part to expanded government programs and increasing federal deficits as the Johnson administration's Great Society programs took hold — led Congress to raise OASDI benefits three times between 1969 and 1972: 15 percent in 1969, 10 percent in 1971, 20 percent in 1972.

In addition, various eligibility requirements for the OASDI program were considerably eased. To finance the increased benefits, the amount of earnings subject to the Social Security tax was substantially increased. The taxable earnings base jumped from $4,800 to $12,000 in 1973. Increases in the tax rate itself, which caused greater hardship for lower-income workers, were not as substantial, rising from 4.6 to 5.85 percent during the period from 1972 to 1978. (Part of this increase was to put the Medicare trust fund on a more stable basis.)

These benefit and tax rate changes were all voted as amendments to bills dealing with other subjects. It was not until 1972 that Congress enacted a substantial Social Security bill authorizing other changes in the program.

Because wages had out-distanced prices in the previous two decades, large surpluses had accrued in the trust funds by the 1970s. These heavy reserves led Congress in 1972 to make basic changes in the way benefit increases were calculated.

Rather than increase benefits on an ad hoc basis that often involved intense political fights, Congress decided to tie future increases in Social Security benefits to the Consumer Price Index (CPI). Convinced that benefits were relatively low and that a healthy economy and rising wages would generate adequate revenues to cover future increases, Congress provided for automatic benefit increases, beginning in 1975, when the cost of living rose more than 3 percent annually. In addition, Congress tied the wage base on which Social Security taxes were levied to a wage index that was also expected to increase.

These decisions made the Social Security system even more dependent on the economy's performance. Although indexing seemed logical at the time, the historical relationship between wages and prices changed drastically during the 1970s and the national economy took a turn for the worse. As a result, benefit increases required by indexing ate up the surpluses faster than originally expected and played a major role in pushing the Social Security system toward the red.

The 1972 legislation also made a revolutionary shift in the structure of Social Security. A new program of assistance to the aged poor — Supplemental Security Income (SSI) — was set up to take the place of the original Old Age Assistance program. Unlike the OAA, the new program was to be fully financed by the federal government from general tax revenues and would set uniform national eligibility requirements. Old Age Assistance had been a joint federal-state program.

The SSI program provided benefits in 1975 to more than 5 million persons compared with 3.2 million under the entire federal-state public assistance program that had preceded it. In 1979 between 8 and 9 percent of persons aged 65 and over received Supplemental Security Income, while approximately 90 percent received Social Security payments.

The result of these developments was a greater intermingling of the welfare benefit concept with the insurance principle intended in the original Social Security Act — and a multitude of financial problems ahead for the benefit-heavy social insurance program. Rising benefit costs outpaced the tax increases provided by the 1972 amendments, and by the mid-1970s the first signs of Social Security's financial troubles were becoming apparent. Since 1975 the OASI trust fund has paid out more to beneficiaries than it collected from payroll taxes. By 1981 the fund had made up that deficit by drawing almost $15 billion from the system's dwindling reserves.

In its 1977 annual report, the Social Security Board of Trustees — the secretaries of the Departments of Labor, Treasury, and Health, Education and Welfare (since 1979, Health and Human Services) — projected that the system's Disability Insurance fund would exhaust its reserves by 1979 and that the retirement and survivors benefits fund would run out in the early 1980s. Although there were other contributing factors, the main cause of these shortfalls was the combination of prolonged inflation and recession, which together raised Social Security benefit costs and reduced program receipts from the payroll tax. Government actuaries and other experts began predicting grave financial strains for the Social Security system.

1977 Reforms

The Carter administration in May 1977 proposed a Social Security rescue plan based on gradual increases in employer but not employee tax contributions into the sys-

Social Security Benefits and Beneficiaries, 1940-80

	1940	1945	1950	1955	1960	1965	1970	1975	1977	1979	1980
Workers in Covered Employment[1]											
Total	35.4	46.4	48.3	65.2	72.5	80.7	93.1	100.2	106.1	*	*
Self-employed	—	—	—	6.8	6.9	6.6	6.3	7.1	7.6	*	*
With maximum earnings	1.2	6.4	13.9	16.7	20.3	29.1	24.2	15.1	15.7	*	*
OASDI Beneficiaries[1]											
Retired workers, dependents and survivors	.2	1.3	3.5	8.0	14.1	19.1	23.6	27.7	29.2	30.3	30.9
Retired workers only	.1	.5	1.8	4.5	8.1	11.1	13.3	16.6	17.8	19.0	19.6
Average Monthly Benefits[2]											
All retired workers	$23	$24	$44	$59	$ 74	$ 84	$118	$207	$243	$294	$341
Maximum to men at age 65	41	43	45	99	119	132	190	316	413	503	572
Maximum to women at age 65	41	43	45	99	119	136	196	334	422	503	572
Minimum at age 65	10	10	10	30	33	44	64	93	108	122	134

* Data not available   [1] In millions   [2] In current dollars

Source: Social Security Administration

Social Security Taxes: 1977 Amendments

Year	OASDHI[2] Tax Rate (%)	Wage Base[1]	$10,000 Wage Earner Annual Contributions Increase Over Prior Year		$20,000 Wage Earner Annual Contributions Increase Over Prior Year		Maximum Wage Earner[1] Annual Contributions Increase Over Prior Year	
1977	5.85	$16,500	$585	—	$ 965.25	—	$ 965.25	—
1978	6.05	17,700	605	$20.00	1,070.85	$105.60	1,070.85	105.60
1979	6.13	22,900	613	8.00	1,226.00	155.15	1,403.77	332.92
1980	6.13	25,900	613	—	1,226.00	—	1,587.67	183.90
1981	6.65	29,700	665	52.00	1,330.00	104.00	1,975.05	387.38
1982	6.70	32,400	670	5.00	1,340.00	10.00	2,170.80	195.75
1983	6.70	35,100	670	—	1,340.00	—	2,331.70	180.90
1984	6.70	38,100	670	—	1,340.00	—	2,552.70	201.00
1985	7.05	41,100	705	35.00	1,410.00	70.00	2,897.55	344.85
1986	7.15	44,100	715	10.00	1,430.00	20.00	3,153.15	255.60
1987	7.15	47,100	715	—	1,430.00	—	3,367.65	214.50
1988	7.15	50,000	715	—	1,430.00	—	3,582.15	214.50

[1] Amounts for 1982-88 are based on economic predictions.
[2] Old Age, Survivors, Disability and Health Insurance

Source: Social Security Administration

tem. The proposal also included countercyclical transfers of general revenues to the dwindling trust funds to make up for revenues lost during periods of high unemployment when fewer workers were paying into the retirement system. Carter's plan was designed to provide an additional $83 billion to the funds by 1982. The president emphasized that his proposals would achieve that goal without raising payroll taxes for low- and middle-income workers, thus fulfilling a 1976 election campaign pledge.

Carter's plan made little headway in the House and Senate, however. After considering some innovative financing schemes, Congress in 1977 relied exclusively on traditional payroll taxes to replenish the shrinking reserves in the trust funds. The 1977 Social Security tax increase — $227 billion over a 10-year period — was the nation's largest peacetime tax increase ever.

The measure set new, steeper tax schedules that steadily increased both the tax rate and the taxable earnings base for both employee and employer equally, beginning in 1979 through 1990. The maximum tax rate was scheduled to more than triple by 1987. In 1977, with payroll taxes set at 5.85 percent each for employer and employee on the worker's earnings up to $16,500, the maximum contribution required from a worker and his employer was $965 each. By 1987, when the tax rate was set to rise to 7.15 percent on income up to $47,100, each could expect to pay more than $3,000 a year into the Social Security system. *(Table, this page)*

The 1977 bill did take a modest step toward reducing Social Security expenditures by including an important administration-backed measure to correct a technical flaw in the formula for computing the starting benefit levels of future retirees. The 1972 amendments had permitted increases in both wage levels and prices to influence benefit schedules for future retirees — an overcompensation for inflation that could have allowed recipients' benefits to exceed their pre-retirement wages and that threatened to send benefits skyrocketing over the next several decades. To correct the problem, Congress in 1977 separated ("decoupled") the process of granting cost-of-living increases to already retired persons from the computation of their initial benefit levels. Under the 1977 law, the benefit structure used for post-retirement computations would not increase.

But Congress in 1977 also eased the "earnings test," allowing elderly persons to earn more money without losing a portion of their benefits, and liberalized the treatment of divorced and widowed beneficiaries. The Carter administration had criticized those changes as costly. *(Details, 1977 law, p. 178)*

As it became evident that the 1977 amendments would not restore the system to financial health, President Carter in 1979 urged Congress to eliminate a number of "unnecessary" Social Security benefits. That the president would even mention the possibility of reducing benefits reflected a major shift in thinking about Social Security, since Congress historically had done little but increase benefits. Among the changes Carter proposed were a phase-out of education benefits for dependent children age 18 and over, a cut-off in surviving parent benefits after the youngest child had reached age 16, and elimination of the minimum benefit guarantee.

Congress in 1980 did adopt a temporary solution to the Social Security system's impending financial crisis when it voted to reallocate some funds from the Disability Insurance fund to the OASI fund in 1980-81 to assure the timely payment of benefits. But under election-year pressures, Congress opted for a more politically appealing "stopgap" measure that merely postponed the potential crisis for a few more years.

Acknowledging that the system was becoming too expensive, Congress in 1980 did make an attempt to roll back the Social Security program slightly by reducing Disability Insurance benefits to workers who became disabled after July 1, 1980. Provisions of the new law were expected to reduce Social Security and welfare spending by $2.6 billion in fiscal 1981 through 1985.

FINANCING PROBLEM: A POTENT TIME BOMB

When it passed the 1977 amendments, Congress thought it had settled the Social Security financing problem once and for all. The Social Security Board of Trustees proclaimed in its 1978 annual report: "The Social Security Amendments of 1977 have restored the financial soundness of the cash benefit program over the short-range and medium-range periods, beginning in 1981, and greatly improved the long-range actuarial status."

But the system's money troubles apparently had only just begun. Unforeseen economic difficulties — double-digit inflation, economic recession and stagnation, low productivity and sustained high unemployment — continued to play havoc with the Social Security trust funds.

Even with the scheduled steep increases in the tax rates and taxable wage base set up in the 1977 amendments, the Reagan administration projected that the Old Age and Survivors Insurance fund could go bankrupt by as much as $111 billion by 1986. Unless major reforms were enacted, the long-term deficit could reach as high as 1.52 percent of total payroll over the next 75 years, warned Health and Human Services Secretary Richard S. Schweiker in 1981.

High inflation has boosted outlays for benefit payments, while high unemployment and the trend toward early retirement have reduced expected revenues generated from the payroll tax. Congress' 1972 decision to index Social Security benefit payment increases to the Consumer Price Index (starting in 1975) turned out to be much more costly than originally anticipated. In 1975, the indexing formula gave retirees a 14.3 percent cost-of-living increase in benefits. In 1980 the cost-of-living payment boosted Social Security benefits by 14 percent; in 1981 they were up by an additional 11 percent.

At the same time, wage increases did not keep pace with inflation. Combined with the high inflationary pressures, that slower wage growth meant a drop in Social Security tax revenues.

Unemployment also cost the system revenues. For every 1 million workers who were laid off for a single month in 1980, approximately $100 million in anticipated employee and employer contributions was not paid into the Social Security trust funds. Most experts agreed that heavy unemployment, on top of high inflation, might also act as an impetus for an increasing number of workers to retire earlier than actuaries originally projected, which would eat up anticipated Social Security revenues and increase benefit payments disproportionately. As retirees seemed to be better protected against rampant inflation than workers paying into the system, it was little wonder that more people had been retiring before age 65.

Other social and economic trends — including low birth and mortality rates, increased participation of women in the work force and the slow rate of economic growth — have also contributed to the financial strains burdening the Social Security system.

Disputed Assumptions

Much of the debate over remedies for the Social Security system's impending financial crisis has been complicated by widely varying economic assumptions used to project the trust fund balances. In 1981 the array of economic assumptions included the "worst-case" economic assumptions on which the Reagan administration based its Social Security proposals, more moderate economic assumptions projected by the Congressional Budget Office and the Social Security Board of Trustees' 1981 report, and the optimistic assumptions the administration used for its fiscal 1982 budget requests.

The Reagan administration decided to base its projections on "worst-case" assumptions because, it said, past administrations had been overly optimistic and, as a result, had been forced to return to Congress repeatedly for additional help in rescuing the funds. "We're trying not to repeat the debacle of 1977," when the Social Security amendments were touted as the solution to the system's financial problems, Secretary Schweiker told the Senate Finance Committee.

But the price of caution, opponents argued, could be painful, unnecessary cuts in benefits for Social Security recipients. They charged that the administration's ulterior motive was to use larger-than-necessary cuts in Social Security benefits to reduce the federal budget deficit. While the administration argued correctly that Social Security funds could not be used for anything but Social Security, general revenue deficits in the so-called "unified" budget were offset by trust fund surpluses in reaching the total deficit figure.

Sen. Bill Bradley, D-N.J., challenged the administration in early 1981 for its use of one set of assumptions for its Social Security request and another, more optimistic set of assumptions for its fiscal 1982 budget and tax program. "You can't have it both ways," he told Secretary Schweiker.

To illustrate the importance of assumptions, under the administration's pessimistic outlook, the combined trust funds of Social Security would have a $111 billion budget deficit by 1986. To solve the problem, the administration recommended $111 billion in Social Security benefit cuts.

However, under the assumptions the administration used in its 1982 budget request, the funds were expected to face only an $11 billion deficit over that same period. This deficit would not be difficult to take care of, some policy makers argued, because Congress in 1981 approved $22.8 billion in Social Security cuts for fiscal 1982-86.

Adequate Reserve Ratios

In addition to deciding which economic assumptions to use, policy makers must also decide what the system's "reserve ratio" should be. The reserve ratio is the amount of money in the trust funds at the beginning of the year expressed as a percentage of that year's anticipated expenditures. Generally, a reserve ratio of between 9 and 13 percent is considered necessary at any one time, and specialists agree that a ratio of about 20 to 25 percent would be the bare minimum needed to cushion the funds against unexpected economic conditions. This means that a "safe" margin of reserves is about one-fourth of anticipated benefit payments for the year — or enough to pay benefits for three months in the absence of additional income to the funds.

However, the Reagan administration's proposals called for a 30 percent reserve ratio by 1990 and a 50 percent ratio by 1995, an amount some critics maintained was too large too soon, especially if it was accumulated through substantial benefit cuts.

The Short-Term Picture

No matter what set of economic assumptions were used, the consensus among experts was that the Old Age and Survivors Insurance trust fund would become insufficient to pay timely benefits sometime during the 1980s. Experts in 1981 generally agreed that the following five years would be critical ones for the Social Security system.

However, there was considerable disagreement over exactly when and by how large a margin benefit outlays would exceed revenues generated from the payroll tax. Depending on whose statistics were used, the urgency of the retirement system's financial troubles ranged from manageable to critical to disaster.

The Social Security Administration estimated that the annual shortfall in Social Security reserves might reach $30 billion by 1985.

The Carter administration had predicted $150 billion paid into the Social Security system from payroll taxes and other receipts — with an expected $160 billion in outlays — for a shortfall of $10 billion under its fiscal 1982 budget assumptions. President Reagan's revised figures for the fiscal year were not much cheerier. The Reagan administration in April 1981 projected that outlays would be $157.7 billion. Expected trust fund balances would be $20.3 billion

at the end of 1982, for a trust fund reserve ratio of only 13 percent (less than two months worth of benefits). Only 10 years earlier, the OASDI funds posted a reserve ratio of over 100 percent. Outlays for OASDI in 1972 were $38.5 billion, with an end-of-year balance of $35.3 billion.

The National Commission on Social Security, a congressional study group created under the 1977 Social Security amendments, indicated in its March 1981 final report that the financial and actuarial estimates used in the 1977 law were overly optimistic and alarmingly outmoded. Milton S. Gwirtzman, chairman of the commission, told the House Ways and Means' Subcommittee on Social Security in February 1981 that by the end of the year "we will be coming very close to the margin of safety."

According to the 1981 annual report of the Social Security Board of Trustees, issued in July, the three Social Security trust funds taken together decreased by $3.3 billion in 1980: the OASI and DI funds were down by $3.8 billion, while the Health Insurance fund had increased by $.5 billion. Overall, income to the three funds in 1980 increased by 13 percent, but outlays were up by 16 percent over the previous year's figures.

According to the board, even if the three trust funds were permitted to borrow from each other on a permanent basis (which would require congressional action), their combined assets would still decline significantly in the short-range picture before 1985. And even if the national economy picked up sharply, the board projected that assets would barely suffice to meet accrued obligations for benefit payments. Combining assets would only serve to postpone the expected shortfall for a few months. "Stopgap" measures such as a reallocation of the payroll tax rate among the funds or interfund borrowing would not produce adequate short-range financing under adverse economic conditions, according to the board.

Hope in Improved Economy?

Other statistics and economic projections were more optimistic. Many experts and members of Congress challenged the assumptions of imminent financial disaster for the Social Security system. The House Select Committee on Aging decided that the trust funds — provided interfund borrowing was allowed — would be actuarially secure through the early 21st century, according to testimony given in hearings it held in 1981. Other experts — including Alicia Munnell, an economist with the Federal Reserve Bank in Boston and author of a book on Social Security reform — have argued that large cuts in benefit payments were not necessary. "We have a short-run problem of reasonable and solvable magnitude," Munnell maintained.

Alice M. Rivlin, director of the Congressional Budget Office, told the Senate Finance Committee in September 1981 that recent CBO figures indicated interfund borrowing possibly could tide the system over until 1990. However, Rivlin warned that relying solely on interfund borrowing would not be "prudent." She pointed out that if economic conditions turned out to be even "slightly worse" than the "moderately optimistic" CBO projections, the funds could be in serious trouble. Rivlin noted that these projections did not account for any "margin of safety" and that the level of economic growth they assumed would require "very good luck indeed."

Assuming that the near-term shortfall of funds would be resolved in some way, some experts predicted the Social

Security system would be in good shape through the "medium term," from 1985 to the 1990s. This was due to certain demographic factors: for a short while the number of retirees, born in the Depression years, will be low compared with the relatively larger number of workers, born during the post-World-War-II "baby boom," who will be at the peak of their active work lives. With the baby-boom generation flooding the work force, analysts expected the scheduled payroll tax increases set up in the 1977 amendments to bring in enough money to put the OASI and DI trust funds back in the black with safe margins through the year 2010.

However, by that time the Health Insurance fund, which ran a surplus of about half a billion dollars in 1980, may be in financial trouble. The HI fund was expected to pay out more cash than it would take in, unless the growth in health care cost was slowed, the Medicare portion of the payroll tax reallocated, benefits cut or taxes raised again.

Since the root of the Social Security system's short-range financial problems lay in the economic troubles of the past few decades, it followed that if the nation's economic health improved, the severity of many of the system's expected short- and medium-term financial troubles could be ameliorated. Economists emphasized that projections were subject to the accuracy of underlying assumptions about the performance of the national economy. Some analysts believed the retirement program could even post surpluses by the mid-1980s, provided the administration's economic projections were close to target.

However, the Reagan administration assumptions were considered optimistic and if the actual improvement in the economy was only slightly worse, as the CBO recommendations pointed out, the trust funds would be unable to pay benefits by the late 1980s. Historically, Congress too had been overly optimistic about economic trends in setting up payroll tax increases to finance the Social Security system.

Social Security Insecurity

In addition to the practical problem of maintaining adequate reserves in the Social Security funds, a complicating factor was the lack of confidence in the soundness of the retirement system generally expressed by the American public. In an April 1981 survey conducted for the National Federation of Independent Business, 68 percent of those persons interviewed said they felt the Social Security program was in trouble financially; only 18 percent expressed confidence that the system was financially sound.

A May 1980 nationwide poll ordered by the National Commission on Social Security found that most U.S. workers under age 55 feared that the system would not have enough money to pay their benefits when they retired. A staggering 73 percent of those interviewed between the ages of 25 and 44 expressed little or no confidence in the system's ability to pay future benefits. Of persons aged 45 to 54, 56 percent lacked confidence in the system, while 58 percent of those between age 55 and 64 — and 74 percent of the elderly — had a great deal of faith.

However, despite lack of faith in the system and increases in the payroll tax, most of the public apparently supported the Social Security system, according to the commission. Pollster Peter D. Hart, who conducted the poll, said it had indicated that the U.S. public generally understood what benefits Social Security offered and how it worked. However, "substantial numbers of Americans

are misinformed" about Social Security in two areas: fewer than 40 percent realized that federal employees did not pay into the system, and only 45 percent knew that benefits rose automatically with inflation. When asked to choose between higher taxes or lower benefits, only 21 percent of those questioned opted for lower benefits and 69 percent opposed lowering them.

In a similar survey conducted by CBS News and *The New York Times* in summer 1981, after President Reagan had announced his proposed cutbacks in the program, approximately 73 percent of those workers aged 18 to 29 felt the retirement income system would not have sufficient funds to pay their benefits. In the 30- to 44-year-old age group, 67 percent said the Social Security system would not be able to pay their benefits. About 40 percent of those aged 45 to 54 agreed. In marked contrast to the 1980 survey, only 54 percent of persons over age 65 showed confidence in the Social Security system, with 13 percent indicating the system would not be able to pay their benefits and 33 percent of those polled expressing no opinion.

The Long-Term Picture

Public concern and distrust of the Social Security system stemmed from the realization that — even if the economy could be stabilized and Social Security costs contained — a much more serious crisis loomed on the horizon for the retirement income system. The basic problem was fewer workers supporting more retirees, which could eventually result in higher Social Security costs per worker.

The fact that the U.S. population was aging much more rapidly than in past decades — compounded by de-

Old Age and Survivors Insurance Trust Fund, 1940-80

In billion dollars

Year	Income	Outgo	Total Assets At End of Period
1940	$ 0.4	$ 0.06	$ 2.0
1945	1.4	0.3	7.1
1950	2.9	1.0	13.7
1955	6.2	5.1	21.6
1960	11.4	11.2	20.3
1965	16.6	17.5	18.2
1970	32.2	29.8	32.5
1972	40.0	38.5	35.3
1975	59.6	60.4	37.0
1977	72.4	75.3	32.5
1979	86.9	90.1	27.7
1980	100.1	103.2	24.6

Source: Social Security Administration

mographic imbalances resulting from the post-World-War-II baby boom — altered the statistical basis on which the system was founded. The declining number of births and increased longevity further complicated the gloomy long-term picture for Social Security. These factors threatened to put nearly intolerable burdens on pension systems — both public and private — by the early 21st century.

Most experts conceded that Social Security revenues certainly would be unable to cover anticipated costs by the early 21st century when the baby-boom generation would begin reaching retirement age. The Board of Trustees' 1981 annual report projected that after 1990 expenditures would rise sharply due to a larger benefit population, mainly because the proportion of the aged population would be increasing drastically.

The Graying of the Population

At the beginning of the 20th century, the average life expectancy was 47 years; only 4 percent of the U.S. population lived beyond age 65. A child born in 1935, when the Social Security system was created by Congress, could expect to live to age 61. By mid-century, the average life span had increased to 68 years. Life expectancy for a child born in 1980 was more than 74 years. The number of workers paying into the Social Security system compared with the number of individuals receiving benefits has been shrinking steadily — and in increasing disproportion — since the system was first set up.

According to a May 1981 Census Bureau report, there were 25.5 million Americans over age 65 in 1980 — a 28 percent increase over 1970. In 1981 nearly 25 million people in the United States were over age 65 — about 11 percent of the total population. Approximately 5,000 people reach age 65 every day; only 3,400 of that age or older die, resulting in a net gain in the elderly population of 1,600.

These numbers were expected to continue to grow steadily through the end of the century, with the aged accounting for 12 percent of the total population by the year 2000, according to Dr. Beth J. Soldo of the Center for Population Research in Washington, D.C. By the year 2020, when the postwar baby-boom generation is retiring, she calculated that there would be 45 milion persons over age 65 — 16 percent of an expected U.S. population of 290 million. *(Graph, below)*

Baby Boom and Baby Bust

In addition to this aging of the already-born population, there has been a sharp decline in the birthrate in the United States. Consequently the median age of the population has been increasing steadily. From 29 years in 1940, when the Social Security program was gearing up, the median age of Americans had climbed to age 30 in 1980. By the century's end it was expected to climb to 36. In year 2010, when the postwar generation begins to reach retirement age, the median age was expected to pass age 38.

Steadily decreasing birthrates have been a recent trend, resulting in the so-called "baby bust" of the 1970s and early 1980s. Contributing factors included improved methods and increased use of contraceptives and postponement of child-bearing until women reach their late 20s or 30s. Moreover, many couples wanted only one or two children compared with larger families of earlier generations.

The birthrate at the height of the postwar baby boom in 1957 was 25.3 births per 1,000 persons; by 1976 it had

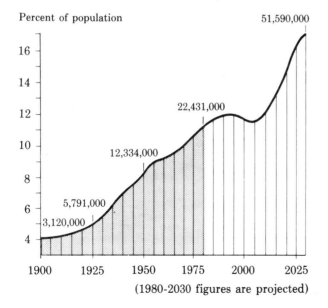

U.S. Population, age 65 and older

Percent of population

51,590,000

22,431,000

12,334,000

5,791,000

3,120,000

1900   1925   1950   1975   2000   2025

(1980-2030 figures are projected)

Source: Department of Commerce, Bureau of the Census

Changes in U.S. demographic trends will place serious strains on the Social Security system when the baby-boom generation begins retiring in the early 21st century. Fewer workers paying into the system will carry a heavier tax burden to support a rapidly increasing number of retirees.

fallen to 14.8, only four points above the all-time low during the 1930s Depression. In 1981 the number of births over deaths in the United States stood at 7 per 1,000 per year, compared with a world rate of increase of 17 per 1,000. While there have been some indications of an increase in fertility trends, demographers do not expect any explosion in future birthrates above the existing low trends.

Clearly, the impact of the baby-boom generation on U.S. society has been profound. The dislocations in government services such as education and Social Security have been marked. During the 1970s the labor force increased by 22 million, compared with 12 million in the 1960s and 7.5 million in the 1950s. This influx of young, inexperienced workers has sometimes been blamed for the slowdown in worker productivity. Some experts have maintained that this labor surplus also helped to depress real income for younger workers.

In future years, as the numbers of elderly persons increased, so would the demands for long-term health care and adequate retirement incomes.

The Dependency Ratio

Barring unforeseen developments in U.S immigration policy and other demographic trends, the plummeting birthrate means there will be far fewer people entering the work force. Therefore, decreasing numbers of active workers will support a much enlarged retired population in the years ahead.

Whereas approximately 10 workers were paying into the Social Security system to support each retiree when the program was getting started in the 1940s, in 1980 the ratio of contributors to beneficiaries was about 3 workers to 1 retiree. This "dependency ratio" — the number of workers paying into the Social Security system in proportion to the number of retirees and dependents receiving benefits out of the trust funds — was expected to decrease steadily through the middle of the 21st century. When the baby-boom generation, born in 1945 through 1959, begins to retire in the year 2010 or so, the dependency ratio was expected to drop dramatically to fewer than 2 workers supporting each retiree.

Other Factors

This gloomy forecast was complicated by two other factors. More and more American workers have been opting for early retirement. In 1977 about 77 percent of the recently retired men and 79 percent of the recently retired women took reduced early retirement Social Security benefits, available before age 65. Although some evidence suggested the trend might be changing in the face of continued inflationary pressures, the early retirement factor has played a big part in shrinking the Social Security funds.

Second, advanced medical developments, better nutrition and other changes in lifestyles have resulted in increased longevity. People are living in retirement for longer periods of time than in past decades. When Social Security was enacted in 1935, the average person who retired at age 65 spent 12.8 years in retirement; according to the February 1981 final report of the President's Commission on Pension Policy, that statistic had jumped to 16 years and was presumably still growing in 1981.

This trend toward early retirement meant that workers, although paying more money into the Social Security system for longer periods of time, were nevertheless more likely to receive benefit payments over an extended period, thus putting additional financial pressures on the rapidly depleting Social Security trust funds.

Because of this imbalance in the age distribution of the population, experts predicted a deficit in Social Security funding of between 5 and 14 percent annually during the years 2030 through 2054.

The President's Commission on Pension Policy summed up the basic alternatives to the impending long-term financial crisis in its final report:

> Only under the optimistic demographic and economic assumptions will the trust funds accumulate to very high levels and then decline when the baby boom [generation] retires. If the more unfavorable, but more likely alternatives develop, more revenue from higher payroll taxes or other revenue sources must be found or benefits must be reduced.

The long-term dilemma of how to make the Social Security system financially secure was one of the biggest challenges facing the president and Congress in the 1980s.

THE SEARCH FOR SOLVENCY

There has been no shortage of reports and studies on why the Social Security program was experiencing money troubles and how they could be solved. In December 1979 the Advisory Council on Social Security — which was required by law to report every four years on the status of the Social Security system — supplied Congress with a long, complicated list of proposals for strengthening the system. In 1981 numerous study panels — then President-elect Reagan's Social Security Task Force, the President's Commission on Pension Policy and the National Commission on Social Security — all offered alternatives for making the retirement income system financially sound.

Many of these proposals for basic changes in the Social Security system, such as funding portions of the program with general tax revenues, have been recommended to Congress by advisory councils since 1938. Although Congress over the years has put many council recommendations into law, significant fundamental changes have failed to win approval.

These study groups have worked for years, holding dozens of public hearings around the country and conducting studies and public opinion polls, to produce some of the best thinking available on American retirement problems and the troubles of the Social Security system.

Most experts and policy makers have agreed that the Social Security system requires fundamental changes to ensure the system's solvency through the coming decades. But these necessary choices in such a popular program would be painful ones — both politically and economicallly — and would affect every citizen in one way or another. The basic dilemma was how to increase revenues or decrease outgo for benefits.

The obvious solution was either to raise taxes steeply, or reduce benefits substantially, or let the federal deficit increase drastically. But there were problems with each proposed solution: increased taxes hindered economic growth; benefit cuts could devastate the elderly who relied on Social Security as their sole source of retirement income.

Revenue Raisers

Policy makers — fearful of the political repercussions of cutting Social Security benefits but eager to meet taxpayers' demands for lower payroll deductions — have been searching for new sources of revenue for the troubled social insurance system.

Payroll Tax Hike

Although it would be a politically distasteful move, some experts have recommended raising the payroll tax rate even higher than those increases already scheduled under the 1977 amendments. The April 1981 final report of the National Commission on Social Security recommended changing the tax rate schedule so the OASDI funds would be adequately financed with a contingency reserve of at least one year's outgo. Others have suggested changing Social Security law so that a covered employee's income from interest, rents and profits — under current law exempt from the payroll tax — would be subject to Social Security taxes, thus generating additional revenues. Still others have recommended reducing the payroll tax rate while increasing the earnings base on which it is levied.

Additional taxes have not been considered a real policy option, however, because legislators fear they would result in a further undermining of public support for the Social Security system. And, in light of the tax cut Congress approved in 1981, it appeared unlikely that taxes would be raised to aid the troubled system in the near future. Furthermore, experts generally conceded that any additional revenues derived from increases in the payroll tax alone would not be sufficient to make up the predicted Social Security deficit of billions of dollars by the mid-1980s.

Critics of a tax hike pointed out that, with scheduled increases in the payroll tax totaling 15 percent between 1981 and 1990, the average worker's tax burden was too heavy already. Raising Social Security taxes any higher to finance current program requirements would be unfair to those workers who had to bear the tax burden. Because the tax rate is regressive, an increase there would disproportionately affect lower-income people. And because lower-paid workers will receive a higher percentage of their past earnings out of the system than will better-paid workers, increases in the wage base would disproportionately affect the wealthy, who would be paying higher taxes to "subsidize" the poor.

Policy makers generally agreed that any benefits from improved economic health for the nation — lower inflation, less unemployment, more stable prices — would indirectly help out the ailing Social Security program. One reason commonly given against financing the predicted future deficit with additional contributions from the payroll tax was that it would only serve to put a drag on the economy and its hoped-for recovery. Since employers pay half of each employee's Social Security contribution, higher tax rates would add to an employer's labor costs and eventually result in increased prices for consumer goods.

The 1979 Advisory Council on Social Security pointed out that in "a time when inflation is a major economic problem, increases in payroll taxes work directly against price stability."

More importantly, higher tax rates might very well discourage further economic growth. Some businesses might be reluctant to hire new workers. Critics pointed out that this "extra" money eaten up by Social Security taxes perhaps could be used more efficiently elsewhere in the economy — as capital investments, for example — to spur new growth.

Payroll Tax Reallocation

Short of a payroll tax increase, some economists and policy makers suggested reallocating the overall Social Security payroll tax rate among the three trust funds.

In 1981 the 6.65 percent payroll tax rate was divided as follows: 5.35 percent going to finance Old Age, Survivors and Disability Insurance benefits and 1.3 for the Health Insurance fund (with the balance of the HI fund financed with general revenues). Some suggested changing this formula to give a full 6 percent to the OASDI fund and only .65 percent to the Medicare fund (covering Medicare's deficit with gradually increasing funds from general revenues). Such a move would not undermine the basic "earned right" concept of Social Security benefits, because health care payments for the elderly had always been based on health needs and not computed on past earnings.

Taxing Benefits

Although chances for enactment were considered unlikely, some experts called for a tax on Social Security benefits to help put the system on secure financial ground. Money derived from such taxes could be channeled back into the trust funds to cover the deficit. Under existing law Social Security benefits were not subject to federal taxes.

The 1979 Advisory Council on Social Security recommended that 50 percent of benefits be considered as taxable income for federal tax purposes. The council pointed out that instead of a gift, the "right to Social Security benefits is derived from earnings in covered employment just as in the case with private pensions." Due to the income tax exemptions for the elderly, the council pointed out that even if benefits were subject to taxation, few persons or couples over the age of 65 would pay any income tax if Social Security were their only source of income.

The council estimated that based on 1978 data taxing half of Social Security benefits would affect 10.6 million tax filings out of 24.2 million persons who were receiving benefits in that year. The average tax increase was estimated to be $350 and the total increase in federal tax collections would be $3.7 billion.

Prospects were slim for Congress to approve the taxation of Social Security benefits, not only because of the anticipated political fallout but also because it would change Social Security from a contribution-based to a need-based system. Critics pointed out that such a tax would be biased against lower-income workers, who received a proportionately higher amount of their retirement income from Social Security than those in higher pay brackets.

General Revenue Financing

Although most members of Congress and other policy makers have been averse to financing the Social Security deficit with funds from general tax revenues, indications were that the American public would probably favor such a move. In a survey by ABC News and *The Washington Post* in May 1981, 68 percent of those polled said Social Security should be protected at all costs even if money had to be taken from other programs; 15 percent favored reducing benefits; 17 percent said paycheck deductions should be raised to protect benefits.

There are many ways that general revenues could be used to defray costs of the retirement system. Some supporters would use general revenues to pay a percentage of Social Security costs; others would provide general revenue financing for Health Insurance or Disability Insurance. Still others wanted to use general revenue funds to cover the costs of benefits for low-income retired workers.

President Carter in 1978 had proposed using income taxes to supplement the payroll tax whenever high unemployment depleted the income of the Social Security trust funds. Such a "countercyclical triggering device" would replace revenue lost to the funds during periods of high inflation or unemployment beyond certain levels.

The 1979 Advisory Council on Social Security recommended such protection against severe economic fluctuations, but only if reserves in the Social Security funds were less than 60 percent of annual outlays. The council unanimously agreed "that the time has come to finance some part of Social Security with non-payroll tax revenues." The council also proposed that the funds be allowed authority to borrow money from the U.S. Treasury if reserves fell below three months' payment of benefits. More radically, the council suggested the OASI and DI funds be merged permanently into a single fund, but retaining separate annual cost analyses.

The National Commission on Social Security appeared to support partial funding of Social Security from general tax revenues. According to the commission, the combined employer/employee payroll tax should not exceed 18 percent, but when deficits occurred at this rate of taxation, general revenues should be allowed to make up the difference. The commission advocated that one-half of the cost of Social Security's Health Insurance fund be financed from general revenues, beginning in 1983. Payroll taxes would be kept at the scheduled rates, with the "extra" money supporting the troubled OASDI funds. To offset the contribution from general revenues, the commission suggested a 2.5 percent surcharge be added to the federal personal income tax. Borrowing from the U.S. Treasury could be used to shore up the funds, but as "an emergency measure only."

Most other industrial nations use some general revenues to pay for social insurance, but the idea has been hard to sell to the U.S. Congress. The traditional conservative argument against general revenue financing was that it would obliterate the original basic insurance aspect of Social Security by breaking the relationship between contributions paid into the system and benefits received. Critics maintained that a Social Security system financed with general tax revenues would be perceived by the public as even more of a welfare program than it already has come to resemble.

Others maintained that general revenue financing would remove an important cost control. Once general funds were made available for Social Security financing, some lawmakers argued, it would become very difficult for Congress to resist proposals to increase benefits and thus drive program costs up.

General revenue financing would not reduce the costs of Social Security, but would shift the burden of financing benefits from the payroll tax to other federal taxes. Advocates argued that this would turn out to be less burdensome and more progressive than the regressive payroll deduction, since the income tax makes up a large proportion of the federal government's revenues. However, some Americans — such as federal employees who have their own pension system and do not participate in Social Security — in effect would be subsidizing other people's retirement benefits.

The principal drawback to all general revenue financing proposals has been the already-heavy federal government deficit. With the Reagan administration attempting to cut back this deficit, the "extra" money was not available in the general Treasury for a transfer of funds to finance anticipated Social Security deficits. Critics maintained that any resort to the general fund without an accompanying income tax hike would swell the federal budget deficit and fuel inflation.

Separate Insurance Systems

The most common — and least controversial — general revenue proposals would take Health and Disability

Payroll Tax Relief?

Although further Social Security tax hikes were unlikely to receive much support in Congress, a concept that did have considerable backing involved helping workers offset the burden of increasing Social Security taxes: income tax credits. The main argument for the tax credit approach was that it would provide relief to employees hurt by the rise in payroll taxes without undoing the 1977 law.

Legislation introduced by Rep. Richard A. Gephardt, D-Mo., in 1980 and again in 1981 would have provided an income tax credit equal to 20 percent of annual contributions to the Social Security system. Other suggestions included allowing taxpayers an income tax credit equal to 15 percent of yearly payroll taxes or letting them claim a dollar-for-dollar income tax credit for all increases in the tax rate above a certain percentage.

Many members of Congress agreed that tax relief for low-income workers — leaving the payroll tax schedule intact — was preferable to financing the system with general tax revenues. They maintained the payroll tax added soundness to the Social Security program as an insurance system, not a welfare program. Since it was levied at a flat rate on only the lower and middle ranges of income, the payroll tax was considered much less progressive than the income tax, which would pay a major share of the program if general funds were used to finance Social Security.

Insurance out of the Social Security system and fund them with general Treasury revenues to lessen pressure on the payroll tax. Some proposals would even allow the payroll tax to be reduced eventually. However, corporate taxes would rise indirectly because businesses would no longer be able to deduct health insurance and disability insurance as a business cost from their taxable income.

Removing programs from the payroll tax for which benefits bear little relationship to past contributions would put the main part of the retirement system on more sound actuarial footing. Such a separation of the welfare and insurance aspects of the Social Security system — with the welfare portions funded from general tax revenues — would allow health and disability payments to be based on need only.

This approach to general revenue financing has captured much attention in Congress. While it would still open the system to general revenues, this alternative was designed to overcome concerns that general revenue financing would reduce fiscal discipline in the Social Security program. Rather than injecting general revenues into the trust funds that pay benefits, these proposals provided that the funds would continue to be financed solely by payroll taxes. That, theoretically, would prevent Congress from increasing retirement benefits without raising payroll taxes.

The 1979 Advisory Council on Social Security recommended a politically appealing way to reduce reliance on the Social Security payroll tax. Part of the Health Insurance payroll tax would be reallocated to the OASDI program to guarantee its financial soundness, with the balance of the HI payroll tax to be repealed. The council recommended that the HI program be financed entirely through earmarked portions of the personal and corporate income tax. These actions would have allowed substantial reductions in future payroll tax rate increases: a 5.60 rate for both 1980 and 1981, as opposed to the 1979 and 1980 rates of 6.13 percent and 1981 rate of 6.65. An individual subject to the maximum tax would pay about $450 a year less, according to the council's estimates.

The advisory council further suggested that, if Congress decided not to adopt this recommendation, further increases in payroll taxes for HI (.25 percent of both employers and employees in 1981) be replaced with general revenue funds. According to the council, if either of these recommendations were implemented, a payroll tax increase would not be necessary until 2005 in order to bring the Social Security program into long-run actuarial balance.

Rep. J. J. Pickle, D-Texas, chairman of the House Social Security Subcommittee, introduced legislation (HR 3207) in 1981 to draw half of the financing of the HI trust fund from general revenues. Pickle estimated that such a change could bring approximately $91 billion into the Social Security system for fiscal 1982-86, a sum that would go a long way toward easing the program's financial woes. Another bill (HR 3393) introduced by House Aging Committee Chairman Claude Pepper, D-Fla., would use general revenues to fund 70 percent of the HI trust fund. *(Legislative action, p. 95)*

Interfund Borrowing

Because the idea of general revenue financing was distasteful to many members of Congress, some experts suggested permanent authority for borrowing among the Social Security trust funds as a less drastic, and perhaps less painful, way to relieve some of Social Security's money troubles. This method would allow a fund with a deficit to borrow from a fund with a surplus, easing temporary cash-flow problems.

Congress in 1980 reallocated some money from the Disability Insurance fund to prop up the ailing OASI fund during 1980 and 1981 but the transfer was only temporary. Other proposals would let the trust funds borrow money from the U.S. Treasury during financial "emergencies" to make timely benefit payments, with the money to be repaid with interest within a certain period.

The National Commission on Social Security and the President's Commission on Pension Policy also endorsed interfund borrowing.

Although generally labeled as only a temporary, "band-aid" solution to Social Security's money troubles, interfund borrowing was almost certain to be part of any package to reform the system. Policy makers have advocated interfund borrowing as the solution to the immediate financial crisis, which would provide the additional time necessary for examination of more complicated long-term solutions. Although some officials, including the Social Security Board of Trustees, have maintained that interfund borrowing would not provide adequate short-range financing under adverse economic conditions, others such as the Congressional Budget Office have indicated that it might tide the system over for 10 years or so.

Increase Retirement Age

A number of economists and policy makers have argued that raising eligibility for full Social Security benefits to those aged 68 or older would resolve a large part of the system's financial problems. Many have suggested gradually phasing in an increase to coincide with the baby-boom generation's retirement when higher taxes would be needed to pay benefits.

The President's Commission on Pension Policy in 1981 proposed phasing in a higher retirement age in increments of three months, starting in the year 2000, so that by 2012 the full retirement age would be 68. According to C. Peter McCollough, chairman of the panel, raising the retirement age to 68 would boost the Social Security dependency ratio to four workers to one beneficiary, compared with the projected 2-to-1 ratio.

The commission encouraged Congress to enact the retirement age increase quickly "to provide sufficient warning to the younger workers that there will be a gradual move upward." The commission also urged fast action before the population aged further and the political pressures to block the retirement age boost increased. Both the Reagan Task Force on Social Security and the National Commission on Social Security agreed that the eligibility age should be increased gradually to age 68. The advisory council did not make specific recommendations, but urged that "serious consideration be given to enactment now of an increase in the normal retirement age under Social Security that would be effective at about the turn of the century."

Those who advocated raising the eligibility age argued that 65 was an arbitrary age limit, set at a time when life expectancy was considerably shorter. As a result, the burden placed on the system was far beyond what its founders ever imagined. Congress in 1978 raised the mandatory retirement age for most private sector workers to age 70 and abolished the age limit for federal employees. Critics maintained some adjustment was also necessary in eligibility for

Inequities in the Social Security System

Recent assessments of Social Security financing problems illuminated other inequities in the system. The national commissions studying Social Security and other experts recommended reforms to update the system to reflect changes in the work force and other social and economic trends.

Various categories of workers complained that the retirement income system was inequitable. Single persons argued that they had to pay heavy Social Security taxes even though they did not expect to benefit from the survivors' and dependents' provisions. Self-employed persons paid a 50 percent higher tax than the rate paid by salaried workers, although the benefits received were the same.

Earnings Test

An often criticized aspect of the Social Security system was the "earnings test," which penalized retired workers aged 65 to 71 who continued to earn salaries after they qualified for Social Security benefits. Under the earnings test rule, workers lost one dollar of Social Security income for every two dollars earned beyond a certain exempted amount. In 1981 retirees could earn up to $5,500 without losing Social Security benefits; this exempted amount was scheduled to increase to $6,000 in 1982.

Critics of the earnings test argued that it most adversely affected lower-income workers who were in need of additional income to supplement their Social Security benefits. Because the test applied only to earned income — and not to income received from investment or other pension plans — it did appear biased in favor of retirees formerly in the higher income brackets. Others defended the test, arguing that Social Security was an insurance system and not a pension plan, which it would be if a beneficiary was permitted to receive unlimited earned income.

Unfair to Women

The Social Security system has been particularly skewed to the disadvantage of women. While society changed rapidly in recent decades — with the massive increase in the female work force and the divorce rate — spouse and survivor benefits have remained about the same since 1940.

Under the existing system, married women generally received Social Security protection as dependents of their husbands. If women did work, they could be covered as dependents of their husbands or on their own right, but not both. If the marriage lasted fewer than 10 years and ended in divorce, the non-working woman lost her coverage. A widowed homemaker under age 60 who had not worked could not receive benefits unless she was either at least age 50 and disabled or caring for minor children.

Because married women could not receive both spouse and worker benefits, the protection they received as workers often duplicated rather than supplemented their coverage as spouses. In addition, benefits were often higher for couples where one spouse earned most or all of the income than for couples where both spouses had roughly equal earnings, even though total family earnings in both cases were the same. The two-income family, however, did draw greater benefits because dependents were protected in the case of either spouses's death or disability. And one spouse could opt for early retirement and draw benefits while the other continued to work.

A February 1978 study issued by the Health, Education and Welfare Department recommended several changes to resolve these inequities for women. The report suggested that 50 percent of the total annual earnings of a couple be credited to each spouse's individual earnings record. The benefits of each spouse then would be based on one-half of the couple's earnings during years of marriage and on individual earnings while unmarried. Or, a two-tier benefit system could be established where everyone would qualify for a flat-dollar benefit, regardless of earnings, with an earnings-related benefit based on income from covered employment.

The 1979 Advisory Council on Social Security concluded that such a system would be the "most promising" way to deal with these issues. "Under earnings sharing," the council report explained, "a husband and a wife, or divorced spouses, each would be entitled to retirement and disability benefits based on half of the couple's total earnings for the years in which they were married and 100 percent of any earnings received outside of marriage."

According to the council, earnings sharing would provide more adequate benefits for widow and widowers; equalize benefits for the survivors of one- and two-earner couples where total earnings were the same; treat marriages lasting at least 10 years as economic partnerships; and eliminate dependency-based benefits for aged surviving spouses, aged divorced spouses and aged surviving divorced spouses.

The Reagan Task Force on Social Security recommended phasing out "extra" spouses' benefits by the year 2015 and surviving spouses' benefits by 2035. Under existing law, non-working spouses (mostly women) were automatically entitled to 50 percent of their working spouses' benefits when both reached retirement age. And a surviving spouse received 100 percent of the deceased's benefits. The panel justified its recommendations on the grounds that more women were earning their own benefits, reducing the need for these special payments.

retirement benefits to preserve the integrity of the Social Security system.

As an alternate solution to bring in additional revenues and to decrease benefit outlays, some proposals advocated encouraging workers to postpone retirement until age 68 or so. Workers would be paying into the system for longer periods of time and, it would be hoped, eventually take out less in benefits later. The Reagan administration advocated encouraging longer work by phasing out the limits on outside earnings for those retired workers aged 65 to 71. Legislation under consideration in 1981 by the House Social Security Subcommittee would eliminate this "earnings test" in 1983 for those aged 68 and older. Incentives such as "bonus" cash payments have been suggested to discourage early retirement. Such a move would amount to an indirect "cut" in full retirement benefits at age 65.

Extension of Coverage

It has been suggested that additional money could be brought into the Social Security system by extending coverage to the approximately 2.8 federal workers and 3.5 million state and local employees who do not participate in the program. About 10 percent of U.S. workers are not covered by Social Security. As Rep. Barber B. Conable Jr., R-N.Y., once put it: "How do you expect people to believe in the Social Security system when the Commissioner of Social Security does not contribute to the system?"

"Universal coverage" would greatly increase the system's cashflow in the short run, although most of the anticipated extra revenue eventually would be paid out to a larger number of people drawing benefits. In the long run, according to most analysts, the system probably would not be any better off with extended coverage.

Legislating universal coverage could prove to be difficult, however. Federal workers were regarded as one of the most formidable Washington lobbies. And they obviously had something to fight for: the government pension system was considered far superior to the Social Security system. Federal retirees received automatic cost-of-living increases

twice a year; Social Security benefit payments were subject to one annual increase. In addition, initial benefit levels under the federal pension system were usually much higher than under Social Security or most private pension systems.

However, some thought civil service employees might be persuaded to accept a merger of the retirement system if Social Security could be used to supplement certain coverage gaps in their own plans.

Other Tax Proposals

Proposals to raise additional revenue for the Social Security system through other kinds of taxes have received comparatively little attention. One plan, offered by Sen. John C. Danforth, R-Mo., proposed adding a 10-cent tax to a package of cigarettes to raise revenues for the Health Insurance trust fund. Others have suggested easing the burden of future Social Security costs with a "value-added tax (VAT), " which is essentially a national sales tax levied on manufacturers at each level of the production and distribution processes.

Efforts in the 97th Congress to bolster the Social Security system with revenues derived from the tax on oil industry profits resulting from the 1981 deregulation of oil went nowhere. Moreover, the Reagan administration was adamantly opposed to increasing taxes for Social Security, and any other such proposals were expected to meet strong resistance.

Spending Cuts

The alternative to increasing revenues is to cut outlays in some way. Expenditures for administering the trust funds could be reduced, or benefit payments could be decreased by either cutting them across the board or tightening eligibility requirements.

Some observers maintained that one way to reduce outgo would be to reduce waste and fraud in the administration of the Social Security program. The Social Security Administration has been criticized for its heavy case backlog and chronic computer problems.

The investment policies of the Social Security trust funds have also been blamed for recent shortfalls. Sen. William Proxmire, D-Wis., charged that Social Security "needlessly" lost $2 billion in 1980 by investing in securities that yielded low — 8.3 percent — interest. He introduced a measure (S 1528) with 17 cosponsors in the 97th Congress to require the system's Board of Trustees to maximize its investments.

But the major question in 1981 was whether to cut benefits. Although President Reagan had promised during his campaign that Social Security benefits would remain inviolate as part of the "social safety net," in May 1981 he proposed major cutbacks in several Social Security programs including early retirement benefits and the minimum benefit guarantee. *(Details of benefit cut proposals, p. 94)*

Proposals to cut benefits faced strong opposition from groups representing the interests of the elderly, whose ever-increasing numbers exerted powerful political pressure. A coalition of 100 national elderly and other groups called Save Our Security (SOS) — representing between 35 and 40 million members and headed by Wilbur E. Cohen, HEW secretary during the Johnson administration — insisted that cutting benefits would amount to a breach of faith with today's workers and would seriously undermine the already-troubled Social Security system.

A major problem in cutting benefits was that there was little agreement about whether the current level of benefits was actually adequate to support the nation's elderly. Although Social Security was originally intended as a supplemental source of income to the aged — meant to provide about 40 percent of total retirement income — Social Security in 1981 remained the sole source of old age income for more than half of U.S. retirees. Experts generally agreed that somewhere between 60 and 80 percent of a retiree's regular wages before retirement was necessary to maintain his or her standard of living. The percentage of pre-retirement earnings provided by Social Security payments ranged from 60 percent for low-income workers to about 30 percent for higher-income workers.

New Benefit Formulas

In the 97th Congress there was strong support for changing the formulas by which Social Security benefits were indexed. One Reagan administration proposal that received widespread attention would indirectly cut benefits for future retirees. That plan entailed a revision of the formula used to determine the monthly payment for a retiree. A newly retired worker's initial benefit level was wage-indexed to reflect changes in wages during his working lifetime. Two figures in the formula — called "bend points" — were indexed to increase at 100 percent of the average annual growth in national wages. The administration proposed changing the index to 50 percent for 1982 through 1987, in effect cutting benefits about 10 percent for all new beneficiaries.

Some experts called for changes in the indexation of annual cost-of-living increases in Social Security benefits to reduce system costs. Under existing law, Social Security benefits were increased each July by 100 percent of the rise in the Consumer Price Index (CPI) of the previous year. The Reagan administration proposed that the annual cost-of-living increases be moved to October of each year, to coincide with the beginning of the government's fiscal year. Expected savings for the three-month delay for fiscal 1982-86 would be about $6.3 billion under intermediate economic assumptions, according to the administration.

Many economists maintained that the CPI distorted the "real" level of inflation. In addition, it was generally agreed that the CPI-based system overstated the expenses of the retired. The government acknowledged that in October 1981 when it announced that it would weight some components of the CPI differently in the future.

The National Commission on Social Security estimated that if the cost-of-living allowance (COLA) had been limited to the lower of either the CPI or a wage index in the 1977 amendments, the Social Security system probably would not be in such dire financial straits in the 1980s. The Reagan task force also advocated that benefits be limited to the average annual increases in prices or wages, whichever was lower. Senate Budget Committee Chairman Pete V. Domenici, R-N.M., proposed capping such COLA increases at 3 percentage points below the CPI increase for a savings of $46 billion in Social Security for fiscal 1982-86, according to Budget Committee estimates.

Economist Martin Feldstein, Harvard University professor and president of the National Bureau of Economic Research, advocated in 1981 a 2 percent floor under the indexation of Social Security benefits. Benefits would continue to be adjusted upward each year, but only by the excess of inflation over 2 percent. For example, if the inflation rate was 10 percent, benefits would increase by only 8 percent.

Professor Feldstein maintained that if a floor was put into effect in 1982, savings by 1985 could reach $15 billion, wiping out the expected short-term deficit. By 1992, payroll tax rates necessary to finance benefits would be 20 percent lower than under current law. This floor could be removed whenever the ratio of benefits to wages had returned to a satisfactory level. Unlike proposals to increase benefits by a fixed fraction of each year's cost-of-living increases, Feldstein maintained this floor would protect beneficiaries from the "uncertainties of changing inflation."

The Social Security commission suggested a "small modification" of the current 100 percent cost-of-living indexing of retirement benefits when prices rose much faster than wages. It said further consideration should be given to the development of a separate cost-of-living index for the retired. The President's Commission on Pension Policy agreed, recommending that the Bureau of Labor Statistics develop a new cost-of-living index — separate from the Consumer Price Index — to be used in adjusting retirement benefits.

POLITICS HAMPER FINDING A SOLUTION

Congress and the White House moved in 1981 to solve Social Security's immediate financing problems. But intense public opposition to President Reagan's proposals for longer-term reform of the system forced the president to put aside those suggestions and propose that a panel study the problems once again.

Congress was quick to fall in with that plan. Public pressure had already forced legislators to overturn the one major action that Congress took to hold down Social Security costs in 1981. By mid-October both houses had voted to restore the $122 minimum monthly benefit Congress had eliminated earlier in the year. The prospect that the elderly would be more than willing to vent their anger at the polls in November 1982 made Democrats and Republicans alike hesitant to talk about major reform of the Social Security system, which most certainly would require either benefit cuts or tax increases.

Budget Cuts

Announcing his program for economic recovery Feb. 18, 1981, President Reagan proposed a "two-track" approach to Social Security. He asked Congress to use the fiscal 1982 budget process to make immediate changes in the program to save money in the short term. More fundamental Social Security reform would be addressed once these initial cutbacks were achieved.

Reagan announced his recommendations for immediate changes in March. While not proposing any cuts in basic Social Security benefits, the administration did request cutbacks in "unearned benefits" in four retirement and disability programs and also asked Congress to eliminate three "add-on" benefit programs and tighten the eligibility for a fourth. *(Text, p. 201)*

However, Reagan's major proposal was to eliminate as of July 1 the minimum benefit program, which provided a floor payment of $122 a month to anyone eligible for Social Security, regardless of employment and wage history. Reagan's proposal was intended to reduce the so-called "windfall" received by many beneficiaries — often retired government workers with generous federal pensions — who worked only a short time in employment covered by Social Security. The 3 million people receiving minimum payments would have their benefits recalculated to reflect their earnings history. Supplemental Security Income payments (SSI) were to replace, dollar for dollar, the benefits lost by the "truly needy," the administration said. It estimated that elimination of the minimum benefits program would save $1.3 billion in outlays in fiscal 1982.

Reform Proposals

Meanwhile, on May 12 President Reagan announced his proposals for longer-range Social Security reform. Those included reduced benefits for those retiring before age 65, an end to existing limitations on outside earnings, tighter disability requirements and a one-time delay of three-months in the 1982 cost-of-living increase for benefits. The administration said the cuts were necessary to pull the old age pension fund back from the brink of bankruptcy. *(Details, box, p. 94)*

The administration estimated that enactment of all its Social Security proposals, including those sent up as part of the March budget package, could save $81.9 billion by the end of 1986.

Reaction on Capitol Hill and across the nation ranged from reservation to outright anger at the Reagan administration's proposals to revise the Social Security system. House Aging Committee Chairman Pepper called the proposals "the most fundamental assault" ever on Social Security. House Speaker Thomas P. O'Neill Jr., D-Mass., said they were "despicable. . . . I for one will be fighting this thing every inch of the way."

Groups representing the elderly voiced immediate opposition to the Reagan package and predicted a major outcry when the American people became aware of what the impact of the proposals would be. The Save Our Security (SOS) lobbying group, which had already decided to fight the March proposed cutbacks, in May vowed to oppose any and all cuts. The administration plan was not only "a breach of contract, but it isn't even necessary," Robert Ball, former Social Security Commission and SOS organizer, said at a press conference on May 27.

SOS argued that the long-term financial stability of the system's trust funds could be ensured without reducing benefits at all. The SOS advocated funding part or all of Medicare benefits with general revenues; increasing the payroll tax with an offsetting income tax credit; or allowing borrowing among the system's three trust funds, until a long-term solution could be found.

The plan to reduce benefits for those who elected to retire early, beginning in January 1982, was the most criticized in the president's package. Under the existing system, those who retired at age 62 received 80 percent of the benefits they would be entitled to if they had retired at age 65. President Reagan wanted those early benefits reduced to 55 percent of full benefits to encourage people to remain in the work force longer. Jim Hacking, assistant legislative counsel of the National Retired Teachers Association/ American Association of Retired Persons, complained that the early-retirement reduction was "too drastic and too soon." Such a change would place an unfair burden on those who were currently planning to retire at age 62 and were counting on higher benefits, he said.

Also widely criticized was the delay in the 1982 cost-of-living increase, which the administration estimated would save at least $6.3 billion over the next five years. "It's clear that the administration has backed off from its commitment not to propose changes that would adversely affect people already on the Social Security rolls," Hacking said.

Retirement Benefits Compared

Earnings[1]	Existing Law	Reagan Proposal[2]
Retire at age 62 in January 1982		
Low	$247.60	$163.90
Average	372.80	246.80
Maximum	469.60	310.50
Retire at age 65 in January 1982		
Low	$355.30	$355.30
Average	535.40	535.40
Maximum	679.30	679.30
Retire at age 62 in January 1987		
Low	$384.40	$225.20
Average	580.70	348.30
Maximum	755.60	430.00
Retire at age 65 in January 1987		
Low	$477.10	$447.40
Average	719.00	691.90
Maximum	942.80	860.30

[1] *"Low earnings" are defined as the federal minimum wage in each past year, and the 1981 minimum increased by the change in average wages in future years. "Average earnings" are defined as the average wage for indexing purposes in each year. "Maximum earnings" denote the contribution and benefit base in each year.*

Figures assume that worker entered covered employment in 1956 and worked steadily thereafter. Future earnings (for retirement in Jan. 1987) follow trend under intermediate assumptions in 1980 Trustees Report.

[2] *Proposed benefits include effect of (1) 55 percent benefit rate (instead of 80 percent) for retirement at age 62, (2) age 65 computation point (instead of age 62) for all ages at retirement, and (3) 50 percent reduction in wage index used in primary benefit formulation for 1982-87. Benefit amounts are for worker only. Worker is assumed to reach exact age shown in January.*

Source: Department of Health and Human Services

Jerry Wurf, president of the American Federation of State, County, and Municipal Employees (AFSCME), called the Reagan proposals a "fiscal hoax." He accused the administration of using the money saved from Social Security to finance its proposed tax cut.

The real danger to the elderly, said Robert Ball, was not the Reagan proposals themselves — "they're so horrendous, it's unlikely they'll be adopted" — but the compromises on Capitol Hill that could result from them. "They'll end up with something that's still terrible," he predicted.

Democratic Attack

Reagan's proposals proved to be a political godsend for Democrats in their search for an issue on which the Reagan administration was vulnerable. Many Democrats charged that the Reagan administration was exaggerating the trust funds' problems and was painting a worse-than-necessary financial picture to balance the federal budget at the expense of Social Security benefits.

Labeling Reagan's bankruptcy talk alarmist, they contended demographic trends in the medium term would bail out Social Security. In the short run, rather than cut benefits, Democrats were more inclined to shuffle money among the various Social Security trust funds and make up any shortages out of general tax revenues.

House and Senate Democrats made the most of initial unfavorable reaction to the president's proposals. In the Senate, Democrats May 20 pushed through the Republican-controlled Senate a non-binding resolution promising that the Senate would not cut early retirement benefits immediately or unnecessarily. The House Democratic Caucus May 20 unanimously adopted a resolution calling the proposed changes an "unconscionable breach of faith" and vowing not to "destroy the program for a generation of retirees."

Minimum Benefit Fight

The following day, Congress completed action on its first budget resolution setting revenue, spending and deficit goals for fiscal 1982. That resolution directed the Senate Finance and House Ways and Means committees to include fiscal 1982 Social Security cuts — including cuts in the minimum monthly benefit — in reconciliation legislation. Passage of the reconciliation measure (HR 3982) would put into effect the $36 billion in budget cuts that Congress had agreed to in its first budget resolution.

Adopting its reconciliation bill June 26, the House voted to end the minimum monthly benefit for all new beneficiaries as of Jan. 1, 1982, and for all beneficiaries as of April 1982. The Senate reconciliation measure, passed June 25, called for an immediate end to the minimum benefit. Both versions also contained several other provisions — many of them modifications of the Reagan budget proposals — cutting fiscal 1982 Social Security costs. The two versions of reconciliation then went to a House-Senate conference.

Almost as soon as they had acted both the House and Senate had second thoughts on the political wisdom of terminating the minimum monthly benefits. House Democrats decided to mount a rescue effort for the minimum benefit during the conference on HR 3982. They argued that its elimination would leave some needy beneficiaries — including an often cited group of elderly nuns — without an alternate source of income. Republicans, armed with data from the Office of Management and Budget, con-

tended that only about 300,000 of the 3 million recipients of minimum benefits would actually be affected by the cutoff. The others would have their regular Social Security or Supplemental Security Income benefits recalculated to make up the difference.

On July 21, a day when thousands of senior citizens were holding a rally on the Capitol steps, House Democrats offered a non-binding resolution (H Res 181) urging reconciliation conferees to take steps "to ensure that Social Security benefits are not reduced for those currently receiving them."

Pronouncing the resolution "meaningless," House Minority Leader Robert H. Michel, R-Ill., freed his members to vote for it and thus avoided, for the moment, having Republicans cast as the "Scrooges" of Social Security. The House adopted the resolution by a 405-13 vote.

A more substantive effort to save the minimum benefit was tabled in the Senate by a vote of 52-46 on July 21. That amendment to the Senate tax bill would have continued minimum benefit payments for those who already received them and for those who would become entitled to them within the 1981 calendar year.

House Democrats made one last-ditch effort. House Rules Committee Chairman Richard Bolling, D-Mo., threatened to refuse to convene his panel to clear the reconciliation bill for final floor action unless the conference was reopened to restore the minimum benefit. Bipartisan House and Senate leaders met behind closed doors to reach an agreement on the issue. That agreement allowed two separate House votes — one on the conference report and one on a bill (HR 4331) that would reinstate the minimum benefits language deleted by the conference report. The House adopted the reconciliation conference bill July 31. That bill eliminated the $122 minimum monthly benefit for all new recipients beginning with the December 1981 payment and for all current recipients for benefits paid after February 1982. *(Provisions, p. 196)*

The House then passed the minimum benefits bill by a 404-20 vote and sent it to the Senate, where an attempt to gain immediate consideration of the measure was rebuffed, 56-30. Finance Committee Chairman Robert Dole, R-Kan., said the issue would be explored at September hearings on Social Security reform.

Even though the July 31 vote did not restore the minimum benefit, Democrats felt they had gained some political mileage on the issue and had put the onus for eliminating the payments squarely on President Reagan and his Republican allies in Congress.

Reagan Backs Off

Reagan had already discovered the political sensitivity of the Social Security issue. The huge outpouring of opposition to his May proposals forced the administration to begin to backpedal on its reform plan within a week of its announcement. Administration officials insisted that almost everthing in the plan was negotiable. Social Security Commissioner John A. Svahn said Reagan was adamant about only two things: that no general revenues be used to rescue the system and that taxes not be increased. "But from that point on we're willing to look at compromise," he said.

In late May administration officials indicated to a House subcommittee areas where President Reagan might be willing to compromise. Health and Human Services Secretary Richard S. Schweiker told the Ways and Means

Subcommittee on Social Security on May 28 that one of the most controversial proposals — to lower benefits for those who elect to retire before age 65 — could be phased in over time instead of going into effect Jan. 1, 1982, as the administration had proposed.

But, Schweiker added, other savings would have to be found to make up the difference. The administration contended that approximately $82 billion would have to be cut from the retirement program over the next five years to help the system through an expected financial shortfall in 1982 and to ensure its long-term solvency. Schweiker also said he might consider some change in the annual cost-of-living allowance for beneficiaries, "as part of a bipartisan compromise." The administration had proposed only to delay a scheduled cost-of-living increase three months, from July 1982 until October 1982, but left the formula unchanged.

Later, David A. Stockman, director of the Office of Management and Budget, told the House panel that the administration would consider an income tax credit for those who continued to work after age 65. That compromise proposal was suggested by Rep. Barber B. Conable

Jr., R-N.Y., ranking minority member of the Ways and Means Committee, as a substitute for a proposal to phase out penalties for Social Security recipients who earn more than a certain amount in outside income.

Weary of all the Democratic potshots, Reagan first said he would defend his views on Social Security as part of his July 27 televised speech on his tax bill. But House Republican Leader Michel and Senate Majority Leader Howard H. Baker Jr., R-Tenn., feared that this would distract attention from the Reagan tax bill, which was the main topic of the upcoming speech, and urged Reagan to delay presenting his case for the cutbacks.

Reagan scratched Social Security from his July script, except to protest that the public was being "needlessly frightened by some of the inaccuracies which have been given wide circulation" and to promise his support for keeping the system fiscally sound. Democratic leaders in a televised response to Reagan's speech nonetheless scored Reagan for breaking his commitment to pensioners and charged he planned to use Social Security cuts to help balance his budget in the future. *(Text of Reagan speech, p. 206)*

Reagan Reform Plan

"The crisis is inescapable," said Health and Human Services Secretary Richard S. Schweiker, in announcing the administration's Social Security reform plan on May 12. "Today we move to face it head-on and solve it. If we do nothing, the system would go broke as early as fall 1982, breaking faith with the 36 million Americans depending on Social Security." The administration predicted that its program would not only allow the system to remain solvent, but would permit the reduction of payroll taxes below the existing 6.65 percent rate by 1990.

Most provisions in the administration plan would affect only workers going on the Social Security rolls after Jan. 1, 1982. "This means that the young person entering the labor force next year would pay an average of $33,600 less in Social Security taxes over his/her lifetime, a reduction of over 10 percent," said Schweiker.

In addition to the delayed cost-of-living allowance increases and reduced benefits for early retirees, major administration proposals would:

● Permanently eliminate "windfall" benefits for retirees, such as government employees, who had worked only a few years under Social Security but could collect relatively high benefits under existing formulas. The administration proposed figuring in other pension receipts for these "double dippers" when calculating their Social Security benefits.

● Phase out the retirement earnings limits by 1986. Current recipients aged 65 through 71 were

losing $1 in benefits for every $2 earned each year over $5,500. The administration proposal would permit $10,000 in outside earnings in 1983, $15,000 in 1984, $20,000 in 1985, and no earnings limits thereafter.

● Revise the formula used to determine a recipient's initial benefit level by using only 50 percent of a wage index, instead of the full index. The purpose, the administration said, was to correct past "over-indexing," and the change would apply only through 1987, when the distortion should be corrected. It was estimated that the change would reduce a recipient's primary benefit by 7 percent.

● End children's benefits for retirees under age 65.

● Place a cap on benefits for families of retired and deceased workers to prevent such benefits from exceeding what had been the worker's net take-home pay.

● Tax sick pay for the first six months of a worker's illness. Sick pay was not subject to the payroll tax.

● Raise from 20 to 30 the number of quarter-years out of the past 40 that a worker must be in the work force to qualify for disability benefits.

● Consider only medical factors — instead of age, education and work experience — in determining if a worker qualifies for disability benefits and extend from 12 to 24 months the anticipated period of disability required.

Long-Range Reform

The heated political rhetoric of the Social Security debate in the summer of 1981 troubled the House and Senate subcommittees that were charged with writing Social Security reform. They emphasized that a bipartisan plan would be necessary to push such politically sensitive legislation through Congress and vowed to give the administration plans a hearing.

In the Senate, Finance Committee Chairman Dole was pushing for a broad Social Security reform package based largely on the president's proposals. Sen. William L. Armstrong, R-Colo., and Rep. J. J. Pickle, D-Texas, chairmen of the subcommittee panels that write Social Security legislation, had been quietly assembling consensus legislation to deal with the long-range financing of Social Security. Their committees were considering the Reagan proposals along with other legislative recommendations.

Congressional Reform Plans

The Senate bill Dole supported was based on a scaled-down version of the May 1981 Reagan proposals. Dole and Armstrong indicated they wanted to enact legislation in 1981 that would address both the long- and short-term problems of the Social Security system. While accepting the Reagan plan as a foundation for markups, Dole attempted to get broad support for his reform package by eliminating the most controversial of the Reagan proposals, including the immediate curtailment of benefits for retirement before age 65.

In the House Pickle, who had consistently emphasized the immediacy of the Social Security financial crisis, had begun markup of a bill (HR 3207) to address Social Security's short- as well as long-term financial difficulties even before the Reagan proposals were announced. His subcommittee had been holding hearings on the Social Security issue since 1980.

As introduced HR 3207 would overhaul the Social Security system but in a less drastic way than the administration's proposals. It would gradually raise the retirement age to 68 by the year 2000, use general revenues to fund part of the Health Insurance trust fund and reduce benefits for those opting for early retirement.

In a floor statement on Sept. 17, Pickle made an emotional plea for comprehensive Social Security reform:

> Our choices are simple. We can hope that the economy has no downturns for the rest of the decade and we can therefore scrape by with little more than we have done now. We can enact deep cuts either all together or piece by piece through the budget process as each year the fund is in trouble once again. Or we can go ahead and shore up the Social Security reserves with general funds for the short term and let the public have some piece of mind on this issue.

Action Postponed

Hopes for passage of a long-term solution to Social Security's financing problems, already dim, were practically extinguished Sept. 24. During the day, the Senate Finance Committee was unable to reach agreement on a comprehensive reform package and instead approved a short-term funding measure that would tide the system over through the mid-1980s.

That evening in a nationally televised speech President Reagan endorsed stopgap legislation similar to the Finance Committee measure. In apparent recognition of his political miscalculation in proposing major Social Security cutbacks in May, the president stressed that he would not make any additional cuts in the Social Security program beyond those he had already submitted to Congress. David Gergen, White House communications director, indicated that Reagan had conceded that chances for enactment of those benefits cutbacks were not good. *(Speech text, p. 209)*

Reagan also asked Congress to form a bipartisan task force — with five members appointed by the House Speaker, five by the Senate majority leader and five by the president himself — to develop by January 1983 a plan to address the long-term "pending insolvency" of the Old Age and Survivors Insurance trust fund.

Significantly, the president, reversing his earlier position, asked Congress to restore the monthly minimum Social Security benefit to lower-income beneficiaries. And Reagan voiced support for a stopgap answer to financing problems by proposing temporary interfund borrowing, "to ensure that checks can continue to be issued for the next several years."

With any realistic chance for passage of major Social Security reform legislation scotched, the Senate went ahead with its stopgap measure. The measure, passed by a 95-0 vote Oct. 15, virtually assured the restoration of some form of the Social Security minimum monthly benefit and at least a short-term solution to any impending crisis.

The Senate measure would permanently reallocate payroll taxes from the healthier Disability Insurance trust fund to the OASI fund. It also would reallocate taxes designated for the Health Insurance trust fund to OASI through 1984. And it would allow OASI to borrow funds from the DI fund through 1990 if the payroll tax reallocations proved insufficient to keep the OASI fund afloat.

The Senate bill also would restore the minimum benefit for all 3 million current beneficiaries except about 300,000 recipients who were living overseas or had government pensions over $300 month. Members of religious orders could continue to start receiving the minimum payment for the next 10 years. Restoration of the benefit was expected to cost the Social Security trust fund $4.5 billion for fiscal 1982-86.

To offset the costs of restoring the minimum benefits, the Senate agreed to apply the payroll tax to the first six months of sick pay; such pay was exempt under existing law. It also lowered the maximum family retirement and survivor benefit to 150 percent of the worker's primary insurance amount. Existing law permitted such benefits to go as high as 188 percent.

The bill then went to conference with the House, which had voted July 31 to restore the $122 minimum monthly payment for all current and future recipients. The House, however, had made no provisions for the short-term health of the system. Nor had it offset the costs of restoring the benefit guarantee. A spokesman for House Speaker O'Neill said the House would continue to push for full restoration. However, the Ways and Means Social Security Subcommittee earlier had recommended elimination of the minimum benefit for future recipients.

On Nov. 4, the same day the House voted to go to conference with the Senate on restoration of the minimum benefits, the House Ways and Means Committee rejected Pickle's reform proposals by an 18-14 vote.

After a month-long conference impasse, Congress agreed to restore the minimum benefit and to patch up the financially troubled retirement system through the end of 1982.

The Senate adopted the conference report December 15 by a 96-0 vote; the House approved it the following day. The final package restored the minimum benefit payment for all three million recipients who already were entitled to receive it but eliminated the benefit for those who became eligible for Social Security after Dec. 31, 1981. To offset part of the cost, Congress agreed to extend the 6.7 percent payroll tax to the first six months of all sick pay, beginning in 1982.

The bill also allowed the financially troubled Old Age and Survivor's Insurance (OASI) trust fund to borrow from the two other, somewhat healthier trust funds. However that provision was only in effect through the end of 1982, which would force Congress to address the sticky issue of Social Security's funding problems again in 1982.

By that time, the Health Insurance trust fund could be in trouble. The Social Security Administration Oct. 21 released updated figures showing that 1981 outlays for that trust fund were $1.1 billion higher than anticipated and therefore could run out sooner than expected.

Policy makers maintain that if Congress does not resolve the short-term problems, they will intensify the anticipated long-term troubles so that even more drastic measures will be needed to save the system from bankruptcy. "I don't know if Congress has the will to make the tough decisions," said Rep. Pickle. "I hope we do the right thing, but I know we have to recognize the world of realities," he added.

7

Side Effects of 'Reaganomics'

Congressional approval of President Ronald Reagan's first round of tax and budget cuts may have shifted the nation toward the supply-side economic philosophy that the president endorsed. While it remained to be seen whether that economic theory would encourage the savings and investment — and the consequent productivity — that its proponents claimed it would, it was already clear that the massive spending and tax cuts would have a substantial impact on several segments of the American public as well as on the relationship between the federal government and the states.

Spending cuts in a series of domestic programs meant that many poor Americans would have to seek help outside the federal government or go without. A natural place for them to turn was to state and local governments. But they too were affected by the budget cuts. At the same time that the Reagan government wanted to return responsibility for many programs to the states, it was cutting back the amount of federal funding channeled to the states. Thus it was unclear whether the states would have the ability to fill the gaps left by eliminations of and cutbacks in federal programs. Meanwhile enactment of Reagan's tax cuts, and his reluctance to increase taxes, meant that further spending cuts were the only way to keep the still mounting federal budget deficit under control.

Budget Cuts

The spending cuts — contained in a massive Omnibus Budget Reconciliation Act (PL 97-35) — slashed nearly $35.2 billion from a fiscal 1982 spending level projected at the time the cuts were enacted to be approximately $740 billion. The budget reductions came largely from domestic social programs and were expected to have their greatest and most immediate affect on the poor and low-income workers. (Reconciliation details, p. 131)

Congress did not give the president everything he wanted. The final bill contained more funding than Reagan had sought for the Export-Import Bank and several other programs. And Congress refused to place an administration-requested "cap" on federal contributions to the states for Medicaid or to create some of the block grants Reagan wanted. The president had called for consolidation of 84 health, education and social service categorical aid programs into six block grant programs.

However, such disappointments were insignificant compared to the overall accomplishment represented by the reconciliation measure — a major change in the direction of government and an abrupt slowdown in the growth of federal spending.

Impact on the Poor

Presenting his economic proposals to the nation Feb. 5, 1981, Reagan said the budget cuts were necessary if the nation was to avoid "an economic calamity of tremendous proportions." At the same time, Reagan stressed that the spending cuts "will not be at the expense of the truly needy.... We can, with compassion, continue to meet our responsibility to those who ... need our help."

The administration said its spending reductions were designed to protect the poor by means of a "safety net" of federal programs spared from cuts. Those seven programs, ranging from Social Security retirement payments to summer jobs for teen-agers, cost about $200 million a year. Administration officials also argued that the proposed changes in such programs as welfare and food stamps would encourage people to work and become self-sufficient.

But studies by the Congressional Budget Office (CBO), the University of Chicago's Center for the Study of Welfare Policy and the Field Foundation's Project on Food Assistance and Poverty attacked both of the administration contentions even before the first budget cuts were enacted. And it appeared that even if the Reagan administration theories proved true in practice, millions of the poor and low-wage earners would lose significant federal benefits during the transition.

According to the Project on Food Assistance and Poverty, most of the safety net programs served mainly middle-income people. Only 21 percent of the benefits went to people with incomes below the poverty line. By contrast, 17 major programs for the poor were targeted for $25 billion in cuts. CBO estimated that up to 25 million people, most of them poor, would lose some benefits because of cuts in just four of those programs: welfare, food stamps, public service jobs and school lunches.

States Feel the Pinch

The budget cuts also made the Reagan administration's "new federalism" something of a double-edged sword for state and local governments. Following through on a long-held belief that states and cities could more wisely and efficiently handle programs affecting their citizens, Reagan proposed transferring power from the federal government back to the states, chiefly through block grants that would enable them to use certain federal funds as they — not Washington — saw fit.

But the administration's budget also reflected the second part of Reagan's philosophy: that the federal government should not be in the business of guaranteeing the incomes and taking care of all the needs of the poor.

Thus, under Reagan's new federalism, the states would have much more flexibility in spending allocated federal dollars. But they would have fewer dollars to spend and in some cases more responsibilities to fulfill, or not fulfill, as they saw fit.

The states found themselves in a bind. For years they themselves had been asking for that kind of flexibility. They had said they were willing to accept 10 percent reductions in federal grant funds in return for grant consolidation and simplification. But at the same time, the states had pushed for the federal government to assume the full burden for welfare and other income maintenance programs.

An analysis by the U.S. Conference of Mayors concluded that 66 percent of the proposed fiscal 1982 cuts in budget authority would come from city and state programs. And the National Governors' Association concluded that the Reagan administration's budget decisions presaged "a substantial cutback on the federal involvement in intergovernmental domestic programs in both the near and long term."

A survey by Congressional Quarterly indicated that the financial position of about half of the states would make accepting new responsibilities difficult. These states, many of them in the East and Midwest, were tightening their belts even before they began to feel the impact of the federal cuts in October.

The energy-rich states of the West and Upper Midwest, on the other hand, were in good financial health, supported by heavy taxes on oil, coal and other natural resources. Those states would have an easier time absorbing the Reagan budget cuts.

Most of the poor states' difficulties were a product of the nation's economic downturn. Rising unemployment and industry cutbacks sliced into tax collections, while inflation increased state expenditures.

In some cases, however, taxpayers had brought on the difficulties. In November 1980, Massachusetts voters passed "Proposition 2-1/2," which limited property taxes to 2-1/2 percent of actual property values. Cities and towns lost an estimated $483 million in local revenues. Similar problems faced California, which in 1981 felt for the first time the full impact of Proposition 13, passed by voters in 1978. Previously a budget surplus had cushioned the impact of the cuts, but that had been exhausted by 1981. Moreover, California had to deal with an estimated $700 million in federal budget cuts.

The states acknowledged that the administration designed its budget cuts, for the most part, so that states and local governments would not be forced to pick up where the federal government left off. Instead they would be able simply to pass on the reductions to the programs' beneficiaries — such as food stamp and Medicaid recipients — provided Congress agreed to give them the necessary administrative flexibility.

Tax Cut

At the same time that it made large cuts in federal program spending, Congress enacted legislation giving American wage earners and businesses the largest tax reduction in history. A number of lawmakers expressed fears that the tax reductions, especially those slated for 1983 and beyond would contribute to the budget deficit and necessitate even further cuts in domestic programs such as food stamps, health services and school lunches. Still others were concerned by some of the side effects of the new law.

Designed to provide a wide variety of incentives for savings and investment by both individuals and businesses, and thus stimulate productivity and economic growth, the tax cut reversed more than a decade of tax reform efforts.

In previous years, Congress had used tax cut legislation as an opportunity to enact reforms in the tax system. Since 1969 those reforms primarily benefited workers at the lower end of the economic scale. The Reagan tax cut gave most of its benefits to businesses and to individual taxpayers at the upper end of the income scale.

Democrats in particular criticized the bill, arguing that the individual reductions should have been targeted toward the poor and middle-income Americans. "[Y]ou...left out a lot of people. Where in your plan will the poor be beneficiaries?" Rep. Charles B. Rangel, D-N.Y., asked John E. Chapoton, Treasury's assistant secretary for tax policy, during the House Ways and Means Committee's markup of the bill in June. Rangel's criticism was echoed in the Senate by Bill Bradley, D-N.J., who introduced unsuccessful amendments to focus individual rate cuts toward the middle- and lower-income classes.

An even more important change in the tax bill, however, might prove to be its provisions for automatically adjusting or "indexing" income taxes to offset inflation. Beginning Jan. 1, 1985, as consumer prices rose, so would the standard tax deduction, the personal exemption and both ends of each tax bracket.

Conservatives who supported the measure argued that indexing tax rates would end unlegislated increases in both taxes and revenues and would automatically limit government spending. Some liberals who favored the measure said that without indexing, lower income taxpayers would continue to be hit hardest by the "tax bracket creep" accompanying rising wages.

But critics charged that indexing would lock the federal government into a system of either perpetual budget deficits or painful spending cuts and would prevent Congress from reforming the tax system through periodic tax reductions.

SPENDING CUTS MEAN LOSSES FOR POOR

While millions of working Americans saw evidence of the tax cuts in their October paychecks, millions of low-income — and some middle-income — Americans began to feel the pinch of the spending cuts in social programs approved by Congress in July.

Even as President Reagan went on television to announce his proposals for a new round of cuts, beneficiaries of federal assistance programs were bracing for the impact of the budget reconciliation bill (HR 3982 — PL 97-35) already enacted.

That legislation went into effect Oct. 1, and as a result:

• Nearly 700,000 families lost all or part of their welfare benefits.

• Food stamps were taken away from 1.1 million recipients.

• School lunch prices were higher, and meals smaller.

• An extra 13 weeks of benefits were denied to 1.5 million unemployed workers, and 900,000 people who would have had public service jobs or job training positions did not get them.

• Hundreds of other changes were to be made in programs affecting the poor. *(Details of cuts, chart, p. 102)*

The legislation revised federal programs to slash nearly $35.2 billion from a projected fiscal 1982 spending level of approximately $740 billion. About $25 billion in cuts — some 70 percent of the budget savings achieved by the entire reconciliation bill — were made in programs affecting the poor. The Census Bureau said nearly 30 million persons in the United States lived on incomes at or below the poverty level.

Just how severely the cuts made by the reconciliation bill would affect those people was a subject of dispute. The Reagan administration, which pushed for the cuts, denied that the "truly needy" would suffer. But critics of the reconciliation changes, such as Tom Joe of the Center for the Study of Welfare Policy, warned that the cuts would deprive the poor of the basic necessities of life. "They're going to eat less and get fewer clothes," he said.

The 'Safety Net'

Reagan repeatedly stressed his determination to protect people who could not help being poor — those who "rely on government for their very existence" — from being left destitute. The safety net programs, as contained in his March 10 budget, and their fiscal 1981 budget authority were:

• Old Age and Survivors Insurance, the core Social Security program, $119.8 billion.

• Medicare health insurance, $44.9 billion.

• Veterans' pension and compensation benefits, $13.3 billion.

• Supplemental Security Income (SSI) for the aged, blind and disabled, $7.3 billion.

• Head Start preschool education, $1.1 billion.

• Summer jobs for disadvantaged youths, $800 million.

• Free school lunches and breakfasts, $2.2 billion.

The first three programs, which made up more than 90 percent of the spending for the seven, did form a safety net protecting large numbers from destitution. But it was a safety net for the elderly, not for the poor.

With their massive numbers of recipients — 31.3 million for Social Security, 28 million for Medicare, 4.6 million for veterans' pensions and compensation — the three programs lifted many elderly people out of poverty. According to a study by former Congressional Budget Office (CBO) analyst G. William Hoagland, Social Security alone reduced the incidence of poverty among white men aged 65 and over to 6 percent, from 46 percent without the benefits.

But those three programs were not targeted to the poor. The Project on Food Assistance and Poverty estimated that 85 percent of their recipients had incomes above the poverty level.

The other four programs were limited to poor people. However, their funding levels were only a small fraction — one-seventeenth — of the total for the three programs for the elderly. Overall, the safety net programs provided little help to much of the poverty population. The food project study estimated that 16 million poor people — 64 percent of America's estimated 25 million poor (the Census Bureau's count) — either received no help at all from the programs or got only a free school meal.

"The safety net is working," said Edwin L. Dale Jr., spokesman for the Office of Management and Budget, in September 1981. Despite administration assurances that the safety net was working, two immediate problems faced those who relied on government help in 1982. First, there was the question of funding for the food stamp program. Although it was not on Reagan's list of safety net programs, food stamps were expected to be a vital source of income for people who lost benefits from other programs.

But congressional spending limits on food stamps — $10.9 billion in the Senate and $11.3 billion in the House — were below the Congressional Budget Office's (CBO) $11.7 billion estimate of what the program would actually cost in fiscal 1982. The Senate passed its food stamp bill (S 1007) in June; the House version was contained in the omnibus farm bill (HR 3603), passed in October.

Second, the complex changes in welfare rules were causing confusion at the local level even before the new fiscal year began and could result in lengthy delays in receiving benefits. "They [Congress and the Department of Health and Human Services] have required states to make a huge number of changes on an impossible timetable. It's going to be a calamity for the next six months. People are going to find it very difficult to get onto the program," predicted Henry Freedman of the Center on Social Welfare Policy and the Law.

In the first few months of fisal 1982, the states, which operated most of the assistance programs, would have to deal with the federal spending cuts. While some states were in good financial condition and could make up the difference with their own funds, others were strapped for funds and would likely reduce services. Definite estimates of the effects of some of the cuts were impossible until states decided what to do. *(State finances, box, p. 106)*

The Working Poor

Very poor people who were totally dependent on welfare programs probably would be spared major losses under the budget cuts. But the "working poor," who had low-paying jobs as well as welfare benefits, faced severe reductions under the new law. In some states, CBO estimated, working welfare mothers would end up with incomes no higher than those who did not work. Furthermore, some welfare recipients would be required to work at community service jobs to "pay" for their benefits.

This new relationship between welfare, primarily Aid to Families with Dependent Children (AFDC), and unemployment reflected Reagan administration philosophy. "I just don't accept the assumption that the federal government has a responsibility to supplement the income of the working poor through a whole series of transfer payments," Office of Management and Budget Director David A. Stockman said on ABC News' "Issues and Answers." "We believe that the guy who takes two jobs and makes $26,000 a year shouldn't be obligated to transfer part of his income and taxes to the guy who's making $10,000," he said.

Hard to Count Overlapping Benefits

Estimates of the effects of budget cuts on individual programs did not give an accurate picture of the loss of income to the poor because many people received benefits from more than one program.

No one really knew how many poor people participated in more than one program. Because of the lack of information about "overlapping" benefits, some poverty experts, such as Tim Smeeding of the Census Bureau, said it was virtually impossible to develop good estimates of the aggregate effects of the cuts on the poor.

For some people, the combined loss of benefits from different programs could produce a devastating loss of income. For others, the loss in one program might be mitigated by a benefit increase from another.

For example, someone who lost his Comprehensive Employment and Training Act (CETA) job would be eligible for unemployment compensation benefits. A cut in Aid to Families with Dependent Children (AFDC) benefits might lead to an increase in food stamps.

When Congress considered the fiscal 1982 budget cuts, the federal government was only beginning to collect accurate data on overlapping benefits. One study, done for the Food and Nutrition Service by Morey MacDonald of the University of Wisconsin's Institute for Research on Poverty, found that food stamp recipients participated heavily in other programs. About half received AFDC; another third were aged and disabled recipients of Social Security or Supplemental Security Income (SSI).

A more comprehensive survey by the Social Security Administration also indicated a high degree of overlap among five programs: Social Security, SSI, AFDC, unemployment compensation and food stamps.

The survey found that 83 percent of households receiving food stamps or SSI, and 77 percent of households on AFDC, got a benefit from at least one of the other programs; 3,000 households received aid from all five programs.

The study did not include other major program overlaps. For example, all AFDC and SSI recipients received Medicaid, and virtually all school-age AFDC children got free lunches at school.

Joe and other welfare experts feared that the reconciliation bill's elimination of federal "work incentives" would discourage welfare recipients from trying to get jobs. (Federal work incentives allowed welfare recipients to retain a large part of their welfare payments, even if they had income from jobs.) But Michael de Marr, acting director for policy of the Department of Health and Human Services' Office of Family Assistance, said the work incentives actually had not increased the percentage of welfare recipients who worked.

Increasing Poverty

The cuts in anti-poverty programs came at a time when the number of poor people in the United States was growing. The Census Bureau said that in 1980, 29.3 million persons — 13 percent of the population — were living below the poverty level: $8,414 for a non-farm family of four. In 1979 the poverty rate was 11.7 percent — 26.1 million poor people.

That spread of poverty would continue through at least the first half of the 1980s, predicted Sheldon Danzinger of the University of Wisconsin's Institute for Poverty Research. "As people have looked in the past for income transfers that will keep them out of poverty, now they're going to look and not find them. Between now and 1985, poverty will increase," he said.

Future spending cuts, particularly if they involved significant reductions in Social Security, could have an even greater impact on the poor. Social Security protected far more people against poverty than any other program. Speculating on promised future budget cuts, Robert Greenstein of the Project on Food Assistance and Poverty said, "What's to come will be far more excruciating than what has already been done. With each succeeding cut, it hurts more and more. In virtually every program, the first billion cut doesn't hurt nearly as much as the second."

Effects of Cuts

CBO, the various federal departments and lobby groups studied the effects of the spending cuts mandated by the reconciliation bill. The following summary uses estimates based on that law only; it does not take into account any future spending reductions.

AFDC. Cuts in the core welfare program, Aid to Families with Dependent Children (AFDC), would fall most heavily on recipient households that had earned income. The Department of Health and Human Services (HHS) estimated that 687,000 of the 3.9 million households receiving AFDC benefits in fiscal 1981 would be hurt by the reconciliation bill; 408,000 would be thrown off the program in fiscal 1982 and 279,000 would receive reduced benefits. Most of the people who would lose benefits had incomes over the poverty line, argued HHS policy analyst Rick Kasten.

CBO had not done an overall analysis of the AFDC cuts, although one study examined the impact of AFDC, food stamp, housing and Medicaid cuts on sample households in different states. The study was based on the original Reagan administration budget proposals but also applied to the reconciliation changes. It found that:

● Households with earnings would lose more than households without earnings.

● Households in states with low benefit levels would lose a larger share of their incomes than those in states with high benefit levels.

● After elimination of federal work incentives, households with low earnings would have no more money than those with no earnings at all.

CBO also predicted major benefit losses for recipients in states that chose to consider food stamps and housing subsidies as income. The reconciliation bill allowed states to do so, but it was not known how many would.

The reconciliation bill also lowered the limit on the assets of welfare households to $1,000 in equity, from $2,000 in market value. If states strictly enforced that provision, the number of households losing benefits could be enormous. However, HHS estimated only a small effect, with a $16 million savings.

Similarly, states would have the option of requiring recipients to work in exchange for their benefits. Several states had expressed interest in the idea, but HHS did not know how many would proceed with it.

Food Stamps. An estimated 1.1 million of the 22.6 million people receiving food stamps lost their stamps entirely under the reconciliation bill; virtually all the rest found their stamps providing less help against rising food costs. The biggest group of people losing all their benefits, according to the Agriculture Department's Food and Nutrition Service (FNS), was the 295,000 households (at an average of three persons each) with incomes over 130 percent of the poverty level. In addition, 145,000 people who lived in boarding houses were dropped from the program, as were some 25,000 households with a member on strike.

The reconciliation bill also required a three-month delay in the inflation adjustment of benefits. That would cost a typical family of four $23 a month for three months. In addition, a delay in the inflation updating of deductions would cost each family an average of $4.50 a month.

The biggest single food stamp savings, according to Agriculture Department estimates, was expected to come from reducing benefits to people during their first month on the program. However, FNS said it did not know how many people signed up for the program in any given month and so could not tell how many people would be affected.

Medicaid. Recipients of Medicaid, the state-federal health care program for the poor, lost some of their freedom to choose their own doctors. But — at least in the short run — they were expected to escape major additional losses in health services under the reconciliation spending cuts.

According to George Washington University's Intergovernment Health Policy Project, states earlier in 1981 were already moving to scale back their Medicaid services because of economic conditions. How they would respond to the reconciliation bill's cut in federal contributions to their programs was not clear.

Groups such as the National Governors' Association were hopeful, however, that other reconciliation provisions would help states avoid further service reductions. The bill gave states freedom to try new ways to hold down the cost of their programs.

To cite one example, Michigan was already considering restricting recipients' "freedom of choice" in selecting physicians, according to state Medicaid expert Vern Smith. Under the proposal, recipients who in the past had visited many different doctors would be assigned one primary physician. That physician would determine any referrals for the patient.

Housing. Fewer new federally subsidized dwellings would be available for the poor and poor people who already lived in subsidized housing would have to pay a bigger share of their income as rent as a result of the reconciliation measure.

The bill limited construction of new public housing to 153,000 units — more than 100,000 units fewer than requested by the Carter administration. According to the National Low-Income Housing Coalition, that would make the search for affordable housing much harder for the poor, since half a million low-income housing units disappeared each year because of rent inflation, condominium conversion and abandonment.

Residents of subsidized housing had been paying 25 percent of their income for rent. Under the new law, their rent would rise to 26 percent in 1982; the amount would go up one point each year until it reached 30 percent.

Jobs, Job Training. Nearly a million people who would have had Comprehensive Employment and Training Act (CETA) jobs or job training positions in fiscal 1982 would have to look for other jobs. The Labor Department estimated that the spending limits in the reconciliation bill would fund CETA positions for 900,000 fewer people than in 1981.

A major part of the reduction was due to the elimination of the CETA public service employment program. There were 306,173 people holding public service jobs on Feb. 28, 1981; by Oct. 1 there were none. The Labor Department estimated in September that it had found unsubsidized jobs for less than half (43.8 percent) of those workers.

School Lunches. The 26 million children who got federally subsidized lunches at school were faced with higher prices, smaller portions and possibly even closed cafeterias. Children from families with incomes below $10,990 a year (for a family of four) continued to receive free lunches. However, schools would be allowed to serve smaller meals, which meant that for some nutrients, the lunches provided one-fourth, rather than one-third, of the children's daily needs.

Children from families with slightly higher incomes (between $10,990 and $15,630 for a family of four) had to pay 40 cents for reduced-price meals, up from 20 cents. Middle-income children (those from families of four with incomes over $15,630) at the least would have to make up the reconciliation bill's 11-cent cut in the basic school lunch subsidy, said George Braley of the FNS. The average lunch price in the 1980-81 school year was 60 cents.

About 500,000 students who had been getting free meals would have to pay 40 cents a day in fiscal 1982; 450,000 who had been paying 20 cents a meal would have to pay 75 cents or more. And the American School Food Service Association worried that the subsidy cuts would cause some schools to close their programs altogether, leaving many poor children without lunch.

College Student Aid. College students from families with incomes over $15,000 a year faced the loss of their Pell grants in the 1982-83 school year, according to CBO. The basic form of federal aid to college students, Pell grants were funded in advance, so the 1982 spending cuts would not be felt until September 1982.

Major Cuts in Programs for the Poor ...

Program, Number of participants before budget cuts *(latest available figures)*	Description of program	Fiscal 1982 baseline*	Fiscal 1982 cuts	How principal savings achieved
		(in billions of dollars)		
Compensatory Education (5.2 million)	Funds to school districts educating children from low-income families.	$ 4	−$ .4	Spending limited to $3.48 billion, but program was not included in Reagan-backed block grant.
Pell Grants (2.6 million)	Grants to low- and middle-income college students; pays up to one-half of educational costs.	$ 3.2	−$ .5	Spending limited to $2.65 billion. Education Department to determine how to reduce program costs.
CETA Public Service Jobs (822,000)	Grants to state and local governments to provide jobs to low-income unemployed.	$ 3.8	−$ 3.8	Program eliminated.
CETA Job Training and Youth Programs (2.8 million)	Grants to state and local governments to provide job training to low-income youths and unemployed.	$ 2.6	−$ .6	Spending for job training limited to $1.43 billion. Youth employment and training capped at $576.2 million.
Medicaid (18.3 million)	State-federal program to pay for medical care for the poor.	$18.5	−$ 1.1	Federal payments to states reduced; however, the Reagan-backed cap on contributions to states was not imposed.
Housing Assistance (2.4 million units)	Rent subsidies for low-income families; aid to public housing projects.	$28.6	−$11.6	Number of new subsidized housing units cut; higher rental contribution from tenants required.
Food Stamps (22.6 million)	Coupons, good for food purchase, issued to low-income households.	$12.3	−$ 1.7	Income eligibility limited; inflation adjustment delayed; benefits to working poor reduced.
Supplemental Feeding for Women, Infants and Children (WIC) (2.2 million)	Food packages provided to low-income mothers and children deemed to be at "nutritional risk."	$ 1	+$ .02	Spending not cut, but limited to $1.017 billion.
School Feeding Programs (26 million)	Subsidies for school meals; additional subsidies for children from low-income families.	$ 4.5	−$ 1.4	Federal subsidies for school meals cut; income eligibility limited; special milk program eliminated; summer feeding program restricted.

... Required by Reconciliation Bill

Program, Number of participants before budget cuts (latest available figures)	Description of program	Fiscal 1982 baseline* (in billions of dollars)	Fiscal 1982 cuts (in billions of dollars)	How principal savings achieved
Aid to Families with Dependent Children (AFDC) (11.1 million)	Matching grants to state programs of cash support to low-income families with children.	$ 6.6	−$ 1.2	Benefits to working recipients reduced; states allowed to establish "workfare" programs.
Energy Assistance (11.7 million households)	Grants to states for distribution to welfare recipients and other low-income persons for help with energy bills.	$ 2.2	−$ .4	Spending limited to $1.875 billion. Program converted into block grant.
Supplemental Security Income (SS1) (4.2 million)	Cash grants to low-income aged, blind or disabled persons; benefits supplemented by states.	$ 7.8	−$ .05	Accounting methods tightened.
Unemployment Insurance (3 million)	Federal-state insurance program providing 26 weeks of benefits to the unemployed; extended benefits available for an additional 13 weeks under certain conditions.	$21	−$ .2	Nationwide extended benefits program eliminated; restrictions placed on conditions under which states can provide extended benefits.
Title XX Social Services	Grants to states for providing services such as day care, foster care and family planning.	$ 3.1	−$ .7	Spending limited to $2.4 billion; program not included in Reagan-backed block grants.
Legal Services (1.5 million)	Grants to local legal aid clinics providing assistance to low-income persons in civil cases.	$ .34	?	Program not included in Reagan-backed block grant; funding to be set by separate legislation.
Community Services Administration	Grants to local community action agencies for social services to low-income persons.	$ .59	−$ .2	Agency abolished; program converted into separate block grant, authorized at $389.4 million.
Social Security Minimum Benefit (3 million)	Ensures that Social Security recipients receive at least $122 a month, regardless of past earnings.	—	−$ .7	Provision eliminated; however Congress had taken steps to restore the benefit.

*The baseline is, generally, the Congressional Budget Office's projection of the amount needed to maintain existing program level in fiscal 1982, based on 1981 spending level adjusted for inflation.

Source of figures: Congressional Budget Office

Students from poorer families would be somewhat protected. Those with family incomes of less than $8,000 a year who received the maximum individual grants probably would get around $1,670, as they did for the 1981-82 school year.

The only students who might benefit from the reconciliation changes were those from families making between $8,000 and $12,000. The formula being worked out by the Education Department for the 1982-83 school year would provide slightly larger grants to those students, CBO predicted.

As the president requested, the final version of the legislation established a "needs test" limiting guaranteed student loans for individual students to the difference between a student's educational costs (tuition, room and board and other expenses) and his financial resources (other forms of student aid plus the expected parental contribution). However, the new test applied only to students from families with incomes over $30,000 a year; the administration had wanted to apply the test to all students.

Social Security. Some 1.3 million people were slated to lose income because of the elimination of the Social Security minimum benefit provision, according to CBO. However, Congress reconsidered its action. In July, the House voted to restore the $122 minimum monthly payment for all current and future recipients, and the Senate passed its version of a restoration in October. Action came after the benefit cut drew intensely hostile public reaction. A House-Senate conference worked out the differences in the two bills and the final version was approved before Congress adjourned for 1981.

Although not strictly a program for the poor, the minimum benefit had gone disproportionately to elderly women, who were more likely to be poor than other Social Security recipients. There was no way to tell how many of the people who would have lost the benefit were poor, CBO said. Of the total, 360,000 had pensions from jobs not covered by Social Security, and about half a million had substantial assets or income from other sources, according to CBO.

Unemployment Compensation. An estimated 1.5 million people lost their extended unemployment benefits under the reconciliation bill, the Labor Department predicted. Under existing law, some 2.6 million people in all states would have received 13 weeks of extended benefits, supplementing their 26 weeks of regular benefits. The reconciliation bill reduced that to 1.1 million in 36 states. The bill cut off extended benefits even in states, such as Michigan, that were experiencing severe unemployment. There were about 46,000 people receiving extended benefits in Michigan in September; their benefits stopped Oct. 1.

Services to the Poor. The reconciliation bill also cut a number of programs that provided services to the poor. Predictions about the effects were difficult because the programs were run by state and local governments that had not yet decided what to do.

The major service programs for the poor were compensatory education; supplemental feeding for women, infants and children (WIC); energy assistance; and social, legal, community and child welfare services. Only WIC and child welfare escaped cuts in reconciliation; legal service funding had not been determined by mid-November 1981.

In addition to reducing funding, the reconciliation bill loosened the strings of federal control over the programs. In the Title I program of compensatory education for low-income children, for example, school officials were freed from "unnecessary" federal supervision. Robert Silverstein, a lawyer who studied Title I for the National Institute of Education, predicted the bill also would let school officials change the focus of the program from the poor to general aid to education.

Similarly, the bill eliminated the requirement that state social service programs financed by Title XX of the Social Security Act be focused on low-income people. Greenstein of the Project on Food Assistance and Poverty said he feared states might direct funds toward politically powerful groups of people who were not necessarily poor, such as the elderly, and reduce help for low-income families.

STATES AND CITIES ASSESS BUDGET CUTS

Under Reagan's economic plan, states, cities and counties had new responsibility for deciding whether to fill the void in government services left by federal budget cuts. Their authority to control some programs had been increased by the enactment of new block grant programs, although not as much as Reagan would have liked. But the reconciliation act trimmed fiscal 1982 federal aid to states and localities by most of what Reagan asked for, about $7 billion below the 1981 level of $95.1 billion. And the president later called for $13 billion in additional spending cuts.

States also stood to lose more than $2 billion in tax revenues and higher borrowing costs because of Reagan's federal tax cut. The combined squeeze was clamped on state and local budgets that already were relatively tight. As of November 1981, there had been no concrete proposal by the administration to fulfill the other part of Reagan's dream, which was to relinquish federal tax sources, such as excise taxes on liquor or gasoline, to states and localities. And the president's intent to remove the federal government from some programs entirely was precisely the opposite of what states and localities would like to see. Many state and local officials liked the sound of the president's "new federalism" but were just finding out what it could entail in practice. They did not like much of that.

"I'm not really sure what the Reagan administration thinks about federalism, separate from what (Budget Director) Dave Stockman thinks about budget cuts," Gov. Richard Snelling of Vermont complained. Snelling, a self-described conservative Republican who headed the National Governors' Association (NGA), described meetings between administration officials and representatives of state and local governments as "pseudo-consultation." He criticized the administration for not coupling its cuts in federal aid with a pragmatic effort to sort out tangled federal, state and local responsibilities. Although he tempered his criticism with praise for Reagan's goals, his remarks resembled those of some Democrats.

Eugene Eidenberg, executive director of the Democratic National Committee and formerly the top aide for intergovernmental affairs in the Carter White House, also complained that the Reagan administration had made no systematic effort to sort out the complex federal system. "The only philosophy they've got is to make the federal government smaller," he charged.

Reagan aides countered that there was a clear philosophy underlying the administration's approach: the same opposition to the "encroaching federal establishment" that Reagan voiced consistently since he ran for governor of California in 1966. "I think it's very, very hard to argue that Ronald Reagan doesn't have a philosophy," said Richard S. Williamson, assistant to the president for intergovernmental affairs.

Reagan contended that cutting the federal budget "is only a first step toward returning power to states and communities." Even if it did seem inconsistent to cut federal aid at the same time, his aides said, it would work out in the long run as the public's willingness to support programs was tested in local political arenas. Meanwhile, they said, states and localities would have more flexibility to manage the aid they did get.

John Gunther, executive director of the U.S. Conference of Mayors, said that after meeting with Reagan he became all too aware of what the president had in mind. "I think the president's made it very clear that it's his goal to get rid of federal aid to state and local government," Gunther said.

Budget Direction

The best description of the administration's direction on federalism came from its budget for fiscal 1982, with projections for years beyond. The Reagan budget, adjusted for inflation, foresaw total federal aid to states and localities dropping by 14.8 percent from fiscal 1981 to 1982, and by 32.5 percent from 1980 to 1986.

Reagan proposed a further 12 percent cut for most aid funds, including the revenue sharing program that was the clear favorite of local officials, in fiscal 1982. There would also be further cuts in entitlement programs, which included several that took the form of grants to states. Grant programs stood to be reduced even further by additional cuts Reagan promised for future years.

Of the shrinking total of federal aid, however, the administration pledged to give a larger portion to states and localities in the form of grants with fewer federal strings. That intent was reflected in Reagan's proposal to create new block grants by combining narrow categorical aid programs that carried rigid federal requirements. Congress approved some of the block grants in the reconciliation act, but in a watered-down form that retained many strings.

The Office of Management and Budget (OMB) provided a rough measure of how much flexibility there is in federal aid. The budget is broken down to show how much of the total aid is provided in programs relatively free of federal strings, such as revenue sharing, block grants and other broad-based programs. The OMB figures showed that the portion of federal aid provided in flexible funds began to decline after fiscal 1978, when it peaked at 27.1 percent. In 1981 the flexible portion stood at 18.5 percent, and President Carter's budget for 1982 projected a further decline to 16.6 percent.

Reagan reversed that trend, mainly through block grants. His budget showed the flexible portion of federal aid rising to 22.2 percent in 1982. "He can look the governors and the mayors in the eye and say, 'You're getting fewer strings than you had before,'" observed John Shannon, assistant director of the Advisory Commission on Intergovernmental Relations (ACIR), a federal panel composed of federal, state and local officials.

But by a different measure, the discretion in state and local budgeting was being reduced. OMB also breaks down the aid total according to whether funds are passed through state and local governments to individual beneficiaries, such as in the Aid to Families with Dependent Children (AFDC), housing-subsidy and Medicaid programs. What is left of the total aid — grants that actually go to the governments as the final recipients — is used for such purposes as community development, public works, highways, mass transit, education, training and jobs programs. Many localities said they used revenue sharing, also included in the grants-to-governments category, for basic operating expenses.

In a political sense, apart from the presence or absence of administrative strings, these grants feed much of states' and localities' discretionary spending. The OMB analysis showed that in this area Reagan was accelerating a trend that began under Carter: Less and less of total federal aid was actually supplied as grants to governments. The rest was eaten up by the income transfer programs for individuals.

The governments' portion of total aid stood at 66.6 percent in fiscal 1978, and dropped to 57.8 percent in 1981.

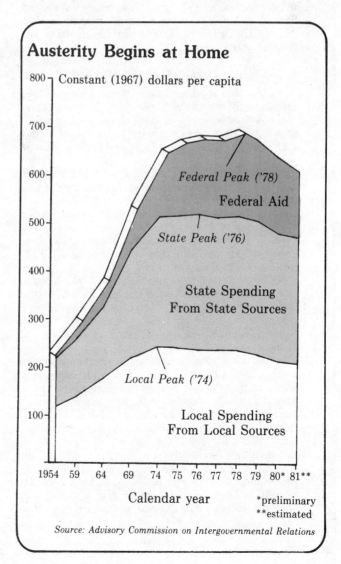

Austerity Begins at Home

800 Constant (1967) dollars per capita

Federal Peak ('78)

Federal Aid

State Peak ('76)

State Spending
From State Sources

Local Peak ('74)

Local Spending
From Local Sources

1954   59   64   69   74   75   76   77   78   79   80*   81**

Calendar year   *preliminary
                     **estimated

Source: Advisory Commission on Intergovernmental Relations

Squeeze on State and Local Finances ...

The fiscal squeeze on state and local governments did not begin with Ronald Reagan. Their own budgets, adjusted for inflation and population, started shrinking in the mid-1970s, and federal aid had been drying up since 1978. But Reagan's spending cuts were a major step in the national march toward government austerity. Because Reagan's deeper cuts in federal aid came when state and local governments already had tightened their budgets, the reductions were that much harder to cope with.

"The big message for our federal system is that Reagan is just dropping the third shoe," said John Shannon, assistant director of the Advisory Commission on Intergovernmental Relations (ACIR).

ACIR figures showed that after a long and steady growth since the mid-1950s, local governments' spending from their own sources, principally taxes, peaked in 1974 and then began to decline. States' spending from state sources peaked in 1976. The ACIR figures were adjusted for inflation and population changes.

Government Spending Decline

State and local governments were able to keep growing only because of a continuing increase in federal aid. But federal aid, in adjusted terms, stopped growing in 1978. Since then, the fiscal curve for state and local governments has been all downhill. *(Graph, p. 105)*

Total spending per capita from state and local sources, plus federal aid, peaked during calendar year 1978 at $693 in inflation-adjusted 1967 dollars, according to the ACIR figures. In 1981, the commission staff estimates, the adjusted level would be down to $608. That trend was evidence of the effects of Reagan's budget cuts. But they would not be felt fully until calendar year 1982.

Between fiscal 1981 and fiscal 1982, which began Oct. 1, 1981, Reagan's budget projected a cut — after adjusting for inflation — of 14.8 percent in total federal aid to state and local governments. The bulk of those cuts already were enacted by October, and Reagan was pressing for more.

The overall figures for federal grants masked an even deeper cut contemplated by the administration. Much of the total aid has been passed through state and local governments directly to individual beneficiaries of such programs as Medicaid or Aid to Families with Dependent Children. The Reagan projections essentially called for leveling off their growth, not turning it around.

But as the whole federal aid pie was shrinking, states and localities were projected to have a smaller portion to keep for their own programs. It was here that the Reagan administration foresaw deep, real

cuts. On top of reductions in federal aid, many state governments would have their own tax revenues reduced by the tax cut (PL 97-34) Congress passed in August 1981 because many state tax systems were linked to federal tax law.

State and local governments also suffered from stubbornly high interest rates, which raised the cost of their other primary financial source, tax-exempt borrowing. The federal tax law passed in 1981 was expected to raise those costs further.

"Taken all together, the combined federal tax and spending policies, and accompanying monetary policies, have represented a triple whammy for state and local government finances," John E. Petersen of the Government Finance Research Center, a study group sponsored by municipal finance officers, told the Joint Economic Committee Sept. 28.

States Feel Pressure

The National Governors' Association (NGA), in its annual survey of state budgets, found that 41 states spent more than they took in during fiscal 1981. For most states, the fiscal year runs from July 1 to June 30. Thirty state budgets projected that spending would outrun revenue during fiscal 1982.

All states but Vermont have legal constraints on incurring deficits in their operating funds. The difference between spending and revenue generally is made up by reducing the cash balances in the funds — much as a household checking account balance is reduced if spending exceeds deposits.

But spokesmen for the governors warned that that reservoir, intended to smooth state cash flows, was dangerously low. According to the NGA survey, the states' total operating balances stood at 6 percent of expenditures at year's end in fiscal 1977, 8.6 percent in 1978, 8.7 percent in 1979, and 9 percent in 1980. By the end of fiscal 1981, the survey said, the figure plunged to 3.3 percent, and it was projected to drop to 1.5 percent in 1982.

The operating budgets covered by the survey generally do not include federal aid, and the survey was taken in the spring of 1981, before the full impact of the federal budget and tax changes was known.

The NGA did find, however, that governors were not planning to increase spending significantly to make up for the loss of federal funds or services. In fact, the survey report said, governors generally had budgeted spending to grow less rapidly than revenue, to build their operating balances up again.

Tax Cut Impact

State revenue was expected to suffer from the effect of the new federal tax act, however, which put

... Did Not Begin With President Reagan

an immediate squeeze on these budgets. In a separate report, the NGA estimated the federal tax changes would cost the states $2.3 billion in corporate tax revenue and higher borrowing costs during 1982.

Another study by Citizens for Tax Justice, a research organization sponsored by labor unions and public interest groups, estimated that the new law's liberalized depreciation rules for business — if matched by the states — would cost them $1.6 billion in 1982.

The total tax loss for the states could be $27.5 billion through 1986, the study said. That figure was based on the assumption that all 45 states with income taxes, plus the District of Columbia, matched the federal law's treatment of business depreciation. Twenty-five states' tax laws are tied automatically to the federal depreciation rules. The study said that in these states alone the tax loss would total more than $15 billion through 1986.

There were signs that states were starting to increase taxes, after several years of net cuts. A study by the Tax Foundation, an independent research group of businesses and individuals, counted tax increases totaling $2.5 billion a year passed by state legislatures during 1981.

But the states avoided significant increases in the potentially lucrative personal or corporate income taxes. Taxes that were raised significantly included sales taxes, the biggest single category of increases, as well as fuel levies raised to compensate for declining usage. States traditionally have been loath to raise taxes levied on business, since they compete among themselves for new commercial and industrial development.

Interest Rates

In addition to the tax squeeze, budget officers feared that their interest costs would be driven up by the 1981-created tax-exempt All Savers' certificates offered by banks and savings and loan institutions, which could siphon away money that might have been used to purchase state and local governments' tax-exempt bonds. And the reduction in federal tax rates tended to make all such tax shelters less attractive to investors.

State and local governments also suffered disproportionately as overall interest rates climbed. Peter C. Trent, chairman of the Public Securities Association, estimated that each percentage point in higher interest rates cost state and local governments $500 million a year.

Not only have rates in the tax-exempt market risen along with general interest rates, but the tax-exempt rates have climbed closer to the rates on taxable issues. Tax-exempt bond rates reached 13 to 14 percent in 1981, nearly 80 percent of the rates charged for long-term corporate bonds. The historical level has been 70 to 75.

Regional Differences

All the bleak statistics on states and localities obscure significant differences among regions. Some areas, especially those with energy resources to tax, are relatively rich.

"If it weren't for the big central cities and the Midwest, and this recession they're having out there right now, you could clearly make a case that the feds are feeling more pressure than the states," said Shannon of the ACIR.

States vary widely not only in per capita income to which many federal aid formulas are indexed but also in the strength of their overall tax bases.

An experimental method developed by the ACIR staff to measure each state's total tax base shows that in 1979 the tax bases varied from 71 percent of the national average in Mississippi to 215 percent in Alaska.

A related index estimating states' tax effort — how much of their theoretical tax base they actually tapped — showed that tax efforts varied from 63 percent of the national average in Texas to 172 percent in New York.

The situation is further complicated when these indexes are compared to similar measurements of states' dependence on federal aid as a share of their total resources.

There is at least a rough correlation between various states' per capita income and their dependence on aid. Relatively poor states, such as those in the South, tend to be more dependent on aid.

But that correlation begins to erode when total tax bases are used for the comparison. Some states that are relatively rich by this measure, such as Wyoming, also are above average in their dependence on federal aid.

And when tax effort is compared to dependence on aid, the correlation disappears. Several states that are below average in tapping their tax bases are above average in their use of aid, while others are below the norm. Some states that bite more deeply into their tax bases are relatively dependent on Washington, while other are not.

Overall, states and localities had a strong stake in the success of Reagan's economic program. If it succeeded, their interest charges and service costs might decline, and their tax revenue might go up.

"But if the president's economic plan does not work, then the states are in deep trouble," said Democratic Gov. Ted Schwinden of Montana.

Carter's last budget projected the governments' share to decline to 55.4 percent in 1984. Reagan's projection called for only 50.3 percent in that year. By 1986, the Reagan budget envisioned that the grants to governments, after adjustment for inflation, would be half of what they were in 1980. State and local officials feared this projection would be reduced further by future cuts. "From everything I've been told in talking to the White House so far, in the budget they send up in January of '84, for fiscal '85, there will not be one nickel for grants to governments," Gunther said.

Whose Responsibility?

Administration officials had not confirmed that prediction. But their statements about Reagan federalism indicated that the programs being financed by grants to governments were the kind he thought the federal government should not be involved in. Interior Secretary James G. Watt said at a House hearing Oct. 6, 1981, "A main administration aim under the new federalism is to return to the state and local level those areas of government responsibility which produce primarily state and local benefits."

Watt, installed by Reagan as chairman of the ACIR panel, was testifying before the House Government Operations Subcommittee on Intergovernmental Relations. He said that before considering whether to ask the federal government for aid for a local purpose, officials should first see if any government should have a program at all.

Local officials in particular were concerned about the outlook for grants to governments, since that category included their favorite programs. Fred Jordan, a spokesman for the National League of Cities, said there were only three major federal aid programs that cities considered "truly flexible": general revenue sharing, Urban Development Action Grants and Community Development Block Grants.

There was almost unanimous opposition from local officials, even those who generally were supporters of Reagan, to his proposed 12 percent cut in revenue sharing. City and county officials also were troubled by Reagan's philosophical commitment to cut their ties to Washington, forcing them to deal with state governments for aid. "I see that as one of the clearer moves, and one that we as mayors are not particularly happy about, even those of us who are supporters of the president," said Columbus, Ohio, Mayor Tom Moody, R. But Moody and other fiscal conservatives were less upset over the long-range cuts in some development aid. "Those pots of money that are being lost by city hall are being lost, but so is the opportunity to boondoggle that money," he said.

The governors' formal position was that they opposed any further cuts in aid in 1981. But in general, they were less strident in opposing long-range cuts in grants to governments than were local officials. Many state executives grudgingly accepted Reagan's intent to have the federal government pull back from this area. "I agree with that, and I think most governors do. But it's the rate of change that's the problem," said Gov. Lamar Alexander, R-Tenn.

For their part, governors were fighting hardest to get the administration to agree to assume entirely some major income-transfer programs that were shared by Washington and the states, such as Medicaid, in exchange for state assumption of other programs such as highways or education. The general notion of such a "sorting out process," embraced by the governors, local government interest groups and the ACIR, collided head-on with Reagan's belief that welfare should be a state responsibility.

Reagan, responding to a backlash against reports in August that the administration was considering a new block grant to replace federal entitlement payments for the AFDC program, assured the governors that no decision was near on that option. But he made no move toward accepting a counterproposal put forth in September by Alexander, vice chairman of the ACIR, and Gov. Bruce Babbitt, D-Ariz. Their plan would have the federal government take over the states' $7 billion to $10 billion contribution to Medicaid while the states assumed the federal government's $6 billion role in education.

Alexander, Snelling and other governors were working to reach an accommodation with the administration soon enough for some proposal to be included in the fiscal 1983 budget due in January 1982. Alexander polled other governors in an attempt to find some specific proposal to put on the table in talks with the administration. "For anything to happen, the president will have to put federalism in his budget, and it will cost something," Alexander said. "We would like to see a revenue turnback, or a [program] swap, or find some new initiative to turn back the resources."

An NGA spokesman said the governors were trying to work out a proposal to give states the resources from the federal gasoline tax. Alexander said he hoped for some program tradeoff. "The president has never rejected out and out the notion of a Medicaid-for-something swap," the governor said. "What the president has always felt is that welfare should not be federalized."

Likewise, Snelling said, governors might be willing to accept more responsibility for welfare, if only some minimum, equalized benefit standard could be devised.

On the issue of turning tax sources over to states and localities, the wheels were turning slowly. The subject was a focus of early work by a new panel — the Presidential Federalism Advisory Committee — created by Reagan and headed by Sen. Paul Laxalt, R-Nev.

Williamson noted that others in the administration, wrestling with the federal deficit and considering "tax enhancements" to increase federal revenues, wanted to move more slowly in giving up taxes. The biggest part of the tax landscape is the tax on individual and corporate income. One option was for the administration simply to declare that because it had cut income taxes, other governments were free to move in.

But there were legal obstacles to raising taxes in many states and localities, and the same anti-tax politics that helped elect Reagan had simmered at their level for years. "I think Proposition 13 is still in the breeze," said Gov. Robert Ray, R-Iowa.

INDEXING CHANGE: TAX POLICY WATERSHED

Although slipped in as almost an afterthought, indexing could turn out to be the most important change made by the 1981 tax cut act. The plan, involving a major shift in how tax policy is made, called for automatic adjustment of income taxes to offset inflation every year beginning in

1985. By limiting the increase in federal revenues, it could curb the growth of government for years.

The indexing provisions of the 1981 law were designed to prevent what happened when inflation pushed taxpayers into higher and higher tax brackets — for every 1 percentage point increase in inflation, the federal government collected approximately 1.5 percent more in revenues. As a result, taxpayers had larger chunks of their incomes eaten away in taxes. Indexing would put a hold on "bracket creep" by revising income tax brackets, the personal exemption and the zero bracket amount (that amount of income on which there was no tax) to reflect, and offset, increases in inflation each year.

Some lawmakers said the change could prove "disastrous." To cover budget deficits, legislators would be forced to either raise taxes or make painful spending cuts, both politically unhealthy choices. More importantly, they claimed, indexing would shield a larger segment of the American public from the destructive effects of inflation and in the process cut their — and the country's — incentive to fight it. "If we are ever going to lick inflation in this nation, it is absolutely essential that everyone feel the pain," John H. Chafee, R-R.I., argued during Senate floor debate.

Those who pushed the indexing provision countered that inflation had given liberal Congresses a relatively painless way — at taxpayer expense — to amass funding for new government programs. They said it was time for Congress to be more "honest" about its spending and tax policies. If spending was to grow, Congress must swallow its medicine and vote to increase taxes.

"Tax indexing does nothing more than redistribute the tax implications of inflation so that consumers no longer bear all of the burden, while government reaps all the benefits," said David Durenberger, R-Minn.

How Indexing Would Work

Indexing was scheduled to begin in 1985 after three across-the-board rate cuts totaling 25 percent were set in place. Individual tax brackets, the personal exemption and the zero bracket rate then would be adjusted annually by the average increase in the Consumer Price Index (CPI) over the 12-month period ending Sept. 30 of the preceding year. In general, indexing meant that if an individual's taxable income increased with inflation, he would continue to pay the same portion of his income in federal taxes. The tax would be higher in actual dollars, but the real value of the tax burden should remain the same.

To illustrate, if the CPI increased 10 percent in 1984, three things would happen in 1985:

● The zero bracket amount (formerly called the standard deduction) would be increased 10 percent, from $2,300 to $2,530 for individuals and from $3,400 to $3,740 for joint returns.

● The $1,000 personal exemption would rise to $1,100.

● The top and bottom numbers of each tax bracket would be increased 10 percent.

For example, a married couple filing jointly in 1984 with $23,000 of taxable income would fall in the $20,200-$24,600 tax bracket. They would owe a tax of $2,497 plus 22 percent of everything over $20,200 — or $3,113, 13.5 percent of their taxable income. Without indexing, if the couple's taxable income increased 10 percent (with inflation) in 1985 to $25,300, they would be pushed up into the $24,600-$29,900 bracket. They would pay $3,465 plus 25

percent of everything over $24,600, or a total tax of $3,640, 14.4 percent of their taxable income.

With indexing, the $20,200-$24,600 tax bracket would be increased 10 percent to $22,220 to $27,060, with a tax of $2,747 plus 22 percent of everything over $22,220. The couple would have a total tax of $3,424, or 13.5 percent of their taxable income, the same percentage they paid in the previous year.

Because higher income was taxed at a higher rate, indexing, advocates pointed out, would keep the income tax system as progressive as it was in 1984.

Budget Worries

Even some of the strongest supporters of indexing acknowledged that, while politically popular, its future could hinge on the economic outlook over the next few years.

"[Indexing] is a very good idea, but I think we'll never see it," said Rudolph Penner, director of tax policy at the American Enterprise Institute. He pointed out that other countries, such as Australia, suspended their indexing programs when budgetary pressures became too great. "And I think we'll suspend ours," he added.

Penner and others expected that the administration would have a difficult time fulfilling its promise of a balanced budget in 1984 and would be looking for new sources of revenue in 1985, rather than additional tax cuts. The elimination of indexing would be a logical solution to that anticipated problem. But other observers believed that once American taxpayers understood what indexing meant to their tax liability, it would become politically difficult, if not impossible, to prevent it from becoming a permanent fixture of tax law. "Economic problems would have to be fairly severe" to repeal indexing, said Rep. Henson Moore, R-La.

Estimates varied on just how much indexing would cost the Treasury, in large part because the numbers were so sensitive to the anticipated rate of inflation. The Joint Committee on Taxation projected that indexing would reduce individual taxes $12.9 billion in fiscal 1985 and $35.8 billion in fiscal 1986. That would come on top of $122.6 billion and $143.8 billion in lower individual taxes for those same years as a result of the across-the-board marginal rate cuts made by July 1, 1983. The administration, using more optimistic economic assumptions, projected that indexing would cost only about $8.6 billion and $22.7 billion for fiscal 1985 and 1986, respectively.

Either way, both proponents and opponents of indexing conceded that the provisions would put a great deal of pressure on the federal budget. The House Budget Committee estimated that the fiscal 1985 budget deficit would be well over $100 billion.

Joseph Pechman, director of economic studies at the Brookings Institution, called indexing "ill advised" in light of the uncertain outlook. "It was a hasty action. I would have preferred that they waited until 1984 before making such a commitment," he said. He and others argued that further efforts should be made to control the spending side of the budget, much of which was also indexed, before indexing the revenue side.

Senate Budget Committee Chairman Pete V. Domenici, R-N.M., warned right before a July 16 vote to include indexing in the Senate version of the tax cut bill that the provision would push the budget "sharply into deficit" in 1985. He chastised his colleagues for setting the country on such an uncharted course during a time of economic uncertainty. "What we are really saying with mangement by formula is that we cannot trust ourselves, the policy makers, to make the hard decisions on tax and spending policy without being bolstered by a formula," he said.

Administration Doubts

Indexing was not included in President Reagan's original tax cut proposal, even though the president was a supporter of the concept. The administration wanted a "clean" bill (calling for individual rate cuts and accelerated business depreciation) without any add-ons that might bog down the package. Several administration officials also expressed doubts about just how wise a step indexing might prove to be and proposed the measure be saved for a later tax bill.

Treasury Secretary Donald T. Regan told the Senate Finance Committee in May 1981 that he opposed indexing because it would be an "indication we're giving in to the inflationary fight."

But congressional support for the measure was strong, with such influential backers as Finance Committee Chairman Robert Dole, R-Kan. The provision was introduced on the Senate floor as a committee amendment to the panel's tax cut package and passed by a vote of 57-40.

Senate adoption of indexing raised the hopes of backers in the House, where an indexing bill by Rep. Bill Gradison, R-Ohio, had 223 cosponsors. Gradison and others urged the administration to add indexing to help defeat a Democratic tax plan that, at the time, was given a narrow chance of winning in the House.

"We all agreed at the time that if something terrible should happen to the economy, we could take it out of the law," said Rep. Moore, a member of the House Ways and Means Committee.

The final version of the administration tax package, submitted to the House July 24, included indexing. The president's package was approved five days later by a 238-195 vote.

The Canadian Experience

Cited often in the debate over indexing was the Canadian experience with such a system. Canada, several other countries and nine U.S. states had adopted some form of tax indexing during the 1970s. But the Canadian system, which adjusted tax brackets, the personal exemption and some deductions for increases in inflation, was most like the indexing provisions enacted by Congress.

While the Canadian government had decreased its growth in spending since indexing was introduced in 1974, budget deficits had "grown to record levels," according to a Congressional Budget Office (CBO) study. In 1974 the Canadian budget had a $1 billion surplus; in 1980 the deficit was $11 billion, or 3.7 percent of its gross national product. The U.S. deficit in 1980 was only 2.4 percent of GNP.

Those such as Penner who predicted large U.S budget deficits by the mid-1980s maintained that indexing would only push the federal government further and further away from a balanced budget, unless the economic picture brightened substantially. But those who supported indexing pointed to other changes in the Canadian budget, in part attributable to indexing. The annual rate of growth of federal spending in Canada dropped substantially from 16.2 percent in 1974 to 4.9 percent in 1980, and inflation dropped slightly.

Some of the same signs of restraint also were evident in the nine U.S. states that adopted some form of tax indexing. The Advisory Commission on Intergovernmental Relations reported in a 1980 study on the state systems: "We can draw one inference with a fairly high degree of confidence — indexation has forced state policy-makers to take a somewhat harder look at their expenditure priorities than ... under a non-indexed system."

That, said proponents, was what indexing was all about. By forcing the government to work with limited revenues, federal spending would not be allowed to mushroom as it had over past decades. Congress either would have to tighten its belt and cut spending or vote to increase taxes.

Inflation Impact

Several other questions remained about how well indexing would work. Many argued that the CPI was not the best index to use to adjust for inflation because it valued increases in housing costs as though everyone bought a new house every year. As a result, the CPI measure could overadjust tax rates for inflation, cutting taxes in real terms and putting an even greater strain on the federal budget. The problem was finding a suitable substitute. Pechman suggested a cost-of-living adjustment that would include a "rental equivalent" component rather than the cost of new housing, but others maintained no index was perfect and that over the long run differences among inflation indexes would be slight.

Members of Congress also argued during the indexing debate that it would aggravate inflation. They said it would make it appear the government had given up its fight against inflation and would put sizable amounts of money in the hands of consumers during times of high inflation, just when consumer spending should be kept down.

But those who advocated indexing argued the opposite: the tax system without indexing would only encourage more government spending, itself inflationary. "Indexing doesn't cause inflation," said Sen. William L. Armstrong, R-Colo., a major backer of the plan, "It's a response to inflation."

According to CBO, however, "evidence on this matter is mixed, at best." Inflation in Canada over the period during which indexing had been in place had not differed substantially from inflation in the United States, it reported.

Congressional Initiative

One of the major arguments against indexing — or for indexing, depending on which side one was on — was that it took from Congress much of its discretion over taxes. Indexing advocates charged that recent Congresses had gone on a spending spree with the extra tax revenues brought in by inflation. In fact, taxes had actually been cut several times since 1967, bringing total taxes to almost the same level they would have been at had they been indexed, according to CBO. It was these periodic tax "cuts," including the one approved in 1981, that members of Congress no longer would be able to bestow on constituents, as indexing ate away at government revenues.

Indexing proponents said that was good, in part because members would no longer be getting credit for cutting taxes when they really were just stopping them from growing any larger. They also argued for a "permanent" tax cut. "I think the economy will be better off if we set the rules of the game. It will make it much easier for businesses and individuals to make decisions over the long run," said Gradison.

Russell B. Long, D-La., ranking minority member of the Senate Finance Committee, argued during floor debate that if an indexing system had been put in place several years ago, Reagan's far-reaching tax program would not have been possible because there would have been little, if any, revenue to cut in 1981.

Long and others maintained indexing would tie Congress down to the existing distribution of taxes, with little leeway for making changes to adjust to fluid economic conditions. Indexing advocates wrote off such statements as the bitter replies of Democrats who had built their careers on government growth. Growth, they said, would no longer be so easy.

"Of course, service on the Ways and Means Committee is going to be a lot less attractive," said Gradison, a member of that panel since 1977. "The possibility of considering tax increases as well as tax cuts will loom real."

Budget Legislation, 1965-81

This chronology is a broad summary of federal budget making between 1965 and 1981. It traces the president's annual requests and Congress' response to those requests.

The succeeding chronology contains economic legislation — including tax, monetary policy, and other measures — enacted to implement the nation's fiscal and monetary policy.

1965

President Johnson in the first federal budget that was fully under his control, stressed health, education and welfare spending and de-emphasized defense outlays. The budget he sent to Congress was for fiscal 1966 and had been under preparation during Johnson's first full year in office in 1964. By the end of the year, however, the increasing U.S. commitment to the war in Vietnam required the Johnson administration to revise substantially its estimates of spending for national defense.

For the rest of Johnson's years in office, increased defense spending was the major factor in the intractable budget problems that plagued his administration. In his January 1965 presentation of the fiscal 1966 budget, he estimated Defense Department outlays at $49 billion; the final total was more than $55 billion. This was to rise to almost $78 billion by the end of fiscal 1968, half a year before Johnson left office, and related outlays pushed the total national defense figure to more than $80.5 billion.

In 1965, however, the budget pinch that was to develop was only in its early stages and caused the administration no more than the usual hardships in Congress as the conservative Appropriations committees reduced spending allotments below requests. Congress during 1965 acted on 17 appropriations bills totaling $107,037,566,896. Requests totaled $109,448,074,896.

Johnson's approach to the budget was noticeably different than that in his first budget message in January 1964. Then he had emphasized the necessity of controlling federal expenditures. In 1965 he stressed the importance of government activity in social programs and hinted at future spending trends, saying that the budget he was sending to Congress "begins to grasp the opportunities of the Great Society."

In other budget developments during the year, Johnson directed heads of federal agencies to introduce a system of budget preparation called planning-programming-budgeting (PPBS). This was described as an extension of the cost-effectiveness budgeting system used in the Defense Department and in a few other agencies. It was intended to permit agencies to better determine goals and alternate methods of achieving them, to measure the anticipated results of each dollar spent under each alternative and to do this throughout the year (rather than just during the few months in the fall when the budget was prepared) and for a period of five years at a time. Government agencies were instructed in March 1965 to begin establishing the system.

1966

President Johnson in the fiscal 1967 federal budget submitted to Congress in January 1966 proposed a substantial increase in spending for the Vietnam War and moderate increases in expenditures on Great Society programs.

During the session, Congress appropriated the defense funds with little change. But it also threatened at various times to appropriate larger sums than requested for other programs and thereby require federal spending substantially in excess of the amount that government officials and private economists believed the nation's economy — already under inflationary pressures — could absorb.

Numerous public statements by the president criticizing the threatened additions resulted in Senate and House cutbacks that produced appropriation totals slightly under the administration's final requests. Congress passed 15 appropriations providing a total of $130,281,568,480 compared to requests of $131,164,926,586.

Spending Limit

The increasing pinch on government finances resulting from the war gave new impetus to Republicans and conservative Democrats to cut spending in other areas of the budget. Attempting to reduce federal spending, particularly for domestic social programs, was nothing new for congressional conservatives. But the financial pressures from the war gave them added ammunition.

Conservative attempts to cut spending were ultimately successful. But in 1966 Republicans failed in their attempts to amend seven fiscal 1967 appropriations bills to limit spending in the agencies covered by each bill to 95 percent of the amounts estimated in the president's budget.

1967

President Johnson's fiscal 1968 budget provoked a yearlong dispute between the president and Congress. Although that argument ended in somewhat of a stalemate, it was a prelude to the 1968 conflict between the two branches, which ended in the imposition of strict mandatory expenditure controls.

Congress sought to impose spending controls in 1967 but with mixed success. It refused to give Johnson the tax increase he wanted and he in turn refused to cut back the spending total estimated in his budget. He did, however, agree to help hold down increases over his January estimates.

In action on appropriation bills, Congress provided $141,872,346,664, which was almost $6 billion less than the president's requests of $147,806,557,929. Republicans tried again to attack the 5 percent spending reduction provision to six regular appropriations bills. In a seventh bill, a GOP proposal would have forced a 5 percent reduction in appropriations as opposed to spending. None of the attempts were enacted.

Spending Limit

The most important and controversial spending limit action in 1967 came on a continuing appropriations resolution. Such resolutions are normally routine bills, enacted as stopgap legislation after the beginning of a fiscal year to provide temporary funds for agencies until their regular appropriations bills are cleared by Congress. In 1967 these resolutions became the vehicle for House Republicans to attempt to force President Johnson to make overall reductions in federal spending.

The Republican effort was in large part a reaction to the president's request for a 10 percent surcharge on corporate and personal income taxes; Johnson forecast a $29 billion deficit if Congress failed to approve it. The Republicans who led the House economy drive felt that holding down federal spending was preferable to raising taxes as a means of reducing the projected deficit and stemming inflationary pressures in the economy.

They finally succeeded, adding language to the final continuing appropriations resolution of 1967 (H J Res 888 — PL 90-218) that required federal agencies to hold fiscal 1968 obligations to a figure about $9.1 billion below budget requests. That had the effect of reducing fiscal 1968 spending by $2.4 billion.

Although the Johnson administration opposed the spending limits, it proposed the limitation formula contained in H J Res 888 in the hopes that it would spur Congress to action on the surcharge. The formula was quickly endorsed by conferees, ending a six-weeks-long conference, and adopted by both chambers.

The formula required that each department and independent agency reduce its budgeted fiscal 1968 obligational authority for salaries and other personnel expenses by 2 percent and its funds for other "controllable" requests by 10 percent. Obligations related to national defense were exempt from the cuts as were cuts in such "uncontrollable" obligations as interest on the national debt, welfare and Medicare payments. Also exempted from the mandatory cuts were the legislative and judicial branches of the government.

1968

The confrontation between Congress and the White House over government spending, which had been developing ever since the United States became deeply involved in the Vietnam War, reached its high point during the Johnson administration in 1968.

The president in January submitted a fiscal 1969 budget that called for more than a $3 billion increase in national defense spending but a "hold-the-line" approach for most domestic programs. Considering the administration's past inaccurate estimates of the Vietnam War costs, Congress did not place too much trust in the defense spending projection. At the same time, the economy was straining under severe inflationary pressures complicated by deep domestic turmoil resulting from racial antagonisms, increasing crime and the plight of the cities. Against that background, the federal budget was the logical focus for the struggle over allocation of the nation's limited resources.

The president and his top aides had previously concluded that the nation could no longer meet from existing financial resources even the most basic responsibilities it had assumed — fighting a costly war, combating inflation and paying for vital social programs — without a tax increase. Johnson had proposed a 10 percent surcharge on personal and corporate income taxes in 1967, which was not acted upon. In 1968 he again urged Congress to impose the surcharge.

On the other hand, many powerful members of Congress believed that the best way to pay for the war and fight inflation was by cutting spending. Thus, for almost a year, the surcharge proposal was held hostage while an agreement was reached on mandatory limits on federal spending.

In the end both sides obtained what they wanted, but Congress got much more than the administration had been prepared to give in the beginning. For its part, the administration obtained the surcharge in a bill (HR 15414 — PL 90-364) enacted June 28. In the same bill, however, Congress added provisions — which were its price for the tax increase — requiring a $6 billion reduction in federal spending in fiscal 1969, an $8 billion rescission of unspent prior-year appropriations and a cut of approximately 245,000 civilian employees in the executive branch. *(Details, p. 150)*

1969

As one of his last acts in office, President Lyndon B. Johnson sent Congress a fiscal 1970 budget calling for a relatively small increase in overall defense spending, modest growth in urban aid and education programs and a sharp increase in spending for public health and welfare. Johnson's budget was designed to produce a $3.4 billion surplus, which the president said would "contain" the inflationary pressures that had been building up in the economy since 1965.

After a three-month study, however, Nixon administration economists decided that even greater surpluses would be necessary to stem the tide of inflation. On April 15, President Richard Nixon sent Congress a revised budget calling for cuts in both the domestic and defense spending projections laid out by President Johnson in January. The result was expected to be a $5.8 billion surplus — fourth largest in the nation's history. If attained, it would be the second surplus in a row after eight consecutive years of deficits, culminating in a deficit of $25.2 billion in fiscal 1968 — the largest deficit since fiscal 1945. (The Johnson budget for fiscal 1969 produced a surplus of $3.2 billion — $800 million more than Johnson had predicted and $2 billion above Nixon's estimates.)

But as fiscal 1970 wore on, actions and inactions by Congress, coupled with increases in uncontrollable spending such as Social Security payments and interest on the national debt, cast doubt on the likelihood of such a large surplus by the end of fiscal 1970. Moves by Congress to increase Social Security benefits by 15 percent and to reduce tax revenues in conjunction with the 1969 Tax Reform Act helped throw the Nixon budget out of alignment. *(1969 tax act, p. 151)*

Congress did cut $5.8 billion from budget requests for defense spending; but it added unrequested funds for a wide range of domestic programs, such as $600 million for pollution control. Failure to enact presidential requests on items like postal rate increases and adjustment of credit programs of the Veterans Administration and Farmers Home Administration also reduced the new revenues that the president had figured into his budget estimates. Worse still, revenues from existing taxes fell below expectations because of the recession that hit in early 1970. By the end of the fiscal year, the projected surplus of almost $6 billion had become a deficit of $2.8 billion.

Spending Limit

In its own move to cool down inflation, Congress in 1969 approved legislation establishing a ceiling on expenditures of $191.9 billion for fiscal 1970. The spending limit, attached to a $4.3 billion supplemental appropriations bill for fiscal 1969 (PL 91-47), appeared to have the effect of ordering a $1 billion reduction in spending because it was $1 billion below the Nixon administration's projections for

the year. In reality, however, the ceiling was adjustable because it could be increased or lowered by any congressional action affecting the budget (such as add-ons for unrequested items) and could be increased by as much as $2 billion by the president to reflect the increased costs for uncontrollable items such as Social Security payments.

As it developed, even the $2 billion cushion for uncontrollables was not enough to cover the sharp increase in spending for these requirements. In a second supplemental appropriations bill (HR 17399 — PL 91-305), passed in mid-1970, Congress increased the fiscal 1970 ceiling to $197.9 billion, plus another $2 billion cushion for uncontrollables. Actual spending for the fiscal year came to $196.6 billion, $3.3 billion less than the revised legal ceiling.

1970

President Nixon in the fiscal 1971 federal budget, the first budget fully under his own control, sought to continue the policy of fiscal restraint that he had outlined in his budget amendments the year before. The new budget, prepared on the assumption that inflation would continue during fiscal 1970 though at a reduced rate, called for a slight spending increase of $2.9 billion and a surplus of $1.3 billion.

By late winter, however, inflation was still rampant and new problems had appeared: creeping recession, growing unemployment (reaching 6 percent by the end of the year), declining stock prices, a rising budget deficit and a dissatisfied public. The Nixon administration, critics charged, had achieved recession, unemployment and inflation simultaneously.

Critics faulted Nixon's original stringent fiscal and monetary policies for the strains they placed on the economy, including the unemployment and rising interest rates. Allocation of credit and controls on wages and prices would have restrained rising prices without the loss of employment and output the administration's program produced, some argued. Democratic leaders in Congress issued a new call for controls on Dec. 3. Congress had passed legislation authorizing controls in December 1969 (PL 91-151) and a wage-price freeze on Aug. 13, 1970 (PL 91-379) over the president's opposition.

Nixon remained opposed to the wage-price controls — commonly known as an "incomes policy" — throughout the year, despite pressure from Federal Reserve Board Chairman Arthur F. Burns that he move in that direction. But by year's end, the president had announced a marked shift in his monetary and fiscal strategy. In a major economic speech Dec. 4, Nixon stressed the obligation of the government to move the economy toward full employment. That would require greater ease in monetary policy, he indicated. And on the fiscal front, the president indicated he would use deficit spending to stimulate economic growth. He said he was planning the new budget "on the basis that it would be balanced if we were at full employment and the economy were producing full revenues." Under impact of the president's new policy, coupled with sluggish revenues, the planned $1.3 billion surplus plummeted to a $23.0 billion deficit by the end of the fiscal year.

In other developments, Congress again disputed the president over spending priorities. For the third consecutive year, it enacted a spending ceiling. Congress sliced funds from Nixon's military, foreign aid and space requests and added money to numerous domestic programs, notably education, health, manpower, training and pollution control. The president responded with vetoes to ward off some of the unwanted spending, but he was not always successful. Of five vetoes cast on budget matters, two were overridden by Congress.

Spending Limit

The limit on spending for fiscal 1971 was embodied in a second supplemental appropriations bill for fiscal 1970 (PL 91-305), the same bill that had placed a limit of $197.9 billion plus a $2 billion cushion for uncontrollable items on the fiscal 1970 budget. The limits for fiscal 1971 were to be $200.8 billion plus a $4.8 billion allowance for uncontrollables and an unlimited ceiling for congressional add-ons. The basic $200.8 billion ceiling was the amount projected by the president in his fiscal 1971 budget.

The only dispute over the spending limit focused on the amount of leeway to be given the administration to handle the controllables. The House voted a $3 billion allotment, and the Senate $6 billion. "In view of the history of increases on uncontrollable items, the committee believed it prudent" to double the cushion, the Senate Appropriations Committee said in its report on the bill. House and Senate conferees compromised on a cushion of $5.5 billion. Congress later approved a series of add-ons to the president's budget, resulting in actual spending of $211.4 billion for the year.

Presidential Vetoes

President Nixon's disputes with Congress over spending priorities led to presidential vetoes of five bills during the 1970 session of Congress (four other bills were vetoed but not primarily because of spending disputes). The bills vetoed over budgeting controversies included HR 13111, appropriating $19.7 billion for the departments of Labor and Health, Education and Welfare (HEW) and the Office of Economic Opportunity for fiscal 1970 (the first veto Nixon cast since becoming president); HR 11102, authorizing $2.79 billion through fiscal 1973 for the Hill-Burton hospital construction programs; HR 16916, appropriating $4.4 billion for fiscal 1971 programs administered by the Office of Education in HEW; HR 17548, appropriating $18 billion for the Department of Housing and Urban Development and other agencies for fiscal 1971; and S 3867, authorizing $9.5 billion in fiscal 1971-74 for federal manpower training and public service employment programs.

The hospital construction and Office of Education vetoes were overridden and the other vetoes sustained (including the four bills vetoed over non-spending issues).

Program Terminations

An effort by President Nixon to reduce, restructure or terminate a number of government programs he considered to be of low priority was blocked by Congress in 1970. Among the president's budget-cutting proposals, designed to save $2.1 billion a year, were the disposal of $750 million in material from the nation's stockpile of strategic and critical materials, reductions in the federal impact-areas school assistance program, and termination of the Agricul-

ture Department's special milk program and agricultural conservation program.

Congress June 29 did approve legislation (in 17 separate bills) authorizing the sale of $150 million worth of materials from the nation's stockpile. But action was never taken on the other requests in the president's package. An effort to cut $1.4 billion from such programs had failed the year before.

Budget Bureau Reorganization

In another key budget development, Congress in 1970 approved a reorganization plan submitted by President Nixon to establish an Office of Management and Budget (OMB) to be built around the nucleus of the Bureau of the Budget, which would be abolished. The changes came in Reorganization Plan No. 2, one of four reorganization plans proposed by the president and accepted by Congress during the year.

The new office did not downgrade the budgeting function but amplified it. The existing responsibilities of the Bureau of the Budget were extended and greater use made of organization and management systems, development of executive talent and a broader career staff, better dissemination of information and appropriate use of modern techniques and equipment. The rationale for these changes was to provide greater executive capability for analyzing, coordinating, evaluating and improving the efficiency of government programs.

1971

In his State of the Union message on Jan. 22, 1971, President Nixon outlined a new economic strategy that was the guiding principle of the budget for fiscal year 1972. Nixon called his new fiscal plan a "full-employment" budget, which meant that the budget, with large deficits projected for both fiscal years 1971 and 1972, would have been in balance if the economy had been at full output and employment. The projected deficits, totaling $18.6 billion and $11.6 billion, respectively, represented the loss of federal revenues caused by economic performance below potential. (Actual deficits came to $23 billion for both fiscal 1971 and fiscal 1972.)

The purpose of the new plan was to stimulate a faster recovery from the recession. "By operating as if we were at full employment," the president said, "we will help to bring about that full employment." Chief among the assumptions underlying the budget was a total output of the economy (gross national product) of $1,065 billion in calendar year 1971. This was approximately $20 billion higher than the consensus of estimates by economists outside the government and about $18 billion more than the economy actually achieved.

As in 1970, Nixon was urged with increasing frequency during the year to adopt an incomes policy, under which the government would influence or intervene in wage and price decisions in the private economy to curb inflation. Nixon maintained an unremitting hostility toward wage and price controls well into the year. Then in a surprise move Aug. 15, the president froze wages and prices and ordered a series of other tough actions, including a 5 percent reduction in federal employment, six months' deferral of a federal pay raise scheduled for early 1972 and postponement of the starting dates for his welfare reform and revenue-sharing program, neither of which was expected to be enacted soon. Nixon's decisive effort to cope with the nation's worsening economic problems gained him the initiative and some relief from criticism — at least until announcement later in the year of Phase Two — the post-freeze period of the new policy. *(Details of the president's stabilization program, p. 158)*

Presidential Vetoes

President Nixon vetoed three bills during the 1971 session, each time largely because of budgetary issues. The measures were S 575, a $5.7 billion public works acceleration and regional development bill; HR 2600, a bill increasing retirement benefits for certain District of Columbia policemen and firemen, U.S. park policemen and members of the Executive Protection Service and the U.S. Secret Service; and S 2007, a $6.3 billion, two-year OEO extension and child development bill. All three vetoes were sustained.

Program Terminations

The Nixon administration again called unsuccessfully for reductions and terminations in what it saw as non-essential federal programs. Nixon in his fiscal 1972 budget proposed $2.9 billion in cuts ($3.7 billion on a one-time, non-recurring basis), including termination of the Agriculture Department's special milk program, sale of $635 million in materials from the national stockpile and cuts and termination of many other programs. As in 1970, the program was only partially approved by Congress.

1972

For the second consecutive year, President Nixon submitted a "full employment" budget in 1972, calling for extensive deficit spending to take up the slack in the economy. The president's economic plan for fiscal 1973 embodied a record quarter-trillion-dollar budget with a $25.5 billion deficit. By midyear, however, indications were that congressional add-ons to the budget could increase the deficit by $10 billion or more. The president responded with veto threats and hints that higher taxes might be necessary to fund the growing deficit.

The economy had been able to absorb the planned budget deficit for fiscal 1972, the president said in his budget message, even though that deficit had swollen to more than three times his January 1971 projections. An expected shortfall of almost $20 billion in tax revenues from the January 1971 projections, combined with $7.4 billion in increased spending above 1971 estimates, would produce an expected deficit of $38.8 billion, which would translate into a full employment deficit of $8.1 billion. (The actual fiscal 1972 deficit came to $23 billion and the full employment deficit to $3.6 billion.) "While our economy can absorb such a deficit for a time, the experience of the

late 1960s provides ample warning of the danger of continued, and rising, full-employment deficits. The lesson of 1966-68, when such deficits led to an intolerable inflation, is too clear and too close to permit any relaxation of control of government spending," the president said.

Holding the year's increase in outlays to $9.7 billion in fiscal 1973 while receipts were expected to rise by $23 billion was designed to reduce the actual deficit in the 1973 budget and keep it just above balance on a full-employment basis. The spending plan also provided less stimulation during fiscal 1973, when the administration forecast that the economy would be expanding vigorously.

Spending Limit

In the final floor battle of the session, Congress dealt the president a scathing defeat by denying authority he had requested to fix a spending limit of $250 billion on federal spending for fiscal 1973. The administration proposal, considered as a rider to the debt limit bill, was accepted intact by the House but was rewritten by the Senate to place strict limits on the nature and size of any proposed cutbacks. Yielding to Senate pressures against broad presidential authority, House-Senate conferees dropped the ceiling altogether.

Deletion of the spending ceiling, which Nixon said was necessary to avoid the need for a tax increase, was the climax of a dramatic series of maneuvers between Congress and the president. In the first of these ploys, the president had withheld his approval of a water pollution control bill (S 2770) awaiting the outcome of the spending controversy. Shortly after the Senate balked on the spending ceiling, Nixon vetoed the water bill; but Congress overrode his action the following day.

At the last minute, the White House had sought to compromise on the issue by backing a conference bill that would have circumscribed the president's authority to dictate spending cuts, although not as severely as under the Senate bill. The Senate rejected the conference report by a 27-39 roll-call vote, leaving the administration with the choice of a spending limit with the Senate's tight restrictions, or no ceiling at all. The president took the latter route.

Throughout the debate on the proposed ceiling, the central issue was the scope of authority to be given the president. Most members of both chambers agreed that some curb was needed on federal outlays, projected to reach $256 billion in fiscal 1973. But key senators objected to Nixon's demand of unlimited discretion to choose the areas where spending would be trimmed.

Powerful political considerations fueled the debate, which developed into a lively sparring match between the White House and Congress in 1972. Nixon had made clear his intention to hold Congress responsible in the upcoming elections for continued inflation and any future tax increases made necessary by unfettered federal spending. Democrats hotly disputed that contention, arguing that the president was equally responsible for the high spending level of the past four years, since he could have vetoed any spending he considered inflationary.

Nixon Vetoes

Reiterating his theme of economy in government, Nixon vetoed 16 bills during the 1972 session, including a mammoth $30.5 billion appropriation for the departments of Labor and Health, Education and Welfare (HEW).

Nine of the 16 vetoes, among them the Labor-HEW measure (HR 16654) came by pocket veto Oct. 27 — nine days after Congress had adjourned. Nixon's post-adjournment rejection of the Labor-HEW money bill marked his second veto of those agencies' appropriations in 1972. An earlier Labor-HEW bill (HR 15417) had been vetoed Aug. 16. Among the other bills vetoed by the pocket route Oct. 27 were the Public Works and Economic Development Act of 1972 (HR 16071), the Flood Control Act of 1972 (S 4018), the Rehabilitation Act of 1972 (HR 8395) and the Veterans' Health Care Expansion Act of 1972 (HR 10880).

In a combined veto message, Nixon said: "If I were to sign these measures into law, I would, in effect, be making promises that could not be kept since the funds required to finance the promised services are not available and would not be available without the higher taxes I have promised to resist."

Nixon said that the bills would have pushed spending over the fiscal 1973 budget by $750 million and over the fiscal 1974 budget by almost $2 billion.

After the House sustained the first Labor-HEW bill veto Aug. 16, Congress cleared a second bill appropriating the same amount of money — $30,538,919,500 — but permitting the president to impound up to $1.2 billion. If he impounded the maximum, the bill would still have been $532 million more than he requested. Thus the president remained opposed to the bill.

1973

Starting his second term as president, Nixon promptly challenged Congress to battle on federal budget issues.

In submitting a $268.7 billion fiscal 1974 budget on Jan. 29, 1973, the president outlined plans for fiscal 1973-74 spending cutbacks through reduction and elimination of more than 100 federal programs. The proposed savings — most to be accomplished by administrative action — were spread across a range of established federal programs that enjoyed wide constituent and congressional support.

Nixon defended the budget as "clear evidence of the kind of change demanded by the great majority of the American people." He asked Congress to endorse the administration's campaign for spending restraints by enacting a firm $268.7 billion ceiling on fiscal 1974 outlays.

In addition to demanding a spending limit, the president's budget message criticized existing congressional budget procedures. It suggested several revisions for consideration by a special Joint Committee on Budget Control that Congress had created in response to Nixon's previous spending limitation proposals in 1972.

The budget also renewed in scaled-down form Nixon's 1971 proposal for consolidating existing federal grant programs into broad-purpose "special revenue sharing" packages. Omitting earlier requests for transportation and rural community development consolidations, Nixon in 1973 urged approval of $6.9 billion in special revenue sharing programs for education, law enforcement, manpower training and urban development.

House and Senate leaders, concerned by the erosion of congressional powers and by Nixon's sweeping interpreta-

tion of presidential authority, quickly protested the president's claim to a re-election mandate for budget curtailments. House Speaker Carl Albert, D-Okla., vowed that Congress "will not permit the president to lay waste the great programs ... which we have developed during the decades past."

Fiscal Policy

The outcry over proposed spending cuts overshadowed the budget's planned shift away from the stimulative fiscal policies that Nixon had followed in 1971-72. With a strong economic recovery apparently getting under way, the president stressed the need to pare down persistent budget deficits to restrain inflationary pressures.

At that point, the deficit for fiscal 1973 — the ongoing year that had started July 1, 1972 — was being estimated at $24.8 billion. That followed two straight $23 billion deficits in fiscal 1971-72.

To hold down the fiscal 1974 deficit — without violating his 1972 campaign pledge opposing tax increases — Nixon sought spending restraints to cut potential outlays by $6.5 billion in fiscal 1973, $16.9 billion in fiscal 1974 and $21.7 billion in fiscal 1975.

Even with those cutbacks, the budget estimated that maintenance of defense spending levels and built-in social and health spending increases would push fiscal 1974 outlays $18.9 billion above expected fiscal 1973 levels. But anticipated economic expansion and previously enacted Social Security payroll tax increases were expected to boost revenues by $31 billion, leaving the fiscal 1974 deficit at $12.7 billion.

To justify that deficit to conservatives, Nixon again used the full employment budget concept that he had embraced in defending his first-term budget policies. On that basis, with revenues and outlays calculated as if the economy were operating with a 4 percent unemployment rate, the budget was viewed as restraining demand by running a $300 million surplus.

Congressional Response

Congress resisted Nixon's budget assault. Stung by the administration's attempted spending cutbacks, the House and Senate fought to increase outlays for specific programs and drew up legislation to limit the impoundment powers that Nixon was trying to wield.

Nonetheless sensitive to Nixon's charges that Congress was fiscally irresponsible, the House and Senate both went on record supporting the fiscal 1974 spending ceiling that Nixon had requested. But none of the spending limit provisions were enacted into law.

The Senate three times approved a $268 billion ceiling, and the House accepted a $267.1 billion limit. Those ceilings were in all cases coupled with impoundment control provisions.

Intended to protect congressional control over federal spending priorities, the impoundment control provisions actually authorized Nixon to impound appropriated funds to meet the spending ceiling. But the impoundments would have been subject to congressionally prescribed conditions; several costly programs would have been protected from impoundments altogether.

However, after passing the spending limit and impoundment provisions, the House and Senate never went to conference to resolve their differences; they concentrated instead on revising their own budget procedures.

Budget Control

With some Republican prodding, the House moved swiftly on budget revision proposals based on the recommendations of the joint House-Senate study panel. Despite the immense implications for committee jurisdictions, members' personal power and time-honored congressional habits, the House by the end of the year had passed a far-reaching budget revision plan.

The Senate drew up a similar plan, but its Government Operations Committee proposals were sidetracked in December for review by the Rules and Administration Committee in 1974. Congress cleared the budget review act in 1974. *(Details, p. 120)*

Spending Measures

By starting the process of revising its budget procedures, Congress in 1973 acknowledged that the uncoordinated, undisciplined system that it used for considering the president's budget proposals had let federal spending escape congressional control.

Those same slipshod procedures stayed in effect during the 1973 session, however, so the House and Senate once again adjusted the fiscal 1974 budget without tying separate spending bills into an overall fiscal framework. Without much regard for eventual total outlays, Congress accordingly reshaped the budget in separate action on 13 regular and one supplemental appropriations bills and through numerous legislative bills that mandated spending levels, including occasional riders to debt ceiling and other minor measures.

In some cases, Nixon responded with vetoes. Of nine regular 1973 vetoes, five were related to the spending controversy, and all of those were sustained.

In other cases, compromises were reached. Nixon Dec. 18 signed a bill (HR 8877 — PL 93-192) that appropriated $32.9 billion for the departments of Labor and Health Education and Welfare (HEW) — nearly $1.4 billion more than the administration's request — after Congress accepted language authorizing the president to impound up to $400 million of the funds.

Budgets respond to other influences, however, most notably economic conditions. By the end of fiscal 1974 on June 30, 1974, total budget outlays for the year had amounted to only $269.6 billion, slightly more than Nixon's original $268.6 billion proposal.

Congress had significantly shifted budget priorities, however, holding defense spending $2.5 billion below Nixon's proposal while allowing income security payments to grow by nearly that amount above the budget projections.

A strong 1973 economic performance, along with the effects of inflation on the tax system, meanwhile pushed fiscal 1974 revenue $8.9 billion above the initial budget projection. That cut the eventual fiscal 1974 deficit to $4.7 billion, $7 billion less than Nixon first had projected.

1974

The recession took hold during the first half of 1974, economic statistics later showed. But federal budget planning, still preoccupied with restraining inflation rates that were reaching double-digit levels, failed to anticipate the yearlong slide that ended in a fourth-quarter collapse.

Nixon Feb. 5 sent Congress a $304.4 billion budget for fiscal 1975, the year that would start July 1, 1974. While seeking "moderate restraint" through a $9.4 billion deficit, the budget stressed fiscal flexibility in dealing with a slumping economy that was plagued by inflation and severe energy shortages.

Nixon accordingly reserved the option of shifting toward greater budgetary stimulus "to support the economy if that should be necessary." And Frederick V. Malek, assistant director of the Office of Management and Budget (OMB), told reporters that administration officials "are prepared to do whatever is necessary to avoid a recession.

"The president is very firm about that," Malek added. "If it means busting the budget, then he will bust the budget rather than keep people out of jobs."

Nixon Policy Drift

Fighting to stay in office as his Watergate scandal involvement unfolded, Nixon took a conciliatory approach to Congress in the budget and abandoned the 1973 attempt to dismantle many domestic programs. He proposed no bold fiscal 1975 initiatives, on the other hand, although built-in increases pushed projected outlays above $300 billion for the first time. No spending ceiling was requested.

The resulting $9.4 billion deficit, Nixon maintained, "will continue a posture of moderate restraint rather than greatly intensifying that restraint." Calculated on a full employment basis, the administration's budget was expected to run an $8 billion surplus.

While promising stimulative measures if necessary, Nixon gave no specific proposals for later implementation. The budget message only suggested that Congress enact his 1973 proposal to raise standards and extend coverage under the unemployment insurance system.

Congressional pronouncements, relying on consultations with Democratic economists who favored stimulative countercyclical measures, generally called for tax cuts and public service jobs programs, along with revenue raising tax revisions. But Congress did not translate them into legislation.

Ford Budget Strategy

Despite President Ford's efforts to come up with more effective economic strategies after Nixon's August resignation, federal budget policy was left largely unchanged for the rest of 1974.

Stiff congressional resistance stymied Ford's Oct. 8 prescription to tighten fiscal restraints still further in 1975 by imposing a 5 percent tax surcharge and cutting fiscal 1975 outlays back to $300 billion. And the House smothered a late-session tax revision bill providing $1.6 billion in tax reductions that Ford had endorsed.

While Congress ignored his budget-restraining proposals, Ford finally accepted congressional initiatives that beefed up federal unemployment programs as the depth of the economic downturn became evident.

On Sept. 11, Ford himself announced release of about $1 billion of additional funding under an existing 1973 employment law to finance about 170,000 public service jobs with state and local governments during the coming winter. And the president's Oct. 8 economic message proposed a new public service jobs program with funding to be released in stages if the unemployment rate climbed.

Congress found Ford's proposal inadequate. It instead passed a three-part legislative package that authorized a $2.5 billion public service jobs program, extended unemployment compensation to another 12 million persons, speeded up existing federal public works projects, gave jobless workers an additional 13 weeks of unemployment benefits and appropriated $4 billion in fiscal 1975 to fund those programs.

Budget Control

After months of intense internal negotiations, Congress cleared legislation (HR 7130 — PL 93-344) in June 1974 creating new procedures for handling budget matters. The procedures were scheduled for full use in 1976. *(Story, p. 57)*

As signed into law, the Congressional Budget and Impoundment Control Act of 1974 included major provisions that:

Budget Committees

● Established House and Senate Budget committees to study the president's budget and recommend changes in fiscal policy and spending priorities.

● Set House committee membership at 23, including five members from the Appropriations Committee, five from the Ways and Means Committee, 11 members from other standing committees, one from the majority party leadership and one from the minority party leadership. No member could serve on the committee for more than two Congresses out of five during a 10-year period.

● Set Senate committee membership at 15, selected by normal assignment procedures.

Budget Office

● Created a Congressional Budget Office (CBO) to assist the Budget committees in studying budget information. To the extent possible, CBO would assist other committees and members as well.

● Provided for appointment of a CBO director by the Speaker of the House and president pro tempore of the Senate upon Budget Committee recommendations. The law set four-year terms for the director and allowed either the House or Senate to remove him by resolution.

● Directed CBO to file a report to the Budget committees by April 1 of each year on alternative fiscal policies and budget priorities among major programs and functional categories.

Budget Timetable

● Set forth a timetable for completing various actions required by the new budget process before Oct. 1, the start of the next fiscal year.

● Required House and Senate standing committees, the Joint Economic Committee and Joint Committee on Internal Revenue Taxation to submit budget recommendations to the Budget committees by March 15.

First Budget Resolution

● Required the Budget committees separately to report by April 15 a concurrent resolution on the budget.

● Required Congress to complete action on the first concurrent budget resolution by May 15.

● Required that the resolution specify appropriate levels for:

1. Total outlays and total new budget authority.
2. Estimated outlays and recommended budget authority within those totals for each major functional budget category, contingencies and undistributed intragovernmental transactions.
3. Level of surplus or deficit, if any, appropriate to economic conditions or other factors.
4. Recommended level of federal revenues, along with the amount that expected total revenues should be increased or cut through legislative action.
5. Level of the public debt, along with any change in the public debt limit that it would require.
6. Other budget matters as appropriate.

● Permitted the House and Senate to revise the budget resolution at any time after enactment.

● Allowed Congress to require through the first budget resolution that no bill providing budget authority or new backdoor spending authority be sent to the president until Congress had completed its budget reconciliation process.

● Directed that the conference report on the first budget resolution be accompanied by a joint statement by the conferees allocating the total budget outlays and new budget authority among the House and Senate committees with jurisdiction over the measures providing the budget authority.

● Directed the Appropriations committees and other committees in turn to subdivide their allocations among their subcommittees, with a further breakdown between controllable and uncontrollable amounts.

Appropriations Process

● Required that all bills authorizing appropriations for the coming fiscal year be reported by May 15.

● Prohibited House or Senate floor consideration of any measure providing new budget authority, new backdoor spending or tax cuts or increases during the following fiscal year until Congress had completed action on the first budget resolution. The bill included procedures for waiving the rule.

● Directed the House Appropriations Committee if practical to complete markup of all regular appropriations bills before it reported any of the measures for floor action. The law required the committee to file a report comparing its appropriations decisions with the first budget resolution's targets.

● Required that Congress complete action by the seventh day after Labor Day in September on regular appropriations bills for the coming fiscal year and on all bills providing new spending authority effective in that year. The law excepted appropriations measures for programs whose authorizing legislation had not been "timely enacted."

Reconciliation

● Required the Budget committees to report a second concurrent resolution to reaffirm or revise the first budget resolution targets — and possibly direct committees to prepare revisions in legislation providing budget authority, new spending authority, revenue levels or the public debt limit.

● Required that Congress complete action on the second resolution by Sept. 15.

● Required that committees so directed by the second budget resolution promptly report a reconciliation bill or resolution making the requested changes. If action by more than one committee in each house were required, the Budget Committee would combine their proposals in a single measure.

● Allowed reconciliation to be accomplished through a concurrent resolution revising previously passed bills that had not yet been sent to the president.

● Required Congress to finish action on any reconciliation measure by Sept. 25.

● Made any subsequent bills or amendments that would violate the second budget resolution levels subject to points of order that would block floor consideration. However, Congress remained free to revise its budget totals.

Backdoor Spending

● Required that funding for new or additional contract or borrowing authority — programs allowing federal officials to sign contracts or take out loans obligating the government to make future payments — be provided through annual appropriations bills for each fiscal year.

● Prohibited congressional action on bills providing new entitlement authority — legislation requiring federal officials to make payments to all persons or governments that met certain standards — that would go into effect before the start of the next fiscal year.

● Provided for Appropriations Committee review of new entitlement authority reported by another committee and effective in the coming fiscal year if the amount of funding would exceed the related allocation within the first budget resolution that the authorizing committee had reported.

● Exempted from these restrictions new budget authority provided from Social Security trust funds, other trust funds financed primarily by designated taxes, general revenue sharing, insured or guaranteed loans, federally owned corporations and gifts to the government for specific purposes.

Fiscal Year

● Shifted the federal government to a fiscal year running from Oct. 1 through Sept. 30.

● Started fiscal 1977 on Oct. 1, 1976, after a three-month transition quarter following the end of fiscal 1976 on June 30, 1976.

President's Budget

● Required the president to submit by Nov. 10 of each year a current services budget for the fiscal year to start on the following Oct. 1.

● Required that administration requests for legislation authorizing programs during a fiscal year be submitted a year in advance of the congressional deadline for reporting the bills. The law required that the requests be made by May 15, 1975, for instance, for fiscal 1977 authorizations that committee would have to report by May 15, 1976, for the fiscal year starting Oct. 1, 1976.

● Required that the administration budget include certain analyses, including tax expenditure estimates and five-year budget projections.

Impoundment Control

● Revised the Anti-Deficiency Act of 1950 to authorize administration officials in allocating appropriated funds to

establish reserves only to provide for contingencies or effect savings made possible by changed requirements or improved efficiency.

● Required the president, if he concluded that budget authority should be permanently eliminated or temporarily withheld from obligation, to send Congress a special message asking that appropriations be rescinded or deferred.

● In the case of proposed rescissions, required the president to make the funds available for spending after 45 days if Congress failed to approve rescission legislation.

● In the case of proposed deferrals, required that the funds be spent if either the House or Senate adopted a resolution disapproving the deferral.

1975

The economy's steep decline forced a belated reappraisal of federal budget policy as 1975 began. Once economic events had shifted the primary policy focus to countering unemployment, the government moved decisively to stimulate demand by cutting taxes.

That meant accepting monumental budget deficits, a painful exercise for a Republican administration that remained committed to restraining inflationary pressures. In proposing a record $349.4 billion fiscal 1976 budget on Feb. 3, President Ford reluctantly projected back-to-back deficits of $34.7 billion in fiscal 1975 and $51.9 billion in fiscal 1976.

The president nonetheless renewed his customary plea for budgetary restraint, proposing a one-shot rebate of 1975 income taxes instead of permanent reductions and once more seeking to hold down built-in budget increases.

But Congress took control of fiscal policy almost from the start. It deepened the tax cuts, shifted the benefits toward lower income levels and provided most of the reduction through 1976 tax withholding changes that later were made permanent.

Putting the new budget procedures into use ahead of schedule, Congress went on to shape Ford's budget to its liking. With overwhelming House and Senate majorities — and with distressing unemployment rates to justify stimulative measures — congressional Democrats resisted most spending cuts and pumped more funds into the domestic programs that they favored.

And although they lost one December veto showdown with the president, the Democrats still pushed through a tax cut extension for the rest of fiscal 1976 with only a symbolic concession to budget restraint.

As a result of those congressional budget changes — along with changing economic trends and unanticipated program fluctuations — the deficits grew to $45.1 billion in fiscal 1975 and an all-time $66.5 billion record in fiscal 1976.

Ford Budget Proposal

Even as he proposed a $51.9 billion fiscal 1976 deficit, Ford cautioned Congress against pushing too fast to lower unemployment through budgetary stimulus that risked reviving inflationary pressures.

Ford's budget message stressed the need to keep in mind the long-run economic dangers posed by inflation and uncertain energy supplies. The nation's serious economic problems could be dealt with, Ford insisted, "if we exercise reasonable patience and restraint."

In the administration's view, overly stimulative policies before inflation had abated could only create worse economic problems for the future. The administration's budget proposed "a set of programs that head us in the right direction," argued outgoing Office of Management and Budget (OMB) Director Roy L. Ash, "without taking us right over the cliff."

The administration accordingly tried to limit the fiscal 1976 budget's stimulative impact to jolt the economy into a turnaround without setting off an irreversible and inflationary budgetary binge.

Key elements included:

• A one-time $16 billion tax cut, through a 12 percent rebate on calendar 1974 individual income taxes and a temporary 12 percent business investment credit.

• Yet another package of spending curbs, designed to trim $17.5 billion from expected outlay increases, including a 5 percent ceiling through the end of fiscal 1976 on federal pay raises and on cost-of-living increases in Social Security and other federal benefits.

• A moratorium on new federal programs, except for energy development, and a clamp on domestic spending, although the budget included an $8 billion increase in defense outlays.

Ford's program also included a $30 billion package of oil and gas taxes designed to discourage consumption by raising energy prices. The administration proposed to offset the drain of those taxes through permanent individual income tax reductions, payments to the poor and a 6 percent cut in the corporate income tax rate.

Tax Cut

Dominated by activist Democrats, the 94th Congress was in no mood for such restraint in fighting unemployment. In writing its tax-cut legislation, proposing various employment measures and starting up its new budget machinery, Congress consistently pushed beyond the fiscal constraints that Ford was seeking.

The House Ways and Means Committee quickly reworked the administration's tax program. Despite extensive Senate changes that tacked on additional stimulative measures — including Social Security bonus payments and extended unemployment benefits — Congress cleared a $22.8 billion tax cut (HR 2166 — PL 94-12) by March 26.

Ford reluctantly signed the bill, which added $6.1 billion to his initial $12 billion tax rebate proposal. *(Tax cut, p. 165)*

Budget Resolution

Congress in 1975 allayed many fears by putting key parts of the budget process to use a year ahead of schedule. Despite two close calls in the House, Congress in December agreed on a $374.9 billion budget resolution that raised the estimated fiscal 1976 deficit to a record $74.1 billion.

The final budget totals dismayed fiscal conservatives and displeased some pro-spending liberals who wanted Congress to take stronger action to reduce unemployment. In spite of their differences, important conservatives and liberals in both the House and Senate supported the new system at critical points and kept it from collapsing.

Fiscal 1976 Process

The 1974 law made its budget procedures mandatory for fiscal 1977, allowing Congress a year to get the feel of the process in 1975 if it chose through a "trial run" consideration of the fiscal 1976 budget. Eager to demonstrate congressional determination to take charge of economic policies, the House and Senate leadership and new Budget committees agreed to implement key parts of the process for the fiscal 1976 budget.

As announced March 3, the 1975 implementation plan called for adoption of a first budget resolution setting budget targets. But the resolution was to specify only overall budget figures, leaving out targets for the 16 functional program categories that could set off heated congressional disputes over spending priorities. Instead, the Budget committees included category targets in reports on the resolution. The plan also left until later a decision on whether to follow through by adopting firm fiscal 1976 ceilings in a second budget resolution.

The Budget committees also agreed to waive the budget law's tight deadlines for committee action on authorization bills and final action on appropriations. The process operated under various handicaps during 1975, moreover, including lack of a functioning Congressional Budget Office (CBO) early in the year. Alice M. Rivlin, an economist and senior fellow at the Brookings Institution, was sworn in as CBO director Feb. 24.

First Resolution

Completing action on the first concurrent resolution (H Con Res 218) May 14, Congress targeted fiscal 1976 spending at $367 billion. The resolution estimated federal revenues at $298.2 billion and the resulting deficit at $68.8 billion.

The first resolution laid out congressional Democrats' plans for additional economic stimulus beyond the emergency tax cuts. The resolution targeted $7.5 billion for programs to encourage expansion, divided among public works, public employment and temporary recovery programs.

Second Resolution

The final congressional budget resolution (H Con Res 466), adopted Dec. 12, estimated the fiscal 1976 budget deficit at $74.1 billion. That was $5.3 billion more than anticipated by the first resolution and $22.2 billion higher than Ford's February budget projection.

Those increases reflected several changes from the administration's budget assumptions, notably the expected continuation of the 1975 tax reductions and spending increases for Social Security, unemployment and other payments that responded to economic conditions. Congress ignored Ford's politically unpopular proposal for a 5 percent limit on Social Security benefit increases, so an 8.7 percent increase was triggered automatically on July 1 by a 1972 law (PL 92-336) that tied benefit increases to the inflation rate.

When fiscal 1976 ended on June 30, 1976, however, the deficit stood at $66.5 billion, $7.6 billion less than Congress had estimated in its budget resolution.

Actual fiscal 1976 outlays amounted to $366.5 billion, well under the $374.9 billion ceiling approved by Congress. Revenues were $300 billion, slightly below the $300.8 billion floor that Congress had specified.

1976

The economy was recovering when 1976 began, and inflation had abated. Congress and the president nonetheless remained sharply divided over appropriate fiscal policies as they began debating the fiscal 1977 budget.

President Ford built his Jan. 21 budget proposal around his 1975 request for a $28 billion tax cut and equivalent spending reductions. The president's budget projected outlays of $394.2 billion, just under his 1975 $395 billion ceiling request, and a still significant $43 billion deficit.

Ford rejected an election-year "policy of the quick fix" for economic troubles, and the administration's long-range economic outlook anticipated slow but steady reduction in unemployment and inflation rates.

The president renewed his traditional Republican theme of restraint, both on the fiscal 1977 deficit and on the built-in momentum of federal spending growth.

In return for stepping up the $18 billion tax cut provided in 1975 by another $10 billion, Ford's budget called for controversial measures to curb outlays. Major proposals, some revivals of earlier ideas that Congress had ignored, included: consolidation of existing education, health, child nutrition and social services programs into block grants for distribution to the states; limits on Medicare rates, increases in Medicare costs paid by most patients along with catastrophic illness protection for aged and disabled persons; and reductions in major unemployment programs in the expectation of continued economic improvement.

While proposing additional income tax reductions, the budget called for payroll tax increases effective in 1977 to put the Social Security and unemployment compensation trust funds on more secure long-range footing. Ford asked for a 0.6 percent Social Security tax increase, divided evenly between employers and workers, and a .15 percent increase in the unemployment insurance tax rate paid by employers.

Congressional Budget

Congress was quick to challenge Ford's contention that fiscal 1977 outlays could — or should — be held below $395 billion. Critics charged that the president's tax and spending combinations would create neither public nor private jobs and generally make the recovery slower than necessary.

Ignoring its December 1975 pledge to consider offsetting spending reductions, Congress May 13 adopted a fiscal 1977 budget blueprint that assumed extension of the existing tax cuts while adding $19.1 billion to the outlays that Ford had budgeted.

Assuming revenues of $362.5 billion, the initial fiscal 1977 budget resolution (S Con Res 109) projected federal spending of $413.3 billion and a resulting deficit of $50.8 billion, or $7.8 billion more than the administration's budget.

Budget Committee economists estimated that the congressional budget would produce one million more jobs than would Ford's. S Con Res 109 also set binding budget totals, leaving a $16.2 billion deficit for the federal government for the July-September 1976 transition quarter cre-

ated by the 1974 budget control law to shift the government onto an October-September fiscal year.

Congress followed through on that budget plan. After completing action on most fiscal 1977 spending measures, the House and Senate Sept. 16 adopted a second budget resolution (S Con Res 139) that limited total fiscal 1977 outlays to $413.1 billion.

That overall spending total, slightly less than contemplated by the initial congressional budget resolution, was $13.1 billion more than the Office of Management and Budget (OMB) had estimated in a July 16 budget revision.

With revenues set at $362.5 billion, the congressional budget estimated the fiscal 1977 deficit at $50.6 billion. That was only $3.1 billion more than OMB's July 16 prediction that the deficit would be $47.5 billion because Congress had turned down an administration tax program that would have reduced expected revenues about $10 billion.

As reworked by Congress, the fiscal 1977 budget therefore sought larger direct stimulus to economic activity through higher federal spending — particularly for education, health and various job-creating programs — with less emphasis on cutting taxes to leave more money for use in private hands.

Spending Measures

Congressional action on fiscal 1977 spending measures also was more orderly in 1976 as the budget authority and outlay totals provided by separate appropriations and authorization measures were fitted within the budget resolution limits.

All regular appropriations bills, along with one modest supplemental measure, had been cleared by Oct. 1, the first day of fiscal 1977. Congress thus had put the basic funding in place by the start of the fiscal year, a significant change dictated by the 1974 budget control law. In earlier years, Congress usually finished the appropriations process well into the fiscal year being funded.

Congress still was forced to clear a continuing resolution to keep funding available for some programs — including several health, education and jobs programs along with the Energy Research and Development Administration — whose fiscal 1977 authorization measures had fallen by the wayside during the 1976 session.

Following the guidelines laid down by the budget process, Congress in passing separate funding legislation ignored Ford's proposals for domestic program cutbacks or consolidations and concentrated new spending on several jobs programs. In some cases, Congress backed up its economic initiatives by overriding presidential vetoes.

After failing in February to overturn Ford's veto of a more expensive public works job measure, Congress July 22 overrode a second veto to enact a $3.95 billion authorization bill (S 3201 — PL 94-369) for state and local public works projects, countercyclical grants to state and local governments and for waste water treatment programs.

Congress followed up Sept. 22 by clearing a $3.7 billion fiscal 1977 appropriations bill (HR 15194 — PL 94-447) for those emergency programs, finally finishing action on a key recession-fighting measure that Democratic leaders had been proposing since the 94th Congress convened in 1975. Ford signed the bill.

In another display of pre-election muscle on budget issues, the House and Senate Sept. 30 overrode the president's veto of a $56.6 billion appropriations bill for the departments of Labor and Health, Education and Welfare (HR 14232 — PL 94-439). Ford termed the measure, which provided nearly $4 billion more than his budget request, "a perfect example of the triumph of election-year politics over fiscal restraint and responsibility."

1977

Congress moved quickly in 1977 to accommodate President Carter's plan to stimulate the sagging economy. But Carter's sudden shift away from proposed recession-fighting tax rebates and deep divisions among House Democrats over defense and social spending nearly threw the fledgling congressional budget process into chaos.

In March Congress adopted an unprecedented third fiscal 1977 budget resolution that adjusted previously approved spending and revenue limits to make room for stimulative measures that Carter proposed shortly after taking office. But by May, after Carter abruptly abandoned his proposed $50 tax rebates and payments, Congress again was forced to change its fiscal 1977 assumptions.

Congress in September backed the new president by approving fiscal 1978 budget goals that were far more expansive that the proposals that Republican President Ford left behind in January. The binding fiscal 1978 budget levels assumed a large increase in federal spending, the second highest deficit ever and a slower economic growth rate than in fiscal 1977.

In the process, congressional faith in the newly designed budget-making procedures was shaken by uncertain economic forecasts, changing Office of Management and Budget (OMB) revenue and outlay estimates and intense debate about proper defense spending levels. In an unusual coalition, Democratic liberals and Republican conservatives combined to defeat for the first time a preliminary fiscal 1978 budget resolution.

In the end, House and Senate Budget Committee leaders settled on a $61.25 billion fiscal 1978 deficit in a final budget resolution that held defense spending low enough to attract liberal support. House Republicans continued to balk at stimulative budget policy. But Democrats eagerly went along with Carter's recession-fighting programs, while resisting the administration's campaign to hold down future growth of outlays for politically popular water projects and other programs.

Carter Budget Revisions

Less than two weeks after taking office in January, Carter began shifting federal fiscal policy to accelerate economic growth and bring unemployment down more rapidly from its 1974-75 recession depths. To inject a quick boost to demand, the new administration January 31 outlined a $31.2 billion two-year plan that combined tax rebates and reductions with increased outlays for federal job programs.

Charles L. Shultze, chairman of Carter's Council of Economic Advisers, Jan. 27 had told the House Budget Committee that the package was designed to combine quick stimulus through tax refunds with sustained support for economic growth that would generate business and consumer confidence. He also noted that the administration wanted to keep permanent tax cuts and spending increases small in order to leave room for new federal initiatives such as health insurance while balancing future budgets.

For fiscal 1977, under way since the previous Oct. 1, the Carter package proposed $13.8 billion in tax cuts, mostly through one-shot, $50 rebates on 1976 taxes, and $50 payments to all Social Security, railroad retirement and supplemental security income recipients, and to low-income taxpayers who were eligible for the earned income credit. The administration also sought to increase outlays by $1.7 billion for a variety of programs, including federally funded public service jobs, public works jobs, training and youth programs, and countercyclical assistance to state and local governments.

For fiscal 1978, the year that would begin on Oct. 1, 1977, the administration's program called for $7.6 billion in additional spending on those programs, along with $8.2 billion in personal and business tax cuts through the permanent changes accompanying the 1976 tax rebates. Carter Feb. 22 incorporated those initiatives in revised fiscal 1978 budget proposals that called for spending $19.4 billion more than President Ford's budget had envisioned. *(Fiscal 1978 budget, p. 125)*

Fiscal 1977 Stimulus Resolution

Congress promptly went to work writing new fiscal 1977 budget targets to fit Carter's initiatives. In September 1976, the 94th Congress had set binding revenue, spending and deficit limits calling for a $50.6 billion federal deficit for the year. Carter's stimulative tax and spending changes would have breached the totals set by the second 1976 budget resolution (S Con Res 139).

For the first time since Congress put its budget process into effect in 1976, the House and Senate therefore had to write a third fiscal 1977 budget resolution to accommodate those changes. S Con Res 10 raised the deficit to $69.75 billion, nearly $2 billion more than the administration estimated in its Feb. 22 budget revisions. Devising the figures while congressional committees still were working on tax and spending measures, the House and Senate Budget committees arrived at aggregate figures that assumed $17.5 billion in additional stimulus for the remaining seven months of the fiscal year. Given final approval on March 3, S Con Res 10 allowed for fiscal 1977 outlays of $417.45 billion, $69.75 billion more than the anticipated revenues of $347.7 billion.

Those figures encompassed Carter's full $13.8 billion tax package, even though doubts were growing in Congress about how much stimulus $50 tax rebates would generate. Convinced that direct government spending would create jobs more quickly than the administration's proposal, Congress nearly doubled planned outlay increases for jobs and countercyclical assistance.

Carter Reversal

Barely a month after Congress put revised fiscal 1977 budget goals in place, Carter abandoned the $50 tax rebates that the administration had proposed for quick stimulative impact. Carter April 14 told reporters that improving economic indicators since the stimulus package was planned in December had made immediate stimulus unnecessary. The administration reversed itself five days before the Senate took up the Finance Committee's tax-cut package in a climate of growing hostility to the $50 rebates from Republicans who favored permanent tax cuts and Democrats who thought spending increases would be more effective in stimulating economic activity. *(Stimulus tax cut, p. 178)*

Carter's surprising withdrawal of the rebate plan — and proposed business tax credits as well — left the third fiscal 1977 budget assumptions far too generous. In writing tentative fiscal 1978 budget targets (S Con Res 19), Congress in May again revised its fiscal 1977 figures, increasing revenue estimates to remove the previously expected cost of the rebate plan. The final revision set the fiscal 1977 deficit estimate at $52.6 billion, just $2 billion more than Congress had approved the previous September.

Fiscal 1978 Budget

Democratic efforts to stimulate the economy were more evident in the fiscal 1978 budget. Working from Carter's Feb. 22 budget revisions, Congress Sept. 15 approved binding budget levels for fiscal 1978 that departed sharply from the previous Republican administration's campaign for fiscal restraints. The final product, reflecting gloomy economic forecasts as well as congressional tax and spending decisions, aimed for a $61.25 billion deficit, which would be the second largest in the nation's history.

Final Ford Budget

Three days before his term ended, Ford sent Congress a $440 billion budget for fiscal 1978 that contemplated a $47 billion deficit. The budget was followed by Ford's economic report to Congress cautioning the incoming administration against stimulative spending increases while urging permanent tax cuts and incentives for business investment.

Both documents reflected the outgoing Republican administration's philosophy of fiscal restraint and limited government involvement in the economy. The budget was in some ways a memorial to Ford's bitter differences with a Democratic Congress during his 30 months in office. It reiterated Ford's past proposals for spending curbs that Congress had ignored, and it renewed an earlier proposal for individual income tax cuts to offset tax increases resulting from inflation. That program stood no chance of being accepted by a Democratic administration or Congress, especially since Carter was even then readying stimulative measures based on one-time tax rebates and accelerated spending on federal jobs programs.

But the $47 billion deficit in Ford's fiscal 1978 proposal, which was nearly $20 billion less than the actual fiscal 1976 shortfall of $65.6 billion and $10 billion less than Ford's estimated fiscal 1977 deficit, posed a challenge to the incoming president who had pledged to balance the budget by 1981.

Carter Revisions

Carter Feb. 22 revised Ford's budget projections upward, calling for $19.4 billion more in outlays than the Republican budget contemplated. Carter's $459.4 billion budget proposal allowed for a 10 percent increase above expected fiscal 1977 outlays, which matched the average annual jump over the previous decade but was well above the 7 percent growth in spending that Ford's budget envisioned. Carter predicted a $57.7 billion fiscal 1978 deficit, $10.8 billion more than Ford's estimate, assuming that federal revenues would rise in response to economic growth rekindled by the Democratic administration's 1977 fiscal stimulus package.

Carter restored most funding reductions sought by Ford. The administration asked for other cutbacks of its own, notably for defense and water project construction.

Congressional Budget Targets

As required by budget-making procedures, Congress in May approved fiscal 1978 budget targets for subsequent tax and spending deliberations. Members agreed on those goals, including a deficit $6.9 billion higher than Carter's revised projection, only after the House resoundingly rejected an initial budget package that displeased conservatives and liberals alike. That defeat, plus OMB re-estimates of likely fiscal 1978 figures, forced the House and Senate Budget committees back to the drawing boards to prepare new congressional targets.

In April, both panels had approved target resolutions (H Con Res 195 — H Rept 95-189; S Con Res 19 — S Rept 95-90) that projected deficits well over $60 billion. The panels based their targets on economic forecasts that were more pessimistic about the speed of recovery than administration expectations and on some policy differences with Carter. For example, the House panel turned down efforts to raise defense spending levels by $2.3 billion, to the level recommended by Carter. The Senate committee, in its separate proposal, approved defense outlays only $300 million less than Carter's request.

House Targets Rejected. House backing for the initial budget targets, usually tenuous at best, unraveled on the House floor. During two days of debate in late April, the House adopted numerous amendments — including committee revisions — that boosted the deficit target to $68.6 billion. On a vote of 225-184, the House approved an amendment to restore defense appropriations and outlays to Carter's proposed levels, thus undercutting the panel's efforts to balance defense and domestic spending. The amended resolution satisfied neither side, and it went down to defeat, 84-320, with only five Budget Committee members supporting its approval.

House Compromise Approved. The House May 5 approved a compromise resolution (H Con Res 214 — H Rept 95-239) that its Budget Committee had fashioned in an effort to satisfy objections to the first measure. This time the House turned down by a 176-233 vote a proposal to raise defense funding to Carter's requested levels. With Democratic leaders warning members that the survival of the budget process was at stake, the House adopted H Con Res 214 by a 213-179 vote. The Senate had passed the panel's resolution May 4 after approving floor amendments that added $7.2 billion in budget authority and $400 million in outlays.

Final Action. House-Senate conferees easily settled most differences, but they spent one full day and half of a second negotiating a compromise defense target that Senate conferees felt was high enough and that House conferees thought was low enough to attract enough liberal votes to pass the entire resolution. Conferees settled on defense goals that nearly matched Carter's proposed fiscal 1978 outlays but scaled back his budget authority request.

The Senate approved the compromise on May 13. The House accepted it on May 17, 221-177. Support from 29 Republicans marked a departure from the minority's nearly unanimous opposition to previous congressional budget resolutions.

Binding Fiscal 1978 Totals

Congress in September approved a final fiscal 1978 budget resolution (H Con Res 341) that assumed a large increase in federal spending and a deficit of slightly more than $61 billion. The binding budget totals were based on predictions that a slowing economy would reduce revenues below and increase outlays above the levels projected by the Carter administration.

In most programs, congressional action on appropriations already had set spending levels that generally fell within the targets Congress had set for itself in May. But the House and Senate Budget committees, writing final budget proposals in August, made important adjustments to accommodate pending energy legislation and higher spending than previously anticipated for farm programs. Both Budget panels were unhappy with congressional decisions that ignored preliminary budget targets in drafting an omnibus farm-food stamp measure. But the Senate committee's attempt to order farm spending restraint was overridden.

During floor debate, both the House and Senate voted to raise spending limits to accommodate the pending farm legislation. The House and Senate also amended the final budget resolution on the floor to make room for revenue-losing tax credits for college tuition that some members were advocating. The Senate turned down Republican tax-cut proposals, while the House defeated a Republican plan to balance the fiscal 1978 budget. The House narrowly approved its version, 199-188, as Republicans again voted nearly unanimously in opposition to the congressional budget figures, particularly the high deficit.

In shaping a conference compromise on binding budget totals (H Rept 95-601, S Rept 95-428), House and Senate conferees split the difference to settle on a 4.8 percent estimate for the expected real growth in economic output on which they based tax and spending projections. Both chambers approved the conference version Sept 15.

1978

The U.S. economy's continuously changing prospects bedeviled federal budget policy again in 1978. Working from President Carter's $500.2 billion fiscal 1979 proposal, Congress began writing its budget targets with high unemployment and possible economic downturn in mind. But inflation soared again during the year, and Congress began responding to an anti-government spending spirit that took hold in national politics.

By September, concern about inflation and high federal spending had eclipsed the early focus on stimulative tax cuts and job-creating measures. As a result, Congress that month approved a $487.5 billion fiscal 1979 budget that sheared Carter's $60.6 billion deficit to less than $39

billion. The binding budget resolution (H Con Res 683) took account of congressional actions reducing tax cuts and federal spending and reflected smaller-than-previously-expected outlays for defense procurement and for medical and unemployment assistance.

In the process, Congress scaled back its own $50.9 billion deficit target set by a first fiscal 1979 budget resolution (S Con Res 80) in May. And the Senate, demonstrating notable support for its Budget Committee's position, held firm in September against House Democratic leaders' pressure to accept $2 billion in new spending for public works projects. The dispute delayed approval of binding budget totals until Sept. 23, a week after the deadline set by the 1974 budget control law.

As usual the Senate gave bipartisan support to budget resolutions. But most House Republicans continued to oppose fiscal recommendations by the Democratic majority, and their votes came close to defeating budget proposals. Republicans tried unsuccessfully to amend budget resolutions to make room for deeper tax cuts. They also challenged House Budget Committee procedures that they maintained simply toted up spending requests for different programs without fitting them to previously designed fiscal policy guidelines.

Fiscal 1979 Budget

Carter's fiscal 1979 budget proposal, released Jan. 23, combined a $24.5 billion tax reduction with markedly slowed growth in federal outlays. By Carter's analysis, judged overly optimistic by some critics, that combination would spur solid, but not spectacular, economic growth and bring a modest drop in unemployment.

The $500.2 billion fiscal 1979 budget was the first produced entirely by Carter's Democratic administration. Despite its $60.6 billion deficit projection, the document hewed to the president's philosophy that government should be limited. That view was revealed by Carter's proud assertion that he was holding real spending growth above current-service levels under 2 percent. Still, the budget contemplated that spending would rise $7.8 billion above the estimated $492.4 billion needed to maintain existing programs. The additional outlays included $1 billion for defense, $2.1 billion for energy and another $1 billion for education, training, employment and social service programs.

First Budget Resolution

By May, when Congress adopted a first budget resolution (S Con Res 80) setting tentative fiscal 1979 targets, inflation was surging and unemployment falling more rapidly than Carter's budget had anticipated. Congress and the administration therefore scaled back the proposed tax cuts to $19.4 billion and agreed to put them into effect on Jan. 1, 1979, three months into the fiscal year. The resulting $15 billion estimated revenue loss, along with downward revision in some outlay projections, produced a $498.8 billion congressional budget goal with a deficit nearly $10 billion less than Carter's January estimate.

Conferees skirted potential tax disputes by remaining silent on Social Security payroll tax rollbacks and leaving room in the budget targets for either the tuition credit or increased student loans and grants. The conferees spent three days in what one budget expert called "a symbolic battle over guns versus butter" before splitting the difference between House and Senate appropriations recommendations for defense and a variety of human services.

The Senate approved the conference report (H Rept 95-1173; S Rept 95-866) by voice vote on May 15. The House, with Republicans protesting the decision to reduce tax cuts rather than limit spending, adopted the targets May 17 by a cliff-hanging 201-198 margin with only two minority members voting for the resolution.

Binding Budget Resolution

The inflation-fighting mood in Congress carried over through the summer, shaping the binding fiscal 1979 budget limits that the House and Senate agreed on in September. Events that followed approval of the first resolution strengthened the trend toward reducing the deficit. Continued inflation confirmed the belief that a smaller tax cut was appropriate. As in the past, July budget re-estimates suggested that federal agencies were unable to spend money as fast as Congress appropriated it. In June, California voters approved a state constitutional amendment slashing property taxes, drawing national attention to a so-called "taxpayers' revolt."

In response, Congress fashioned a final fiscal 1979 resolution that cut the $50.9 billion deficit target to $38.8 billion. Final approval came, however, only after Senate budget negotiators, with unprecedented backing from the full Senate, made a determined stand in conference against a House plan to add $2 billion for new public works.

Budget Committee Chairman Edmund S. Muskie, D-Maine (1959-80), with strong backing from the panel's top-ranking Republican, Henry Bellmon, R-Okla. (1969-81), contended that the $2 billion public works program would stimulate an already healthy construction sector, driving up wages and building material prices. In conference negotiations, Muskie refused to accept House conferees' compromise proposals; while Speaker Thomas P. O'Neill Jr., D-Mass., urged House Budget Committee Chairman Robert N. Giaimo, D-Conn. (1959-81), to take a tough stand for public works spending.

With negotiations stalemated, Muskie asked the Senate to back up his stand. By a 63-21 margin, the Senate complied Sept. 14 by instructing its conferees to insist on no new public works spending at all. The impasse blocked a conference agreement for several days, until the conferees accepted a face-saving solution that allowed the House and Senate to interpret the budget limits differently.

Conferees also compromised on the fiscal 1979 revenue floor, agreeing on a $448.7 billion figure that left room for an additional $2 billion in tax cuts for calendar 1979. The final version of the tax cut bill was then written to accommodate that goal. *(Tax bill, p. 180)*

The House adopted the compromise Sept. 21; the Senate approved it Sept. 23.

1979

Congressional budget making faltered in 1979, troubled by a sagging economy and political disarray in the House.

Congress managed to hold its binding fiscal 1980 deficit estimate to less than $30 billion, meeting a goal that President Carter had set the year before. But the House, sharply divided over where spending should be cut, defeated two budget resolutions before settling on the final compromise. As a result, Congress did not put its binding fiscal 1980 budget resolution into place until nearly two months after the fiscal year began.

In the Senate, the Budget Committee continued to make impressive strides in encouraging fiscal discipline. The Senate in September insisted on large defense funding increases, but it went along with the Budget panel's plan to order Appropriations and authorizing committees to trim $3.6 billion to live within budget spending limits. The House, however, backed away from enforcing strict outlay curbs.

As it was, the final budget resolution met the deficit goal only because inflation-generated revenues partly kept pace with rising federal outlays. With recession threatening, Congress abandoned the $23 billion deficit target it had set in its first budget resolution in May. The final budget figures provided an extra $5.7 billion for defense that senators had demanded as their price for supporting the SALT II arms limitation treaty. But House liberals put their own price tag — more spending for domestic social programs — on support for more military funds.

Fiscal 1980 Budget

The president in 1979 sent Congress a "lean and austere" $531.6 billion fiscal 1980 budget proposal. That budget planned to reduce government services in all but three major areas — defense, Social Security and interest on the national debt — while holding the deficit to $29 billion. "The policy of restraint...is an imperative if we are to overcome the threat of accelerating inflation," the president declared Jan. 22.

Carter's tight-fisted approach allowed fiscal 1980 outlays of $531.6 billion, a 7.7 percent increase over fiscal 1979 levels. His $502.6 billion revenue estimate assumed no general tax cuts or Social Security payroll tax relief. The budget provided for a 3 percent rise in real defense outlays, but it scaled back planned administration initiatives, cut back anti-recession public service job programs and chipped away at social program benefits while tightening eligibility requirements.

Fiscal 1980 Budget Targets

Pressure to balance the budget built up early in the year. Some state legislatures and potential presidential candidates clamored for a constitutional amendment forbidding federal deficits, and conservatives stalled debt limit legislation until congressional leaders assured them a chance to vote for balancing the budget.

Congress responded, after a long and arduous battle, by writing a first budget resolution (H Con Res 107) that promised to bring the fiscal 1980 deficit down to $23 billion, $6 billion less than Carter's proposal. In the process, the Senate Budget Committee laid out a strategy for balancing the next fiscal year's budget — but only if Congress provided no tax cuts until 1982.

In the same resolution, Congress revised the binding fiscal 1979 budget figures it had adopted the previous September. The revisions lifted outlays to $494.45 billion, allowing room for nearly $7 billion in higher-than-expected costs and for various supplemental appropriations for defense and other functions. But the resolution also raised the revenue estimate by more than $12 billion, allowing Congress to reduce its projected deficit by $5 billion, to $33.45 billion.

The $23 billion fiscal 1980 deficit target was set even though the Senate insisted on approving most of Carter's defense spending request. House Democratic liberals, who had persuaded the House to include substantial defense reductions in its original budget resolution, mounted a successful campaign to defeat the initial conference report. They demanded that funds be shifted from defense to social programs. Senate conferees refused to budge, although they mollified the House by accepting increased appropriations targets for education, training, employment and social service programs. That concession satisfied enough House liberals for the House to approve the revised compromise May 24 by a six-vote margin, 202-196.

Binding Budget Levels

Congress approved binding fiscal 1980 budget levels (S Con Res 53) on Nov. 28, more than two months after the Sept. 15 deadline. The House Sept. 19 had rejected its budget committee's initial binding recommendations, the first time a second budget resolution had been turned down by either the House or Senate. Eight days later, on Sept. 27, the House accepted a revised resolution, but conferees then haggled for a record 23 days before agreeing to increase both defense and social spending.

The final resolution raised the fiscal 1980 outlay ceiling to $547.6 billion, but kept the expected deficit at $29.8 billion by assuming rising revenues. But the House refused to go along with the Senate Budget Committee's plan to enforce those limits by instructing congressional authorizing and Appropriations committees to pare $3.6 billion from spending. S Con Res 53 did carry compromise language warning committees that Congress would not bail them out by approving a third fiscal 1980 resolution to cover spending increases. As it turned out, Congress bumped up against the binding levels by March of 1980 and, overlooking the warning, added $19.4 billion to its fiscal 1980 budget as part of its 1981 budget process.

1980

Alarmed by an election-year surge in prices, Congress and President Carter worked hard together in 1980 to balance the federal budget. But just as the House and Senate set that as their goal for fiscal 1981, a volatile economy and rising defense costs wrenched the budget back toward a deep and growing deficit.

A discouraged Congress put off final budget decisions until after the November elections, then quietly approved a $27.4 billion projected deficit. The final fiscal 1981 budget resolution (H Con Res 448) left to newly elected Republican President Ronald Reagan and a conservative-minded 97th Congress the hard task of slowing the rapid growth of the federal budget.

Carter began the year in January by proposing a "prudent and responsible" fiscal 1981 blueprint that contemplated a $15.8 billion deficit. But by year's end the administration had revised its fiscal policies three times to reflect changing economic conditions and Carter had been swept from office by voters demanding a president who would be more frugal with tax dollars.

Even as Carter announced his budget, the January inflation rate soared to an annual rate of nearly 18.2 percent, and U.S. bond markets came close to collapse. Republicans grabbed at the grim economic news, blaming the Democratic controlled government for driving prices upward through continued budget deficits. Democratic congressional leaders quickly went to work with the Carter administration to chisel the budget into balance. Even before the White House first revised its requests in mid-March, the House and Senate Budget committees were drafting congressional budget targets to meet the president's 1976 campaign pledge to balance the budget during his first term in office.

Congress followed up in June — despite a brief revolt by young House liberals against domestic spending cuts — by adopting for the first time a budget resolution calling for a slim fiscal 1981 surplus. By then, however, the entire budget process had fallen a month behind schedule.

Six months later, Congress used budget reconciliation procedures for the first time to cut $8.2 billion from potential fiscal 1981 spending. But it adjourned without finishing appropriations bills for the year for several federal agencies.

Fiscal 1980 Revisions

Even as it set a balanced budget goal for fiscal 1981, Congress acknowledged that its fiscal 1980 budget figures had been wide of the mark. In passing its first budget resolution in June, Congress accordingly revised the fiscal 1980 budget limits it had set in November 1979. The fiscal 1980 revisions, as approved June 12, boosted the $29.8 billion deficit that Congress had agreed to in November to $47 billion. The new spending limit added $25.1 billion to the November 1979 estimate of $547.6 billion to take account of inflation-linked outlays for Social Security, food stamps, Medicaid, Medicare and public debt interest.

Fiscal 1981 Budget

Carter Jan. 28 sent Congress a $615.8 billion campaign-year budget calling for large defense and energy spending increases without offsetting cuts in social programs. The fiscal 1981 budget spared most programs the kind of politically unpopular reductions that Carter had sought in the previous year's "lean and austere" budget. The fiscal 1981 proposal allowed spending to rise $3.7 billion above "current service" levels, evidently abandoning Carter's pledge to balance the budget in 1981. Uncharacteristically for an election year it left no room for tax cuts to counter a predicted recession, even though inflation was pushing revenues up rapidly.

Barely two months later, the administration reworked its budget proposal to fit a hastily devised anti-inflation strategy prompted by the January price surge. Carter's budget revisions, submitted to Congress March 31, were built around $15 billion in spending reductions that White

House economic advisers had worked out in several days of consultations with Democratic lawmakers. Because inflation was boosting automatic spending on existing programs, the March 31 budget trimmed only $4.3 billion from the $615.8 billion in outlays the administration had estimated in January. But by assuming a $28 billion revenue increase — including $12.6 billion from a proposed surcharge on oil imports — Carter nonetheless predicted that the changes would produce a $16.5 billion fiscal 1981 surplus.

First Budget Resolution

By the time Carter's updated budget arrived on Capitol Hill, Congress was far into its 1980 budget-making process. But because Democratic leaders had participated in the spending cut deliberations, the House and Senate Budget Committee resolutions followed the president's revisions closely on most matters.

Both the House and the Senate turned back floor amendments that would have made major changes in the Budget committee recommendations. The House rejected an amendment that would have allowed additional spending for several domestic programs, while the Senate turned back an effort to transfer $2 billion from the Pentagon to social programs.

House-Senate conferees May 22 approved compromise budget targets setting fiscal 1981 spending at $613.3 billion, leaving a $500 million estimated surplus. The compromise set defense spending at $153.7 billion, $2 billion less than the Senate figure but $5.8 billion more than the House resolution provided. The compromise cut $1.2 billion from House education and training levels and substantial amounts from other domestic program targets.

The resulting $18 billion defense spending increase was a victory for defense-minded senators. But five moderate-to-liberal Democratic House conferees refused to sign the conference report and campaigned for the House to turn down the compromise resolution.

The day before the House voted, the president himself said the conference agreement was too generous to the military. House Speaker Thomas P. O'Neill Jr., D-Mass., had a change of heart hours before the vote, telling reporters that "this budget goes against my philosophy." Although other House leaders stayed behind the budget compromise, the House defeated the conference report, 141-242, with 146 Democrats siding with most Republicans in opposition.

No sooner had the compromise been defeated, however, than the House turned around and instructed its Budget Committee members to insist on retaining the conference report's record-high defense figures. Two weeks later, conferees agreed on a second compromise that increased outlays for transportation and low-income energy assistance by $300 million, cutting the projected budget surplus to $200 million from $500 million. In addition, conferees switched $800 million in budget authority from defense to social programs. The House June 12 accepted those changes, 205-195, and the Senate cleared the resolution by a 61-26 vote the same day.

Binding Budget Deficit

Within a month, however, events made it clear that congressional budget-balancing struggles would prove futile. The first budget resolution's economic foundation was shifting, with inflation easing and a long-predicted recession apparently taking hold. In July, when the administration revised its fiscal 1981 budget outlook for the second time, the $16.5 billion surplus that Carter sought in March had turned into a whopping $29.8 billion deficit.

A chastened Congress adjusted its binding fiscal 1981 budget accordingly, although it held off the politically unpalatable task until after the November elections.

The final version essentially split the difference between the House and Senate resolutions, winding up with $632.4 billion in spending and a $27.4 billion deficit. The conference agreement provided for a $30 billion to $40 billion tax cut in calendar 1981, reducing expected revenues to $605 billion. Its outlay and revenue figures assumed that Congress eventually would enact the reconciliation legislation that the first budget resolution had ordered.

Even so, many members acknowledged that the final fiscal 1981 deficit would probably turn out double the congressional goal, due to increased inflation, government borrowing costs and a possible jump in unemployment. And, as retiring Sen. Henry Bellmon, R-Okla., ranking Republican on the Senate Budget Committee, pointed out, Congress already had approved appropriations bills that exceeded the spending total by $2.5 billion. The House and Senate approved the compromise Nov. 20.

Reconciliation Bill

Two weeks after finishing its binding fiscal 1981 budget resolution, Congress in 1980 approved "reconciliation" legislation to cut the expected deficit by more than $8.2 billion. It was the first time in the six-year history of the congressional budget process that Congress made use of reconciliation procedures to adjust ongoing federal programs to fit congressional budget limits.

Congress cleared the measure (HR 7765 — PL 96-499) Dec. 3, responding to instructions that it had tacked onto the first fiscal 1981 resolution (H Con Res 307) adopted in June. While falling short of the savings that the first budget resolution had targeted, HR 7765 did contain $4.6 billion in spending cutbacks and $3.6 billion in revenue increases.

By using the reconciliation mechanism — at the end of a year in which budget-balancing efforts had collapsed — Congress salvaged some hope that the budget-making process it created in 1974 could in fact discipline federal program spending.

In its final form, the measure cut back spending for federal programs already on the books — for education, transportation, health, federal retirement, unemployment compensation and other services — to save $4.6 billion in outlays for the fiscal year that had started Oct. 1. Its revenue-raising provisions were expected to yield $3.6 billion in added tax receipts through various tax-law changes, duties and excise taxes. HR 7765 combined in one bill provisions that eight House and 10 Senate committees had drafted to meet budget goals. Its approval, despite protests from some powerful congressional committee chairmen, bolstered the House and Senate Budget committees' influence over appropriations and authorization legislation.

Background

The 1974 Congressional Budget Act (PL 93-344) established the reconciliation process, but Congress previously had been reluctant to use it. The Senate in 1977 backed its Agriculture Committee by knocking out a Budget Committee reconciliation proposal to force cuts in pending farm legislation. In 1979, House Budget Committee leaders refused to challenge other committees and instead forced the Senate to abandon reconciliation instructions it had approved in its second budget resolution.

The 1974 law permitted reconciliation orders only as part of the binding second resolution. But in the spring of 1980, with Congress determined to approve a balanced budget as congressional elections approached, the House and Senate Budget committees agreed to add reconciliation instructions to the non-binding targets set by the first budget resolution. Cleared June 12, H Con Res 307 accordingly ordered House and Senate panels to recommend $6.4 billion in fiscal 1981 spending cuts to fit the balanced budget. It also directed the tax-writing House Ways and Means and Senate Finance committees to draft measures to raise $4.2 billion in new revenues.

The largest conference in the history of Congress convened on the reconciliation bill Sept. 18, with more than 100 senators and representatives taking part. The conferees subsequently split up into small groups representing the authorizing committees involved, but deliberations took two months to resolve all House and Senate differences.

The knottiest issues — involving cost-of-living increases for military and federal retirees, changes in Medicare and Medicaid, child nutrition programs, mortgage subsidy bonds and the crude oil windfall profits tax — delayed a final compromise until late November.

Provisions

As cleared by Congress Dec. 3, HR 7765 provided for spending reductions in the following categories:

● Education and labor, $840 million in budget authority and $826 million in outlays.

● Post Office and Civil Service, $429 million in budget authority and $463 million in outlays.

● Highway, rail and airport programs, $375 million in budget authority and $917 million in outlays.

● Small business, $800 million in budget authority and $600 million in outlays.

● Health, $12 million in budget authority and $915 million in outlays.

● Unemployment compensation, $32 million in budget authority and $147 million in outlays.

● Social Security and public assistance, $117 million in budget authority and $270 million in outlays.

The bill also raised revenues of:

● $256 million by phasing out tax-free mortgage bonds issued by state and local governments.

● $3.06 billion by requiring large corporations to pay estimated taxes equal to at least 60 percent of current year tax liability.

● $42 million by imposing capital gains taxes on real estate sold by foreigners.

● $44 million by treating employer payment of employees' Social Security and unemployment payroll tax contributions as wages subject to those taxes.

● $358 million by delaying a scheduled reduction and elimination of the federal telephone excise tax.

● $12 million by imposing duties on ethyl alcohol used as fuel.

HR 7765 also lost $180 million in revenues by easing the new windfall profits tax on oil for royalty owners.

1981

Offering his formal budget March 10, President Reagan issued a blunt warning to Congress to adopt his sweeping spending and tax cuts or risk angering voters who instructed Washington in the 1980 elections to put "America's economic house in order."

In a message accompanying the details of his budget for fiscal 1982, Reagan claimed that his plan to reduce federal spending by $48.6 billion in fiscal 1982 and lower taxes by $53.9 billion would help move the nation "back toward economic sanity." Combined with a "stable" monetary policy and a rollback in federal regulations, Reagan said the budget reductions would result in a quick drop in inflation and a "return to prosperity."

Reagan recommended that total federal spending be held to $695.3 billion in fiscal 1982, with budget authority of $772.4 billion, revenues of $650.3 billion and a deficit of $45 billion. Reagan's broad spending cuts, which spared only military and so-called "social safety net" programs, would reduce the growth of spending to 6.2 percent in fiscal 1982, compared to the 11.6 percent rate proposed by Carter.

First Budget Resolution

Giving the president most of what he wanted, Congress passed its fiscal 1982 non-binding budget resolution May 21. The resolution (H Con Res 115) called for $770.9 billion in budget authority, $695.45 billion in outlays, $657.8 billion in revenues and a $37.65 billion deficit. That amounted to $150 million more than Reagan requested for outlays and $7.35 billion less than his projected deficit.

In calling for a $51.3 billion reduction in revenues, the resolution assumed enactment of a $53.9 billion tax cut, partially offset by $2.6 billion in additional user fees. In reality, Congress in August enacted a tax bill that would cut fiscal 1982 revenues by an estimated $37.7 billion. *(1981 tax cut, p. 191)*

The budget resolution also included instructions requiring 14 Senate committees and 15 House committees to make $36 billion in fiscal 1982 spending cuts.

After final congressional action on the resolution, White House Deputy Press Secretary Larry Speakes said the president was "extremely pleased that the Congress has acted in record time."

In contrast to past budget resolutions, the disagreements between the House and Senate resolutions were fairly narrow. Close to $8 billion of the difference between the two chambers' spending figures resulted from differences in economic assumptions — chiefly the difference in assumptions about interest rates. The chambers split the difference on the interest assumptions, and the Senate accepted the House measure's more optimistic growth rates for the remainder of fiscal 1981 and fiscal 1982, as well as the House's higher revenue figures. Both helped to lower the anticipated deficit.

The House and Senate also were very close on their reconciliation figures. The Senate called for $36.9 billion in cuts and the House resolution required $36.6 billion. But technical differences arose because of different assumptions and discrepancies in committee jurisdictions.

Final Reconciliation Savings

The final version of the reconciliation package (HR 3982) altered existing programs to achieve the following budget savings *(by House committee jurisdiction, in millions of dollars)*:

Committee	Fiscal 1982 Budget Authority Cuts	Fiscal 1982 Outlay Cuts	Fiscal 1983 Budget Authority Cuts	Fiscal 1983 Outlay Cuts	Fiscal 1984 Budget Authority Cuts	Fiscal 1984 Outlay Cuts
Agriculture	$ 2,449	$ 3,264	$ 3,042	$ 3,878	$ 3,930	$ 4,661
Armed Services	846	882	767	731	374	374
Banking, Finance and Urban Affairs	13,566	481	15,954	1,154	18,402	2,115
District of Columbia	39	40	56	58	72	69
Education and Labor	10,088	7,297	12,414	10,749	14,261	13,881
Energy and Commerce	7,955	7,115	7,457	7,710	6,686	6,961
Foreign Affairs	376	286	524	463	538	515
Interior and Insular Affairs	820	736	+236[1]	111	68	5
Judiciary	72	30	70	71	59	66
Merchant Marine and Fisheries	242	106	242	212	265	253
Post Office and Civil Service	4,706	5,163	6,253	6,690	7,214	7,555
Public Works and Transportation	6,606	1,411	5,070	3,136	6,371	5,418
Science and Technology	1,395	828	961	1,016	1,209	1,065
Small Business	504	823	540	517	527	506
Veterans' Affairs	110	116	122	127	124	128
Ways and Means	4,140	8,981	4,455	9,822	4,763	10,803
Total Cuts[2]	**$51,900**	**$35,190**	**$55,734**	**$44,033**	**$61,721**	**$51,353**

[1] *Increase in budget authority attributable to an increase in the cap on Interior Department funding; conferees' elimination of a provision to increase the price of government uranium enrichment services; and increased funding for the Naval Petroleum Reserve, requested by the administration.*
[2] *Adjusted for jurisdictional overlap.*

In an unprecedented use of the reconciliation process, Congress in 1981 cut $35.2 billion from the fiscal 1982 budget. In so doing, it dramatically altered the scope and shape of many government programs. House Budget Committee Chairman James R. Jones, D-Okla., called passage of the reconciliation measure "clearly the most monumental and historic turnaround in fiscal policy that has ever occurred."

The final version of the budget resolution required reconciliations of about $36 billion; that figure, however, could include savings resulting from fiscal 1981 rescissions. Conferees agreed to resolve differences in four disputed program areas in reconciliation by: providing more money for child nutrition and the supplemental feeding program for women, infants and children (WIC); cutting out funds for the Small Business Administration's direct loan program; and adding $300 million for Medicare programs.

Reconciliation Bill

As soon as it completed action on the non-binding budget resolution, Congress began work on the reconciliation measure. Little more than two months later, it sent President Reagan an omnibus reconciliation package that cut $35.1 billion from the fiscal 1982 budget and dramatically altered the scope and shape of many government programs.

Final action on what House Budget Chairman James R. Jones, D-Okla., called "clearly the most monumental and historic turnaround in fiscal policy that has ever occurred" came July 31, just two days after both the House and the Senate approved the other major element of Reagan's economic recovery program, a three-year tax relief package. *(Tax cut, p. 191)*

The Congressional Budget and Impoundment Control Act of 1974 created the reconciliation mechanism as a way for Congress to reconcile spending and revenues by altering existing programs. In conjunction with its biannual budget resolutions, Congress could instruct certain authorizing and Appropriations committees to recommend changes in programs already on the books that would reduce outlays or increase revenues by specific amounts. The Senate and House budget committees would then combine the various reconciliation proposals and take them to the floor as a single omnibus bill. The drafters of the 1974 bill designed the procedure in hopes that lawmakers would be more willing to vote for a package of savings than for a number of separate spending cut measures.

Reconciliation was used for the first time in 1980, trimming existing programs to achieve outlay savings of $4.6 billion and provide new revenues of $3.6 billion. *(Story, p. 129)*

In its fiscal 1982 non-binding budget resolution, Congress directed 15 Senate committees and 14 House committees to come up with about $36 billion in fiscal 1982 spending cuts. The Republican-controlled Senate easily passed its reconciliation measure June 25 that differed only slightly from the Reagan plan. The House version, which was nearly a complete reflection of the Reagan administration's budget and program-slashing desires, passed June 26 after a crucial handful of conservative Democrats joined Republicans on the key procedural and substantive votes.

During the conference to reconcile the two measures, Reagan lost more than he gained. Congress refused to place a "cap" on federal contributions to the states for Medicaid and declined to create some of the block grants for state and local governments that Reagan wanted. In addition, funding was continued for several programs — such as the Economic Development Administration and the non-highway programs of the Appalachian Regional Commission — that Reagan wanted to eliminate.

However, such disappointments were insignificant compared to the overall accomplishment represented by the reconciliation measure — a major change in the direction of government and an abrupt slowdown in the growth of federal spending.

Economic Legislation, 1964-81

1964

The assassination of John F. Kennedy in November 1963 brought to the presidency a man uniquely qualified to lead a reluctant Congress to the enactment of much of the program his predecessor had urged without success. Lyndon B. Johnson promptly dedicated all his skills in the politics of consensus to winning quick approval of the Democratic administration's tax cut bill and other pending economic and welfare legislation. Mindful that opposition to these measures stemmed from the ranks of conservatives, the president wooed their support with pledges of fiscal frugality, while at the same time summoning the nation's conscience to a war on poverty.

Johnson's techniques were remarkably effective. The centerpiece of administration economic policy, the tax cut, moved quickly through Congress; Johnson signed the bill into law Feb. 26, just three months after he entered office. The measure was designed to encourage the rapid conversion of tax savings into consumer spending by providing for immediate reduction in the withholding rate to 14 percent, from 18 percent, thereby giving full economic effect to the cut in individual rates in 1964.

The Economic Opportunity Act of 1964 authorized a $1 billion start on Johnson's anti-poverty program. Other major requests honored by the 88th Congress in 1964 included a mass transit bill, several natural resource measures, new wheat and cotton legislation, an extension of excise tax rates, improved regulation of the securities industry and an "interest equalization tax" on foreign securities.

But Congress failed to complete action on aid to public schools, "medicare" for the elderly, increased funds for depressed areas and a special program of aid for Appalachia. All told, Congress appropriated almost $106 billion in 1964, or about $4.1 billion less than requested.

Fueled by the tax cut, the economy performed well in 1964. Business fixed investment rose by 9 percent, retail sales by 8.5 percent. Gross national product for the year amounted to $622 billion, up 6.5 percent from 1963, while prices remained fairly stable. Unemployment dropped to 5 percent in December and averaged 5.2 percent for the year,

as the number of new jobs (1.5 million) more than matched the number of new entrants to the labor market. By the beginning of 1965, the nation had experienced four years of expansion at an average gain of 5 percent in real GNP per year, and the immediate outlook was for more of the same. But the "interim" goal of 4 percent unemployment was not in sight, and there was growing doubt whether it could be attained in the light of rising productivity and a more rapidly expanding labor force. With Johnson's landslide victory at the polls in 1964, however, the continuation of expansionary fiscal and monetary policies was assured.

1964 Revenue Act

Congress early in the year completed action on the Revenue Act of 1964 (HR 8363 — PL 88-272), an $11.5 billion omnibus tax reduction and reform bill that was intended to promote economic growth in the United States. The legislation had been requested by President Kennedy in his Jan. 14, 1963, State of the Union message and was strongly endorsed by Johnson when he succeeded the assassinated president in November. Upon signing the bill on Feb. 26, 1964, President Johnson called it "the single most important step that we have taken to strengthen our economy since World War II."

Although the final version of HR 8363 differed greatly in detail from President Kennedy's proposals, it accomplished the same basic aim: to leave with taxpayers some $10 to $11 billion of their annual earnings that they had been paying to the federal government in taxes. Both the Kennedy and Johnson administrations hoped that the spending of these additional dollars would push the economy to new heights, increase profits, reduce unemployment, increase business investment and create and sustain long-range economic growth.

Encountering sharp ideological debate and considerable partisan wrangling, the tax bill made slow progress in 1963 and was little more than halfway toward enactment when the session ended. In marked contrast, Congress swiftly enacted the bill in 1964, permitting larger take-home pay for workers beginning in March.

A major reason for the faster pace was Johnson's friendly persuasion of key senators, particularly top mem-

Summary of Bill

To accomplish the desired economic growth, the Revenue Act of 1964 contained many provisions for tax reductions, capital gains revisions, and revenue-raising and revenue-losing reforms:

● Individual tax liabilities were cut $6.1 billion in 1964 and $9.1 billion in 1965. Rate reductions and reforms combined were expected to cut tax liabilities an average of 19.4 percent in 1965.

● Corporate tax liabilities were cut $1.6 billion in 1964 and $2.4 billion in 1965, representing a 7.7 percent reduction when fully effective. The rates also were revised to give special benefit to small businesses.

● A minimum standard deduction aided lower-income families and removed 1.5 million persons from the tax rolls. Broader tax deductions were authorized for medical expenses of persons 65 or older, for dependent care expenses, for the cost of moving to a new job location and for some types of charitable contributions.

● Deductions were tightened for certain state and local excise taxes and for casualty losses.

● Higher taxes were imposed on the value of premiums for certain employer-paid insurance, on pay received while sick, on income earned by Americans living abroad and on some oil and gas income.

● The 4 percent dividend credit was repealed but the $50 dividend exclusion was doubled.

● Real estate tax loopholes were closed a little, but persons over 65 who sold their homes received a tax break under certain conditions.

● Individuals with widely fluctuating annual incomes were provided with a new income-averaging formula.

● Business benefited from a broadening of the value of the 7 percent investment tax credit.

---

bers of the Senate's tax-writing Finance Committee. The president's influence was enhanced not only by his long working relationships with these senators during his service in that body, but also by his reduction in government expenditures that lowered estimated fiscal 1965 spending below the total outlay expected during fiscal 1964.

Background

Major tax cut proposals in 1963 had become a certainty as early as August 1962. At that time President Kennedy pledged to submit "permanent and basic reform and reduction" proposals to Congress in 1963. His statement was intended to cool down proposals for a "quickie" tax cut that summer. Congress was then in the midst of work on Kennedy's 1961 proposals for tax revision, which were aimed principally at helping the business community.

The Revenue Act of 1962 had contained a number of tax reforms, many of which were designed to close loopholes. However, the centerpiece of the law was a new tax break for the business community — a 7 percent investment tax credit that, the administration argued, would promote new and expanded investment to modernize the nation's industrial plant. In addition, the administration in 1962, by executive action, had revised the government's schedule of depreciation allowances. The new schedule generally shortened the time period over which a business could recover the cost of a productive asset. The credit and the new depreciation allowances provided income tax savings to business in 1962 of about $2.3 billion. This 1962 assistance to business was a key reason that the Kennedy administration's 1963 tax package emphasized tax help for the consumer.

Kennedy submitted his tax program to Congress Jan. 24, 1963, and indicated that it was his top priority request for the year (although it was later to share that spot with civil rights). The key to the program was a substantial cut in the tax rates on individual and corporate incomes. But in addition, it included structural reforms; many would have reduced the revenue losses from the tax cut, but some, designed to relieve hardship, would have increased revenue losses.

Kennedy proposed a net tax reduction of $10.3 billion, beginning July 1, 1963, and spread over the following two calendar years. Tax liabilities were to be cut $13.6 billion — $11 billion for individuals and $2.6 billion for corporations. Tax reforms would have increased tax liabilities by $3.3 billion. (By contrast, the bill as enacted in 1964 cut tax liabilities $11.5 billion annually, composed of an $11.7 billion decrease from lower rates and about a $180 million increase from reform provisions and capital gains changes.)

Throughout the 1963-64 debate on the tax proposals the administration repeatedly emphasized one point: the existing tax structure was drawing from the economy too much of the nation's resources, was taking too large a share of personal and business purchasing power and was reducing "the financial incentives for personal effort, investment and risk-taking."

Controversies

President Kennedy sought to win support for his tax program from both conservative and liberal groups with much the same approaches that he used, with considerably more success, in gaining enactment of the Trade Expansion Act of 1962. As later events proved, the president did receive wide support for the principle of tax reduction. But beyond this basic agreement, divergences of opinion engulfed the tax program in controversy immediately upon its presentation to Congress and contributed heavily to the delay in enactment until 1964.

Though most major interest groups were in favor of tax reductions, each had its own view of how the cuts should be distributed. Labor labeled the program "altogether inadequate" and called for bigger and quicker cuts for low-income persons. Business groups demanded bigger cuts in the upper-income brackets "to promote investment."

The basic disagreement was over consumption versus investment. Although it was generally agreed that the tax program was designed primarily to release consumer spending dollars, labor said it did not provide enough, while business said it placed too much emphasis on consumption and badly discriminated against middle-income taxpayers. But as passage neared in both chambers, most interest groups found enough merit in the proposed rate structure to urge adoption of the bill.

Plans for structural changes in the tax system were a major complication in enactment of HR 8363. In his 1962 statements, Kennedy stressed that tax reform would be an important part of his program, as it was. Nevertheless, during the early part of 1963 when the economy remained sluggish, there was some feeling that the administration might be willing to trade reform for early enactment of an economy-stimulating tax cut.

Continued improvement in the economy in the following months removed the basic reason the administration could have advanced for dropping the reform package. In addition, the influential chairman of the House Ways and Means Committee, Wilbur D. Mills, D-Ark. (1939-77), supported tax revision combined with reductions.

Whether or not to attempt reform was a minor issue compared to the storm caused by the actual reforms that were proposed. The Ways and Means Committee spent about two months receiving testimony — mostly on the proposed reforms — and then devoted five months to preparing the complex language to implement the structural revisions. No small amount of this period was consumed in discussions and log-rolling by lobbyists for special groups, by Treasury and administration lobbyists and by members of Congress as they haggled about with proposals were or were not equitable and which ones should or should not be included in the bill.

One of the principal reasons for the delay in enactment, in addition to the controversy over tax cut distribution and tax reforms, was the widespread opposition to President Kennedy's spending proposals. This was the subject that most aroused participants in the 1963 tax debate, dominated the discussion of federal fiscal policy and prevented many politicians from supporting tax cuts that they claimed they otherwise would welcome. The unexpectedly low budget of President Johnson for fiscal 1965 brought a sharp reversal on all of these points; the speed-up of the bill in the Senate following the president's budget reductions was eloquent testimony to the delaying influence that fiscal policy had on tax reduction in 1963.

Provisions

As signed into law Feb. 26, HR 8363, the Revenue Act of 1964:

Individual Tax Rates

● Reduced personal income tax rates from the existing range of 20 to 91 percent to 16 to 77 percent for 1964 and to 14 to 70 percent for 1965 and thereafter.

● Lowered the tax withholding rate from the existing 18 percent to 14 percent; provided that the new withholding rate take effect one week after enactment.

● Divided the existing lowest income tax bracket ($2,000 for single persons; $4,000 for married couples) into four single brackets of $500, $1,000, $1,500 and $2,000 (each bracket doubled for married couples). Tax rates would be 14, 15, 16 and 17 percent, respectively for each higher step beginning with the 14 percent rate on the first $500 of taxable income (or the first $1,000 for married couples).

● Applied that highest rate of 70 percent (when fully effective) to incomes over $100,000 for single persons or $200,000 for married couples.

Corporate Tax Rates

● Reduced corporate income tax rates over a two-year period to 48 percent from the existing 52 percent and rearranged the normal and surtax rates to benefit small business. Effective Jan. 1, 1964, the normal tax rate — applicable to the first $25,000 of corporate profits — would drop to 22 percent from 30 percent while the surtax rate — which was added to the normal tax for profits over $25,000 — would increase to 28 percent from 22 percent, providing a combined 50 percent tax rate for 1964. Effective Jan. 1, 1965, the surtax would decline to 26 percent and the normal tax would remain at 22 percent, for a combined rate of 48 percent.

● Required a gradual speedup in the payment of corporate taxes over a seven-year period beginning in 1964, so that in 1970 and subsequent years all of a corporation's tax liability in excess of $100,000 would be paid in the year in which the income was earned

Capital Gains Revisions

● Allowed individuals suffering capital losses an indefinite number of years in which to credit the losses against other forms of income.

● Approved tighter tax rules governing the operation of stock option plans.

● Increased taxes on the gain from the sale of a building when the gain resulted from "accelerated" depreciation practices that allowed faster write-offs in a property's book value in the early years of its life.

● Allowed capital gains tax rates to be applied to royalties received from the mining of iron ore except in the cases of foreign leases and property owned and operated by substantially the same parties.

● Reduced the capital gains tax that a person 65 or older had to pay when he sold his home for more than he paid for it. If the home was the taxpayer's personal residence for at least five of the past eight years before sale, the owner would not have to pay a tax on any capital gain attributable to the first $20,000 of the sales price. For a sale above $20,000 the portion of the gain that would not be taxed would be the same proportion as $20,000 was of the total sales price.

Revenue Raising Reforms

● Disallowed deductions on federal income tax returns for various state, local and foreign excise taxes, including those on cigarettes, alcoholic beverages and poll taxes and various miscellaneous sales taxes and fees for auto registration and licenses; provided that the followung taxes would continue to be deductible: gasoline, diesel fuel and other motor fuels; state and local real and personal property; income; war profits; excess profits and general sales taxes; and foreign real property, income, war profits and excess profits taxes.

● Eliminated from existing law the provision that allowed a taxpayer to claim as a credit against his tax liablity an amount equal to 4 percent of his income from dividends above $50 that were received from domestic corporations.

● Allowed a taxpayer to exclude from his taxable income the first $100 of such dividends ($200 for married persons), rather than the first $50 as under existing law.

● Allowed exclusion from taxable income of pay received (up to $100 a week) while sick or injured and absent from work only when the absence was for more than 30 consecutive days.

• Limited tax deductions for casualty and theft losses to the amount of each loss in excess of $100.

• Eliminated from existing law, with certain exceptions, the privilege of grouping oil and gas properties for tax purposes in a manner providing extra benefits from depletion allowances.

• Approved the imposition of a new penalty tax on the earnings of certain affiliated corporations that filed separate tax returns; the rate of the penalty tax would be 6 percent on the first $25,000 of taxable income.

• Provided, with certain exceptions, that no tax deductions would be allowed for interest payments on money borrowed to purchase or continue life insurance, endowment or annuity contracts under a plan of "systematic" borrowing from the policy or other source.

• Required a taxpayer to include in his taxable income the value of employer-paid premiums for group term life insurance for the employee in excess of $50,000.

Revenue Losing Reforms

• Allowed, as an alternative to the standard 10 percent deduction, a taxpayer to claim a standard deduction of $300 plus $100 for each additional $600 personal exemption he claimed on his tax return, up to existing $1,000 maximum standard deduction.

• Removed from existing law a limitation on the 7 percent investment tax credit, enacted in 1972, which stipulated that the depreciation basis of a new asset had to be reduced by the amount of the tax credit taken (that is, restricted the depreciation basis to 93 percent of costs if the full credit was taken). In the case of property on which the basis already had been reduced, the taxpayer was allowed to increase the basis in the future to compensate; no tax refunds would result.

• Extended the investment tax credit to purchases of elevators and escalators.

• Permitted deductions of the following moving expenses for new employees of a firm and for existing employees of a firm who were not reimbursed for such expenses: the cost of transporting household goods and personal effects; transportation charges; and the cost of meals and lodging of the employee and his family while in transit. Allowed the deduction in such a manner as to permit the taxpayer to either itemize other deductions or use the standard 10 percent deduction.

• Provided a new income-averaging formula for individuals, such as artists and lawyers, whose income fluctuated widely from year to year. To be eligible for the new formula, a taxpayer had to have income in the current (taxable) year that was one-third higher than his average taxable income for the prior four years. In addition, the income subject to averaging would have to exceed $3,000.

• Liberalized existing deductions allowed taxpayers for care of children or incapacitated dependents when the taxpayer worked.

• Repealed an existing 2 percent penalty tax imposed on consolidated returns of affiliated corporations; allowed corporations in certain affiliated groups, that gave up certain tax benefits, to take a 100 percent deduction for corporate dividends received from other members of the group, this eliminating an existing tax on such dividend transfers.

• Allowed persons over age 65 unlimited deductions for medical expenses.

• Adjusted the retirement income credit to conform to the new tax rates; provided that the credit in 1964 would be equal to 17 percent of retirement income and in 1965 and thereafter to 15 percent of retirement income.

• Permitted individuals or businesses, such as department stores, to defer tax payments on profits from revolving credit sales (with certain exceptions) from the time the sale was made until the payments actually were received.

Other Reforms

• Set a tax deduction limitation of 30 percent of income (rather than the existing 20 percent) on contributions to publicly supported and controlled organizations; retained the 20 percent figure for contributions to private foundations and trust funds.

• Allowed a taxpayer who contributed more than 30 percent of his income in any single year to carry the excess into the following five years and receive tax deductions to the extent that contributions in those years were under 30 percnt.

• Restricted unlimited charitable contribution deductions (used by wealthy taxpayers to considerably reduce or eliminate federal income taxes) to contributions to publicly supported organizations unless the private foundation was actively distributing money to charitable causes or organizations.

• Gave the Treasury Department general authority to specify that pension trust plans qualified (retroactively to the date of their creation under certain circumstances) for federal tax exemptions and for employer deductions for contributions on the behalf of employees.

• Lowered from $35,000 to $25,000 the maximum amount of overseas earned income that may be excluded from U.S. taxation by an American who maintained permanent residence abroad for more than three consecutive years.

Excise Tax Extension

Congress in 1964 extended for another year — through June 30, 1965 — $1.9 billion in existing excise tax levies. Senate amendments to the House-passed administration bill would have repealed or reduced numerous permanent excises, at a cost of $525 million, but none of the tax-paring amendments survived the Senate-House conference. Republicans in the House had unsuccessfully pressed for similar cuts. The final bill (HR 11376 — PL 88-348) provided only for the extension of expiring taxes and rates — the eleventh annual extension of most of the taxes.

If HR 11376 had not been enacted, the 10 percent tax on general telephone service and the 5 percent tax on air passenger travel would have expired on July 1. In addition, the following levies would have declined: cigarettes to 7 from 8 cents a pack; liquor to $9 from $10.50 a gallon; beer to $8 from $9 a barrel; wines, from varying rates, by approximately 11 percent; automobiles to 7 from 10 percent of the manufacturer's price; and auto parts and accessories to 5 from 8 percent of the manufacturer's price.

Background

Most of the excises in force during 1964 were imposed originally during wartime as temporary sources of revenue that would be eliminated when conditions returned to normal. A number of World War I excises were re-introduced in 1932 to compensate for plummeting income tax collections. The Revenue Act of 1941 made the 1932 excises permanent and imposed numerous other levies, including those on general telephone service and the transportation of persons by railroad, bus, plane and water. The latter taxes were made subject to annual extension in 1959.

The Revenue Act of 1950 was conceived as a measure to cut the annual $7.5 billion excise intake by about $1 billion, but the outbreak of the Korean War in June 1950 forced an extension of the old taxes and imposition of new ones. Faced by expanding defense expenditures, Congress in 1951 increased excise taxes by $1.2 billion. Among the new levies was the package extended in 1964 by HR 11376.

In 1954, a number of the World War II excises were slashed; however, all of the 1951 rate increases were extended for one year. Since 1954, the emergency rate increases of 1951 have been re-extended for one-year periods in every session of Congress.

The annual extensions of all the taxes met strong opposition in the Senate in 1960. After unsuccessful efforts in both chambers in 1961 to repeal the passenger transportation taxes, the levies on passenger travel by railroad, bus and water were eliminated in 1962 and the tax on air travel cut to 5 from 10 percent. In 1963, Congress extended the existing rates for another year, after an attempt in the Senate to eliminate the tax on air travel was defeated.

President Johnson in his budget message Jan. 21, 1964, called for extension of existing excise levies. Treasury Secretary Douglas Dillion Jan. 20 said, however, that the entire federal excise tax structure should undergo "a thorough overhaul" in the next few years. Congress responded in 1965 by eliminating a number of the taxes. *(Details, p. 138)*

Provisions

As enacted into law, HR 11376, the Excise Tax Rate Extension Act of 1964:

● Extended for one year, through June 30, 1965, the existing rates of excise tax on cigarettes, distilled spirits, beer, wines, automobiles, auto parts and accessories, general telephone service and passenger travel by air.

● Corrected and amended a provision in the Revenue Act of 1964 (HR 8363 — PL 88-272) to make retroactive to the beginning of 1959 a casualty loss tax deduction to individuals whose property had been confiscated by Cuba; limited application of this provision to individuals who were U.S. citizens on Dec. 31, 1958; extended its application to include intangible property; provided that it apply only to losses before Jan. 1, 1964, of property held by the taxpayer and located in Cuba on Dec. 31, 1958; and stipulated that a loss could be carried back three years or carried forward five years instead of being carried forward 10 years as provided in the Revenue Act of 1964.

1965

The first session of the 89th Congress, starting early and working late, passed more major legislation than most Congresses pass in two sessions. The scope of the legislation was even more impressive than the number of major new laws. Measures, which taken alone would have crowned the achievements of any Congress, were enacted in a seemingly endless stream.

In the course of the year, Congress approved major programs that had long been on the agenda of the Democratic Party — in the case of medical care for the aged under Social Security, for as long as 20 years. Other longstanding objectives were met by enactment of aid to primary and secondary schools; funding for college scholarships; a broad housing program that included rent subsidies to low-income families and grants for beautifying city parks and streets; and bills to promote regional economic planning and development and rebuild the Appalachian region. Congress also eliminated most federal excise taxes and extended and revised the manpower training and antipoverty laws.

Other measures revised the feed grains, wheat and cotton commodity programs; increased Social Security benefits and taxes; removed silver from coins and gold backing from Federal Reserve deposits; reduced the tourist duty exemption and took other steps to combat the balance-of-payments deficit; enabled U.S. participation in the International Coffee Agreement; and put into effect a U.S.-Canadian agreement on auto tariffs.

A major defeat for Johnson was his failure to secure repeal of section 14(b) of the Taft-Hartley Act, which permitted states to enact laws banning the union shop. The bill bogged down in a Senate filibuster at the end of the session and was laid aside by a weary Congress eager for adjournment. Congress also failed to get around to passing Johnson bills to expand minimum wage coverage, reform the unemployment compensation system and provide the president with standby tax cut authority.

Meanwhile, the U.S. economy continued into its fifth consecutive year of expansion — the longest boom since the end of World War II. By the end of the year, the expansion — which began in February 1961 — was 59 months old. Performing beyond expectations, the economy set records in most areas. The gross national product totaled $675.6 billion, up $47 billion from 1964 and $9.4 billion above the original government estimate.

As 1965 began, tax cuts enacted the previous year continued to stimulate the economy, as did the recovery from automobile strikes in late 1964. Throughout 1965, however, the administration was not indifferent to wage and price developments. Officials continued to emphasize the importance of the administration's wage-price guideposts, which sought to define non-inflationary limits for wage and price increases. Although voluntary, government officials sometimes resorted to direct efforts to enforce the guidelines.

In January 1965, Johnson urged Congress to establish counter-recessionary procedures to permit quick action on temporary income tax cuts and appropriation of funds for immediate "job-creating public programs." No action occurred on these requests.

In December, the Federal Reserve Board increased the discount rate to 4.5 percent from 4 percent in an effort to control inflation. The move brought the rate to its highest level since March 1930.

The U.S. balance of payments, in deficit since 1957, moved toward equilibrium in 1965. The deficit was down to $1.4 billion as measured on the liquidity basis, compared with $2.8 billion in 1964. By the end of the year, however, the problem remained serious enough to require increased efforts to reduce the dollar drain during 1966. The 1965 improvement in the payments account was attributable, in considerable part, to administration efforts to keep dollars at home, repatriate liquid funds held abroad and attract foreign capital to the United States. The program was announced by President Johnson Feb. 10 in a special message to Congress. The administration's program was aimed at net capital outflows, which had risen from $4.5 billion in 1963 to $6.6 billion in 1964 and to an annual rate of upwards of $9 billion in the fourth quarter of 1964. To stem the flow of dollars abroad, the president called on businessmen and bankers to exercise "voluntary restraint" in overseas lending and investment operations. Widespread compliance held 1964 net outflows of capital to about $3.8 billion.

In other key features of his program, the president proposed further reductions of U.S. government expenditures abroad and outlined a legislative program that included proposals to extend and expand the 1964 interest equalization tax, continue authority of U.S. banks to pay higher rates of interest on time deposits (short-term investments) of foreign governments than on domestic deposits and provide antitrust exemptions for bankers who cooperated to cut down on overseas dollar movements. All of these requests were enacted.

Excise Tax Cuts

Congress in 1965 repealed a variety of federal excise taxes that had annoyed businesses, consumers and tax collectors for years.

The bill (HR 8371 — PL 89-44) completely eliminated many levies and reduced others to a low level. Some levies were left untouched; they were largely specialized items such as user taxes (primarily for highway construction), sumptuary taxes on alcoholic beverages and tobacco products, and regulatory taxes on marijuana, opium, gambling and similar items.

In total, the bill provided a $4.7 billion cut in federal excise taxes between June 22, 1965, the effective date of the law, and Jan. 1, 1969, when the last stage of the reductions was to go into effect. In 1970, Congress extended the tax on telephone service and automobiles. *(Details, p. 156)*

Provisions

As signed into law, PL 89-44, the Excise Tax Reduction Act of 1965, established a five-stage timetable for excise cuts by Jan. 1, 1969. The phases of reduction, with the taxes reduced or eliminated and the annual revenue lost, were as follows:

First Stage

The first of the five phases reduced excise levies by $1.8 billion, effective June 22, 1965, or in certain cases, July 1, 1965. Excises repealed June 22:

● All retail taxes except those on diesel fuel and special motor fuels. The items covered were handbags and luggage, toilet articles, jewelry and furs. $550 million.

● Manufacturers' taxes on: business machines; sporting goods (except on fishing equipment); photographic equipment; radios; television sets; phonographs and phonograph records; musical instruments; refrigerators; freezers; air conditioners; electric, gas and oil appliances; fountain pens; ball point pens; mechanical pencils; lighters; matches and playing cards. $608 million.

The June 22 cuts also:

● Reduced the manufacturers' tax on passenger automobiles from 10 percent to 7 percent. $570 million.

● Provided refunds of the 3 percent automobile tax and the entire air conditioners tax paid on purchases made after May 14, 1965.

● Made the manufacturers' excises on trucks and truck parts and accessories inapplicable to camper coaches, the bodies of mobile homes, certain farm vehicles and school buses purchased by independent operators for their use under contract to transport school children. $10 million.

● Authorized floor stock refunds to retailers and wholesale dealers for inventories of previously taxable items they had on hand on the reduction date.

● Excise taxes repealed July 1 were those on safe deposit boxes, initiation fees paid by members of clubs organized after the repeal date, coin-operated amusement devices, bowling alleys, and billiard and pool tables. $20 million.

● Exempted, effective July 1, U.S. servicemen from the 5 percent excise on air travel when international flights were made under certain circumstances. Negligible revenue effect.

Second Stage

On Jan. 1, 1966, PL 89-44 provided an additional $1.6 billion in excise tax reductions, as follows:

● Reduced from 10 percent to 3 percent the levy on local and long-distance telephone service, including teletypeprinter service. $639 million.

● Repealed the excise on admissions. This tax included the levies on general admissions (concerts, movies, theater performances, and athletic events and racing), cabarets and club dues. (Repeal of the general admissions and cabaret levies was to take effect at noon on Dec. 31, 1965, to accommodate New Year's Eve festivities.) $187 million.

● Repealed the manufacturers' excises on cutting oil, lubricating oil (except that used in highway vehicles), electric light bulbs and automobile parts and accessories (except those used primarily for trucks). $303 million.

● Reduced the automobile tax to 6 percent. $190 million.

● Repealed the documentary stamp tax on issuances or transfers of stocks and bonds. $153 million.

● Repealed the excise levy on manufactured tobacco (chewing, smoking and snuff). $18 million.

● Repealed the excises on telegraph and wire service. $32 million.

● Repealed the telephone excise tax on private communications systems linked with general telephone networks. $130 million.

● Provided floor stock refunds on goods held by wholesalers and retail dealers on the date of reduction.

Remaining Stages

PL 89-44 provided an additional $1.3 billion in excise tax reductions between 1967 and 1969, as follows:

● Further reduced the manufacturers' excise tax on passenger automobiles to 4 percent on Jan. 1, 1967, to 3 percent on Jan. 1, 1968, and to a permanent level of 1 percent on Jan. 1, 1969. $950 million.

● Further reduced the tax on local and long-distance telephone service and teletypeprinter service by one percentage point annually beginning Jan. 1, 1967, culminating in complete repeal on Jan. 1, 1969. $274 million.

● Repealed the tax on real estate conveyances, effective Jan. 1, 1968. $42 million.

Other Provisions

● Made permanent the temporary rates imposed during the Korean War on cigarettes (8 cents a pack), liquor ($20.50 a gallon), beer ($9 a barrel), and wines (varying rates). Under existing law, these levies had to be extended at the beginning of each fiscal year or the rates fell to lower levels.

● Made permanent the 5 percent excise on the transportation of persons by air, which required annual extension under existing law.

● Transferred $70 million in highway user taxes from general revenues to the Highway Trust Fund. These included levies on truck parts and accessories ($20 million) and on lubricating oil used by highway motor vehicles ($50 million).

● Extended the excise on automobile parts from July 1, 1965, through Dec. 31, 1965.

Economic Development Act

With the passage of the Public Works and Economic Development Act (S 1648 — PL 89-136) Aug. 26, 1965, the federal government launched a major program to help the approximately 27 million people living in economically depressed areas throughout the nation. Depressed areas were classified as areas of chronic, long-term high unemployment and low living standards, usually due to structural faults in the local economy, the absence of basic public facilities needed to sustain commerce and industry, or the decay or obsolescence of formerly active business enterprises.

The act, requested by President Johnson as part of his "Great Society" program, provided $3.25 billion over fiscal years 1966-70 for grants and loans for public works, development and technical assistance and other projects, to stimulate long-term and lasting economic growth in areas plagued by chronic unemployment. It also established a new agency in the Commerce Department — the Economic Development Administration — to administer the act.

As enacted into law, S 1648 relied on three basic federal approaches toward aiding depressed areas:

(1) Encouraging economically depressed communities to draft and carry out economic development plans that would help them emerge into a condition of healthy economic growth. Wherever possible, such plans were to be on a regional or multi-county basis, rather than a single-county basis.

(2) Helping depressed communities to finance construction of the basic public facilities (such as harbors, sewage plants, access roads, industrial parks) that would make the community attractive to private investment and would thus help foster economic growth.

(3) Providing special financial aid to private firms to encourage them to build plants and businesses in depressed areas.

The large-scale spending for public facilities authorized by the bill also had the effect of creating immediate job opportunities in areas of high unemployment and low economic levels.

One important new departure in the bill was the provision to foster the growth of economically sound towns and small cities that had a potential for substantial economic growth, which would help nearby depressed areas. It was believed that, in many cases, a depressed area would benefit far more if expansion were encouraged in a nearby area with a potential for "healthy" growth than if government aid went solely for projects in the depressed area itself.

The final provisions of S 1648 constituted in part a reenactment and broadening of the Kennedy administration's 1961 Area Redevelopment Act, which had been temporarily extended and then expired Aug. 31, 1965. However, the provisions for construction of public works in depressed areas also were based on the approach used in the 1962 Public Works Acceleration Act (which had provided $900 million in federal aid for immediate acceleration of job-creating public works projects in high-unemployment areas). In addition, the emphasis on regional and multi-county economic planning in S 1648 followed a pattern set in a separate Appalachia-aid bill passed earlier in 1965.

Provisions

Following are the major provisions of The Public Works and Economic Development Act:

Development Grants

● Provided $500 million a year in fiscal years 1966-69 for federal matching grants to local public agencies and non-profit groups for construction of public works and development facilities that would foster the economic growth of economically depressed areas and help provide job opportunities. Only areas that had drawn up an overall economic development plan acceptable to the secretary of commerce were eligible for aid, and only for projects consistent with the plan.

Examples of public works and development facilities that could be built or obtained with development grants: water works, water and sewer lines, waste treatment plants and health facilities; streets and roads needed for commercial and industrial development; harbor facilities, reservoirs, railroad sidings, airports and industrial parks (land improvement and site utilities); tourist facilities; area vocational schools; land for the above. Funds would not be available for construction of court houses, town halls, swimming pools unrelated to tourism or playgrounds.

Development Loans

● Provided $170 million a year in fiscal years 1966-70 for (1) federal loans for the same purposes, agencies and facilities covered by development grants; and (2) federal loans and loan guarantees to both public and private borrowers for acquisition and development of land, buildings, machinery and equipment for industrial and commercial use in economically depressed areas.

Technical Assistance

● Provided $25 million a year in fiscal 1966-70 for federal technical assistance, research and informational aid to economically depressed areas and to other areas needing such aid to improve their economic position.

Development Districts

● Provided $50 million a year in fiscal 1967-70 in federal grants, loans and loan guarantees for growth projects in towns, small cities and other "economic development centers" that had a population of less than 250,000, that (even if not in a depressed condition themselves) had a potential for economic growth that would aid nearby economically depressed areas, and that were associated with such areas in multi-county economic development districts having over-all development plans.

Regional Planning

● Encouraged the states to set up multi-stage regional commissions to plan and foster economic development programs in depressed regions (such as northern New England), and provided $15 million a year in fiscal 1966-70 for federal technical advice and planning aid to the commissions.

Social Security, Medicare

Congress in 1965 passed the bill that was not only the most important welfare legislation of the Johnson administration, but was also generally considered the most important welfare measure since passage of the original Social Security Act in 1935. The bill (HR 6675 — PL 89-97) established a medical care program for the aged under the Social Security system, a goal of liberals throughout the postwar period. But the Medicare program finally enacted was much more far-reaching than the plan which liberals had proposed unsuccessfully for years. Moreover, HR 6675 made a multitude of other changes in the Social Security law, including a 7 percent increase in retirement benefits.

The Medicare program called for compulsory hospital insurance for the aged covering spells of hospital and post-hospital care, financed through an increase in the Social Security tax.

The basic health plan provided in the bill benefited about 19 million aged. It provided up to 90 days of hospital care, 100 days of nursing-home care and 100 home-health care visits and outpatient diagnostic services. The supplementary health plan benefited about 16.9 million aged and paid about 80 percent of the cost of a variety of health services, including services of doctors, after a $50 deduction.

Medical assistance to the elderly poor was extended to needy persons under all public assistance programs, and federal funds for the programs were increased. About 8 million persons would be benefited. Federal funds were increased for existing child health care programs, and new programs were added.

Social Security cash benefits for about 20 million persons were increased by 7 percent, and regulations were liberalized to provide further benefits. Coverage was extended to self-employed doctors.

The increased Social Security benefits and most of the basic health program were financed by payroll taxes. The supplementary health plan was financed by contributions from participants and general revenue. All other benefits in the bill would be financed by general revenues.

1966

Spiraling U.S. involvement in the Vietnam War and the inflationary trend in the nation's economy were dominant themes of the 1966 session of Congress. Simply stated,

the issue of the year was "guns versus butter" — a policy choice between stepped-up war efforts and expansion of President Johnson's domestic social scheme, the "Great Society."

Johnson said the country could afford both. Congress was not quite so sure. Most members supported "guns" but differed on how much "butter" the country could afford.

In his Jan. 24 budget presentation, the president called for a $15.2 billion expansion of the war during fiscal years 1966-67 — but not at the expense of his Great Society. A $3.3 billion increase in proposed domestic spending brought the fiscal 1967 budget to $112.8 billion — the first time in history budget expenditures had been projected at more than $100 billion. Republicans revived the "guns and butter" catchword and set out to pare almost every aspect of the president's domestic program.

As 1966 began, the U.S. economy was strained to its non-inflationary limit. After four years of stable economic growth, it was near full employment. Plant capacity was in full use. Any sizable increase in demand under those conditions would be bound to result in inflation.

That was precisely what occurred under pressure of the defense spending spiral, which was not offset sufficiently by measures to cut back on other purchasing power. The cost-of-living index jumped from 111.0 percent in January to 113.8 percent in August, compared to the 1957-59 average. The president early in the year asked for and received rapid congressional approval of a $5.9 billion bill to accelerate certain types of tax payments and reimpose 1965 excise levies, but the measure was hardly adequate to counter the Vietnam spending boom. Almost every leading economist in the nation called for a general tax increase, but Johnson refused to ask for one.

Toward the end of the session, the president sought and received legislation suspending incentives to business investment, but no one was calling the measure a panacea. Congress, responding to rising interest rates, a tightening of the money market and a growing shortage of mortgage money in the homebuilding industry, passed administration-backed bills increasing the purchasing authority of the Federal National Mortgage Assn. to provide more mortgage capital and regulating maximum interest rates paid by banks and other institutions on deposits or share accounts.

Congress rejected many of the president's proposed spending reductions for domestic programs and increased spending above his requests for other programs. Despite strong persuasive efforts by the president, numerous priority bills became casualties, among them repeal of section 14(b) of the Taft-Hartley Act authorizing state "right to work" laws. Languishing in conference was a bill to overhaul the unemployment compensation system. Among other measures killed for the year were East-West trade incentives, "truth in lending" and broadened picketing rights for construction unions.

Although the landmark social measures passed in 1965 alone made the 89th Congress one of the most productive on record, the second session made its mark as well. Major legislation cleared included a substantially higher minimum wage, new educational incentives, continuation of the war on poverty and a "demonstration cities" plan to counter urban blight.

The U.S. balance-of-payments deficit was not eliminated or reduced to a satisfactory level in 1966. The administration continued its program of voluntary controls on foreign investment and lending to help solve the problem, and Congress enacted a bill to induce foreign investment in the United States. That bill, however, became one of the best known of the year because it was loaded with extraneous amendments to give tax breaks to a multitude of individuals and organizations ranging from hearse owners to presidential candidates. It was known, accordingly, as the Christmas tree bill.

Tax Revenue Increases

The increasing costs of the war in Vietnam and accompanying signs of inflation in the domestic economy led President Johnson, in his first 1966 message to Congress, to ask for a quick $6 billion increase in tax revenues. He did not ask for higher income or corporate taxes, saying these were "not clearly required at this time." The president continued to hold back throughout the session in requesting tax increases, which Congress was bound to be reluctant to impose in an election year. In September Johnson asked for suspension of the investment tax credit in an effort to discourage what he called the "exaggerated boom in business investment" in plants, equipment and commercial construction.

The president's September request was a clear admission that the revenue increases he had recommended in January and the clampdown he sought on federal spending were not sufficient to dampen the inflationary trend. The revenue increases enacted in March in the Tax Adjustment Act of 1966 (HR 12752 — PL 89-368) were expected to raise $1.13 billion in fiscal 1966 and $4.8 billion in fiscal 1967. Almost all the funds were to be raised from a speedup in corporate income tax payments ($4.2 billion) and a two-year suspension of recently instituted cuts in telephone and automobile excise taxes ($790 million and $480 million, respectively). In addition, the bill increased tax withholding on most individuals' income taxes.

In addition, the final version of HR 12752 contained several important sections that had not been requested by the administration. These included a House provision designed to prevent overwithholding from persons with heavy deductions and a Senate provision prohibiting tax deductions for tickets to political dinners and advertising in political publications. Another Senate-added provision, modified in the final bill, temporarily extended Social Security benefits to persons over 72 who had no Social Security coverage. The fiscal 1967 cost was estimated at $95 million.

Other provisions of the Tax Adjustment Act of 1966:

● Required self-employed persons to pay Social Security and hospital insurance taxes in quarterly installments in the year liabilities became due. (Existing law permitted payment of such taxes in a lump sum on April 15 of the following year.)

● Required taxpayers to pay at least 80 percent (up from 70 percent) of their estimated tax liability throughout the year.

● Amended U.S. tariff law to increase the duty-free exemption for gift packages shipped by members of the Armed forces serving in combat zones.

Investment Tax Credit

As part of the administration's program to stem rising inflation in the United States, Congress in 1966 enacted a bill (HR 17607 — PL 89-800) suspending existing tax incentives for business investment.

HR 17607 was designed to reduce inflationary pressures in the capital goods industry by temporarily suspending both the 7 percent investment tax credit on the purchase of machinery and equipment and certain methods of accelerated depreciation of industrial and commercial buildings. The suspensions were to last almost 15 months.

The final version of HR 17607 embodied essentially the same provisions sought by President Johnson when he proposed the measure Sept. 8 as a key part of his anti-inflation drive. Although House and Senate conferees agreed to certain minor exemptions from the suspensions, they delivered the president a major victory by deleting Senate-passed exemptions for railroad and other transportation interests. The president had sought an across-the-board suspension.

Throughout 1966, the president's Council of Economic Advisers (CEA) had urged suspension of the investment incentives, but this had been opposed by the Treasury Department. The CEA had contended that monetary policy alone was not sufficient to diminish inflationary pressures, while the Treasury asserted that permanent tax measures such as investment credit should not be altered to influence economic trends of a temporary nature. President Johnson, who had accepted the Treasury's fiscal arguments until late summer, sought suspension after it became apparent that business was making record investments despite tight money and high interest rates. One survey, conducted jointly by the Securities and Exchange Commission and Commerce Department, estimated planned business investment in plant and equipment at $60.8 billion for the year — an increase of 17 percent over 1965. The projected increase compared with actual increases of 15.7 percent in 1965, 14.5 percent in 1964, and average annual increases of only 6.8 percent in 1962 and 1963.

Strong opposition to investment credit suspension came from business interests, whose general position was that a cutback in investment might more than offset inflationary trends. However, qualified support came from three of the nation's largest corporations — the Campbell Soup Co., American Telephone and Telegraph Co., and the Pennsylvania Railroad — which made their support contingent on a coupling of suspension with a substantial cutback in federal spending, as had been promised by the president in his anti-inflation plan.

Suspension of accelerated depreciation was opposed by homebuilders and real estate interests, who contended the plan would further depress the housing industry, already ailing from a lack of loan funds. After intensive lobbying, these interests won an exemption for buildings costing $50,000 or less.

The Commerce Department early in 1967 announced that business interests had cut back their investment plans by an estimated $300 million in the last three months of 1966 as a result of the investment credit suspension. For the full year 1967, the department projected, suspension would induce a $2.3 billion cutback in investment plans. Even with the projected cutbacks, however, a survey by the McGraw-Hill Co. predicted that business investment in 1967 would increase by 7 percent over the level in 1966.

Provisions

As signed into law, PL 89-800 contained the following major provisions:

Investment Tax Credit

• Suspended, for a period beginning Oct. 10, 1966, and terminating Dec. 31, 1967, a provision of the Revenue Act of 1962 (PL 87-834) permitting a credit against tax liability of up to 7 percent of investments in new and used machinery and equipment.

• Stipulated that the suspension would not apply to investment of less than $20,000 (allowing taxpayers to continue to claim a tax deduction of up to $1,400). Existing law provided no ceiling on investments eligible for the tax credit.

• Made the suspension applicable to equipment *ordered* as well as received during the suspension period.

• Allowed the full credit on costs of a machine or piece of equipment when a firm, prior to Oct. 10, 1966, had placed a binding order for more than 50 percent of the machine's components.

• Allowed the full credit for purchase of facilities to control air and water pollution.

• Provided for a broadening of the investment credit upon its restoration Jan. 1, 1968, to increase the maximum amount of the tax credit to 50 percent of tax liabilities above $25,000, and to allow investors to carry unused balances forward for a period of up to seven years. Existing law limited the maximum tax credit to $25,000, plus 25 percent of the taxpayer's liability over $25,000. Any unused portion of the credit could be used in any of the following five years.

Accelerated Depreciation

• Suspended, for the same period as the investment tax credit, a provision of the 1954 Internal Revenue Code authorizing two methods of accelerated tax write-off on industrial and commercial buildings — the "double declining balance" and "sum of the years digits" techniques — both of which allowed larger tax deductions for depreciation during the earlier years of a building's use than in its later years.

• Allowed each taxpayer, however, to continue use of all accelerated depreciation techniques for buildings valued at $50,000 or less (up to a maximum total exemption of $50,000, regardless of the number of buildings purchased).

• Stipulated that the two suspended methods would not be available after their 1968 restoration for any non-exempt building constructed or ordered during suspension. Provided, however, that either method could be used for a building whose construction was begun prior to suspension, or had been committed under terms of a binding contract in effect before Oct. 10, 1966.

Combined Exemption

• Continued the investment credit and/or accelerated depreciation on the full cost of a building constructed or equipped during the suspension period when a firm, prior to Oct. 10, 1966, had placed a binding order or was otherwise committed for 50 percent or more of the project's total cost. Specifically stipulated that the exemption covered outdoor plants, such as drydocks and oil pipelines.

Foreign Investors Bill

The U.S. balance-of-payments deficit was not eliminated or reduced to a satisfactory level in 1966. Congress enacted a bill (HR 13103 — PL 89-809) in late 1966 to induce foreign investment in the United States.

As a result of intensive lobbying efforts by special interest groups, HR 13103 was loaded with extraneous amendments to give tax breaks to a multitude of individuals and organizations including presidential candidates, big-time investors, self-employed persons, mining interests, an aluminum company and even hearse owners. The legislation was known, accordingly, as the Christmas tree bill.

President Johnson signed the bill into law on Nov. 13, but his remarks indicated that except for a few important provisions — the foreign investors section and the precedent-setting campaign finance plan — he would have vetoed it. (As it turned out, the campaign finance plan never got off the ground: with second thoughts about its hasty action, Congress in early 1967 suspended the provision.)

As passed, the investors tax provisions of the bill, part of the administration's long-range program to combat the U.S. balance-of-payments deficit, were designed originally to induce more foreign investment in U.S. stocks and bonds through favorable tax treatment. During the 19-month study accorded the measure, however, Congress rewrote the administration bill to provide a comprehensive overhaul of relevant tax structures. Thus the bill in its final form tightened tax "loopholes" that allegedly permitted foreigners to escape U.S. taxation, in addition to carrying out its original purpose of providing investment incentives.

Participation Certificates

At President Johnson's request, Congress in 1966 authorized the federal government to "pool" certain mortgages and other loan assets held by six federal agencies as a result of their having made direct loans to farms, colleges and others under various federal programs, and then to sell shares in the pool to the public, in the form of interest-bearing "participation" certificates.

The new program (S 3283 — PL 89-429) was intended to convert $3.2 billion in paper assets held by the government into ready cash in fiscal 1967 (and more later), and also, in effect, shift part of the burden of federal credit to private hands. The funds obtained by the six federal agencies through the sale of participation certificates based on their paper assets could be used by the agencies to finance further direct-loan operations under their existing program authorizations, in lieu of new appropriations from the Treasury that would otherwise be needed.

Mechanics of Program

The mechanics of the new program were as follows:

Under various existing programs, a large number of federal agencies were authorized to make direct loans to individuals, colleges, local public agencies and other institutions to help them build facilities and carry on activities that the federal government considered desirable to encourage. Such activities included home purchases by veterans and other special groups, construction of college dormitories and academic facilities, and farm housing and farm operating costs.

In many cases, these loans were made at very low interest rates in order to subsidize a particular type of activity. The total federal portfolio of mortgages and repayment commitments on all direct loans was about $33 billion as of mid-1966.

In some cases, if the government wished to obtain cash for the mortgages and loan repayment commitments, it simply sold them outright to private banks and other investors. However, loans that bore very low interest rates or were made to high-risk borrowers were extremely difficult to sell to banks and other private investors.

Consequently, S 3283, the Participation Sales Act of 1966, authorized the government, as an alternative to selling the mortgages and other loan assets held by six specified agencies, simply to put them into a pool that was retained in the government's hands and that was used as the backing for sale by the government of participation certificates. The transaction was to be handled by the Federal National Mortgage Association (FNMA). The participation certificates were permitted to bear whatever interest rates were necessary to assure their sale, and could be either of short- or long-term maturities. The certificates were to be guaranteed both as to principal and interest by the FNMA. This guarantee together with the fact that the certificates were to be sold at an attractive rate of interest made the certificates easy to sell to private investors.

By selling the participation certificates, the federal agencies participating in the pool obtained cash — in effect — for their paper assets. Each agency would receive an amount of cash equal to the amount of paper assets it had put into the pool as backing for the participation certificates. These funds could be used to make additional direct loans under existing authorized lending programs, or to reduce Treasury advances to the agency.

Both the principal and interest owed to purchasers of the participation certificates were to be paid off by the FNMA with the proceeds it obtained from repayments on those mortgages, loan repayment commitments and other paper assets that were in the pool. However, because of the low interest rates borne by many of the paper assets in the pool, such proceeds would not be large enough to fully service the participation certificates. Therefore, the government would simply make up the deficit by appropriating enough funds to cover the difference. It was estimated that, on the amount of participation certificate sales that the administration planned for fiscal 1967 ($3.2 billion), the deficit would be about $10 to $14 million a year.

Because the participation certificates were issued by the FNMA, rather than the Treasury directly, the certificates were not counted as part of the national debt. Their sale would not be subject to the debt limit. Moreover, the financing of new direct loans by federal agencies with funds obtained from the sale of participation certificates was not classified as spending in the federal budget, whereas the use of new appropriations would have been. Use of participation certificates therefore had the effect of reducing the ostensible size of the federal budget deficit. These aspects of the certificates were eliminated in a 1967 debt limit bill and in the fiscal 1969 budget.

Republican Criticisms

Voting on the bill largely followed partisan lines with only 5 Republicans supporting it in the Senate and no Republicans supporting the original House version.

Republicans charged that the whole idea of selling participation certificates was simply a gimmick to obtain funds for further broadening federal spending without substantial congressional supervision and without having such spending show up as deficits in the federal budget or subject to the national debt limit.

Democrats conceded that the use of proceeds from participation certificates to finance new federal loans would have the effect of "dressing up" the appearance of the federal budget and federal debt position. But they said the real purpose of the new program was to find a way to continue to finance desirable federal social programs by the conversion of paper assets into cash, without having to raise taxes, without cutting back the programs, and without surpassing the debt limit. It was not desirable to go to the Treasury for further appropriations, they said, when federal agencies were sitting on a tremendous pile of paper assets that could readily be converted into cash. Administration spokesmen also said that it was the government's policy, wherever possible, to use private credit rather than federal credit to finance desirable loan programs. The sale of participation certificates would convert part of the credit burden now resting on the federal government into private credit.

Bank Interest Rates

An extremely tight policy of credit restraint maintained by the Federal Reserve Board required Congress in 1966 to enact an administration-backed bill (HR 14026 — PL 89-597) giving flexible authority to federal bank regulatory agencies to set different limits on the interest rates banks and other financial institutions might pay on different types and amounts of fixed maturity (time) deposits.

The purpose of the bill was to protect savings and loan institutions (S&Ls), traditional source of financing for home loans, from the competition of high-interest certificates of deposit (CDs) issued by commercial banks.

Despite the Federal Reserve Board's policy to reduce inflationary pressures by limiting availability of loan funds and increasing loan interest rates, a high demand for loans prevailed throughout 1966. Consequently, banks and savings and loan institutions began competing vigorously for the savings dollar — a major source of loan money.

To acquire funds to meet a high demand for industrial and consumer loans, the banks had begun to offer the certificates in amounts far smaller than in the past and at interest rates higher than S&Ls could afford to pay. The result was that persons with relatively small amounts of money to invest were taking funds out of S&Ls (or not going there in the first place) and instead buying small denomination CDs from banks. This in turn limited the funds available to S&Ls and dried up the major source of home financing; a sharp downturn in the housing industry was one of the most prominent imbalances in the economy during 1966.

The "rate war" for savings arose because existing law required federal authorities to set a single general limit on time deposits, with variations permitted only with respect to differing maturities and other related factors. Thus, when banks began offering CDs in low denominations, authorities could make them less attractive only by lowering the rates on time deposits across the board. Because this would have included large-denomination CDs, an obligation bought in substantial quantities by major corporations, it would have cut into a major source of funds available to banks for lending.

The discretionary rate controls authorized by PL 89-597 were to expire one year after the bill's enactment. (However, they were extended in stages through March 31,

1973). Agencies given the new powers were the Federal Reserve Board (Fed), the Federal Deposit Insurance Corp. (FDIC) and the Federal Home Loan Bank Board (FHLBB). Together, these three agencies regulated all banks and savings and loan institutions insured by the federal government.

As signed into law on Sept. 21, the 1966 act also gave the FHLBB authority for the first time to directly establish interest and dividend rates that S&Ls could pay their depositors, increased the reserves that the Fed could require member banks to hold against time deposits and enlarged the types of government securities that the Fed could buy and sell. The reserves provision (not subsequently implemented) was designed to crimp CD operations by banks even further, while the authority to deal in a broadened portfolio of securities was designed to enlarge the Fed's role in economic management by moving funds in and out of sensitive areas of the economy. The FHLBB authority was extended in stages through March 31, 1973, and the other two provisions were made permanent in 1968.

1967

Frustration over the Vietnam War, rioting in the nation's urban ghettos and rising government spending marked the first session of the 90th Congress. Confused over priorities, members found it difficult to move affirmatively in any direction. Consequently, the session was one of the longest on record and the least productive of Johnson's years in the White House.

Pointing to the enormous costs of the war and the "incongruity" of "rewarding" the ghetto rioters with new federal aid, House Republicans set out to emasculate most aspects of the president's domestic program. With the help of Southern Democrats, they met with notable successes.

Although the president's requests were modest when compared with those of the last three sessions, few administration bills except war appropriations moved through Congress unscathed. Johnson's major legislative proposal — a 10 percent income tax surcharge to pay for the war and fight domestic inflation — never moved out of House committee. In addition, funds for existing programs were scaled back drastically from the president's requests. Johnson suffered major setbacks on a truth-in-lending bill, mutual funds regulation, rural development aid, East-West trade and a number of other proposals.

Qualified victories could be claimed for enactment of Social Security and anti-poverty bills. The first carried welfare restrictions the administration objected to, while poverty funds were cut below the requested level. One part of Johnson's economic program was enacted quickly. It was a bill to restore the investment tax credit and accelerated depreciation earlier than had been planned. The bill was delayed slightly by addition of a rider to suspend the presidential election campaign financing law that was enacted in 1966.

Buoyed by increased defense spending, the U.S. economy in December entered a record 82nd consecutive month of expansion. The cost-of-living index in October rose to a

record 117.5 percent of the 1957-59 average, a 2.6 percent increase over the October mark of a year before. In a related development, interest rates — which had fallen earlier in the year after reaching near-record highs in 1966 — moved substantially upward throughout the fall. Economists consequently feared a new credit squeeze that could result in another recession in housing (although few thought it would be as serious as the housing recession of 1966). Economists earlier in the year had been almost unanimous in predicting runaway inflation for 1968, but by year's end some were predicting a tapering off of the expansion in the months ahead.

The balance-of-payments deficit took a major turn for the worse late in the year and prompted a new program by the administration in early 1968 to lower the dollar outflow. No major new efforts were made in 1967, but two existing laws dealing with the problem were extended.

Investment Credit

One of the first major laws enacted in the 90th Congress was an important part of President Johnson's economic program for 1967. The bill (HR 6950 — PL 90-26) provided for restoration of the 7 percent investment tax credit and certain accelerated depreciation practices, which had been suspended Oct. 10, 1966, in an effort to curb inflationary pressures by reducing new business investments. Restoration had not been scheduled to take place until Jan. 1, 1968. *(PL 89-800, p. 141)*

Enactment of HR 6950's tax provisions could have occurred in much less time because there was general support for them in Congress. However, quick action was prevented when the Senate for more than five weeks debated a non-germane rider to repeal the 1966 Presidential Election Campaign Fund Act. After much confused voting, the Senate in the end agreed to make the 1966 law inoperative until Congress by law had adopted guidelines governing the distribution of money to candidates and their parties. The House had not considered the issue at all, but House conferees accepted the Senate provision without change and it was included in the final bill.

As President Johnson had requested, PL 90-26 ended the suspension of the 7 percent investment tax credit on the purchase of machinery and equipment and of certain methods of accelerated depreciation of industrial and commercial buildings after March 9, the day of the president's message. In requesting early restoration, the president told Congress the suspension had already "done the job" and that "excessive pressure" on machinery industries had "eased very dramatically." Administration officials denied that restoration was necessary to head off a recession; rather they simply argued that the suspension was no longer necessary.

The House and Senate agreed on the March 9 termination date for the suspension. However, there was a major difference between the House and Senate relating to treatment of property that was built or ordered during the Oct. 10-March 9 suspension period.

House-Senate conferees agreed on a bill that was essentially along the lines of the more liberal House measure. Conferees allowed the tax credit on property, which was ordered during the suspension period but delivered on or after May 24, the day they reached agreement. Fast depreciation and the tax credit were allowed on the portion of construction done after May 24 even though construction had begun during the suspension.

House Members argued that their more liberal provisions were fairer and administratively more workable. The administration objected to the revenue loss and said the provision was unfair to those taxpayers who supported the administration in holding off on projects or orders during the suspension period.

Tax Relief

Congress late in December 1967 sent to the president a bill (HR 4765 — PL 90-225) granting special tax relief to three private companies. The measure provided tax relief to stockholders of the Financial General Corp., a large holding company; an estimated $22 million tax rebate to American Motors Co., which was in financial difficulties; and a tax adjustment for the Jefferson Standard Life Insurance Co.

As originally passed by the House, the bill provided only the tax relief for Financial General stockholders. The Senate Finance Committee added amendments to the bill allowing American Motors a $2 million investment tax credit, resolving tax problems of mortgage guaranty insurance companies, permitting a taxfree "spin-off" of stock of a controlled life insurance company (Jefferson Standard), and altering the tax treatment of unfunded pension plans of universities and other tax-exempt groups.

The Senate passed the bill after adopting three floor amendments. One required that Financial General shareholders pay a capital gains tax when the corporation carried out the divestiture of non-banking interests required under the 1966 amendments to the Bank Holding Company Act (PL 89-485). The second amendment added a $20 million tax break to the committee's $2 million provision benefiting American Motors. This permitted the financially troubled company to carry back operating losses for five years, instead of the existing three years. The third amendment limited to one year the effect of the committee's provision for mortgage guaranty insurance companies.

House-Senate conferees on the bill insisted on the original House treatment of Financial General stock divestiture, but accepted the two American Motors amendments and the life insurance company provision. They dropped the pension plan provision and recommended that the mortgage guaranty insurance company provision be enacted on a permanent basis in a separate bill. (The mortgage guaranty insurance company provision was finally enacted in early 1968 as PL 90-240). President Johnson signed HR 4765 into law on Dec. 27.

Social Security Amendments

Congress in 1967 enacted a bill raising Social Security benefits and making major changes in the Social Security system. Two years previously, Congress had made sweeping changes in the bill by establishing a medical care program (Medicare) for the aged under Social Security (PL 89-97). The 1967 measure (HR 12080 — PL 90-248) also wrote major new restrictions into the nation's welfare program. *(1965 law, p. 140)*

In its Social Security provisions, HR 12080 provided a 13 percent across-the-board increase in benefits under the Old Age, Survivors and Disability Insurance (OASDI) programs. The administration had requested 15 percent. It also raised the monthly minimum benefits, liberalized the retirement test and liberalized the definition of blindness for disability payments. The first full year (1969) cost of the bill was put at $3.7 billion.

The bill also made changes in the Medicare program. Some extra days of hospitalization were provided, and hospital outpatient diagnostic services were transferred to the supplementary Medicare plan. Another provision of the bill attempted to limit federal participation in the fast-growing Medicaid program for the "medically needy" poor who did not qualify for welfare payments. The bill also made substantial increases in maternal and child health and child welfare authorizations. It earmarked at least 6 percent of all maternal and child health appropriations for family planning services.

The final bill did not include a number of major provisions requested by President Johnson in his first special message to the 90th Congress. These included extension of Medicare to the 1.5 million disabled who received Social Security benefits but who were under 65 and a new system of tax treatment for the elderly. Also missing from the final bill were a number of costly Senate floor amendments such as a big increase in the amount a person could earn and still receive Social Security, liberalized Medicare reimbursement to hospitals and nursing homes, restoration of the full income tax deduction for medical expenses of the elderly, and a provision to adopt a method for bringing down the cost of drugs purchased under federally aided programs.

The conference report was cleared for the president Dec. 15, the final day of the 1967 session, after a threatened filibuster by Senate liberals against the welfare provisions was averted. President Johnson signed the bill into law (PL 90-248) Jan. 2, 1968. He said, "Measured in dollars of insurance benefits, the bill . . . is the greatest stride forward since Social Security [was enacted] in 1935." But he criticized the welfare restrictions, said the welfare system was "outmoded" and in need of major change, and appointed a commission to look into it.

Provisions

As signed into law PL 90-248 made the following amendments to the Social Security retirement and Medicare programs:

OASDI

Provided an across-the-board increase of 13 percent to all beneficiaries under the Old Age, Survivors and Disability Insurance (OASDI) programs, effective Feb. 1, 1968. Raised the monthly minimum benefit from $44 to $55. The first full year (1969) cost of all improvements in benefits was estimated at $3.7 billion.

● Increased the special benefits to persons 72 and over who had not met Social Security requirements from $35 to $40 a month for a single person and from $52.50 to $60 a month for a couple. The annual cost was about $50 million.

● Liberalized the retirement earnings test, allowing a beneficiary to earn $1,680 a year, or $140 a month, instead of $1,500 a year, or $125 a month, without loss of benefits. The 1969 cost was $220 million.

● Provided graduated cash for some 65,000 disabled widows or widowers between 60 and 62 years old at an estimated cost of $60 million for the first 12 months. Provided a stricter definition of disability. Liberalized the definition of blindness for purposes of disability. Improved benefits for children adopted by disabled persons.

● Provided $83 million in additional benefits for 175,000 dependent children whose mother was covered by OASDI but died, retired or became disabled.

● Provided cash benefits for some 100,000 young workers who were disabled before age 31 and had been covered by OASDI for at least six quarters. The first year cost was $70 million.

● Financed higher benefits and other changes in OASDI through existing trust funds and increases in Social Security tax payments. Raised the taxable wage base to $7,800 from $6,600, beginning Jan. 1, 1968. Raised the 4.4 percent payroll tax which the employee and employer each contributed to the employee's OASDI and Medicare benefits to 4.8 percent in 1969, 5.2 percent in 1972, 5.65 percent in 1973, 5.7 percent in 1976, 5.8 percent in 1980 and 5.9 percent in 1987 and thereafter.

Medicare

● Permitted Medicare reimbursements under the doctor-bill plan to a doctor or directly to a patient on the basis of an itemized bill, whether paid or unpaid, submitted by a patient. Permitted Medicare payments for certain ancillary hospital and extended care facility services which previously were not reimbursable. Included coverage of podiatrists' services for non-routine foot care under Medicare.

● Allowed full "reasonable charges" for inpatient radiological and pathological services. Permitted reimbursement for outpatient physical therapy services and out-patient diagnostic x-rays.

● Permitted an annual enrollment period for the supplementary plan rather than enrollment only in odd-number years. Permitted a person becoming 65 in 1968 to be covered by Medicare if he or she had three quarters of Social Security coverage. This requirement would increase by three quarters each year for persons becoming 65 after 1968.

● Provided each Medicare beneficiary with a total "lifetime reserve" of 60 days of added hospital coverage to be used whenever the 90 days covered in a "spell of illness" had been exhausted. The patient would pay $20 a day for each day of the additional protection.

● Transferred hospital outpatient diagnostic services to coverage under the supplementary insurance plan, subject to a $50 annual deductible and a 20 percent coinsurance provision.

● Required the secretary of health, education and welfare to make a study of the cost of including under Medicare reimbursement of all prescription drugs and the establishment of a method of controlling the cost and quality of drugs purchased under federally aided programs. The report was due Jan. 1, 1969. The secretary also would study ways to improve the earnings test and the feasibility of increasing payments on delayed retirements.

1968

Congress was in a conservative mood in 1968, preoccupied chiefly with inflation and crime and disorders in the streets and on college campuses. Lawmakers were divided

on how to respond to rioting, the multiple problems of the cities that riots had highlighted — unemployment, poor education and inadequate housing — and the underlying racial issues.

Although Congress enacted a landmark housing and urban development bill, it also imposed a deep reduction in government spending in general and gave no serious consideration to appropriating the vastly increased sums of money that some members and private citizens contended were needed to relieve the nation's urban problems.

Congress insisted on setting a spending ceiling for the administration in fiscal 1969 as the price for passing a federal income tax increase which the administration had sought since the beginning of 1967. The ceiling, as enacted, required cuts of $6 billion in estimated 1969 expenditures; the figure later rose to $7 billion as actual spending rose, but Congress acted to exempt some programs from the cuts.

Congress was even less cooperative with the other over-riding tax-related issue of 1968: the balance-of-payments deficit. After some improvement in 1965 and 1966, the deficit took a bad turn for the worse in 1967 and prompted the administration in 1968 to propose a wide-ranging program of controls to halt the outflow of dollars. Stiff mandatory controls on foreign investment, replacing voluntary controls that were in existence, were put into effect by administrative action. The president also asked Congress for various pieces of legislation, the primary one being a travel tax, to help reduce the deficit.

Congress rejected most of the proposals. Nevertheless, the nation's payments balance improved during the year. But it was not certain as 1969 began that the improvements made in 1968 were anything more than temporary changes that would not be repeated.

Although the crisis of the cities was the central social issue in 1968, few major new proposals to aid the cities were considered with the exception of the housing bill. There was greater emphasis than in earlier years on involving the private sector in alleviating the cities' problems. The housing bill contained a number of provisions designed to encourage industry and non-profit groups to build or rehabilitate low- and moderate-income housing. In addition, the administration's major manpower proposal in 1968 was based on federal support for private industry training of the hardcore unemployed.

Inflation became a more acute threat in 1968 with sharper cost-of-living increases and a large budget deficit. The continuing expansion of the national economy brought production closer to capacity and prices edged upward as demand grew. The Consumer Price Index increase for June-July 1968 was the steepest two-month advance in 11 years — the equivalent of an average annual rate of 3.6 percent in August compared with an annual average of 1.3 percent from 1961-65 and 2.9 percent from 1965-67.

Income Tax Surcharge

Congressional action on taxes was dominated by a single issue in 1968: a 10 percent surcharge on personal and corporate income taxes to help finance the Vietnam War and to reduce inflationary pressures in the U.S. economy. After a bitter and prolonged fight Congress in June 1968 finally sent the president the tax increase he said was essential to economic stability.

But Congress attached to the legislation mandatory reductions in spending, appropriations and federal employment levels that Johnson at one point said "would really bring chaos to the government." The struggle over enactment of the legislation (HR 15414 — PL 90-364) pitted powerful political forces against one another and cut through to a basic economic issue — the level of government spending.

In passing the tax-increase bill, Congress completed action on the first general income tax increase since the Revenue Act of 1951 (PL 82-183).

In economic terms, the tax increase contained in the act represented the other side of the fiscal coin of the tax cut contained in the 1964 Revenue Act (PL 88-272). Taken together, the two bills represented the first complete test of the "New Economics" — a theory that government fiscal policy should be used to guide the national economy through budget deficits in a recession and budget surpluses (or at least smaller deficits) during inflation. Both bills, however, were enacted long after they had been requested. The time-lag between request and enactment of the fiscal measures led President Kennedy in 1962 to ask specifically for standby authority to reduce certain taxes and President Johnson in 1965, 1966 and 1968 to seek to "develop procedures to assure the timely adjustment of fiscal policy...." (*1964 tax cut, p. 133*)

When the 1968 tax increase was enacted, the economy was in the 88th month of an unprecedented period of expansion, but strong inflationary pressures were overriding the expansion. The gross national product, which had risen more than $16 billion in the third and fourth quarters of 1967, jumped more than $20 billion in the first quarter of 1968 and an estimated $19.6 billion during the second quarter. Prices were rising steadily, and the unemployment rate dropped from 4.1 percent in September 1967 to 3.5 percent in May 1968. Provisions of HR 15414 — to cut fiscal 1969 spending by $6 billion, to rescind $8 billion of unspent prior-year appropriations and to cut back civilian employment in the executive branch — were designed to exert further restraint on the economy.

Federal spending and employment limitations in the bill apparently were only partially successful in actually curbing government spending and employment, however.

Background

In an August 1967 message to Congress, Johnson asked for a 10 percent surcharge as well as some other lesser tax measures to raise extra revenues. The bill went nowhere in 1967 but prompted a major debate about the state of the economy and government spending.

In 1968 the president again asked for the surcharge and warned that failure to act would lead to "an accelerating spiral of price increases, a slump in home building and a continued erosion of the American dollar...." Suddenly, bypassing the tax-writing House Ways and Means Committee, the Senate in early spring 1968 added the surcharge and the $6 billion spending cut (and other floor amendments) to a comparatively innocuous House-passed bill (HR 15414) extending some soon-to-expire excise tax rates.

Uncertainty hung over the House and Senate conference on HR 15414. Time passed while conservative members opposed to higher taxes and liberals opposed to spending cuts were sounded out. More time was lost awaiting indications that President Johnson, who very much wanted the surcharge, was willing to accept the spending cut and

other restrictions added by Congress to get the tax increase.

The trigger to congressional action on the tax increase, according to most observers, was a rapidly developing crisis in the international gold market. The crisis became so critical in mid-March (when the tax increase began to make headway) that the United States was forced to abandon its traditional single-price system for gold and to adopt a new, two-price system. The links between the gold crisis and the tax increase were a rush of gold speculation, a dwindling supply of U.S. gold reserves, and a growing and persistent U.S. balance-of-payments deficit. Advocates of a tax increase said it would help reduce the balance-of-payments deficit. (*Gold cover, p. 149; balance of payments problems, box, p. 148*)

It was estimated that the bill's tax provisions would produce an additional $15.5 billion in government revenues. The surcharge was expected to produce about $11.6 billion of that total.

By the time Congress finished work on HR 15414, it had become a highly complex measure with 18 sections broken down among three titles. The bulk of the provisions represented one-time Senate floor amendments. What once had been merely a bill to extend certain excise taxes had become one of the most important bills of the 90th Congress.

Provisions

As signed into law, PL 90-364 contained the following major provisions:

● Continued the existing 10 percent excise tax on telephone service and the 7 percent tax on manufacturers' prices of new cars through Dec. 31, 1969. Gradual reductions in both excise tax rates were set up for 1970, 1971 and 1972, with elimination of both taxes scheduled for Jan. 1, 1973.

● Repealed provisions of existing tax law that required corporations to file a declaration of estimated tax for the current taxable year. The portion of corporate income taxes that were to be paid during the year in which the liability was incurred was raised to 80 percent from 70 percent.

● Reduced from $100,000 to $40,000 the amount of corporate tax liability on which payment could be postponed until April 15 of the year after the liability was incurred was to be phased in over a ten-year period. Corporations using the existing $100,000 tax deferral provision were given a ten-year transitional period to become current in their tax payments. The act also established certain conditions under which a corporation could apply for a tax refund immediately after the close of a taxable year.

● Imposed a 10 percent surcharge on individual and corporate income taxes, effective April 1, 1968, for individuals and Jan. 1, 1968, for corporations, both through July 1, 1969. The first $1,000 of taxable income for a single person and $2,000 for joint returns was exempted from the surcharge. Increased withholding was scheduled to begin 15 days after enactment. For individuals filing declarations, the increase was to be reflected in declarations filed Sept. 15 for calendar-year taxpayers; for corporations the surcharge was to be applied before the application of tax credits.

● Set a ceiling of $180.1 billion on fiscal 1969 spending and a ceiling of $191.7 billion on new obligational authority requested for fiscal 1969. However, spending and appropri-

Unsettled International Economic System . . .

An unsettled international economic system contributed to U.S. problems in 1973-77 and complicated government policies dealing with them. Throughout the non-communist nations rapid inflation rates and steep recession paralleled and reinforced the extreme U.S. economic cycle. Counteracting government fiscal and monetary policies, along with adjustments to massive oil price increases and crop failures, strained new international trade and financial arrangements that came into use following severe currency exchange disruptions in early 1973.

A series of extraordinary economic shocks — including grain harvest shortfalls, critical commodity shortages and petroelum price increases dictated by a producing nations' cartel — helped set off a worldwide round of inflation in 1972-73. Their effects were boosted by simultaneous stimulative actions by all the major trading nations that fed a short-lived boom in early 1973. The ravages of the resulting rising prices, along with concurrent deflationary efforts by governments, then helped bring on a cumulative 1974-75 recession. An uneven recovery followed, but the pace faltered in mid-1976 even in those relatively strong economies. Recovery lagged behind in other nations, notably Great Britain and Italy, where inflation persisted at higher levels that forced governments to tighten restraints on demand.

Oil Price Demands

All the western industrialized nations, and most less developed countries as well, spent 1973-77 making painful adjustments to skyrocketing fuel costs. The most deeply felt international economic development of the period was the four-fold crude oil price increase that the Organization of Petroleum Exporting Countries (OPEC) cartel imposed in stages. The OPEC nations' determination to multiply their earnings from production of their vital petroleum reserves — and willingness to use oil as a political weapon as demonstrated by the 1973 export embargo imposed after war broke out between Arab nations and Israel — produced severe energy shortages and inflationary reverberations that contributed heavily to recession. Even as other raw material producing nations considered similar cartel tactics, the petroleum crisis made

the industrialized nations all too aware of their disturbing dependence on dwindling supplies of critical materials that often were beyond their direct control.

Rising oil import bills created severe imbalances in the flow of goods, services and capital among nations. Energy-consuming nations ran up heavy trade and international payments deficits as oil payments flowed to the OPEC nations.

In 1974 alone OPEC countries accumulated $70.5 billion in payments surpluses. Because the producing nations could absorb relatively few imports, and had not begun to invest oil earnings in other countries, that wealth was not returned to reverse flows back to the industrialized economies.

The resulting payments drain eased in 1975 when recession curtailed energy demand in industrialized nations and when OPEC countries stepped up imports and foreign investments. But the trend was expected to reverse with economic recovery and additional oil price increases. And the financing of continued oil deficits threatened to exhaust the ability of some nations, such as Great Britain, to borrow foreign funds to cover rising government debt and domestic consumption. The resulting financial problems were forcing retrenchment in domestic economic goals in some countries while rising oil prices fueled inflation in all nations and discouraged needed investment in energy-intensive industries.

International Monetary Structure

Those painful adjustments were thrust upon an improved international monetary system that began evolving from the ruins of the post-World-War-II structure. That previous system, negotiated at the 1944 Bretton Woods, N.H., conference and centered on a strong U.S. dollar, fell apart in 1971-73 in long-delayed recognition of new world economic realties.

The Bretton Woods system, which assigned each nation's currency a fixed value pegged to the f[dollar and through it to gold, began unraveling during the 1960s when the United States encountered chronic outflows in its balance of payments.

The turning point came in 1971 when President Nixon suspended the long-standing U.S. commitment to exchange its gold reserve assets for unwanted

ations for the Vietnam War, payment of interests on the federal debt, and payments for veterans' and Social Security benefits were exempted from the spending reductions. The president was also required to make specific recommendations for rescinding $8 billion in unspent prior-year appropriations for the fiscal 1970 budget.

● Stipulated that not more than 75 percent of the vacancies in the executive branch were to be filled until the

number of full-time persons employed there was reduced to the June 30, 1966, level of 2,366,000 persons. Limits were also placed on the number of temporary and part-time employees in the departments and agencies. Certain categories of employees, such as presidential appointees, were exempted.

● Eliminated the existing tax exemption on the interest from certain industrial development bonds issued after

...Contributed to U.S. Problems in 1973-77

dollars accumulated by other nations, in effect allowing the dollar to float. He then negotiated a currency exchange rate realignment that devalued the dollar to a level that more realistically reflected international assessment of the U.S. economy's strength.

The 1971 currency realignment failed to end international payments problems, however, and a wave of speculation against the dollar forced another 10 percent devaluation in February 1973. Shortly thereafter inflationary pressures and volatile flows of capital among nations led governments to give up all attempts to maintain fixed exchange rates through market intervention. The Bretton Woods structure was replaced by a *de facto* system of floating exchange rates, in which supply and demand forces on international exchanges were left free to determine the relative values of currencies. The International Monetary Fund (IMF) nations meanwhile continued negotiations on devising a new monetary system to replace the Bretton Woods arrangements.

Floating Exchange Rates

In theory the floating exchange rate system was expected to help correct international payments imbalances through largely automatic adjustments. Market judgments would cause the currency of a country with a weak economy, high inflation and persistent payment outflows to float downward in value against other currencies. With the currency costing less in terms of other currencies and the country's products therefore cheaper in other nations, demands for its exports would strengthen, more costly imports from other countries would decline, its domestic output would increase and its payments balance would swing back toward equilibrium. A country with a payments surplus, on the other hand, could expect its currency to appreciate, cutting back foreign demand for its exports while making imports more attractively priced.

In practice the system worked less smoothly. Despite large currency fluctuations in response to inflation rate differntials, countries such as Great Britain and Italy whose currencies had depreciated were unable to maintain their export market shares as world trade began expanding with recovery from the recession. Germany and Japan, with much stronger currencies, increased their exports, perhaps because their lower inflation rates and amicable management-labor relations promised better performance in fulfilling contracts. Critics contended that exchange rate fluctuations worsened price pressures in inflation-plagued nations as depreciation made imports more costly; defenders of the system argued that exchange rates could be held steady only if a government took adequate measures to curb underlying inflation pressures at home.

Regardless of such problems, the floating rate system weathered the fluctuating worldwide economic fortunes without disastrous strains. Along with special arrangements by the IMF for directing OPEC surpluses to deficit nations, the system was beginning to accommodate to the redistribution of economic power and assets resulting from oil price increases.

Following a 1975 understanding between France and the United States, the IMF drew up revised international monetary agreements that in effect confirmed the floating system. Congress in 1976 approved U.S. ratifications of the agreement, under which IMF nations agreed to avoid exchange rate manipulation except to counter disorderly conditions, provided for possibile reinstitution of fixed rates in the future, replaced gold with IMF special drawing rights (SDRs or paper gold) as the medium of settlement in IMF transactions, and authorized sale of part of IMF gold reserves to finance a trust fund to help poor nations adjust to higher oil costs.

Trade Negotiations

The major industrial nations in the meantime were engaged in wide-ranging trade negotiations aimed at further reductions in tariffs and other barriers to international commerce. Congress in 1974 authorized U.S. participation by giving the president authority to negotiate and implement some trade barrier reductions, ignoring organized labor support for strong protectionist measures to curb competition from foreign imports. Despite the unemployment that accompanied the recession, the industrialized nations for the most part resisted drastic trade curbs designed to bolster domestic production.

May 1968. However, certain bonds issued for certain residential properties and public facilities were exempted from the new taxable status.

● Postponed certain provisions of the 1967 Social Security amendments relating to the Aid to Families with Dependent Children (AFDC) program and the cutoff date for federal matching payments to states under the Medicaid program.

Gold Cover

Congress voted in March 1968 to remove the remaining gold backing from U.S. currency. The bill (HR 14743 — PL 90-269) eliminated the existing requirement that each Federal Reserve bank maintain reserves in gold certificates of not less than 25 percent of its Federal Reserve notes (currency) in circulation.

Like similar legislation in 1965 (PL 89-3), HR 14743 was necessary because of the continued actual and threatened drain on the U.S. gold stock as a result of balance-of-payments deficits. President Johnson had requested the legislation in his 1968 State of the Union message. *(Balance of payments problems, box, p. 148)*

In 1968 the current U.S. gold stock was about $12 billion, but approximately $10.7 billion of that total was earmarked to meet the 25 percent backing requirement. The balance was available for sale to foreign countries at $35 an ounce.

The administration said that the $10.7 billion also had to be made available for sale to assure other nations that there would be ample gold available to exchange for dollars that they had been accumulating as a result of the U.S. balance-of-payments deficit. The hope was to encourage these nations to retain their dollars rather than demand gold and, by so doing, to emphasize that the strength of the dollar depended on the strength of the U.S. economy and not upon a legal 25 percent gold backing for the currency.

Federal Reserve Requirements

The Federal Reserve Act of 1913 had required that the 12 Federal Reserve banks created by the act maintained a reserve of gold certificates valued at no less than 35 percent of the amount of commercial bank deposits held by each. In addition it required that Federal Reserve notes issued by the government be backed by gold bullion holdings amounting to no less than 40 percent of value.

The coinage of gold was ended in 1934, when the United States went off the gold standard as a form of commercial exchange. After that gold was used chiefly as a reserve for meeting international obligations; the United States maintained the gold value of the dollar at $35 an ounce.

The reserve provisions of the 1913 act remained unchanged until 1945, when both the required Federal Reserve holdings of gold certificates and the gold backing for Federal Reserve notes were reduced to 25 percent. Early in 1965, Congress passed legislation ending the requirement that the Federal Reserve bank maintain a 25 percent reserve of gold certificates against bank deposits.

The 1968 removal of the 25 percent gold cover was opposed, mainly by Republicans, as offering only temporary relief for the widespread economic problems that were contributing to the nation's growing balance-of-payments deficit.

Concern also was expressed by members of Congress from Western gold-producing states who sought to strengthen confidence in the dollar by stimulating increased gold production. Although HR 14743 did become law quickly, it passed by narrow margins in both the House and Senate. President Johnson signed the bill March 18.

1969

The first session of the 91st Congress, the sixth longest in history, adjourned with the lowest legislative output in 36 years. The major piece of legislation passed during the session was the tax reform bill, the most comprehensive revision of the tax code since the income tax was established in 1913.

The administration had proposed tax code revisions aimed mainly at tightening preferences used by wealthy persons and removing the poor from the tax rolls. Congress, however, approved a sweeping reform bill, which went beyond the administration's requests in some areas but added a revenue-losing increase in the personal income tax exemption to $750, from $600, and tacked on a 15 percent increase in Social Security benefits to the tax bill.

A key issue in the year-long debate on tax reform was President Nixon's request for extension of the income tax surcharge past its June 30, 1969, expiration date. Another major issue was retention for tax purposes of the 27.5 percent depletion allowance for oil and gas companies. The final bill reduced the figure to 22 percent.

In other important economic legislation, Congress cleared a bill granting states broader authority to tax; extended the Interest Equalization Tax; and raised the permissible interest rate on Series E and H savings bonds to 5 percent, from 4.25 percent. Economic legislation left pending at the end of the session included Nixon's proposal to share federal revenue with states and a House-passed bill placing holding companies that control a single bank under the regulating authority of the Federal Reserve Bank.

The most important congressional action in the area of international economics in 1969 was passage of a new Export Control Act. The act replaced the 1949 Export Control Act, a restrictive measure affecting U.S. trade with communist countries, with a new law which had the effect of encouraging East-West trade.

In the area of monetary policy, the Federal Reserve Board in 1969 continued the policy of tight money and high credit it had begun late in the Johnson administration. It held the money supply almost constant through 1969 despite warnings by some economists that inadequate monetary expansion was likely to cause a recession. Investment capital — particularly mortgage money for housing — grew scarce, and interest rates climbed to the highest level in 100 years.

Gross national product rose at an annual rate of $66 billion to $897.6 billion in 1969, measured in current prices. Measured in constant (1958) prices, GNP increased by less than one-third that amount. The average inflation of consumer prices was 5.4 percent. Thus at the end of his first year, President Nixon had had no success at all in meeting his number one domestic goal — control of inflation.

Surtax Extension

Following intense infighting in Congress, President Nixon sought and won continuation of the 1968 income tax surcharge as a means of curbing economic activity that was contributing to runaway inflation. Congress agreed to compromise legislation to extend for six months the 10 percent surcharge on personal and corporate income taxes. Total revenue from the surtax extension was estimated at $5.6 billion for fiscal 1970.

On March 26, Nixon had requested extension of the surtax for a year beyond the scheduled June 30, 1969, expiration date. He modified that request April 21 in announcing his tax reform proposals. Under his revised plan, the surtax was to be extended at 10 percent through Dec. 31, 1969, and at 5 percent through June 30, 1970. In addition Nixon sought repeal of the 7 percent investment tax credit for business. Under both plans the scheduled reduction in automobile and telephone exise taxes was postponed for one year. *(Excise taxes, p. 138; excise tax extension, tax reform bill, this page)*

House Democratic liberals, unconvinced that the administration and congressional leaders really wanted tax reform, waged a campaign against extension of the surtax until passage of a comprehensive tax reform bill was assured. Many opponents of the extension contended the surtax had not acted as a curb on inflation but was itself inflationary because the surtax had been passed along to the consumer in the form of higher prices. Congressional opposition to the surtax was bolstered as constituents made it clear they were unhappy with what they considered already unreasonably high taxes.

The administration and many economists, on the other hand, said inflation would have been much worse had there been no surtax. Responding to opponents of the surtax extension, the administration June 12 agreed to add tax relief for the poor to the surtax bill and to speed up its own timetable for other tax reform proposals. House Democratic leaders, too, said they would speed up consideration of the tax reform bill.

Despite these efforts, a surtax extension bill (HR 12290) squeaked through the House by five votes. The controversy then continued in the Senate — where liberals were even more adamant about holding up the surtax extension until floor consideration of tax reform was assured.

The deadlock was broken when Senate Democratic and Republican leaders reached a compromise by agreeing to a six-month extension of the surtax with a promise by the Democrats to take up the rest of the tax package contained in the House-passed bill after they agreed on tax reform. Meanwhile, the House Ways and Means Committee had attached the rest of Nixon's tax package to the committee's tax reform bill (HR 13270).

The Senate voted Nov. 1 to attach the surtax amendment to HR 9951, which had passed the House in May. The House concurred in the Senate amendment Aug. 4, clearing the bill for the president's signature.

As signed into law, the act (HR 9951 — PL 91-53) contained these major provisions:

● Extended the surtax at 10 percent through Dec. 31, 1969.

● Required that federal unemployment taxes be paid quarterly rather than annually; exempted employers whose cumulative tax liability was $100 or less.

● Made certain other changes to ensure that the accelerated revenues collected could be used for state and federal administrative purposes.

Tax Reform

In a move initiated on Capital Hill instead of by the president, Congress in 1969 passed legislation providing comprehensive reform of the nation's tax statutes and the largest tax cut since the Revenue Act of 1964. The Tax Reform Act of 1969 (HR 13270 — PL 91-172), passed over the threat of a presidential veto, coupled tax reforms worth $6.6 billion a year when fully effective with cuts of $9.1 billion — an annual loss to the Treasury of $2.5 billion.

The bill, cleared by both houses of Congress Dec. 22 and signed by the president Dec. 30 despite some major reservations, also provided a 15 percent increase in the basic Social Security benefits. Those increases, estimated at $4.4 billion a year, were to be paid for out of surpluses in the Social Security trust funds and did not require an immediate increase in Social Security taxes. (Because of the financing from their own trust fund, the increased Social Security benefits were not included in the above estimates for the bill's revenue effects.)

Impetus for tax revision came just before President Nixon took office Jan. 20, when retiring Treasury Secretary Joseph W. Barr warned Congress of an emerging "taxpayer's revolt" spurred on by increased public awareness of existing tax inequities. While middle-income persons were bearing the brunt of taxation, Barr said, some millionaires were able to avoid taxes altogether through investment in tax-exempt securities and use of other tax shelters. Tax reform became a major issue almost overnight and on Feb. 18 the House Ways and Means Committee opened the most extensive hearings on the subject in a decade. Finally, in mid-April, the Nixon administration introduced its own tax proposals but few were adopted by Congress.

House-Senate Differences

Significant differences between the House and Senate versions of the bill threatened late in the session to hold up final action until 1970. The House bill, passed Aug. 7, would have provided $9.3 billion a year in tax reductions when fully effective and $6.9 billion in tax reform. The Senate measure, cleared Dec. 11, carried $11 billion in eventual reductions and $5.6 billion in reform. President Nixon threatened to veto the bill if it included both the Senate's increase in Social Security benefits (the president had proposed a 10 percent increase) and a Senate-proposed increase of $200 in the personal income tax exemption allowed each taxpayer and dependents. The 15 percent increase in Social Security benefits remained intact in the final bill, but the personal exemption was modified. As sent to the White House, the bill increased the exemption by only $150 over a three-year period rather than the Senate's two-year proposal.

In its final form, HR 13270 produced a projected surplus of $3.7 billion in tax increases over cuts during fiscal 1970 and $2.7 billion in fiscal 1971. Including the increase in Social Security benefits, there would be a surplus of only $1.9 billion in fiscal 1970 and a deficit of $1.6 billion for fiscal 1971.

But this was a major restoration in revenue that would have been lost under the original Senate version of the bill. The Senate measure would have produced a deficit of about $900 million for fiscal 1970 and $7.6 billion for the following year. The president had been counting on a revenue surplus from the bill in fiscal 1970 to help produce a surplus, originally estimated close to $6 billion, for all government operations together. Similarly, he needed a surplus from the tax bill to hold the budget in balance during fiscal 1971.

In signing the measure Dec. 30, the president called it "an unbalanced bill that is both good and bad." He said the decision to sign it had not been easy.

Provisions

As signed by the president, HR 13270, the Tax Reform Act of 1969, contained the following provisions:

Private Foundations

- Defined private operating and non-operating foundations.
- Prohibited self-dealing between foundations and disqualified persons. Defined disqualified persons to include substantial contributors, foundation managers, owners of substantial interests in businesses or other activities that were substantial contributors, members of families of persons in the previous categories, businesses or trusts or estates of which disqualified persons owned 35 percent in aggregate, and government officials.
- Defined self-dealing in general as almost any use of the assets, income, credit, or facilities of a foundation for the benefit of disqualified persons, including transactions with undisqualified third parties for the purpose of benefiting disqualified persons, and also payments to government officials in most circumstances.
- Required foundations to distribute annually for charitable, educational, or other exempt purposes their total income, but not less than 6 percent of their total assets.
- Limited combined stock holdings of a foundation and its contributors and officers to 50 percent of any single business and the foundation itself to 25 percent, requiring divestiture of excess holdings generally within 10 years, with exceptions for certain conditions.
- Prohibited use of foundation funds to finance attempts to influence legislation or the outcome of specific elections. Specifically permitted financing of non-partisan voter registration drives carried on in five or more states, with certain financing limits.
- Made foundations responsible, within limits, for activities carried on by recipients of their grants.
- Prohibited investment of foundation assets in ways that jeopardized carrying out their tax-exempt purposes.
- Provided three levels of sanctions: moderate taxes on the amounts involved in violations; confiscatory taxes on the amounts involved in uncorrected violations; and loss of tax-exemption and assessment of taxes equivalent to the aggregate tax benefits previously enjoyed, plus interest, as under the change of status provisions below.
- Required repayment of aggregate tax benefits if a foundation changed its status to avoid compliance but permitted change of status if a foundation operated as a public charity or another type of exempt organization other than a private foundation for five years or gave all its assets to public charities.
- Required foundations to change their governing instruments by 1972 to conform to the requirements of the act.
- Levied an audit tax of 4 percent on net annual investment income.

Other Tax-Exempt Organizations

- Required tax-exempt organizations with income over $5,000, other than churches and their auxiliaries and associations, to file annual information returns and financial reports.
- Required organizations claiming exemption for the first time, other than churches and educational and charitable organizations with income of less than $5,000, to notify and provide information to the Internal Revenue Service (IRS).
- Subjected to tax the income from debt-financed property that was unrelated to the tax-exempt purpose of an organization.
- Made taxable the income of unrelated businesses owned by all exempt organizations except religious orders and their educational institutions.
- Broadened application of the unrelated business tax to include such income as that from advertising in publications of exempt organizations and from interest, rent, royalties, etc. of subsidiaries owned 80 percent or more by exempt organizations.
- Made investment income of social and employee benefit organizations taxable to a limited extent.

Charitable Contributions

- Increased the allowable deduction for charitable contributions from 30 percent of income to 50 percent.
- Phased out the unlimited charitable contribution, eliminating it in 1974.
- Taxed the appreciation in value of charitable gifts of certain property.
- Made income from property placed in short-term trusts taxable.
- Restricted deductible charitable gifts of less than full interest in property, except for undivided and remainder interests.
- Generally denied deductions to non-exempt trusts for income set aside for — but not yet given to — charity, except for pooled income funds.
- Restricted and in some cases disallowed deductions for charitable contributions of remainder interests in trusts.
- Limited or disallowed charitable deductions for contributions of income interests given in trust.
- Imposed on non-exempt charitable trusts restrictions similar to those imposed on private foundations relating to self-dealing, holdings, and investments.
- Allowed charitable deductions for gifts to community foundations.

Farm Income

- Restricted paper farm losses that could be offset against non-farm income where losses exceeded $25,000 and non-farm income exceeded $50,000.
- Disallowed deduction of losses from farm operations not engaged in for profit.
- Recaptured depreciation previously allowed for livestock sold at a capital gain.
- Recaptured deductions for soil and water conservation expenditures on land sold at a gain, with a phaseout after five years.
- Provided that a farmer could report insurance compensation for damaged crops in either the year when compensated or the following year.
- Required that costs of planting and establishing citrus groves be depreciated over the useful life of the groves.
- Set required holding periods for livestock to qualify for capital gains treatment: two years for breeding, sporting, dairy and draft animals; one year for other livestock as under existing law.
- Specified that breeding livestock did not qualify for tax-free "like-kind" exchange treatment if of different sexes.

Corporate Reforms

- Limited multiple corporations to a single surtax exemption and a single tax credit for accumulated earnings rather than credits and deductions for each subsidiary.

● Disallowed deductions for interest on convertible bonds issued by a corporation to acquire assets of another.

● Authorized the Treasury to issue guidelines for distinguishing between debt and equity for tax purposes.

● Made readily negotiable bonds of a purchaser, given to a seller as installment payments, taxable in the year they were received.

● Adjusted the tax treatment of purchasers of original-issue discount bonds to make it consistent with that of issuing corporations.

● Limited deductions to the actual cost of borrowing for corporations repurchasing their own convertible bonds.

● Taxed common stock dividends where a cash distribution to some shareholders resulted in an increase in the proportionate share of other shareholders.

● Standardized depreciation rules applicable to regulated industries and utilities except oil pipelines.

● Provided that domestic corporations must use straight-line depreciation in computing earnings and profits.

● Allowed special deductions in certain circumstances for compensation provided under the Clayton Antitrust Act for injured parties in antitrust, breach of contract, patent infringement and other settlements.

● Codified court decisions disallowing deductions for payment of fines or similar penalties resulting from violations of any law, for bribes and kickbacks, and for two-thirds of treble damages assessed for criminal violations of antitrust laws.

● Excluded "foreign base company" income from taxable income where the creation, organization, acquisition, and transactions of controlled foreign corporations were not for tax-avoidance purposes.

● Provided that the appreciation of property given to a shareholder by a corporation in a stock-redemption transaction was to be taxable, with a number of exceptions.

● Redefined the "reasonable needs" exception under which accumulated corporate property became tax-exempt.

● Allowed deduction of interest on special group contingency reserves of insurance companies.

● Provided new rules applying to taxation of the "spinoff" of a subsidiary of a life insurance company to its parent holding company.

● Allowed a limited carryover and deduction for insurance companies with net operating losses when change in organization changed their tax status.

● Permitted a cooperative to deduct or exclude from income the payment of "per-unit-retain" allocations in cash (as well as in certificates, as under existing law) to patrons for goods marketed for the patrons.

● Restricted deductions for expenses incurred in providing services and goods to members of non-exempt membership organizations.

● Increased from 10 to 20 percent the margin of earnings that personal holding companies were not required to distribute within a tax year.

● Permitted "tacking on" of previous owners' holding periods of securities to reduce the capital gains recognized for tax purposes in the liquidation of controlled corporations, chiefly personal holding companies.

Financial Institutions

● Reduced allowable deductions for bad-debt reserves for commercial banks, mutual savings banks, savings and loan associations, and cooperative banks.

● Allowed new small business investment corporations to base their allowable bad-debt reserves on the industry average during their first 10 years.

● Required banks to treat their gains and losses from corporate and government bonds as ordinary income.

● Clarified existing law regarding restoration of bad-debt reserve funds to income in mergers of savings and loan associations.

● Provided that until after 1975 bank deposits of non-resident aliens and foreign corporations in American banks would continue to be regarded as non-U.S. property (and interest on them as non-U.S. income) unless effectively connected with the conduct of business in the United States.

● Permitted special banks for cooperatives a 10-year loss carryback for net operating losses.

● Treated periodic payment mutual fund plans as if the stock shares held by a custodian were owned directly by the investors.

Oil and Other Minerals

● Reduced the percentage depletion allowance on oil and gas from 27.5 percent to 22 percent for both foreign and domestic production.

● Reduced percentage depletion on minerals receiving 23 percent to 22 percent, raised molybdenum from 15 to 22 percent, and reduced minerals receiving 15 percent to 14 percent except for silver, gold, copper, oil shale and iron ore.

● Allowed depletion for minerals other than salt extracted from domestic saline lakes.

● Permitted application of depletion to oil shale after partial refinement (rather than at the source).

● Eliminated use of mineral production payments for tax avoidance by treating them as loans for tax purposes.

● Applied general recapture rules to deductions for mining exploration expenditures.

● Provided that mineral operations within the U.S. continental shelf (recognized as U.S. territory for mineral operations purposes) were to be treated as domestic operations.

● Prohibited use of excess foreign tax credits attributable to the percentage depletion allowance on mineral income from one foreign country to reduce the U.S. tax payable on other foreign income.

Capital Gains and Losses

● Retained the "alternative" (maximum) 25 percent capital gains tax rate for individuals (not including surtax) on gains up to $50,000 and raised the rate on gains above that figure in stages to 35 percent.

● Increased the alternative capital gains rate for corporations from 25 percent to 30 percent (without surtax).

● Retained the holding period on property eligible for long-term capital gains treatment at six months.

● Limited individual capital losses which could be offset against ordinary income to 50 percent, up to the existing $1,000 limit.

● Provided a three-year carryback and extended existing "quickie" refund procedures for capital losses of corporations.

● Taxed as ordinary income the gain from sale of letters, memoranda, and other papers by the producer or by persons for whom they were produced.

• Provided that the entire amount received from sale or other disposition of a life-estate was to be taxed, rather than limiting the tax to the gain.

• Provided that casualty losses of property used to produce income were to be netted with casualty gains.

• Denied capital gains treatment for income from the sale of a franchise if the seller retained significant rights to the subject matter of the asset.

• Deferred recognition of gains from sale of property in federally assisted housing projects where the gain was reinvested in similar projects.

• Extended to two years the period that individuals were allowed to hold property that was compulsorily or involuntarily converted to replacement status (due to loss, condemnation, etc.) before reinvesting it without becoming subject to tax.

• Treated employer contributions to pension, profit-sharing, and similar funds, when paid to the beneficiary in a lump sum, as ordinary income.

Real Estate Depreciation

• Limited double-declining-balance and sum-of-the-years-digits accelerated depreciation to new residential housing from which at least 80 percent of income was rental.

• Allowed 150 percent accelerated depreciation on new commercial and industrial real estate.

• Allowed 125 percent depreciation of used residential rental property with an expected lifespan of 20 years or more.

• Provided a special five-year amortization deduction for expenses of rehabilitating used residential housing for rental to low- and moderate-income families.

• Provided that accelerated depreciation which exceeded straight-line depreciation at the time property was sold at a gain would be recaptured as ordinary income, but with a phaseout of excess depreciation for rental housing.

• Limited depreciation on real estate not otherwise covered to straight-line.

• Applied new depreciation and recapture provisions to real estate acquired on or after July 25, 1969, unless it was subject to a binding contract before that date.

Municipal Bonds

• Preserved the non-taxability of income from municipal and state bonds except those issued for arbitrage.

• Made income taxable from municipal and state arbitrage bonds — those issued in order to acquire other higher-yielding securities.

Investment Credit Repeal

• Repealed the 7 percent tax credit for business investment, effective April 19, 1969 (two days before the president's April 21 proposal for repeal), with provisions maintaining it in force where there were binding contracts for facilities entered into before the effective date.

• Allowed five-year amortization deductions for pollution-control facilities installed in existing plants and placed in service before 1975.

• Allowed four-year amortization deductions for new railroad rolling stock owned by railroads or subsidiaries and placed in service before the end of 1970, five-year amortization for new rolling stock owned or leased by railroads and placed in service before 1975, and 50 year amor-

tization of gradings and tunnels placed in service after 1968.

• Allowed five-year amortization for certain coal mine equipment required by the Coal Mine Health and Safety Act of 1969 and placed in service before 1975.

Individual Tax Reform

• Established a 10 percent minimum tax on otherwise tax-free income (except that from municipal and state bonds) and on income offset by certain major deductions, to the extent that the income exceeded $30,000 plus normal tax liability on taxable income, applicable to individuals, personal holding companies, and "Subchapter S" corporations (those with 10 or fewer stockholders, each owning 5 percent or more of the stock and all taxed more or less as partners).

• Made individual (executive) compensation, such as stock, which was subject to restrictions, taxable at the time received unless it was subject to substantial risk of forfeiture.

• Required shareholder-employees of Subchapter S corporations to include in their taxable income the amount of corporate contributions to their retirement plans which exceeded 10 percent of salary, or $2,500, whichever was less, after 1970.

• Taxed income of accumulation trusts, including multiple trusts, as if it had been received by the trusts instead of by the beneficiaries.

• Limited deductions for interest on money borrowed to finance investments, when the deductions exceeded investment income plus capital gains plus $25,000, to half the excess interest.

Individual Tax Relief

• Increased the personal income tax exemption from $600 to $750 in $50-dollar increments taking effect in mid-1970, 1971, and 1972.

• Replaced the minimum standard deduction with a low-income allowance of $1,100 per taxpayer in 1970, which was reduced to $1,050 for 1971 and $1,000 in 1972.

• Set new rates to reduce taxes paid by single persons to 20 percent more than the amount couples filing joint returns on the same income would pay, and provided new head-of-household rates midway between the two.

• Lowered the amount by which an individual's income must have increased — from 33-1/3 percent of income to 20 percent — in order for him to average his income for taxes.

• Liberalized deductions for moving expenses to include additional expenses up to a total of $2,500.

• Provided that deductions for accrued vacation pay could not be denied under an IRS ruling before 1971 if a consistent accounting method had been used by the taxpayer.

• Excluded from taxable income the insurance compensation for temporary living expenses paid to a person whose home was destroyed by fire or natural disaster.

• Permitted treatment of foster children as dependents for tax purposes.

• Permitted cooperative housing projects to retain that status, and tenant-stockholders to deduct their proportionate shares of interest and taxes paid, despite the degree of ownership of projects by government agencies.

• Increased the standard deduction to 15 percent of income with a $2,000 ceiling, in three stages with full effect in 1973.

● Established a maximum tax rate on earned income at 50 percent, except that earned income equivalent to the amount by which tax preferences exceeded $30,000 would be subject to higher existing rates.

Withholding

● Allowed employers to use more flexible procedures in withholding taxes from employees' wages in order to withhold the correct amount of tax for the year.

● Liberalized requirements for claiming additional exemptions to reduce withholding in order to reflect excess itemized deductions.

● Permitted acceptance of certificates of non-taxability from students and part-time employees whose income would not reach a taxable level, in order to eliminate withholding from wages of persons with no tax liability.

● Required the payer of supplemental employment compensation benefits to withhold federal income tax from the payments.

● Required the Treasury to prescribe withholding rates and tables incorporating the low-income allowance, surcharge, personal exemption increase, standard deduction increase, and reduced rates for single persons and heads of households.

Administrative

● Relieved taxpayers of the requirement to file income tax returns if their income was less than the low-income allowance plus the total of their personal exemptions.

● Liberalized restrictions and authorized the Treasury secretary to waive remaining restrictions on the amount and source of income, deductions, status, etc., of taxpayers eligible to have IRS compute their taxes.

● Provided a monthly penalty of ½ of 1 percent — up to a maximum of 25 percent — on taxes not paid when due and a flat penalty of 5 percent for failure to make deposits of tax on time.

● Waived interest and penalty for underpayment of tax due to any amendment made by the act.

● Changed the tax return filing date from Feb. 15 to March 1 for farmers and fishermen.

● Exempted sufficient income from IRS levies due from divorced fathers for them to cover support payments ordered by divorce courts.

● Permitted a taxpayer to change from the installment accounting method back to the accrual method without increased tax liability, provided certain conditions were met.

● Made several changes and clarifications in the administration, procedures, and powers of the Tax Court and in the terms of service and retirement of its judges.

● Created simplified Tax Court small claims procedures that could be used, at a taxpayer's option, when litigation involved $1,000 or less.

Surtax and Excises

● Extended the income tax surcharge at 5 percent from Jan. 1 to June 30, 1970. The original 10 percent surcharge expired Dec. 31, 1969.

● Extended the 10 percent excise tax on local and toll telephone service (which was to have been reduced to 5 percent during 1970) and the 7 percent excise on passenger automobiles (which was to have dropped to 5 percent on Jan. 1) until Jan. 1, 1971, and postponed scheduled reduc-

tions and ultimate repeal of both by one year. (The excise tax was again extended in 1970.)

● Added two rules for determining fair market price in situations where a manufacturer or importer regularly sold items subject to excise taxes to affiliated corporations for resale to independent retailers.

Social Security

● Increased Social Security retirement, disability and dependents' benefits by 15 percent across the board beginning in January 1970.

● Guaranteed every recipient of both public assistance and Social Security a minimum increase of $4 per month in benefits until July 1970 by limiting state readjustments of public assistance following the Social Security increase; prohibited state reduction of public assistance benefits to offset Social Security benefit increases to be paid in April for previous months of the year.

Consumer Credit

Congress laid the first, modest step in its groundwork for an incomes policy at the close of the 1969 session when it approved legislation (S 2577 — PL 91-151) empowering the president to place controls on consumer credit or, as an alternative, to reinstate a system of Korean War-era controls in which he could urge the credit industry to work out the restraints voluntarily.

Both provisions were opposed by the administration and were not used in 1969 or 1970. In 1971, however, as part of his new economic policy, Nixon did urge banks not to raise interest rates. But he did not formally invoke a voluntary credit control program.

Impetus for the bill came when Nixon's policy of fiscal restraint failed to make inroads in the pace of inflation during the president's first 10 months in office. Democrats saw the credit controls as a mild step that, if taken quickly, might stave off the need for wage, price and rent controls. Republicans opposed the controls as an affront to Nixon's economic program.

Provisions

As enacted, the bill in its major provisions:

● Authorized the president to instruct the Federal Reserve Board to regulate the terms, amounts and interest rates of all forms of credit when he deemed it necessary to combat inflation.

● Permitted the establishment of the voluntary controls by repealing a prohibition in the Defense Production Act against reactivating the voluntary restraints and restoring the president's authority to do so.

● Raised maximum insurance protection on deposits in federally chartered banks and savings and loan institutions from $15,000 to $20,000.

● Extended through March 22, 1971, the existing authority for federal regulatory agencies to set different limits on the interest rates that banks and other financial institutions could pay on different types and amounts of time deposits.

● Increased the supply of home mortgage money by increasing the Federal Home Loan Bank Board's authority to borrow from the Treasury by $3 billion, to $4 billion.

1970

In his first State of the Union address, delivered in January 1970, President Nixon said, "When I speak of actions which would be beneficial to the American people, I can think of none more important than for Congress to join this administration in the battle to stop the rise in the cost of living." He specifically avoided blaming either business or labor, but said U.S. deficit spending in the 1960s was the primary cause of inflation.

To fight inflation, the president again called for the restrictive fiscal policies he had supported in 1969 — a budget in surplus with federal spending held down. The Federal Reserve Board, however, moved to a more expansive monetary policy.

As proposed, the president's fiscal 1971 budget called for a surplus of $1.3 billion. When the fiscal year came to an end, however, he had a deficit of $23 billion instead. There were a number of reasons for this. Tax revenues were $13.7 billion lower than projected because of the continuing recession. The economy had begun to pick up slowly in mid-1970, but was thrown back again by a two-month General Motors strike. In addition the president indicated late in the year that he was converted to the theory that deficit spending was a valuable tool for countering recession and the administration consequently made less of an attempt to hold the lid on spending.

There was, however, as in 1969, a continuing struggle between the president and Congress over federal spending priorities. Nixon vetoed five bills on economy grounds; two of the vetoes were overridden. There was no major request or action on taxes in 1970. Congress did pass an administration bill extending excise taxes.

Monetary policy in 1970 was quite different from the restrictive tight money policy of 1969. The Federal Reserve Board permitted the money supply to expand at a relatively high average of about 5.5 percent during the year. Both the discount rate at which the Federal Reserve system lends money to member banks and the prime rate — the interest rate banks charge their best customers — underwent successive reductions. Mortgage interest rates stabilized, and other interest rates fell sharply. The Federal Reserve Board continued this kind of expansionary monetary policy for the rest of Nixon's first term.

During the year as the recession and inflation continued and unemployment began to climb, a number of economists urged the president to adopt some sort of system of wage-price controls. The new Federal Reserve Board Chairman, Arthur F. Burns, publicly supported adoption of an "incomes policy," a term that came into fashionable use. It referred to a broad range of activities, from guideposts to wage and price controls, to influence incomes through wages and prices parallel to other policy efforts to influence the money supply through fiscal and monetary policy.

On June 17 in a televised address, the president declared, "I will not take this nation down the road of wage and price controls, however politically expedient they may seem." However, during 1970 the president did change his economic policies somewhat. He moved toward "jawboning" (administration persuasion of business and labor to hold down prices and wages) with the issuance of two "inflation alerts" to publicize excessive wage and price increases.

At year's end, the economic figures for 1970 were dreary. GNP for the year reached $974.1 billion but in constant prices totaled 0.5 percent less than in 1969. Consumer price increases above 1969 levels averaged 5.9 percent, more than in 1968-69 increase. And unemployment, which had been 3.5 percent of the labor force in December 1969, skyrocketed past the traditional 4 percent "full employment" to 6.2 percent in December 1970. The only really good economic news of the year was that the stock market slide that had begun in December 1968 bottomed in June.

The only international economic issue on which Congress spent much time was the president's trade bill. By the end of the session the bill had been altered almost unrecognizably into a protectionist measure. But before the president had to make up his mind whether to sign the bill, Senate liberals succeeded in having it recommitted.

Excise, Gift Taxes

Two days before adjournment, Congress in 1970 sent the president a bill (HR 16199 — PL 91-614) that was expected to produce an estimated $4 billion in tax revenues over fiscal 1971 and 1972. The bill, cleared Dec. 31, extended excise taxes on telephone service and automobiles, speeded up collection of estate and gift taxes and established a working capital fund for the Treasury Department.

HR 16199 also opened a new tax loophole for certain persons and businesses that in previous years had legally avoided most or all federal income tax liability but were made subject to taxation in 1970 by the minimum income tax provision in the 1969 Tax Reform Act.

The bill's excise taxes were expected to produce $630 million in additional revenue in fiscal 1971 and $1.9 billion in fiscal 1972. The collection speedup was expected to produce $100 million in fiscal 1971 and $1.5 billion the next fiscal year. These revenues would be reduced by $100 million a year, however, by the loophole-opening amendment modifying the "minimum tax" provision of the 1969 act. President Nixon had requested the excise extension in his January budget message and the accelerated estate and gift tax payments in a separate statement on April 2.

Provisions

As signed into law, HR 16199 contained the following major provisions:

Excise Taxes

● Postponed reductions in automobile and telephone service excise taxes, which were to have gone into effect Jan. 1, 1971, for two years.

● Phased out both taxes over a 10-year period beginning Jan. 1, 1973, and repealed both as of Jan. 1, 1982.

Estate and Gift Taxes

● Required filing of estate tax returns and payment of such tax nine months after death.

● Provided for discharge of executors and fiduciaries from liability for a decedent's taxes.

● Permitted extensions up to 12 months (instead of the six months allowed by existing law) for filing estate tax returns in cases of hardship.

● Required donors to file quarterly (instead of annual) gift tax returns and pay gift taxes on the same basis — returns and payments to be due in the middle of the quarter after the quarter in which gifts were given.

● Retained the structure of existing law concerning gifts, including the $3,000 maximum annual exemption per person and the $30,000 maximum lifetime exemption.

● Exempted fully deductible charitable gifts from the requirement.

Working Capital Fund

● Established a $1 million working capital fund in the office of the secretary of the Treasury.

● Authorized the office of the secretary to furnish, on a reimbursable basis, various centralized services, such as printing, procurement and telecommunications services, to Treasury Department bureaus financed under separate appropriations.

Minimum Income Tax

● Allowed a seven-year carryover of normal income taxes in excess of tax preferences over $30,000 to offset income in future years that would be subject to the 10 percent minimum income tax (established by the Tax Reform Act of 1969 — PL 91-172).

Wage-Price Controls

In an effort to curb inflation, Congress in summer 1970 passed legislation (S 3302 — PL 91-379) authorizing the president to freeze wages, prices, rents and salaries at existing or higher levels. President Nixon signed the bill but opposed the freeze provisions and said emphatically that he would not use them.

Exactly a year later, Nixon reversed himself. On Aug. 15, 1971, the president ordered a 90-day freeze on wages, prices, salaries and rents. (Details, p. 158)

The Democratic Congress avoided a veto of the wage-price control authority only by attaching it to a bill extending the Defense Production Act of 1950 to June 30, 1972. The controls, called the Economic Stabilization Act of 1970 (a separate title of S 3302), gave the president discretionary authority thorugh Feb. 28, 1971, to freeze wages, prices rents and salaries at levels not lower than those prevailing on May 25, 1970. The bill also authorized use of injunctions to enforce the controls and provided for $5,000 fines for violations.

The controls section was added to the Senate bill by the House Banking and Currency Committee, which said in reporting the measure: "...If the Congress, in its wisdom, enacts this legislation, the president will have all of the necessary weapons needed to control inflation."

Republicans charged that the controls were an election-year gimmick by Democrats to place the onus on President Nixon for either imposing or not imposing the controls — whichever seemed the greatest political liability.

In the key legislative test on the controls — a House vote on the conference report on S 3302 — Republicans opposed the measure, 23-144. Democrats favored it, 194-9.

President Nixon issued a blistering attack on the bill when he signed it into law Aug. 15. Nixon said that if it were not for some important provisions in the Defense Production Act, he would have vetoed the measure. The president said he had no intention of using the authority to freeze wages and prices because such action "simply does not fit the economic conditions which exist today." He added that if Congress felt that wage-price controls should be mandatory it should "face up to its responsibilities and make such controls mandatory."

Extension of Controls

At the insistence of the House Banking and Currency Committee, Congress in December approved a rider to a Small Business Administration bill (S 4536 — PL 91-558) that extended the president's wage-price control authority for another month, through March 31, 1971.

The purpose of the brief extension was to give Congress more time to act on a longer extension after the 92nd Congress convened in January 1971. President Nixon signed the bill Dec. 17 despite his continued opposition to controls.

The administration remained lukewarm toward extension of the authority. Nonetheless, Congress May 5, 1971, passed an extension of the act (HR 4246 — PL 92-15) until April 30, 1972. While studying that measure, Congress March 29 had cleared a bill (S J Res 55 — PL 92-8) temporarily extending the authority to June 1, 1971.

However, faced with rising budget and balance of payments deficits and continued high inflation, Nixon Aug. 15 announced his "new economic policy;" it imposed a 90-day wage-price freeze and a 10 percent surtax on imports. Consistent with that policy, Nixon asked for and received a year's extension, through April 30, 1973, of the stabilization authority. The measure (S 2891 — PL 92-210), signed Dec. 22, 1971, also broadened the president's stabilization powers to cover interest rates and corporate dividends. (Nixon economic policy, below)

1971

Despite the govenment's growing budgetary deficit, tax cuts to stimulate the economy were the centerpiece of Nixon's fiscal policy in 1971. Early in the year the president used his administrative authority to give businesses a tax break worth more than $3 billion a year by permitting them an accelerated tax writeoff of their depreciation costs. (The program was known as ADR for "asset depreciation range.") And in his Aug. 15 announcement of his new economic program, the president called for additional tax cuts averaging $5.7 billion a year over the next three years and indeterminate amounts after that. Congress modified the ADR program and provided a tax cut of $8.6 billion a year, including the ADR benefits.

Nixon's tax proposals were coupled with a program to fight inflation and strengthen the nation's balance of payments position on one hand and to move the country out of recession on the other. By early 1972 it appeared that the program was making headway on each of these fronts.

The president's original budget for fiscal 1972, submitted in January, gave little indication of the bold tax moves that were in store for late summer. If there was a hint of what was to come it was in the president's January announcement that he would move by administrative order to institute the ADR program in hopes of stimulating business investment. Otherwise, the president asked for relatively routine tax measures: a two-year extension of the Interest Equalization Tax, an increase in the taxable wage base for Social Security, airline user charges to pay the costs of air marshals to guard against aircraft hijackings, higher user charges on automotive diesel fuel and a change in the existing fixed-rate use tax on heavy trucks to a graduated scale based on weight.

Congress provided the broader Social Security tax and the Interest Equalization Tax extension but turned down the user charge proposals.

The sweeping economic program announced in August came largely as a surprise. To combat inflation, the program called for a 90-day wage, price and rent freeze to be followed by a "Phase Two" program of controls. To bring the U.S. balance of payments under control, the president suspended convertibility of the dollar to gold and announced a temporary 10 percent surtax on imports. This led to a series of major foreign currency negotiations with other countries and culminated in what the president described as a "historic" December international agreement, signed at the Smithsonian Institution in Washington, in which the surtax was dropped and the dollar in effect devalued 8.57 percent in return for concessions by foreign countries.

The Phase Two program that replaced the wage-price freeze was announced Oct. 7. It involved establishing a Pay Board and a Price Commission with authority to set guidelines for wage and price increases. The largest businesses and unions were to be controlled most stringently and had to receive prior approval for pay and price increases. The Pay Board set a general guideline of 5.5 percent per year for wage increases and 2.5 percent for price increases.

At year's end it was too early to tell how well the new policy would work. The rate of unemployment hovered at around 6 percent all year, but the economy was clearly out of the 1970 recession. GNP expanded vigorously in the fourth quarter of the year, bringing the total to $1,065 billion — an increase of approximately 9.5 percent over the 1970 total. About $60 billion of the increase was in actual gain or output. The remainder represented price increases. The cost of living increase was 4.6 percent for the year. It had begun to level off in July.

Omnibus Tax Bill

Congress Dec. 9 cleared for the president's signature the Revenue Act of 1971 (HR 10947 — PL 92-178), cutting tax liabilities by $25.9 billion over a three-year period (and indeterminate amounts in later years) to stimulate the economy. The bill, requested by President Nixon to implement his new economic policy, was the first major tax legislation passed by Congress since the Tax Reform Act of 1969 (PL 91-172). *(p. 151)*

Legislative History

President Nixon announced his new economic program Aug. 15, on a suddenly scheduled telecast after a weekend of intensive planning with advisers at Camp David, Md., the presidential retreat. The program included a broad range of actions, some of which would be accomplished by executive order and others by legislation.

Acting on his own authority, the president, among other actions, ordered a 90-day freeze on all wages, prices and rents, freed the dollar from its historic $35-an-ounce gold price, imposed a temporary 10 percent surcharge on most imports, ordered a 10 percent cut in foreign economic aid, and ordered a 5 percent reduction in federal executive branch employment.

The president asked Congress to provide: a 10 percent investment tax credit for business machinery (dubbed "job development" credit by the president instead of its traditional title) retroactive to Aug. 15, to be reduced to 5 percent after one year; repeal of the 7 percent excise tax on automobiles; tax incentives for U.S. firms engaged primarily in the export business; and an advance to Jan. 1, 1972, of the income tax cuts already scheduled to become effective Jan. 1, 1973, through an increase in the personal income tax exemption and the standard deduction.

Most of the provisions of the measure that Congress cleared in December were identical or similar to Nixon's requests. In that sense, they were a victory for the president but in another they were a defeat: Congress put more emphasis on individual tax cuts than it did on tax breaks for business. The final bill provided $3.8 billion more in individual tax relief than the president had requested over the 1971-73 period but $5.9 billion less for business than he had sought. Altogether the bill reduced individual and business taxes by an average of $8.6 billion a year over the 1971-73 period.

In addition to its tax provisions, the bill contained a non-germane amendment authorizing taxpayers to allot $1 of their annual taxes for use by the party of their choice in presidential election campaigns. The rider, favored by Democrats and opposed by Republicans, aroused the threat of a presidential veto of the tax bill. Congress then amended the measure to put off the effective date of the campaign fund until after the 1972 election — a provision satisfactory to President Nixon.

Provisions

As signed into law, HR 10947 contained the following major provisions:

Individual Taxes

● Increased the personal exemption per taxpayer and dependent to $675, from $650, for 1971; moved up the scheduled increase to $750 from 1973 to 1972.

● Moved up to 1972, from 1973, the effective date of an increase in the standard deduction to 15 percent of income with a maximum of $2,000.

● Raised the minimum income levels at which taxpayers must file tax returns to correspond to increases in the personal exemption and low-income allowance.

● Eliminated a scheduled 1972 reduction in the low-income allowance from $1,050 to $1,000; increased the allowance for 1972 and subsequent years to $1,300.

● Revised withholding rates and schedules to prevent underwithholding, effective Jan. 15, 1972.

● Raised the minimum level of total income not withheld and the tax levels at which declarations of estimated tax were required; waived penalties for failure to declare estimated taxes for some taxpayers for 1971.

● Allowed increased deductions for care of disabled children and other children up to age 15, in or outside the home, beginning in 1972, up to $400 per month for single parents, parents treated as single, couples of whom one was disabled, and working couples with combined incomes of $18,000 or less after the deduction; included a 50 percent phaseout of the deductions for incomes over $18,000 and required that the deductions be itemized.

Excise Tax Repeal

● Repealed the 7 percent excise tax on foreign and domestic automobiles and light trailers effective Aug. 16, 1971.

● Authorized refunding of excise tax on vehicles sold between Aug. 15 and the date of enactment of the bill (Dec. 10, 1971), including floor stocks of vehicles sold but not delivered by Aug. 15.

Investment Credit

● Reinstated the 7 percent tax credit for business investment (repealed in 1969) applicable generally to tangible property integrally involved in the functioning of a business (not real estate) and effective for property ordered on or after April 1, 1971, or acquired after Aug. 15, 1971.

● Denied the credit for foreign-produced property for the duration of the 10 percent import surcharge imposed by the president on Aug. 15, 1971, but allowed the credit for foreign property ordered between April 1 and Aug. 16, 1971.

● Authorized the president to continue to deny the credit to foreign property under certain conditions after termination of the surcharge.

● Allowed the president by executive order to permit the credit retroactively for up to two years to any date after Aug. 15, 1971, for foreign property otherwise denied the credit.

● Established specific provisions and limits on application of the credit to certain types of property, businesses, conditions and situations, including the useful life of the property, carryover of unused credits, public utilities, antipollution equipment, transmission facilities and equipment, storage facilities, used property, amortized property, leased property, livestock, recapture, depreciation and accounting.

● Modified effective Jan. 1, 1972, the first-year depreciation allowed for property under the Asset Depreciation Range (ADR) system put into effect in 1971 by the Treasury Department.

● Established a tax credit of 20 percent of the wages paid by a business to persons employed for two years or more under the Work Incentive program (WIN) administered by the Department of Labor.

Exports and Imports

● Exempted from taxation the profits of businesses engaged primarily in exporting that qualified (under the criteria below) as Domestic International Sales Corporations (DISC) and provided for taxation of half the profits of such businesses when distributed to shareholders, effective for a period of five years beginning in 1972.

● Required that, for a business to qualify as a DISC, 95 percent of its gross receipts must arise from export sales, leases, investments and related activities and that 95 percent of its assets must be export-related.

Political Contributions

● Established, effective in 1973, a tax credit of $12.50 for an individual ($25 for a married couple filing a joint return) and as an alternative a deduction of $50 for an individual ($100 for a married couple) for contributions to candidates for federal, state or local political office in general, primary or special elections.

● Authorized taxpayers starting in 1973 to designate on their tax returns that $1 ($2 for a joint return) be paid into a public campaign fund for the presidential and vice presidential candidates of a qualified major or minor party or alternatively into a general public campaign fund to be distributed among qualified candidates.

Miscellaneous Provisions

● Increased to $1 million from $250,000 the limit on spending from private sources for unanticipated expenses allowed on any project financed by tax-exempt bonds. Under existing law, a municipality was allowed to issue up to $5 million in tax-exempt bonds to build a plant or other facility provided that total expenditures on the project did not exceed the value of the bonds, plus $250,000 for unanticipated expenses required by inaccurate estimates or similar problems.

Social Security Tax

In a bill increasing the federal debt ceiling (HR 4690 — PL 92-5), Congress in 1971 raised the taxable wage base for Social Security levies to $9,000 from $7,800. The higher taxes became effective in January 1972. President Nixon had sought a January 1971 effective date.

The bill also increased Social Security benefits by 10 percent and increased the Social Security tax rates on employees and employers to 5.15 percent from 5 percent beginning in 1976. Under existing law, the tax rate was scheduled to remain at 4.6 percent through 1972 and to increase to 5 percent in 1973. The president had requested a 6 percent increase in Social Security benefits; he had not requested the higher 1976 tax rates.

Lockheed Loan Guarantee

By close votes in both houses, Congress in summer 1971 cleared legislation (HR 8432 — PL 92-70) authorizing a federal guarantee of up to $250 million in bank loans for the Lockheed Aircraft Corporation, one of the nation's largest defense contractors.

The main purpose of the measure was to prevent a Lockheed bankruptcy. The company's problems developed soon after Rolls-Royce Ltd., the British manufacturer of engines for Lockheed's L-1011 (Tristar) commercial airliner, declared bankruptcy Feb. 4, 1971. Already reeling from large penalties assessed by the Defense Department for cost overruns on the C-5A transport aircraft and other defense contracts, Lockheed needed additional credit to go into production with its Tristar. And the company needed the Tristar to stay in business.

The administration, which requested the loan guarantee, argued that the free enterprise issue should be cast aside in Lockheed's case because of the unique nature of the problem. Although the government did not need the Tristar, the argument went, it did need to take measures to maintain Lockheed's defense production capability. Another argument that scored points for loan proponents was that Lockheed bankruptcy would worsen the nation's already serious unemployment problem. Critics of the loan guarantee, led by Sen. William Proxmire, D-Wis., countered that since the government already owned much of Lockheed's production facilities, another company could simply step in and take over Lockheed's defense work. The only persons who would lose their jobs, the critics said, were Lockheed's top executives.

The possibility of a government loan guarantee for Lockheed had been considered briefly in 1970 by leaders of a group of 24 banks that eventually agreed to lend the company $400 million, without a guarantee, to complete development of the Tristar. The idea was raised again, soon after Rolls-Royce went bankrupt, when the banks indicated they would not extend further credit to Lockheed.

Cautious support and determined opposition met the legislation that the Nixon administration sent to Congress May 13 to guarantee $250 million in bank loans to the beleaguered company. The employment aspect of the Lockheed loan guarantee made the administration's proposal difficult for many members of Congress to oppose. Yet a number hedged their support. Some posed conditions: that Lockheed be required to use American engines on the Tristar; that the legislation be broadened so that it would apply to future cases involving other companies; or that Lockheed's management be required to resign.

The position of organized labor was crucial to many members. George Meany, president of the AFL-CIO, publicly announced support for the loan guarantee. But some labor spokesmen regarded Lockheed as a "runaway" because of its contract with foreign-based Rolls-Royce.

President Nixon at San Clemente, Calif., May 5 told a news conference the major factor in his view was the unemployment that would be caused by a Lockheed bankruptcy and consequent abandonment of the L-1011 program. Treasury Secretary John Connally said Lockheed had employed 17,000 persons in the airbus program, of whom some 7,000 had been laid off because of financial difficulties and the uncertainty of the project. The payroll for the 17,000, he said, was $5 million per week. In addition, 14,000 persons were employed by the principal suppliers for the L-1011. Lockheed had 35,000 subcontracting companies, most of which were small businesses. If Lockheed went bankrupt, the secretary said, the $1.4 billion invested in the L-1011 would be written off "as best it can be" by the investors, with a substantial loss in revenues to the government, and an important defense capability would be lost.

Drafted in general terms, HR 8432 did not mention Lockheed by name. If Congress had increased the dollar total of guarantees permitted, the bill would have authorized the same kind of assistance to other major companies.

The House passed the bill July 30 by a vote of 192-189. The Senate passed the identical measure Aug. 2, 49-48. President Nixon signed the bill into law Aug. 9.

1972

Administration economic policy in 1972 continued along the lines established in 1971. The president submitted another "full employment" expansionary budget and

the Phase Two controls continued throughout the year. The rate of inflation was reduced substantially and unemployment dropped a little. The economy expanded rapidly, earning approval for the president's domestic economic policies.

On the international side, however, the dollar devaluation had not improved the balance of payments situation as much as had been hoped. The deficit was $10.1 billion in 1972, the second largest in the nation's history (after 1971). A major contributor to this was a tripling — from $2.7 billion to $6.9 billion — in the deficit in the U.S. balance of trade (the excess of imports over exports). The administration, divided by conflicting trade philosophies, did not develop an over-all coordinated trade policy and submitted no major trade proposals to Congress during its first term.

Although Congress had some quarrels with the administration over fiscal policy, the general public seemed satisfied with economic policy as a whole. It was not an issue in the November 1972 elections and approval of Nixon's decisive 1971 policies was undoubtedly a factor in his huge re-election victory.

The year-end figures for 1972 showed that GNP for the year averaged $1,152.1 billion — 9.7 percent over 1971. Real growth averaged 6.5 percent and inflation just over 33 percent. The growth figure was slightly higher and the inflation rate slightly lower than the 6.0 and 3.25 percent targets that the administration set for itself in January. The unemployment rate was considered less satisfactory, but fell to 5.2 percent from 6 percent the year before. There were also certain other remaining problems hidden in the figures. In December, the wholesale price index rose at a seasonally adjusted annual rate of 19.2 percent, with a continuing jump in food prices a major factor in the gain.

Social Security Changes

In June 1972 Congress cleared a bill (HR 15390 — PL 92-336) granting a 20 percent increase in Social Security benefits. The cost of the increased benefits would be financed by increases in both the Social Security taxable wage base and the tax rate.

The taxable wage base would rise to $10,800 from $9,000 beginning Jan. 1, 1973, and to $12,000 beginning Jan. 1, 1974. The Social Security tax rate would rise to 5.5 percent from 5.2 percent, effective Jan. 1, 1973. The bill also authorized an automatic increase in the taxable wage base whenever the cost of living rose more than 3 percent in any calendar year, beginning with 1975.

Later in the year Congress made other changes in the Social Security system. That bill (HR 1 — PL 92-603) had originally contained President Nixon's controversial family welfare reform plan, but in conference all family welfare provisions were dropped. In addition to containing welfare provisions federalizing and consolidating adult relief programs for the needy blind, aged and disabled in a new Supplementary Security Income (SSI) program, and substantially increasing benefits, HR 1 made important amendments to the 1935 Social Security Act.

Amendments to the Old Age, Survivors and Disability Insurance program included: increased benefits for widows and widowers; an increase in the amount an OASDI beneficiary could earn; and an increase in Social Security benefits for persons who delayed retirement past age 65. Medicare extensions included extension of coverage to OASDI disability benefits recipients and establishment of professional standards review organizations to oversee certain program operations. The bill also repealed the requirement that states have comprehensive Medicaid programs by 1972. HR 1 raised the Social Security tax rate to 5.85 percent for 1973 through 1977. Of that, 1 percent was set aside for Medicare. The tax rate would increase to 6.05 percent in 1978, to 6.15 percent in 1981 and to 6.25 percent in 1986.

General Revenue Sharing

Congress Oct. 13, 1972, completed action on a bill (HR 14370 — PL 92-512) establishing a five-year program to share $30,236,400,00 in federal revenues with state and local governments.

Final action came when the Senate, by a 59-19 roll-call vote, adopted a conference report (S Rept 92-1229) on the bill. The House had approved the report Oct. 12 by a 265-110 roll-call.

As cleared the bill appropriated $30,236,400,000 to a special trust fund for distribution among state and local governments. The program, retroactive to Jan. 1, 1972, at an initial annual level of $5.3 billion, would run until Dec. 31, 1976.

The conference agreement represented a unique compromise between conflicting House and Senate provisions for allocating revenue-sharing funds. The conference agreement gave states the greater of two amounts available under the different formulas approved by the House and the Senate.

The compromise averted a possible stalemate in choosing between the House formula, which generally favored more populous and industrial states, and the Senate formula, which favored less populous states.

To distribute each state's revenue-sharing funds among state and local governments, however, the conference agreement generally followed the Senate bill. By stressing relative income and the extent of government taxing efforts as well as population — and dropping the House bill's emphasis on urbanization — the conference compromise favored poor central city and rural areas at the expense of more affluent suburbs.

Accepting a principle included in the House-passed version of HR 14370, the conference agreement included a list of spending priorities for revenue-sharing funds turned over to local governments. The conference version, less restrictive than the House bill, allowed local governments to use federal revenues for capital expenditures authorized by law and for ordinary operating and maintenance expenditures on public safety, environmental protection, public transportation, health, recreation, libraries, social services for the poor and aged and for financial administration.

Background

During the early years of President Johnson's administration, it appeared that by the late 1960s there would be large surpluses of federal revenue in the Treasury. One proposal advanced was a program of payments to aid state and local governments with no strings attached — revenue sharing. The concept was never publicly accepted by President Johnson, who by the end of his term faced mounting budget deficits brought on by U.S. involvement in the Vietnam War.

By the late 1960s, a system of sharing tax revenues with the states was firmly part of the Republican program. Endorsed by President Nixon when he took office, general revenue sharing fell neatly among other Nixon proposals to shift many government responsibilities to the state and local levels and drew wide support from governors and mayors. Revenue sharing was a major departure from federal aid programs of the past. It meant more federal dollars with no strings attached, no narrow-purpose guidelines and significantly less red tape.

President Nixon in 1969 first proposed a revenue sharing plan that would have made $500 million in federal revenues available to state and local governments in fiscal 1971, with the total rising to $5 billion by fiscal 1976. Congress did not act on it.

In his 1971 State of the Union address, the president unveiled a second revenue sharing plan that exceeded the scope of previous proposals, including his own. The second proposal included two elements:

● $5 billion annually for allocation to the states, counties, municipalities and the District of Columbia.

● $11 billion annually for "special revenue sharing" programs created by consolidating about 105 existing federal aid programs into six broad purposes with fewer federal specifications.

Under the general revenue sharing proposal, 90 percent of the $5 billion would be allocated according to each state's percentage of total U.S. population with adjustments reflecting a state's tax effort. The remaining 10 percent would be available to states that had negotiated a formula for sharing federal funds with local governments. About 50 percent of each state's total share would be passed on to local governments, with school districts and other special purpose government units excluded. The local shares would be distributed according to the ratio of local revenues to state revenues — at least until a negotiated local sharing formula had been adopted.

The House Ways and Means Committee held extensive hearings in June 1971 on the administration's bill. But Chairman Wilbur D. Mills, D-Ark., who fought the plan, announced that his purpose was to expose the dangers and weaknesses of the revenue sharing concept and to kill the bill.

But midway through the hearings Mills decided he favored a revenue sharing plan that would give most of its benefits to urban areas. On Nov. 30, 1971, Mills and nine other members of the Ways and Means Committee introduced HR 11950, a $5.3 billion revenue sharing bill that provided two-thirds of its funds for local governments and one-third for states.

Mills' endorsement of the revenue sharing concept set legislative wheels turning and one year later, Oct. 20, 1972, President Nixon signed the State and Local Fiscal Assistance Act of 1972 (PL 92-512).

The president's program for special revenue sharing, which would have combined categorical grant programs into large block grants for education, urban community development and several other purposes, was never enacted.

Provisions

As signed by President Nixon Oct. 20, the act:

● Created a State and Local Government Fiscal Assistance trust fund, to remain available without fiscal year limitation.

● Appropriated $30,212,500,000 to the trust fund from federal income tax revenues for the period Jan. 1, 1972, through Dec. 31, 1976.

● Appropriated to the trust fund $23,900,000 from income tax collections for adjustments in allocations to noncontiguous states (Alaska and Hawaii) for the periods Jan. 1, 1972, through Dec. 31, 1976.

● Allocated to each state for each time period the greater of two amounts computed by the following methods:

1) A three-factor formula allocating to each state an amount in the same ratio of $5.3 billion (the initial annual rate) as the figure produced by the state's population multiplied by its state and local government tax effort multiplied by its relative income was to the figure produced by the same factors for the nation as a whole.

2) A five-factor formula allocating (at an initial annual level of $5.3 billion) $3.5 billion among the states according to population (one-third), urbanized population (one-third) and population weighted by per capita income (one-third) and the remaining $1.8 billion according to individual income tax collections by state governments (one-half) and the general tax effort of state and local governments (one-half).

● Allocated one-third of each state's entitlement to the state government and the remaining two-thirds to local governments within the state. The local governments' two-thirds would be divided as follows:

1) Allocated to each county within a state an amount computed on the basis of population, tax effort and relative income.

2) Allocated to each county government an amount determined by the ratio of its tax collections to total tax collections by all governments in the county.

3) Allocated among all township governments within a county a total amount determined by their combined share of tax collections, with each township's amount determined by population, tax effort and relative income.

4) Allocated the remainder of the county's share among municipal governments according to population, tax effort and relative income.

5) Allocated part of a county area's allotment to the governing bodies of local Indian tribes or Alaskan native villages on the basis of population.

● Permitted states to legislate optional formulas for distributing local government funds by population and tax effort or by population and relative income, or both.

● Increased revenue sharing entitlements for Alaska and Hawaii by the same percentage as cost-of-living adjustments given federal employees in those non-contiguous states.

● Required that a state government's revenue sharing entitlement be reduced if it reduced transfers of state funds to local governments. (The penalty could be reduced or offset if the state had assumed responsibility for expenditures previously made by local governments or had conferred new taxing authority on local governments to provide the funds.)

● Required each government receiving revenue sharing funds to submit to the secretary of the Treasury and publish in local newspapers reports on the planned and actual uses of shared revenues.

● Prohibited discrimination by race, color, national origin or sex in any activity or program funded in whole or in part with revenue sharing money.

● Required local governments to use revenue sharing funds only for "priority expenditures": capital expenditures authorized by law or maintenance and operating expenditures on public safety, environmental protection, public transportation, health, recreation, libraries, social services for the poor and aged, and financial administration.

● Provided for collection by the federal government's Internal Revenue Service of state income taxes.

● Placed a $2.5 billion ceiling on annual, federal 75 percent matching grants to state and local governments for social services, with each state limited to the same percentage of $2.5 billion as the percentage of its population to total U.S. population.

● Required that not more than 10 percent of each state's federal matching grants be used for assistance to persons not receiving welfare. Programs for child care, family planning, the mentally retarded, drug addicts, and alcoholics and foster homes for children would be exempted from the 10 percent limit.

1973

Safely re-elected to a second term, President Nixon in 1973 abruptly abandoned economic policy initiatives he had taken in mid-1971 to speed economic growth. Nixon Jan. 11 lifted most of the wage and price controls that had been used to slow inflation, then submitted a restrictive $268.7 billion fiscal 1974 budget featuring wholesale spending cuts in federal domestic programs.

The mandatory wage-price controls of Phase Two were to be replaced by Phase Three — voluntary guidelines backed by the threat that the government would intervene to roll back wage and price increases it considered inflationary. Controls were left in force only for three "particularly troublesome" areas: processed agricultural products, health costs and the construction industry.

While dropping most mandatory controls, the president said that he was returning to fiscal and monetary policies as the principal weapons to continue to attack inflation. He set an overall inflation rate of 2.5 percent as his goal for 1973 and said its attainment would depend on federal budgetary restraint. He called on Congress to cooperate in holding federal spending down to avoid the inflationary impetus of a large government deficit.

Phase Three was widely criticized from the beginning — especially in Europe — as being too weak. This led to unexpectedly strong pressure on the dollar abroad, and the administration Feb. 12 announced the second devaluation of the dollar in 14 months. The dollar was officially devalued 10 percent, but as pressure continued it was allowed to float in relation to other currencies, bringing the effective rate lower.

Nixon's return to the fundamentalist economic policy stance of the first years of his administration proved to be ill-timed. The largely voluntary Phase Three wage and price controls system he adopted was overwhelmed by a burst of inflationary pressures that had been building up in a booming economy throughout 1972. Reinforced by growing worldwide demand — and compounded by food and critical materials shortages and industrial capacity bottlenecks — the resulting price spiral forced the administration to reimpose a 60-day freeze and then undertake more gradual decontrol.

Federal fiscal policy turned less stimulative during 1973, although Congress resisted most of Nixon's program reductions. Concerned by the administration's budget assault, the House and Senate both passed legislation to curb presidential impoundment powers, then shelved it to concentrate on updating their own budget-making procedures.

Federal Reserve monetary policy also turned more restrictive. The narrowly defined money supply, which includes currency plus demand deposits, increased by 6 percent from December 1972 to December 1973, down from the 9.2 percent in 1972. The more broadly defined money supply, also including bank time deposits, increased by 8.8 percent, down from 11.4 percent in 1972.

For the year as a whole real gross national product grew by 5.5 percent. Unemployment fell to 4.6 percent in October before rising again. After devaluation the dollar gained strength against other currencies, which were floating against each other on international monetary markets, and the U.S. trade and payments positions recovered strongly to record slight surpluses.

But those figures disguised the trouble for which the economy was heading. The boom in output that carried over from 1972 spent itself in a frantic first quarter, and actual growth slowed drastically during the rest of the year. Inflation festered: the Consumer Price Index rose 8.8 percent and the wholesale price index a disturbing 15.4 percent for the year despite the freeze and subsequent slower decontrol. Interest rates jumped; stock prices fell throughout most of the year; unemployment started back up; and shortages developed.

By the end of 1973, those troubles were being compounded by energy shortages that were severely amplified by the October Arab oil embargo. Led by fuel oil and gasoline, energy prices began accelerating in response; the embargo resulted in widespread shortages of gasoline and other petroleum products by early 1974. The higher crude oil prices brought a massive flow of wealth from industrialized and developing energy-consuming nations to the petroleum-producing nations that were members of the Organization of Petroleum Exporting Countries (OPEC). That development severely strained international monetary mechanisms, leaving consuming nations with large balance of payments deficits because the Arab producing nations' economies could not return the flow of wealth by increasing imports or investments in other economies. Energy price increases raised inflation rates throughout the world and made industrial and agricultural processes requiring intensive energy use uneconomic.

At the same time, mounting worldwide demand for food contributed to a 20 percent increase in U.S. consumer food prices. Poor 1972 harvests in many countries, along with continued rising international demand, prompted a rapid growth in U.S. exports. The dollar devaluation made U.S. farm products cheaper overseas, moreover. Athough farm products were exempt, U.S. price controls contributed to domestic shortages.

Federal Financing Bank

Congress took one step in 1973 designed to reduce the potentially disruptive impact of federal government borrowing in U.S. financial markets by establishing a Federal Financing Bank. Cleared on Dec. 19, the legislation (HR 5874 — PL 93-224) set up the special bank within the Treasury Department to coordinate borrowing by federal agencies that were authorized to raise funds by selling debt securities.

In approving expanded federal assistance to various economic sectors over the years, Congress had resorted in many cases to creating semi-independent agencies outside the federal budget to make loans or loan guarantees to encourage private development. Those agencies — such as the Federal Home Loan Bank Board, Federal National Mortgage Association and the Export-Import Bank — raised funds for their operations by selling their own bonds to the public on financial markets. As these types of agency issues proliferated, they competed with each other and the Treasury's own debt instruments as well as private bonds for the available supply of investment savings. As a result, the interest costs that the federal government paid to attract investors were forced upward.

The Federal Financing Bank was set up to cut federal borrowing costs and prevent financial market disruptions by buying securities offered by other federal agencies. In turn, the bank would sell securities to the public to finance its purchases.

Congress wrote several exemptions and limitations into the bank legislation requested by the Nixon administration. In general, those provisions were intended to prevent the administration from using the Treasury's power to disapprove agency borrowing proposals to curtail or eliminate programs created by Congress.

As enacted, major provisions of PL 93-224:

● Established the Federal Financing Bank within the Treasury Department to coordinate federal borrowing by buying and selling any obligation issued by a federal agency.

● Authorized the bank to sell up to $15 billion in its own obligations to the public to finance its operations and authorized appropriation of up to $100 million without fiscal year limitation as a loan from the Treasury to provide initial capital.

● Required advance approval by the Treasury secretary of the timing, terms and other conditions carried by any obligations sold by federal agencies.

● Directed the secretary to approve or disapprove a federal agency's securities issue within 120 days and report reasons for delay to Congress if he had not acted within 60 days.

● Exempted Farmers Home Administration rural housing securities from prior Treasury approval.

● Prohibited the secretary, if he determined that some federal financing should be delayed because of market conditions, to force one agency or activity to bear a disproportionate burden by curtailing its borrowing drastically while allowing others to proceed.

1974

The forces that had gathered during 1973 came together in the following year to send the U.S. economy reeling into its worst recession since World War II brought the nation out of the Great Depression of the 1930s. Although output fell throughout the year, it took a fourth-quarter collapse to make clear how drastic the downturn would be.

For most of the year, attention focused on inflation, which reached double-digit rates before slackening as demand deteriorated late in the fall. Severe petroleum shortages, resulting in long lines at gasoline filling stations and curtailed production and consumption that undercut first-quarter activity, perhaps helped disguise the general weakness that was spreading throughout the economy.

In the meantime, the federal government floundered in a fruitless search for policies to correct those dismal economic trends. Preoccupied with the Watergate revelations that finally forced him from office in August, Nixon let the economy take its course while stressing fiscal and monetary restraints on inflationary pressures. The Federal Reserve Board bore most of the burden of fighting inflation through efforts to hold down monetary growth, and its restrictive policies sent interest rates to record levels before being eased late in the year.

Wage and price controls were abandoned, except for oil price restrictions, when Congress refused Nixon's request for continued limited controls and for inflation-monitoring powers. Fiscal policy remained restrictive and the fiscal 1974 budget wound up with a slight $4.7 billion deficit.

After replacing Nixon, President Ford continued the restrictive stance against inflation but moved to bolster confidence in the economy. Congress quickly granted his request for renewed inflation-monitoring authority — but no controls — and the president tried to enlist congressional and public support for an expanded anti-inflation program through a series of domestic summit conferences on the economy.

But Ford's Oct. 8 economic program that resulted from those deliberations was made irrelevant by the economy's accelerating plunge. The president tried a down-the-middle approach, balancing tax and spending assistance to hard-pressed industries and individuals with anti-inflationary fiscal restraints built around a 5 percent tax surcharge on 1975 federal taxes.

Congress ignored the program, but neither did it act on most economic policy proposals that House and Senate Democrats drew up during the year as alternatives to administration strategies. With Ford's support, Congress rushed through a public service jobs program in its post-election session; but the House Ways and Means Committee failed after two years of trying to produce comprehensive legislation to toughen petroleum taxes, relieve hard-pressed taxpayers and make revenue-raising tax revisions.

Some significant economic measures were given final approval, however. Congress approved new House and Senate budget procedures devised to strengthen its control over fiscal policy and budget priorities. After lengthy delay caused by Soviet trade issues, Congress also granted presidential authority for international trade negotiations. *(Details, budget act, pp. 56, 120)*

While government policy remained ineffective, economic performance deteriorated. The first-quarter decline in output moderated slightly during the spring and summer months, but spread into a general collapse in the final three months of the year. Real gross national product fell at a 7.5 percent annual rate during the final quarter, ending the year 1.7 percent below its 1973 level. Personal consumption fell sharply in the October-December quarters. Automobile sales collapsed due to 1975 model price increases, energy problems and general uncertainty. The industry began large-scale lay-offs of workers. Business fixed investments fell off; a coal mine strike undercut activity; and purchases by the federal, state and local governments held steady, providing no countercyclical stimulus to demand. Real disposable income fell for the first time since 1947 as price increases outpaced wage and salary gains. The unintended workings of the federal tax system helped undercut consumer purchasing power as inflation boosted taxpayers into higher brackets and Social Security tax wage base increases continued payroll tax deductions from workers' paychecks later into the fall.

Unemployment jumped as a result, reaching 7.2 percent in December, up from 5 percent in May. Civilian employment started falling in August, and steady reductions in available jobs left more than 6.6 million workers out of work by December.

While the severe lag in demand brought some fourth-quarter relief, prices continued rising throughout the year at annual rates of more than 10 percent. The most comprehensive inflation measure, the gross national product price deflator, rose 10 percent above its 1973 level; the Consumer Price Index increased 12.2 percent for the year and the wholesale price index by a whopping 20.9 percent.

The cost of borrowing money reached the highest levels ever recorded in the United States in response to money supply constrictions and to expectations for continued high inflation. The prime rate that commercial banks charged their best corporate customers reached 12 percent by mid-year before declining in the fall. Demand for business credit rose during the year as industries found themselves short of cash to finance capacity expansion and inventory accumulation. Profits rose substantially but for the most part reflected huge inventory value adjustments due to inflation that did not provide additional internal funds for reinvestment. Equity investment fell as stock prices continued their general plunge.

The combination of monetary stringency and business loan demand severely squeezed credit markets, and high interest rates drew funds away from the thrift institutions that provide most mortgage financing; residential construction fell 27 percent, its worst decline since World War II.

Before shifting policy late in the year to ease monetary growth to counteract the recession, the Federal Reserve kept the clamps on the money supply. The narrowly defined money supply grew only 4.7 percent for the year, with the broader supply increasing 7.2 percent.

The U.S. trade and payments balances swung back into deficit, partly in response to oil import price increases and to a worldwide recession that cut demand for U.S. exports. The pattern of inflation and recession was repeated in other nations, reinforcing U.S. economic troubles.

1975

The recession of 1974 reached its nadir during the first few months of 1975. The downturn climaxed with a drastic first-quarter drop, recording the fifth straight quarterly fall in actual gross national product.

Recovery followed, prodded by tax cuts enacted after surging unemployment spurred a divided federal government to agree on stimulative countermeasures. Although inventory corrections produced a misleading third-quarter spurt, the expansion's pace was dismayingly slow but evidently steady.

The unemployment rate still stood at 8.3 percent in December 1975, down only slightly from its 8.9 percent peak in May. More than 7.7 million workers were out of jobs at year's end.

On the other hand, the nation's stubborn inflation rate, a confidence-sapping force that had helped undercut economic activity, fell to half the postwar record "double-digit" levels that it had reached in 1974. Further moderation was predicted even though food and fuel prices still were rising uncomfortably at the end of the year.

Although they had compromised by extending 1975 tax reductions through the first six months of 1976, a strongly Democratic Congress and the Republican Ford administration still were locked in their prolonged debate over the federal government's strategy for curing both rising prices and lagging economic output. Ford asked for a one-shot tax rebate. Congress complied but approved business tax relief as well. It also tacked on $50 bonus payments to federal benefit recipients as a further stimulative measure.

Fiscal policy turned decisively stimulative. The fiscal 1975 budget wound up with a $45.1 billion deficit as strong growth in transfer payments through Social Security, unemployment and other programs replenished personal income. The emergency tax measure went into effect in April, pumping $8.1 billion back into the economy through rebates and another $1.8 billion through bonus benefits. Lower tax withholding rates, put into effect on May 1, reduced tax collections by $7.8 billion through the rest of the year.

The Federal Reserve Board continued to go its own way in guiding monetary growth, generally sticking to a restrictive stance against inflation despite congressional pressure to accelerate money supply expansion to accommodate a faster recovery. The House backed away from proposals by Rep. Henry S. Reuss, D-Wis., the activist new chairman of its Banking, Currency and Housing Committee, to dictate money supply goals.

By the end of the year, the narrow money supply had grown only 4.1 percent and the broader supply 8.5 percent. The money supply had accelerated sharply in the second quarter as the Treasury paid out tax rebates and bonus payments, but the pace slowed markedly during the second half of the year.

After bottoming in April, output began recovering at a 5.6 percent annual rate in the second quarter of the year. Inventory liquidations that had started in the first quarter continued at high levels. Recovery quickened in the summer months, and actual GNP grew at a boom-like 11.4 percent rate in the July-September quarter. That pace was not sustained, however, as personal consumption slowed, government purchases moderated and business fixed investment continued to lag. In the fourth quarter, actual output rose by only 3.3 percent.

The slow rebuilding of demand allowed a slowdown of inflation, although the GNP deflator still hung at 9.3 percent. The Consumer Price Index increased by 7 percent for the year, while the wholesale price index rose a more moderate 4.2 percent.

Despite general monetary stringency, interest rates

continued the decline that had begun late in 1974 through most of 1975. Stock prices climbed steadily during the first half of the year, then fluctuated well below pre-recession levels. Early in the year, Congress completed action on legislation to encourage securities industry competition and modernization.

The U.S. recovery was followed by economic improvement in other nations. Still, the volume of world trade fell significantly for the first time in 30 years and the worldwide recovery was uncertain as consuming nations continued adjusting to energy price increases.

The U.S. trade and payments balances recorded strong surpluses, partly because imports fell off more drastically than exports to other nations. Agricultural exports remained strong, although the government temporarily embargoed Soviet grain sales that threatened to push food prices upward.

Emergency Tax Cuts

In a sharp shift to stimulative fiscal policies, Congress rushed through an emergency tax reduction measure as its first priority of business in 1975.

As cleared in late-night March 26 sessions, the legislation (HR 2166 — PL 94-12) provided $22.8 billion in individual and business tax cuts along with $1.9 billion in special countercyclical government spending. A cutback in the oil depletion allowance coupled with foreign oil tax benefit curbs offset part of the Treasury loss by raising the petroleum industry's taxes by $2 billion.

President Ford signed HR 2166 on March 29, clearing the way for the Treasury to start paying out $8.1 billion in 1974 tax rebates and to put $10 billion in lower 1975 tax withholding rates into effect on May 1. Those refunds and paycheck withholding reductions were intended to pump sorely needed spending power back into the private economy.

With the economy in deep recession, the president accepted the measure despite reservations about congressional decisions that reworked his own one-shot tax cut proposals and added $50 bonus payments to Social Security and federal welfare recipients. In its rush to clear HR 2166 before its April recess, the president complained, Congress included "a lot of extraneous changes in our tax laws, some well-intentioned but very ill-considered, which should have waited for deliberate action" as part of a comprehensive tax law review.

House leaders themselves had supported a straightforward Ways and Means Committee version of a tax cut measure, trying to keep the emergency bill free from controversial proposals that could delay final action. But the House Democratic Caucus, eager to crack down on oil industry taxes, overrode that cautious advice to force the depletion curbs to the floor.

The Senate took the $19.9 billion House-passed bill and raised its impact to $30.4 billion through committee and floor amendments. Conferees carved that back to $22.8 billion but preserved most Senate initiatives. The final result raised and redistributed the administration's $16 billion proposal for cutting personal and business taxes to replenish lagging economic activity.

Congress enacted additional legislation later in 1975 that extended the emergency tax cuts beyond the end of the year. *(Story, p. 167)*

Provisions

As signed by President Ford March 29, HR 2166 contained the following provisions:

Individual Taxes

● Provided a 10 percent rebate on 1974 individual income taxes up to a maximum of $200. Each taxpayer would receive a refund of at least $100 — or his total tax payment if less than $100 — with the $200 maximum phased downward for taxpayers with incomes of $20,000 or more. At incomes of $30,000 or more, the rebate would be $100.

● Increased the low-income allowance — a minimum standard deduction designed to free poverty level families from paying federal taxes — to $1,600 for single persons and $1,900 for joint returns during 1975.

● Increased the percentage standard deduction for 1975 to 16 percent of adjusted gross income with a maximum of $2,300 for single persons and $2,600 for joint returns.

● Allowed a $30 credit against taxes owed on 1975 income for each taxpayer and dependent.

● Provided a refundable 10 percent tax credit up to $400 on earned income of $4,000 or less for a family with at least one dependent child. The credit would be phased down on higher earnings and eliminated at $8,000.

● Allowed a 5 percent credit up to $2,000 against taxes for the purchase of a newly built home that was finished or under construction by March 26, 1975. The credit was available for principal residences bought between March 13, 1975, and Dec. 31, 1976. This provision was modified in subsequent action on legislation (PL 94-45) extending jobless benefits.

● Increased to $35,000 from $18,000 the income level at which the $4,800 limit on itemized deductions allowed by existing law for child-care or household services would start being phased down $1 for every $2 in additional income.

● Extended to 18 months from 12 months the period in which a taxpayer who sold one house after Dec. 31, 1974, must reinvest his proceeds in another home to qualify for deferral of taxes on his capital gain. The limit for the purchase of a new house being built by the taxpayer was increased to 24 months from 18 months.

Business Taxes

● Increased the business investment tax credit to 10 percent in 1975 and 1976 from the existing levels of 4 percent for public utilities and 7 percent for other businesses.

● Allowed corporations to take an 11 percent credit on investments during 1975 and 1976 provided that benefits from the additional 1 percent credit were contributed to an employee stock ownership plan.

● Increased the existing $50,000 limit on the amount of used property qualifying for the credit to $100,000 effective for 1975 and 1976.

● Increased the existing limit on the amount of the investment credit taken by a utility during one year to 100 percent of tax liability in 1975 and 1976 from the existing ceiling of 50 percent of tax liability above $25,000. After 1975 and 1976, the limit would phase back to 50 percent over a five-year period.

● Allowed businesses to claim the investment credit for progress payments made during one year toward construction of investments taking several years to complete.

● Allowed public utilities that had elected immediately to pass along the benefits of the 4 percent credit reinstated in 1971 to consumers through lower rates to choose to keep for their own purposes the benefit of the additional credit provided by the increase to 10 percent. If a state regulatory agency required that the benefits be channeled to customers immediately, the increased credit would be denied.

● Increased the amount of corporate income exempt from the 26 percent corporate tax surcharge to $50,000 in 1975 from the existing $25,000 level.

● Reduced the normal 22 percent corporate income tax rate during 1975 to 20 percent on the first $25,000 in income.

● Increased to $150,000 from $100,000 the amount of earnings that a corporation could accumulate instead of distributing it to stockholders without being subject to a special tax imposed on earnings kept in a business for the purpose of avoiding individual income taxes.

Individuals and Business

● Allowed a tax credit for 20 percent of wages paid between the date of enactment and July 1, 1976, to hire a recipient of federal Aid to Families with Dependent Children (AFDC) benefits. For individual taxpayers who hired AFDC recipients for personal services rather than for a business, the amount of the credit would be limited to $1,000 for each employee the taxpayer hired.

● Allowed self-employed persons to deduct from their 1975 taxable incomes contributions to qualified pension plans made after the end of the year but before their 1975 tax returns were filed.

Oil and Gas Depletion

● Repealed the 22 percent depletion allowance on oil and gas production retroactive to Jan. 1, 1975.

● Retained the 22 percent allowance until July 1, 1976, for natural gas sold under federal price regulations (or until the controlled price was raised to take account of repeal of depletion).

● Retained the allowance for natural gas sold under fixed-price contracts until the price was raised.

● Provided a permanent small producer exemption that allowed independent oil companies to continue taking the depletion allowance on a basic daily output of oil and natural gas.

● Allowed an initial small producer exemption retaining a 22 percent depletion allowance on an average daily production of 2,000 barrels of oil or 12 million cubic feet of natural gas or an equivalent quantity of both oil and gas.

● Reduced the daily production eligible for depletion by 200 barrels a day for each year between 1976 and 1980, leaving the small producer exemption at a permanent level of 1,000 barrels of oil per day or 6 million cubic feet of natural gas.

● Reduced the depletion rate available on the small producer exemption to 20 percent in 1981, 18 percent in 1982, 16 percent in 1983 and to a permanent 15 percent rate in 1984.

● Kept the depletion rate at 22 percent until 1984 for production of up to 1,000 barrels a day through costly secondary or tertiary recovery methods used to extract remaining oil and gas from wells that were mostly pumped out.

● Limited the deduction taken under the small producer exemption to 65 percent of the taxpayer's income from all sources.

● Denied the small producer exemption to any taxpayer that sold oil or gas through retail outlets or operated a refinery processing more than 50,000 barrels of oil a day.

Foreign Income

● Limited the amount of foreign tax payments on oil-related income that an oil company could take as a credit against U.S. taxes to 52.8 percent of its 1975 income from foreign oil operations. The limit would be reduced to 50.4 percent in 1976 and 50 percent theraffter.

● Allowed use of excess credits within those limits only to offset U.S. taxes on foreign oil-related income, not on income from other foreign sources.

● Denied oil companies after 1975 the use of the per-country limitation option that allowed a company to compute its maximum foreign tax credits on a country-by-country basis.

● Required recapture of foreign oil-related losses that were deducted from income subject to U.S. taxes by taxing an equivalent amount of subsequent foreign oil-related profits as if earned in the United States (and therefore not eligible for deferral until transferred to the United States). The credit for foreign taxes on the subsequent profits also would be reduced in proportion to the amount treated as U.S. profits.

● Denied the foreign tax credit for any taxes paid to a foreign country in buying or selling oil or gas from property that the nation had expropriated.

● Denied the investment tax credit for drilling rigs used outside the northern half of the Western Hemisphere.

● Denied deferral of taxes on half of the profits from exports of natural resources and energy products by domestic international sales corporations (DISCs).

● Repealed effective in 1976 certain existing exemptions from a 1962 law requiring current U.S. taxation of profits earned by subsidiaries set up by U.S. corporations in tax haven countries that imposed little or no taxes.

● Allowed deferral of U.S. taxes on all earnings by a foreign subsidiary if less than 10 percent of its income was defined as tax haven income.

Other Provisions

● Granted a $50 bonus payment out of general Treasury revenues to each recipient of Social Security retirement, railroad retirement or Supplemental Security Income (SSI) benefits.

● Provided an additional 13 weeks of emergency unemployment benefits to jobless workers in nine states who had exhausted their available 52 weeks of regular and extended benefits.

Tax Cut Extension

Before adjourning for Christmas, Congress kept emergency 1975 tax cuts in effect beyond the end of the year (HR 9968 — PL 94-164), but only after a session-ending showdown with President Ford that nearly blocked the extension. *(Emergency Tax cuts, p. 165)*

Although the 1975 tax cuts were temporary, Congress clearly intended from the start to keep them in effect indefinitely. That foregone conclusion, along with the political and economic risks of allowing taxes to rise in 1976, presented the Ford administration with a tough dilemma

as it tried to bring the federal budget closer into balance after massive fiscal 1975-76 deficits. Allowing the tax cuts to expire on Jan. 1, 1976, as scheduled in the original law, would have raised paycheck withholding rates while the strength of economic recovery still was in doubt.

Ford had positioned himself for a fight over continuing the tax reductions in an Oct. 6 proposal for a permanent $27.7 billion 1976 tax cut conditioned on equivalent fiscal 1977 spending reductions. In making that offer, the president vowed to veto any tax cut extension unless linked to "a clear affirmative decision" by Congress to hold fiscal 1977 outlays to $395 billion, roughly $28 billion below administration projections.

Ford's program was a bold but somewhat desperate bid to retake the budget policy initiative that Congress had held since early 1975 when it reworked the administration's one-shot tax rebate plan. By tying taxes and spending together in taxpayers' minds — and offering larger tax cuts in return for spending cuts — the president hoped to pressure Congress to take a stand on continuing Republican campaigns for budget restraint. He also built a case for vetoing extended 1976 tax reductions on anti-inflationary grounds.

The legislation (HR 5559) agreed to by House-Senate conferees on Dec. 16 allowed an $8.4 billion six-month extension. It provided a 16 percent standard deduction, with maximums of $2,400 for single persons and $2,800 for joint returns. The bill set the low-income allowance at $1,700 for single taxpayers and $2,100 for couples. And it boosted the $30 individual tax credit to $35 or 2 percent of the first $9,000 of taxable income, whichever was greater.

As promised, President Ford vetoed the initial bill within a few hours. In a tense, politically charged vote the House Dec. 18 stunned Democratic leaders by falling 17 votes short of the two-thirds majority needed to overturn Ford's veto. Aided by southern Democratic conservatives, House Republicans stood unexpectedly firm behind Ford's demand that extended tax cuts be accompanied by some kind of congressional commitment to hold down the growth of future federal spending.

After a one-day standoff, congressional leaders worked out compromise spending restraint language that rescued the tax cuts. The compromise (HR 9968) pledged Congress to cut fiscal 1977 outlays dollar for dollar if it extended the tax cuts, but it specified that Congress reserved the right to ignore the pledge if it concluded through the budget process that changing economic conditions or other circumstances required higher or lower spending levels. The pledge was all but forgotten by the time Congress worked on the budget in 1976.

The pledge and the tax cut extension were quickly added to HR 9968, which cleared Dec. 19. Ford signed the measure into law Dec. 23.

Social Security Amendments

Congress Dec. 19 cleared for the president a bill (HR 10727 — PL 94-202) aimed at reducing the large backlog of cases appealing the government's denial of Social Security benefits and making other minor and technical changes in the Social Security laws.

As signed into law, HR 10727 (PL 94-202):

● Gave applicants for Supplemental Security Income benefits the same administrative and judicial rights enjoyed by applicants for Social Security and Medicare benefits.

● Authorized hearing examiners for the Supplemental Security Income and black lung benefits programs to hear Social Security and Medicare claims cases.

● Decreased, after Feb. 29, 1976, to 60 days, from six months, the amount of time an applicant had to appeal denial of a Social Security or Medicare benefits claim; increased to 60 days, from 30 days, the time period for appealing denial of a Supplemental Security Income claim.

● Allowed annual, rather than quarterly, reporting of Social Security wages after Jan. 1, 1978, but did not alter dates on which the tax payments were due.

● Required the Department of Health, Education and Welfare to give 18 months' notice before making any changes in the way state and local governments deposited Social Security contributions.

● Exempted certain state payments to Alaskans from the definition of income to allow them to receive their full Social Security benefits.

● Made technical changes regarding Social Security coverage for certain police and fire safety personnel in West Virginia.

Federal Reserve Policies

Stopping far short of dictating monetary policy goals, Congress in 1975 cleared a resolution (H Con Res 133) that offered general congressional guidelines for Federal Reserve Board money supply decisions.

As a concurrent resolution, the measure did not require the president's signature and was not legally binding. Its monetary policy goals were vaguely worded, although the resolution imposed one concrete requirement by directing Federal Reserve officials to outline their own objectives in regular semiannual testimony before the House and Senate banking committees.

In sum, the sense-of-Congress resolution was far less than Democratic leaders aimed for in their economic poicy statements at the start of the 1975 session. It nonetheless underscored continuing congressional unhappiness with the Federal Reserve's restrictive monetary stance against inflation among Democrats who preferred to fight unemployment first.

The House Banking, Currency and Housing Committee blocked tougher monetary policy legislation. As first proposed by Chairman Henry S. Reuss, D-Wis., the proposal would have directed the Federal Reserve to expand the money supply at a rate of 6 percent a year and allocate private banking credit to specific useful purposes. However, a panel subcommittee split the plan into two bills: HR 3160 setting monetary growth goals and HR 3166 conferring credit allocation powers. The subcommittee also dropped the specific 6 percent target figure for monetary growth and substituted language directing the Federal Reserve to conduct monetary policy in the first six months of 1975 "so as to lower long-term interest rates, and thus do its part in promptly and steadily reducing unemployment." The full committee rejected the modified HR 3160 by a 19-20 margin and approved instead the sense-of-Congress resolution (H Rept 94-20), which the full House adopted.

In the Senate, the Banking, Housing and Urban Affairs Committee reported a revamped resolution (S Rept 94-38) that added the requirement that Federal Reserve officials appear at semiannual House or Senate hearings to outline monetary policy objectives for the coming year. Conferees combined the two versions, and the conference agreement was adopted by both houses in March.

Aid to New York City

Although many members opposed the move, Congress agreed late in 1975 to lend financially ailing New York City the cash it needed to avoid going bankrupt.

Legislation (HR 10481 — PL 94-143) cleared Dec. 6 allowed the Treasury secretary to make federal loans of up to $2.3 billion a year through mid-1978 to help the city meet its seasonal cash needs. The city was required to repay the loans and interest of about 8 percent by June 30 of each year. A fiscal 1976 supplemental appropriations bill (HR 10647 — PL 94-157), passed Dec. 15, funded the loan program.

Enactment of the legislation ended, at least temporarily, a harrowing string of money crises for the nation's largest city. New York had faced financial default for many months, but used a variety of rescue measures to stave it off. By December, however, the city had run out of ways to pay its bills except by getting some form of aid from the federal government.

The New York aid issue provoked one of the most heated battles of the legislative year. Supporters argued that the federal government could not let the nation's financial capital collapse. Opponents objected vehemently to the precedent of "bailing out" a city that had mismanaged its financial affairs for years.

Prospects for federal aid were remote when city officials first petitioned Ford for his help in May. Throughout the summer, Congress showed no interest in the issue and Ford administration officials were adamantly opposed to federal aid.

Although the president remained opposed, key members of Congress began to push for federal help in September and October as events started to wear down traditional congressional hostility toward New York. The city tottered dramatically on the edge of default on Oct. 17, but managed once again to scrape up the cash to continue operating through November.

The Senate and House banking committees accelerated their work on aid legislation after the near-default and eventually both committees developed legislation that would have allowed the federal government to guarantee bonds issued to help the city meet its expenses. In the meantime, however, Ford had vowed Oct. 29 to veto any bill designed to "bail out" New York before a default.

After the state had taken several new steps to raise the city's taxes and reduce its immediate spending needs, Ford agreed to support federal loans to help New York meet its seasonal cash needs on Nov. 26. Ford argued that New York had bailed itself out by approving those steps and insisted that his hard-line stance on the aid issue had prodded the city into approving them.

Faced with an impending default deadline, supporters of aid to New York then threw out the guarantee proposals the banking committees had spent several weeks preparing and rushed the president's plan through Congress in five days.

Despite the president's position, many members of Congress, particularly from southern and farm states, remained opposed to aid to New York. They argued that their constituents would not stand for any use of their tax dollars to help a city that had been living beyond its means for more than a decade.

But the fact that a number of Republicans supported the legislation indicated that political sentiment on the issue had shifted dramatically in seven months. During this period, New York City's financial problems were widely publicized, with some economic experts predicting that a New York default would have a serious impact on the national economy and financial markets. The inevitable pressure for some kind of federal action pushed the issue to the top of the congressional agenda.

Provisions

As signed into law, HR 10481:

● Authorized the Treasury secretary to make loans to New York City or a financial agent authorized by the state to administer the city's financial affairs; limited the total value of loans outstanding at any one time to $2.3 billion.

● Required the city or its financial agent to repay the loans made in any fiscal year by the last day of the city's fiscal year (June 30) at an interest rate 1 percent higher than the prevailing Treasury borrowing rate.

● Barred the secretary from making loans unless he determined that there was a reasonable prospect of repayment; authorized the secretary to set terms and conditions for the loan that he deemed appropriate to assure repayment.

● Authorized the secretary, to the extent allowed in appropriation acts, to withhold other federal funds due the city to offset the amount of any unrepaid loans.

● Barred the secretary from making loans unless all prior loans had been repaid on time.

● Authorized the General Accounting Office to audit the state's and city's financial records.

● Ended authority to make loans to the city on June 30, 1978.

1976

The economic recovery sputtered in 1976. After growing at a 9.2 percent annual rate in the first three months, actual output slowed progressively during the rest of the year. In the final quarter, actual GNP grew only 2.6 percent, below the rate of expansion considered sufficient to provide jobs for a growing work force. After falling to 7.3 percent in May, unemployment in fact edged back up to 8 percent in November before settling down to 7.8 percent in December.

Ford and the Democratic Congress continued their fiscal policy struggles through the year. Pressures for stimulus to reduce the politically sensitive unemployment rate were heightened by the approach of the Nov. 2 presidential and congressional elections, and Ford's narrow defeat by Democratic candidate Jimmy Carter was partly due to continued economic sluggishness. The Federal Reserve Board maintained its cautious monetary policy course despite continued grumbling in Congress.

Although Ford opposed stimulative measures that risked long-term inflation, Congress enacted increased fis-

cal assistance through public works and countercyclical aid to state and local governments. The tax cuts again were extended and Congress enacted a long-promised tax revision measure. But actual federal outlays fell inexplicably short of intended levels at critical junctures during the year, perhaps contributing to the recovery's slowdown, and the incoming Carter administration made stepped-up stimulus to speed the recovery one of its 1977 priorities.

By any measure, federal fiscal policy was stimulative in 1976. The fiscal 1976 budget wound up with a $66.5 billion deficit, less than the $74.1 billion projected by Congress but more than the $51.9 billion that Ford had proposed in 1975.

The Federal Reserve Board maintained its monetary expansion goals for the upcoming year in the 4.5 percent to 7 percent range for the narrowly defined money supply, after lowering the upper target to 6.5 percent. That signaled continued caution about price pressures.

For the year, real GNP grew by 6.1 percent, despite the slowdown of expansion in the last nine months. Interest rates fell steadily throughout 1976 with short-term rates reaching their lowest levels since 1972, but were starting to climb again in early 1977. Corporate profits improved, and business fixed investment showed some signs of reviving after lagging behind the levels needed to help lead a stronger recovery.

Price increases generally were moderate, but the GNP deflator still measured at 5.1 percent for the year. By the fourth quarter, the Consumer Price Index had risen by 5 percent from its 1975 fourth-quarter level, and the wholesale price index had gone up by 4.1 percent over the same period. All three measures reached their highest rates of increase during the second half of the year, however.

With inflation moderating, real wages rose by 2 percent in 1976 after declining during the two previous years. After rapid first-quarter starts, real disposable income and personal consumption slowed through the middle of the year before reviving in the final three months. Strong Christmas season activity helped boost retail sales in the final quarter. Housing starts and residential investment held up well during the year and accelerated significantly in the fourth quarter of 1976.

The U.S. trade and international payments balances swung back into deficit as rising domestic demand brought in more imports. Most of the import volume increase was due to rising fuel imports as the nation's energy use increased about 3.5 percent after falling for two years.

Tax Revision

It took four years — and fundamental shifts in House and Senate power — for Congress to start following up on its frequently stated pledge to revise the U.S. tax laws.

But Congress finally finished part of that task in 1976, wrapping up a massive measure (HR 10612 — PL 94-455) that affected the federal taxes of every individual and business. The law provided its most widely distributed benefit by continuing $17.3 billion in individual and business tax cuts.

The final tax revision product was the most extensive tax measure since 1969. Its 28 titles included major provisions that restricted tax shelter investments, made the first major gift and estate tax changes in more than 30 years, revised capital gains taxes, increased the existing minimum tax on the very wealthy, simplified individual income tax preparation, repealed outmoded tax code "deadwood," added safeguards in tax law administration and tightened taxation of foreign income.

Prodded by the young and ambitious House Democratic freshmen elected in 1974, Congress in 1975 had taken a portentous first step toward tax revision by tying curbs on the oil and gas depletion allowance to the emergency tax cut bill.

Many Democrats had pledged tax revision action in their 1974 campaigns, and the depletion allowance was among the most visible of tax preferences in an era of sharp energy price increases.

But another year and one-half — and tough House and Senate infighting over the power of the tax-writing committees and their chairmen — were required before Congress completed work on the extensive tax law redrafting that it had started in 1973.

'Legislative Miracle'

Termed a "legislative miracle" by some participants, the 1976 tax revision package was a major achievement for the House Ways and Means and the Senate Finance committees, the two tax-writing panels that control congressional action on the complex and convoluted Internal Revenue Code.

The measure was a special accomplishment for the Ways and Means Committee and its new chairman, Rep. Al Ullman, D-Ore. The House panel had spent most of 1975-76 adjusting to the less dominant leader, expanded liberal bloc and more open procedures that the House had imposed at the start of the 94th Congress.

House Democrats dictated those changes after the panel had spent two unproductive years in 1973-74 unable to write tax revision and energy tax legislation acceptable to the full House. The committee ran into difficulty in those years as then-Chairman Wilbur D. Mills, D-Ark., once the unquestioned master of House tax deliberations, encountered personal troubles and slipped from power.

Mills resigned as chairman at the end of 1974, then retired from Congress in 1976. His downfall left Senate Finance Committee Chairman Russell B. Long, D-La., to dominate congressional tax action through most of the 1975-76 session.

Long fended off most tough tax revision proposals that liberals brought up in Senate committee and floor maneuvering on HR 10612. But Congress began to challenge the Finance Committee chairman's authority through new budget procedures it put into effect in 1975-76.

Budget Link

Using the revised budget process it created in 1974, Congress adopted fiscal 1976 and fiscal 1977 budget resolutions that directed the tax-writing committees to raise additional revenues through tax revision legislation. In 1975, that requirement was dropped at the end of the budget process after House tax revision action dragged on into December.

In 1976, however, the budget process had more effect. The Senate defeated a floor challenge to Long by Senate Budget Committee Chairman Edmund S. Muskie, D-Maine, who contended that the Finance Committee's tax revision package failed to comply with congressional budget targets. But House-Senate conferees, in negotiating a tax revision compromise as the session drew to a close, felt obliged to tailor its revenue effects to fit the final $1.6 billion budget goal.

Provisions

As signed into law, HR 10612 (PL 94-455):

Tax Shelters

● Limited, for real estate ventures, the deductible losses of limited partners to the amount a partner had or would have at risk; limited deductions for construction-period interest and taxes on commercial and residential real-estate investments, with a gradual shift to amortization over 10 years of the costs; recaptured excess depreciation deductions for residential real estate and subsidized housing by treating equivalent amounts of the proceeds from selling such property as ordinary income instead of capital gains, which are taxed at a lower rate.

● Limited deductions for losses from investments in farming operations, except trees other than fruit or nut trees, to the amount an investor actually had at risk; required farming syndicates to deduct expenses for supplies when they were used rather than when purchased, to capitalize costs for poultry, thereby precluding immediate tax deductions, and to capitalize orchard costs before an orchard actually became productive; required farm corporations to use accrual accounting methods matching deductible expenses against subsequent income for tax purposes. Family corporations, as well as those in which a family owned at least 50 percent of the stock, and corporations with gross annual receipts of less than $1 million could continue to use cash accounting methods, deducting expenses in the year incurred regardless of when the resulting income was earned.

● Limited, for oil and gas investments, deductions for losses to the amount an investor actually had at risk, excluding loans for which the individual was not personally responsible; recaptured excess depreciation deductions by treating equivalent sales proceeds as ordinary income rather than capital gains.

● Limited, for investments in motion pictures, deductions for losses to the amount a taxpayer actually had at risk; required individuals and corporations which were at least 50 percent owned by a family that produced films, books, records and similar property to capitalize the production costs and deduct them over the period that income was produced.

● Limited, for equipment leasing activities, deductions for losses to the amount a taxpayer actually had at risk, excluding loans for which he was not personally at risk.

● Curtailed the amount of the purchase price of a sports franchise that could be allocated to depreciable player contracts and required recapture of player contract depreciation if the franchise was sold or exchanged.

● Revised rules for allocating income, losses and tax deductions among members of a partnership; restricted deductions for losses by a limited partner in any investment to the amount the individual had or would have at risk.

● Limited individuals' deductions for interest on investment debts to $10,000 plus net investment income, although interest payments above that amount could be deducted in future years.

The limitation would not apply to interest on investment debts incurred before Sept. 11, 1975, or under a contract in effect then.

Minimum-Maximum Taxes

● Increased the existing minimum tax on individuals' income from activities that received preferential tax treatment to 15 percent from 10 percent.

● Reduced the amount of preference income exempt from the minimum tax to $10,000 or one-half the amount paid in regular federal income taxes, whichever was greater. (Existing law provided a $30,000 exemption and a deduction for regular taxes.)

● Expanded the list of tax preference income subject to the minimum tax to include the amount of itemized deductions (other than medical and casualty deductions) exceeding 60 percent of adjusted gross income, intangible drilling costs for gas and oil in excess of deductions if costs were capitalized, and accelerated depreciation on equipment leases.

● Increased the minimum tax on corporations to 15 percent from 10 percent; reduced the amount of preference income exempt from the minimum tax to $10,000 or the amount of regular taxes paid, whichever was greater; eliminated a provision of existing law that permitted corporations with more than enough regular taxes to offset preference income subject to the minimum wage during one year to carry the excess over to reduce preference income in seven subsequent years; required timber companies to include two-thirds of their capital gains in the minimum-tax base, in effect excluding them from the changes.

● Extended the 50 percent maximum tax rate to pensions and annuities, redefined "earned income" as "personal service income" and reduced the amount of income eligible for the maximum tax rate by all preference income. (Under existing law, income eligible for the 50 percent rate was reduced by the amount of preference income over $30,000.) Also, the list of preference income items was increased to correspond to the minimum tax list.

Personal Tax Cuts

● Made permanent 1975 tax law changes that raised the standard personal deductions to 16 percent of adjusted gross income to maximums of $2,800 for joint returns and $2,400 for single taxpayers.

● Also made permanent 1975 provisions that increased the minimum standard deduction (low income allowance) to $1,700 for single taxpayers and $2,100 for joint returns.

● Extended through 1977 a credit against taxes owned equal to $35 per individual or 2 percent of the first $9,000 of taxable income, whichever was greater.

● Extended through 1977 a tax credit for individuals with children equal to 10 percent of the first $4,000 of earnings that was phased out as adjusted gross income rose from $4,000 to $8,000; directed that federal cash payments made to families under the refundable tax credit be disregarded determining eligibility for any federal benefits and assistance if the individual was a beneficiary the month before receiving the refund.

Tax Simplification

● Replaced 12 optional individual tax tables based on adjusted gross income up to $10,000 with 4 tables based on taxable income up to $20,000, effective in 1976.

● Changed the existing deduction for alimony payments from an itemized deduction to a deduction from gross income, making it available to taxpayers who use the standard deduction, effective in 1977.

● Revised the existing 15 percent tax credit on retirement income to apply it to earned income as well as pensions or other forms of retirement income of persons age 65 and older. The revised credit would be available on income up to $2,500 for single persons and $3,750 for joint returns. The credit would be phased down $1 for each $2 by which total adjusted gross income exceeded $7,500 for single persons and $10,000 for joint returns.

● Replaced an existing itemized deduction with a 20 percent tax credit for child care within or outside the home necessary to allow an individual to work. Allowed on expenses of up to $2,000 a year for one dependent and $4,000 for two or more dependents, the credit against taxes could amount to $400 for one child or $800 for more than one. The bill also eliminated the existing $35,000 income limit, extended the credit to married couples where one spouse works part-time or is a student and to divorced or separated parents with custody of a child. It also made payments to relatives for child-care costs eligible for the credit.

● Revised the existing sick pay exclusion to provide a maximum $5,200 a year exclusion available only to retired taxpayers under age 65 who were permanently and totally disabled. The exclusion would be reduced dollar-for-dollar on income above $15,000.

● Revised the existing moving expense deduction to make it available if a new place of work were at least 35 miles instead of at least 50 miles from the old residence. Existing limits would be raised to $1,500 from $1,000 for house-hunting and temporary living expenses before the move and to $3,000 from $2,500 for overall expenses of selling the old home and buying or renting a new one.

● Expanded the moving expense deductions for military personnel to include the cost of moving a spouse to a U.S. location when the member was stationed overseas and to include the cost of storing personal belongings of military personnel forced to relocate. The bill also exempted service personnel being transferred from the mileage limitation and from non-military employment requirements, and would not require them to count in-kind moving services provided by the federal government as moving allowances included in gross income for tax purposes.

Business Deductions

● Restricted deductions for using a home for business purposes to that part of a dwelling unit or separate structure used exclusively on a regular basis as the taxpayer's principal place of business or for meeting with patients, clients or customers in the normal course of business. Deductions would be permitted for inventory storage in some cases; employees could take deductions only if the business use was for the employer's convenience. In all cases, the deduction would be limited to the amount of income earned by business conducted in the home.

● Applied limits to business deductions for a vacation home rented to others if the taxpayer used it for personal purposes for more than two weeks or 10 percent of the days it was rented out. If the vacation home was rented less than 15 days a year, then no business deductions could be taken for it, nor would rental income be taxed.

● Prohibited deductions for expenses of attending more than two foreign conventions a year, and limited deductible expenses for those two conventions to coach or economy air fares and to daily subsistence allowances provided for federal government employees stationed where the convention was held. Transportation and living expenses would be deductible only if a specific proportion of time was spent on business-related activities.

● Treated as ordinary income a qualified stock option granted to an employee if the stock's market value could be readily determined. (If no fair value could be assigned, when the option was exercised the increase in the stock's price over the option price would be taxed as ordinary income.)

● Required an individual who paid off a loan he had guaranteed personally but not as part of his trade or business to treat his loss as a short-term capital loss rather than an ordinary loss.

● Directed the Internal Revenue Service (IRS) to set rules for limiting reasonable deductions by members of state legislatures for the cost of living away from home (defined as the districts they represent) while serving in state capitals.

Corporate Taxes

● Extended through 1980 the temporary 10 percent investment tax credit provided in 1975-76. Under permanent law, the credit was limited to 7 percent for most businesses and 4 percent for utilities.

● Extended through 1980 temporary 1975-76 provisions that increased the limit on used property purchases eligible for the investment tax credit to $100,000 from $50,000.

● Extended through 1980 an additional 1 percent investment credit (making it 11 percent) for firms that contributed the extra amount to an employee stock ownership plan (ESOP). The temporary 1 percent credit would have expired at the end of 1976. Another .5 percent credit would be available to firms that matched a .5 percent contribution by employees. Also adopted were a series of technical rules designed to correct problems that had emerged in the stock ownership plans.

● Specified rules allowing the investment credit to be taken for the production costs of movie and television firms.

● Increased the period that businesses may choose to use net operating losses to offset taxable income. The three-year carryback period was left unchanged, while the carryforward was extended to seven years from five for most businesses and to nine years from seven for regulated industries. Companies also could elect to skip the carryback and apply a loss to future years. New rules were specified for companies that purchased unprofitable businesses in order to apply the loss carryovers to their profits.

● Extended through 1977 temporary 1975 law that increased the amount of corporate income exempt from the 26 percent corporate tax surcharge to $50,000 from $25,000, and also reduced the normal 22 percent corporate tax rate to 20 percent on the first $25,000 of income, leaving the 22 percent rate in effect on income between $25,000 and the new $50,000 surtax exemption cut-off.

Foreign Income

● Lowered the exclusion taxpayers may apply to income earned abroad against U.S. taxes to $15,000 from $20,000. The existing $20,000 exclusion would continue to apply to employees of U.S. charitable organizations who work overseas. Modifications also were made in the tax rate, foreign tax credit and income eligible for the exclusion.

● Allowed U.S. taxpayers married to non-resident aliens to file joint U.S. returns with their spouses if they agreed to pay U.S. taxes on their total worldwide income.

● Tightened tax rules governing foreign-based trusts set up by Americans for U.S. beneficiaries.

● Extended the existing excise tax on transfers of stocks and securities to foreign entities to cover transfers of all other property, and increased the tax rate to 35 percent from 27½ percent.

● Repealed the per-country limitation option allowing U.S. companies to compute the limit on the credit for foreign taxes on a country-by-country basis.

● Required that foreign losses used to reduce overall income subject to U.S. taxes in one year be recaptured in subsequent years.

● Required U.S. corporations receiving dividends from corporations in less-developed nations to include the foreign taxes paid from those dividends in computing income subject to U.S. taxes before credits for the foreign tax were taken, thus ending a double tax allowance for ventures in less-developed countries.

● Discounted capital gains from sale of property in a foreign country in determining foreign income for computing the foreign tax credit limit if no substantial foreign taxes were paid on the capital gains.

● Reduced to 48 percent from 50 percent the percentage of foreign income taxes creditable against U.S. taxes on foreign oil and gas income, on an overall rather than country-by-country basis.

● Exempted from taxes bank deposit interest paid to non-resident aliens and foreign corporations. The exemption had been set to expire at the end of 1976.

● Phased out over four years existing preferential tax treatment for Western Hemisphere Trade Corporations; over three years for China Trade Act Corporations; substituted a tax credit for an existing income exclusion allowed for income earned in Puerto Rico and possessions by U.S. corporations.

● Denied tax deferral and reductions-in-earnings benefits for foreign bribes paid by U.S. corporations.

● Denied the foreign tax credit, deferral of taxes on earnings of foreign subsidiaries and deferral of taxes on portions of export income to firms participating or cooperating in an international boycott. The benefits would be denied in the same proportion as the income from the boycott activity to the firm's foreign business. The change would not apply to existing contracts until 1978 and 30 days after enactment for new ones.

DISC Curbs

● Restricted use of existing provisions allowing a corporation to indefinitely defer taxes on 50 percent of income from exports through a domestic international sales corporation (DISC). Between 1976 and 1979, the tax deferral would be allowed only on the amount of a DISC's gross export receipts that exceeded 67 percent of its average annual receipts in the period 1972-75. Beginning in 1980, the four-year base period would move forward a year, with the 1980 base period 1973-76.

● Permitted half the ordinary DISC benefits for exports of military equipment.

● Allowed DISC benefits to continue until March 18, 1980, on fixed contract sales of natural resource products, despite the repeal of the benefit in 1975.

Administrative Provisions

● Established additional rules for the disclosure of tax returns and return information, and for public inspection of IRS letter rulings giving tax law interpretations to specific taxpayers.

● Imposed identification and reporting requirements on persons and firms that prepare income tax returns for others, and imposed penalties for negligent or fraudulent preparation of returns.

● Specified procedures for the IRS in making summary assessments of additional tax to correct mathematical or clerical errors on tax returns, with remedies available to individual taxpayers.

● Required federal withholding of state income taxes for members of the military, and withholding of state and local income taxes from the drill and training pay of National Guard and Reserve personnel.

● Permitted federal withholding of state income taxes from federal employees in states where withholding was voluntary if the employees requested it.

● Required tax withholding of 20 percent on gambling winnings of more than $1,000, including racetracks and other forms of gambling, and on state lottery winnings of more than $5,000. Exempted from the requirement were winnings from slot machines, keno and bingo.

● Exempted all state lotteries from the 2 percent federal wagering tax.

● Gave taxpayers the right to block banks or other third parties from complying with IRS administrative summonses for financial records.

● Permitted state and local governments to require the use of Social Security numbers for identifying individuals in administering the tax, welfare, motor vehicle and driver licensing laws.

Technical Provisions

● Allowed political consultants to deduct bad debts owed by political parties or campaign committees.

● Allowed publishers to continue to deduct prepublication expenses, despite an IRS ruling to the contrary, until IRS issued new regulations.

● Increased the tax credits available to employers hiring welfare recipients and reduced the time such employees must work in order for the employer to receive the credits.

● Postponed until Jan. 1, 1979, an IRS ruling requiring employers to report separately tips received by employees on charge account payments, even if not reported by the employees.

● Extended through 1980 five-year amortization for firms that installed pollution control equipment in an existing plant, and an additional 5 percent investment credit for equipment installed after 1976.

● Modified the rules under which oil and gas producers were exempt from repeal of the percentage depletion allowance in 1975.

● Provided a deduction of up to $25,000 for the removal of architectural and transportation barriers to the handicapped and elderly in business facilities and vehicles.

● Restricted tax depreciation and deductions that could be taken on new buildings built where a certified historic structure was torn down or substantially changed, and permitted accelerated depreciation to be taken on the acquisition and rehabilitation of historic buildings.

Capital Gains and Losses

● Lengthened to one year from six months the period for which an asset must be held to qualify for long-term capital gains treatment. The holding period would be increased in two stages, to nine months in 1977 and a full year in 1978. Gains on agricultural commodity futures contracts would be excepted from the longer period.

● Increased to $3,000 from $1,000 the amount of ordinary income against which a capital loss could be deducted. The limit would rise in stages, to $2,000 in 1977 and $3,000 in 1978.

● Allowed mutual funds with capital losses in a year starting with 1970 to carry them forward against capital gains in eight subsequent years.

Retirement Accounts

● Expanded existing law on individual retirement accounts (IRAs) to cover non-working spouses. A qualified individual could contribute up to $1,750 to a joint IRA account or up to $875 into separate accounts for the individual and the spouse, or up to 15 percent of compensation, whichever was less.

● Allowed National Guard and Reserve personnel to qualify for IRA contributions if they had less than 90 days active duty during a year, and also volunteer firemen.

Specialized Provisions

● Adopted a series of technical changes in the tax treatment of real estate investment trusts (REITs).

● Permitted railroads and airlines to take investment credits of up to 100 percent of their tax liabilities for 1977 and 1978, with annual reductions of 10 percent each year after that until their investment credit returned to the normal 50 percent in 1983.

● Repealed nearly 150 sections of the Internal Revenue Code and amended 850 additional sections to eliminate obsolete or rarely used "deadwood" provisions.

Tax-Exempt Organizations

● Permanently reduced to 5 percent from 6.75 percent the mandatory percentage of non-charitable assets that private foundations must pay out for charitable and other purposes.

● Exempted tax-exempt organizations from paying the unrelated business income tax on certain income they might receive from fairs and expositions, conventions and trade shows.

● Established procedures for organizations to petition the federal district court for the District of Columbia, the U.S. Court of Claims and the U.S. Tax Court for declaratory judgments to settle their tax situation, if the IRS denied or revoked their tax-exempt status as charitable, religious or eligible to receive tax deductible donations.

Estate and Gift Taxes

● Unified the tax rate schedules for estates transferred at death and gifts given during lifetime, with rates ranging from 30 to 70 percent.

● Changed the existing exemptions for gifts and estate transfers to a credit applied to taxes. The unified credit would be $30,000 in 1977, rising to $34,000 in 1978, $38,000 in 1979, $42,500 in 1980 and $47,000 in 1981. (The credits would be the equivalent of increased exemptions.)

● Increased the size of the estate a person could leave tax-free to a spouse to $250,000 or half the estate, whichever was greater, from the existing half of the estate. For gifts, the first $100,000 would be tax-free; there would be no deduction for gifts between $100,000 and $200,000, and a deduction for half the gifts over $200,000.

● Provided that under certain conditions, farm property or a closely held business in an estate could be valued on the basis of its current use, rather than its potential "highest and best use." The special valuation could not reduce the estate more than $500,000. The tax benefits from such valuation would be recaptured by the government if the farm or closely held business passed out of the family within 15 years.

● Increased to 15 years from the generally applicable 10 years the period for the payment of estate taxes on farms and closely held businesses. The interest rate on the extended period was reduced to 4 percent from 7 percent and qualified estates would be eligible for the extension if they showed "reasonable cause" rather than the existing "undue hardship."

● Changed the basis on which inherited property was taxed if sold to its value on Dec. 31, 1976, from the existing fair market value at the time of death. For property acquired after Dec. 31, the basis for valuation would be the original purchase price, with adjustments. There would be a $10,000 exemption for household and personal effects, and a minimum basis of $60,000 was provided per estate. The changes applied to property of persons dying after Dec. 31, 1976.

● Imposed a new tax on "generation skipping" transfers under trusts or similar arrangements, but provided an exemption of $250,000 on transfers to each grandchild.

Miscellaneous Provisions

● Clarified the authority of Congress to override presidential decisions on remedies recommended by the International Trade Commission when U.S. businesses were injured by foreign imports.

● Allowed public charities that chose to meet new tests for expenditures for lobbying to retain their tax-exempt and tax-deductible status, and required disclosure of the lobbying expenditures of the organizations choosing the new spending rules.

● Excluded from an individual's taxable income any employer contributions or benefits received from qualifying group prepaid legal services plans. The benefits would be tax-free until 1981 and a study of the fringe benefit by the Treasury and Labor Departments would be due in 1980.

● Increased the deductions available on inventory contributed to public charities or private operating foundations for use in caring for the sick, poor or children.

● Allowed a parent who did not have custody of children to receive a tax exemption for a child if he or she contributed at least $1,200 for each of the children, and if the parent with custody did not clearly provide more support.

● Increased, for taxpayers over 65, the exemption from capital gains taxes on the sale of a home. The gain from the sale of the home would not be taxed if the sales price was less than $35,000, an increase from the existing $20,000. For sales over $35,000, only the gain over that would be taxed.

General Revenue Sharing

Congress in 1976 approved a $25.6 billion extension of the federal revenue sharing proram through fiscal 1980. The measure (HR 13367 — PL 94-488) provided up to $6.85 billion a year through Sept. 30, 1981, for distribution to the nation's state and local governments.

Cleared by Congress Sept. 30, the legislation retained the basic format of the program that the federal government began in 1972 to strengthen the federal system by sharing a portion of its tax collections with the states and their counties, cities and other local jurisdictions. *(1972 programs, p. 161)*

President Ford in 1975 had proposed a longer and more expensive revenue sharing extension to keep the program going for five and three-quarter years at a total cost of $39.85 billion. Ford asked for the extension a year ahead of the law's scheduled expiration at the end of 1976 to give state and local governments assurance that the funds still would be available in planning their budgets for 1977 and beyond.

The $25.6 billion extension for not quite four years was both less generous and less lengthy than Ford had requested, demonstrating that Congress clearly had doubts about the "new federalism" concept of sharing federal tax revenues without federal control over their use.

That doubt coupled with a desire to cut federal spending prompted the Carter administration to propose that revenue sharing for the states be dropped. Congress complied in 1980, extending revenue sharing programs only to local governments for three years. *(1980 action, p. 190)*

Provisions

As signed into law, major provisions of the 1976 legislation:

Extension

● Extended the revenue sharing program for three and three-quarter years from Jan. 1, 1977, through Sept. 30, 1980, thus moving the program to a fiscal-year basis from a calendar-year basis.

● Authorized entitlements to qualifying state and local governments up to $6.85 billion for each full fiscal year and an additional adjustment allowance up to $4,923,759 each fiscal year for the non-contiguous states of Alaska and Hawaii. The entitlement was based on a formula geared to federal income tax collections.

The effect of the langauge was to provide entitlements of $4,987,500,000 for the last nine months of fiscal 1977 ($6.65 billion on an annual basis) and $6.85 billion each for fiscal 1978-80. In addition, the effect for non-contiguous states was to provide $3,585,000 for the remainder of fiscal 1977 ($4.78 million on an annual basis) and $4,923,759 for each of fiscal years 1978-80. The grand total was $25,555,856,277.

Distribution of Funds

● Continued the original act's formulas for distributing the funds to local governments, as well as the one-third share for state governments and two-thirds for local governments, and the minimum and maximum levels for local government payments.

● Required each state government to maintain assistance to local governments equal to a two-year average of their intergovernmental transfers. The average had to equal or exceed the average of the transfers for the immediately preceding two years.

● Repealed the 1972 act's prohibition on using revenue sharing assistance to match federal grants received under other programs.

● Required that the tax data used in calculating grants cover a period ending before the beginning of an entitlement period.

● Barred adjustments in payments unless the local government or Treasury secretary made the demand for an adjustment within one year of the end of the entitlement period in question. Additional payments or refunds were to be made to or from an adjustment reserve fund to be established by the Treasury secretary from 0.5 percent of each state's entitlement.

Citizen Participation

● Required state and local government reports to the Treasury secretary at the close of the local fiscal year on the actual use of the shared revenues, as well as their relationship to the local budget and to the proposed use of the funds.

● Required information on the proposed use of the grant to be published in local newspapers before budget hearings and after budget adoption and to be available for public inspection, and provided a waiver authority for the Treasury secretary.

● Required public hearings on the proposed use of the revenue sharing funds and also on the local budget, with waiver authority for the Treasury secretary.

● Required information on local compliance with the public participation and non-discrimination provisions in the Treasury secretary's annual report to Congress on the program.

● Urged that senior citizens and their organizations be given an opportunity for comment, to the extent possible.

Non-discrimination

● Widened the existing prohibition on discrimination on the basis of race, color, national origin or sex to include age, under the provisions of the 1975 Age Discrimination Act; handicapped status, under the provisions of the 1973 Rehabilitation Act; and religion, under the Civil Rights Acts of 1964 and 1968.

● Provided the anti-discrimination provisions would apply to any program or activity of state and local governments receiving revenue sharing assistance except those the jurisdiction could show by clear and convincing evidence had not been funded in whole or in part with revenue sharing aid.

● Established a procedure and timetable that could lead to the suspension of revenue sharing aid to jurisdictions 50 days after a notice of non-compliance was issued by the Treasury secretary, following the secretary's investigation, or a finding by a federal or state court or federal administrative law judge.

● Authorized the attorney general to bring civil action in cases of alleged discrimination.

● Provided that individuals could file private civil suits alleging violations of the act, after administrative remedies were exhausted.

● Permitted courts to award reasonable attorneys' fees to the prevailing party in private citizen suits brought to enforce the non-discrimination provisions.

Miscellaneous Provisions

● Required an independent financial and compliance audit of recipient governments, with certain exceptions, at least every three years.

● Directed the Advisory Commission on Intergovernmental Relations to conduct a three-year study of the federal fiscal system, particularly the allocation of public resources among federal, state and local governments.

● Prohibited state and local governments from using any revenue sharing funds to lobby on legislation related to the act.

Anti-recession Aid

Congress spent nearly two years battling with the administration over an anti-recession assistance (also called countercyclical aid) program for state and local governments. President Ford vetoed the first $6.1 billion proposal, but Congress followed up by authorizing a $3.95 billion replacement over a second presidential veto.

Congressional enactment of the scaled-down measure (S 3201 — PL 94-369) in 1976 established a three-pronged stimulative package that channeled $2 billion to state and local governments for public works construction, $1.25 billion through countercyclical grants over 15 months, and $700 million in additional funding for wastewater treatment plant construction. After authorizing those efforts, Congress appropriated $3.7 billion to begin their operations in fiscal 1977.

1975 Action

The anti-recession assistance program took shape as Congress prepared its own proposals for stimulating the economy out of recession through increased federal spending. President Ford, while asking for temporary tax cuts that Congress eventually deepened and continued indefinitely, opposed any new spending initiatives in an effort to hold down potentially inflationary federal budget deficits.

House Democratic leaders in March 1975 unveiled a $5 billion proposal for increased spending on state and local public works projects as part of a package of emergency economic legislation. The plan included $3.5 billion for unfunded projects already authorized by Congress along with $1.5 billion for newly proposed projects. Although urban officials lobbied actively for the countercyclical assistance concept, the Ford administration opposed the bill as too expensive and inflationary.

The House passed HR 5247 on May 20. The Senate agreed to the House bill after combining in the measure the provisions of scaled-down public works and countercyclical assistance bills reported separately by two committees. Final action on the legislation was delayed for several months by conference disputes over a water pollution fund redistribution amendment added on the Senate floor. The Senate adopted the final conference report on Dec. 17, in the final days of the 1975 session, but House leaders postponed action until Congress reconvened in 1976.

First 1976 Veto Sustained

Those 1975 deliberations set the stage for crucial 1976 veto battles between President Ford and Congress over the stimulative public works/countercyclical aid package. The president won the first fight, but Congress was successful the second time around.

The House Jan. 29 set up the initial confrontation by adopting the conference report on HR 5247, despite Ford's veto threats. The House margin was 53 votes more than the two-thirds majority that would be required to override the expected veto.

Ford vetoed HR 5247 on Feb. 13, calling the measure "little more than an election year pork barrel." Instead of the 600,000 jobs that Democrats contended the public works program would create, Ford argued that HR 5247 would produce at most 250,000 jobs whose costs per job would be "intolerably high, probably in excess of $25,000." The president also criticized the countercyclical aid program, contending that it favored governments that imposed high taxes without distinguishing between jurisdictions that used the funds efficiently and those that followed wasteful practices. Ford supported instead a Republican-backed alternative to channel $780 million to local governments through the community development block grant mechanism created by 1974 housing legislation.

The House Feb. 19 voted 319-98 to override the veto — 41 votes more than the required two-thirds majority. Fifty-six House Republicans voted to override the president; their defection was attributed to the pressure of upcoming 1976 congressional elections.

Less than three hours later, however, the Senate sustained the veto in a 63-5 roll call that fell three votes short of the required two-thirds. With fewer senators up for re-election, Republicans held firm behind the veto, some citing economic improvement and declining unemployment in switching to back the president after voting to pass the measure in 1975.

Resurrected Measure

The Senate resurrected the vetoed bill in April, paring the total authorizations down somewhat to a maximum of $5.2 billion. After behind-the-scenes negotiations attempting to broaden Democratic support for the concept, the Senate again wrote a revised countercyclical aid program into the public works legislation. Sponsors of S 3201 warned that the countercyclical package would risk another veto, but the Senate passed the rebuilt bill by a 54-28 vote.

The House was eager to follow suit although Government Operations Committee opposition to countercyclical aid posed a potential obstacle. Speaker Carl Albert, D-Okla., therefore avoided referral to the Government Operations panel, while the Public Works and Transportation Committee drew up new public works project legislation (HR 12972). That bill authorized $2.5 billion for public works projects along the lines of the vetoed measure. The House passed HR 12972 without change on May 13. In a tactic that assured the Senate's countercyclical provisions would be considered in conference, the House then wrote the provisions of HR 12972 into S 3201.

The conference agreement basically settled on the House public works program, the Senate's countercyclical aid program and a scaled-down water pollution control proposal. The Senate approved the conference agreement June 16 by a 70-25 vote, the largest Senate margin the stimulative package had received. The House gave its approval by an overwhelming 328-83 vote on June 23.

Ford vetoed the $3.95 billion package on July 6, arguing that "bad policy is bad whether the inflation price tag is $4 billion or $6 billion." The president estimated that S 3201 would create 160,000 jobs at most, compared to congressional projections of 300,000 to 350,000 jobs.

But this time Congress was prepared to shrug off the president's opposition. The Senate assured the outcome July 21, voting to override the veto in a 73-24 roll call.

The House confirmed the override with 39 votes to spare in a 310-96 vote on July 22.

Action on the Bill in 1977-80

Congress in 1977 extended and expanded the program. But determined congressional resistance scuttled President Carter's request for a five-year extension as part of his economic stimulus program. The countercyclical aid was attached to legislation (HR 3477 — PL 95-30) enacting remnants of Carter's tax stimulus plans. However, Congress let the grants lapse in 1978 and again in 1980 refused to revive the program.

Provisions

As finally enacted into law over the president's veto, PL 94-369:

Public Works

● Authorized $2 billion through Sept. 30, 1977, for three types of grants for public works projects on which on-site labor could begin within 90 days of project approval: 1) direct grants providing full federal funding for state and local public works projects or the completion of plans for such projects, 2) grants to bring the federal share of financing up to 100 percent for projects already authorized by federal law that had not begun because of lack of required state and local matching funds and 3) grants to cover either the state or local share of projects authorized under state or local law.

● Required the secretary of commerce, in awarding grants, to give priority to local government projects.

● Required the secretary to consider the duration and extent of unemployment in a particular area, as well as the potential contribution of a public works project to the reduction of unemployment, when awarding grants; stipulated that a grant application would be approved automatically unless rejected by the secretary within 60 days of receipt.

● When the national unemployment rate for the three previous months was at least 6.5 percent, reserved 70 percent of available appropriations for grants to state and local governments with unemployment rates higher than the national level and 30 percent of available funds for grants to state and local governments with unemployment rates below the national level and above 6.5 percent.

● Barred use of grant funds for acquisition of real estate, project maintenance or projects affecting natural waterways or canals.

● Guaranteed each state 0.5 percent of all available appropriations; limited a single state's share of available funds to 12.5 percent.

● Allowed the secretary to make grants for projects that would benefit or provide employment for residents of communities suffering high unemployment that were located within cities experiencing little unemployment as a whole.

● Stipulated that all laborers and mechanics hired for projects assisted by the act should be paid at the wage prevailing for work on similar construction in the area under the terms of the Davis-Bacon Act.

● Barred job discrimination on the basis of sex on projects funded under the bill.

State and Local Government Grants

● Authorized the Treasury secretary to make grants for five calendar quarters (beginning July 1, 1976) to help state and local governments maintain services, avert layoffs of public service employees and avoid tax increases.

● For each quarter, authorized payments totaling $125 million plus $62.5 million for each 0.5 percent by which the national unemployment rate for the quarter ending three months earlier exceeded 6 percent; authorized no funds if the national unemployment rate did not exceed 6 percent during the quarter that ended three months earlier or the last month of that quarter.

● Limited the aggregate authorization for the five calendar quarters beginning July 1, 1976, to $1.25 billion.

● Reserved one-third of available funds for grants to state governments and two-thirds for grants to local governments.

● Barred grants to any state or local government unless its own average unemployment rate for the quarter ending three months earlier was at least 4.5 percent and its rate during the last month of that quarter exceeded 4.5 percent.

● Based the amount of a grant to a state on a formula comparing its fiscal 1976 general revenue sharing funds and its "excess" unemployment rate (the difference between its existing rate and a 4.5 percent rate) to similar data for all states.

● Based the amount of a grant to a local government on an identical formula.

● Required the secretary to set aside one lump sum for grants to local governments within states for which verified unemployment data was not available; allowed the states to allocate these funds under a plan submitted to the secretary.

● Allowed state and local governments to use the grants to maintain customary basic services; barred use of funds for construction or acquisition of materials used unless needed to maintain services.

● Required governments to submit statements providing assurances that funds would be used to maintain public employment levels and basic services; required governments to comply with federal labor standards and anti-discrimination requirements in the use of funds.

● Required governments to notify the secretary of any increase or decrease in their taxes, reductions in public employment levels or cuts in services.

● Required the General Accounting Office to investigate the impact of the grants on state and local government operations and the national economy.

Water Pollution Control

● Authorized $700 million in fiscal 1977 in additional funding for the construciton of publicly owned wastewater treatment plants; allocated the funds to states that had received inadequate allotments under an old formula used to distribute water pollution control funds released in 1975.

1977

The nation's economy continued on an uncertain course in 1977. As in 1976, the economy grew rapidly in the first half of the year but slowed in the second, and 1977 ended as it began — with calls for new economic stimulus to maintain the recovery from the 1974-75 recession.

President Carter was widely criticized for his handling of economic issues in 1977. Critics faulted the administration for failing to weigh individual programs within the framework of an overall economic policy. They said Carter's failure to pursue consistent policies had created a damaging crisis of confidence in the business community.

By year's end Carter had committed himself to development of a comprehensive economic program. And he postponed his long-awaited tax package until 1978 so that it could reflect the impact of pending Social Security and energy legislation, as well as the need for stimulus tax cuts.

Meanwhile, skepticism grew about Carter's pledge to balance the budget by fiscal 1981, and administration officials started hedging. There had been doubts right along that the president could redeem all his promises for welfare reform, health insurance, aid to the cities and other costly programs without increasing expenditures faster than revenues would rise.

In addition, the pace of economic growth fell behind the administration's expectations and independent analysts doubted that the economy would expand vigorously enough to provide the revenues needed to balance the budget, even if spending could be held down. Tax cuts to stimulate the economy would put a balanced budget even further beyond reach, it was contended.

Administration officials qualified the budget-balancing pledge. They specified that the administration intended to balance the budget in a high-employment economy. That is, if economic growth and employment fell below targets, budget deficits would continue.

The economy spurted dramatically during the first quarter of 1977. The real gross national product, adjusted for seasonable variations and inflation, increased at a 7.5 percent annual rate, up from 1.2 percent in the last quarter of 1976. The GNP tapered off later in the year, though not so sharply as in 1976.

Consumer spending, which made up roughly two-thirds of the GNP, continued to climb steadily. Business investment in plants and equipment posted smaller gains than some observers felt was necessary. Inflation as measured by the GNP price deflator increased at a 7.1 percent annual rate in the second quarter but abated later in the year.

Consumer prices rose faster than in 1976, when the increase in the Consumer Price Index was 4.8 percent. The average worker's take-home pay increased faster than prices through most of 1977, maintaining moderate gains in purchasing power.

Although the growth rate during the first three quarters stayed above the 4 percent level economists believed was necessary to prevent unemployment from rising, the unemployment rate hovered around 7 percent during most of 1977, after dropping from 7.8 percent in December 1976.

Business confidence in the economy was a matter of concern during 1977. There were complaints that inflation was eroding true profits and that uncertainties about taxes and government policies made business commitments too risky. Industries produced at a relatively low 82 to 83 percent of plant capacity during much of the year, according to the Federal Reserve Board.

Bucking some other business trends, the housing industry recorded its best year since 1973. New housing starts increased from 1.5 million units in 1976 to about 2 million units, despite the fact that the median new home price exceeded $49,000, according to the National Association of Home Builders.

Uncertainty over government policies, concern about rising interest rates and recession fears were blamed for sharp declines in the stock market. Administration officials remained moderately optimistic about the economic outlook and said the gloom on Wall Street was exaggerated.

Tax Stimulus

Congress began its first session of the 96th Congress with prompt action on President Carter's request for tax cuts to stimulate the economy. By May 16 Congress had sent the new president a three-year, $34.2 billion tax reduction package (HR 3477 — PL 95-30) providing three-fourths of its benefits to individual taxpayers.

Carter's economic stimulus plan, unveiled in a Jan. 31 message to Congress, was based on four tax components. Those elements were: a one-time $50 rebate on 1976 taxes for each taxpayer and dependent; a $50 payment to every recipient of Social Security, Supplemental Security Income or federal railroad retirement benefits; a permanent change in the standard deduction; and a reduction in corporate income taxes.

The House and the Senate molded the measure into a traditional Democratic device to fight unemployment by pumping up consumer demand. But five days before the Senate took up the bill, Carter withdrew his plan for one-shot $50 individual tax rebates that had formed the heart of the administration's stimulus program.

Carter claimed that the $50 rebates, along with proposed $50 payments to recipients of Social Security and other federal benefits, no longer were needed as economic recovery took hold. The president's rebate plan had faced stiff Senate resistence from Democrats who preferred stepped-up government spending and Republicans who pressed permanent tax cuts.

To attack unemployment, estimated at 7 percent in April, the bill established an innovative tax credit for employers who hired new workers. It also extended through calendar 1978 the temporary recession-fighting tax reductions that Congress had enacted in 1975 (PL 94-12). And to simplify tax preparation — while providing additional tax cuts — the measure set flat dollar amounts for individual and joint standard deductions that resulted in lowered federal tax withholdings. *(1975 tax law, p. 165)*

Other provisions delayed for one year the effective date of several 1976 tax law changes. After considerable debate in the Senate, the bill also carried amendments to extend countercyclical assistance to state and local governments. Congress created the aid program in 1976 as a recession-fighting measure. *(1976 tax law, p. 169); countercyclical aid, p. 175)*

By extending 1975 business tax rate cuts, the bill reduced federal revenues $1 billion in fiscal 1978 and $1.3 billion in fiscal 1979. The new job-creating credit, targeted at small- and medium-sized firms, was estimated to cost the Treasury $689 million in fiscal 1977, $2.5 billion in fiscal 1978 and $1.9 billion in fiscal 1979. All told, the estimated tax cuts amounted to $2.2 billion in fiscal 1977, $17.7 billion in fiscal 1978, and $13.8 billion in fiscal 1979.

Provisions

As signed into law May 23, major provisions of HR 3477:

Individual Taxes

● Set the standard deduction at $2,200 for single persons and at $3,200 for joint returns effective with the 1977 tax year. Under existing law the standard deduction had ranged from $1,700 to $2,400 for individuals and from $2,100 to $2,800 for joint returns.

● Adjusted the tax table and rates to reflect the change, with new withholding rates to take effect June 1, 1977.

● Extended through 1978 the general tax credit of $35 per person or 2 percent of the first $9,000 of taxable income, whichever was larger.

● Made the $35 per capita tax credit available for the extra age and blindness exemptions.

● Limited married persons filing separately to the $35 credit.

● Extended through 1978 the earned income credit of 10 percent of the first $4,000 of earned income. The credit was phased out as income rose to $8,000 from $4,000 and was available only to families with children.

Business Taxes

● Extended through 1978 corporate tax reductions first enacted in 1975 that set the corporate tax rate at 20 percent on the first $25,000 of taxable income, 22 percent on the second $25,000 and 48 percent on the excess of $50,000.

● Provided a tax credit to employers in 1977 and 1978 of $2,100 (50 percent of the first $4,200 of wages) for each new worker. To be eligible, an employer's total wage base would have to increase by 2 percent from the previous year to account for "normal" growth. The employer's deductions for wages would be reduced by the amount of the credit claimed, and no employer could claim more than $100,000 per year in credits. Employers hiring handicapped persons could receive an additional 10 percent credit.

Social Security Financing

To cover rising benefits, Congress in 1977 raised Social Security payroll taxes by $227 billion over a 10-year period. The Social Security measure (HR 9346 — PL 95-216) imposed the largest peacetime tax increase in the nation's history.

After considering some innovative financing schemes, Congress in the end relied exclusively on traditional payroll taxes to replenish dwindling balances in the Social Security retirement and disability trust funds. Because benefits increased as inflation rose, the Social Security system since 1975 had paid out more to recipients than it collected from payroll taxes paid by workers and employers.

Cleared by Congress on Dec. 15, the measure set new schedules that steadily increased both the Social Security tax rate and the amount of each worker's wages on which the levy was imposed. That meant all covered workers would pay higher Social Security taxes beginning in 1979. The bill more than tripled the maximum taxes that middle- and upper-income workers and their employers would pay by 1987. In 1977, with Social Security taxes set at 5.85 percent on earnings up to $16,500, the maximum contribution by a worker and employer was $965 each. By 1987, with the tax rising to 7.15 percent on income up to $47,100 under the bill's provisions, each could pay more than $3,000 a year into the Social Security system.

President Carter, aware of probable economic side effects from rising payroll taxes, quickly pledged to design income tax cuts to offset the drain on workers' purchasing power. The administration in May had outlined a Social Security rescue plan coupling less severe payroll tax boosts with temporary infusions of general Treasury revenues. But proposals for fundamental changes in the program made little headway during House and Senate debate on HR 9346.

The House voted overwhelmingly against requiring Social Security coverage of government workers and summarily dismissed proposals to finance Medicare from Treasury revenues, freeing substantial hospital insurance taxes for Social Security benefits. An administration proposal requiring a higher taxable wage base for employers than for employees only narrowly survived in the Senate, and conferees later discarded it.

The final bill did include administration-backed procedures for correcting a defective inflation adjustment formula, which had threatened to drive benefits sharply upward over the next several decades. But Congress also decided to ease the "earnings test," allowing elderly persons to earn more without losing a portion of their benefits, and liberalize the treatment of divorced and widowed beneficiaries. The administration had criticized all of those changes as costly.

Provisions

As signed into law by President Carter Dec. 20, major provisions of PL 95-216:

Short-Term Funding

● Raised the Social Security wage base for employers and employees above levels provided automatically under existing law in each of the years 1979 to 1982. Under the new schedule, the base would increase from the 1978 level of $17,700 to $22,900 in 1979, and in stages to $31,800 in 1982; after that, to keep pace with inflation, automatic adjustments would occur annually, to a projected base of $47,100 by 1987.

● Raised payroll tax rates, starting in 1979. Coupled with increases already scheduled under existing law, Social Security tax rates would climb from the 1978 level of 6.05 percent each for employees and employers to 6.13 percent in 1979, 6.65 percent in 1981, 6.70 percent in 1982, 7.05 percent in 1985, 7.15 percent in 1986, and 7.65 percent in 1990.

● Set the Social Security tax rate paid by self-employed individuals at 1.5 times the employee rate, beginning in 1981.

● Shifted revenues from the retirement and survivors programs to the Disability Insurance trust fund, beginning in 1978.

Inflation Adjustment

● Adopted "decoupling" procedures to correct a flaw in the existing benefit formula that overadjusted for inflation. The new techniques, which changed only the starting benefit levels of future retirees, guaranteed the average worker initial benefits equal to 43 percent of pre-retirement wages.

Earnings Test

● Eased restrictions on outside earnings by Social Security recipients over age 65, setting new limits of $4,000 in

1978, $4,500 in 1979, $5,000 in 1980, $5,500 in 1981 and $6,000 in 1982. (Over those amounts, individuals would continue to lose 50 cents in benefits for each dollar earned.)

● Required subsequent yearly increases in the limits to reflect general wage trends.

● Dropped the test entirely, beginning in 1982, for Social Security recipients aged 70 and 71. Existing law already exempted persons aged 72 and over.

Marital Status

● Guaranteed pre-existing levels of benefits to persons over age 60 who marry or remarry, effective January 1979; permitted reapplications after that date by persons whose dependents' benefits were cut off because of changes in marital status.

● Permitted persons to qualify for Social Security benefits based on their spouses' earnings after 10, rather than 20, years of marriage.

● Reduced Social Security benefits to a dependent spouse by the amount of any federal, state or local civil service pension received by the spouse; established a five-year transition period, to protect women who retired early from government service, or had been planning to, in expectation of collecting spouses' benefits under Social Security according to the old rules.

Other Benefit Adjustments

● Froze the initial level of the "minimum benefit," currently claimed by persons with minimal coverage under Social Security, at the 1978 level of $121 a month; made adjustments for inflation each year for individuals actually drawing the benefit.

● Raised the "special minimum" benefit, available to persons with lengthy covered work experience at low wage levels, to allow as much as $230 a month for an individual and $345 a month for a couple, beginning in January 1979; provided for cost-of-living adjustments.

● Increased a bonus added to the entitlements of workers who delay their retirement beyond age 65, from the level of 1 percent to 3 percent per year; assured the same benefit bonus to widows or widowers of workers who postpone their retirement.

1978

The state of the economy in 1978 gave Carter reasons both for good cheer and for concern. It had recovered doggedly from the worst recession since the 1930s — in the process outstripping the recovery of the other industrialized Western nations. But that performance was clouded by several persistent problems. Despite the strong recovery, unemployment stayed at high levels. Business confidence seemed as yet not fully restored, with the result that new investment was at discouragingly low levels. That gave rise to concerns that the economy would be unable to continue the strong expansion. Inflation appeared to be stuck at a level of 6 percent or higher. Finally, there were indications that the economic recovery was about to run out of steam, even though joblessness was still far above levels traditionally acceptable to Democratic administrations.

Trying to balance the various competing forces represented by his presidency, Carter proposed a budget that he proudly asserted was "lean and tight" but still "compassionate" enough to meet the social needs of the nation. It included a call for a substantial tax cut, which Carter said was necessary to continue the economic recovery and help reduce unemployment.

The promised tax cut and other social program proposals seemed to be in keeping with the traditional Democratic philosophy. The tax cut was consistent with the approach of past Democratic administrations in aiming more relief at lower income groups while at the same time proposing tax reforms which would close loopholes that benefit the well-to-do.

The budget also included an ambitious proposal to reform the welfare system. Later, under pressure from urban groups, Carter sent Congress a new package designed to help the nation's deteriorating cities to rebuild. He also said he would work to develop other prized liberal programs — including national health insurance.

While some Democrats continued to doubt Carter's liberal credentials, developments through 1978 appeared to suggest that a conservative trend was even stronger than the president had believed. One of the first indications came from California, where voters June 6 overwhelmingly approved Proposition 13, a state constitutional amendment sharply limiting property taxes. While the meaning of the vote was subject to debate, it appeared to reflect a fairly widespread belief that government spending had grown too rapidly — at least given the results that government was achieving.

The "taxpayer's revolt," as it was dubbed, had a distinctly middle class flavor as it was expressed in Congress. A surprisingly large number of lawmakers denounced Carter's tax proposals on the grounds that they failed to recognize that the time had come to help the middle class, rather than lower income people. The result was that Carter's tax proposal was significantly skewed — most notably by a large cut in capital gains taxes — so that it did relatively more for the well-to-do than any tax bill in recent memory.

In the meantime, the welfare reform proposals floundered, the urban policy was picked apart, and national health insurance was postponed. Growing increasingly concerned about inflation as unemployment dipped and the rise in prices appeared to accelerate — and as an election drew near — Congress chipped away at the budget and scaled back the size of the tax cut.

As the year went on, the economy performed in ways not entirely anticipated. Most surprisingly, employment rose much more than expected. That, combined with a new surge of inflation, served to shift the attention of economic policy makers away from the feared downturn and back to inflation.

Other forces prodded the administration to take steps to curb inflation. The dollar remained under pressure on international money markets, in part because of the nation's relatively high inflation rate as well as costly oil imports, lagging overseas economies and the competitive edge that European and Japanese companies had achieved over aging American industries.

In April, Carter strengthened his commitment to fight inflation by promising federal fiscal restraint and renewing a request that business and labor hold price and wage increases below the rate for the two previous years. Pres-

sured by other Western nations, and by domestic political realities as well, Carter Oct. 24 adopted a sterner stance by calling for voluntary wage and price guidelines, proposing "real wage insurance" tax rebates for workers and promising to hold the fiscal 1980 deficit to $30 billion.

Despite the administration's changing emphasis, the Consumer Price Index shot up 9 percent during the year and producer price increases foreshadowed further inflation. Real GNP growth ebbed to 4.8 percent, leaving unemployment near 6 percent. By the end of 1978 warnings were sounded that continued fiscal and monetary restraints could tip the economy into a recession in 1979.

1978 Tax Cut

Congress in 1978 cut federal taxes $18.7 billion for the following year. One of the last measures approved by the 95th Congress, the tax cut bill (HR 13511 — PL 95-600) reduced individual income taxes to offset part — but not all — of the 1977 Social Security tax increases. The measure also included substantial reductions in the tax on capital gains paid mainly by middle- and upper-income people. The legislation cut corporate taxes, especially for smaller businesses, and expanded investment tax credits to encourage purchase of new plants and equipment.

In its final form, HR 13511 cut taxes by $18.7 billion in calendar 1979, with further reductions in following years that would reach $34.1 billion a year by 1983. In summary, major components of the measure included:

● Individual income tax cuts accomplished by adjusting tax brackets, increasing the personal exemption to $1,000 from $750, and expanding the earned income credit for low-income taxpayers.

● Business tax reductions through revised corporate income tax schedules setting reduced rates for businesses with $100,000 or less in income. Other measures included a permanent 10 percent investment tax credit, with more lenient rules for its use, and a revamped "targeted jobs credit" for wages paid to hire certain disadvantaged persons.

● Capital gains tax reductions, granted by increasing the amount of capital gains that could be excluded from ordinary taxes to 60 percent from the existing 50 percent limit. A separate provision gave homeowners over age 55 a one-time exclusion from taxes for up to $100,000 in capital gains from the sale of personal residences that had gone up in value.

● A host of other tax law changes dealing with diverse arrangements such as retirement plans, profit sharing, industrial development bonds, small business corporations and the tax problems of various businesses and individuals. The measure also carried provisions stepping up federal payments to state and territorial welfare programs.

Shift in Policy

In drafting HR 13511, the House and Senate sharply turned away from the tax-law philosophy that recent Democratic Congresses had followed. Earlier tax cuts had directed most benefits to low-income taxpayers and had generally curtailed special treatment for the kinds of income — such as capital gains from the sale of assets whose value had risen — most often earned by the wealthy.

President Carter's Democratic administration offered a traditional tax cut package in January, but the final measure bore little resemblance to that proposal. It skewed tax reduction benefits much more toward higher-income brackets than Carter had recommended. And despite repeated presidential veto threats, Republicans and conservatives wrote into the bill capital gains tax cuts for about 4.3 million investors in an effort to spur new investment in productive enterprises.

Furthermore, Congress scrapped almost all of Carter's proposed reforms, including his celebrated 1976 campaign pledge to crack down on business's tax breaks for "three-martini lunches." Indeed, lawmakers, riding the crest of a middle-class "taxpayers' revolt," wound up reversing some 1976 tax reforms that congressional liberals prized highly.

Although Congress concentrated on spreading tax cut relief among Americans at all income levels, both the House and the Senate turned down a Republican plan — authored by Rep. Jack F. Kemp, R-N.Y., and Sen. William V. Roth Jr., R-Del., — to cut federal taxes by 30 percent across-the-board over three years. While strong doubts about the Kemp-Roth plan remained, congressional action on the 1978 tax cuts suggested growing support for easing the federal income tax burden on American families and business. Congress cleared HR 13511 Oct. 15 and Carter signed the bill without comment Nov. 6.

Even with the 1978 reductions, most Americans paid more taxes in 1979 because previously approved Social Security payroll tax increases were deducted from their paychecks. At the same time, rampant price and wage inflation pushed many into higher brackets, forcing them to pay stiffer taxes even though their actual buying power was stagnant. With Treasury Secretary W. Michael Blumenthal working actively with House and Senate conferees to hold tax revenue losses within administration budget objectives, lawmakers found themselves too constrained by budget concerns to make tax cuts deep enough to completely cancel the built-in overall increases.

Provisions

As signed into law, the Revenue Act of 1978 (HR 13511 — PL 95-600) included the following tax provisions (all were effective Jan. 1, 1979, unless otherwise noted):

Individual Taxes

Rates and Brackets. Increased the zero bracket amount — the level of income not subject to income tax — to $2,300 from $2,200 for single persons; to $3,400 from $3,200 for married people filing joint returns; and to $1,700 from $1,600 for married people filing separate returns.

● Reduced the number of tax brackets and widened the remaining ones to slow the rate at which inflation-induced salary increases pushed taxpayers into higher brackets. Rates were reduced in some brackets. For single people, the 25 brackets were replaced with 16 wider ones, ranging from the 14 percent bracket with taxable income between $2,300 and $3,400, to the 70 percent bracket with taxable income above $108,300. For married people, the 15 new brackets ranged from 14 percent on taxable income between $3,400 and $5,500 to 70 percent on taxable income above $215,400.

● Increased the personal exemption to $1,000 from $750, in place of the expiring general tax credit.

Earned Income Credit. Made the earned income credit permanent, and expanded it to 10 percent of the first $5,000 of income (maximum of $500), to be phased out at a

12.5 percent rate as income rose to between $6,000 and $10,000 (previously, the credit was equal to 10 percent of income up to $4,000 and it phased out at a 10 percent rate between $4,000 and $8,000).

● Enabled employees to elect to receive the credit in their paychecks each pay period, instead of when they filed annual tax returns. Employers would reduce their income tax withholding and Social Security tax liabilities by the amount of advance payments made to their employees. Effective July 1, 1979.

Itemized Deductions and Credits. Repealed the itemized deductions for state and local taxes for motor fuels not used in business or investment activities.

● Repealed the itemized deduction for political contributions, and increased the maximum political contributions credit to $50 for single returns and $100 for joint returns (the credit equaled 50 percent of contributions up to those maximum levels).

● Provided that payments to grandparents for the care of their grandchildren qualified for the child care tax credit.

Unemployment Compensation. Provided that unemployment compensation benefits be taxable to the extent they equaled one-half the amount by which a taxpayer's adjusted gross income exceeded $20,000 for single people and $25,000 for married people.

Other Individual Tax Provisions. Established or clarified rules for taxing employees' deferred compensation, profit-sharing plans and "cafeteria" plans giving workers a choice among a package of employer-provided fringe benefits.

● Permitted firms offering no retirement plans for workers to make tax deductible contributions to individual retirement accounts (IRAs) set up by employees.

● Changed rules governing pension, profit-sharing, stock-bonus and annuity plans for various groups and organizations.

● Extended existing tax exemptions for military health services scholarships, for canceled student loans for persons who took work in certain areas (for instance, a nurse who agreed to work in a rural area), and for amounts that employers paid workers for education.

Future Spending, Tax Cuts. Stated, but did not require, that the growth in federal spending should not exceed 1 percent per year, adjusted for inflation, between fiscal year 1979 and fiscal year 1983; that federal outlays as a percentage of gross national product (GNP) should decline to below 21 percent in fiscal 1980, 20.5 percent in fiscal 1981, 20 percent in fiscal 1982 and 19.5 percent in fiscal 1983; and that the federal budget should be balanced in fiscal years 1982 and 1983.

● Stated that if those conditions were met, the tax-writing committees would intend to report legislation providing "significant" tax reductions for individuals to the extent they were justified in light of prevailing and expected economic conditions.

Business Taxes

Corporate Tax Rates. Reduced the top federal corporate income tax rate to 46 percent from 48 percent and established a five-tier graduated rate schedule in place of the reduced rates imposed by existing law on income below $50,000. The graduated schedule, designed to benefit small business corporations, taxed earnings as follows:

Taxable Income	Previous Rate (percent)	New Rate (percent)
0 to $25,000	20	17
$25,000 to $50,000	22	20
$50,000 to $75,000	48	30
$75,000 to $100,000	48	40
Over $100,000	48	46

Investment Tax Credits. Made permanent the 10 percent investment tax credit.

● Increased to 90 percent from 50 percent the amount of regular tax liability the credit could offset, to be phased in at 10 additional percentage points per year beginning with taxable years that ended in 1979.

● Allowed the credit for the full investment, rather than one-half the investment, for pollution control facilities where five-year amortization was elected — provided the facility was not financed with tax-exempt industrial development bonds. Effective for facilities constructed or acquired after Dec. 31, 1978.

● Made the investment credit available for rehabilitating 20-year-old commercial buildings; building poultry, egg, livestock or plant production structures; and for investments by cooperatives.

Targeted Jobs Credit. Replaced the expiring general jobs tax credit with a "targeted jobs credit" for 1979-81.

● Set the credit at 50 percent of wages up to $6,000 in the first year of employment and 25 percent in the second year.

● Made the credit available to employers for wages paid to hire welfare recipients, Supplemental Security Income (SSI) recipients, handicapped people undergoing vocational rehabilitation, Vietnam veterans under age 35, released convicts, disadvantaged individuals age 18-25 and certain students age 16-18.

Other Business Changes. Disallowed business deductions for any entertainment facility, including dues to social, athletic or sporting clubs other than country clubs.

● Extended to all activities except real estate the "specific at risk rule," whereby taxpayers were prevented from sheltering income from taxes by claiming tax deductions for losses larger than their actual economic investment.

● Increased to $10 million from $5 million the amount of "small issue" industrial development bonds that could be issued tax exempt for acquisition, construction or improvement of land or depreciable property over six years for projects costing no more than that.

● Made various changes in tax laws dealing with small business partnerships, farms, regulated gas and electric utilities, railroad car rentals and industrial development bonds.

General Tax Changes

Capital Gains Tax. Increased to 60 percent from 50 percent the amount of individual capital gains that could be excluded from ordinary taxation. Effective Nov. 1, 1978.

● Repealed the alternative tax for capital gains, whereby taxpayers could elect to pay a tax of 25 percent on the first $50,000 of gains if their rate would otherwise be higher. Effective Nov. 1, 1978.

● Reduced to 28 percent from 30 percent the tax rate that corporations could elect to pay on capital gains if that rate was less than their regular tax rate.

● Provided that taxpayers 55 years or older could completely exclude from taxation up to $100,000 in gain from the sale of a personal residence once. Effective July 26, 1978.

● Allowed individuals to "roll over" capital gains from home sales (reinvest them in new homes without paying capital gains taxes) more often then the once every 18 months allowed by previous law, if they were required to relocate for work purposes.

Minimum Tax. Removed capital gains and excess itemized deductions (deductions other than medical and casualty loss deductions that exceeded 60 percent of adjusted gross income) from the list of items subject to the minimum tax of 15 percent on the sum of tax preferences in excess of $10,000.

● Established a new alternative minimum tax, payable only if it exceeded the sum of a taxpayer's regular tax and his minimum tax, levied on taxable income, plus excluded capital gains and excess itemized deductions. After a $20,000 exemption, the tax would equal:

Tax Base Levels	Percent
$0 to $40,000	10
$40,000 to $80,000	20
Over $80,000	25

● Removed capital gains from the list of preference items that reduced, dollar-for-dollar, the amount of personal service income subject to the 50 percent maximum rate on "earned" income.

Other Tax Provisions. Delayed until 1980 the effective date of provisions of a 1976 law (PL 94-455) establishing that heirs must pay capital gains taxes on the entire gain on inherited property they sold, rather than just the gain that occurred during their ownership. The "carryover basis" provision, originally due to take effect in 1977, thus applied to estates of decedents dying after Dec. 31, 1979.

● Authorized creation of general stock ownership corporations, exempt from corporate taxes, chartered by state governments with stock owned by state residents. The provision was designed to enable Alaska residents to acquire ownership interests in that state's natural resources.

● Nullified an Internal Revenue Service ruling requiring restaurant operators to report employee tips added to checks by charge-account customers.

● Ended the "widows tax" on farms and other businesses by assuming that a surviving spouse who jointly owned a business with a person who died had acquired an interest in the business for estate tax purposes at a rate of 2 percent for every year they held the business together.

● Reduced to 2 percent from 4 percent the excise tax on private foundations' net investment income, effective Oct. 1, 1977.

● Phased out the federal tax on slot machines by June 30, 1980.

● Provided special tax treatment for a variety of interests, made technical corrections in the Tax Reform Act of 1976, and made other minor tax law changes.

Full Employment

Working against the clock, a diverse group of senators produced a last-minute version of the Humphrey-Hawkins full employment bill (HR 50) that was able to gain final congressional approval.

The Senate passed the compromise version of the bill Oct. 13, 1978, by a 70-19 vote. The House agreed to the compromise without a conference Oct. 15, the last day of the session.

The eleventh-hour efforts rescued from what had seemed certain defeat organized labor's only remaining hope for a major legislative victory in 1978. Passage was also a victory for the Carter administration, which had worked hard in the dwindling days of the 95th Congress to move the bill to the Senate floor.

Still, the final outcome was a bittersweet victory for the bill's labor and civil rights supporters who were forced to accept a measure that, to a considerable extent, was dictated by some of their most vocal legislative opponents — especially Sen. Orrin G. Hatch, R-Utah. By the end, some wags were calling HR 50 the Humphrey-Hawkins-Hatch bill.

As cleared HR 50 bore only a faint resemblance to the massive federal jobs and economic planning bill introduced by Sen. Hubert H. Humphrey, D-Minn., and Rep. Augustus F. Hawkins, D-Calif., during the depths of the mid-1970s recession.

The bill that President Carter signed Oct. 27 (PL 95-523) was stripped of its original provisions calling for government "last resort" jobs for the unemployed, although it still retained the central goal of reduction of the unemployment rate to 4 percent by 1983.

In addition, the final version contained a new national goal by calling for a reduction of the inflation rate to 3 percent by 1983 and 0 percent by 1988.

Unemployment during 1978 hovered around 6 percent, while inflation as measured by the Consumer Price Index edged toward double-digit levels.

Although the bill was diluted at each step of the legislative process, it retained a strong emotional impact with black and labor groups, who lobbied intensively for it as a symbol of concern for the jobless. Democratic leaders worked to preserve the bill as a major element of the party program for the November elections. Another factor in support was the desire to create an enduring legislative monument to Sen. Humphrey, who had died in January 1978.

Coretta Scott King, a leader of the Full Employment Action Council, conceded that "we did not get all of the provisions in the bill that we would have liked. But there is no question that this is a major victory and an important first step in the struggle for full employment. Those who call it symbolic just don't understand how important it is."

Organized labor took a somewhat less sanguine view of the final bill. "It does represent a small symbolic step forward," said Kenneth Young of the AFL-CIO, "but the Senate weakened it severely."

Background

The Humphrey-Hawkins bill traced its origins to the 1946 Employment Act (PL 79-304), which established a national policy of providing "useful employment opportunities" for all persons "able, willing and seeking work."

But the 1946 act provided no mechanism by which the federal government could guarantee such opportunities and so the full employment goal remained little more than a paper promise.

The most recent legislative effort to translate that promise into a government-backed reality began June 20, 1974, when Hawkins introduced the first version of the full employment bill. Humphrey first introduced the Senate measure in October 1974.

Both men held extensive hearings on the legislation in 1975. In 1976 the House Education and Labor Committee reported a revised version of HR 50. But the bill made some unexpected enemies among liberal economists who said it was vague, inflationary and generally unworkable. The full House never considered it and the Senate counterpart never emerged from committee.

Although President Carter endorsed HR 50 during his 1976 campaign, it took considerable prodding from black leaders and other Humphrey-Hawkins supporters to win Carter's backing in 1977. Even after the campaign pledge, Carter kept his distance from the controversial bill and his top economic advisers were openly hostile to it.

It was not until November 1977 that the bill's supporters were able to produce a version of the bill that Carter would endorse. The revised version set a five-year target of 4 percent unemployment among workers aged 16 and over (3 percent among workers aged 20 and older) and guaranteed public employment as a last resort if other methods failed.

To win Carter's approval, the proposal left the choice of approaches to unemployment open and gave the president a chance to revise the numerical goals at a later date. Although HR 50 supporters endorsed this latest revision, many observers suggested that it was toothless, little more than a broad statement of national policy reminiscent of the 1946 act that had proved insufficient.

Provisions

As signed into law, HR 50, the Full Employment and Balanced Growth Act of 1978 (PL 95-523):

National Goals and Priorities

● Declared a national policy of promoting full employment, increased real income, balanced growth, a balanced federal budget, growth in productivity, an improved balance of trade and price stability.

● Stated that the purpose of the bill was to better coordinate and integrate federal economic policy through improved management, increased efficiency, attention to long-range problems and a balanced federal budget.

● Stipulated that provisions of the act did not provide authorization for federal controls on wages and prices, production or resource allocation in order to achieve the goals of the act.

● Declared a policy of primary reliance on the private sector, and gave the following order of priority for job creation: regular private sector jobs, private sector jobs with federal assistance, conventional public sector jobs and a last-resort government employment reservoir.

● Encouraged adoption of fiscal policies that would reduce federal spending as a percentage of the gross national product to the lowest possible level consistent with national needs.

● Required the president to include in his annual economic report to Congress numerical goals for the current year (short-term goals) and each of the three succeeding years (medium-term goals) for unemployment, production, real income, productivity and prices.

● Required the president to set the medium-term goals so as to achieve reduction of the unemployment rate to 3 percent among persons aged 20 and over, and 4 percent for persons aged 16 and over, within five years.

● Required further that the medium-term goals be directed toward achieving a 3 percent inflation rate within five years, provided that steps taken to reduce inflation not impede achievement of the unemployment goal. Further required that, after the 3 percent goal had been achieved, succeeding economic reports contain the goal of achieving 0 percent inflation by 1988.

● Allowed the president, beginning with the second economic report after enactment, to propose modifications in the timetables for achieving the unemployment and inflation goals.

● Recommended that the president consider, along with other policies for achieving the goals, development of an agricultural policy aimed at providing full parity for farm prices.

●Required the annual budget of the president to reflect the goals set forth in the economic report.

● Required the Federal Reserve Board to report twice a year on its monetary policies and their relationship to the goals of the act, with the second report each year to include predictions for economic conditions in the next calendar year.

● Required the president to undertake policies to reduce the rate of inflation, including price monitoring, alleviation of product shortages, establishment of commodity stockpiles, increased productivity, increased private sector competition, removal of unnecessary government restrictions and increased exports.

Structural Economic Policies

● Required the president to propose such structural economic policies as he deemed appropriate to achieve the goals of the act, including consideration of countercyclical employment policies, coordination with state and local governments, assistance to economically depressed regions, youth employment policies and efforts to achieve a high rate of capital formation.

● Permitted the president to establish reservoirs of public employment, if he found that other policies were failing to achieve the full employment goals.

● Required that any reservoir jobs be useful and in the lower ranges of skill and pay, be targeted on individuals and areas with the worst unemployment problems and be set up so as not to draw workers from the private sector.

Congressional Review

● Established procedures for congressional review of goals and policies in the economic report and Federal Reserve Board reports.

● Directed the Joint Economic Committee to report to the Senate and House Budget committees by March 15 annually on the short-term and medium-term goals and policies in the economic report, after holding hearings and receiving reports from other committees on their views.

● Gave the congressional Budget committees the option of including in the first congressional budget resolution for the fiscal year recommended economic goals the resolution was designed to achieve.

● Gave Congress the option, if the president declared that the unemployment goals could not be met within five years, of including in the first budget resolution for the fiscal year a congressional determination of when the full employment goal could be reached.

General Provisions

● Prohibited discrimination on account of sex, race, age, religion or national origin in any program under the bill.

● Provided that workers in reservoir jobs established under the act be given equal pay for equal work, but not less than the federal minimum wage; stipulated that none of the jobs be of the type covered by the Davis-Bacon Act's provisions requiring payment of locally prevailing wages on federal construction projects.

New York City Aid

Congress in 1978 approved up to $1.65 billion in long-term loan guarantees to continue federal aid to financially troubled New York City. By authorizing 15-year Treasury guarantees for bonds sold by the city government, Congress agreed to city officials' pleas to extend and enlarge the financial backing that the federal government began in 1975 to keep the city government solvent. *(1975 aid law, p. 168)*

The new law (HR 12426 — PL 95-339) shifted New York City assistance into a long-term program to allow the city government to raise needed capital, regain fiscal health and thus restore investor confidence to the point where the city could borrow on public credit markets. As in 1975, many members of Congress were reluctant to set a precedent by "bailing out" New York City. Both supporters and critics maintained that the new program was the last time that the federal government would come to the city's aid. The conditions Congress wrote into the bill were intended to discourage other cities from seeking similar assistance through what opponents considered an unfortunate federal involvement in local affairs.

Nonetheless, congressional approval demonstrated belief that New York City was making significant strides in putting its fiscal house in order. It acknowledged that short-term loans were inadequate to see the city government through — and that making long-term guarantees was preferable to risking the bankruptcy of the nation's largest city. The Carter administration March 2 endorsed extension of aid beyond the June 30 expiration date.

By most accounts the city made substantial improvements in its finances after the 1975 crisis. The city pared its work force by 60,000 employees, negotiated a wage freeze, eliminated its operating deficit and converted $4 billion in short-term notes into long-term bonds. Other measures increased mass transit fares, imposed tuition for the first time at city colleges and set up a management information and expense control system. Treasury Secretary W. Michael Blumenthal told the Senate Banking Committee in 1977 testimony that the city had repaid each federal seasonal loan with interest on time or ahead of schedule.

Still, a city plan to sell more than $200 million in six-month notes collapsed in November 1977 after Moody's Investors Service gave its lowest rating to the issue. Officials projected large revenue shortfalls in fiscal 1979 through 1982. Taking office in January 1978, newly elected Democratic Mayor Edward I. Koch announced what he called a "candid and realistic" four-year plan of job reductions and management improvements. Under the plan, a $283 million gap left after those cost-cutting measures would be filled by continued seasonal loans from the federal government, plus new federal and state loan guarantees.

In its final form, HR 12426:

● Authorized the secretary of the Treasury to issue federal loan guarantees totaling up to $1.65 billion for as long as 15 years on New York City bonds.

● Limited the amount that could be guaranteed during fiscal year 1979 to $750 million. Of that total, guarantees up to $500 million could be extended to long-term city bonds (maturing in one year or more), and guarantees up to $325 million could be extended to seasonal loans (maturing in one year or less) to the city.

● Limited loan guarantees during fiscal year 1980 to $250 million, plus any unused or repaid amount from the sum authorized for fiscal year 1979. Only long-term bonds could be guaranteed during the year.

● Limited loan guarantees during fiscal year 1981 to $325 million, plus any unused or repaid amount from the sum authorized for fiscal years 1979 and 1980. Only long-term bonds could qualify.

● Limited loan guarantees during fiscal year 1982 to $325 million, plus any unused or repaid amount from the sum authorized for fiscal years 1979, 1980 and 1981. Only long-term bonds could qualify.

● Restricted federal loan guarantees only to bonds purchased and held by city and state pension funds.

● Provided that either the House or the Senate could veto proposed guarantees during fiscal 1980 and 1981.

● Terminated the secretary's authority to issue guarantees on June 30, 1982.

1979

"The year in which recession refused to arrive" was how one administration economist characterized 1979. Others fretted that the year had seemed bent upon confounding the predictions and plans of economic policy makers.

The final year of the decade was to have been the year that the economy cooled to no-growth, boosting the jobless rolls and easing consumer demand. Instead Americans continued spending at impressive rates, fueling the economy and holding down the unemployment rate.

It was to have been the year that President Carter brought inflation under control, through restrained federal spending and a successful wage-price program. Instead energy prices doubled and home mortgage interest rates skyrocketed — helping to push the inflation rate into the double-digit range for 12 straight months.

And it was to have been the year that the dollar improved on foreign currency markets after the Federal Reserve cracked down on credit. Instead international uncertainty kept the dollar low.

Carter began the year by sending Congress a "lean and austere" fiscal 1980 budget that he said would help bring inflation under control and slow the growth of government. In that annual budget, Carter proposed sharp cuts in such popular programs as housing and jobs, arguing that "the policy of restraint . . . is an imperative if we are to overcome the threat of accelerating inflation." By year's end, however, Congress had rejected a number of administration measures for trimming the costs of programs such as Medicare-Medicaid or veterans' health care.

In addition, Carter's wage-price guidelines fizzled as it became clear that he would not impose sanctions against violators of the pay standards.

The final evidence that the administration's anti-inflation program had failed arrived in January 1980: The rate of inflation was 13.3 percent for 1979, the Labor Department reported — the highest rate since President Truman lifted wage-price controls after World War II. A year earlier, Carter had predicted consumer prices would rise 7.4 percent.

The administration blamed the painfully high rate of inflation mostly on external factors — such as international crises and the doubling of energy costs. It also argued that Americans seemed to have accepted inflation as a fact of economic life, which led them to buy ahead to beat further price hikes.

But critics maintained that Carter's economic policy had not been tough enough. Some opponents even suggested that he should have imposed mandatory controls. Still others noted that while Carter talked a hard line against inflation, he often supported price-raising actions by the government, such as restrictions on imports.

Economists had begun — and ended — the year predicting a recession. But they qualified their year-end forecasts by noting that the economy had proved stronger than anticipated and perhaps would resist a downturn again. At midyear signals had pointed towards a recession. The GNP declined during the second quarter at a 2.3 percent annual rate. While unemployment remained relatively stable, economists predicted that it would rise.

During the third and fourth quarters, however, Americans dipped into their savings and sharply increased consumer debt. That allowed them to continue spending at high levels, despite a decline in after-tax personal income, adjusted for inflation. That surprising strength in spending helped the GNP blossom into a 3.1 percent rate of growth in the third quarter. In the fourth quarter, it increased again, by 2.1 percent — bringing the growth for the year to 2.3 percent.

Chrysler Aid

Congress in late 1979 approved $1.5 billion in federal loan guarantees for the financially ailing Chrysler Corporation. That pledge was part of a $3.5 billion package that staved off bankruptcy, at least temporarily, for the nation's third largest auto maker.

Congress cleared the measure (HR 5860 — PL 96-185) Dec. 21 just before recessing for Christmas, spurred by market reports that Chrysler otherwise would run out of cash in January 1980. The House and Senate agreed on the aid package during three days of marathon sessions that worked out the amount of wage concessions that the plan demanded from Chrysler employees.

As enacted, HR 5860 authorized $1.5 billion in federal loan guarantees only if Chrysler officials agreed to:

● Win $462.5 million in wage concessions from the company's unionized workers plus a $125 million wage concession from non-union management workers.

● Obtain $500 million in new credit from U.S. banks, $125 million in new loans from foreign banks and other creditors, $250 million in aid from state and local governments, and $180 million in aid or credit from dealers and suppliers.

• Sell off $350 million of company assets or other equity.

• Develop an energy-saving plan.

• Issue $162.5 million of new common stock to its employees.

• Make another $100 million of new common stock available for sale to its employees. Any worker purchase of such stock would count against the required wage concessions.

Despite the wage concessions, the auto union employees still would receive $600 million in raises over the three-year period. The legislation made it necessary for the union to renegotiate its recently concluded three-year contract with Chrysler, which contained a $203 million concession, to accommodate the new requirement. Union members ratified the contract changes in early 1980.

Administration of the guarantees was assigned to a three-person board composed of the secretary of the Treasury, the comptroller general and the Federal Reserve chairman. The secretaries of labor and transportation were to sit on the panel as non-voting members.

Under the legislation, the board could begin providing government backing for loans to the company once it had "adequate assurance" of commitments by all parties under the private financing plan.

The Chrysler "bail-out," like previous federal financial aid to Lockheed Aircraft Corp. and New York City, grew into a major controversy over the federal government's role in propping up financially troubled enterprises. But by the time Congress began rushing the loan guarantee plan through, most members were convinced that the government had to try to save the nation's 10th largest corporation with its $4.1 billion payroll.

Plagued by plummeting car sales — and heavy retooling costs to begin production of small, fuel-efficient models — Chrysler lost $721.5 million in the first nine months of 1979, then the largest loss in U.S. corporate history. The company first sought federal aid in August, asking for a $1 billion Treasury advance against future U.S. tax credits. The Carter administration rejected Chrysler's initial proposals. But as Chrysler reported a record third-quarter loss of $460 million, the White House Nov. 1 agreed to sponsor aid legislation.

The administration plan was contingent upon Chrysler's ability to raise a matching $1.5 billion by selling assets and winning pledges of aid from creditors, workers and localities. The administration had hoped to have those commitments in hand when it recommended its bill, an aide said, but finally decided to proceed without them because the company's situation was deteriorating so rapidly.

1980

The nightmare of "stagflation" — spiraling prices accompanied by a stagnant economy and severe unemployment — came true in 1980 as the long-awaited recession failed to wring inflation from the economy.

The state of the economy spelled disaster for dozens of politicians — including President Carter — who were turned out of office by voters demanding relief from an inflation rate that neared 20 percent in the first quarter and averaged 13.5 percent for the year. Indeed, if 1980 proved nothing else, it showed that getting control of the economy was a more difficult task than many politicians imagined. Outside forces, such as rising oil prices, put upward pressure on the inflation rate — pressure that could not be relieved by domestic policy.

By year's end, advisers for Republican President-elect Ronald Reagan were warning that it might take more time than originally anticipated to put his economic plan into effect. They indicated that his goal of balancing the federal budget might be postponed to permit an increase in military spending and phased-in tax cuts.

The year had begun as 1979 had ended — with economists predicting a recession that would put millions of Americans out of work but ease consumer demand, thus reducing inflation. Their forecast of an economic downturn was confirmed: A sharp "V" shaped recession began in January and reached its low point in early summer.

The GNP plummeted at an annual rate of 9.9 percent in the second quarter and began its upward climb in the next, rising at a 5 percent rate in the final quarter of the year. Unemployment increased from 6.2 percent in January to 7.6 percent in May, ending the year at 7.4 percent.

But economists were wrong about the stickiness of the inflation rate, as measured by the Consumer Price Index (CPI). It reached a peak annual rate of 18.2 percent during the first three months of the year, then fell off sharply as a result of the recession. The relief was only temporary, however: December figures showed the CPI had increased 12.4 percent during the year.

The continuing upward spiral in prices prompted the Federal Reserve to continue its squeeze on the money supply, thereby sending interest rates to record highs. In December, the prime rate — the interest rate banks offer their best corporate customers — reached 22.5 percent, and economists were predicting the steep cost of credit could trigger a second economic downturn.

Hardest hit by the financial ups and downs were the automobile and housing industries. Domestic car sales ended the year down 24 percent from 1979, with all manufacturers reporting major losses. And with mortgage rates hitting almost 17 percent in April and ending the year at nearly 15 percent, new housing construction plummeted.

Experts said a second downturn would be even more devastating than the first because firms which had barely weathered the 1980 recession would enter the 1981 slump in weakened condition.

Much of the burden of fighting inflation was left to the Federal Reserve in 1980 as Congress and the administration wavered on fiscal policy. Late in 1979, the Fed announced it was adopting a new, more efficient way of regulating the money supply, a change it said would help bring inflation under control. It reaffirmed that policy in 1980 and also instituted controls on credit as part of the administration's March 14 anti-inflation package.

That squeeze on borrowing — accomplished primarily through restraints on consumer credit — quickly sent the economy into a tailspin. And little more than two months after the controls were put into effect, the Fed began dismantling them. All controls were lifted July 3.

The Fed's actions had short-term positive effects. Consumer prices held steady in July and the economy began recovering that same month. But by year's end, the money supply — and the cost of living — resumed their upward climb.

The Fed again clamped down on the money supply, an action that threatened to abort the recovery from the recession. But officials of the central bank maintained they had no choice if inflation was to be checked.

President Carter's wage-price policy fizzled in 1980, as the advisory committee he established to recommend voluntary limits on wage increases urged its own disbandment.

In March, Carter accepted the recommendation of the Pay Advisory Committee that wages be permitted to rise a maximum of 9.5 percent. And as part of his anti-inflation program, he announced he would ask Congress for authority to double the staff of the Council on Wage and Price Stability (COWPS) to better monitor pay and price increases around the country.

Congress denied that request, however, voting to fund the agency in fiscal 1981 and the 1980 level. And after a General Accounting Office study found that the guidelines had little discernible effect in slowing inflation, COWPS decided against issuing a third year of new pay and price standards. That action came as Reagan pledged to eliminate the agency when he took office.

Bank Deregulation

Congress in 1980 restructured the nation's financial industry, removing most federal regulatory distinctions between commercial banks and savings and loan associations. The broad bank deregulation measure also extended Federal Reserve Board power over the bank deposits that made up a large part of the nation's money supply. Treasury Secretary G. William Miller called the new law (HR 4986 — PL 96-221) "the most important legislation dealing with banking and finance in nearly half a century."

When it cleared HR 4986, Congress had been weighing proposals to revamp the U.S. banking system for nearly a decade. In 1971 President Nixon's Commission on Financial Structure and Regulation recommended abolishing interest rate ceilings, expanding bank and thrift institution powers, offering direct housing investment incentives, and reorganizing the bank regulatory functions shared by the Federal Reserve Board, the comptroller of the Currency and the Federal Home Loan Bank Board. The Senate in 1975 passed legislation embodying some key proposals, but the House never acted on the measure.

In the meantime, the federal bank regulatory agencies began edging away from the prohibition, in effect since 1933, against interest-bearing checking accounts. From 1972 to 1978, the agencies authorized several innovative services that allowed financial institutions to pay interest on what amounted to checking deposits. But in 1978, a court ruling forced Congress specifically to authorize those services — and paved the way for the far-reaching changes.

The court decision coincided with the completion of work by a Carter administration task force assessing "Regulation Q" interest rate limits. After reviewing the task force's work, President Carter May 22 urged Congress to enact "comprehensive financial reform legislation." Carter specifically proposed allowing all federally insured institutions to offer interest-paying checking accounts, letting deposit interest rates rise to market levels, allowing federally chartered savings institutions to make variable rate mortgage loans, and giving federally chartered savings institutions authority to invest up to 10 percent of their assets in consumer loans.

Major Provisions

The new law's major innovations set the stage for broad changes in the nation's banking industry. Both commercial banks and thrift institutions — savings and loan associations, mutual savings banks and credit unions — played key economic roles as financial intermediaries that attracted savings from businesses and individuals and lent that money to finance business and consumer activities.

Previously, banks provided most financing for business ventures and consumer purchases, while savings and loan associations specialized in home mortgage financing. However, the new law offered customers of financial institutions wider choices for earning larger returns on their savings — and gave financial institutions more flexibility to compete for funds and adjust loan portfolios to inflation and wide interest-rate fluctuations. Since the mid-1960s, inability to make those adjustments occasionally had disrupted the flow of funds to housing, small business and other industries that depended on banks and thrift institutions for financing.

To ease those problems, HR 4986 permitted financial institutions to diversify the services they offered to attract deposits. The measure also set in motion a gradual lifting of the interest rate ceilings that prevented financial institutions from paying the going market rate on savings deposits. Finally, the measure dismantled federal regulations that had locked banks and thrift institutions into limited loan portfolios and kept them from competing effectively with high-yielding investment opportunities such as money market funds.

Major changes made by HR 4986:

● Ordered a six-year phase-out of federal Regulation Q interest rate ceilings that limited savings account interest to 5.25 percent at banks and 5.5 percent at savings and loan associations. When completed, the phase-out was scheduled to end the .25 percent interest rate advantage that Regulation Q limits gave to savings institutions.

● Authorized all federally insured financial institutions — savings and loans as well as banks — to offer interest-paying negotiable-order-of-withdrawal (NOW) accounts. The law also permanently authorized other services, previously approved by regulatory agencies, that paid interest on what amounted to checking accounts. Those provisions ended a 1933 ban on paying interest on checking accounts while permitting thrift institutions to offer checking as well as savings services.

● Allowed savings and loan associations to offer consumer loans, checking accounts, credit cards and trust services previously reserved for commercial banks. The measure left unchanged existing law that gave banks exclusive power to make corporate loans and hold corporate checking accounts.

The other major component of HR 4986 was an effort to tighten the Federal Reserve Board's control over monetary policy. The measure set uniform reserve requirements for all depository institutions whether or not they belonged to the Federal Reserve System. That step was taken to stem what Federal Reserve Chairman Paul A. Volcker termed an "avalanche" of banks defecting from the system to escape Federal Reserve requirements that members maintain non-interest-bearing reserves against the deposits they held.

Other provisions of HR 4986 changed federal truth-in-lending laws, overrode state usury laws on certain loans and raised the maximum federal deposit insurance to $100,000.

President Carter signed the measure on March 31, beating a deadline that Congress had set in 1979 when it approved a 90-day extension of popular checking-type services that a federal court had ruled illegal. HR 4986 provided permanent authority for financial institutions to offer those services, thus reversing the court decision that bank regulatory agencies had no power to permit them.

Windfall Profits Tax

Congress in 1980 responded to public unhappiness with recurring energy shortages, rising energy prices and reports of record profits for the major oil companies by passing legislation (HR 3919 — PL 96-223) that imposed a tax on the windfall profits of the domestic oil industry. Intended to produce more than $227 billion in revenue for the federal government over the decade of the 1980s, the tax was the largest ever levied on a single U.S. industry.

The tax was the crucial element in President Carter's energy plan, a necessary counterpoint to his decision to lift the federal price controls that had held down the price of domestic oil during the 1970s while the price of foreign oil skyrocketed. The purpose of the windfall tax was to recapture for general use some of the profits the oil companies were expected to receive as a result of price decontrol. The new tax was not levied on all income from domestic oil production, but only that portion attributable to the difference between a certain base price for each barrel of domestic oil and the actual sale price of that oil.

The idea of a windfall profits tax coupled with an end to price controls did not originate with Carter. President Ford had proposed such a move in 1975, but Congress chose to retain price controls and gave scant attention to the tax proposal.

In 1979, Carter's move to decontrol domestic oil prices drew little more than rhetorical opposition in Congress. As world oil prices soared and, along with them, the profits of domestic oil producers, even the oil industry and other staunch opponents of the windfall tax realized they were fighting a losing battle. Recognizing that Congress would enact some sort of tax, the industry and other opponents of such a measure concentrated their efforts on weakening it.

The final version of the tax differed in three major respects from that proposed by Carter. The president had proposed a permanent tax, which, in the view of the industry, was the most onerous aspect of his plan. Congress decided to phase out the tax over a 33-month period. The earliest the tax would end was the beginning of October 1990; the latest would be the beginning of October 1993. When the phase-out would begin depended on how long it took the tax to generate the agreed-upon total of $227.3 billion. (Future Congresses, however, could vote to extend the life of the oil tax.)

Carter proposed that revenue from the tax be channeled into a special energy security trust fund. From there it would be allocated for aid to low-income families hit with high fuel bills, for development of synthetic fuels, and for mass transportation. Congress, however, decided to allow the additional revenue to go directly into the general revenue fund. From there Congress could allocate the money as it wished. Congress did make some suggestions in PL 96-223 about how the money from the tax might be used, but

without future legislation, those suggestions carried little weight.

The third difference between Carter's proposal and the final version of the tax measure was the tax rate. Carter had proposed a flat tax rate of 50 percent. Congress decided to vary the rate, depending upon the type of production and the time at which the well began producing.

Final congressional action on HR 3919 came in March, after moves to send it back to conference were defeated in both houses. Despite the difficulty of the bill's passage through the legislative process, the House finally agreed to the conference report by a wide margin of 302-107 and the Senate gave its final approval by a 66-31 vote.

Provisions

As finally signed into law, the Crude Oil Windfall Profits Tax Act established a new federal tax to be imposed solely upon the income from domestically produced oil. In addition to its windfall tax provisions, the law provided various incentives for individuals and businesses to cut back on their use of oil and natural gas and set up a program to aid poor families with rising energy bills.

The Tax

The law provided for a new tax to be imposed upon a portion of the income that oil producers received from the sale of domestic oil. The tax would be imposed upon the portion of that income that could be attributed to the difference between a base price and the actual selling price for each barrel.

The tax was imposed at a different rate — and the base price varied — depending upon the type of oil, the date upon which the well from which it came was first tapped, the method of its production and its producer. The tax rate varied from 30 percent to 70 percent and the base ranged between $12.81 and $16.55. (The base price was to be adjusted each year for inflation.)

The tax applied to income from all oil produced from wells after 1 a.m. on March 1, 1980.

In addition, PL 96-223:

● Limited the tax to a maximum of 90 percent of the net income from a property.

● Defined the tax as a deductible business expense for income tax purposes.

● Provided that the windfall profit subject to the tax could be reduced by the amount of state severance taxes on the windfall profit. Specified that if a state increased its severance tax after March 31, 1979, the deduction would still be allowed only if the state increase applied equally to the entire price of the barrel and only if the state severance tax did not exceed 15 percent.

● Provided a 33-month gradual phase-out of the tax that would begin in January 1988, if $227.3 billion in revenues had been raised by the tax. Specified that if that revenue target were not reached, the phase-out was to begin one month after the Treasury secretary estimated that $227.3 billion had been raised. Provided that even if the $227.3 billion had not been raised by Jan. 1, 1991, the phase-out was to start on that date.

Spending Guidelines

PL 96-223 set out some general standards for the use of revenues from the windfall profits tax, including provisions that:

● For accounting purposes only, allocated revenues from the windfall profits tax to a separate account of the Treasury. Allocated net revenues under the price assumption as follows: 25 percent for aid to low-income families; 60 percent for income tax reductions; and 15 percent for energy and transportation programs.

● Allocated revenues in excess of $227 billion one-third to the poor and two-thirds for income tax reductions.

● Specified that the energy tax incentives provided in the windfall tax legislation and any synthetic fuels programs were to be funded by general revenues. (The actual distribution of revenues from the tax was dependent on future legislation.)

Other Tax Provisions

PL 96-223 also made some changes in the general income tax law. They included provisions that:

● Repealed the provision of existing law, scheduled to take effect after Dec. 31, 1979, that would have required persons who inherited property to pay capital gains tax on the difference between the original purchase price and the price when it was sold by the heir. The repeal left in effect existing law that required payment of capital gains tax only on the difference between the value of the property when it was inherited and when it was sold.

● Increased to $200 from $100 (to $400 from $200 for married couples) the existing exclusion from taxable income of dividends, and broadened the exclusion to include interest earned from domestic sources. Eligible interest included that from a bank, savings and loan or other thrift institution, certain types of corporate debt, government, and a share in a trust established and maintained by a corporation. Thus, qualifying obligations included interest-bearing bank deposits, certificates or notes of deposit, commercial paper, bills, notes and bonds.

● Authorized a tax break for companies that involuntarily liquidated inventories in response to a government regulation or request.

● Tightened the method for taxing the inventory of a liquidating corporation.

Social Security Earnings

Congress Oct. 2, 1980, completed action on a bill (HR 5295 — PL 96-473) changing the Social Security earnings test to rectify a problem resulting from the 1977 Social Security legislation. Before enactment of the 1977 law, two earnings tests were used to determine Social Security benefit size and eligibility. One was an annual test, the other monthly. The 1977 law eliminated the monthly test except for the first year of retirement. *(1977 law, p. 178)*

HR 5295 reinstated eligibility for benefits to several classes of individuals who were inadvertently disqualified by elimination of the monthly earnings test. Beneficiaries of the change included surviving children who left the benefits program in midyear and teachers who worked only part of a year before they fully retired.

Reconciliation Tax Bill

Congress in 1980 changed federal tax laws to boost fiscal 1981 revenues by $3.6 billion. The House and Senate wrote those changes into a budget reconciliation bill (HR

7765 — PL 96-499) to meet fiscal objectives Congress set for itself through its fiscal 1981 budget resolution. *(1980 reconciliation bill, p. 130)*

In the process, congressional tax-writing committees resolved several tough tax-code issues that they had been previously weighing. Signed into law on Dec. 5, the omnibus spending-cut/revenue-raising measure thus carried provisions to phase out tax-exempt mortgage subsidy bonds, impose capital gains taxes on foreign real estate investments and speed up corporate income tax payments.

The measure also raised non-beverage alcohol duties, extended telephone excise taxes and revised treatment of employer-paid payroll taxes. One disputed provision, which actually lost fiscal 1981 revenues, eased the impact of the newly enacted oil windfall profits tax on landowners who received oil-well royalties.

Mortgage Bonds

Ending a months-long House-Senate stalemate, lawmakers included in HR 7765 provisions phasing out by Dec. 31, 1983, use of tax-free bonds to subsidize home mortgages.

The bonds were a home financing tool that Congress sanctioned in 1968 when it enacted the Revenue and Expenditure Control Act (PL 90-364). That law permitted state and local governments to subsidize home mortgages by selling low-yield bonds that were attractive to investors because they were exempt from federal taxes. Government agencies then loaned the money to home buyers at below-market interest rates.

In 1979 the Ways and Means Committee drafted legislation (HR 5741 — H Rept 96-678) to curb rising revenue losses resulting from expanded use of the housing bonds. The panel, unable to settle on a single answer to the problem, offered the House a choice between phasing out the bonds or replacing them immediately with tax incentives for savings accounts providing funds for mortgage lending. The House March 26 adopted an amendment that continued the tax exemption for two years but in the meantime limited bond use to aiding low-income homebuyers. The House then passed the revised measure, 238-178.

The Senate, generally more responsive to requests from the housing industry to hold off action on mortgage bonds, June 27 adopted an appropriations bill rider saying the rules governing issuance of the bonds should not be changed before Jan. 1, 1981.

The Senate took no further action on the issue, but the Ways and Means Committee subsequently included the provisions of HR 5741 in the House version of the reconciliation bill, thus picking up $400 million in savings.

The compromise that ultimately was fashioned phased out the subsidy in three years rather than two as the House had proposed. It deleted all income limitations the House had imposed in order to qualify for a subsidized mortgage and softened some other restrictions in the House bill. But it nonetheless saved an estimated $256 million in revenues in fiscal 1981, while providing some temporary relief for the housing industry and some certainty to governments and the bond market.

Foreign Realty Taxes

Following up on legislation (HR 2297) that the Senate Finance Committee had drafted in 1979, Congress added provisions that were expected to bring in $42 million in fiscal 1981 by taxing capital gains that foreigners earned by selling real estate in the United States. Under previous law, most foreigners paid no capital gains taxes on profits realized on U.S. real property.

The tax would be imposed at a minimum rate of 20 percent of property gains. Generally the rates would follow the U.S. graduated capital gains rates allowing full use of deductions for any connected losses. Conferees dropped provisions in the original measure requiring persons who bought real estate from foreigners to withhold part of the purchase price to cover U.S. capital gains taxes. Instead, they opted to try to enforce the tax by requiring foreign owners to report real estate holdings and transactions to the Treasury Department.

Corporate Tax Payments

The reconciliation bill altered the rules under which corporations paid their estimated taxes so that any company whose taxable income exceeded $100 million in any of the three preceding years would be required to pay an estimated tax of at least 60 percent of its current year's tax liability, regardless of its prior year's liability.

Under previous rules, corporations were required to pay 80 percent of their estimated annual tax liability in quarterly payments. And they were exempt from any penalty for underpayment for the current year as long as their estimated taxes equaled 100 percent of their prior year's tax liability.

The alteration, which did not actually change tax law, speeded up payments to bring in an additional $3.06 billion in revenues in fiscal 1981.

Windfall Profits Credit

The controversial windfall profits tax change granted a credit or refund to roughly two million royalty owners who owned land on which an oil well had been drilled. While usually not actively involved in drilling and producing oil, landowners received a share of profits from production in the form of royalty payments. *(Windfall tax, p. 188)*

The provision, written into HR 7765 by the Senate, allowed royalty owners a tax credit or refund of up to $1,000 against the windfall profits tax imposed on oil production. The credit could be used by individuals, estates and family farm corporations.

Revenue Sharing Extended

In an end-of-session burst of parliamentary maneuvering, Congress in 1980 approved a three-year reauthorization of general revenue sharing, the no-strings federal grant program for state and local governments.

The Senate completed action on the bill (HR 7112 — PL 96-604) Dec. 12 when it accepted a take-it-or-leave-it package put together by the House Dec. 10.

As cleared, the bill provided a mandatory entitlement of $4.6 billion annually for local governments for the next three fiscal years (1981-83). It barred state participation in the program in fiscal 1981, but authorized $2.3 billion annually for the states in fiscal 1982-83, subject to congressional approval of the necessary appropriations for the program.

The final version of the bill included a number of amendments the Senate had adopted before it had passed

the bill Dec. 9. It also included a House provision forcing states, in fiscal 1982-83, to give up one dollar of categorical grants — grants designated for specific purposes — for each dollar of revenue sharing funds they accepted.

Background

The general revenue sharing program originally was enacted in 1972 as part of Republican President Richard M. Nixon's "new federalism." Congress in 1976 extended the program through fiscal 1980. Although that extension expired Sept. 30, 1980, the first grants to the states and localities under the new revenue sharing bill were not due until January 1981. *(1972 law, p. 161; 1976 extension, p. 175)*

While revenue sharing was exceedingly popular among constituents, many members of Congress, especially some influential House members, contended that the states and some local governments were in better financial shape than the federal government and should not continue to receive these huge no-strings grants.

On Jan. 3, 1980, the Carter administration announced it would support a reauthorization of general revenue sharing for both state and local governments at the existing overall funding level of $6.9 billion annually. But three months later, as part of the effort to balance the budget, the White House dropped the states from its proposal. Instead it asked Congress to provide $500 million in transitional funds for local governments — which in many cases received sizable amounts from the states' share of revenue sharing — in fiscal 1981 and 1982.

In acting on its fiscal 1981 budget resolutions for the federal government, Congress made no allowance for state revenue sharing. Nor did it provide for the $500 million in transitional funds requested by the president.

Major Provisions

As enacted, the revenue sharing bill:

• Extended the general revenue sharing program for three years, fiscal 1981-83.

• Provided a mandatory entitlement of $4.6 billion annually for local governments in fiscal 1981-83; authorized discretionary appropriations of $2.3 billion annually in fiscal 1982-83 for state governments.

• Required states to choose between categorical grant money designated for specific purposes or the "no-strings" revenue sharing money, if appropriated by Congress. If a state chose revenue sharing funds, it would have to decline or refund categorical grants in an amount equal to its revenue sharing payment.

• Redistributed excess funds, created because general revenue sharing payments to local governments could not exceed 50 percent of their adjusted taxes plus governmental transfers, to local governments not affected by the limitation, rather than to the states as under previous law.

• Wiped out $28 million in debts states had owed the federal government dating back to 1836.

• Directed the Census Bureau to adjust census figures to include a reasonable estimate of the number of resident persons not counted in the 1980 census or its revisions.

• Modified certain audit requirements so that if a state had entered into an agreement with the federal government to conduct audits on behalf of a local government, the local government would still be considered in compliance with the revenue sharing requirements and eligible to receive funds.

1981

Barely six months after he took office, President Reagan was assured of enactment of the principal elements of his economic recovery program — a 33-month across-the-board reduction in individual income tax rates and a massive reconciliation package that pared an estimated $35.1 billion from the federal budget in fiscal year 1982.

Reagan officials consistently painted tax legislation as a far more difficult concept to sell than their budget cuts. But one member of the House Democratic leadership said, "Too much was made earlier this year of the notion that conventional political wisdom was reversed and that you could now sell budget cuts more easily than tax cuts."

What the administration offered his House colleagues — and Americans — was an offer too good to refuse, the member said. The White House urged people to "step forward and do something patriotic for your country; help the economy, and you can have a tax cut, too."

Reagan also was helped by events beyond his control, such as a slowing of the inflation rate because of the oil glut and because food price increases had moderated. Polls showed earlier in 1981 that Americans who opposed a tax cut did so because they thought it would add to inflation.

Internal problems among House Democrats also enhanced the effect of Reagan's lobbying machinery. Liberal Democrats and moderate Republicans from the Northeast disliked the oil tax provisions and other sections that the House Ways and Means Committee accepted in the bidding war to win tax bill votes.

Rep. Dan Glickman, D-Kan., cited a newspaper editorial that said the Republican position was stronger because the GOP tax bill was connected to a larger concept, while the Democrats had no similar goal. "We offered a mishmash," he said.

One sign of Reagan's power was the number of members who voted for the tax bill against their own convictions. Glickman, however, cited a prominent House Republican who wondered aloud after the key tax vote, "Do you think it will work?"

That question had even more meaning later in 1981. President Reagan's September call for even more cuts in federal spending was greeted with little enthusiasm on Capitol Hill. Congress had not completed action on the second, binding budget resolution, nor had it completed work on most of the fiscal 1982 appropriations bills. Those it had approved exceeded Reagan's spending goals.

By November the administration acknowledged that the economy had slipped into a recession. And Reagan admitted that the budget might not be balanced by 1984 — as he had promised throughout his campaign. He also announced that he would defer any requests for major economic policy changes until 1983.

Economic Recovery Tax Act

The tax bill Reagan signed into law Aug. 13, 1981, reflected a wide range of concessions made to ensure enactment of his revolutionary tax cut policies. But none of the many changes and add-ons to the legislation did damage to the heart of the Reagan supply-side plan — across-the-board reductions in individual income taxes and faster write-offs for capital investment to spur productivity.

The form of the package changed substantially. Reagan had originally wanted a "clean" bill with other popular tax plans saved for a second tax measure later in the year. But, bowing to the realities of politics, the president reshaped the package several times, giving in on some details but standing firm on the central theme. By doing so, Reagan forced Democrats, intent on passing their own alternative tax plan, to move closer and closer to the administration position.

"This is President Reagan's economic tax recovery plan," Treasury Secretary Donald T. Regan told reporters Aug. 1 after a conference agreement was reached on the two versions of the bill (HR 4242) passed by the House and Senate earlier in the week.

Regan boasted that the administration received "95 percent" of what it had sought. Democrats, still hurting from their recent legislative loss, were more than happy to agree and shift all responsibility for the economic consequences to the president.

The Economic Recovery Tax Act of 1981 would put an estimated $749 billion — more money than the federal government was expected to spend in fiscal 1982 — back in the hands of business and individual taxpayers over the next five years. Opponents feared the plan would aggravate inflation and lead to uncontrollable budget deficits.

The Senate gave its final approval to the measure Aug. 3 by a vote of 67-8. The House cleared the package the following day on a 282-95 vote.

Background

Reagan's tax legislation originated with a bill that until mid-1981 was given little serious chance of passage. The measure, introduced simultaneously in 1977 by Sen. William V. Roth Jr., R-Del., and Rep. Jack F. Kemp, R-N.Y., called for a three-year average income tax cut of approximately 33 percent, future indexing of taxes to offset the effects of inflation and reductions in business taxes.

Interestingly, what became known as the Kemp-Roth plan originally called for rate cuts that targeted more of the relief to those in the lower- and middle-income brackets, not unlike the alternative tax plans Democrats tried so desperately to persuade Reagan and the majority of Congress to accept. Such targeting had been a longstanding tenet of Democratic tax policy.

It was not until the Republican Party and its presidential candidate Ronald Reagan latched onto Kemp-Roth during the 1980 campaign that the proposal was given serious attention.

On the steps of the Capitol June 25, 1980, Senate and House Republicans unanimously pledged their support to a revised version of Kemp-Roth: a one-year, 10 percent, across-the-board tax cut for individuals and a plan to allow business faster write-offs of investment in plant and equipment. The accelerated depreciation plan was one business groups and several members of Congress had been working on since passage of the 1978 tax bill.

Simultaneously, Reagan backed such a tax cut for Jan. 1, 1981, followed by additional 10 percent cuts in individual income taxes in each of the next two years and indexing. But soon after, Reagan began changing, if not his tune, at least the words of his song.

On Feb. 18, 1981, Reagan announced his tax plans to Congress. He called for $53.9 billion in tax cuts in 1982,

White House Lobbying Apparatus...

Reaching deep into members' districts, President Reagan's formidable lobbying apparatus produced his stunning victory on tax legislation and solidified his hold on the nominally Democratic House. Reagan's July 29, 1981, victory was composed of elements familiar from his earlier budget successes, tuned to a crescendo that left many members awed.

"They've been giving us the works," said Rep. Claude Pepper, D-Fla., who said he could recall nothing like the tax lobbying during his 33 years of Senate and House service.

GOP Whip Trent Lott of Mississippi declared with a broad grin, "I've got the best whip organization because Ronald Reagan is in it."

A key element was Reagan's televised appeal two days before the House vote, which prompted many Americans to lobby on the president's behalf. The Capitol switchboard reported double the usual number of calls the day after Reagan's July 27 address. Individual members, such as Dan Glickman, D-Kan., whose office received 1,500 calls, were swamped. Western Union said Mailgrams were running at four times the customary volume. "The bottom line is, the president blew them away," said White House Chief of Staff James A. Baker III.

Business organizations and corporations greatly extended the reach of administration efforts by setting up telephone banks to call members and by urging their members and employees to do the same. Campaign contributors reminded members — gently or forcibly — that they wanted a pro-Reagan vote. An exasperated Speaker Thomas P. O'Neill Jr., D-Mass., told the House that such corporate giants as "Phillip Morris, Paine Webber, Monsanto Chemical, Exxon, McDonnell Douglas ... were so kind to allow the use of their staff to the president of the United States in flooding the switchboards of America."

In Washington, the White House invited dozens of lawmakers to drop by for a chat with the president. Fifteen on-the-fence members were flown to Camp David July 26 for hot dogs, hamburgers and tax talk. Later, 12 of them voted with Reagan. Others who were clearly committed to the president also were favored with White House visits. Newly-elected Rep. Michael Oxley, R-Ohio, in town less than a week, was asked his strategy opinions. "And it was a nice photo opportunity," he said. Rep. Eugene Johnston, R-N.C., also was invited to the Oval Office to talk tactics. Earlier, Johnston said, he had resisted a suggestion that he try to persuade recalcitrant North Carolinians to vote with the president but changed his mind when Lott promised to report his reluctance to the White House.

Reagan also journeyed to the Capitol July 24 to cheer on the House Republican Caucus. In their negotiations, administration officials again displayed their fine-grained appreciation of each House member's personal style and the individual needs of his district. And the White House artfully dispensed such rewards as promises not to end the controversial peanut program and to oppose a windfall profits tax on natural gas. Arm-twisting was left to Reagan supporters in Congress, and the communities of business and campaign contributors.

Dispensing Favors

Most members were touchy about suggestions that they traded their votes for special favors. But a few of them, such as Rep. Bill Goodling, R-Pa., frankly acknowledged that they used the leverage of their votes to bring rewards to their districts. Goodling held off announcing his support for Reagan because, he said, "I don't want them to think I'm a patsy." His strategy paid off. Goodling won administration pledges not to close a military installation in his district and to support $37 million worth of legislation to clean up the Three Mile Island nuclear plant in his district.

---

starting with a 10 percent cut in individual income tax rates July 1, 1981 (six months later than he originally had proposed), and additional 10 percent cuts on July 1 in each of the two succeeding years. Indexing was dropped, but his business depreciation plan remained intact. Reagan promised a second tax bill for such measures as relief from the "marriage penalty" tax.

However, on June 4, 1981, bowing to the pressures of a tight budget and a Congress less than enthusiastic about the original tax cut package, Reagan offered an alternative. He proposed $37.4 billion in tax cuts for 1982, reduced the first rate reduction to 5 percent, delayed it until Oct. 1, 1981, and put in some popular "sweeteners."

Business groups remained cool toward the plan, so before the package was introduced in Congress, the administration added more tax advantages for business. With a close vote on the House floor only a few days away, the administration July 24 proposed its final version. The basic concept remained — across-the-board cuts and investment incentives — but the floodgate on "sweeteners" was opened in an attempt to win a handful of swing House votes.

Compromise Agreement

The final agreement was the product of an all-night session July 31 during which House and Senate conferees

...Produces Impressive Tax Vote Victory

Others reported varying reasons for siding with the president.

● Peanuts were the lifeblood of freshman Democrat Charles Hatcher's Georgia district, but Hatcher "knew we were in trouble the moment I came to Washington." Reagan's farm bill proposed to phase out the restrictive program that prohibited all but a few farmers from growing the lucrative crop. Hatcher buttonholed every administration official he could on the subject. "They are savvy enough to know that I would really appreciate it" if the program were to continue unchanged, he said. "And," Hatcher added, "I'm smart enough to know that they would really appreciate my vote."

Baker confirmed that the Office of Management and Budget had abandoned earlier opposition to the peanut provisions in the pending House reauthorization of farm programs (HR 3603), which preserved the acreage allotment system and boosted peanut price supports. Hatcher, by his own report, was "ecstatic."

● Marge Roukema, R-N.J., intensely disliked both the Reagan and the Democratic tax bills. But "I couldn't vote 'no' on both," she said, so she went with the president.

Instead of inviting her to the White House, the administration arranged telephone calls to her from two personal friends — Vice President George Bush and William E. Brock III, U.S. trade representative. Roukema said she was impressed with the "artful, gracious style" of White House work. The friendships dated from 1978 when Brock, then chairman of the Republican National Committee, and Bush, heading his own political action committee, backed her first, unsuccessful run for a congressional seat.

Roukema perceived Reagan officials as both savvy and "reasonable," citing a personal visit from Budget Director David A. Stockman to work out final budget bill language on guaranteed student loans that would be acceptable to colleges in her district.

There was, however, no relationship between that and her vote on the tax bill, Roukema said.

● Glenn English, D-Okla., once an opponent of the GOP bill, continued to worry about the effects of a tax cut. But Reagan backed estate tax and oil tax sections that were critical to farmers and oil producers in his district, he said.

"It's the first time in years that these people had a chance to get their problems addressed, and it's going to be the last time for maybe 20 years," English remarked. He also received a note from Reagan promising to veto "with pleasure" legislation to impose a windfall profits tax on natural gas. Gas producers were prominent in English's district.

● Glickman said he made no deals but was impressed with the number of calls from back home, from Democrats as well as Republicans, urging him to "give Reagan's economic program a chance — because nothing else has worked."

Glickman himself saw little difference between the two bills. But he believed that the indexing feature of the Republican bill, by keeping federal revenues from growing with inflation in future years, could check excessive spending on defense. And he also felt the Republican victory took Democrats off the hook if Reagan's tax and budget initiatives failed to produce.

"I feel like Martin Luther King Jr. when he said 'Free at last'," Glickman said.

● Rep. Bo Ginn, D-Ga., voted with Reagan because, according to an aide, "The constituents broke our door down. It wasn't very subtle."

Many other members also cited the avalanche of pro-Reagan mail, telegrams and telephone calls, which were not targeted only on Reagan opponents. Lott's home telephone started ringing just after Reagan's July 27 speech: two Marines, a doctor and a rural letter carrier called to make sure he was on board.

---

worked out the differences between the two versions of the tax cut bill passed earlier that week. Major disagreements were few, with the exception of oil-related tax breaks, in large part because both bills had been written with strong White House influence.

The Senate accepted House provisions to give oil royalty owners more generous exemptions from the windfall profits tax and to totally exempt "stripper" wells — those that produce 10 barrels or less of oil a day — from the tax after 1982. The two measures were expected to cost $8.4 billion through fiscal 1986.

House plans to freeze the oil depletion allowance at 22 percent and to allow a tax credit for wood-burning stoves

were dropped, as was a Senate provision to give tax credits for home heating costs. Both measures reduced the windfall profits tax on newly discovered oil from 30 percent to 15 percent by 1986, a $3.2 billion tax break.

The House accepted Senate-passed child-care credits, stricter restrictions on a tax loophole called the commodity tax straddle and increased tax benefits for employee stock ownership plans (ESOPs). The Senate accepted House-passed tax breaks for homes sold but rejected a provision to reduce to six months from one year the holding period for capital gains.

A number of miscellaneous special-interest provisions were dropped from the final bill.

Major Provisions

As signed by President Reagan, the Economic Recovery Tax Act (HR 4242 — PL 97-34) included the following major provisions (all effective Jan. 1, 1982, unless otherwise noted).

Individual Tax Cuts

● Reduced all individual income tax rates by 5 percent Oct. 1, 1981, 10 percent July 1, 1982, and an additional 10 percent July 1, 1983. Each cut would be applied to marginal tax rates, or those rates imposed on the last dollar of income. The changes would be reflected in lower withholding in paychecks beginning Oct. 1.

The overall 1981 cut would be just over 1 percent for the entire year because the 5 percent rate change would only be in effect for the last three months of the year. The cuts would average 10 percent for 1982, 19 percent for 1983 and 23 percent for 1984, when the program would be fully phased in. The final cut was only 23 percent instead of 25 percent because the rate reductions each succeeding year were applied to a smaller base.

● Reduced the top rate on investment, or "unearned," income from 70 percent to 50 percent, the existing maximum for earned income.

● Reduced the maximum rate on capital gains — which are taxed at 40 percent of the investment income rate — from 28 percent to 20 percent, effective June 10, 1981.

● Increased individual income tax brackets, the zero bracket amount and the personal exemption to reflect annual increases in the Consumer Price Index (CPI), beginning with the 1985 tax year. For example, if the CPI increased 10 percent during the preceding year, the lowest tax bracket, currently $3,400 to $5,500, would be changed to $3,740 ($3,400 plus 10 percent) to $6,050 ($5,500 plus 10 percent). The tax rates would remain the same.

● Allowed two-earner married couples filing joint returns in 1982 to deduct 5 percent of up to $30,000 (a maximum deduction of $1,500) of the lesser of their two incomes. The deduction would increase to 10 percent (a maximum of $3,000) in 1983 and after.

● Increased to 30 percent from 20 percent the tax credit for child and dependent day care expenses in connection with the taxpayer's employment, for those earning $10,000 or less. The credit would be reduced one percentage point for each $2,000 in additional income, up to $28,000. Those earning over $28,000 would be eligible for a 20 percent credit.

● Increased the maximum amount of expenses eligible for the credit from $2,000 to $2,400 for one dependent and from $4,000 to $4,800 for two or more dependents.

● Allowed individuals who did not itemize deductions on their tax returns to deduct charitable contributions as follows: up to 25 percent of contributions of $100 or less (a $25 maximum deduction) in 1982 and 1983; 25 percent of up to $300 in 1984 (a $75 maximum); 50 percent with no cap in 1985; and 100 percent in 1986. The provision would expire after 1986.

● Extended from 18 months to 24 months the period an individual was allowed to defer taxes on proceeds from the sale of a primary residence if that money was used to buy another home at the same or greater cost. The provision applied to all sales after July 20, 1981, and in cases where the 18-month "rollover" period had not expired by July 20, 1981.

● Increased from $100,000 to $125,000 the one-time exclusion from tax of capital gains from the sale of a home by those aged 55 and over, effective July 21, 1981.

● Allowed an individual working overseas to exclude from tax up to $75,000 of foreign earned income in 1982. The exclusion would increase $5,000 each year over the next four years to $95,000 in 1986 and after. The provision, if elected by the taxpayer, would replace existing tax breaks for the excess living costs of those working abroad.

● Provided an allowance for "reasonable" housing costs in excess of a base amount, 16 percent of the salary of a grade GS-14, Step 1, government worker (the existing base amount would be $6,059).

Business Tax Cuts

● Replaced the complex existing system for depreciating assets over their "useful" lives with a more simplified approach called the Accelerated Cost Recovery System (ACRS). Under ACRS, investments in plant and equipment would be grouped in four classes, each having a standard schedule of deductions that could be taken over a fixed recovery period. Businesses could write off the value of an asset over three, five, 10 or 15 years at an accelerated rate. The provisions were made retroactive to Jan. 1, 1981.

● Classified assets as follows:

Three years: Automobiles, light trucks, equipment used in research and development, racehorses, and machinery and equipment that under existing law had a depreciation range of up to four years. A one-time, 6 percent investment tax credit would be allowed.

Five years: All other machinery and equipment, public utilities with a current depreciation range of 18 years or less, single-use farm structures (such as hen houses) and some petroleum storage facilities. A 10 percent investment tax credit would be allowed.

Ten years: Public utility property with a current depreciation range from 18.5 years to 25 years, railroad tank cars, some mobile homes and other structures (such as theme parks). A 10 percent investment credit would be allowed.

Fifteen years: Public utility property with a current depreciation range of more than 25 years and all other buildings. A 10 percent investment tax credit would be available for the public utility property only.

● Permitted taxpayers to depreciate an asset over a period of time longer than that designated in one of the four depreciation classes.

● Allowed through 1984 all assets except 15-year real estate to be written off using an accelerated depreciation system that combined what were called the 150 percent declining balance and straight-line methods. The declining balance method allowed a firm to deduct 15 percent of the total value of the investment the first year and 15 percent of the undepreciated value in each subsequent year. Under the straight-line method, assets were depreciated an equal percentage each year — for example, 10 percent for each of 10 years.

● Allowed all assets except 15-year real estate to be depreciated in 1985 at an even faster rate using 175 percent declining balance (17.5 percent of the undepreciated value is written off in the early years) and after 1985, using 200 percent declining balance (20 percent of the undepreciated value written off in the early years).

● Allowed structures other than low-income housing to be depreciated using the 175 percent declining balance method, with straight-line depreciation for the later years; 200 percent declining balance could be used for low-income housing.

● Gave taxpayers the option of substituting straight-line depreciation for all of the above methods.

● Allowed "expensing," or the immediate deduction by small businesses of the cost of new or used machinery and equipment, of up to $5,000 in 1982 and 1983, $7,500 in 1984 and 1985, and $10,000 after 1985.

● Increased from $100,000 to $125,000 in 1981 through 1984, and to $150,000 in 1985, the maximum amount of used property eligible for an investment tax credit.

● Extended from 7 to 15 years the period over which businesses could carry forward unused tax credits and offset them against future tax liability.

● Liberalized leasing laws to make it easier to transfer investment tax credit and accelerated depreciation benefits from businesses that were not profitable enough to use such benefits to businesses that could use them.

● Increased the existing 10 percent investment tax credit for the rehabilitation of old buildings to 15 percent for buildings 30-39 years old, 20 percent for buildings 40 years and older, and 25 percent for certified historic structures.

● Allowed more rapid depreciation (175 percent declining balance instead of straight-line) for buildings constructed on the site of a demolished historic structure.

● Allowed a 25 percent tax credit for new spending on research and development above and beyond the average annual amount spent on such activities over the three preceding years. The provision applied to all expenditures made after June 30, 1981, through Dec. 31, 1985.

● Increased deductions for corporate contributions of new equipment to a university or college to be used for research.

● Allowed firms to offset all of their U.S. research and development expenses against U.S. income, instead of against both foreign and U.S. income. The provision aimed to prevent the moving abroad of U.S. corporate research activities.

● Increased from $150,000 to $250,000 the amount of earnings a business could accumulate without paying an accumulated earnings tax.

● Exempted from the provision service corporations in health, law, engineering, architecture, accounting, actuarial science, performing arts and consulting.

● Increased from 15 to 25 the maximum number of shareholders a small business could have and still retain the option of having its individual shareholders, not both the corporation and the shareholders, taxed on income.

● Simplified the use of "last in, first out" (LIFO) accounting. LIFO was generally an attractive accounting method to use during times of high inflation, but, under existing law, had been considered too complex for small businesses to undertake.

● Reduced the lowest corporate income tax rates from 17 percent on the first $25,000 of income to 16 percent in 1982 and 15 percent in 1983, and from 20 percent on the next $25,000 to 19 percent in 1982 and 18 percent in 1983.

● Created so-called "incentive" stock options for employees to buy their employer's stock and for which the employee would be taxed only when the stock purchased under the option was sold. Currently, employees are taxed on ordinary income at the time they are granted such options.

● Extended for one year the targeted jobs tax credit program due to expire at the end of 1981 and expanded the group of disadvantaged workers for which employers could receive the credit.

● Provided preferential tax treatment for mutual savings banks that converted into stock associations.

● Allowed trucking firms a five-year deduction for the loss in value of their operating licenses resulting from the 1980 trucking deregulation bill.

Energy Provisions

● Increased to $2,500 from $1,000 the tax credit allowed small oil royalty owners to offset the windfall profits tax in 1981.

● Provided an exemption from the windfall profits tax on oil production of two barrels a day for 1982-84 and three barrels of oil a day for 1985 and after. (Although the values of the barrel-a-day exemptions would vary with the price of oil, they were likely to be substantially higher than the $2,500 credit.)

● Exempted from the windfall profits tax all independently produced oil from "stripper" wells — those that produced an average of 10 barrels of oil a day or less. The provision would begin in 1983.

● Reduced from 30 percent to 15 percent by 1986 the windfall profits tax on newly discovered oil. The reduction would be phased in: 27.5 percent in 1982; 25 percent in 1983; 22.5 percent in 1984; 20 percent in 1985; and 15 percent in 1986 and after.

● Expanded the existing exemption from the windfall profits tax for charitable organizations to include homes for disadvantaged children.

Savings Incentives

● Increased to the lesser of $2,000 or 100 percent of compensation (from $1,500 or 15 percent of compensation) the amount an individual could deduct for annual contributions to an IRA.

● Increased from $1,750 to $2,250 the deduction for contributions to "spousal" IRAs, those set up by a working spouse for both himself, or herself, and a non-working spouse. A requirement that contributions must be equally divided between the two spouses was dropped.

● Allowed deductible IRA contributions both for those not covered and for those covered by an employer-sponsored plan. In cases where an individual was covered by an employer-sponsored plan, voluntary contributions to that plan would be deductible up to $2,000.

● Permitted divorced spouses to contribute at least $1,125 a year to an IRA that had been set up for them by the other spouse. Under existing law, such persons could no longer contribute to such an IRA after divorce.

● Increased from $7,500 to $15,000 the amount a self-employed individual could deduct for contributions to his or her own retirement plan.

● Repealed as of Jan. 1, 1982, the existing $200 exclusion ($400 for couples) allowed for interest and dividend income, and reinstated a previous $100 ($200 for couples) exclusion for dividend income only.

● Allowed taxpayers, beginning in 1985, to exclude 15 percent of up to $3,000 ($6,000 for couples) of interest income.

● Allowed banks, savings and loans, credit unions, and other depository institutions to issue one-year savings certificates that would earn interest at 70 percent of the one-year Treasury bill rate (about 14 percent in 1981).

• Permitted individuals to exclude up to $1,000 of the interest on such certificates; couples could exclude up to $2,000.

• Permitted the certificates to be issued only from Oct. 1, 1981, through Dec. 31, 1982, and stipulated that they must be offered in denominations of $500 or greater.

• Required institutions, other than credit unions, issuing the certificates to make at least 75 percent of their net new savings available for home or agricultural loans.

• Replaced the existing additional 1 percent investment tax credit allowed employers for contributions to tax credit ESOPs with a payroll-based tax credit. The new credit would be phased in gradually up to .75 percent of compensation of employees covered by the plan in 1985. The provision would expire Dec. 31, 1987.

• Increased from 15 percent of payroll to 25 percent the tax deductions allowed employers for contributions to an ESOP that borrows money to buy stock in the company, provided the contribution is used to pay off the loan.

• Repealed a requirement that voting rights be transferred to employees participating in a profit-sharing ESOP.

• Allowed public utilities shareholders who elect to receive dividends in the form of newly issued common stock rather than cash to exclude from tax up to $750 a year ($1,500 for joint returns). The provision would expire at the end of 1985.

• Extended through Dec. 31, 1984, the current exclusion from employee income of employer contributions to, and the value of benefits received from, a prepaid legal service plan for employees. The existing provision would have expired Dec. 31, 1981.

Estate and Gift Taxes

• Increased to $600,000 from $175,625 by 1987 the total amount of estate and gift transfers that would be exempt from estate and gift taxes. The change would be phased in as follows: $225,000 in 1982; $275,000 in 1983; $325,000 in 1984; $400,000 in 1985; $500,000 in 1986; and $600,000 in 1987 and after. By 1987 less than 1 percent of all estates would be taxed.

• Made it easier to base the value of an estate on its current use rather than to use its generally higher fair market value when determining taxes.

• Reduced the top estate and gift tax rate from the current 70 percent to 50 percent by 1985. The rate was set at 65 percent in 1982, 60 percent in 1983 and 55 percent in 1984. When fully phased in, the top rate would apply to gifts and estates over $2.5 million.

• Repealed existing limits on tax-free estate and gift transfers between spouses.

• Increased the annual gift tax exclusion from $3,000 to $10,000 per donee, with an unlimited exclusion for tuition and medical expenses; allowed gift taxes to be paid on an annual rather than quarterly basis.

• Extended for one year, to Jan. 1, 1983, existing transitional exemptions from the tax on generation-skipping transfers.

Commodity Tax Straddles

• Restricted the use of a tax shelter technique called the commodity tax straddle by imposing a maximum 32 percent tax on the net gain of an individual's commodity futures holdings as of the last day of a tax year, even if the gain has yet to be realized. The straddle, which involved the purchase of offsetting futures contracts, had been used widely to avoid or defer taxes.

• Exempted professional hedgers — those who bought or sold futures as a protection against price fluctuations in commodities they used or supplied — from the annual tax on straddles.

Administrative Changes

• Increased Railroad Retirement System taxes 2.25 percentage points for rail management and two percentage points for employees to keep the troubled fund from going broke.

• Increased from 60 percent to 80 percent the amount of estimated tax a large corporation must pay in the current tax year. The percentage increase would be phased in gradually: 65 percent in 1982; 75 percent in 1983; and 80 percent in 1984.

• Increased from $100 to $500 by 1985 the minimum amount of income tax liability over the amount withheld that requires an individual to declare or pay estimated taxes for the following year.

• Increased from $10 to $60 the fee for filing a petition in U.S. Tax Court.

• Increased miscellaneous penalties, including the penalty for filing a false W-4 form, on which deductions are claimed for tax withholding. The civil fine for that offense was increased from $50 to $500.

• Clarified existing law to ensure that the Internal Revenue Service could refuse to disclose information used to develop standards for auditing tax returns if it would impair tax-collecting operations.

Miscellaneous Provisions

• Allowed state legislators to deduct per diem expenses during legislative sessions, even if they did not stay overnight in the state capital, provided they lived more than 50 miles away. The provision was made retroactive to Jan. 1, 1976.

• Extended the existing prohibition on the taxation of fringe benefits until Dec. 31, 1983.

• Reduced taxes on the income, such as interest income, of a congressional candidate's principal campaign committee. All such income had been taxed at 46 percent; under the bill, it would be taxed at the graduated corporate rate, from 15 percent to 46 percent.

• Allowed volunteer fire departments to issue tax-exempt bonds for the purchase or improvement of a firehouse or fire truck.

• Extended the telephone excise tax at 1 percent through 1984.

• Allowed employees a deduction of up to $400 per item for awards given by their company for length of service, productivity or safety.

• Allowed a deduction of up to $1,500 for expenses incurred in the adoption of a disadvantaged or hard-to-place child.

Social Security Cutback

A reconciliation agreement to eliminate the $122 minimum monthly Social Security benefit caused a public uproar — and a political predicament — that cast doubt on whether the change would go into effect.

Just before final approval of the conference report on the monumental budget-cutting reconciliation package (HR 3982) July 31, the House passed by a 404-20 vote a bill (HR 4331) to restore the minimum benefit paid to workers whose past earnings would make them eligible for less than $122 a month. The Senate Oct 15 approved restoration of the minimum benefit as part of an overall revision in the ailing Social Security system and went to conference with the House. *(Reconciliation bill, p. 130)*

In an effort to defuse strong public opposition to virtually any change in Social Security, President Reagan and congressional leaders vowed to consider revising the provision to ensure that those who depended on the benefit would not be left stranded. "What we want to do is get rid of those people for whom [the minimum] benefit is not a necessity," Reagan said Aug. 4. The administration claimed many of the 2.7 million recipients were former government employees who already were receiving adequate pensions. Those who depended on the minimum benefit should be eligible to collect Supplemental Security Income (SSI) for the poor, it maintained.

The Senate version of HR 4331 would restore the benefit for most of the three million beneficiaries and also called for a stopgap funding plan to see the financially troubled system through the next few years. Under the existing law, the Old-Age and Survivors Insurance (OASI) was expected to go broke near the end of 1982. The Senate bill would eliminate the full minimum payment for those on the rolls who also received a government pension over $300 a month. *(Social Security background, p. 73)*

Elimination of the minimum benefit was only one of a number of changes proposed by the administration as part of its 1982 budget reductions and as part of an overall plan to keep the Social Security system solvent. Total Social Security cuts in the reconciliation bill were expected to save $2.2 billion in fiscal 1982, $3.8 billion in fiscal 1983 and $4.6 billion in fiscal 1984.

The unpopularity of the Social Security proposals proved to be a political asset for Democrats in their search for an issue on which the Reagan administration was vulnerable. The House vote on restoring the benefit was considered a minor victory for the party in its attempt to place the full burden of cutting Social Security benefits, especially for current recipients, on Republican shoulders.

Provisions

As cleared by Congress, the Omnibus Reconciliation Act made the following cutbacks in Social Security programs:

● Eliminated the $122 minimum monthly payment for all new recipients beginning with the December 1981 payment and for all current recipients for benefits paid after February 1982. Such recipients would instead receive benefits based on prior earnings.

● Changed the age limitations on Supplemental Security Income to allow individuals aged 60 to 64 who would be eligible for the minimum benefit before December to qualify for offsetting SSI payments if they met other eligibility requirements.

● Eliminated the $255 lump-sum death payment for deaths occurring after Aug. 31, 1981, in cases where there were no surviving spouses or dependent children.

● Required that those electing to retire at age 62, and their dependents, begin to receive Social Security benefits in the first full month of their entitlement. Under existing law, if a worker retired in the middle of the month, he or she received benefits for the entire month. The provision was scheduled to go into effect for September 1981 benefits.

● Extended for one year, until Jan. 1, 1983, existing limits on outside earnings for those under 72 years of age. The age cap had been scheduled to drop to 70 in 1982.

● Eliminated payments for a parent caring for a child receiving benefits when the child reached age 16. Under existing law, these benefits ended when the child turned 18. The provision did not apply to parents caring for a disabled child. It was to go into effect for current recipients two years after the bill was signed into law; for all new recipients, the provision was effective two months after enactment.

● Eliminated benefits for new postsecondary students aged 18 to 22 after August 1982. Payments for current recipients and those eligible for such benefits before Sept. 1, 1981 — who entered postsecondary school before May 1, 1982 — would be phased out gradually, 25 percent each year through July 1985. Cost-of-living adjustments and payments for summer months would be eliminated for all recipients.

● Reduced disability benefits by the amount received from other federal, state or local disability programs if benefits from the combined programs exceeded 80 percent of the worker's prior earnings. Existing law only offset disability benefits with workers' compensation payments.

● Made the offset provision applicable to workers aged 64 and under and their dependents, instead of those under 62 as existing law required. The offsets were to be made as soon as the non-Social Security payments began. The provision, which affected only new recipients, applied to those who become disabled no more than five months before the bill was signed into law.

● Eliminated reimbursement of state vocational rehabilitation programs, except in cases where it could be shown that the program had resulted in taking a disabled person off the Social Security rolls.

● Required rounding to the next lowest 10 cents at each stage of the benefit calculation except for the final benefit amount, which would be rounded to the next lowest dollar. Benefits at the time were rounded to the next highest 10 cents.

Reagan Economic Texts

In his first eight months in office, President Reagan addressed the country five times on the condition of the economy. The first was a televised address to the nation in which he described the situation as "the worst economic mess since the Great Depression" and outlined his program of spending and tax cuts. The last came Sept. 24 when he urged Congress to make a second round of spending cuts.

In between, the former movie star effectively used television to help persuade Congress to enact his program. On April 28, he made a successful appeal to Congress to approve the "bipartisan" House substitute budget resolution instead of the Democratic plan. Two months later on July 27 he sought public support for his tax cuts; the approved measure was on his desk in less than two weeks.

FEBRUARY 5
ADDRESS TO THE NATION

Following is the text of President Reagan's report to the nation on the economy, as broadcast February 5, 1981:

Good evening. I am speaking to you tonight to give you a report on the state of our Nation's economy. I regret to say that we are in the worst economic mess since the Great Depression. A few days ago I was presented with a report I had asked for — a comprehensive audit if you will of our economic condition. You won't like it, I didn't like it, but we have to face the truth and then go to work to turn things around. And make no mistake about it, we can turn them around.

I'm not going to subject you to the jumble of charts, figures, and economic jargon of that audit but rather will try to explain where we are, how we got there, and how we can get back.

First, however, let me just give a few "attention getters" from the audit. The Federal budget is out of control and we face runaway deficits, of almost $80 billion for this budget year that ends September 30. That deficit is larger than the entire Federal budget in 1957 and so is the almost $80 billion we will pay in interest this year on the national debt.

Twenty years ago in 1960 our Federal Government payroll was less than $13 billion. Today it is $75 billion. During these twenty years, our population has only increased by 23.3 percent. The

Federal budget has gone up 528 percent.

Now, we've just had two years of back-to-back double digit inflation, 13.3 percent in 1979 — 12.4 percent last year. The last time this happened was in World War I.

In 1960 mortgage interest rates averaged about 6 percent. They are 2-1/2 times as high now, 15.4 percent. The percentage of your earnings the Federal Government took in taxes in 1960 has almost doubled. And finally there are 7 million Americans caught up in the personal indignity and human tragedy of unemployment. If they stood in a line — allowing 3 feet for each person — the line would reach from the Coast of Maine to California.

Inflation Impact

Well, so much for the audit itself. Let me try to put this in personal terms. Here is a dollar such as you earned, spent, or saved in 1960. Here is a quarter, a dime, and a penny — 36¢. That's what this 1960 dollar is worth today. And if the present inflation rate should continue three more years, that dollar of 1960 will be worth a quarter. What initiative is there to save? And if we don't save we are short of the investment capital needed for business and industry expansion. Workers in Japan and West Germany save several times the percentage of their income than Americans do.

What's happened to that American dream of owning a home? Only ten years ago a family could buy a home and the monthly payment averaged little more than a quarter — 27¢ out of each dollar earned. Today it takes 42¢ out of every dollar of income. So, fewer than 1 out of 11 families can afford to buy their first new home.

Regulations adopted by government with the best of intentions have added $666 to the cost of an automobile. It is estimated that altogether regulations of every kind, on shopkeepers, farmers, and major industries add $100 billion or more to the cost of the goods and services we buy. And then another $20 billion is spent by government handling the paperwork created by those regulations.

I'm sure you are getting the idea that the audit presented to me found government policies of the last few decades responsible for our economic troubles. We forgot or just overlooked the fact that government — any government — has a built-in tendency to grow. Now, we all had a hand in looking to government for benefits as if government had some sources of revenue other than our earnings. Many if not most of the things we thought of or that government offered to us seemed attractive.

In the years following the Second World War it was easy (for awhile at least) to overlook the price tag. Our income more than doubled in the 25 years after the War. We increased our take-home pay in those 25 years by more than we had amassed in all the preceding 150 years put together. Yes, there was some inflation, 1 or 1-1/2 percent a year, that didn't bother us. But if we look back at those golden years we recall that even then voices had been raised warning that inflation, like radioactivity, was cumulative and that once started it could get out of control. Some government programs seemed so worthwhile that borrowing to fund them didn't bother us.

By 1960 our national debt stood at $284 billion. Congress in 1971 decided to put a ceiling of $400 billion on our ability to borrow. Today the debt is $934 billion. So-called temporary increases or extensions in the debt ceiling have been allowed 21 times in these 10 years and now I have been forced to ask for another increase in the debt ceiling or the government will be unable to function past the middle of February and I've only been here 16 days. Before we reach the day when we can reduce the debt ceiling we may in spite of our best efforts see a national debt in excess of a trillion dollars. Now this is a figure literally beyond our comprehension.

We know now that inflation results from all that deficit spending. Government has only two ways of getting money other than raising taxes. It can go into the money market and borrow, competing with its own citizens and driving up interest rates, which it has done, or it can print money, and it's done that. Both methods are inflationary.

We're victims of language, the very word "inflation" leads us to think of it as just high prices. Then, of course, we resent the person who puts on the price tags forgetting that he or she is also a victim of inflation. Inflation is not just high prices, it is a reduction in the value of our money. When the money supply is increased but the goods and services available for buying are not, we have too much money chasing too few goods.

Wars are usually accompanied by inflation. Everyone is working or fighting but production is of weapons and munitions not things we can buy and use.

Taxes

One way out would be to raise taxes so that government need not borrow or print money. But in all these years of government growth we've reached — indeed surpassed — the limit of our people's tolerance or ability to bear an increase in the tax burden.

Prior to World War II, taxes were such that on the average we only had to work just a little over one month each year to pay our total Federal, state, and local tax bill. Today we have to work four months to pay that bill.

Some say shift the tax burden to business and industry but business doesn't pay taxes. Oh, don't get the wrong idea, business is being taxed — so much so that we are being priced out of the world market. But business must pass its costs of operation and that includes taxes, onto the customer in the price of the product. Only people pay taxes — all the taxes. Government just uses business in a kind of sneaky way to help collect the taxes. They are hidden in the price and we aren't aware of how much tax we actually pay. Today, this once great industrial giant of ours has the lowest rate of gain in productivity of virtually all the industrial nations with whom we must compete in the world market. We can't even hold our own market here in America against foreign automobiles, steel, and a number of other products.

Japanese production of automobiles is almost twice as great per worker as it is in America. Japanese steel workers out-produce their American counterparts by about 25 percent.

Now this isn't because they are better workers. I'll match the American working man or woman against anyone in the world. But we have to give them the tools and equipment that workers in the other industrial nations have.

We invented the assembly line and mass production, but punitive tax policies and excessive and unnecessary regulations plus government borrowing have stifled our ability to update plant and equipment. When capital investment is made it's too often for some unproductive alterations demanded by government to meet various of its regulations.

Excessive taxation of individuals has robbed us of incentive and made overtime unprofitable.

We once produced about 40 percent of the world's steel. We now produce 19 percent.

We were once the greatest producer of automobiles, producing more than all the rest of the world combined. That is no longer true, and in addition, the big 3, the major auto companies, in our land have sustained tremendous losses in the past year and have been forced to lay off thousands of workers.

All of you who are working know that even with cost-of-living pay raises you can't keep up with inflation. In our progressive tax system as you increase the number of dollars you earn you find yourself moved up into higher tax brackets, paying a higher tax rate just for trying to hold your own. The result? Your standard of living is going down.

Over the past decades we've talked of curtailing government spending so that we can then lower the tax burden. Sometimes we've even taken a run at doing that. But there were always those who told us taxes couldn't be cut until spending was reduced. Well, you know, we can lecture our children about extravagance until we run out of voice and breath. Or we can cure their extravagance by simply reducing their allowance.

Turning Point

It is time to recognize that we have come to a turning point. We are threatened with an economic calamity of tremendous proportions and the old business as usual treatment can't save us.

Together, we must chart a different course. We must increase productivity. That means making it possible for industry to modernize and make use of the technology which we ourselves invented; that means putting Americans back to work. And that means above all bringing government spending back within government revenues which is the only way, together with increased productivity, that we can reduce and, yes, eliminate inflation.

In the past we've tried to fight inflation one year and then when unemployment increased turn the next year to fighting unemployment with more deficit spending as a pump primer. So again, up goes inflation. It hasn't worked. We don't have to choose between inflation and unemployment — they go hand in hand. It's time to try something different and that's what we're going to do.

I've already placed a freeze on hiring replacements for those who retire or leave government service. I have ordered a cut in government travel, the number of consultants to the government, and the buying of office equipment and other items. I have put a freeze on pending regulations and set up a task force under Vice President Bush to review regulations with an eye toward getting rid of as many as possible. I have decontrolled oil which should result in more domestic production and less dependence on foreign oil. And I am eliminating that ineffective Council on Wage and Price Stability.

But it will take more, much more and we must realize there is no quick fix. At the same time, however, we cannot delay in implementing an economic program aimed at both reducing tax rates to stimulate productivity and reducing the growth in government spending to reduce unemployment and inflation.

On February 18th, I will present in detail an economic program to Congress embodying the features I have just stated. It will propose budget cuts in virtually every department of government. It is my belief that these actual budget cuts will only be part of the savings. As our Cabinet Secretaries take charge of their departments, they will search out areas of waste, extravagance, and costly administrative overhead which could yield additional and substantial reductions.

Now at the same time we're doing this, we must go forward with a tax relief package. I shall ask for a 10 percent reduction across the board in personal income tax rates for each of the next three years. Proposals will also be submitted for accelerated depreciation allowances for business to provide necessary capital so as to create jobs.

Now, here again, in saying this, I know that language, as I said earlier, can get in the way of a clear understanding of what our program is intended to do. Budget cuts can sound as if we are going to reduce total government spending to a lower level than was spent the year before. This is not the case. The budgets will increase as our population increases and each year we'll see spending increases to match that growth. Government revenues will increase as the economy grows, but the burden will be lighter for each individual because the economic base will have been expanded by reason of the reduced rates.

Balanced Budget

Now let me show you a chart I've had drawn to illustrate how this can be. Here you see two trend lines. The bottom line shows the increase in tax revenues. The red line on top is the increase in government spending. Both lines turn upward reflecting the giant tax increase already built into the system for this year 1981, and the increases in spending built into the '81 and '82 budgets and on into the future.

As you can see, the spending line rises at a steeper slant than the revenue line. And that gap between those lines illustrates the increasing deficits we've been running including this year's $80 billion deficit.

Now, in the second chart, the lines represent the positive effects when Congress accepts our economic program. Both lines continue to rise allowing for necessary growth but the gap narrows as spending cuts continue over the next few years, until finally the two lines come together meaning a balanced budget.

I am confident that my Administration can achieve that. At that point tax revenues in spite of rate reductions will be increasing faster than spending which means we can look forward to further reductions in the tax rates.

Now, in all of this we will of course work closely with the Federal Reserve System toward the objective of a stable monetary policy.

Our spending cuts will not be at the expense of the truly needy. We will, however, seek to eliminate benefits to those who are not really qualified by reason of need.

As I've said before, on February 18th, I will present this economic package of budget reductions and tax reform to a joint session of Congress and to you in full detail.

Our basic system is sound. We can, with compassion, continue to meet our responsibility to those who through no fault of their own need our help. We can meet fully the other legitimate responsibilities of government. We cannot continue any longer our wasteful ways at the expense of the workers of this land or of our children.

Since 1960 our government has spent $5.1 trillion; our debt has grown by $648 billion. Prices have exploded by 178 percent. How much better off are we for all that? We all know, we are very much worse off.

Need to Act

When we measure how harshly these years of inflation, lower productivity, and uncontrolled government growth have affected our lives, we know we must act and act now.

We must not be timid.

We will restore the freedom of all men and women to excel and to create. We will unleash the energy and genius of the American people — traits which have never failed us.

To the Congress of the United States, I extend my hand in cooperation and I believe we can go forward in a bipartisan manner.

I found a real willingness to cooperate on the part of Democrats and members of my own Party.

To my colleagues in the Executive Branch of government and to all Federal employees I ask that we work in the spirit of service.

I urge those great institutions in America — business and labor — to be guided by the national interest and I'm confident they will. The only special interest that we will serve is the interest of all the people.

We can create the incentives which take advantage of the genius of our economic system — a system, as Walter Lippmann observed more than 40 years ago, which for the first time in history gave men "a way of producing wealth in which the good fortune of others multiplied their own."

Our aim is to increase our national wealth so all will have more not just redistribute what we already have which is just a sharing of scarcity. We can begin to reward hard work and risk-taking, by

forcing this government to live within its means.

Over the years we've let negative economic forces run out of control. We've stalled the judgment day. We no longer have that luxury. We're out of time.

And to you my fellow citizens, let us join in a new determination to rebuild the foundation of our society; to work together to act responsibly. Let us do so with the most profound respect for that which must be preserved as well as with sensitive understanding and compassion for those who must be protected.

We can leave our children with an unrepayable massive debt and a shattered economy or we can leave them liberty in a land where every individual has the opportunity to be whatever God intended us to be. All it takes is a little common sense and recognition of our own ability. Together we can forge a new beginning for America.

Thank you and good night.

FEBRUARY 18 BUDGET PROPOSALS

Following is the text of the address delivered by President Reagan to a joint session of Congress on February 18, 1981, in which he presented his administration's proposals to cut government spending:

Mr. Speaker, Mr. President, distinguished Members of Congress, honored guests, and fellow citizens. Only a month ago, I was your guest in this historic building and I pledged to you my cooperation in doing what is right for this Nation that we all love so much.

I am here tonight to reaffirm that pledge and to ask that we share in restoring the promise that is offered to every citizen by this, the last, best hope of man on earth.

All of us are aware of the punishing inflation which has, for the first time in some 60 years, held to double digit figures for 2 years in a row. Interest rates have reached absurd levels of more than 20 percent and over 15 percent for those who would borrow to buy a home. All across this land one can see newly built homes standing vacant, unsold because of mortgage interest rates.

Almost eight million Americans are out of work. These are people who want to be productive. But as the months go by, despair dominates their lives. The threats of layoffs and unemployment hang over other millions, and all who work are frustrated by their inability to keep up with inflation.

One worker in a Midwest city put it to me this way: He said, "I'm bringing home more dollars than I ever believed I would possibly earn, but I seem to be getting worse off." And he is. Not only have hourly earnings of the American worker, after adjusting for inflation, declined 5 percent over the past 5 years, Federal personal taxes for the average family increased 67 percent.

We can no longer procrastinate and hope that things will get better. They will not. Unless we act forcefully, and now, the economy will get worse.

National Debt

Can we who man the ship of state deny it is somewhat out of control? Our national debt is approaching $1 trillion. A few weeks ago I called such a figure — a trillion dollars — incomprehensible. I've been trying ever since to think of a way to illustrate how big a trillion is. The best I could come up with is that if you had a stack of $1,000 bills in your hand only four inches high you would be a millionaire. A trillion dollars would be a stack of $1,000 bills 67 miles high.

The interest on the public debt this year we know will be over $90 billion. And unless we change the proposed spending for the fiscal year beginning October 1, we'll add another almost $80 billion to the debt.

Adding to our troubles is a mass of regulations imposed on the shopkeeper, the farmer, the craftsman, professionals and major industry that is estimated to add $100 billion to the price of things we buy and it reduces our ability to produce. The rate of increase in American productivity, once one of the highest in the world, is among the lowest of all major industrial nations. Indeed, it has actually declined in the last 3 years.

I have painted a pretty grim picure but I think that I have painted it accurately. It is within our power to change this picture and we can act with hope. There is nothing wrong with our internal strengths. There has been no breakdown in the human, technological, and natural resources upon which the economy is built.

Four-point Proposal

Based on this confidence in a system which has never failed us — but which we have failed through a lack of confidence, and sometimes through a belief that we could fine tune the economy and get a tune to our liking — I am proposing a comprehensive four-point program. Let me outline in detail some of the principal parts of this program. You will each be provided with a completely detailed copy of the entire program.

This plan is aimed at reducing the growth in Government spending and taxing, reforming and eliminating regulations which are unnecessary and unproductive or counterproductive, and encouraging a consistent monetary policy aimed at maintaining the value of the currency.

If enacted in full, this program can help America create 13 million new jobs, nearly 3 million more than we would have without these measures. It will also help us gain control of inflation.

Tax Increase Rate Reduction

It is important to note that we are only reducing the rate of increase in taxing and spending. We are not attempting to cut either spending or taxing levels below that which we presently have. This plan will get our economy moving again, increase productivity growth, and thus create the jobs our people must have.

And I am asking that you join me in reducing direct Federal spending by $41.4 billion in fiscal year 1982, along with another $7.7 billion user fees and off-budget savings for a total savings of $49.1 billion.

This will still allow an increase of $40.8 billion over 1981 spending.

Full Funding for Truly Needy

I know that exaggerated and inaccurate stories about these cuts have disturbed many people, particularly those dependent on grant and benefit programs for their basic needs. Some of you have heard from constituents, I know, afraid that Social Security checks, for example, were going to be taken away from them. I regret the fear that these unfounded stories have caused and I welcome this opportunity to set things straight.

We will continue to fulfill the obligations that spring from our national conscience. Those who through no fault of their own must depend on the rest of us, the poverty stricken, the disabled, the elderly, all those with true need, can rest assured that the social safety net of programs they depend on are exempt from any cuts.

The full retirement benefits of the more than 31 million Social Security recipients will be continued along with an annual cost-of-living increase. Medicare will not be cut, nor will supplemental income for the blind, aged, and disabled, and funding will continue for veterans' pensions.

School breakfasts and lunches for the children of low-income families will continue, as will nutrition and other special services for the aging. There will be no cut in Project Head Start or summer youth jobs.

All in all, nearly $216 billion worth of programs providing help for tens of millions of Americans — will be fully funded. But government will not continue to subsidize individuals or particular business interests where real need cannot be demonstrated.

And while we will reduce some subsidies to regional and local governments, we will at the same time convert a number of categorical grant programs into block grants to reduce wasteful administrative overhead and to give local government entities and States more flexibility and control. We call for an end to duplication in Federal programs and reform of those which are not cost effective.

Restore Programs to States and Private Sector

Already, some have protested that there must be no reduction in aid to schools. Let me point out that Federal aid to education amounts to only eight percent of the total educational funding. For this eight percent the Federal Government has insisted on a tremendously disproportionate share of control over our schools. Whatever reductions we've proposed in that eight percent will amount to very little in the total cost of education. They will, however, restore more authority to States and local school districts.

Historically the American people have supported by voluntary contributions more artistic and cultural activities than all the other countries in the world put together. I wholeheartedly support this approach and believe that Americans will continue their generosity. Therefore, I am proposing a savings of $85 million in the Federal subsidies now going to the arts and humanities.

There are a number of subsidies to business and industry that I believe are unnecessary. Not because the activities being subsidized aren't of value but because the marketplace contains incentives enough to warrant continuing these activities without a government subsidy. One such subsidy is the Department of Energy's synthetic fuels program. We will continue support of research leading to development of new technologies and more independence from foreign oil, but we can save at least $3.2 billion by leaving to private industry the building of plants to make liquid or gas fuels from coal.

We are asking that another major industry, business subsidy I should say, the Export-Import Bank loan authority, be reduced by one-third in 1982. We are doing this because the primary beneficiaries of tax payer funds in this case are the exporting companies themselves — most of them profitable corporations.

High Cost of Government Borrowing

This brings me to a number of other lending programs in which Government makes low-interest loans, some of them at an interest rate as low as 2 percent. What has not been very well understood is that the Treasury Department has no money of its own. It has to go into the private capital market and borrow the money. So in this time of excessive interest rates the government finds itself borrowing at an interest rate several times as high as the interest rate it gets back from those it lends the money to. This difference, of course, is paid by your constituents, the taxpayers. They get hit again if they try to borrow because Government borrowing contributes to raising all interest rates.

By terminating the Economic Development Administration we can save hundreds of millions of dollars in 1982 and billions more over the next few years. There is a lack of consistent and convincing evidence that EDA and its Regional Commissions have been effective in creating new jobs. They have been effective in creating an array of planners, grantsmen and professional middlemen. We believe we can do better just by the expansion of the economy and the job creation which will come from our economic program.

Welfare and Unemployment Programs

The Food Stamp program will be restored to its original purpose, to assist those without resources to purchase sufficient nutritional food. We will, however, save $1.8 billion in fiscal year 1982 by removing from eligibility those who are not in real need or who are abusing the program.

Even with this reduction, the program will be budgeted for more than $10 billion.

We will tighten welfare and give more attention to outside sources of income when determining the amount of welfare an individual is allowed. This plus strong and effective work requirements will save $520 million in the next year.

I stated a moment ago our intention to keep the school breakfast and lunch programs for those in true need. But by cutting back on meals for children of families who can afford to pay, the savings will be $1.6 billion in fiscal year 1982.

Let me just touch on a few other areas which are typical of the kinds of reductions we have included in this economic package. The Trade Adjustment Assistance program provides benefits for workers who are unemployed when foreign imports reduce the market for various American products causing shutdown of plants and layoff of workers. The purpose is to help these workers find jobs in growing sectors of our economy. There is nothing wrong with that. But because these benefits are paid out on top of normal unemployment benefits, we wind up paying greater benefits to those who lose their jobs because of foreign competition than we do to their friends and neighbors who are laid off due to domestic competition. Anyone must agree that this is unfair. Putting these two programs on the same footing will save $1.15 billion in just 1 year.

Federal Regulation Burden

Earlier I made mention of changing categorical grants to States and local governments into block grants. We know, of course, that the categorical grant programs burden local and State governments with a mass of Federal regulations and Federal paperwork.

Ineffective targeting, wasteful administrative overhead — all can be eliminated by shifting the resources and decision-making authority to local and State government. This will also consolidate programs which are scattered throughout the Federal bureaucracy, bringing government closer to the people and saving $23.9 billion over the next 5 years.

Our program for economic renewal deals with a number of programs which at present are not cost-effective. An example is Medicaid. Right now Washington provides the States with unlimited matching payments for their expenditures. At the same time we here in Washington pretty much dictate how the States are going to manage these programs. We want to put a cap on how much the Federal Government will contribute but at the same time allow the States much more flexibility in managing and structuring the programs. I know from our experience in California that such flexibility could have led to far more cost-effective reforms. This will bring a savings of $1 billion next year.

Space and Postal Agencies

The space program has been and is important to America and we plan to continue it. We believe, however, that a reordering of priorities to focus on the most important and cost-effective NASA programs can result in a savings of a quarter of a billion dollars.

Coming down from space to the mailbox — the Postal Service has been consistently unable to live within its operating budget. It is still dependent on large Federal subsidies. We propose reducing those subsidies by $632 million in 1982 to press the Postal Service into becoming more effective. In subsequent years, the savings will continue to add up.

The Economic Regulatory Administration in the Department of Energy has programs to force companies to convert to specific fuels. It has the authority to administer a gas rationing plan, and prior to decontrol it ran the oil price control program. With these and other regulations gone we can save several hundreds of millions of dollars over the next few years.

Defense Spending

I'm sure there is one department you've been waiting for me to mention, the Department of Defense. It is the only department in our entire program that will actually be increased over the present budgeted figure.

But even here there was no exemption. The Department of Defense came up with a number of cuts which reduced the budget increase needed to restore our military balance. These measures will save $2.9 billion in 1982 outlays and by 1986 a total of $28.2 billion will have been saved. Perhaps I should say will have been made available for the necessary things that we must do. The aim will be to provide the most effective defense for the lowest possible cost.

I believe that my duty as President requires that I recommend increases in defense spending over the coming years.

I know that you are aware but I think it bears saying again that since 1970, the Soviet Union has invested $300 billion more in its military forces than we have. As a result of its massive military buildup, the Soviets have made a significant numerical advantage in strategic nuclear delivery systems, tactical aircraft, submarines, artillery and antiaircraft defense. To allow this imbalance to continue is a threat to our national security.

Notwithstanding our economic straits, making the financial changes beginning now is far less costly than waiting and having to attempt a crash program several years from now.

We remain committed to the goal of arms limitation through negotiation. I hope we can persuade our adversaries to come to realistic balanced and verifiable agreements.

But, as we negotiate, our security must be fully protected by a balanced and realistic defense program.

Let me say a word here about the general problem of waste and fraud in the Federal Government. One government estimate indicated that fraud alone may account for anywhere from 1 to 10 percent — as much as $25 billion — of Federal expenditures for social programs. If the tax dollars that are wasted or mismanaged are added to this fraud total, the staggering dimensions of this problem begin to emerge.

New Inspectors General

The Office of Management and Budget is now putting together an interagency task force to attack waste and fraud. We are also planning to appoint as Inspectors General highly trained professionals who will spare no effort to do this job.

No administration can promise to immediately stop a trend that has grown in recent years as quickly as Government expenditures themselves. But let me say this: waste and fraud in the Federal budget is exactly what I have called it before — an unrelenting national scandal — a scandal we are bound and determined to do something about.

Tax Proposals

Marching in lockstep with the whole program of reductions in spending is the equally important program of reduced tax rates. Both are essential if we are to have economic recovery. It's time to create new jobs. To build and rebuild industry, and to give the American people room to do what they do best. And that can only be done with a tax program which provides incentive to increase productivity for both workers and industry.

Our proposal is for a 10-percent across-the-board cut every year for three years in the tax rates for all individual income taxpayers, making a total cut in tax rates of 30 percent. This 3-year reduction will also apply to the tax on unearned income, leading toward an eventual elimination of the present differential between the tax on earned and unearned income.

I would have hoped that we could be retroactive with this, but as it stands the effective starting date for these 10-percent personal income tax rate reductions will be called for as of July 1st of this year.

Again, let me remind you that while this 30 percent reduction will leave the taxpayers with $500 billion more in their pockets over the next five years, it's actually only a reduction in the tax increase already built into the system.

Unlike some past "tax reforms," this is not merely a shift of wealth between different sets of taxpayers. This proposal for an equal reduction in everyone's tax rates will expand our national prosperity, enlarge national incomes, and increase opportunities for all Americans.

Some will argue, I know, that reducing tax rates now will be inflationary. A solid body of economic experts does not agree. And tax cuts adopted over the past three-fourths of a century indicate these economic experts are right. They will not be inflationary. I have had advice that in 1985 our real production of goods and services will grow by 20 percent and will be $300 billion higher than it is today. The average worker's wage will rise (in real purchasing power) 8 percent, and this is in after-tax dollars and this, of course, is predicated on a complete program of tax cuts and spending reductions being implemented.

The other part of the tax package is aimed directly at providing business and industry with the capital needed to modernize and engage in more research and development. This will involve an increase in depreciation allowances, and this part of our tax proposal will be retroactive to January 1st.

The present depreciation system is obsolete, needlessly complex, and is economically counterproductive. Very simply, it bases the depreciation of plant, machinery, vehicles, and tools on their original cost with no recognition of how inflation has increased their replacement cost. We are proposing a much shorter write-off time than is presently allowed: a 5-year write-off for machinery; 3 years for vehicles and trucks; and a 10-year write-off for plant.

In fiscal year 1982 under this plan business would acquire nearly $10 billion for investment. By 1985 the figure would be nearly $45 billion. These changes are essential to provide the new investment which is needed to create millions of new jobs between now and 1985 and to make America competitive once again in the world market.

These won't be make-work jobs, they are productive jobs, jobs with a future.

I'm well aware that there are many other desirable and needed tax changes such as indexing the income tax brackets to protect taxpayers against inflation; the unjust discrimination against married couples if both are working and earning; tuition tax credits; the unfairness of the inheritance tax, especially to the family-owned farm and the family-owned business, and a number of others. But our program for economic recovery is so urgently needed to begin to bring down inflation that I am asking you to act on this plan first and with great urgency. Then I pledge I will join with you in seeking these additional tax changes at the earliest date possible.

Over-regulation

American society experienced a virtual explosion in Government regulation during the past decade. Between 1970 and 1979, expenditures for the major regulatory agencies quadrupled, the number of pages published annually in the *Federal Register* nearly tripled, and the number of pages in the *Code of Federal Regulations* increased by nearly two-thirds.

The result has been higher prices, higher unemployment, and lower productivity growth. Over-regulation causes small and independent businessmen and women, as well as large businesses, to defer or terminate plans for expansion, and since they are responsible for most of our new jobs, those new jobs just aren't created.

We have no intention of dismantling the regulatory agencies — especially those necessary to protect [the] environment and to ensure the public health and safety. However, we must come to grips with inefficient and burdensome regulations — eliminate those we can and reform the others.

I have asked Vice President Bush to head a Cabinet-level Task Force on Regulatory Relief. Second, I asked each member of my Cabinet to postpone the effective dates of the hundreds of regulations which have not yet been implemented. Third, in coordination with the task force, many of the agency heads have already taken prompt action to review and rescind existing burdensome regulations. Finally, just yesterday, I signed an executive order that for the first time provides for effective and coordinated management of the regulatory process.

Much has been accomplished, but it is only a beginning. We will eliminate those regulations that are unproductive and unnecessary by executive order, where possible, and cooperate fully with you on those that require legislation.

The final aspect of our plan requires a national monetary policy which does not allow money growth to increase consistently faster than the growth of goods and services. In order to curb

inflation, we need to slow the growth in our money supply.

We fully recognize the independence of the Federal Reserve System and will do nothing to interfere with or undermine that independence. We will consult regularly with the Federal Reserve Board on all aspects of our economic program and will vigorously pursue budget policies that will make their job easier in reducing monetary growth.

A successful program to achieve stable and moderate growth patterns in the money supply will keep both inflation and interest rates down and restore vigor to our financial institutions and markets.

'Economic Recovery' Proposed

This, then, is our proposal. "America's New Beginning: A Program for Economic Recovery." I don't want it to be simply the plan of my Administration — I'm here tonight to ask you to join me in making it our plan. [Applause, members rising]

I should have arranged to quit right there.

Well, together we can embark on this road, not to make things easy, but to make things better.

Our social, political and cultural as well as our economic institutions can no longer absorb the repeated shocks that have been dealt them over the past decades.

Can we do the job? The answer is yes, but we must begin now.

We are in control here. There is nothing wrong with America that we can't fix. I'm sure there will be some who will raise the familiar old cry, "Don't touch my program — cut somewhere else."

I hope I've made it plain that our approach has been evenhanded; that only the programs for the truly deserving needy remain untouched.

The question is, are we simply going to go down the same path we've gone down before — carving out one special program here, another special program there. I don't think that is what the American people expect of us. More important, I don't think that is what they want. They are ready to return to the source of our strength.

The substance and prosperity of our Nation is built by wages brought home from the factories and the mills, the farms and the shops. They are the services provided in 10,000 corners of America; the interest on the thrift of our people and the returns for their risk-taking. The production of America is the possession of those who build, serve, create and produce.

For too long now, we've removed from our people the decisions on how to dispose of what they created. We have strayed from first principles. We must alter our course.

The taxing power of government must be used to provide revenues for legitimate government purposes. It must not be used to regulate the economy or bring about social change. We've tried that and surely must be able to see it doesn't work.

Spending by Government must be limited to those functions which are the proper province of Government. We can no longer afford things simply because we think of them.

Next year we can reduce the budget by $41.4 billion, without harm to Government's legitimate purposes or to our responsibility to all who need our benevolence. This, plus the reduction in tax rates, will help bring an end to inflation.

In the health and social services area alone the plan we are proposing will substantially reduce the need for 465 pages of law, 1,400 pages of regulations, 5,000 Federal employees who presently administer 7,600 separate grants in about 25,000 separate locations. Over 7 million man and woman hours of work by State and local officials are required to fill out government forms.

I would direct a question to those who have indicated already an unwillingness to accept such a plan. Have they an alternative which offers a greater chance of balancing the budget, reducing and eliminating inflation, stimulating the creation of jobs, and reducing the tax burden? And if they haven't, are they suggesting we can continue on the present course without coming to a day of reckoning?

If we don't do this, inflation and the growing tax burden will put an end to everything we believe in and our dreams for the future. We don't have an option of living with inflation and its attendant tragedy, millions of productive people willing and able to work but unable to find a buyer for their work in the job market.

We have an alternative, and that is the program for economic recovery. True, it will take time for the favorable effects of our proposal to be felt. So we must begin now.

The people are watching and waiting. They don't demand miracles. They do expect us to act. Let us act together.

Thank you and good night.

APRIL 28 ECONOMIC ADDRESS TO CONGRESS

Following is the text of a televised speech made by President Reagan April 28, 1981, to a joint session of Congress.

Mr. Speaker, Mr. President, distinguished Members of the Congress, honored guests and fellow citizens.

I have no words to express my appreciation for that greeting.

I have come to speak to you tonight about our economic recovery program and why I believe it is essential that the Congress approve this package which I believe will lift the crushing burden of inflation off of our citizens and restore the vitality to our economy, and our industrial machine.

Acknowledgment of Get Well Wishes

First, however, and due to events of the past few weeks, will you permit me to digress for a moment from the all important subject of why we must bring Government spending under control and reduce tax rates. I would like to say a few words directly to all of you and to those who are watching and listening tonight. Because this is the only way I know to express to all of you on behalf of Nancy and myself our appreciation for your messages, your flowers, and most of all, your prayers, not only for me, but for those others who fell beside me.

The warmth of your words, the expression of friendship and, yes, love, meant more to us than you can ever know. You have given us a memory that we will treasure forever. And you have provided an answer to those few voices that were raised saying that what happened was evidence that ours is a sick society.

The society we heard from is made up of millions of compassionate Americans and their children from college age to kindergarten.

As a matter of fact, as evidence of that I have a letter with me. The letter came from Peter Sweeney. He is in the second grade in the Riverside School in Rockville Center. And he said, "I hope you get well quick or you might have to make a speech in your pajamas." [Laughter.] He added a postscript. "P.S. If you have to make a speech in your pajamas, I warned you." [Laughter.]

Well, sick societies do not produce men like the two who recently returned from outer space. Sick societies do not produce young men like Secret Service Agent Tim McCarthy, who placed his body between mine and the man with the gun simply because he felt that is what his duty called for him to do. Sick societies do not produce dedicated police officers like Tom Delahanty or able and devoted public servants like Jim Brady.

Sick societies do not make people like us so proud to be Americans and so very proud of our fellow citizens.

'Economic Mess'

Now, let us talk about getting spending and inflation under control and cutting your tax rates.

Mr. Speaker and Senator Baker, I want to thank you for your cooperation in helping to arrange this joint session of the Congress. I won't be speaking to you very long tonight, but I asked for this meeting because the urgency of our joint mission has not changed.

Thanks to some very fine people, my health is much improved. I would like to be able to say that with regard to the health of the economy. It has been half a year since the election that charged all of us in this Government with the task of restoring our economy. Where have we come in these 6 months? Inflation as measured by the Consumer Price Index has continued at a double-digit rate. Mortgage interest rates have averaged almost 15 percent for these 6 months, preventing families across America from buying homes. There are still almost 8 million unemployed. The average worker's hourly earnings after adjusting for inflation are lower today than they were 6 months ago, and there have been over 6,000 business failures.

Six months is long enough. The American people now want us to act, and not in half measures. They demand, and they have earned, a full and comprehensive effort to clean up our economic mess. Because of the extent of our economy's sickness, we know that the cure will not come quickly, and that even with our package, progress will come in inches and feet, not in miles. But to fail to act will delay even longer, and more painfully, the cure which must come.

And that cure begins with the Federal budget. And the budgetary actions taken by the Congress over the next few days will determine how we respond to the message of last November 4.

That message was very simple. Our Government is too big and it spends too much.

Budget Timetable

For the past few months you and I have enjoyed a relationship based on extraordinary cooperation. Because of this cooperation we have come a long distance in less than 3 months. I want to thank the leadership of the Congress for helping in setting a fair timetable for consideration of our recommendations, and committee chairmen on both sides of the aisle have called prompt and thorough hearings.

We have also communicated in a spirit of candor, openness, and mutual respect. Tonight, as our decision day nears, and as the House of Representatives weighs its alternatives, I wish to address you in that same spirit.

The Senate Budget Committee, under the leadership of Pete Domenici, has just today voted out a budget resolution supported by Democrats and Republicans alike that is in all major respects consistent with the program that we have proposed.

Now we look forward to favorable action on the Senate floor. But an equally crucial test involves the House of Representatives.

Approves House Bipartisan Plan

The House will soon be choosing between two different versions or measures to deal with the economy. One is the measure offered by the House Budget Committee. The other is a bipartisan measure, a substitute introduced by Congressmen Phil Gramm of Texas and Del Latta of Ohio.

On behalf of the Administration, let me say that we embrace and fully support that bipartisan substitute.

It will achieve all the essential aims of controlling Government spending, reducing the tax burden, building a national defense second to none, and stimulating economic growth and creating millions of new jobs.

At the same time, however, I must state our opposition to the measure offered by the House Budget Committee.

It may appear that we have two alternatives. In reality, however, there are no more alternatives left. The committee measure quite simply falls far too short of the essential actions that we must take. For example, in the next 3 years:

• The Committee measure projects spending $141 billion more than does the bipartisan substitute.

• It regrettably cuts over $14 billion in essential defense funding — funding required to restore America's national security.

• It adheres to the failed policy of trying to balance the budget on the taxpayer's back. It would increase tax payments by over a third — adding up to a staggering quarter of a trillion dollars. Federal taxes would increase 12 percent each year. Taxpayers would be paying a larger share of their income to Government in 1984 than they do at present.

• In short, that measure reflects an echo of the past rather than a benchmark for the future. High taxes and excess spending growth created our present economic mess; more of the same will not cure the hardship, anxiety, and discouragement it has imposed on the American people.

Let us cut through the fog for a moment. The answer to a Government that is too big is to stop feeding its growth. Government spending has been growing faster than the economy itself. The massive national debt which we accumulated is the result of the Government's high spending diet. Well, it is time to change the diet and to change it in the right way.

Tax Proposal

I know the tax portion of our package is of concern to some of you. Let me make a few points that I feel have been overlooked. First of all, it should be looked at as an integral part of the entire package, not something separate and apart from the budget reductions, the regulatory relief, and the monetary restraints.

Probably the most common misconception is that we are proposing to reduce Government revenues to less than what the Government has been receiving. This is not true. Actually, the discussion has to do with how much of a tax increase should be imposed on the taxpayer in 1982.

Now, I know that over the recess in some informal polling some of your constituents have been asked which they would rather have, a balanced budget or a tax cut. And with the common sense that characterizes the people of this country, the answer of course has been a balanced budget. But may I suggest with no inference that there was wrong intent on the part of those who asked the question, the question was inappropriate to the situation. Our choice is not between a balanced budget and a tax cut. Properly asked, the question is, do you want a great big raise in your taxes this coming year, or at the worst a very little increase with the prospect of tax reduction and a balanced budget down the road a ways.

With the common sense that the people have already shown, I am sure we all know what the answer to that question would be. A gigantic tax increase has been built into the system. We propose nothing more than a reduction of that increase. The people have a right to know that even with our plan they will be paying more in taxes, but not as much more as they will without it.

The option I believe offered by the House Budget Committee will leave spending too high and tax rates too high. At the same time, I think it cuts the defense budget too much. And by attempting to reduce the deficit through higher taxes, it will not create the kind of strong economic growth and the new jobs that we must have.

Let us not overlook the fact that the small, independent business man or woman creates more than 80 percent of all the new jobs and employs more than half of our total work force. Our across-the-board cut in tax rates for a 3-year period will give them much of the incentive and promise of stability they need to go forward with expansion plans calling for additional employees.

Asks for Cooperation

Tonight I renew my call for us to work as a team, to join in cooperation so that we find answers which will begin to solve all our economic problems and not just some of them. The economic recovery package that I have outlined to you over the past few weeks is, I deeply believe, the only answer that we have left. Reducing the growth of spending, cutting marginal tax rates, providing relief from over-regulation, and following a noninflationary and predictable monetary policy are interwoven measures which will ensure that we have addressed each of the severe dislocations which threaten our economic future. These policies will make our economy stronger and the stronger economy will balance the budget which we are committed to do by 1984.

When I took the oath of office, I pledged loyalty to only one special interest group — "We the people." Those people — neighbors and friends, shopkeepers and laborers, farmers and craftsmen — do not have infinite patience. As a matter of fact, some 80 years ago Teddy Roosevelt wrote these instructive words in his first message to the Congress: "The American people are slow to wrath, but when their wrath is once kindled, it burns like a consuming flame."

Calls for New Solutions

Well, perhaps that kind of wrath will be deserved if our answer to these serious problems is to repeat the mistakes of the past. The old and comfortable way is to shave a little here and add a little there. Well, that is not acceptable any more. I think this great and historic Congress knows that way is no longer acceptable. [Applause] Thank you very much. Thank you.

I think you have shown that you know the one sure way to continue the inflationary spiral is to fall back into the predictable patterns of old economic practices.

Isn't it time that we tried something new?

When you allowed me to speak to you here in these Chambers a little earlier, I told you that I wanted this program for economic recovery to be ours, yours and mine. I think the bipartisan substitute bill has achieved that purpose. It moves us toward economic vitality.

Praises Shuttle Astronauts

Just 2 weeks ago you and I joined millions of our fellow Americans in marveling at the magical historical moment that John Young and Bob Crippen created in their space shuttle Columbia. The last manned effort was almost 6 years ago, and I remembered on this more recent day over the years how we had all come to expect technological precision of our men and machines. And each amazing achievement became commonplace, until the next new challenge was raised.

With the Space Shuttle, we tested our ingenuity once again, moving beyond the accomplishments of the past into the promise and uncertainty of the future. Thus we not only planned to send up a 122-foot aircraft, 170 miles into space, but we also intended to make it maneuverable and return it to Earth landing 98 tons of exotic metals delicately on a remote dry lake bed.

The Space Shuttle did more than prove our technological abilities. It raised our expectations once more. It started us dreaming again. The poet Carl Sandburg wrote, "The Republic is a dream. Nothing happens unless first a dream."

And that is what makes us as Americans different. We have always reached for a new spirit and aimed at a higher goal. We have been courageous and determined, unafraid and bold. Who among us wants to be first to say we no longer have those qualities, that we must limp along doing the same things that have brought us our present misery?

I believe that the people you and I represent are ready to chart a new course. They look to us to meet the great challenge, to reach beyond the commonplace and not fall short for lack of creativity or courage.

Someone, you know, has said that he who would have nothing to do with thorns must never attempt to gather flowers.

But we have much greatness before us. We can restore our economic strength and build opportunities like none we have ever had before.

As Carl Sandburg said, all we need to begin with is a dream that we can do better than before.

All we need to have is faith, and that dream will come true.

All we need to do is act, and the time for action is now.

Thank you and good night.

JULY 27
SPEECH ON TAX BILL

Following is the text of the televised speech given by President Reagan on July 27, 1981:

Good evening. I'd intended to make some remarks about the problem of Social Security tonight, but the immediacy of Congressional action on the tax program, a key component of our economic package, has to take priority. Let me just say, however, I've been deeply disturbed by the way those of you who are dependent on Social Security have been needlessly frightened by some of the inaccuracies which have been given wide circulation. It's true that the Social Security system has financial problems. It's also true that these financial problems have been building for more than twenty years, and nothing has been done.

I hope to address you on this entire subject in the near future. In the meantime, let me just say this: I stated during the campaign and I repeat now, I will not stand by and see those of you who are dependent on Social Security deprived of the benefits you've worked so hard to earn. I make that pledge to you as your President. You have no reason to be frightened. You will continue to receive your checks in the full amount due you. In any plan to restore fiscal integrity of Social Security, I personally will see that the plan will not be at the expense of you who are now dependent on your monthly Social Security checks.

Economic Situation

Now, let us turn to the business at hand. It's been nearly six months since I first reported to you on the state of the nation's economy. I'm afraid my message that night was grim and disturbing. I remember telling you we were in the worst economic mess since the Great Depression. Prices were continuing to spiral upward, unemployment was reaching intolerable levels, and all because government was too big, and spent too much of our money.

We're still not out of the woods, but we've made a start. And we've certainly surprised those long-time and somewhat cynical observers of the Washington scene, who looked, listened, and said, "It can never be done, Washington will never change its spending habits." Well, something very exciting has been happening here in Washington, and you're responsible. Your voices have been heard. Millions of you, Democrats, Republicans, and Independents from every profession, trade and line of work, and from every part of this land. You sent a message that you wanted a new beginning. You wanted to change one little two little word — two letter word, I should say. It doesn't sound like much but it sure can make a difference — changing "by government" — "control by government" to "control of government."

In that earlier broadcast you'll recall I proposed a program to drastically cut back government spending in the 1982 budget which begins October 1st and to continue cutting in '83 and '84. Along with this I suggested an across-the-board tax cut spread over those same three years and the elimination of unnecessary regulations which were adding billions to the cost of things we buy.

All the lobbying, the organized demonstrations and the cries of protest by those whose way of life depends on maintaining government's wasteful ways were no match for your voices which were heard loud and clear in these marble halls of government.

And you made history with your telegrams, your letters, your phone calls and, yes, personal visits to talk to your elected representatives. You reaffirmed the mandate you delivered in the election last November — a mandate that called for an end to government policies that sent prices and mortgage rates skyrocketing while millions of Americans went jobless.

Government Cutbacks

Because of what you did, Republicans and Democrats in the Congress came together and passed the most sweeping cutbacks in the history of the federal budget. Right now, Members of the House and Senate are meeting in a conference committee to reconcile the differences between the two budget cutting bills passed by the House and the Senate. When they finish, all Americans will benefit from savings of approximately $140 billion in reduced government costs over just the next three years. And that doesn't include the additional savings from the hundreds of burdensome regulations already cancelled or facing cancellation.

For 19 out of the last 20 years, the federal government has spent more than it took in. There will be another large deficit in this present year which ends September 30th. But with our program in place, it won't be quite as big as it might have been and starting next year, the deficits will get smaller until in just a few years the budget can be balanced. And we hope we can begin whittling at that almost $1 trillion debt that hangs over the future of our children.

Economic Recovery

Now, so far, I've been talking about only one part of our program for economic recovery — the budget cutting part. I don't minimize its importance. Just the fact that Democrats and Republicans could work together as they have, proving the strength of our system, has created an optimism in our land. The rate of inflation is no longer in double-digit figures. The dollar has regained strength in the international money markets and businessmen and investors are making decisions with regard to industrial development, modernization and expansion, all of this based on anticipation of our program being adopted and put into operation.

A recent poll shows that where a year and a half ago only 24 percent of our people believed things would get better, today 46 percent believe they will. To justify their faith, we must deliver the other part of our program. Our economic package is a closely knit, carefully constructed plan to restore America's economic strength and put our nation back on the road to prosperity.

Each part of this package is vital. It cannot be considered piecemeal. It was proposed as a package and it has been supported as such by the American people. Only if the Congress passes all of its major components does it have any real chance of success. This is absolutely essential if we are to provide incentives and make capital available for the increased productivity required to provide real, permanent jobs for our people.

Let us not forget that the rest of the world is watching America carefully to see how we'll act at this critical moment.

I have recently returned from a summit meeting with world leaders in Ottawa, Canada, and the message I heard from them was quite clear. Our allies depend on a strong and economically sound America and they're watching events in this country, particularly those surrounding our program for economic recovery, with close attention and great hopes.

In short, the best way to have a strong foreign policy abroad is to have a strong economy at home.

The day after tomorrow, Wednesday, the House of Representatives will begin debate on two tax bills and once again they need to hear from you. I know that doesn't give you much time but a great deal is at stake. A few days ago I was visited here in the office by a Democratic Congressman from one of our southern states. He'd been back in his district and one day one of his constituents asked him where he stood on our economic recovery program. I outlined that program in an earlier broadcast, particularly the tax cut. Well, the Congressman, who happens to be a strong leader in support of our program, replied at some length with a discussion of the technical points involved, but he also mentioned a few reservations that he had on certain points. The constituent, a farmer, listened politely until he had finished, and then he said, "Don't give me an essay. What I want to know is are you for him or agin' him?"

Well, I appreciate the gentleman's support and suggest his question is a message your own representatives should hear.

Let me add, those representatives honestly and sincerely want to know your feelings. They get plenty of input from the special interest groups. They'd like to hear from their home folks.

Reagan Program

Now, let me explain what the situation is and what's at issue. With our budget cuts we've presented a complete program of reduction in tax rates. Again, our purpose was to provide incentive for the individual, incentives for business to encourage production and hiring of the unemployed, and to free up money for investment. Our bill calls for a 5 percent reduction in the income tax rate by October 1st, a 10 percent reduction beginning July 1st, 1982, and another 10 percent cut a year later, a 25 percent total reduction over three years.

But then to ensure the tax cut is permanent, we call for indexing the tax rates in 1985 which means adjusting them for inflation. As it is now, if you get a cost-of-living raise that's intended to keep you even with inflation, you find that the increase in the number of dollars you get may very likely move you into a higher tax bracket and you wind up poorer than you would. This is called bracket creep.

Bracket creep is an insidious tax. Let me give you an example. If you earned $10,000 a year in 1972, by 1980 you had to earn $19,700 just to stay even with inflation. But that's before taxes. Come April 15th, you'll find your tax rates have increased 30 percent. Now, if you've been wondering why you don't seem as well-off as you were a few years back, it's because government makes a profit on inflation. It gets an automatic tax increase without having to vote on it. We intend to stop that.

Time won't allow me to explain every detail. But our bill includes just about everything to help the economy. We reduce the marriage penalty, that unfair tax that has a working husband and wife pay more tax than if they were single. We increase the exemption on the inheritance or estate tax to $600,000 so that farmers and family-owned businesses don't have to sell the farm or store in the event of death just to pay the taxes.

Tax Incentives

Most important, we wipe out the tax entirely for a surviving spouse. No longer, for example, will a widow have to sell the family source of income to pay a tax on her husband's death. There are deductions to encourage investment and savings. Business gets realistic depreciation on equipment and machinery. And there are tax breaks for small and independent businesses which create 80 percent of all new jobs.

This bill also provides major credits to the research and development industry. These credits will help spark the high technology breakthroughs that are so critical to America's economic leadership in the world.

There are also added incentives for small businesses, including a provision that will lift much of the burden of costly paperwork that government has imposed on small business.

In addition, a short-term but substantial assistance for the hard pressed thrift industry, as well as reductions in oil taxes that will benefit new or independent oil producers and move our nation a step closer to energy self-sufficiency.

Our bill is, in short, the first real tax cut for everyone in almost 20 years. Now, when I first proposed this — incidentally, it has now become a bipartisan measure co-authored by Republican Barber Conable and Democrat Kent Hance — the Democratic leadership said a tax cut was out of the question. It would be widely inflationary. And that was before my inauguration. And then your voices began to be heard and suddenly the leadership discovered that, well, the one-year tax cut was feasible. We kept on pushing our three-year tax cut and by June the opposition found that a two-year tax cut might work. Now it's July and they find they could even go for a third year cut provided there was a trigger arrangement that would only allow it to go in effect if certain economic goals had been met by 1983.

But by holding the peoples' tax reduction hostage to future economic events they will eliminate the people's ability to plan ahead. Shopkeepers, farmers, and individuals will be denied the certainty they must have to begin saving or investing more of their money, and encouraging more savings and investment is precisely what we need now to rebuild our economy.

Democratic Tax Plan

There's also a little sleight of hand in that trigger mechanism. You see, their bill, the Committee bill, ensures that the 1983 deficit will be $6-1/2 billion greater than their own trigger requires. As it stands now, the design of their own bill will not meet the trigger they've put in. Therefore, the third year tax cut will automatically never take place.

If I could paraphrase a well-known statement by Will Rogers that he had never met a man he didn't like, I'm afraid we have some people around here who never met a tax they didn't hike.

Their tax proposal, similar in a number of ways to ours, but differing in some very vital parts, was passed out of the House Ways and Means Committee and from now on I'll refer to it as the Committee bill and ours as the bipartisan bill. They'll be the bills taken up Wednesday. The majority leadership claims theirs gives a greater break to the worker than ours, and it does. That is, if you're only planning to live two more years. The plain truth is our choice is not between two plans to reduce taxes; it's between a tax cut or a tax increase. There is now built into our present system, including payroll, Social Security taxes, and the bracket creep I've mentioned, a 22 percent tax increase over the next three years.

The Committee bill offers a 15 percent cut over two years. Our bipartisan bill gives a 25 percent reduction over three years. Now, as you can see by this chart, there is the 22 percent tax increase. Their cut is below that line. But ours wipes out that increase and with a little to spare, and there it is, as you can see. The red column. That is the 15 percent tax cut and it still leaves you with an increase. The green column is our bipartisan bill which wipes out the tax increase and gives you an on-going cut.

Incidentally, their claim that cutting taxes for individuals for as much as three years ahead is risky rings a little hollow when you realize that their bill calls for business tax cuts each year for seven years ahead.

It rings even more hollow when you consider the fact the Majority leadership will keenly endorse its federal spending bills that project years into the future, but objects to a tax bill that will return your money over a three year period.

Now, here is another chart which illustrates what I said about their giving a better break if you only intend to live for two more years. Their tax cut, so called, is the dotted line. Ours is the solid line. As you can see, in an earning bracket of $20,000, their tax cut is slightly more generous than ours for the first two years. Then as you can see, their tax bill, the dotted line, starts going up and up and up. On the other hand, in our bipartisan tax bill, the solid line, our tax cut keeps on going down, and then stays down permanently.

This is true of all earning brackets, not just the $20,000 level I've used as an example, from the lowest to the highest. This red space between the two lines is the tax money that will remain in your pockets if our bill passes. And it's the amount that will leave your pockets if their tax bill is passed.

I take no pleasure in saying this, but those who will seek to defeat our Conable-Hance bipartisan bill, as debate begins Wednesday, are the ones who have given us "five" tax cuts in the last ten years. But, our taxes went up $400 billion in those same ten years. The lines on these charts say a lot about who is really fighting for whom. On the one hand, you see a genuine and lasting commitment to the future of working Americans, on the other, just another empty promise.

Those of us in the bipartisan coalition want to give this economy, and the future of this nation, back to the people. Because putting people first has always been America's secret weapon. The House Majority leadership seems less concerned about protecting your family budget, than with spending more on the federal budget.

Our bipartisan tax bill targets three-quarters of its tax relief to middle-income wage earners who presently pay almost three-quarters of the total income tax. It also indexes the tax bracket to insure that you can keep that tax reduction in the years ahead. There also is, as I said, estate tax relief that will keep family farms and family-owned businesses in the family, and there are provisions for personal retirement plans and individual savings accounts.

Because our bipartisan bill is so clearly drawn and broadly based, it provides the kind of predictability and certainty that the financial segments of our society need to make investment decisions that stimulate productivity and make our economy grow.

Even more important, if the tax cut goes to you, the American people, in the third year, that money returned to you won't be available to the Congress to spend, and that, in my view, is what this whole controversy comes down to. Are you entitled to the fruits of your own labor or does government have some presumptive right to spend and spend and spend?

I'm also convinced our business tax cut is superior to theirs because it's more equitable and it will do a much better job promoting the surge in investment we so badly need to rebuild our industrial base.

There is something else I want to tell you. Our bipartisan coalition worked out a tax bill we felt would provide incentive and stimulate productivity, thus reducing inflation and providing jobs for the unemployed. That was our only goal. Our opponents in the beginning didn't want a tax bill at all. So what is the purpose behind their change of heart? They've put a tax program together for one reason only, to provide themselves with a political victory. Never mind that it won't solve the economic problems confronting our country. Never mind that it won't get the wheels of industry turning again or eliminate the inflation which is eating us alive. This is not the time for political fun and games. This is the time for a new beginning.

Request for Public Support

I ask you now to put aside any feelings of frustration or helplessness about our political institutions and join me in this dramatic but responsible plan to reduce the enormous burden of federal taxation on you and your family.

During recent months many of you have asked what can you do to help make America strong again. I urge you again to contact your senators and congressmen. Tell them of your support for this bipartisan proposal. Tell them you believe this is an unequalled opportunity to help return America to prosperity and make government again the servant of the people.

In a few days the Congress will stand at the fork of two roads. One road is all too familiar to us. It leads ultimately to higher taxes. It merely brings us full circle back to the source of our economic problems, where the government decides that it knows better than you what should be done with your earnings and, in fact, how you should conduct your life. The other road promises to renew the American spirit. It's a road of hope and opportunity. It places the direction of your life back in your hands where it belongs.

I'm not taking your time this evening merely to ask you to trust me. Instead, I ask you to trust yourselves. That's what America is all about. Our struggle for nationhood, our unrelenting fight for freedom, our very existence, these have all rested on the assurance that you must be free to shape your life as you are best able to, that no one can stop you from reaching higher or take from you the creativity that has made America the envy of mankind. One road is timid and fearful. The other bold and hopeful.

In these six months we've done so much and have come so far. It's been the power of millions of people like you who have determined that we will make America great again. You have made the difference up to now. You will make the difference again. Let us not stop now.

Thank you. God bless you. Good night.

SEPT. 24
BUDGET ADDRESS

Following is the text of President Reagan's Sept. 24 televised address to the nation reporting on the country's economic situation and requesting public support for further budget cuts and adjustments in Social Security payments:

Good evening. Shortly after taking office I came before you to map out a four-part plan for national economic recovery: tax cuts to stimulate more growth and more jobs, spending cuts to put an end to continuing deficits and high inflation, regulatory relief to lift the heavy burden of government rules and paperwork, and, finally, a steady, consistent, monetary policy.

We've made strong, encouraging progress on all four fronts. The flood of new governmental regulations, for example, has been cut by more than a third. I was especially pleased when a bipartisan coalition of Republicans and Democrats enacted the biggest tax cuts and the greatest reduction in federal spending in our nation's history. Both will begin to take effect a week from today. These two bills would never have passed without your help. Your voices were heard in Washington and were heeded by those you've chosen to represent you in government. Yet, in recent weeks we've begun to hear a chorus of other voices protesting that we haven't had full economic recovery. These are the same voices that were raised against our program when it was first presented to Congress. Now that the first part of it has been passed, they declare it hasn't worked. Well, it hasn't. It doesn't start until a week from today.

Inflation Easing Up

There have been some bright spots in our economic performance these past few months. Inflation has fallen and pressures are easing on both food and fuel prices. More than a million more Americans are now at work than a year ago, and recently there has even been a small crack in interest rates. But let me be the first to say that our problems won't suddenly disappear next week, next month, or next year. We're just starting down a road that I believe will lead us out of the economic swamp we've been in for so long. It'll take time for the effect of the tax rate reductions to be felt in increased savings, productivity, and new jobs. It will also take time for the budget cuts to reduce the deficits which have brought us near runaway inflation and ruinous interest rates.

The important thing now is to hold to a firm, steady course. Tonight I want to talk with you about the next steps that we must take on that course, additional reductions in federal spending that will help lower our interest rates, our inflation, and bring us closer to full economic recovery.

I know that high interest rates are punishing many of you, from the young family that wants to buy its first home to the farmer who needs a new truck or tractor. But all of us know that interest rates will only come down and stay down when government is no longer borrowing huge amounts of money to cover its deficits.

These deficits have been piling up every year and some people here in Washington just throw up their hands in despair. Maybe you'll remember that we were told in the spring of 1980 that the 1981 budget, the one we have now, would be balanced. Well, that budget, like so many in the past, hemorrhaged badly and wound up in a sea of red ink.

More Cuts in Federal Spending

I have pledged that we shall not stand idly by and see that same thing happen again. When I presented our economic recovery program to Congress, I said we were aiming to cut the deficit steadily to reach a balance by 1984.

The budget bill that I signed this summer cut $35 billion from the 1982 budget and slowed the growth of spending by $130 billion over the next three years. We cut the government's rate of growth nearly in half.

Now we must move on to a second round of budget savings — to keep us on the road to a balanced budget.

Our immediate challenge is to hold down the deficit in the fiscal year that begins next week. A number of threats are now appearing that will drive the deficit upward if we fail to act. For example, in the euphoria just after our budget bill was approved this summer, we didn't point out immediately as we should have that while we did get most of what we'd asked for, most isn't all. Some of the savings in our proposal were not approved; and since then, the Congress has taken actions that could add even more to the cost of government.

The result is that without further reductions, our deficit for 1982 will be increased by some $16 billion. The estimated deficit for '83 will be increased proportionately. And without further cuts, we can't achieve our goal of a balanced budget by 1984.

Now, it would be easy to sit back and say, "Well, it will take longer than we thought. We got most of what we proposed, so let's stop there." But that's not good enough.

Must 'Face Up' to Cuts

In meeting to discuss this problem a few days ago, Senator Pete Domenici of New Mexico, Chairman of the Senate Budget Committee, recalled the words of that great heavy-weight champion and great American Joe Louis just before he stepped into the ring against Billy Conn. There had been some speculation that Billy might be able to avoid Joe's lethal right hand. Joe said, "Well, he can run but he can't hide."

Senator Domenici said to me, "That's just what we're facing on runaway federal spending. We can try to run from it but we can't hide. We have to face up to it."

He's right, of course. In the last few decades we started down a road that led to a massive explosion in federal spending. It took about 170 years for the federal budget to reach $100 billion. That was in 1962. It took only eight years to reach the $200 billion mark and only five more to make it $300 billion. And in the next five we nearly doubled that.

It would be one thing if we'd been able to pay for all the things government decided to do, but we've only balanced the budget once in the last 20 years.

Trillion Dollar National Debt

In just the past decade, our national debt has more than doubled. And in the next few days it will pass the trillion dollar mark. One trillion dollars of debt — if we as a nation needed a warning, let that be it.

Our interest payments on the debt alone are now running more than $96 million a year. That's more than the total combined profits last year of the 500 biggest companies in the country; or to put it another way, Washington spends more on interest than on all of its education, nutrition and medical programs combined.

In the past, there have been several methods used to fund some of our social experiments. One was to take it away from national defense. From being the strongest nation on earth in the post World War II years, we've steadily declined, while the Soviet Union engaged in the most massive military buildup the world has ever seen.

Now, with all our economic problems, we're forced to try to catch up so that we can preserve the peace. Government's first responsibility is national security and we're determined to meet that responsibility. Indeed, we have no choice.

Well, what all of this is leading to is — what do we plan to do? Last week I met with the Cabinet to take up this matter. I'm proud to say there was no hand-wringing, no pleading to avoid further budget cuts. We all agreed that the "tax and tax, spend and spend," policies of the past few decades lead only to economic disaster. Our government must return to the tradition of living within our means and must do it now. We asked ourselves two questions — and answered them: "If not us — who? If not now — when?"

Let me talk with you now about the specific ways that I believe we ought to achieve additional savings — savings of some $16 billion in 1982 and a total of $80 billion when spread over the next three years. I recognize that many in Congress may have other alternatives and I welcome a dialogue with them. But let there be no mistake: We have no choice but to continue down the road toward a balanced budget — a budget that will keep us strong at home and secure overseas. And let me be clear that this cannot be the last round of cuts. Holding down spending must be a continuing battle for several years to come.

Here is what I propose. First, I'm asking Congress to reduce the 1982 appropriation for most government agencies and programs by 12 percent. This will save $17.5 billion over the next several years. Absorbing these reductions will not be easy, but duplication, excess, waste and overhead is still far too great and can be trimmed further.

Defense Budget to be Cut

No one in the meeting asked to be exempt from belt-tightening. Over the next three years, the increase we had originally planned in the defense budget will be cut by $13 billion. I'll confess, I was reluctant about this because of the long way we have to go before the dangerous window of vulnerability confronting us will be appreciably narrowed. But the Secretary of Defense assured me that he can meet our critical needs in spite of this cut.

Reduce Federal Staff

Second, to achieve further economies, we'll shrink the size of the non-defense payroll over the next three years by some 6½ percent, some 75,000 employees. Much of this will be attained by not replacing those who retire or leave. There will, however, be some reductions in force simply because we're reducing our administrative overhead. I intend to set the example here by reducing the size of the White House staff and the staff of the Executive Office of the President.

As a third step, we propose to dismantle two Cabinet departments, Energy and Education. Both secretaries are wholly in accord with this. Some of the activities in both of these departments will, of course, be continued either independently or in other areas of government. There's only one way to shrink the size and cost of big government and that is by eliminating agencies that are not needed and are getting in the way of a solution. Now, we don't need an Energy Department to solve our basic energy problem. As long as we let the forces of the marketplace work without undue interference, the ingenuity of consumers, business, producers and inventors will do that for us.

Similarly, education is the principal responsibility of local school systems, teachers, parents, citizen boards and state governments. By eliminating the Department of Education less than two years after it was created, we cannot only reduce the budget, but ensure that local needs and preferences rather than the wishes of Washington determine the education of our children. We also plan the elimination of a few smaller agencies and a number of boards and commissions, some of which have fallen into disuse or which are now being duplicated.

Loan Guarantee Reductions

Fourth, we intend to make reductions of some $20 billion in federal loan guarantees. These guarantees are not funds that the government spends directly. They're funds that are loaned in the private market and insured by government at subsidized rates. Federal loan guarantees have become a form of back door, uncontrolled borrowing that prevent many small businesses that aren't subsidized from obtaining financing of their own. They are also a major factor in driving up interest rates. It's time we brought this practice under control.

Welfare and Entitlement Reform

Fifth, I intend to forward to Congress this fall a new package of entitlement and welfare reform measures, outside Social Security, to save nearly $27 billion over the next three years. In the past two decades we've created hundreds of new programs to provide personal assistance. Many of these programs may have come from a good heart but not all have come from a clear head. And the costs have been staggering.

In 1955 these programs cost $8 billion. By 1965 the cost was $79 billion. Next year it will be $188 billion. Let there be no confusion on this score. Benefits for the needy will be protected, but the black market in food stamps must be stopped, the abuse and fraud by beneficiaries and providers alike cannot be tolerated, provision of school loans and meal subsidies to the affluent can no longer be afforded.

In California when I was Governor and embarked upon welfare reform, there were screams from those who claimed that we intended to victimize the needy. But in a little over three years we saved the taxpayer some $2 billion at the same time we were able to increase the grants for the deserving and truly needy by an average of more than 40 percent. It was the first cost of living increase they'd received in 13 years. I believe progress can also be made at the national level.

We can be compassionate about human needs without being complacent about budget extravagance.

Tax Reform

Sixth, I will soon urge Congress to enact new proposals to eliminate abuses and obsolete incentives in the tax code. The Treasury Department believes that the deficit can be reduced by $3.0 billion next year and $22 billion over the next three years with prompt enactment of these measures.

Now that we've provided the greatest incentives for saving, investment, work and productivity ever proposed, we must also ensure that taxes due the government are collected and that a fair share of the burden is borne by all.

Finally, I am renewing my plea to Congress to approve my proposals for user fees — proposals first suggested last spring, but which have been neglected since.

When the federal government provides a service directly to a particular industry or to a group of citizens, I believe that those who receive benefits should bear the cost. For example, this next year the federal government will spend $525 million to maintain river harbors, channels, locks, and dams for the barge and maritime industries. Yacht owners, commercial vessels and the airlines will receive services worth $2.8 billion from Uncle Sam.

My spring budget proposals included legislation that would authorize the federal government to recover a total of $980 million from the users of these services through fees. Now, that's only a third of the $3.3 billion it will cost the government to provide those same services.

None of these steps will be easy. We're going through a period of difficult and painful readjustment. I know that we're asking for sacrifices from virtually all of you. But there is no alternative. Some of those who oppose this plan have participated over the years in the extravagance that has brought us inflation, unemployment, high interest rates and an intolerable debt. I grant they were well intentioned but their costly reforms didn't eliminate poverty or raise welfare recipients from dependence to self-sufficiency, independence and dignity. Yet in their objections to what we've proposed they offer only what we know has been tried before and failed.

I believe we've chosen a path that leads to an America at work, to fiscal sanity, to lower taxes and less inflation. I believe our plan for recovery is sound and it will work.

Tonight I'm asking all of you who joined in this crusade to save our economy to help again. To let your representatives know that you'll support them in making the hard decisions to further reduce the cost and size of government.

Social Security

Now, if you'll permit me, I'd like to turn to another subject which I know has many of you very concerned and even frightened. This is an issue apart from the economic reform package that we've just been discussing, but I feel I must clear the air. There has been a great deal of misinformation and for that matter pure demagoguery on the subject of Social Security.

During the campaign I called attention to the fact that Social Security had both a short and a long range fiscal problem. I pledged my best to restore it to fiscal responsibility without in any way reducing or eliminating existing benefits for those now dependent on it.

To all of you listening and particularly those of you now receiving Social Security, I ask you to listen very carefully: First to what threatens the integrity of Social Security and then to a possible solution.

Some thirty years ago, there were 16 people working and paying the Social Security payroll tax for every one retiree. Today that ratio has changed to only 3.2 workers paying in for each beneficiary.

For many years we've known that an actuarial imbalance existed and that the program faced an unfunded liability of several trillion dollars.

Now, the short range problem is much closer than that. The Social Security retirement fund has been paying out billions of dollars more each year than it takes in and it could run out of money before the end of 1982 unless something is done.

Some of our critics claim new figures reveal a cushion of several billions of dollars which will carry the program beyond 1982. I'm sure it's only a coincidence that 1982 is an election year.

The cushion they speak of is borrowing from the Medicare fund and the disability fund. Of course doing this would only postpone the day of reckoning. Alice Rivlin of the Congressional Budget Office told a congressional committee the day before yesterday that such borrowing might carry us to 1990, but then we'd face the same problem. And as she put it, we'd have to cut benefits or raise the payroll tax. Well, we're not going to cut benefits and the payroll tax is already being raised.

In 1977, Congress passed the largest tax increase in our history. It called for a payroll tax increase in January of 1982, another in 1985, and again in 1986 and in 1990.

When that law was passed we were told it made Social Security safe until the year 2030. But we're running out of money 48 years short of 2030.

For the nation's work force, the Social Security tax is already the biggest tax they pay. In 1935 we were told the tax would never be greater than 2% of the first $3,000 of earnings. It is presently 13.3% of the first $29,700 and the scheduled increases will take it to 15.3% of the first $60,600. And that's when Mrs. Rivlin says we would need an additional increase.

Some have suggested reducing benefits. Others propose an income tax on benefits, or that the retirement age should be moved back to age 68 and there are some who would simply fund Social Security out of general tax funds as welfare is funded. I believe there are better solutions. I am asking the Congress to restore the minimum benefit for current beneficiaries with low incomes. It was never our intention to take this support away from those who truly need it.

Possible Solutions

There is, however, a sizable percentage of recipients who are adequately provided for by pensions or other income and should not be added to the financial burden of Social Security.

The same situation prevails with regard to disability payments. No one will deny our obligation to those with legitimate claims. But there's widespread abuse of the system which should not be allowed to continue.

Since 1962, early retirement has been allowed at age 62 with 80 percent of full benefits. In our proposal we ask that early retirees in the future receive 55 percent of the total benefit, but, and this is most important, those early retirees would only have to work an additional 20 months to be eligible for the 80 percent payment. I don't believe very many of you were aware of that part of our proposal.

The only change we proposed for those already receiving Social Security had to do with the annual cost of living adjustment. Now, those adjustments are made on July 1st each year, a hangover from the days when the fiscal year began in July. We proposed a one-time delay in making that adjustment, postponing it for three months until October 1st. From then on it would continue to be made every 12 months. That one time delay would not lower your existing benefits but would, on the average, reduce your increase by about $86 one time next year.

By making these few changes, we would have solved the short and long range problems of Social Security funding once and for all. In addition, we could have cancelled the increases in the payroll tax by 1985. To a young person just starting in the work force, the savings from cancelling those increases would, on the average, amount to $33,000 by the time he or she reached retirement, and compound interest, add that, and it makes a tiny nest egg to add to the Social Security benefits.

However, let me point out, our feet were never imbedded in concrete on this proposal. We hoped it could be a starting point for a bipartisan solution to the problem. We were ready to listen to alternatives and other ideas which might improve on or replace our proposals. But, the majority leadership in the House of Representatives has refused to join in any such cooperative effort.

I therefore am asking, as I said, for restoration of the minimum benefit and for interfund borrowing as a temporary measure to give us time to seek a permanent solution. To remove Social Security once and for all from politics I am also asking Speaker Tip O'Neill of the House of Representatives and Majority Leader in the Senate Howard Baker to each appoint five members and I will appoint five to a task force which will review all the options and come up with a plan that assures the fiscal integrity of Social Security and that Social Security recipients will continue to receive their full benefits.

I cannot and will not stand by and see financial hardship imposed on the more than 36 million senior citizens who have worked and served this nation throughout their lives. They deserve better from us.

Well now, in conclusion, let me return to the principal purpose of this message, the budget and the imperative need for all of us to ask less of government, to help to return to spending no more than we take in, to end the deficits and bring down interest rates that otherwise can destroy what we've been building here for two centuries.

Requests Volunteer Help

I know that we're asking for economies in many areas and programs that were started with the best of intentions and the dedication to a worthwhile cause or purpose, but I know also that some of those programs have not succeeded in their purpose. Others have proven too costly, benefiting those who administer them rather than those who were the intended beneficiaries. This doesn't mean we should discontinue trying to help where help is needed. Government must continue to do its share. But I ask all of you, as private citizens, to join this effort too. As a people we have a proud tradition of generosity.

More than a century ago a Frenchman came to America and later wrote a book for his countrymen telling them what he had seen here. He told them that in America when a citizen saw a problem that needed solving he would cross the street and talk to a neighbor about it and the first thing you know a committee would be formed and before long the problem would be solved. And then he added, "You may not believe this, but not a single bureaucrat would ever have been involved." . . . I believe the spirit of voluntarism still lives in America. We see examples of it on every hand, the community charity drive, support of hospitals and all manner of non-profit institutions, the rallying around whenever disaster or tragedy strikes.

The truth is we've let government take away many things we once considered were really ours to do voluntarily out of the goodness of our hearts and a sense of community pride and neighborliness. I believe many of you want to do those things again, want to be involved if only someone will ask you or offer the opportunity. Well, we intend to make that offer.

We're launching a nationwide effort to encourage our citizens to join with us in finding where need exists and then to organize volunteer programs to meet that need. We've already set the wheels of such a volunteer effort in motion.

As Tom Paine said 200 years ago, "We have it within our power to begin the world over again."

What are we waiting for?

God bless you, and good night.

Glossary

Appropriations Bill — Grants the actual monies approved by authorization bills, but not necessarily to the total permissible under the authorization bill. An appropriations bill must, under the Constitution, originate in the House and normally is not acted on until its authorization measure is enacted. General appropriations bills are supposed to be enacted by the seventh day after Labor Day before the start of the fiscal year to which they apply, but in recent years this has rarely happened. See also Continuing Appropriations. In addition to general appropriations bills, there are two specialized types: see Deficiency and Supplemental Appropriations.

Authorization Bill — Authorizes a program, specifies its general aim and conduct, and unless "open-ended," puts a ceiling on monies that can be used to finance it. Usually enacted before the related appropriations bill is passed. See also Contract Authority.

Automatic Stabilizer (Built-in Stabilizer) — A mechanism having a countercyclical effect that automatically moderates changes in incomes and outputs in the economy without specific decisions to change government policy. Unemployment insurance and the income tax are among the most important of the automatic stabilizers in the United States.

Backdoor Spending Authority — Budget authority provided in legislation outside the normal appropriation process. The most common forms of backdoor authority are borrowing authority, contract authority and entitlements.

Balanced Budget — A budget where the receipts are equal to or greater than outlays.

Balance of Payments — The relationship between total flows of assets into or out of a country, including not only trade but also transfers of capital, defense spending, foreign aid and transfers of monetary reserve assets such as gold.

Balance of Trade — The relationship between a nation's total exports and imports of goods and services, with an excess of exports producing a trade surplus and an excess of imports a trade deficit.

Borrowing Authority — Budget authority that permits a federal agency to incur obligations and make payments for specified purposes with borrowed money.

Budget Authority (BA) — Authority to enter into obligations that will result in outlays involving federal funds. The basic forms of budget authority are appropriations, contract authority and borrowing authority. BA is divided into new obligational authority (NOA) and loan authority (LA).

Budget Outlays — The actual spending of money as distinguished from the appropriation of it. Outlays, also called expenditures, are made by the disbursing officers of the administration; appropriations are made only by Congress. The two are rarely identical in any fiscal year; outlays may represent money appropriated one, two or more years previously. Total budget outlays for a fiscal year exclude outlays for off-budget federal entities. See Off-budget Outlays.

Budget Surplus or Deficit — The difference between budget receipts and outlays.

Business Cycles — The recurrent phases of expansion and contraction in overall business activity, as indicated by fluctuations in measures of aggregate economic activity, especially real gross national product. Although business cycles are recurrent, both the duration and the magnitude of individual cycles vary considerably.

Capital — In addition to land and labor, the third major factor of production. Capital refers either to physical capital, such as plant and equipment, or to the financial resources required to purchase physical capital.

Capital Gain — Profit from the sale of capital investments, such as stock and real estate. Captial gains are taxed at a lower rate than other income.

Concurrent Resolution on the Budget — A resolution passed by both houses of Congress (not requiring the president's signature) that sets forth, reaffirms, or revises the congressional budget for the U.S. government for a fiscal year. The first concurrent resolution (scheduled by law to be passed by May 15) establishes congressional budget targets for the fiscal year; the second concurrent resolution (due by September 15) puts a ceiling on budget authority and outlays and sets a floor on receipts. Additional concurrent resolutions revising the budget levels may be passed by Congress at any time.

Constant Dollar — A dollar value adjusted for changes in prices. Constant dollars are derived by dividing current dollar amounts by an appropriate price index ("deflating"). The result is a dollar value that would exist if prices and transactions were the same in all subsequent years as in the base year. Any changes therefore reflect only changes in the real volume of goods and services produced.

Consumer Price Index (CPI) — Either of two measures of the price change of a fixed "market basket" of goods and services typically purchased by urban consumers. CPI-U is based on a market basket determined by expenditure patterns of all urban households, while the market basket for CPI-W is determined by expenditure patterns of urban wage-earner and clerical-worker families. The level of the CPI indicates the relative cost of purchasing the specified market basket compared to the cost in a designated base year, while the current rate of change in the CPI measures how fast prices are currently rising or falling. Although the consumer price index is often used as the "cost-of-living index," the CPI measures only price changes, which are just one of several important factors affecting living costs. The CPI is published monthly by the Labor Department's Bureau of Labor Statistics.

Continuing Appropriations — Legislation enacted by Congress to provide budget authority for specific ongoing activities in cases where the regular appropriation has not been enacted by the beginning of the fiscal year. The continuing resolution usually specifies a maximum rate at which the agency may incur obligations, based on the rate of the prior year, the president's budget request or an appropriations bill passed by either or both houses of Congress but not yet cleared.

Contract Authority — Budget authority that permits the federal government to let contracts or obligate itself for future payments from funds not yet appropriated. The assumption is that funds will be available for payment when contracted debts come due.

Controllability — The ability of Congress and the president to increase and decrease budget outlays or budget authority during the year in question without changing the basic law authorizing the program. Relatively uncontrollable spending is that which the government cannot increase or decrease without changing existing substantive law. Uncontrollable spending includes outlays for open-ended programs and fixed costs such as interest on the public debt and Social Security benefits.

Cost-Benefit Analysis — An analytical technique that measures the costs of a proposed program or policy action against its presumed benefits, stated in terms of dollars.

Countercyclical — Deliberate government actions aimed at smoothing out swings in economic activity, including monetary and fiscal policy (such as countercyclical revenue sharing or public jobs programs). See also Automatic Stabilizer.

Current Dollar — The dollar value of a product or service in terms of prices existing at the time the product or service was sold.

Current Services Estimates — Estimated budget authority and outlays for the upcoming fiscal year based on continuation of existing level of service without policy changes. These estimates, accompanied by the underlying economic and programmatic assumptions upon which they are based, are transmitted by the president to Congress when the budget is submitted.

Deferral of Budget Authority — Any action or inaction by an employee of the United States that withholds, delays or effectively precludes the obligation or expenditure of budget authority. The 1974 budget law requires a special message from the president to Congress reporting a proposed deferral of budget authority. Deferrals may not extend beyond the end of the fiscal year in which the message reporting them is transmitted and they may be overturned by passage of a resolution by either house of Congress.

Deficiency Appropriations — An appropriation to cover the difference between an agency's regular appropriation and the amount deemed necessary for it to operate for the full fiscal year. In recent years deficiency bills have usually been called Supplemental Appropriations.

Deflation — A decrease in the general price level, usually accompanied by declining levels of output, increasing unemployment and a contraction of the supply of money and credit. Declines in output with increases in unemployment are sometimes referred to as deflationary changes.

Devaluation — The lowering of the value of a country's currency in relation to gold, or to the currency of other countries, when this value is set by government intervention in the exchange market. Devaluation usually refers to fixed exchange rates. In a system of flexible rates, if the value of the currency falls, it is referred to as depreciation; if the value rises, it is called appreciation.

Discount Rate — The interest rate that a commercial bank pays when it borrows from a Federal Reserve bank. The discount rate is one of the tools of monetary policy used by the Federal Reserve System to affect economic conditions. The Fed raises or lowers the discount rate to signal a shift toward restraining or easing its money and credit policy.

Disposable Personal Income — Personal income less personal taxes and non-tax payments to the federal government. It is the income available for consumption or saving.

Economic Growth — An increase in a country's productive capacity leading to an increase in the production of goods and services. Economic growth is measured by the annual rate of increase in real (constant dollars) gross national product.

Economic Indicators — A set of statistical series issued by the government that have had a systematic relationship to the business cycle. Each indicator is classified as leading, coincident, or lagging, depending on whether the indicator generally changes direction in advance of, coincident with, or subsequent to changes in the overall economy. Taken as a whole, the economic indicators are valuable tools for identifying and analyzing changes in business cycles.

Employment — In economic statistics, employment refers to all persons who, during the week when the employment survey was taken, did any work for pay or profit, or who worked for 15 or more hours without pay on a farm or in a business operated by a member of the person's family. Also included as employed are those people who did not work or look for work, but had a job or business from which they were temporarily absent during the week.

Entitlement Programs — A federal program that guarantees a certain level of benefits to persons who meet the requirements set by law. It thus leaves no discretion to Congress as to how much money to appropriate. Entitlement programs include Social Security and veterans' benefits.

Expenditures — See Budget Outlays.

Federal Debt — The federal debt consists of public debt, which occurs when the Treasury or the Federal Financing Bank borrows funds directly from the public or another fund or account, and agency debt, which is incurred when a federal agency other than Treasury or the FFB is authorized by law to borrow funds from the public or another fund or account. The public debt comprises about 99 percent of the gross federal debt.

Fiscal Policy — Federal government policies with respect to taxes, spending and debt management, intended to promote the nation's economic goals, particularly with respect to employment, gross national product, price level stability and equilibrium in balance of payments.

Fiscal Year — Financial operations of the government are carried out in a 12-month fiscal year, beginning on Oct. 1 and ending on Sept. 30. The fiscal year carries the date of the calendar year in which it ends. (Prior to fiscal 1977, the federal fiscal year began on July 1 and ended on June 30. The period June 30 through Sept. 30, 1976, is usually included as a separate accounting period commonly referred to as the "transition quarter.")

Gross National Product (GNP) — The market value of all final goods and services produced by labor and property supplied by residents of the United States in a given calendar or fiscal year. Depreciation charges and other allowances for business and institutional consumption of fixed capital goods are subtracted from GNP to derive net national product. GNP comprises the purchases of final goods and services by persons and governments,

gross private domestic investment (including the change in business inventories) and net exports. GNP can be expressed in current dollars or in constant dollars ("real GNP").

Implicit Price Deflator (GNP Deflator) — A price index for all final goods and services produced in the economy, derived by calculating the ratio of the gross national product in current prices to the gross national product in constant prices. It is a weighted average of the price indexes used to deflate the component of current-dollar GNP, the implicit weights being expenditures in the current period.

Impoundment — Any action or inaction by an employee of the United States that precludes the obligation or expenditure of budget authority provided by Congress. Impoundments may be disapproved by either house of Congress. See Deferral of Budget Authority.

Indexing — The practice of adjusting (wages, interest rates, Social Security benefits, tax rates) automatically to reflect changes in the cost of living.

Inflation — A persistent rise in the general price level that results in a decline in the purchasing power of money. Frequently defined as "too much money chasing too few goods."

Labor Force — Those persons who are employed plus those who are seeking work but are unemployed. The total U.S. labor force consists of civilians plus members of the armed forces stationed at home or abroad.

Marginal Tax Rate — The tax rate imposed on the last dollar of income.

Monetary Policy — Policies, which affect the money supply, interest rates and credit availability, that are intended to promote national economic goals — particularly with respect to employment, gross national product, price level stability and equilibrium in balance of payments. Monetary policy is directed primarily by the Board of Governors of the Federal Reserve System and its Federal Open Market Committee. Monetary policy works by influencing the cost and availability of bank reserves. This is accomplished through open-market operations (the purchase and sale of securities, primarily government securities), changes in the ratio of reserves to deposits that commercial banks are required to maintain and changes in the discount rate.

Money Supply — The amount of money in the economy. There are several definitions of money. M1-A consists of currency (coin and paper notes) plus demand deposits at commercial banks, exclusive of demand deposits held by other domestic banks, foreign banks and official institutions and the U.S. government. M1-B is M1-A plus other checkable accounts, including negotiable orders of withdrawal and automatic transfers from savings accounts at commercial banks and thrift institutions, credit unions share draft accounts and demand deposits at mutual savings banks. M-2 consists of M1-B plus savings and small denomination time deposits at all depository institutions, overnight repurchase agreements at commercial banks, overnight Eurodollars held by U.S. residents other than Caribbean branches of member banks, and money market mutual fund shares. M-3 is M-2 plus large denomination time deposits at all depository institutions and term repurchase agreements at commerical banks and savings and loan associations.

Off-budget Outlays — Transactions of certain federally owned or controlled agencies that have been excluded from the budget totals under provisions of law even though these outlays are part of total government spending. Spending activities of off-budget entities, such as the Federal Financing Bank, are not included in outlay totals but are presented in a separate part of the budget and as memorandum items in various tables in the budget.

Prime Rate — The rate of interest charged by commercial banks for short-term loans to their most creditworthy customers.

Producer Price Indexes (PPI) — A set of measures of average changes in prices received in all stages of processing by producers of commodities in the manufacturing, agriculture, forestry, fishing, mining, gas and electricity, and public utilities sectors. Published monthly by the Labor Department's Bureau of Labor Statistics. (Formerly known as "wholesale price indexes.")

Recession — A decline in overall business activity that is pervasive, substantial and of at least several months' duration. Historically, a decline in real gross national product for at least two consecutive quarters has been considered a recession.

Reconciliation — The process used by Congress to reconcile amounts determined by tax, spending and debt legislation for a given fiscal year with the ceilings enacted in the second required concurrent resolution on the budget for that year. Changes to laws, bills and resolutions, as required to conform with the binding totals for budget authority, revenues and the public debt, are incorporated into either a reconciliation resolution or reconciliation bill. In 1981 Congress used the reconciliation process to cut $36 billion from the fiscal 1982 budget before it enacted its fiscal 1982 binding budget totals.

Rescission — An item in an appropriation bill rescinding, or canceling, funds previously appropriated but not spent. Also, the president may request rescission of a previous appropriation to cut spending. Congress must approve such proposed rescissions under procedures in the Budget and Impoundment Control Act of 1974 for them to take effect.

Reserve Requirements — The percentage of deposit liabilities that U.S. commercial banks are required to hold as a reserve at their Federal Reserve bank, as cash in their vaults or as directed by state banking authorities. The reserve requirement is one of the tools of monetary policy. Federal Reserve officials can control the lending capacity of the banks (thus influencing the money supply) by varying the ratio of reserves to deposits that commercial banks are required to maintain.

Spending Authority — A designation for borrowing authority, contract authority and entitlement authority, for which the budget authority is not provided in advance by appropriation acts. See also Backdoor Authority.

Stabilization — The maintenance of high-level economic activity with an absence of severe cyclical fluctuations. Stability is usually measured by an absence of fluctuations in production, employment and prices, three aspects of economic activity that tend to change in a cyclical fashion.

Stagflation — Simultaneous high unemployment and high inflation.

Supplemental Appropriations — Normally, these are passed after the regular (annual) appropriations bills, but before the end of the fiscal year to which they apply. See Deficiency Appropriations.

Tax Credits — Tax credits include any special provision of law that results in a dollar-for-dollar reduction in tax liabilities that would otherwise be due.

Tax Expenditures — Revenue losses attributable to provisions of the federal income tax laws that allow a special exclusion, or deduction from gross income, or that provide a special credit, preferential tax rate, or deferral of tax liability. Tax expenditures may be considered federal government subsidies provided through the tax system to encourage certain activities and to assist certain groups. The U.S. Treasury forgoes some of the receipts that it otherwise would have collected and the beneficiary taxpayers pay lower taxes than they would otherwise have had to pay.

Trust Funds — Funds collected and used by the federal government for carrying out specific purposes and programs according to terms of a trust agreement or statute, such as the Social Security and unemployment compensation trust funds. Trust funds are administered by the government in a fiduciary capacity and are not available for the general purposes of the government.

Unemployment Rate — The number of unemployed persons expressed as a percentage of the civilian labor force. Unemployed persons are those who, during a specified week, had no employment but were available for work and had sought employment within the past 4 weeks, were laid off from a job or were waiting to report to a new job within 30 days.

Source: *This glossary of budget and economic terms was adapted by Congressional Quarterly from General Accounting Office, "Terms Used in the Budgetary Process," March 1981.*

Selected Bibliography

Books

Aaron, Henry J., ed. *Inflation and the Income Tax.* Washington, D.C.: Brookings Institution, 1976.

Aaron, Henry J. and Boskin, Michael, J., eds. *The Economics of Taxation.* Washington, D.C.: Brookings Institution, 1980.

Aaron, Henry J. and Pechman, Joseph A., eds. *How Taxes Affect Economic Behavior.* Washington, D.C.: Brookings Institution, 1981.

Aliber, Robert Z. *Monetary Reform and World inflation.* Beverly Hills, Calif.: Sage Publications, 1973.

Anderson, James E. *Politics and Economic Policymaking.* Reading, Mass.: Addison-Wesley, 1970.

Angell, James W. *Financial Foreign Policy of the United States.* New York: Russell & Russell, 1965.

Bach, G. L. *Making Monetary and Fiscal Policy.* Washington, D.C.: Brookings Institution, 1971.

Baker, Howard H., Jr. *No Margin for Error: America in the Eighties.* New York: Times Books, 1980.

Ball, Robert M. *Social Security Today and Tomorrow.* New York: Columbia University Press, 1979.

Berman, Larry. *The Office of Management and Budget and the Presidency, 1921-1979.* Princeton, N.J.: Princeton University Press, 1979.

Bethick, Martha. *Policymaking for Social Security.* Washington, D.C.: Brookings Institution, 1979.

Blechman, Barry M. and others. *Setting National Priorities: The 1975 Budget.* Washington, D.C.: Brookings Institution, 1974.

———. *Setting National Priorities: The 1976 Budget.* Washington, D.C.: Brookings Institution, 1975.

Bodkin, Ronald G. *The Wage-Price-Productivity Nexus.* Philadelphia: University of Pennsylvania Press, 1966.

Booth, Phillip. *Social Security in America.* Ann Arbor: University of Michigan Press, 1973.

Boskin, Michael J., ed. *The Crisis in Social Security.* San Francisco: Institute for Contemporary Studies, 1977.

———, ed. *Federal Tax Reform: Myths and Realities.* San Francisco: Institute for Contemporary Studies, 1976.

Boskin, Michael J. and others. *The Impact of Inflation on U.S. Productivity and International Competitiveness.* Washington, D.C.: National Planning Association, 1980.

Burns, Arthur F. and Samuelson, Paul A. *Full Employment, Guideposts and Economic Stability.* Washington, D.C.: American Enterprise Institute, 1967.

Cagan, Philip and others. *Economic Policy and Inflation in the Sixties.* Washington, D.C.: American Enterprise Institute, 1972.

Campbell, Colin D., ed. *Financing Social Security.* Washington, D.C.: American Enterprise Institute, 1979.

Campbell, Rita R. *Social Security, Promise and Reality.* Stanford, Calif.: Hoover Institution Press, 1977.

Carrington, John C. and Edwards, George T. *Reversing Economic Decline.* New York: St. Martin's Press, 1981.

Case, John. *Understanding Inflation.* New York: William Morrow, 1981.

Collins, Lora S. *The 1980 Recession in Perspective.* New York: The Conference Board, 1980.

Coyle, David C. *Breakthrough to the Great Society.* Dobbs Ferry, N.Y.: Oceana Publications, 1965.

Darby, Michael R. *The Effects of Social Security on Income and the Capital Stock.* Washington, D.C.: American Enterprise Institute, 1979.

Denison, Edward F. *Accounting for United States Economic Growth, 1919-1969.* Washington, D.C.: Brookings Institution, 1974.

Desler, I. M. *Making Foreign Economic Policy.* Washington, D.C.: Brookings Institution, 1980.

Dworak, Robert J. *Taxpayers, Taxes, and Government Spending: Perspectives on the Taxpayer Revolt.* New York: Praeger Publishers, 1980.

Eccles, Marriner S. *Economic Balance and a Balanced Budget.* New York: Da Capo Press, 1973.

Economic Impact of the Vietnam War. Washington, D.C.: The Center for Strategic Studies, Georgetown University, Special Report Series, No. 5, 1967.

Ely, Richard T. *The Past and the Present of Political Economy.* Baltimore, Md.: The Johns Hopkins University Press, 1978.

Feldstein, Martin. *The American Economy in Transition.* Chicago, Ill.: University of Chicago Press, 1980.

———. *Inflation, Capitol Taxation and Monetary Policy.* Cambridge, Mass.: National Bureau of Economic Research, 1981.

Fellner, William J. *Correcting Taxes for Inflation.* Washington, D.C.: American Enterprise Institute, 1975.

Fenno, Richard F., Jr. *The Power of the Purse: Appropriations Politics in Congress.* Boston: Little, Brown & Co., 1966.

Fisher, Louis. *Presidential Spending Power.* Princeton, N.J.: Princeton University Press, 1975.

Flash, Edward S., Jr. *Economic Advice and Presidential Leadership: The Council of Economic Advisers.* New York: Columbia University Press, 1965.

Friedman, Irving S. *Inflation: A World-Wide Disaster.* Boston, Mass.: Houghton Mifflin, 1980.

Friedman, Milton. *Dollars and Deficits: Inflation, Monetary Policy and the Balance of Payments.* Englewood Cliffs, N.J.: Prentice Hall, 1968.

Gilder, George. *Wealth and Poverty.* New York: Basic Books, 1981.

Hamilton, Walton and others. *Price and Price Policies.* New York:

Arno Press, 1973.

Harrington, Michael. *Decade of Decisions*. New York: Simon & Schuster, 1980.

Havemann, Joel. *Congress and the Budget*. Bloomington: Indiana University Press, 1978.

Heller, Walter. *New Dimensions of Political Economy*. Cambridge, Mass.: Harvard University Press, 1966.

——, ed. *Perspectives on Economic Growth*. New York: Random House, 1968.

Ippolito, D. S. *The Budget and National Politics*. San Francisco: W. H. Freeman, 1978.

Janeway, Eliot. *The Economics of Crisis: War, Politics, and the Dollar*. New York: Weybright & Talley, 1968.

Jones, Edward D. *Economic Crises*. Westport, Conn.: Hyperion Press, 1971.

Kaplan, Robert S. *Indexing Social Security: An Analysis of the Issues*. Washington, D.C.: American Enterprise Institute, 1977.

Kemp, Roger L. *Coping With Proposition 13*. Lexington, Mass.: Lexington Books, 1980.

Kristensen, T. *Inflation and Unemployment in the Modern Society*. New York: Praeger Publishers, 1981.

Kristol, Irving and Weaver, Paul, eds. *The Americans, 1976: Critical Choices for Americans*. Lexington, Mass.: Lexington Press, 1976.

Laffer, Arthur B. and Seymour, Jan P. *The Economics of the Tax Revolt*. New York: Harcourt Brace Jovanovich, 1979.

Lanzillotti, Robert F. and others. *Phase II in Review: The Price Commission Experience*. Washington, D.C.: Brookings Institution, 1975.

LeLoup, Lance. *The Fiscal Congress*. Westport, Conn.: Greenwood Press, 1981.

Leveson, Irving. *Economic Future of the United States*. Boulder, Colo.: Westview Press, 1981.

Lewis, Wilfred, Jr. *Federal Fiscal Policy in the Postwar Recessions*. Washington, D.C.: Brookings Institution, 1962.

Lindberg, Leon N. *Inflation and Political Change*. Elmsford, N.Y.: Pergamon Press, 1980.

Lynn, James T. *The Federal Budget: What Are the Nation's Priorities*. Washington, D.C.: American Enterprise Institute, 1976.

McAllister, Eugene J., ed. *Agenda for Progress: Examining Federal Spending*. Washington, D.C.: Heritage Foundation, 1981.

——. *Congress and the Budget: Evaluating the Process*. Washington, D.C.: Heritage Foundation, 1979.

McCracken, Paul W. and Weidenbaum, Murray L. *Fiscal Responsibility: Tax Increases or Spending Cuts?* New York: New York University Press, 1973.

Manley, John F. *The Politics of Finance: The House Committee on Ways and Means*. Boston: Little, Brown & Co., 1970.

Mayer, Martin. *The Fate of the Dollar*. New York: Times Books, 1980.

Melman, Seymour. *The Permanent War Economy: American Capitalism in Decline*. New York: Simon & Schuster, 1974.

Miller, Roger L. *The New Economics of Richard Nixon: Freezers, Floats, and Fiscal Policy*. New York: Harper's Magazine Press, 1972.

Mitchell, Daniel J. B. *Unions, Wages and Inflation*. Washington, D.C.: Brookings Institution, 1980.

Morrison, Rodney J. *Expectations and Inflation: Nixon, Politics and Economics*. Lexington, Mass.: Lexington Books, 1973.

Müller, Ronald E. *Revitalizing America: Politics for Prosperity*. New York: Simon & Schuster, 1980.

Munnell, Alicia H. *The Future of Social Security*. Washington, D.C.: Brookings Institution, 1977.

Myrdal, Gunnar. *Against the Stream: Critical Essays on Economics*. New York: Pantheon Books, 1973.

Neustadt, Richard. *Presidential Power, the Politics of Leadership with Reflections on Johnson and Nixon*. New York: John Wiley & Sons, 1976.

Okun, Arthur M. *Curing Chronic Inflation*. Washington, D.C.: Brookings Institution, 1978.

——. *The Political Economy of Prosperity*. Washington, D.C.: Brookings Institution, 1970.

Okun, Arthur M. and Perry, George L., eds. *Brookings Papers on Economic Activity*. Washington, D.C.: Brookings Institution, 1970.

Ott, David J. and others. *Public Claims on United States Output: Federal Budget Output Options in the Last Half of the Seventies*. Washington, D.C.: American Enterprise Institute, 1973.

Owen, Henry and Schultze, Charles L., eds. *Setting National Priorities: The Next Ten Years*. Washington, D.C.: Brookings Institution, 1976.

Pechman, Joseph A., ed. *Comprehensive Income Taxation*. Washington, D.C.: Brookings Institution, 1977.

——. *Federal Tax Policy*. Washington, D.C.: Brookings Institution, 1977.

——, ed. *Setting National Priorities: Agenda for the 1980s*. Washington, D.C.: Brookings Institution, 1980.

——, ed. *Setting National Priorities: The 1978 Budget*. Washington, D.C.: Brookings Institution, 1977.

——, ed. *Setting National Priorities: The 1979 Budget*. Washington, D.C.: Brookings Institution, 1978.

——, ed. *Setting National Priorities: The 1982 Budget*. Washington, D.C.: Brookings Institution, 1981.

Pechman, Joseph A. and others. *Social Security: Perspectives for Reform*. Washington, D.C.: Brookings Institution, 1968.

Perlman, Richard, ed. *Inflation: Demand-Pull or Cost Push?* Lexington, Mass.: D. C. Heath & Co., 1965.

Pfiffner, James P. *The President, the Budget, and Congress: Impoundment and the 1974 Budget Act*. Boulder, Colo.: Westview Press, 1979.

Porter, Roger B. *Presidential Decision Making: The Economic Policy Board*. Cambridge, Mass.: Harvard University Press, 1980.

Reuss, Henry S. *The Critical Decade: An Economic Policy for America and the Free World*. New York: McGraw-Hill, 1964.

Rostow, James M. *Productivity Prospects for Growth*. New York: Van Nostrand Reinhold, 1981.

Samuels, Warren J. and Wade, Larry L., eds. *Taxing and Spending Policy*. Lexington, Mass., Lexington Books, 1980.

Schick, Allen. *Congress and Money: Budgeting, Spending and Taxing*. Washington, D.C.: Urban Institute, 1980.

——. *The Congressional Budget Act of 1974: Legislative History and Analysis*. Washington, D.C.: Congressional Research Service, Library of Congress, 1976.

Schultze, Charles L. *The Politics and Economics of Public Spending*. Washington, D.C.: Brookings Institution, 1968.

Schultze, Charles L. and others. *Setting National Priorities: The 1971 Budget*. Washington, D.C.: Brookings Institution, 1970.

——. *Setting National Priorities: The 1972 Budget*. Washington, D.C.: Brookings Institution, 1971.

——. *Setting National Priorities: The 1973 Budget*. Washington, D.C.: Brookings Institution, 1972.

——. *Setting National Priorities: The 1974 Budget*. Washington, D.C.: Brookings Institution, 1973.

Sharkansky, Ira. *The Politics of Taxing and Spending*. New York: Bobbs-Merrill Co., 1969.

Shultz, George P. *Guidelines, Informal Controls, and the Market Place: Policy Choices in a Full Economy*. Chicago: University of Chicago Press, 1966.

Siegan, Bernard H., ed. *Government, Regulation, and the Economy*. Lexington, Mass.: Lexington Books, 1980.

Silk, Leonard S. *Nixonomics: How the Dismal Science of Free Enterprise Became the Black Art of Controls*. New York: Praeger Publishers, 1973.

Smith, Warren L. and Teigen, Ronald L., eds. *Readings in Money, National Income and Stabilization Policy*. Homewood, Ill.: Richard D. Irwin, 1965.

Smithies, Arthur. *The Budgetary Process in the United States*. New York: McGraw-Hill Book Co., 1955.

Sommers, Albert T. *Inflation: The Crucial Challenge in the 1980s*. New York: Conference Board, 1980.

Stein, Herbert. *The Fiscal Revolution in America*. Chicago: University of Chicago Press, 1969.

Surrey, Stanley S. *Pathways to Tax Reform*. Cambridge, Mass.: Harvard University Press, 1973.

Thurow, Lester C. *The Zero-Sum Society: Distribution and the Possibilities for Economic Change*. New York: Basic Books, 1980.

Tobin, James. *National Economic Policy: Essays*. New Haven, Conn.: Yale University Press, 1966.

U.S. Government Finances: A Twenty-Two Year Perspective, 1950-1971. Washington, D.C.: American Enterprise Institute, 1970.

Van Gorkom, J. W. *Social Security: The Long Term Deficit*. Washington, D.C.: American Enterprise Institute, 1976.

Wagner, Richard E. and Tollison, Robert D. *Balanced Budgets, Fiscal Responsibility, and the Constitution*. San Francisco, Calif.: Cato Institute, 1980.

Wallace, Robert A. *Congressional Control of Federal Spending*. Detroit: Wayne State University Press, 1960.

Weber, Arnold R. *In Pursuit of Price Stability: The Wage Price Freeze of 1971*. Washington, D.C.: Brookings Institution, 1973.

Weidenbaum, Murray L. *Federal Budgeting: The Choice of Government Programs*. Washington, D.C.: American Enterprise Institute, 1964.

——. *Matching Needs and Resources: Reforming the Federal Budget*. Washington, D.C.: American Enterprise Institute, 1973.

Whitman, Marina N. and McInally, William K. *U.S. Economic Policy in an Era of Détente*. Ann Arbor: University of Michigan Press, 1973.

Wildavsky, Aaron. *Budgeting*. Boston: Little, Brown & Co., 1974.

——. *The Politics of the Budgetary Process*. Boston: Little, Brown & Co., 1974.

Williams, Walter. *The Congressional Budget Office: A Critical Link in Budget Reform*. Seattle: Institute of Government Research, University of Washington, 1974.

Wilmerding, Lucius Jr. *The Spending Power*. New Haven, Conn.: Yale University Press, 1943.

Wynne, Edward. *Social Security: A Reciprocity System Under Pressure*. Boulder, Colo.: Westview Press, 1980.

Articles

Annable, James E., Jr., "Inflation and Politics." *National Forum*, Spring 1981, pp. 36-37.

Balz, Daniel J. "Juice and Coffee and the GNP: The Men Who Meet in the Morning." *National Journal*, April 3, 1976, pp. 426-433.

Barber, Clarence L. "Inflation Distortion and the Balanced Budget." *Challenge*, September/October 1979, pp. 44-47.

"The Behavior of Prices, Labor Cost, and Profits in an Inflationary Economy." *Capital Goods Review*, June 1977, pp. 1-8.

Benoit, E. "Cutting Back Military Spending: The Vietnam Withdrawal and Recession." *Annals of the American Academy of Political and Social Science*, March 1973, pp. 73-79.

Blumberg, Daniel A. "Higher Productivity: The Only Lasting Answer to Spiraling Inflation." *Financial Planning Today*, July 1980, pp. 59-65.

Bonafede, Don. "The Making of the President's Budget: Politics and Influence in a New Manner." *National Journal*, January 23, 1971, pp. 151-165.

Boretsky, Michael. "Trends in U.S. Productivity: A Political Economist's Views." *The American Scientist*, January/February 1975, pp. 70-82.

Brennan, Geoffrey. "Inflation, Taxation, and Indexation." *Policy Studies Journal*, Spring 1977, pp. 326-332.

Brimmer, Andrew J. "The Political Economy of Limitations on Federal Spending." *Challenge*, March/April 1980, pp. 6-11.

Bryan, William R. "Recession and Unemployment, Inflation and High Interest Rates." *Business Review*, July 1980, pp. 1-3.

Byrne, James S. "The Future of Tax Reform: Role of the President." *Tax Notes*, October 4, 1976, pp. 3-6.

Calleo, David P. "Inflation and American Power." *Foreign Affairs*, Spring 1981, pp. 781-812.

Cameron, Juan. "Jimmy Carter Gets Mixed Marks In Economics 1." *Fortune*, June 1977, pp. 98-104.

Colander, David C. "An Overview of Inflation Theory and Policy." *Review of Business*, Winter 1980/1981, pp. 16-19.

Dale, Edwin L., Jr. "Vote Limits to Federal Spending as Percentage of GNP." *Financier*, May 1979, pp. 46-49.

Derber, Milton. "The Wage Stabilization Program in Historical Perspective." *Labor Law Journal*, August 1972, pp. 453-462.

Diebold, William. "The Economic System at Stake." *Foreign Affairs*, October 1972, pp. 167-180.

Domenici, Peter. "Can Congress Control Spending?" *Policy Review*, Fall 1980, pp. 49-65.

Dumbrell, John. "Strengthening the Legislative Power of the Purse: The Origins of the 1974 Budgetary Reforms in the U.S. Congress." *Public Administration*, Winter 1980, pp. 479-496.

Early, John F. and others. "Double Digit Inflation Today and in 1973-74: A Comparison." *Monthly Labor Review*, May 1980, pp. 3-20.

Ellwood, John W. and Thurber, James A. "The Politics of the Congressional Budget Process." In *Congress Reconsidered*, 2d. ed., edited by Lawrence C. Dodd and Bruce I. Oppenheimer, pp. 246-271. Washington, D.C.: Congressional Quarterly Press, 1981.

Fisher, C. William. "The New Congressional Budget Establishment and Federal Spending: Choices for the Future." *National Tax Journal*, March 1976, p. 12.

Fisher, Louis. "Congressional Budget Reform: The First Two Years." *Harvard Journal of Legislation*, April 1977, pp. 413-457.

——. "Impoundment of Funds: Uses and Abuses." *University of Buffalo Law Review*, Fall 1973, pp. 141-200.

——. "Presidential Spending Discretion and Congressional Controls." *Law and Contemporary Problems*, Winter 1972, pp. 135-172.

Freedman, David H. "Inflation in the United States, 1959-1974: Its Impact on Employment." *International Labour Review*, August/September 1975, pp. 125-147.

Fusfeld, Daniel R. "The Next Great Depression II: The Impending Financial Collapse." *Journal of Economic Issues*, June 1980, pp. 493-503.

Galbraith, James K. and Reuss, Henry S. "Fighting Inflation and Recession: 1980 Was a Good Test of the Federal Reserve's Monetary Economics." *Working Papers for a New Society*, September/October 1980, pp. 12-16.

Georgescu-Roegen, Nicholas. "Energy and Economic Myths." *Ecologist*, August/September 1975, pp. 242-252.

"Getting a Grip on the Federal Purse." *Morgan Guaranty Survey*, January 1973, pp. 6-11.

Gittings, Thomas A. "The Inflation-Unemployment Trade Off." *Economic Perspectives*, October 1979, pp. 3-9.

Glass, Andrew J. "The Fight Over Funding." *New Leader*, March 19, 1973, pp. 4-5.

——. "Money Games Presidents Play." *New Leader*, May 3, 1971.

Gooding, Elmer R. and Sandler, Todd M. "Dollars, Deficits, and Devaluation." *Arizona Business*, May 1973, pp. 10-16.

Gramley, Lyle E. "The Role of Supply-Side Economics in Fighting Inflation." *Challenge*, January/February 1981, pp. 14-18.

Haberler, Gottfried. "Oil, Inflation, Recession, and the International Monetary System." *Journal of Energy and Development*, Spring 1976, pp. 177-190.

Haney, Richard L., Jr. and others. "Hidden Cost of Federal Energy Legislation." *California Management Review*, Fall 1979, pp. 13-22.

Hashim, Jawad. "The Future Relationship Among Energy Demand, OPEC, and the Value of the Dollar." *Journal of Energy and Development*, Autumn 1980, pp. 61-71.

Harris, T. G. "Vietnam's Economic Lesson: Peace Can Yield Fatter Profits Than War." *Look*, May 31, 1966, p. 14.

Havemann, Joel. "Zero-Base Budgeting." *National Journal*, April 2, 1977, p. 514.

Hazlitt, Henry. "Why Inflation is Worldwide." *Freeman*, June

1977, pp. 332-339.

Heclo, Hugh. "OMB and the Presidency: The Problem of Neutral Competence." *The Public Interest*, Winter 1975, pp. 80-98.

Heller, Walter W. "Shadow and Substance in Inflationary Policy." *Challenge*, January/February 1981, pp. 5-13.

Hemel, Eric. "The Expensive Myth of 'Uncontrollable' Spending." *Contemporary Studies*, Winter 1981, pp. 15-26.

Higgs, Robert. "Carter's Wage-Price Guidelines: A Review of the First Year." *Policy Review*, Winter 1980, pp. 97-113.

Hudson, Philip. "Business Depressions: Past and Present." *Arizona Review*, October 1974, pp. 1-6.

"Impoundment of Funds." *Harvard Law Review*, June 1973, pp. 1505-1535.

Jones, William K. "Government Price Controls and Inflation: A Prognosis Based on the Impact of Controls in the Regulated Industries." *Cornell Law Review*, March 1980, pp. 32-36.

Kumins, Lawrence. "Energy Shock: Oil and the Economy." *Current History*, November 1975, p. 189.

Laffer, Arthur B. and Turney, James C. "Global Monetary Policy: Implications for the U.S. Dollar and Gold." *Journal of Social and Political Studies*, Spring/Summer 1980, pp. 3-38.

Lee, L. Douglas. "Balancing the Budget: Does It Matter?" *Journal of the Institute for Socioeconomic Studies*, Winter 1980, pp. 25-35.

Leiserson, Avery. "Coordination of Federal Budgetary and Appropriations Procedures Under the Legislative Reorganization Act of 1946." *National Tax Journal*, June 1948, pp. 118-126.

Lekachman, Robert. "Great Society." *Commentary*, June 1965, pp. 37-42.

Levy, Michael E. and Smith, Delos R. "The Congressional Budget Process Again Reformed." *Conference Board Record*, March 1975, pp. 12-17.

Lockwood, Robert M. "The Energy Economy: Energy in Perspective." *Texas Business Review*, June 1973, pp. 134-136.

McCracken, Paul W. "Revitalizing the American Economy: A Strategy for the 1980s." *Journal of Social, Political and Economic Studies*, Spring 1981, pp. 3-18.

McCornack, Reuben. "A New Opportunity: The Congressional Budget Process." *Journal of Current Social Issues*, Winter 1975, pp. 28-30.

Martin, William McChesney, Jr. "Monetary History and International Policy." *Columbia University Forum*, vol. 8, Summer 1965, pp. 4-9.

Melman, S. "Great Society Priorities: Military Budget and Vietnam War Funded at Cost of Social Investments." *Commonweal*, August 5, 1966, pp. 494-497.

Minareck, Joseph J. "Who Wins, Who Loses from Inflation?" *Challenge*, January/February, 1979, pp. 26-31.

Moore, Geoffrey H. "Sequences in the Inflation Cycle." *Morgan Guaranty Survey*, April 1980, pp. 12-14.

Mork, Knut Anton and Hall, Robert E. "Energy Prices and the U.S. Economy in 1979-1981." *Energy Journal*, April 1980, pp. 41-53.

Mowery, David C. and others. "Presidential Management of Budgetary and Fiscal Policymaking." *Political Science Quarterly*, Fall 1980, pp. 395-425.

Niskanen, William A. "Improving U.S. Budget Choices." *Tax Review*, November 1971, pp. 41-44.

"Oil Greases the Skids for the World Economy." *Commerce*, January 1980, p. 24.

Okun, Arthur M. "An Efficient Strategy to Combat Inflation." *The Brookings Bulletin*, no. 4, Spring 1979, pp. 1-2.

———. "The Formulation of National Economic Policy." *Perspectives in Defense Management*, December 1968, pp. 9-12.

Passer, Harold C. "The Effects of the Economic Stabilization Program." *Akron Business and Economic Review*, Winter 1972, pp. 5-8.

Penner, Rudolph G. "Federal Budget Dilemmas in the 1980s." *AEI Economist*, October 1979, pp. 1-8.

Rockoff, Hugh. "Price and Wage Controls in Four Wartime Periods." *Journal of Economic History*, June 1981, pp. 381-401.

Rudder, Catherine E. "Committee Reform and the Revenue Process." In *Congress Reconsidered*, 1st ed., edited by Lawrence

C. Dodd and Bruce I. Oppenheimer, chapter 6. New York: Praeger Publishers, 1977.

Saulnier, Raymond J. "Policies That Ended Inflation, 1956-1961." *Academy of Political Science Proceedings*, no. 4, 1975, pp. 105-113.

Schick, Allen. "The Battle of the Budget." In *Congress Against the President*, edited by Harvey Mansfield, pp. 51-70. New York: Academy of Political Science, 1975.

———. "The Budget Bureau That Was: Thoughts on the Rise, Decline and Future of a Presidential Agency." *Law and Contemporary Problems*, Summer 1970, pp. 519-539.

———. "The Road to PPB: The Stages of Budget Reform." *Public Administration Review*, December 1966, pp. 43-258.

Schwartz, Anna J. "Inflation in the United States." *Current History*, November 1975, pp. 170-174+.

Segal, Harvey H. "The Politics of Inflation, or the Inflation of Politics." *Business Economics*, January 1975, pp. 31-35.

Smith, W. Stephen. "Federal Tax and Spending Reform." *Economic Perspectives*, May/June 1981, pp. 13-19.

Stark, John R. "The Economic Case for the Great Society." *Challenge*, January/February 1967, pp. 22-25.

———. "Great Society: Concept and Cost." *University of Missouri Business and Government Review*, September/October 1966, pp. 5-13.

Stein, Herbert. "The Failure of Carter's Anti-Inflation Policy." *Fortune*, March 24, 1980, pp. 50-52.

Stephens, David B. "Improving Productivity During Inflationary Recession: An Assessment of the Prospects." *Southwest Business and Economic Review*, February 1981, pp. 21-28.

Swobolda, Alexander K. "Inflation, Oil, and World Economic Crisis." *Journal of World Trade Law*, March/April 1976, pp. 97-109.

"Top Secret: Vietnam War Cost." *Nation*, October 31, 1966, pp. 434-435.

Tybout, A. "Prices, Costs, and the Energy Crisis." *Bulletin of Business Research*, June 1973, pp. 4-8.

Vidich, Arthur J. "Inflation and Social Structure: The United States in an Epoch of Declining Abundance." *Texas Business Review*, July/August 1980, pp. 206-209.

Wagner, Richard E. "Spending Limitation, the Constitution and Productivity: A Response to James Tobin." *Taxing and Spending*, Winter 1980, pp. 59-71.

Ways, M. "Creative Federalism and the Great Society: More to L.B.J.'s Domestic Policies Than Meets the Eye." *Fortune*, January 1966, p. 120.

Weintraub, Sidney. "Carter's Economic Doodling: A Little New Deal." *New Leader*, September 22, 1980, pp. 3-5.

Williams, Harold R. "Wage and Price Controls: Efficiency, Equity, and Decontrol." *Nebraska Journal of Economics and Business*, Autumn 1972, pp. 87-100.

Wetzel, James N. "The Federal Role in the Economy." *Current History*, November 1975, p. 179.

Wilson, John O. "Reducing the Role of the Federal Government: Rhetoric versus Reality." *Business Economist*, May 1976, pp. 11-17.

Wilson, Marilyn. "Inflation Fears and Facts." *Dun's Business Month*, October 1981, pp. 37-40.

Documents

America's New Beginning: A Program for Economic Recovery. Washington, D.C.: Executive Office, February 18, 1981.

U.S. Congress, Congressional Budget Office. *Economic Policy and the Outlook for the Economy.* Washington, D.C.: Government Printing Office, 1981.

———. *Financing Social Security: Issues for the Short and Long Term*, July 1977. Washington, D.C.: Government Printing Office, 1977.

———. *Tax Expenditures: Current Issues and Five-Year Budget Projections, Fiscal Years 1981-1985.* Washington, D.C.: Government Printing Office, 1980.

U.S. Congress, House. Committee on Banking, Finance and Urban Affairs. Subcommittee on Economic Stabilization. *Productivity Performance and the American Economy: Hearings, June 24, July 31, August 27, 1980.* 96th Cong., 2nd sess. Washington, D.C.: Government Printing Office, 1981.

U.S. Congress, House. Committee on the Budget. *Controlling Inflation: Hearing, April 1, 1981.* 97th Cong., 1st sess. Washington, D.C.: Government Printing Office, 1981.

——. *Indexing and the Federal Budget: Hearings, March 10-16, 1981.* 97th Cong., 1st sess. Washington, D.C.: Government Printing Office, 1981.

U.S. Congress, House. Committee on Foreign Affairs. Subcommittee on Foreign Economic Policy. *New Realities and New Directions in U.S. Foreign Economic Policy.* 92nd Cong., 2nd sess. Washington, D.C.: Government Printing Office, 1972.

——. Subcommittee on International Economic Policy and Trade. *U.S. International Influence: Agenda for the Future: Hearing, February 24, 1981.* 97th Cong., 1st sess. Washington, D.C.: Government Printing Office, 1981.

U.S. Congress, House. Committee on Interstate and Foreign Commerce. Subcommittee on Oversight and Investigations. *The Energy Inflation Crisis: Sources, Consequences, and Policy Options; Report, December 1980, together with Minority Views.* 96th Cong., 2nd sess. Washington, D.C.: Government Printing Office, 1980.

——. *Impact of Energy Inflation: Hearings, December 13, 20, 1979.* 96th Cong., 1st sess. Washington, D.C.: Government Printing Office, 1980.

U.S. Congress. Joint Economic Committee. *Economic Effect of Vietnam Spending: Report, July 7, 1967, together with Supplementary Views.* 90th Cong., 1st sess. Washington, D.C.: Government Printing Office, 1967.

——. *Government Regulation: Achieving Social and Economic Balance. Special Study on Economic Change, vol. 5.* 96th Cong., 2nd sess. Washington, D.C.: Government Printing Office, 1980.

——. *Inflation and Growth: The Economic Policy Dilemma. Report, July 1978.* 95th Cong., 2nd sess. Washington, D.C.: Government Printing Office, 1978.

——. *The International Economy: U.S. Role in a World Market. Special Study on Economic Change, vol. 9.* 96th Cong., 2nd sess. Washington, D.C.: Government Printing Office, 1980.

——. *Price and Wage Control: Evaluation of a Year's Experience; Report, together with Supplemental and Additional Views.* 92nd Cong., 2nd sess. Washington, D.C.: Government Printing Office, 1972.

——. *Productivity and Inflation: A Study.* 96th Cong., 2nd sess. Washington, D.C.: Government Printing Office, 1980.

——. *Proposition 13: Its Impact on the Nation's Economy, Federal Revenues, and Federal Expenditures, July 1978.* 96th Cong. 2nd sess. Washington, D.C.: Government Printing Office, 1978.

——. *The State of the Economy: Hearings, July 23, August 1, 1980.* 96th Cong., 2nd sess. Washington, D.C.: Government Printing Office, 1980.

——. *Tax Policy and Core Inflation: A Study, April 10, 1980.* 96th Cong., 2nd sess. Washington, D.C.: Government Printing Office, 1980.

——. *Thirtieth Anniversary of the Employment Act of 1946: A National Conference on Full Employment: Hearings, March 18-19, 1976.* 94th Cong., 2nd sess. Washington, D.C.: Government Printing Office, 1977.

——. *U.S. Economic Growth from 1976 to 1986: Prospects, Problems and Patterns.* 95th Cong., 1st sess. Washington, D.C.: Government Printing Office, 1977.

——. Subcommittee on Economic Growth. *Long Term Economic Growth: Hearings, May 8, 9; June 11, 12, 26, 1974.* 93rd Cong., 2nd sess. Washington, D.C.: Government Printing Office, 1975.

——. Subcommittee on Economic Growth and Stabilization. *Wage and Price Controls: Hearing, December 6, 1978.* 95th Cong., 2nd sess. Washington, D.C.: Government Printing Office, 1978.

——. Subcommittee on Energy. *Economic Impact of Oil Decontrol: Hearing, April 25, 1979.* 96th Cong., 1st sess. Washington, D.C.: Government Printing Office, 1979.

——. Subcommittee on Fiscal Policy. *The Federal Budget, Inflation, and Full Employment: Hearings, October 7-9, 13, 14, 22, 23, 1969.* 91st Cong., 1st sess. Washington, D.C.: Government Printing Office, 1970.

——. Subcommittee on Priorities and Economy in Government. *American Productivity: Key to Economic Strength and National Survival.* 92nd Cong., 2nd sess. Washington, D.C.: Government Printing Office, 1972.

U.S. Congress. Joint Committee on Taxation. *Summary of Testimony of Witnesses Regarding Tax Proposals at Public Hearings before the Senate Committee on Finance, July 23-31, 1980.* 96th Cong., 2nd sess. Washington, D.C.: Government Printing Office, 1980.

U.S. Congress. Senate. Committee on Banking, Housing and Urban Affairs. *The State of the Economy: Hearings, January 7-8, 1981 to Discuss Recent Monetary and Economic Development and the Prospects for 1981 and Beyond.* 97th Cong., 1st sess. Washington, D.C.: Government Printing Office, 1981.

U.S. Congress. Senate. Committee on the Budget. *Economy and the Federal Budget: Hearings, January 11-13, 1977.* 95th Cong., 1st sess. Washington, D.C.: Government Printing Office, 1977.

——. *Economy and Fiscal Policy, 1974: Hearings, December 11, 12, 17-19, 1974.* 93rd Cong., 2nd sess. Washington, D.C.: Government Printing Office, 1975.

——. *The Present State of the Economy: Strategies to Restore Stability: Hearings, January 21-22.* 97th Cong., 1st sess. Washington, D.C.: Government Printing Office, 1981.

U.S. Congress. Senate. Committee on Finance. Subcommittee on Energy. *Fiscal Policy and the Energy Crisis: Hearings, November 27-29, 1973.* 93rd Cong., 1st sess. Washington, D.C.: Government Printing Office, 1974.

——. Subcommittee on Social Security. *Social Security Financing: Hearings, April 5, 6, 1978.* 95th Cong., 2nd sess. Washington, D.C.: Government Printing Office, 1979.

U.S. Congress. Senate. Committee on Foreign Relations. *Impact of the War in Southeast Asia on the U.S. Economy: Hearings, April 15, 16, 1970.* 91st Cong., 2nd sess. Washington, D.C.: Government Printing Office, 1970.

——. Subcommittee on International Economic Policy. *The U.S. Stake in the Global Economy: Hearings, February 25, 27, 1981.* 97th Cong., 1st sess. Washington, D.C.: Government Printing Office, 1981.

U.S. Congress. Senate. Committee on Government Operations. Subcommittee on Budgeting, Management, and Expenditures. *Improving Congressional Control of the Budget: Hearings, May 1-9, 1973.* 93rd cong., 1st sess. Washington, D.C.: Government Printing Office, 1973.

U.S. Congress. Senate. Committee on the Judiciary. *Constitutional Amendment to Balance the Federal Budget: Hearings, January 14, February 22, 1980.* 96th Cong., 2nd sess. Washington, D.C.: Government Printing Office, 1981.

——. Subcommittee on the Constitution. *Proposed Constitutional Amendment to Balance the Federal Budget: Hearings, March 12, November 1, 1979.* 96th Cong., 1st sess. Washington, D.C.: Government Printing Office, 1980.

U.S. Congress. Senate. Committee on Labor and Public Welfare. *Unemployment and the Economy: Hearings, February 12, 13; March 3, 17; April 2, 22, 1975.* 94th Cong., 1st sess. Washington, D.C.: Government Printing Office, 1979.

U.S. General Accounting Office. *Proposition 13: How California Governments Coped With a $6 Billion Revenue Loss; Report to the Congress by the Comptroller General of the United States.* Washington, D.C.: Government Printing Office, September 1979.

U.S. President's Commission for a National Agenda for the Eighties. Panel on the American Economy: Employment, Productivity and Inflation. *The American Economy: Employment, Productivity, and Inflation in the Eighties, Report.* Washington, D.C.: Government Printing Office, 1980.

Index